FEMINIST JUDGMENTS IN INTERNATIONAL LAW

The emergence of feminist rewriting of key judgments has been one of the most interesting recent developments in legal methodology. This unique enterprise has seen scholars collaborate in the 'real world' task of reassessing jurisprudence in light of feminist perspectives. This important new volume makes a significant contribution to the endeavour, exploring how key judgments in international law might have differed if feminist judges had sat on the bench. This collection asks whether feminist perspectives can offer meaningful and viable alternatives to international law norms; and if so, whether that application results in distinguishable differences in outcomes. It answers these questions with particular reference to sources of international law, the public and private divide, State responsibility, State immunities, treaty law, State sovereignty, human rights protection, global governance, and the concept of violence in international law. This landmark publication offers a truly innovative reassessment of international law.

Feminist Judgments in International Law

Edited by
Loveday Hodson
and
Troy Lavers

•HART•
OXFORD • LONDON • NEW YORK • NEW DELHI • SYDNEY

HART PUBLISHING

Bloomsbury Publishing Plc

Kemp House, Chawley Park, Cumnor Hill, Oxford, OX2 9PH, UK

HART PUBLISHING, the Hart/Stag logo, BLOOMSBURY and the Diana logo are trademarks of Bloomsbury Publishing Plc

First published in Great Britain 2019

A catalogue record for this book is available from the British Library.

Library of Congress Cataloging-in-Publication data

Names: Hodson, Loveday, editor. | Lavers, Troy, editor.

Title: Feminist judgments in international law / edited by Loveday Hodson, Troy Lavers.

Description: Oxford, UK ; Chicago, Illinois : Hart Publishing, 2019. | Includes bibliographical references and index.

Identifiers: LCCN 2019009092 (print) | LCCN 2019009390 (ebook) | ISBN 9781509914432 (EPub) | ISBN 9781509914456 (hardback)

Subjects: LCSH: International law and human rights—Cases. | Women's rights—Cases. | Women—Legal status, laws, etc.—Cases. | Feminist jurisprudence. | BISAC: LAW / International. | LAW / Jurisprudence.

Classification: LCC KZ1266 (ebook) | LCC KZ1266 .F46 2019 (print) | DDC 341.4/858—dc23

LC record available at https://lccn.loc.gov/2019009092

ISBN: HB: 978-1-50991-445-6
ePDF: 978-1-50991-442-5
ePub: 978-1-50991-443-2

Typeset by Compuscript Ltd, Shannon

This book is dedicated to the memory of the first feminists in our lives, our mothers, Jane and Marie.

FOREWORD

Feminist Judgments in International Law is a welcome and very impressive addition to the catalogue of feminist judgment collections, joining previous publications from Canada, England & Wales, Australia, the USA, Ireland and Northern Ireland, and New Zealand. Within the growing tradition of reimagining judicial decisions from a feminist perspective, this book introduces a number of innovative features. Unlike the earlier projects which focused on particular national jurisdictions (or, in the case of the Northern/Irish project, two jurisdictions with much in common), the feminist international judgments project has turned its attention to international law and the judgments of supra-national courts and tribunals, with participants re-writing judgments from a range of such bodies, each with its own procedural rules, litigation practices and judicial conventions.

A convention applying in some of these international fora is that the court speaks with one voice and thus produces a single judgment, by contrast with the individual opinions familiar in common law countries. Consequently, most of the judgments in this volume have been written collectively by 'chambers' of feminist judges. This raised the challenge of agreeing on a common position and approach, sometimes involving negotiation and compromise, as the authors explain in their reflections following each judgment. In one case (*Ruusunen v Finland*), the authors intriguingly produce both a majority opinion and a concurring individual opinion, while in another (*Şahin v Turkey*), a 'devil's advocate' dissenting judgment taking an alternative feminist position is included. The collaborative writing process adopted in the majority of cases, however, answers one of the ongoing questions about the feminist judgments projects – whether the methodology is transferrable to civil law jurisdictions. This collection demonstrates that it is possible for a court to speak the law with a single *feminist* voice. Moreover, it demonstrates that the single judgment format, while sometimes requiring compromise, may also have an amplifying effect. As the authors of *Kell v Canada* put it in their concluding reflections, 'we have forged a new narrative identity that unites the merits of our individual voices into what we hope is one sonorous, highly enriched stereo-voice'.

The addition of authorial reflections at the end of each judgment is another of this volume's innovations. These reflections are notably thoughtful and illuminating – the authors have taken the task of reflexivity as seriously as that of writing their judgments. The reflections allow us to see the process behind the product, the decisions taken along the way, and the values underpinning them. They add a great deal to the theoretical analysis of the feminist judgments enterprise, particularly in foregrounding the tensions involved in attempting to re-write judgments in a way that is both conventional and critical. But at the same time, they show how it is possible to live with those tensions rather than having to resolve them. Further innovations include cross-referral between re-written judgments (the feminist judgment in the *Lockerbie* case links back to the feminist judgment in the *Bozkurt* case), and the inclusion of a re-written judgment in a case that is still under appeal (*Prosecutor v Karadžić*), and which therefore has a chance of influencing the final decision by showing the judges both how feminist methodology can be applied and the important effects of doing so.

The subject-matter of the re-written judgments includes familiar feminist topics such as reproductive rights, domestic and sexual violence, forced marriage, parental leave and pay equity, and Islamic headscarves, as they have appeared in cases before international courts and tribunals. In some of these cases, the authors re-write judgments considered 'good' for women in that women's claims were successful (eg *Opuz v Turkey*, *Kell v Canada*), but the feminist judgments demonstrate how much better their reasoning could have been if a thorough-going feminist analysis had been applied. A number of cases deal with less obvious subject-matters, including fundamental principles of public international law – the nature of sovereignty, international relations and the international legal order, treaty law and state immunity – and human rights such as freedom of expression and the right to housing. These cases demonstrate that a feminist analysis can be applied well beyond typical 'women's issues', and indeed that feminist reasoning is an essential resource in international decision-making and capable of universal application.

Alongside their original contributions, the re-written judgments in this volume deploy a toolbox of feminist theories and methods held in common with the other feminist judgment projects, and which have been well honed in earlier feminist judgment collections. Theories such as relationality, substantive equality and intersectionality, and the quest for gender, racial and socio-economic justice are prominent in these judgments. The methods adopted to pursue these goals include: paying specific attention to the voices and experiences of the individuals involved in the cases, particularly those traditionally marginalised and silenced in law (and especially in international law where abstract entities have traditionally been the central actors); telling the story differently; renaming and reframing; contextualisation; feminist practical reasoning; attention to the operations of power and the material effects of law; deconstructing binaries and hierarchies; combating gender bias; and drawing on contemporary feminist arguments and literature.[1] The accounts of individual experience are carefully nuanced and

[1] For detailed accounts of these feminist methods and their application to judicial decision-making, see KT Bartlett, 'Feminist Legal Methods' (1990) 103 *Yale Law Journal* 829; R Hunter, 'Can *Feminist* Judges Make a Difference?' (2008) 15 *International Journal of the Legal Profession* 7; R Hunter, 'An Account of Feminist Judging' in R Hunter, C McGlynn and E Rackley (eds), *Feminist Judgments: From Theory to Practice* (Oxford, Hart Publishing, 2010); E Rackley, 'The Art and Craft of Writing Judgments: Notes on the Feminist Judgments Project' in Hunter, McGlynn and Rackley, ibid.

varied. The experience recounted is often one of victimisation, but women are not reduced to victim status – their agency and pleasure are also well represented. In addition to alternative accounts and analyses of the facts, the judgments offer new but equally viable legal reasoning, often featuring more inclusive interpretations of legal principles and treaty provisions, and giving full scope and effect to progressive legislation and Conventions.

This book deserves to be read and its methods followed by all international judges, lawyers and scholars. I hope it will inspire the production of more feminist judgments in international law, both imagined and real.

Rosemary Hunter
25 July 2018

ACKNOWLEDGEMENTS

In true feminist style, this book has been a collective effort. There are so many people whose contribution to it we wish to acknowledge, it's hard to know where to start.

Firstly, to the contributing authors who participated in this project and who have helped us to see international law differently: we thank you, and we salute your insights, creativity, patience and laughter. Gina Heathcote has been a tremendous supporter of the project; not only did she help the project get off the ground with the resources of the Centre for Gender Studies at SOAS, she has been a tireless champion of the project throughout. Without Gina's support and encouragement, this collection could not have been written. Special thanks are owed to the inspirational Erika Rackley and Rosemary Hunter, who not only led the way with the English/Welsh Feminist Judgments Project, but also took time out of their busy schedules to share their experiences with us. Rosemary offered unfailing encouragement to us throughout and continues to be a hugely energetic global ambassador for feminist judgments projects. Judge Howard Morrison gave of his time so we could hear from a 'real live judge' about the ups and downs of judging. His reflections reinforced the contextual approach adopted in many of the judgments in this collection.

We are grateful to our own university, the University of Leicester, whose financial support made the project workshops possible. Leicester Law School has a vibrant cluster of international law scholars who are great colleagues and friends who are always ready to lend an ear. A particular 'thank you' is owed to Mandy Burton for encouraging us in this project from the very beginning.

We also would like to thank our discussants, Louise Arimatsu, Yoriko Otomo, Patricia Palacios Zuloaga, Noelle Quenivet, Jule Mulder, Vivienne Hayes, Keina Yoshida, Samia Bano, Jonathan McCully, Flora Renz, Daniela Nadj, Wade Mansell and Gina Heathcote. These people were extraordinarily generous with their time in reviewing draft judgments and sharing their thoughts on them, and we all benefitted tremendously from their insights and contributions.

Finally, we turn to our families and to all those who supported, encouraged, consoled, and pushed us along the road to completion when we needed it most. Loveday wishes in particular to thank Kim and Tegan for making it all worthwhile, and Sonny the cat for her questionable but attentive research assistance. Troy thanks the long-suffering and always supportive Adrian, her tremendous feminist father Jack, her brother John, and her furry friends Bosun and Leah.

CONTENTS

PART III
HUMAN RIGHTS

PART IV
INTERNATIONAL CRIMINAL LAW

PART V
CONCLUSION

NOTES ON CONTRIBUTORS

Amel Alghrani is a Reader in Law in the School of Law and Social Justice at the University of Liverpool.

Amal Ali is a Senior Lecturer in Law in Lincoln Law School at the University of Lincoln.

Zoi Aliozi is a human rights lawyer and activist. She is a lecturer at the Cinema, Human Rights and Advocacy school at the European Inter-University Centre, Venice.

Merris Amos is a Professor of Human Rights Law in the Department of Law at Queen Mary, University of London.

Nicola Barker is a Professor in the School of Law and Social Justice at the University of Liverpool.

Sara Bengtson is currently a Fulbright scholar and LLM candidate at Columbia Law School.

Yassin M. Brunger is a Lecturer in Human Rights Law in the School of Law at Queen's University Belfast.

Lolita Buckner Inniss is a Professor of Law and the Robert G Storey Distinguished Faculty Fellow in the Southern Methodist University Dedman School of Law.

Maribel Canto-Lopez is a Lecturer in Law in Leicester Law School at the University of Leicester.

Marta Carneiro is a Post-Doctoral Researcher at the Faculty of Law, NOVA University of Lisbon.

Hilary Charlesworth is a Melbourne Laureate Professor at Melbourne Law School and a Distinguished Professor at the Australian National University. She served as judge ad hoc in the International Court of Justice in the Whaling in the Antarctic Case (2011–14).

Christine Chinkin is Emerita Professor of Law and currently Professorial Research Fellow and former Director of the Centre for Women, Peace and Security at the London School of Economics and Political Science.

Shazia Choudhry is a Professor of Law in the Department of Law at Queen Mary, University of London.

Helen Fenwick is Professor of Law in the Durham Law School at the University of Durham.

Damian Gonzalez-Salzberg is a Lecturer in Law in the School of Law, University of Sheffield.

Kathryn Greenman is a Lecturer in the Faculty of Law, University of Technology Sydney.

Celestine Greenwood is a Barrister and currently an Adjunct Professor at the American University Washington College of Law.

Wendy Guns is a Lecturer in Law at the Open University, Netherlands.

Gina Heathcote is a Reader in Gender Studies and International Law at the School of Oriental and African Studies, University of London.

Jonathan Herring is a Professor of Law and Fellow of Exeter College, Oxford University.

Loveday Hodson is an Associate Professor in Leicester Law School at the University of Leicester.

Jessie Hohmann is Associate Professor in the Faculty of Law, University of Technology Sydney.

Emma Irving is an Assistant Professor of Public International Law at the Grotius Centre for International Legal Studies, Leiden University.

Nani Jansen Reventlow is a Lecturer in Law at Columbia Law School. She is also the founding Director of the Digital Freedom Fund and an Associate Tenant at Doughty Street Chambers, London.

Paul Johnson is a Professor of Sociology and Head of Department at the Department of Sociology at the University of York.

Emily Jones is a Lecturer in Law in the School of Law and Human Rights Centre at the University of Essex.

Henry Jones is an Assistant Professor in Law in the Durham Law School at the University of Durham.

Olga Jurasz is a Senior Lecturer in Law at the Open University Law School.

Kirsten Ketscher is a Professor of Social Security, Welfare and Discrimination Law in the Faculty of Law at the University of Copenhagen.

Sheri Labenski is a Research Officer in the Centre for Women, Peace and Security at the London School of Economics and Political Science.

Troy Lavers is an Associate Professor in Leicester Law School at the University of Leicester.

Jill Marshall is a Professor of Law in the School of Law at Royal Holloway, University of London and a qualified solicitor.

Kasey McCall-Smith is a Lecturer in Public International Law and Programme Director for the LLM in Human Rights in the Edinburgh Law School at the University of Edinburgh.

Solange Mouthaan is an Associate Professor of Law in the School of Law at the University of Warwick.

Diana Sankey is a Lecturer in the School of Law at Liverpool John Moores University.

Bérénice K. Schramm is a Postdoctoral Researcher affiliated with the Centre d'études sur le droit international et la mondialisation at UQÀM and the Centre for Gender Studies at the School of Oriental and African Studies, University of London.

Dawn Sedman is a Senior Lecturer in Nottingham Law School at Nottingham Trent University.

Freya Semanda is a Lecturer in Law at University College Absalon.

Rhona Smith is Professor of International Human Rights and Head of School in Newcastle Law School at the University of Newcastle.

Enzamaria Tramontana is Assistant Professor of International Law at the School of Law of the University of Palermo.

Ben Warwick is a Lecturer in the Birmingham Law School at the University of Birmingham.

Ekaterina Yahyaoui Krivenko is a Lecturer at the Irish Centre for Human Rights, School of Law and Vice-Dean for Research in the College of Business, Public Policy, and Law, at the National University of Ireland, Galway.

PART I

Introduction

1

Feminist Judgments in International Law: An Introduction

LOVEDAY HODSON AND TROY LAVERS

I. Beginnings

As feminists who have been engaged in international law scholarship for a number of years, we are constantly driven to think creatively and optimistically of ways that we might do international law differently. We are among a growing number of academic feminists who are challenged by our students and by our own ethical and political commitments to push the discipline in new directions; simply put, many of our discussions focus on the question of how the theory and practice of international law might be done better. International law scholarship is prone to utopian thinking that can often contrast cruelly with the reality of its daily application.[1] Yet feminists have insisted that imagination, hope and activism have a crucial role to play in the study, understanding and application of international law.[2] We have also witnessed first-hand the remarkable creative energy generated, and the insights that emerge, when a group of feminists with an interest in international law are brought together and given space to strategise, critique, encourage and reflect. This book is borne from a paradoxical position that encompasses both optimism about international law's transformative potential and frustration at its frequent failure to bring about meaningful change.

The process of writing *Feminist Judgments in International Law* began a number of years ago. The project from which this book evolved – a project we referred to as the feminist international judgments project (FIJP) – brought together almost

[1] M Koskenniemi, *From Apology to Utopia: The Structure of International Legal Argument* (Cambridge, Cambridge University Press, 2005).

[2] For further discussion, see, for instance: H Charlesworth and C Chinkin, *The Boundaries of International Law: A Feminist Analysis* (Manchester, Manchester University Press, 2000); S Kuovo and Z Pearson (eds), *Feminist Perspectives on Contemporary International Law: Between Resistance and Compliance?* (Oxford, Hart Publishing, 2011); C O'Rourke, 'Feminist Strategy in International Law: Understanding its Legal, Normative, and Political Dimensions' (2017) 28(4) *European Journal of International Law* 1019.

50 international legal scholars and some activists, and asked them to collaborate in the task of (re-)writing key international judgments from a feminist perspective. Participants were asked to imagine what those international judgments might look like viewed through a feminist lens. Applying theory in such a practical way required us to consider the concrete ways in which feminist perspectives can change international law. This book, then, is the result of a collaborative exercise that involved demonstrating the practical application of alternative (feminist) values to international law practice. During the incredible journey that culminated in this collection, our positions have been challenged and our understanding of the value of feminist thinking in international law has deepened.

In undertaking this project, we have followed in the footsteps of some remarkable feminist legal scholars. The idea of a project in which key legal judgments are re-written from a feminist perspective can be traced to the Women's Court of Canada, in which six academics individually re-wrote a Supreme Court judgment.[3] That Canadian project was followed by a larger-scale English/Welsh project that generated considerable interest among legal scholars and beyond, resulting in a high-profile collection of published judgments.[4] Interest in the methodology has now generated a significant number of domestic projects. An Australian collection of feminist judgments was published in 2014;[5] a Northern/Irish feminist judgments project in 2017;[6] and a New Zealand one followed also in 2017.[7] In the US, a series of collections is being written, each focussed on a particular area of law.[8] Scottish,[9] Indian[10] and African[11] projects are currently underway. These projects have enriched thinking about how feminist theory might serve to influence legal outcomes and, to some extent, have also raised questions about the significance that can be attached to women judges.[12] Importantly, they are also generating

[3] These judgments are available at: www.thecourt.ca/decisions-of-the-womens-court-of-canada. There is currently a second Canadian project underway. See also DG Reaume, 'Turning Feminist Judgments into Jurisprudence: The Women's Court of Canada on Substantive Equality' (forthcoming, 2019) *Oñati Socio-Legal Series*.

[4] R Hunter, C McGlynn and E Rackley (eds), *Feminist Judgments: From Theory to Practice* (Oxford, Hart Publishing, 2010).

[5] H Douglas, F Bartlett, T Luker and R Hunter (eds), *Australian Feminist Judgments: Righting and Re-writing Law* (Oxford, Hart Publishing, 2014).

[6] M Enright and J McCandless (eds), *Northern/Irish Feminist Judgments: Judges' Troubles and the Gendered Politics of Identity* (Oxford, Hart Publishing, 2017).

[7] E McDonald, R Powell, M Stephens and R Hunter (eds), *Feminist Judgments of Aotearoa New Zealand: A Two-Stranded Rope* (Oxford, Hart Publishing, 2017).

[8] For details about this series of projects, see the US Feminist Judgments Project website at: https://sites.temple.edu/usfeministjudgments.

[9] Further information on the Scottish Feminist Judgments Project is available at: www.sfjp.law.ed.ac.uk.

[10] Further information on the Feminist Judgments Project India is available at: https://fjpindia.wixsite.com/fjpi.

[11] Further information on the African Feminist Judgments Project is available at: www.lawandglobaljustice.com/the-african-feminist-judgments-project.

[12] See, for example: E Rackley, *Women, Judging and the Judiciary: From Difference to Diversity* (Abingdon, Routledge, 2013); S Kenney, *Gender and Justice: Why Women in the Judiciary Really Matter* (Abingdon, Routledge, 2013).

a network of feminist legal scholars across jurisdictions: in 2017, for instance, organisers of various projects met at the International Institute for the Sociology of Law in Oñati, Spain, to share our experiences and to consider ways in which the methodology might develop.[13] Unexpectedly, then, embarking on a feminist judgments project brought with it from the outset a comforting sense of being supported by a loose network of feminists sharing a creative academic endeavour.

II. Towards an International Law Project

Motivated by the English/Welsh project, we recognised that the methodology of re-writing judgments could have particular importance in an international law context. While feminist scholarship and activism is rich in its complexity and diversity and does not represent a single unified approach, feminists are increasingly at the forefront of critical international legal scholarship. Inspired by the ground-breaking work of MacKinnon in *Towards a Feminist Theory of the State*[14] and Chinkin, Wright and Charlesworth's 1991 article 'Feminist Approaches to International Law'[15] and subsequent monograph,[16] the challenge of laying bare the patriarchal structures upon which the discipline is founded and its consequent blind-spots has been taken up enthusiastically by a growing number of international scholars.[17] However, feminists have discovered that the obstacles

[13] The publications from this meeting are forthcoming in the *Oñati Socio-Legal Series*. See also S Cowan et al, 'Feminist Judging: From Margin to Centre' (*Social and Legal Studies Blog*, 21 November 2018) https://socialandlegalstudies.wordpress.com/2018/11/21/feminist-judging-margin-centre.

[14] C MacKinnon, *Towards a Feminist Theory of the State* (Cambridge MA, Harvard University Press, 1989).

[15] H Charlesworth, C Chinkin and S Wright, 'Feminist Approaches to International Law' (1991) 85(4) *American Journal of International Law* 613.

[16] Charlesworth and Chinkin, above n 2.

[17] K Engle, 'International Human Rights and Feminism: When Discourses Meet' (1991–92) 13 *Michigan Journal of International Law* 517; D Dallmeyer, *Reconceiving Reality: Women and International Law* (Washington DC, American Society of International Law, 1993); H Charlesworth, 'Alienating Oscar? Feminist Analysis of International Law' (1993) 25 *Studies in Transnational Legal Policy* 1; K Knop, 'Re/Statements: Feminism and State Sovereignty in International Law' (1993) 3 *Transnational Law and Contemporary Problems* 293; G Binion, 'Human Rights: A Feminist Perspective' (1995) 17(3) *Human Rights Quarterly* 509; H Charlesworth, 'Feminist Methods in International Law' (1999) 93(2) *American Journal of International Law* 379; A Orford, 'Feminism, Imperialism and the Mission of International Law' (2002) 71 *Nordic Journal of International Law* 275; B Meyersfeld, 'Reconceptualizing Domestic Violence in International Law' (2003–04) 67 *Albany Law Review* 371; D Buss and A Manji (eds), *International Law: Modern Feminist Approaches* (Portland OH and Oxford, Hart Publishing, 2005); D Otto, 'Lost in Translation: Re-scripting the Sexed Subjects of International Human Rights Law' in A Orford (ed), *International Law and its Others* (Cambridge, Cambridge University Press, 2006); C MacKinnon, *Are Women Human? And Other International Dialogues* (Cambridge MA and London, Harvard University Press, 2006); A Orford, *Reading Humanitarian Intervention: Human Rights and the Use of Force in International Law* (Cambridge, Cambridge University Press, 2007); D Otto, 'The Exile of Inclusion: Reflections on Gender Issues in International Law over the Last Decade' (2009) 10 *Melbourne Journal of International Law* 11; M Fineman and E Zinsstag, *Feminist Perspectives on Transitional Justice: From International and Criminal to Alternative Forms of Justice* (Cambridge, Intersentia, 2013); Kuovo and Pearson, above n 2; G Heathcote, *The Law on the Use of Force: A Feminist Analysis* (London, Routledge, 2012).

they face are considerable. Their work brings into question the very structure of international law, its methods and values. Decision-making in international law traditionally prioritises abstract logic and hard (formal) law, thereby reducing the potential importance of conciliation, negotiation, soft law and equity.[18] Traditional scholarship in international law also has the State as its key focal point, raising questions about the power of the State, the sovereignty of States and the use of force by States. Consequently, issues of importance to women all too often fall into the blind spots of international law's gaze. Hilary Charlesworth, for example, has wondered why there is 'a whole series of treaties obsessed with straddling stocks, when the use of breast milk substitutes, which is a major health issue for women in Africa, remains subject to voluntary W.H.O. codes?'[19]

A feminist international judgments project was therefore both timely and relevant. Indeed, frustrated by the confines of traditional international law, feminists have frequently sought to create alternative spaces in which to express their perspectives. There is a long tradition of feminists responding creatively to the discipline's narrow confines by reaching beyond them, perhaps most famously in the form of women's tribunals that aim to address the devastating failure of more formal fora to address crimes and gross human rights violations against women.[20] Other examples that have particularly inspired us include Buchanan and Johnson's use of popular film to expose the binaries created in traditional approaches to the sources of international law,[21] and the work of Yoriko Otomo, whose poetry includes *Her proper name: a revisionist account of international law*, which relates an imagined (absent) account of the signing of the Treaty of Westphalia from the perspective of Maria von Helfenstein (Lady Landgravine):

> Lady Landgravine, they call me. Madame the Landgravine. They gift me so they can guarantee Manne's humanity, Law's masculinity. Their passage to Life and Immunity seduces with promises of Security. But for me? What Virtue is left with no body to keep?[22]

Adopting inventive methods has been a crucial part of feminist attempts to disrupt and challenge the discipline's normative foundations. While the creativity and vision that feminists demonstrate in their engagements with international

[18] Charlesworth and Chinkin, above n 2, 62–71. For example, see R Buchanan and R Johnson, 'The "Unforgiven" Sources of International Law: Nation Building, Violence and Gender in the West(ern)' in Buss and Manji, ibid, 131.

[19] H Charlesworth, 'The Hidden Gender of International Law' (2002) 16(1) *Temple International and Comparative Law Journal* 93, 97.

[20] See, for instance, CM Chinkin, 'Women's International Tribunal on Japanese Military Sexual Slavery' (2001) 95(2) *American Journal of International Law* 335; T Dolgopol, 'The Judgment of the Tokyo Women's Tribunal' (2003) 28(5) *Alternative Law Journal* 242; R Sakamoto, 'The Women's International War Crimes Tribunal On Japan's Military Sexual Slavery: A Legal and Feminist Approach to the "Comfort Women" Issue' (2001) 3(1) *New Zealand Journal of Asian Studies* 49.

[21] Buchanan and Johnson, above n 18.

[22] Y Otomo, 'Her Proper Name: A Revisionist Account of International Law' (March 2014) 2(1) *London Review of International Law* 149.

law continue to inspire and encourage us, in practice, feminists' work has arguably struggled to make an impact on mainstream international law and in judicial thinking. International law as a discipline is deeply rooted in patriarchal thought, and it is notoriously dominated by male perspectives. This collection adopts an innovative approach – one that at once engages with and side-lines law's authority – in order to join those efforts that aim to produce a counter-narrative. The weight of international law's norms is such that the simple yet powerful fact that the law might be otherwise can frequently be overlooked. In re-writing key international judgments, we aimed to demonstrate in accessible and meaningful ways possible alternatives to the structural inequalities of traditional international law.

Simply creating a space in international law that is dominated by women is remarkable. Aside from the scholarly dominance of male voices, it is very apparent that women are excluded from international decision-making and, in particular, are frequently being overlooked for appointment to international courts and tribunals. According to recent research by Nienke Grossman:

> [O]n nine of twelve international courts of varied size, subject-matter jurisdiction, and global and regional membership, women made up 20 percent or less of the bench in mid 2015. On many of these courts, the percentage of women on the bench has stayed constant, vacillated, or even declined over time. Women made up a lower percentage of the bench in mid 2015 than in previous years on two-thirds of the courts surveyed.[23]

As Grossman rightly concludes, such disparity brings the legitimacy of international tribunals' decision-making into question.[24] To some extent, this judgment re-writing project touches on the question of what other tangible differences would follow if gender parity on international benches were achieved, and we acknowledge that women's participation is a vital subject for international lawyers to address. Nonetheless, this project is premised on the idea that it is not enough to call for gender parity: in seeking decisions that make a tangible difference and that address injustice, we pinned our hopes on self-consciously adopting feminist approaches to international law and judging as a driving force for meaningful change.[25]

A further motivation for commencing this project was the opportunity it offered to explore the question of how far (international) law is amenable to feminist ends.[26] From Carol Smart's caution that 'law is so deaf to core concerns of

[23] N Grossman, 'Achieving Sex-Representative International Court Benches' (January 2016) 110(1) *The American Journal of International Law* 82–95, 82. See also the work of GQUAL Campaign for Gender Parity in International Representation: www.gqualcampaign.org.

[24] ibid, at 84.

[25] N Torbisco-Casals, 'Why Fighting Structural Inequalities Requires Institutionalizing Difference: A Response to N Grossman' (2016) 110 *American Journal of International Law Unbound* 92. For an interrogation of what difference feminist judges can make, see R Hunter, 'Can Feminist Judges Make a Difference?' (2008) 15 *International Journal of the Legal Profession* 7.

[26] On governance feminism, see: J Halley, *Split Decisions: How and Why to Take a Break from Feminism* (Princeton NJ, Princeton University Press, 2006); J Halley et al, *Governance Feminism: An Introduction* (Minneapolis MN, University of Minnesota Press, 2018).

feminism that feminists should be extremely cautious of how and whether they resort to law',[27] feminists have not been uncritical of law's potential to bring about radical change. Smart's specific concern is that 'in accepting law's terms in order to challenge law, feminism always concedes too much'.[28] As coordinators of a project that places formal legal process at its centre, we were alive to these concerns yet persisted in the hope that feminist theory and methodology could offer alternative perspectives that illuminate pathways to doing law differently.

III. Designing the Project

As stated above, the aim of the project in straightforward terms was to take the feminist re-writing methodology and apply it to the decisions of international tribunals. Feminist judgment projects, as Hunter has written, provide an important platform for scholars and others to come together and challenge legal doctrine though the process of 'telling the story differently' and highlighting law's silences through the use of contextual materials.[29] In the words of the coordinators of the English/Welsh law project: 'The [project] challenges the notion that judgment-writing is or ought to be an expertise confined to judges, and seeks to develop the practice of writing judgments as a form of critical scholarship.'[30]

In many respects, the value and innovation of this current collection lies in its replication of the feminist judging re-writing methodology and applying it in a novel (international law) context. However, it goes without saying that each jurisdiction presents its own questions and challenges for feminists; consequently, the FIJP took a unique form.

Beyond the innovation of its jurisdictional context, the current project contributes to the development of the feminist judgment re-writing methodology in two specific respects. The first contribution of our project to the judgment-writing methodology is the way in which participants have been encouraged to adopt a reflective stance. The format of other (domestic law) projects has been to include a commentary written by someone other than the author of the judgment. In this collection, participants were asked to reflect and write on their experience of the judgment-writing process and the project itself. The aim of specifically encouraging reflective practice in this project was to disrupt the apparent finality of the judgment-writing process: reflective practice suggests a continual process of learning, un-learning and change.[31] In the words of Brooke Ackerly and Jacqui True: 'Feminist theory has made empirical work particularly challenging because

[27] C Smart, *Feminism and the Power of Law* (London, Routledge, 1989) 2.

[28] ibid at 5.

[29] R Hunter, 'An Account of Feminist Judging' in Hunter, McGlynn and Rackley, above n 4, 35–40.

[30] R Hunter, C McGlynn and E Rackley, 'Feminist Judgments: An Introduction' in Hunter, McGlynn and Rackley, above n 4, 5.

[31] M Ortlipp, 'Keeping and Using Reflective Journals in the Qualitative Research Process' (2008) 13(4) *The Qualitative Report* 695.

feminist theories reveal the politics in every aspect of the research process. Feminist theories commit feminist researchers to exploring absences, silence, difference, oppression and the power of epistemology.'[32]

Consequently, they argue, the '*feminist research ethic* is a commitment to inquiry about how we inquire'.[33] Reflection and reflexivity can also reveal the ways in which power – including our own situatedness – shapes the research process and knowledge formation (and, in this case, judgment-writing), which opens up the possibility of mitigating its abuse. In this context, it can therefore help to underline the value-laden nature of legal judgment-writing. In this collection, participants' reflections form the final section of their chapters and provide insight into the judgment-writing process.

Secondly, this project adds to the judgment-writing methodology by foregrounding a collaborative approach. Whereas earlier projects have generally adopted an individual approach to judgment-writing in which the feminist judgment acts as a separate and additional voice that is 'added' to the original judgment, the international project foregrounded a collaborative methodology. As all of the feminist judgments to date have emerged from common law jurisdictions, the blueprint they provided us with required some re-thinking when applied outside of that legal context. Tribunals such as the European Court of Human Rights typically issue one joint judgment, while leaving open the possibility of individual judges delivering separate or dissenting judgments in their own name.[34] Others, such as the Court of Justice of the European Union, leave no scope at all in their procedures for delivering individual judgments. When embarking on this project, our perspective was therefore somewhat different from those that preceded us: collectively writing a single judgment, which effectively stands in place of the original judgment, seemed to be an obvious approach to take.

With the exception of two separate decisions written by individual judges (*Burden v the United Kingdom* and *Prosecutor v Radovan Karadžić*), the judgments in this collection were written by chambers composed of two to four judges. We anticipated that working in this way would enable participants to experience more closely the 'real-world' nature of international judgment writing, where judgments are generally written in a collective voice and the views of individual judges are not identified. In their contributions, several participants reflect on the nature of delivering judgment and some examine its (in)compatibility with feminist methodology. The very nature of judgment-writing appeared to set us on a quest for a 'single truthful narrative' that sat uncomfortably with many participants. In all cases where a judgment was written jointly, our participants, bringing to the chamber their own feminist views, were faced with the compromises inherent in

[32] B Ackerly and J True, 'Reflexivity in Practice: Power and Ethics in Feminist Research' (Dec 2008) 10(4) *International Studies Review* 693, 694.

[33] ibid, 695.

[34] For a discussion of the significance of separate judgments, see R White and I Boussiakou, 'Separate Opinions in the European Court of Human Rights' (2009) 9(1) *Human Rights Law Review* 37–60.

the process of their individual voices becoming subsumed into a group output. Each met this challenge in different ways. Chambers' reflections on the judgment-writing process show that for several of our groups the answer was to reveal more overtly the contingent nature of their decisions and to face head-on the politics informing them. For some, a degree of 'incoherence' was viewed as a feminist tool that disrupted the 'rationality' and 'neutrality' of typical judgment-writing that conceals the choices made and the politics at work in reaching those decisions. In the words of Hilary Charlesworth, 'Feminist methods emphasize conversation and dialogue rather than the production of a single, triumphant truth'.[35] Working collaboratively was also intended as a strategic act of political unity that we hoped might offer an alternative to placing emphasis on, and rewarding of, isolated individual work that characterises our experiences of academia. We further hoped that working together closely in this way might lay foundations for future collaborations among feminists working in international law, whose geographical spread and disciplinary specialisms, in our experience, makes forging professional partnerships and networks particularly challenging.

Participants in the project have interests in a number of different areas of international law, and include established scholars, PhD students, and some activists. The nature of this project meant that, while 41 people contributed fully to the judgment-writing, participation was much wider than our list of authors suggests: more academics, lawyers and judges than we can mention individually contributed in various ways to the project. We would make two observations about this. Firstly, it was immediately apparent to us that these projects are unique in so far as their capacity to capture people's imaginations and inspire their passion. Secondly, this project brought to the fore questions about the feasibility of treating academic authorship as a form of ownership over knowledge that has been gained in isolation. As Lisa Ede and Andrea Lunsford have commented (and a point that emerged in many of the conversations that took place in the duration of this project), 'success in the academy depends largely on having one's work recognized as an individual accomplishment'.[36] We certainly did not set out with the view that collaboration is an *essential* methodological tool: intersectional feminism has shown the importance of being attuned to individual voices and sensitive to difference, particularly where those voices are marginalised and silenced.[37] What we hoped for in this project was a reflective process in which those dynamics were exposed and reflected on as the group worked towards a decision that was

[35] H Charlesworth, 'Feminist Methods in International Law' (2004) 36 *Studies in Transnational Legal Policy* 159, 159.

[36] L Ede and A Lunsford, 'Collaboration and Concepts of Authorship' (2001) 116(2) *PMLA* 354–69, 357.

[37] For a discussion, see, for instance: R Kapur, 'The Tragedy of Victimization Rhetoric: Resurrecting the "Native" Subject in International Post-Colonial Feminist Legal Politics' (2002) 15 *Harvard Human Rights Journal* 1; J Bond, 'International Intersectionality: A Theoretical and Pragmatic Exploration of Women's International Human Rights Violations' (2003) 52 *Emory Law Law Journal* 71.

composed in a single voice. This of course opened up questions about how this hope could be reconciled with the imperatives and norms of establishing academic authorship.

The practical challenges of working collaboratively were considerable: we now reflect wryly on Ede and Lunsford's remark that, 'the seemingly simple paperwork requirements for a large collaborative project can daunt the most enthusiastic group member'.[38] While we started this project with our eyes open to the obstacles we faced, we were certainly not completely successful in overcoming the practical challenges of collaboration. The project undoubtedly took longer than we anticipated and, unfortunately, some participants (particularly NGO workers) were unable to see the judgment-writing process through to completion. In terms of the steps we took to mitigate these issues, we were keenly aware of how important it was to ensure that participants were clear about what was expected of them; as such, all chambers were assigned a President who was the main point of contact for us and was tasked with ensuring that the collaboration was as successful and productive as possible. In the event that not all participants agreed on (all) points of law raised in the judgment, a separate or dissenting judgment (where allowed by the rules of the relevant court) was permitted. In the end, only one chamber actually took advantage of this option (Judge Merris Amos in *Ruusunen v Finland*). Interestingly, another chamber (*Leyla Şahin v Turkey*) took it upon themselves to invent an additional member of their chamber (Judge Dost Düşman Ayırt Etmek) who acted as foil and devil's advocate in his dissenting judgment.

Effectively co-ordinating the number and geographical spread of participants was a considerable challenge. Chambers were encouraged to make good use of available technology for sharing files and group discussions. Participants were predominantly based in European countries (and mainly the UK), although the project also included participants based in North America. Following an open planning meeting in Leicester, the project began with a one-day introductory workshop that was attended by all participants, a judge of the International Criminal Court and coordinators of the English/Welsh feminist judgments project. Two further two-day workshops followed, during which time was allocated to presenting and providing feedback on each judgment individually. All meetings and workshops were held in London for reasons of (relative) accessibility for the group of (mostly European) participants involved. Experts were invited to attend workshops as discussants on individual judgments, which gave participants the opportunity to further interrogate and reflect upon their judgments. For a project that aimed to open up international law to alternative perspectives and silenced voices, recognising that it is Euro-centric is an important point of reflection. Some of this can be explained by our involvement in European scholarly networks and by our need to ensure that participants could meet face-to-face. But nonetheless, it was incumbent upon us to make greater efforts to offer a different account of

[38] Above n 36, 363.

international law from that which emerges from a heavy dominance of Europe and the West over the discipline's normative values and institutions.

IV. The Structure of this Book

Ultimately, 15 international judgments were (re-)written during the project and form this collection (by which short-hand, we also refer to the decisions of international tribunals in the form of Views, Advisory Opinions and Orders). Following this introductory chapter by the editors, Part II focuses on general international law, and includes one re-written judgment of the Permanent Court of International Justice (commonly referred to as the *Lotus Case*, but retitled the *Bozkurt Case* here), one judgment (*Germany v Italy*) and one order of the International Court of Justice (The *Lockerbie Case*) as well as an Advisory Opinion (Reservation to the Genocide Convention). That section concludes with a judgment from the Court of Justice of the European Union (*Gómez-Limón Sánchez-Camacho v Instituto Nacional de la Seguridad Social*). Part III of this book, in which we turn to human rights, includes five rewritten judgments of the European Court of Human Rights (*Goodwin v the United Kingdom*; *Leyla Şahin v Turkey*; *Opuz v Turkey*; *A, B and C v Ireland*; *Ruusunen v Finland*) and a further individual separate judgment from that Court (*Burden v the United Kingdom*). Part III ends with the Views of the Committee on the Elimination of Discrimination against Women adopted in *Kell v Canada* re-written. The subsequent Part of this book contains a judgment from the Special Court for Sierra Leone (*AFRC Trial Judgment*); another from the International Criminal Court (*The Prosecutor v Lubanga Dyilo*); and ends with a separate opinion in a case from the International Criminal Tribunal for the former Yugoslavia (*Prosecutor v Radovan Karadžić*). The concluding chapter of this collection is written by Hilary Charlesworth, who reflects on the role of judgment re-writing as a form of prefigurative politics.

The judgments in this collection were primarily chosen from those proposed by people responding to our call for participants and were selected to reflect the diversity and range of international law, although of course we could not hope to capture its full breadth. Our hope is that the possibilities that the re-writing methodology offers for critical engagement with international law are sufficiently indicated by this collection to inspire future projects that focus in greater depth on specific tribunals and specific areas of international law.

Each of the judgment chapters comprises three main parts. These chapters begin with an Authors' Note that introduces the key aims and distinguishing features of the re-written judgment. As there is not a separate commentary on the judgments written by someone other than the judgment writer(s) – which, as mentioned above, has been the usual practice with other projects – the Authors' Notes aim to make the re-written judgments accessible. To this end, they place the judgment in its legal context, outline the relevant facts/background to the judgment, and address the legal and social responses to, and consequences of, the original judgment. Finally, these Notes explain the aims of the re-written judgment and the contribution it makes to the feminist reimagining of international law.

The Authors' Note is followed by the judgment itself. In several instances, chambers were not able to re-write the entire original judgment, and were certainly not expected to do so. Many chambers therefore agreed upon the relevant part of the judgment to be re-written and have focused their attention accordingly. Re-written feminist judgments are not bound by strict rules. However, because in this project we wanted to demonstrate feminist alternatives in a concrete and meaningful way, a basic rule for our chambers was that the judgment they wrote must be one that *could* have been one written by the relevant tribunal at the time. The primary consequence of this was that chambers' judgments could only refer to material available at the time the original judgment in question was written: for many, this was a considerable frustration and limitation. The process was not intended to act as an appeal of the original decisions, and chambers were therefore not bound by the points of law decided in the original decisions. Inevitably, however, chambers faced frustrating evidential gaps when trying to make novel points but drawing primarily on the facts and arguments from the original judgments. As long as the re-written judgment *could* have been produced by the specific tribunal, chambers were free to respond to such gaps in a creative way. They were also free to play creatively with the judgment-writing style and conventions of their tribunals, as long as they paid deference to the relevant rules of procedure. Writing a judgment is, of course, a very different discipline to writing an academic paper, where an author's theoretical commitments will be laid bare and opened up for examination. Nonetheless, the feminist judgments are at times highly political in tone. As editors, we celebrated this and did not ask participants to strive for 'objectivity' or 'neutrality'. In the words of Hunter, 'Fairness, independence and impartiality do not – indeed cannot – require the judge to become a blank slate upon which the evidence and arguments in each case are written afresh.'[39]

Finally, in terms of chapter structure, a Reflection follows each judgment that pools the thoughts of chamber members on the judgment-writing process and creates a record of their experiences of the project and its methodology. As we mentioned previously, the reflective writing is one element that sets *Feminist Judgments in International Law* apart from other judgment re-writing projects, and one we ultimately found to be a revealing and useful part of the methodology. The Reflections also provide a space for participants to discuss their experiences of what it was like to re-write a judgment from a feminist perspective. As Hilary Charlesworth notes in her concluding chapter, these Reflections – rife as they are with emotional language, contradictions, conflict and uncertainties – act to destabilise the authoritative voice in which the judgments have typically been re-written.

[39] Hunter, above n 29, 31.

They make an important contribution to revealing the contingent nature of international decision-making and the challenges of trying to use international law as a feminist tool to bring about meaningful change.

V. The Judgments

This collection includes judgments that span a period of time from 1927 to 2012. While some of the later judgments raise issues that are particular to women, several contributions address general questions of international law, the gendered dimension of which are not always immediately apparent. The judgments in this collection therefore serve to demonstrate the relevance of feminism to a wide range of international law subjects and questions. The judgments in Part II in particular bring a fresh approach to normative questions. They demonstrate how a feminist chamber may: place greater emphasis on the context of a dispute; highlight the impact of power and politics on international law decision-making; foreground the experiences of individuals; offer a different interpretation of rules and rights; show less deference to the formal sources of international law; and, crucially, challenge the centrality of the State in international law. The collection also turns to the decisions of human rights tribunals. The distinctiveness of much feminist scholarship of international human rights law lies in, among other things, its challenge to the apparent neutrality and universality of human rights law's normative principles. Feminist method can also reveal 'a distorted picture of pattern of human rights abuses'[40] in which the experience of women is overlooked. While drawing on such insights, the contributors to this collection were not entirely untroubled in their commitment to rights. In practice, most feminists juggle an insider-outsider position, and our contributors in Part III juggle these contradictions and dilemmas in fascinating ways. Part IV, on international criminal law, offers particular insights on the ways in which grave harms done to women and girls, particularly in the context of conflict, are marginalised.

A. General International Law

The judgment chapters begin with a rewriting of the *Bozkurt Case* (*France v Turkey*, aka the *Lotus Case*). Dating from 1927, this judgment of the Permanent Court of International Justice is the oldest in the collection and is often one of the first cases read by students when learning about State sovereignty as a fundamental principle of the international legal system. The chamber in this collection re-imagines the

[40] A Byrnes, 'Women, Feminism and International Human Rights Law – Methodological Myopia, Fundamental Flaws or Meaningful Marginalisation: Some Current Issues' (1988–89) *Australian Yearbook of International Law* 205, 211.

now infamous *Lotus* principle: that the rules of international law emanate from the free will of States. In challenging this principle, the chamber exposes the gendered nature of (Western) sovereignty and the gendered personification of States. Strikingly, for their judgment, the feminist chamber decided to adopt the name of the Turkish vessel, 'the Bozkurt', that had collided with the French vessel, 'the SS Lotus', thereby directing us to think about the way in which power structures operate in international decision-making. The re-written judgment also places the case in historical context and opens up questions about the rights of women that were not posed by the original tribunal. In finding that Turkey's exercise of jurisdiction did not violate international law, the 'Bozkurt Principle' de-centres State sovereignty and establishes international co-operation as a hallmark of international society.

The de-centring of State sovereignty continues in chapter three, which offers a feminist rewriting of the *Reservations to the Genocide Convention* advisory opinion of the International Court of Justice (ICJ). The original opinion dates from 1951, and was the first international decision to address the legal effect of reservations to multilateral treaties. The ICJ in its opinion established the 'object and purpose' test for determining the validity of reservations, a test that came to be included in the Vienna Convention on the Law of Treaties 1969. The original advisory opinion places State consent at the heart of treaty law. The feminist chamber puts forward an alternative normative vision, identifying a different, concrete means for determining the validity of reservations that does not rest on State approval. The de-centring of States is a priority of much feminist engagement with international law, challenging the assumption that States are unbiased and will, for instance, protect human rights and promote humanitarian values. The re-written advisory opinion recommends specific mechanisms for determining the validity of reservations, recognising that those mechanisms will be imperfect, but arguing that they will nonetheless offer better oversight of States' reservations. The chamber was clear that the existing system, that largely relies on State-monitoring of reservations, is insufficiently rigorous, particularly in human rights and humanitarian contexts, and that their proposed alternative would lead to greater State accountability.

At the heart of chapter four is a forensic examination of the allocation of power within the international system. *Libyan Arab Jamahiriya v Unites States of America* (aka the *Lockerbie* case), concerns an ICJ order for provisional measures sought by Libya in order to prevent the United States from applying economic sanctions in retaliation for the so-called harbouring of terrorists responsible for the bombing of Pan Am flight 103 that had exploded over Lockerbie, Scotland in 1992. In seeking to add pressure on Libya to extradite the suspects, the United States, with the support of the United Kingdom and France, had succeeded in getting economic sanctions against Libya authorised by the Security Council. Libya's challenge to the lawfulness of those sanctions raised a crucial question about whether the Court has jurisdiction to review a binding decision of the Security Council. In its original decision, the ICJ denied Libya's request. In its re-written order, the feminist chamber grants Libya's request and stakes a claim for the international rule of law by calling for a more activist ICJ with jurisdiction to review Security Council

Resolutions, stipulating that the Security Council's powers cannot be unrestricted. In reaching its decision, the chamber adopts an ethical position that foregrounds the victims of atrocities and challenges the exercise of state power without accountability. Further, the feminist chamber calls attention to the fact that the situation arose from the United States seeking to use its position as a permanent member of the Security Council in order to effectively circumvent their legal obligations.

Chapter five addresses the customary law governing State immunities. In *Germany v Italy*, the question to be answered was how far State immunities extend in civil suits for human rights violations before national courts. Italian courts had granted compensation to Italians who had been forcibly deported from their homes during World War II and suffered from crimes such as forced labour. The compensation awarded included the seizure of German State property; in response, Germany instigated a case against Italy before the ICJ, alleging that the German State's immunity should have shielded it from these claims before national courts. The ICJ in its original decision agreed that the Italian courts should have recognised German immunity and should not have allowed civil claims to be brought. The re-written judgment puts the case in historical context and places at its centre the rights of the victims who had claimed compensation, highlighting their suffering as opposed to simply reaffirming a State-centred approach to international law. As a result of their feminist analysis, in which close attention is paid to power dynamics and hierarchies, the chamber did not recognise Germany's immunity from these human rights claims.

The section ends with a decision of a regional court, the Court of Justice of the Justice of the European Union (CJEU). *Gómez-Limón Sánchez-Camacho v Instituto Nacional De La Seguridad Social (INSS)* is a case brought by a Spanish national who had reduced her working hours in order to care for her child, and who, while taking advantage of parental leave provisions, developed a permanent disability that prevented her from undertaking paid work. The calculation of her invalidity pension was based on the reduced hours she worked while taking parental leave instead of being calculated on the full-time hours that she ordinarily worked. This case, then, has a clear gender dimension at its core, raising the specific question of whether the calculation of Ms Gómez-Limón's pension constituted direct or indirect gender/sex discrimination contrary to EU law. In its original judgment, the CJEU adopted an analytically selective view of discrimination and found that the reduced calculation of the invalidity pension was not unlawful; conversely, however, the re-written judgment adopts an approach, informed by an intersectional understanding of discrimination, that departs from the equal treatment model. The feminist chamber achieves this different outcome by confronting the reality that more women take parental leave in the form of reduced working hours in order to care for children than men and are consequently more likely to have reduced pension contributions in the circumstances of this case. The feminist chamber acknowledges the social imbalances and stereotypes that underpin the facts in this judgment and, in adopting its approach to discrimination, argues that the laws in question are specifically aimed to tackle these.

B. Human Rights

Chapter seven, *Christine Goodwin v the United Kingdom*, touches on intimate questions concerning the construction of gender in international law. Christine Goodwin, a trans woman, sought legal recognition of her lived gender before the European Court of Human Rights (ECtHR). The original judgment, which recognised that Ms Goodwin's Article 8 (right to private life) and 12 (right to marry) rights under the European Convention on Human Rights (ECHR) had been violated, was considered a progressive victory for trans rights; however, the feminist chamber's rewriting of the judgment shows that the original judgment served to reinforce a binary understanding of gender and was silent on a number of important issues. Echoing earlier chapters, a key method adopted by the feminist chamber was to pay greater attention to the lived experiences of Christine Goodwin and the marginalisation, challenges and humiliations she endured because of the incongruence between her lived and legal gender. Significantly, the rewritten judgment frames the obligation on the State as a negative one; that is, the State must refrain from imposing a gender on an individual that she does not identify with. Placing her suffering at the heart of its reasoning, the feminist judgment also takes Convention jurisprudence into new territory by finding that the State violated Ms Goodwin's right to be free from inhuman and degrading treatment.

Chapter eight, *Leyla Şahin v Turkey*, foregrounds autonomy in its reasoning. Leyla Şahin, a student, challenged the ban on wearing the Islamic headscarf in Turkish universities on the basis that it interfered with her right to freedom of religion and right to education under the ECHR. In its original judgment, the ECtHR found no violation, arguing that the prohibition was valid as a means of preserving the secular, democratic State. The re-written judgment defines the right to a private life as a right to autonomy, identity and integrity. The feminist chamber argues that the restriction penalises women and fails to take women's interests seriously; its judgment asserts women's freedom to make decisions on religious clothing as a matter of personal autonomy. A fictitious dissenting judge joins this chamber and operates to voice concerns that the wearing of headscarves symbolises the subordination of women. The Majority in the feminist chamber rejected the view that women need protection and a State rule to set them free, instead relying on arguments about women's individual freedom of choice.

Chapter nine imagines a further separate but concurring opinion in *Burden v the United Kingdom*, another case from the ECtHR that raises questions about how law privileges certain relationships. The Burden sisters, who had lived together all their lives without partners or children, wanted the inheritance tax exemptions enjoyed by married spouses or civil partners to be extended to them as co-habiting siblings. The sisters claimed they were being discriminated against with respect to the enjoyment of their property rights under the ECHR, in so far as they were denied a benefit available to heterosexual and homosexual spouses and partners. The Chamber and Grand Chamber rejected their application. The ECtHR found that the inheritance tax exemptions aimed to promote stable family life and that the UK had consequently not exceeded its margin of appreciation. The original Grand Chamber judgment found that sibling relationships were qualitatively different from that of spouses and civil partners. The re-written separate opinion in this collection departs from the original judgment in the way it views the special legal status of spouses and civil partners; the feminist judgment finds that the privileging of romantic intimate relationships over other relationships of care amounts to unlawful discrimination. Nonetheless, the re-written judgment, taking into account the relative wealth of the Burden sisters, argues that the State was within its margin of appreciation to not grant them exemption from inheritance tax in this case.

The collection next turns to a case in which the ECtHR was faced with facts arising from a situation of domestic violence, *Opuz v Turkey*. Nahide Opuz suffered abuse throughout her marriage and, after repeated attempts to gain help and assistance for the police and other authorities, she was stabbed and run over by her ex-husband and her mother was fatally shot by him. After being convicted of the murder, he was released pending appeal. The abuse had taken place over the course of some time, and the authorities largely treated it as a private matter. The original judgment, as the feminist chamber acknowledges, was ground-breaking in so far as it brought domestic violence within the ambit of the ECHR. However, in an effort to transcend the individualism of the human rights judgments, the re-written judgment in chapter ten highlights the structural causes of domestic violence, which the feminist chamber argues are rooted in patriarchal social structures that are not exclusive to 'other' cultures. As such, domestic violence is treated by the feminist court as a prevalent, global phenomenon.

The *A, B and C v Ireland* case from the ECtHR, the subject of chapter eleven, was brought by three women who had been unable to obtain the abortions they sought, respectively, for personal, financial or medical reasons and had been required to travel to the UK for the procedure. The applicants claimed that (the then) Irish law governing abortions, which was extremely restrictive in European terms in light of the constitutional protection of the right to life of the unborn, violated a number of their Convention rights. The original court dismissed the women's claims with the exception of the Article 8 (right to private life) claim of applicant 'C', who had sought an abortion on medical grounds. The first striking aspect of the re-written judgment in this collection lies in its approach to interpretation; the suffering and the discrimination the women experienced is placed at the centre of the chamber's decision-making. The feminist chamber found the harm caused to the women by the restrictive laws on abortion in Ireland could not be ignored, and that the gendered nature of the discrimination they suffered needed to be exposed. The margin of appreciation, a tool of interpretation that can operate to restrict the court's review of national legislation, is set aside in the rewritten judgment: gender discrimination is deemed a major goal of the Convention and Irish law deemed to exceed the State's margin of appreciation.

The final case in this collection from the ECtHR is *Ruusunen v Finland*. Susan Ruusunen wrote a book about her romantic relationship with the then

Prime Minister of Finland, Matti Vanhanen. He was aware that the book was being written and, indeed, consented to be photographed for its cover. Susan Ruusunen was nonetheless convicted of the dissemination of information violating personal privacy and fined. She made an application to the ECtHR claiming that Finland had violated her right to freedom of expression. The original court in its judgment found that Finland had a certain margin of appreciation with respect to placing limitations on the right to free speech, and concluded that the interference with Ms Ruusunen's freedom of speech in this case pursued a legitimate aim and was proportionate. The re-written judgment grants Finland a narrower margin of appreciation. It further criticises the gender bias that operated against Ms Ruusunen in the media and government circles, arguing strongly for her right to tell her story of a romantic relationship and not to be silenced and stereotyped as a gold-digger. A separate opinion to the feminist judgment emphasises the particular difficulties faced by single parents on limited incomes when facing criminal charges.

The human rights section of this collection ends with a decision from the Committee on the Elimination of Discrimination against Women, *Kell v Canada*. Cecilia Kell, an indigenous woman living in northern Canada, had secured housing under a scheme for indigenous people. Kell suffered serious abuse from her common law partner and had to leave her home for her safety; her partner, in response, had the locks changed and managed to place the lease of Kell's home in his name alone, abusing his position on the housing board. Kell attempted to regain access to her home through numerous and lengthy domestic legal challenges, but was unsuccessful in her efforts. In many respects, the target of the rewritten decision is the law itself. Cecilia Kell endured years of fruitless legal battles in her efforts to retain her property. In their Views, the feminist chamber argues that her 'intersectional marginality' served to make her invisible to the Canadian legal system; she was a single parent, an indigenous woman and a domestic abuse survivor. Although the original Committee found that Canada had violated certain articles of the Convention, the re-written Views foreground the blind spots of legal process in its analysis and adopts an intersectional approach that highlight in particular the role that Ms Kell's indigeneity played in her experience of discrimination and marginalisation.

C. International Criminal Law

The *AFRC* Trial Judgment, formally known as the *Prosecutor v Brima, Kamara and Kanu*, rewritten in chapter fourteen, emanates from the Special Court for Sierra Leone. The defendants were high-ranking members in the Armed Forces Revolutionary Council, charged with 14 counts of various war crimes and crime against humanity, including acts of sexual violence and the use/recruitment of child soldiers. All three men were found guilty of a number of crimes and sentenced to between 45 and 50 years. While the judgment arguably raised awareness of sexual crimes, sexual slavery and forced marriage, it failed to convict the defendants on those counts. The re-written judgment in this collection consequently addresses crucial gaps in the original judgment concerning gender-based crimes. The first important step the feminist chamber takes is to expand the definition of rape in international criminal law. By explicitly recognising that women can be perpetrators of crimes committed during conflict and that men can be victims of sexual crimes, their account disrupts the usual gendered narratives of conflict. The feminist judgment next turns to refining the contours of forced marriage, framing it as a form of sexual slavery. In sum, the chamber presents a more complex account of women's and girls' experiences during conflict that are not confined to victimhood. The re-written judgment engages with the silences in the original judgment and paints a more complex vision of child soldiering that is built on the actual experience of those involved.

Thomas Lubanga Dyilo, whose trial is the subject of chapter fifteen, has the distinction of being the first person to be convicted by the International Criminal Court. His crimes were part of the conflict in the Democratic Republic of the Congo, in which context Lubanga led a large group of rebels during the Ituri conflict. His charges largely related to the conscription and enlisting of child soldiers under the age of 15 as part of the rebel group. He was convicted of those war crimes charges in 2009. The re-written judgment clarifies the relationship between the crimes of conscription and enlistment, drawing on feminist insights on the notion of consent. It also highlights the silences of the original judgment in terms of the experiences of the girl child, revisiting what it means to 'actively participate in hostilities'. Finally, it foregrounds the particular, gendered experiences of sexual violence that were marginalised in the original judgment. The re-written judgment contextualises the experiences of girl and boy child soldiers and emerges with a more gender-sensitive approach to the questions raised.

The final judgment in this collection is *Prosecutor v Radovan Karadžić*, a judgment of the International Criminal Tribunal for the former Yugoslavia. Karadžić was a political leader and President of Republika Srpska during the conflict in former Yugoslavia in the 1990s. He was convicted by the Trial Chamber of war crimes, crimes against humanity and genocide, namely the genocide committed in Srebrenica during the Bosnian war. However, he was acquitted of genocide in the Municipalities of Bosnia Herzegovina because the court found that the genocidal intent had not been proven. In this partly dissenting opinion, the judge carefully examines the evidence relating to the sexual violence perpetrated in the Municipalities. At the time of writing, both parties had filed notices of appeal. The feminist opinion considers the pattern of evidence of sexual violence, recognising its communicative value as part of its reasoning with regard to establishing genocidal intent. In asking 'the woman question', the dissenting opinion challenges the silences in the Majority judgment on sexual crimes in the Municipalities and recognises the profound nature of the resulting harm. The opinion argues that the legal reasoning on intent to commit genocide was wrongly interpreted by the Majority, and the nature of the harm done to victims of sexual violence was largely overlooked.

VI. Concluding Thoughts

We hope that this rich and diverse collection of judgments plays a part in continuing the conversation about how feminists can harness the transformative potential of international law, in spite of the challenges that this work presents. We have certainly been inspired and awed by the outcome of the chambers' efforts: the judgments in this collection have, in turn, moved us, made us laugh out loud at times, and they have galvanised us to continue to strive to challenge injustice and entrenched power relations in our various interactions with international law. Ultimately, they demonstrate without ambiguity that international law can be done differently. At times our chambers found international law to be a limited tool when seeking significant reform. The understandable conclusion that might be drawn from this is that law and legal method alone is unlikely to be sufficient to meet feminist ends; whilst this is undoubtedly an important observation, we have also observed in this collection the possibilities offered by creatively harnessing law. In short, international law – whilst clearly not a panacea for injustice, especially in its traditional guise – perhaps inhabits space of greater potential than feminist and critical thinkers, worn down by its apparent intransigence, might usually concede. The collaborative method we adopted in *Feminist Judgments in International Law* has contributed to the forging of a network of supportive friendships that are, we have come to believe, an essential part of feminist survival and success. The question of what wider impact this collection will have is part of the next chapter in this project's unfolding story.

We further hope that this project will inspire on-going conversations about the ways in which feminist judgment projects can continue to develop and to adapt to different jurisdictions and contexts. Feminists' relationship with law has often been an ambivalent one, and feminist judgments have proven a useful way to both engage with law and to reject law's values and practices that are damaging to feminist ends. We have found the methodology to be a remarkable tool for creating dynamic, creative and passionate exchanges between feminists working in, and with, law; we have little doubt that they will continue to be an important part of feminists' tool kits. Participants in these projects are forced to think about their feminism in practical ways, and to demonstrate the utility of that which is usually thought about in abstract terms. This is a powerful method and incentive, and we experienced it as having something of an energising effect on participants. On a personal level, we have been moved by the commitment and camaraderie of the women and men who came together to share their vision of how international law might do better. The challenges are undoubtedly significant, but the commitment we have witnessed from so many people during this project, on the road to the completion of *Feminist Judgments in International Law*, makes overcoming those challenges seem more possible.

PART II

General International Law

Permanent Court of International Justice

2

Bozkurt Case,[1] aka the *Lotus Case* (*France v Turkey*): Ships that Go Bump in the Night

CHRISTINE CHINKIN, GINA HEATHCOTE,
EMILY JONES AND HENRY JONES

Authors' Note

The *Lotus Case* was decided in 1927 by the Permanent Court of International Justice (PCIJ), the predecessor to the International Court of Justice (ICJ). The PCIJ held its inaugural sitting in 1922 and had issued five judgments prior to the *Lotus Case*.[2] Although seemingly a case about the collision of two ships at sea – the *Bozkurt*,[3] a Turkish collier,[4] and the *SS Lotus*, a French steamer ship – for international lawyers the *Lotus Case* has come to be understood as the statement of 'perhaps the most powerful principle of State sovereignty within international law'[5] through the articulation of the following passage:

> International law governs relations between independent States. The rules of law binding upon States therefore emanate from their own free will as expressed in conventions or by usages generally accepted as expressing principles of law and established in order to regulate the relations between these co-existing independent communities with a view to the achievement of common aims.[6]

[1] Whilst this case is famously known as the *Lotus Case* within the 'West', in Turkey, the case of the *Bozkurt* was, at least at the time, very famous under this name. The Minister of Justice of Turkey at the time, Mahmout Esat Bey, in fact became subsequently so popular for winning this case that he later added the name Bozkurt to his own.

[2] The PCIJ had also issued 13 Advisory Opinions.

[3] We use the spelling 'Bozkurt' rather than as it appears in the judgment 'Boz-Kourt', in line with the way Turkish speakers would spell the word in English. See, eg: U Özsu, 'De-territorializing and Re-territorializing Lotus: Sovereignty and Systematicity as Dialectical Nation-Building in Early Republican Turkey' (2009) 22 *Leiden Journal of International Law* 29.

[4] A collier is a bulk cargo ship designed to carry coal.

[5] S Mendlovitz and M Daton, 'Judge Weeramantry's Grotian Quest' (1997) 7 *Transnational Law and Contemporary Problems* 401, 406.

[6] *SS 'Lotus' Case (France v Turkey)* PCIJ 1927 Series A No 10 Sept 7th, 18.

In re-writing the *Lotus Case* as a feminist judgment we have worked to re-imagine the *Lotus* principle through engagement with a number of issues from a feminist perspective and through drawing on documents available at the time of the judgment.[7] As a feminist chamber, we also responded in the re-written judgment to a sense of dissatisfaction with the manner in which the facts of the case were reduced and the judgments[8] presented in the original. Accordingly, the feminist judgment raises questions about the reporting of facts to the Court and the manner in which the history of Turkish-French relations, with the various power relations and inequalities embedded in that history, were rendered irrelevant. Primarily, however, the feminist judgment re-imagines how sovereignty might be perceived, with the permissive model of international State sovereignty, as encapsulated in the *Lotus* case, giving way to a preference for co-operation and peaceful measures.

The original *Lotus* judgment marked the first time the Permanent Court was required to deal with a general matter of international law rather than to respond to an issue within a specific treaty regime. The actual outcome with respect to the jurisdiction of States relating to collisions of vessels on the high seas has since been superseded and clarified through the adoption of the 1958 Convention on the High Seas.[9] We do not cover this aspect of the case in the feminist judgment. The case has come to be understood as central to understanding the nature of the international legal system as defined by the sovereign equality of its primary members, States. The International Court of Justice has continued to rely on the *Lotus* judgment in contemporary cases, in particular, the *Nuclear Weapons Advisory Opinion.*[10] In drafting the feminist judgment, the authors agreed that a different model of international relations, one inspired by feminist histories and writing, would need to be at the centre of the legal reasoning in developing what we have called '*the Bozkurt Principle: Ships that go bump in the night*'.

The authors found the feminist rewriting of the *Lotus* judgment challenging in that there were no issues that were evidently relevant to women or women's rights. It therefore required us to think more broadly about feminist methodologies and recognition of the gendered assumptions underlying the international legal order

[7] In particular, we draw on the resolutions adopted at the 1915 International Congress of Women at The Hague. See further: F Baetens, 'International Congress of Women (1915)' in R Wolfrum (ed), *Max Planck Encyclopedia of Public International Law* (Oxford, Oxford University Press, 2010). The resolutions are available online at: www.ub.gu.se/kvinndata/portaler/fred/samarbete/pdf/resolutions_1915.pdf.

[8] The judgment is supplemented by six dissenting opinions. See, eg www.icj-cij.org/pcij/serie_A/A_10/30_Lotus_Arret.pdf.

[9] Convention on the High Seas (adopted 29 April 1958, entered into force 30 September 1962) 450 UNTS, art 11; United Nations Convention on the Law of the Sea (adopted 10 December 1982, entered into force 16 November 1994) 1833 UNTS 3 (UNCLOS), art 97. This is notwithstanding specific disputes that have emerged with similar issues before the International Tribunal on the Law of the Sea. See, eg *Dispute Concerning the Enrica Lexia Incident (The Italian Republic v The Republic of India)*, (Provisional Measures, Order of 24 August 2015) ITLOS Case No 24.

[10] *Legality of the Threat or Use of Nuclear Weapons* (Advisory Opinion) 1996 ICJ Rep 226.

of the 1920s and the Court's approach. The key questions the chamber identified from these perspectives were:

- How have both these States been personified (as sovereign subjects but also as gendered subjects) and what is the relevance of this to the case and the structure of international law?
- What is the context (feminist, historical, internal/external, boundaries) in which the case arose, in particular of France and Turkey?
- What were the feminist voices available within the international arena at the time relating to these issues?
- Are there any other relevant issues to consider? For example, the rights of women and minorities?
- What is the outcome based upon this reasoning? What is the content of '*the Bozkurt Principle: Ships that go bump in the night*'?

When considered with these questions in mind, a feminist judgment on the *Lotus* case raises a range of issues about the nature of sovereignty and international society, the socio-cultural context of relations between France and Turkey, and the possibility of incorporating feminist voices into the Court and a newly crafted *Bozkurt* judgment.

We also engage with two preliminary questions in the feminist judgment. The first addresses the facts of the case, which as presented highlighted a range of silences that were of interest to the chamber. The chamber determined that there was space to revisit the facts with a view to identifying the gaps and/or silences, engaging a feminist methodology centred on the politics of the everyday, the role of narratives in excluding women's and feminist voices/versions and the use of States (or ships) as abstract legal subjects that can dislodge the concerns of individuals.[11] To accommodate this view, and write something that still fits the form of a judgment, the structure of the feminist judgment follows that of the *Lotus* judgment. It begins with a discussion of the Special Agreement which Turkey signed acknowledging the jurisdiction of the PCIJ and under which both States agreed the specific question the PCIJ was charged to answer. This is followed by a discussion of the facts of the case, where the silences and question of how these are narrated are raised. In line with the original *Lotus*, we also present a short summary of the submissions made by each party, before exploring the historical relations between the two States before the Court.

The second preliminary question centred on the chamber's desire to dislodge the assumption that Western sovereignty constituted the measure of civilisation. The chamber sought to explore the nexus between feminist methodologies and these larger engagements with power relations. As a first step toward this, the

[11] For a classic, feminist account of the limitations of the objectivity of law, see: PJ Williams, 'On Being the Object of Property' (1988) 14 *Signs* 1, 5.

chamber decided relatively early on to re-name our judgment the *Bozkurt* case, with the principle it established to be known as *the Bozkurt Principle: Ships that go bump in the night*. Not only did this address the locating of the longstanding European and Christian State (France) at the centre of the original judgment (and by inference Turkey at the periphery), renaming the judgment acknowledges the violence enacted on the *Bozkurt* and its passengers and crew, as well as the fact that the case actually centres on events in Turkey, not in France. Unlike the *Lotus Case* which focuses on sovereignty as territorially defined via 'free will', the *Bozkurt Case* establishes the means to create an international legal structure that prioritises the pacific settlement of disputes and co-operation between States. It potentially re-configures sovereignty as dependent in both its internal and external relations. This is reminiscent of the International Congress of Women's resolutions for permanent peace, which preceded the judgment by over a decade, and also focuses on the pacific settlement of disputes and co-operation between States as the foundations of a functioning international order.[12]

In constructing the feminist judgment our desire was to provide a template and guidance on how it might remain temporally relevant (both today and to the 1920s). Accordingly, the texts we relied on were legal instruments, feminist documents and historical papers that were not necessarily developed through women's work, women's writing or women's activity. Nevertheless, the majority of our source texts were authored by women. But it was not the sex of the author that made them relevant, rather the texts' feminist potential and, in most cases, legacy.

Whilst, of course, greater representation of women can make a difference and is often touted as a feminist goal and strategy, it does not necessarily produce feminist outcomes. This may be due to the restraints of the systems and structures established prior to women's entry and participation, or the further privilege that women who are invited to participate often share with existing male counterparts. Importantly for this project one of the central principles of the International Congress of Women (IWC) outcome document was the requirement that women be granted equal political rights. All of the principles articulated by the IWC have a contemporary equivalent in international law,[13] including the requirements of gender equality in the application of political rights; the single exception has been the principle of disarmament where considerable gains have been made with respect to chemical and biological weapons but the implementation of a full disarmament model, as envisaged in 1915, is yet to be fully achieved.

Interestingly, attempts were made in the early institutionalisation of international law to take account of these questions of diversity. The IWC's concern for gender representation (as well as its own blindness with respect to the patronising and devastating effects of colonialism) is seen in some appointments to international institutions at the time.[14] For example, the Permanent Mandates Commission

[12] Above n 7.

[13] ibid.

[14] Although the IWC itself was problematic in terms of the diversity of the participants and the views espoused with regard to colonised States, see Baetens, above n 7.

had a (token?) female member. Madame Anna Bugge-Wicksell was the Swedish representative on the Mandate Commission for the League and was described at the time as 'a well-known Swedish women, wife of a Professor of Stockholm'.[15] However in looking beyond the League records, the chamber found Madame Bugge-Wicksall to be an eminent Norwegian feminist with a history of work in the Women's Suffrage Alliance, writing on women's economic liberation, as well as on health and education reforms in Sweden. Bugge-Wicksell was 'a veteran women's suffrage and peace campaigner who made it her "particular business to care for and speak for" the "helpless" women and children of the mandated territories'.[16] Bugge-Wicksall was succeeded on the Mandate Commission by 'the like-minded Valentine Dannevig … the director of a Norwegian school for girls and one of the founders of the Norwegian branch of the Women's International League for Peace and Freedom'.[17] As feminists connected to the feminist alliances that led suffrage struggles during the period, both of these women would likely also have been aware of the resolutions drafted at the International Congress of Women in 1915 and 1919 and which were a key influence on the drafting of the *Bozkurt* judgment. In contrast to the inclusion of these women, there was no woman judge on either the PCIJ or its successor the ICJ until 1995 when Professor Rosalyn Higgins was elected. We felt this did not preclude a feminist judgment as we were largely interested in the range of feminist ideas that moved in international spaces at the time: in this sense, Madame Bugge-Wicksall and Dannevig are excellent indicators of feminist knowledge traversing a range of transnational spaces and represent the types of accomplished feminist women who might have been nominees to the PCIJ had States considered such nominations to be necessary (or even desirable) during the life of that Court.

It is not necessary to be 'female' to write a feminist judgment, just as not all women judges would necessarily support feminist arguments, or even consider themselves feminists. However, it must be noted that, whilst identity does not necessitate politics, it still plays a role, in particular in establishing the spaces of intersectional privilege. Baetens notes that the principles adopted by the International Congress of Women also reflected race relations at the time, in particular colonial politics in that 'they spoke in rather patronizing terms about the people in the colonies; "protecting the locals" who are not capable of governing their lands themselves'.[18] International feminism in the 1920s took a certain form: it was white, European or American, liberal and often embedded in colonial relations and law-making. It was, however, a recognisable and recognised force of which a Court could potentially take account. For instance, the International Council for Women, the International Congress of Women and the Women's International

[15] DP Myers, 'The Mandate System of the League of Nations' (1921) 96 *The Annals of the American Academy of Political and Social Science* 74, 77.

[16] S Pedersen, *The Guardians: The League of Nations and the Crisis of Empire* (Oxford, Oxford University Press, 2015) 62, quoting from Bugge-Wicksall's correspondence.

[17] ibid.

[18] Baetens, above n 7, para 16.

League for Peace and Freedom, engaged with and challenged the League of Nations and the international community more broadly. Organisations such as the International Abolitionist Federation or the International Women's Suffrage Alliance campaigned for specific women's rights, in these cases the criminalisation of prostitution and the extension of the franchise.[19] This backdrop, despite limitations, did allow us to reason in a way which while still unfamiliar in the ICJ today, never mind in the foundations of international law, reflects the possible.

A further curious attempt at furthering diverse representation during the life of the PCIJ and the League can be seen in the election of Judge Didrik Nyholm to the Court. Nyholm had previously worked as a judge in the Mixed Courts of Egypt at Cairo.[20] To this day, Nyholm remains the only Dane to have served at the PCIJ or its successor. But it is not this minority status or nationality that rendered Nyholm as a favourable member of the Court. Instead, British Foreign Office records stated that, 'having been some years in Egypt, he [Nyholm] would be an adequate representative for the Mussulman'.[21] Thus on this ground he had French and British support and that of Scandinavian nations. His colleague on the PCIJ, the American Judge, John Bassett Moore, wrote that 'Nyholm is openly discontent. He loved his position at Cairo, and gave it up for the present place on the insistence of his Government'.[22] It was later said in the State Department in Washington DC that Nyholm was 'rather pessimistic but not forceful enough to influence the Court'.[23] However, like the women at the International Congress of Women, this attempt at inclusiveness ultimately represents the colonial politics that informed and infiltrated international law at the time (and since).

As authors we felt a need to recognise such limitations and to integrate this backdrop within other contemporary literatures and opinions relating inter alia to race and class so as to situate this feminist judgment within wider feminist concerns. There is therefore a tension that we had to navigate. This judgment is required to be a feminist judgment which could have been written at the time. Throughout the feminist judgment, the chamber also wished (and in line with feminist methods more broadly) to remain sensitive to various power imbalances, not just to gender per se. Intersectionality is a key feminist method and thus as a chamber we tried at least to understand and incorporate within the judgment analyses of race and colonialism as well as gender. We have not only drawn on feminist literature of the time but rather on a broader array of literature, in order

[19] See J Connors, 'NGOs and the Human Rights of Women at the United Nations' in P Willetts (ed), *The Conscience of the World: The Influence of Non-Governmental Organizations in the United Nations System* (Washington DC, Brookings Institution Press, 1996) 147.

[20] These Courts applied a 'mix' of foreign and local law to settle disputes between foreigners of different nationalities or between foreigners and Egyptians.

[21] As quoted in O Spiermann, 'A Permanent Court of International Justice' (2003) 72 *Nordic Journal of International Law* 399, 404.

[22] ibid.

[23] ibid.

to ensure the *Bozkurt* judgment considers context; a necessity in contemporary feminist thinking although less realised in transnational feminist politics and strategies in the earlier twentieth century. In this it contrasts strongly with the *Lotus* judgment. The key difference between the original judgment and our feminist judgment is simply to re-read the foundational principle of sovereignty as being about community rather than formal equality.

JUDGMENT

THE CASE OF THE SS BOZKURT
France v Turkey

Publications of The Permanent Court of International Justice.
SERIES A.-No 70

Judges: Chinkin, Heathcote, E Jones and H Jones

The Court would like to thank its expert witnesses: Louise Arimatsu, Umut Özsu, and the members of Law and Global Justice Durham (Gleider Hernandez, Konstantina Tzouvala, Jane Rooney, Ben Warwick, Verity Adams, Tom Sparks, Ruth Houghton, Maeve O'Rourke)

September 7th, 1927

THE SPECIAL AGREEMENT

By special agreement signed at Geneva on October 12th, 1926, between the Governments of the French and Turkish Republics, and in accordance with the Rules of the Court, the Governments have submitted the question of jurisdiction which has arisen between them following upon the collision which occurred on August 2nd, 1926, between the steamships *Bozkurt* and *Lotus*.

According to the special agreement, the Court was asked to decide the following questions:

(1) Has Turkey, contrary to Article 15 of the Convention of Lausanne, respecting conditions of residence and business and jurisdiction, acted in conflict with the principles of international law – and if so, what principles – by instituting, following the collision on the high seas and upon the arrival of the French steamer at Constantinople – as well as against the captain of the Turkish steamship – joint criminal proceedings in pursuance of Turkish law against M Demons, officer of the watch on board the *Lotus* at the time of the collision, in consequence of the loss of the *Bozkurt* having involved the death of eight Turkish citizens?

(2) Should the reply be in the affirmative, what pecuniary reparation is due to M. Demons, provided, according to the principles of international law, reparation should be made in similar cases?

THE FACTS

The facts are undisputed, in that the case involves a collision on the High Seas between the Turkish collier, the *Bozkurt*, and the French ship, the *SS Lotus*, that occurred just before midnight on 2 August 1926 between five to six nautical miles to the North of Cape Sigri. The *Bozkurt* was cut in two and in sinking eight Turkish nationals died. The exact conditions and identities of these persons have not been submitted to the Court, although it is known that both sailors and passengers perished during the sinking of the *Bozkurt*. The officer of the watch on board the *SS Lotus* was Monsieur Demons, a French citizen. The Captain of the *Bozkurt* was Hassan Bey, a Turkish citizen, who was saved from the wreck with ten other Turkish nationals. The *Lotus* subsequently resumed its course to Constantinople, where it arrived on 3 August, 1926.

Upon arriving in Turkey, both Monsieur Demons and Hassan Bey were arrested pending trial for involuntary manslaughter, following complaints made by the families of the victims.

The case was first heard by the Criminal Court of Stamboul. The two cases were heard jointly and simultaneously, Turkish criminal law treating these offences as being in 'connexité'/'connexity'. This is a concept which links offences that occurred, for example, at the same time and place. According to the Turkish submissions, this principle was taken from the French Code. From the Turkish standpoint, therefore, these two men were to be tried together due to their responsibility arising from a series of interconnected events.

On behalf of Monsieur Demons, it was submitted that the Turkish Courts had no jurisdiction. This was overruled by the Criminal Court of Stamboul. Monsieur Demons was released on bail until the Court's final decision. Monsieur Demons was sentenced to eighty days' imprisonment and a fine. Hassan Bey was sentenced to a slightly more severe penalty.

These are the facts as presented to the Court. This Court believes that, in order to make a fair and reasonable judgment, it is necessary to consider the broader context in which the events occurred.

First, this is not only a case of two ships that go bump in the night. The Court is concerned to expose a series of silences in the facts as they have been presented by the parties to this case. The identities and stories of the victims are missing. As passengers and as crew, the perished will have left behind families and dependents, none of whom have been given voice either before this Court or in Stamboul. What satisfaction is gained for these poor souls, now departed, and their loved ones, through the exercise of power being played out by France in its attempt to halt the processes of justice in Turkey? Would an exercise of jurisdiction by France, separate to the exercise of jurisdiction based on his nationality over the acts of Hassan Bey, have offered any condolence or peace to the women and children likely made destitute by the deaths of their husbands and fathers? Or would it have assuaged the grief of parents who waved their child off on a journey aboard the *Bozkurt* believing they would see their offspring again? The Court wishes to note the lived and real experience of the victims and their families and to address the poverty of an international legal system that cannot see beyond the artificial entity of the State to understand the living human beings who feel its effects.

Second, the facts must be regarded in light of the history of relationships between Turkey and other European powers, including especially France. The capitulations regime that formed the longer history between the two States, as well the (aborted) Treaty of Sèvres, 10 August, 1920 and the arrangements made by the Convention of Lausanne, 24 July, 1923, place Turkey in a position of younger 'brother' to the established European powers. As such, France epitomises an out-dated masculine model of sovereignty, which prioritises economic and colonial power as a mechanism to achieve gains and perpetuate power. This Court is ready to disregard this out-dated model in favour of a contemporary conception of international sovereignty, solidarity and co-operation, as sought by the Covenant of the League of Nations. In configuring international co-operation at the centre of this judgment, and at the centre of international relations, we wish to demonstrate the commitment of the Court to peace and the pacific settlement of disputes, as established in the Hague Conventions of 1899 and 1907 – forerunners to our own establishment – and as the key to the functioning of international society. In this matter the Court has also been particularly inspired by the resolutions adopted by the International Congress of Women at The Hague in 1915 and Zurich in 1919. The resolutions affirm the importance of international co-operation and the place of women in international affairs, in particular in achieving that co-operative approach.

Third, while noting the admirable advances of the recent reforms of the citizenship laws in Turkey, the Court takes particular interest in the legal situation of women and protection of minorities in the two States parties, in line with the recently adopted Minority Treaties. Further, The Hague and Zurich resolutions of 1915 and 1919 find the model of equality for citizens an important international aspiration.

Prior to discussing these matters, the Court will review the submissions from the two States and then reflect on the history of the relationship between the two States before it.

RE-STATEMENT OF FRENCH AND TURKISH SUBMISSIONS

The French Government in its submission asks for judgment, under the Treaty of Lausanne and the general principles of international law, establishing that criminal jurisdiction over a French officer on board a French ship is acknowledged as belonging exclusively to the French Courts. The Turkish Government initially asked the Court to 'give judgment in favour of the jurisdiction of the Turkish Courts'. The French Government's counter-case sets out the conclusions it wishes this Court to reach, and the arguments. These are summarised as follows:

> Whereas the substitution jurisdiction of the Turkish Courts for that of the foreign consular courts in criminal proceedings against foreigners is the outcome of the consent given by the Powers in the Treaty of Lausanne; as this consent, far from having been given as regards criminal proceedings against foreigners for crimes or offences committed abroad, has been definitely refused

> by the Powers and by France in particular; … the Treaty then does not allow Turkish Courts to take cognisance of criminal proceedings directed against a French citizen for crimes committed outside Turkey; Furthermore, whereas, according to international law as established by the practice of civilised nations, … a State is not entitled … to extend the criminal jurisdiction of its Courts to include an offence committed by a foreigner abroad solely in consequence of the fact that one of its nationals has been a victim; Whereas acts performed on the high seas … are amenable only to the jurisdiction of the courts of the State whose flag the vessel flies; As that is a consequence of the principle of the freedom of the seas …; As, according to existing law, the nationality of the victim is not sufficient ground to override this rule …; Whereas there are special reasons why the application of this rule should be maintained in collision cases, where the culpability of the acts must be judged against the national regulations which apply on board the ship;

The Turkish Government, in its counter-case added a short statement, summarised as follows:

> The Treaty, as regards the jurisdiction of the Turkish Courts, refers simply to the principles of international law; the relevant part of the Turkish Penal Code, taken as it is word for word from the Italian Penal Code, is not contrary to the principles of international law; Vessels on the high seas form part of the territory of the nation whose flag they fly, and in this case the place where the offence took place, where the effects were felt, was the SS *Bozkurt* flying the Turkish flag, so Turkey's jurisdiction is as clear as if the case had occurred on her territory; The *Bozkurt* – *Lotus* case being a case involving 'connected' offences, the Code of criminal procedure for trial – which is borrowed from France – lays down that the French and Turkish officers should be prosecuted jointly. Turkey is entitled to jurisdiction from this standpoint; No provision of international law exists to debar Turkey from exercising jurisdiction;

A SHORT HISTORY OF TURKISH/FRENCH RELATIONS

Turkey is a relatively new State yet a very old civilisation; Byzantium stood alongside Rome when large parts of Europe, including France, were still in the dark ages. It is worth reflecting here on the recent emergence of the Turkish State in order to contextualise the claims of both parties, as well as this judgment, and in order to understand better the relations between Turkey and France.

The Treaty of Peace was signed at Sèvres in 1920 following the defeat of the Central Powers in the Great War, and carved the former Ottoman Empire up into territories. The frontiers of Turkey were determined and detailed in the Treaty, with Turkish control over all other regions being renounced. The remaining area was divided up into new States or into mandate territories bestowed upon the Allied Powers in accordance with the League Covenant; for example, the region of Syria became a Mandate Territory of France.

There is some evidence that the Treaty of Sèvres angered the Turkish national movement. The Turkish War of Independence had raged since 1919 and continued until 1923. In the midst of the fighting, on 1 November, 1922, the Ottoman Sultanate was abolished by the Grand National Assembly of Turkey and, on the 11 November, 1922, the Conference of Lausanne was held. The Conference directly recognised the transference of sovereignty, which previously had been embodied in the dynasty of Osman I, to the newly created Turkish Grand National Assembly. This legal position was formally recognised by the international community through the Treaty of Lausanne, dated 24 July, 1923, and, on 29 October, 1923, the Republic of Turkey was officially declared. Prior to the creation of the Republic of Turkey, France had played a key role in the recognition of the Turkish State, being the first major Western State to recognise Turkey in 1921.

Turkey, as Mahmout Essat Bey has confirmed in his submissions of behalf of the State, is eager to be seen as a modern nation State. And, of course, as a member of the international community of States, developments within the Republic of Turkey are to be accorded equivalent weight as developments within already existing States. The Republic of Turkey has, since establishment, made multiple, progressive claims towards exercising its sovereignty and enjoying Statehood. This has not only been through the declaration and international recognition of such sovereignty and Statehood but also directly through legal policy developments internal to the Republic and its various legal reforms. These have included, as Mahmout Essat Bey has emphasised to the Court, the modelling of domestic law on European models of the State, including the secularisation and unification of the education system. Turkey's penal law is now largely based on various European legal systems. In fact, the law which was used in order to claim jurisdiction over Monsieur Demons is one example of this, modelled as it is on the equivalent Italian Code. Furthermore, the Turkish Civil Code of 1926, adopted from the Swiss Civil Code, secularised family law in Turkey, making significant advances in legal equality for women in issues such as inheritance, divorce and custody of children. This Code was introduced into Turkish law through the work of Mahmout Essat Bey, the Minister of Justice who has appeared for Turkey before this Court. Without presupposing the European model of statehood as determinative, these examples, for the Court, demonstrate the reforms and interests of a sovereign State, concerned for the welfare of all of its citizens, providing protections and rights to all people, women and men, and thus incurring responsibilities as well as privileges. These actions demonstrate the Republic of Turkey to be well deserving of the status of a sovereign and equal State.

In this regard, the Court notes that whilst Turkey has established itself as an independent State in these many ways, even now, capitulations continue through an open door policy, albeit unofficially. France, in the meantime, is still living in the colonial past, using the Mandate system to hide behind while continuing to use its intensive firepower against the Syrian people, its Mandate Territory. Up until the Treaty of Lausanne, Turkey had been subject to a regime of capitulations and extra-territorial jurisdiction, which in practice meant that the justice system within Turkey was not deemed by countries, such as France, to be sufficiently mature and robust to administer disputes involving non-nationals. The question then before this Court must be seen in the context of asking whether general principles of international law would reinstate this system of hierarchy, or rather would recognise Turkey as the sovereign equal of a long time independent State, including France. Should the order preferred and imposed by an elder of the international community always dictate the conditions of the community's newer members?

This Court has held in mind this larger context and history of inequality between the two States appearing before it. This story of inequality through the domination of Empire, and France's expectations that States in the region capitulate to its demands, mocks the idea of State sovereignty. This Court also considers it necessary to consider the changing configuration of, in particular, the Turkish State with respect to its legal reforms after the Treaty of Lausanne. With the emergence of new States in the international order, recognised by international law, this Court is of the belief that ensuring real, *de facto* equality between States, old and new, is instrumental to the successful advancement and the peaceful co-existence of the international community of States.

THE APPLICATION OF GENERAL PRINCIPLES OF INTERNATIONAL LAW

As France submits, this case raises issues far beyond the simple collision of two ships. This is the first time the Court has been asked to rule on a general principle of international law. In particular, this case provides an opportunity to re-define and re-negotiate international space in line with the changing sovereign members of the international community. International law governs relations between independent States. While the Court might be expected to emphasise the independence of States at this point, the history of the two parties before this Court demonstrates the fallacy of any approach that focuses on the independence of a State to the detriment of identifying and clarifying the relational nature of Statehood on the international plane and within the international space. We assert that while the rules of law are binding on States as they emanate from their own free will (as expressed in accordance with the Statute of the Court through international conventions, custom and general principles of international law), we must also remember that international law is established to regulate the relations between States with a view to achieving common aims and promoting international co-operation. This Court considers that the free will of States is meaningless without attention to those common aims of the international community, the promotion of 'international co-operation' and the desire for 'open, just and honourable relations between nations' (Preamble, Covenant of the League of Nations). As such, while a nineteenth century international lawyer may have chosen to prioritise the free will of States as commanding the contours of international law, twentieth century developments have dawned an international space for mutual co-operation and interdependence that can no longer be subsumed as secondary to the independence of States. The Hague Conventions, the Covenant of the League, and the French Minister of Foreign Affairs, Aristide Briand's, open letter for peace, published last April, all demonstrate the international community's desire for the peaceful settlement of disputes.

This Court plays a vital and central role in settling disputes peacefully through international law, not just in the name of individual States, but also for the sake of the stability and security of the international community as a whole.

From the above reflections, the Court considers the classic configuration of State sovereignty to be outmoded and no longer adequate to describe the society of nations. The Court's approach relies on an understanding of sovereignty, and thus the general principles of international law, as built on the spirit of co-operation, community and pacific settlement of disputes. This approach, as indicated above, is in line with contemporary international documents, in particular, the Covenant of the League and the instruments negotiated at The Hague Conferences, including the 1915 Peace Conference of the International Congress of Women and the subsequent resolutions. If international law is to live up to its stated credentials, namely being international and universally applicable, its substance must reflect the diversity of the contemporary international order, comprising States new and old. As such, the Court conceives of sovereignty as no longer simply a shield. As the facts before the Court demonstrate, the time is ripe for international law to evolve mechanisms for guaranteeing the rights of citizens and individuals within a State. International law's growing concern for the individual is well established, as demonstrated by The Hague Conventions of 1899 and 1907 and their constraints on warfare, the creation of the International Labour Organisation, the principle that 'the well-being and development' of peoples in mandate territories is a 'sacred trust of civilisation' and the recently concluded Convention to Suppress the Slave Trade and Slavery. With this in mind, the Court finds it necessary to add some additional comments regarding the status of women and minorities in France and in Turkey, before addressing the relationship between individual rights and sovereignty. A review of international law as a space of co-operation for the international community of States is required.

INTERNATIONAL LAW AS A SPACE OF CO-OPERATION

The emergence of the Republic of Turkey is indicative of a new era in international law, one where new States are claiming their sovereignty and thus their entitlement to sit within the international community of nations. This marks the end of an old European Order, an order drenched in the blood of 1914–18. The world is changing and modernising and so, too, must the conception of the international community so as to reflect shifting power relations and the rise of new States, such as the Republic of Turkey. New conceptualisations of international law and of sovereignty are needed that better fit the way the world is currently constituted. This Court accordingly wishes to disrupt the traditional model of Statehood, in line with the Resolutions and the spirit of the 1915 Hague Peace Conference of the International Congress of Women. Turkey's history alone, with the former (but still *de facto* existing) capitulations system and the division of the Ottoman Empire by the Treaty of Sèvres rebukes the European myth of the independent and territorially bounded sovereign State. The Court reflects that Turkey has in effect been 'feminised' by France and other European powers, through capitulations, formal and informal, and through the type of pressure France is asserting via the raising of this case. The Court notes with concern international law's history as one which persistently feminises weaker and primitive peoples, that is non-white non-Europeans. This is just as men, including white men from 'civilised nations', have subordinated women and historically failed to give their sisters, mothers and wives full suffrage 'and the full equality of women with men politically, socially and economically.' (Resolution, 2nd Congress of Women, Zurich 1919). They thus equate femininity with powerlessness and lack of voice. The Court considers, in line with the Covenant of the League, that it shares the obligation to further the 'sacred trust of civilisation' and to assist Turkey, and other new States (as well as others that may emerge), in being treated as equal at the international level. In so doing it draws an analogy with the brave individuals who have shown the world that women's suffrage is a matter of equality. This Court relies on an understanding of sovereignty as built on the spirit of co-operation, community and pacific settlement of disputes; one that resists inequalities in power relations between those recognised as States and thereby also challenges nineteenth century and positivist conceptions of free will, which assume a formal equality without considering the substantive inequalities between States. Instead the international community must function to produce real equality rather than undermine it through permitting more powerful States to assert continued privileges.

The international legal world consists of strictly demarcated spaces: sovereign spaces within defined territories; empires, less clearly defined, territorially expansive, contested and made up of different sovereign forms; international spaces, for instance the High Seas and airspaces. In this case the Court regards it to be its duty to see beyond these spaces to acknowledge the people within sovereign spaces, territories and empires. In the colliding of these two ships sovereign borders did not just clash, they vanished, and meant nothing to those who drowned, and those whom they left behind. This Court rejects the useful legal fiction of strictly demarcated territories to limit the more fundamental need for accountability for wrongdoing. The artificial boundary between two sovereign States, according to the facts, was disrupted through the very act of the *SS Lotus* dividing the *Bozkurt* in two. For the hapless individuals who lost their lives six nautical miles from the Turkish coast and safety, the territorially defined sovereign State need never have existed, whether in 1648, or 1927. This case constitutes an opportunity to acknowledge real sovereign equality using and through the general principles of international law. International law is moving beyond its conception of itself as a system between formally equal sovereign (European) States who are territorially bounded, individual personalities in international law, towards a system based on connection and co-operation. International law is about how we live internationally, how we encounter each other in international spaces and how a wide array of (different) voices may be considered when trying to understand what international law could be, and is becoming. As evidence of this emerging shift towards co-operation in international law, this judgment itself may be presented.

Turkey is not yet a State party to the Statute of the PCIJ, nor a member of the League of Nations but it has accepted the jurisdiction of the Court to resolve this dispute. The Court commends France's decision to turn to the Court as a mechanism for the pacific settlement of the dispute, which is in contrast to France's decision to use military force in nearby Syria. The Court welcomes this willingness to co-operate and build consensus on the part of both States, despite the historical exploitation by France of its relationship with Turkey. Whilst, in their submissions to the Court, the Turkish State seems eager to persuade the Court of its 'European-ness,' the Court would like to suggest that European States, such as France, should instead learn from Turkey's lead, whilst urging Turkey to forge its own path as a State and not to assume that what constitutes a State and the essence of Statehood are to be derived from its European counterparts. The Turkish State is already recognised as a State under international law as demonstrated by its presence before this Court. As a State newly emerged from Empire, Turkey has an opportunity, shared with others, to recast Statehood. The Court therefore urges Turkey to lead and not simply to model itself upon European States. The Court is of the opinion that the Turkish State can provide a new perspective and configure a change in international law born of the true spirit of a society of nations. The Court also encourages France to consider this model. For example, the promotion of secularism and equality are key configurations within the Turkish Republic that older States might also wish to adopt.

In the words of the women at The Hague in 1915, there is a need to fully recognise 'the interests and rights not only of the great Powers and small nations but also those of weaker countries'. As expressed by the founder of the Women's International League for Peace and Freedom, Jane Addams, 'a new birth of internationalism … designed to protect and enhance the fruitful processes of cooperation in the great experiment of living together in a world become conscious of itself'. The need for a re-configured sovereignty that is relational and inclusive – the new internationalism – is perceived by the Court as personifying a larger series of issues around the equality of sovereign entities. With respect to Turkey and France, Turkey has previously been cast as the female subject, a new sovereign, not dissimilar to a woman with her newly earned right to vote (at least in those countries where this has been achieved), claiming her position amongst a history of masculinist, self-defined 'civilised' nations who have long used economic and military power to assert their right over citizens and others, States and those territories not yet deemed worthy of Statehood.

THE NEED FOR GREATER INCLUSIVITY AND SOVEREIGNTY AS GUARANTEEING RIGHTS

The Court regards France as the epitome of this masculinist State, who must not only acknowledge the sovereign rights of Turkey but also the changing understanding of sovereignty that we outline in this judgment. The Court then sees a need for the Turkish desire to epitomise the traditional masculine State that France represents, to be discarded for a model of sovereignty that is drawn from contemporary understanding of equal rights, such as those in Turkey that include rights for all citizens, not just men, and movements around minority rights.

Turkey's legal reforms do not only show an establishment of sovereignty through legal authority. Turkey's legal reforms have also been aimed at creating a secular and more equal State. Turkey, through these legal reforms, is leading the way in showing that sovereignty is no longer solely a shield but also a mechanism for guaranteeing rights for citizens.

In this world of greater equality between States, it is a necessary precondition that this is matched by the pursuit of greater equality within States. The Court will now have regard to the current status of women's rights in France and Turkey, respectively, to demonstrate how the personification of sovereignty, discussed above, has material dimensions within States. Equality goes both ways: it is needed at the international level but also at the domestic level and this is applicable to all States in the international order, including both Turkey and France.

Women's equality has been emphasised in Turkey under the new Government led by President Kemal Atatürk. Women are encouraged to enter the workforce and public life while being given increased educational opportunities. The 1926 Turkish Civil Code, modelled on the Swiss Civil Code, has given women equal footing in terms of marriage, divorce and inheritance. The Turkish Civil Code also abolished the practice of polygamy. All this must be applauded. However, a number of women's groups within Turkey, whilst welcoming these reforms, have criticised the form of State feminism being promoted by the Government whereby women's rights are being bestowed, according to the Government, so that women will be better able to serve their State and in order to prove to the West that Turkey is the West's equal. There is a general rejection from the Turkish Government of anything related to femininity with President Kemal Atatürk representing the ultimate, masculine figure. Whilst Turkish reforms have benefited women's equality and lives greatly, much is left to be done to ensure real equality, with these reforms, in many ways, forming a facade under which Turkish society has merely reorganised itself to ensure the power of men remains intact. In France, Olympe de Gouge (1748–1793) challenged male authority and demanded rights for women as long ago as her tract, the *Declaration of the Rights of Woman and the Female Citizen* (1791). Women's right to inherit property was granted in the eighteenth century and many of the above listed rights were given in the late nineteenth century. However, in France, as in Turkey, women remain unable to vote and they may not work without their husband's consent. Men are still considered the heads of the household in both countries.

This Court emphasises that equality within States is an integral part of sovereignty in the contemporary world. There is a lot to do, in both Turkey and in France, to ensure that women's political, social and economic equality becomes a reality. The women who came together so courageously to call for peace in 1915 expected that the international community would 'only recognise as democratic a system which includes the equal representation of men and women'. The principle of cooperation, which, this Court today asserts, is to be seen as an aspect of sovereignty. It thereby calls for sovereign States to guarantee rights for all citizens in line with the resolutions drafted at The Hague in 1915 and Zurich in 1919. Cooperation and peaceful resolution of disputes form one aspect of guaranteeing these rights. Both States need to extend suffrage to all women. The Court further urges France to return to considering the status of its own citizens rather than implying that other systems and other States are somehow more primitive than they are.

In the same vein, the Court asks Turkey to reflect upon and change its policies with respect to its treatment of minorities within the State. By this, the Court refers specifically to the Kurdish population of Turkey. Just as Turkey's politics on women are being adopted through a policy of State feminism, – furthered in the name of the State and State progress – the Kurdish question is also being pursued through the lens of State nationalism. The Kurdish people are being treated as an entity that can be absorbed by the State; Turkish national pride thus linking the people of Turkey across all other divides – religious, historical, linguistic and sex. At the same time, this Turkish national identity, which is to be superimposed, is specific and very much based around the Turkish language and a so-called Turkish identity. The Court commends Turkey's limited recognition of minority rights through various legislative changes adopted in 1923 and 1924 but further recommends that Turkey continues to consider this issue in more depth; not by erasing history and difference but through respecting it and working towards true equality through allowing Kurdish citizens to celebrate their language and culture. The Court sees it as appropriate to take every opportunity to uphold the status and rights of minorities.

There is a need to learn from the past, to look towards a new era of internationalism and a broadened understanding of the international community that encompasses new States. Turkey represents both the need to do this as well as the chance to reconfigure citizenship and sovereignty from within the State. However, this goes both ways: with sovereign power comes sovereign responsibility. States must work to protect minorities and women and work towards equality with the same vigour as they assert their international claims. The Court, in this sense, praises the sentiment of the Turkish leader, President Kemal Atatürk, who has articulated that sovereignty belongs to the people. The Court feels it necessary to assert that sovereignty belongs unconditionally to all people, including women and minority groups; and it is this internal equality that has the potential to create the blueprint for an international society comprising sovereign equals, without the power games reminiscent of the era of Empire.

CONCLUSIONS OF THE COURT

The Court finds that no internationally wrongful act has occurred. Turkey was acting within the principles of international law when it exercised jurisdiction over Monsieur Demons. Turkey had jurisdiction because the victims were Turkish, and the harm was felt in Turkey. This is not territorial jurisdiction, as will be explained below, but is instead a new, *international* jurisdiction.

International Jurisdiction

The society of nations requires States to recognise each other as sovereign equals that freely meet to create a space of co-operation. This is not a system premised on free will that promotes State exceptionalism. In the dispute before this Court, France's unwillingness to acknowledge the Turkish exercise of jurisdiction is ill founded. The principles of equality and co-operation between States mean that Turkey must not be denied jurisdiction. Responsibility for international co-operation vests in all States as a consequence of the need for peaceful relations and achievement of common aims; this is the reasoning underpinning the Court's order, stated below.

The Court also recalls the need for internal equality within States, as demonstrated by the women at The Hague in 1915 and Zurich in 1919 who recognised the nexus between national and international equality, as well as setting out and arguing for steps for their attainment. Turkey's exercise of jurisdiction to bring justice for its own nationals need not be something that France fears. Turkish jurisdiction to act needs to be embraced by France as an assurance of sovereign equality and that justice can be achieved through co-operation.

Access to justice

The Court has the following additional comments to make with respect to access to justice. The demands of international justice still apply to acts and misdeeds that occur at sea, even where jurisdiction is not self-evident. The international community must build on the developments at Versailles, with regard to the notion the individuals may bear responsibility for their acts within the international realm. The logical corollary to this principle is that States too have responsibilities to individuals, not just within their territory but internationally. As such this Court, and twentieth century international law, must be animated by a spirit of responsibility for international wrongful acts and accountability for their commission, no matter where they are committed. International spaces such as the High Seas must be peaceful, and that peace will come through law. Turkey has jurisdiction not based on any territorial rule but based on the needs of the victims. The Court has learned nothing of the suffering and hardship experienced by the families of those who lost their lives. It is the Turkish people who perished and their families, ultimately, who have been wronged. Through, on the one hand, establishing the High Seas – and other international spaces – as peaceful zones of freedom for States and, on the other hand, honouring Turkey's right to exercise criminal jurisdiction; it is the grieving families in Turkey who can be given recognition as the victims of the *Bozkurt* tragedy. Lives lost on the High Seas are a concern for the international community at large and all States and their citizens have an interest in seeing justice secured for the victims and their families. By international jurisdiction the Court refers to jurisdiction on the basis of international law, that should include jurisdiction over harms experienced by individuals when those harms are caused by a breach of an international obligation especially when harms occur within international spaces, such as at sea.

DECLARATORY ORDER

Consequently, there is no occasion to give judgment on the question of the pecuniary reparation which might have been due to Lieutenant Demons if Turkey, by prosecuting him as above stated, had acted in a manner contrary to the principles of international law.

While the Court determines that neither State has breached international law in this case the Court nevertheless recommends that:

> The parties provide more information on the fatalities and their families, as well as any compensation or reparations dependents have received from either State. In particular, the Court asks the parties to provide further information with regard to the fatalities that resulted from the collision of the two vessels, including the names, of those perished and their dependents. Further the Court asks France to explain why it is attempting to exercise jurisdiction over the nationals of Turkey who died, or at least the follow up proceedings that attempt to bring justice to those who have suffered the real injustice here; the loss of family members.

On receipt of this information the Court will consider a further order.

Although the Court has not found a breach of international law in Turkey's exercise of jurisdiction, this in no way undermines the importance it attaches to the *Bozkurt* principle of international co-operation as the hallmark of international society as articulated herein and strongly encourages States to build their international relations in line with the principles in this judgment.

Reflections

Writing a feminist judgment posed a series of unexpected joys and difficulties that we will reflect on in this final section of the submission. Prior to writing about the questions and concerns writing the judgment raised, we address a couple of notes on process. First, it is fair to say that being given an early twentieth century case from a now defunct institution on a central structural issue in international law (sovereignty and state consent) that did not speak directly to women's lives and concerns was a daunting task! All four authors arrived at our first joint meeting with some trepidation. This first meeting was held at Durham Law School and we were joined by colleagues from the Law and Global Justice research cluster, who enriched the project considerably with their knowledge of legal developments in the League era. A second important aspect of that meeting was the decision to write the complete judgment jointly – which meant as authors we sat together and first recorded our joint ideas and later edited those thoughts into what is now our re-written judgment. This collaborative method, while initially daunting, provided two features of the judgment. First, we all wrote all of the judgment. Second, the productive space that happens 'between' the words spoken in a dialogue informed the text. That is, rather than individually writing sections of the text that we pieced together the judgment captures what happened when we worked together. This was the most rewarding aspect of the process and definitely captured something none of us might have written absent the collaborative process.

In this final authors' note we reflect on the specific methodological issues raised by the specificity of the PCIJ, questions about the relationship between feminism and law, a comment on the tension in feminist judgments between the feminine voice and feminist voices and a final note on the role of collaborative projects in contemporary higher education settings.

The Specific Methodological Issues Raised by the PCIJ

When drafting the judgment, we were unsure about how much we would use the judgment to challenge judicial methodologies. We asked ourselves, how self-aware could the Court be? This emerged in our discussions as a feeling of discomfort due to the need to jettison personal political commitments to gender fluidity resorting to the language of the gender binary. A further source of discomfort was determining how to express an internationalist politics in a time that was dominated by European colonisation.

Additional questions included: did/would the Court know how foundational this judgment would be? Can we re-imagine the international and turn to documents from the women's peace movement, as international documents? As the chamber was re-writing a judgment that was not clearly connected to women's issues this led us towards materials that we would not usually read or engage with. These materials were largely in connection with familiarising ourselves with the PCIJ and the history of Turkish-French relations, including the capitulations system, the history of women's equality in France and Turkey, the composition of the PCIJ and its nexus to other international bodies, such as the Mandate Commission to help us get a sense with respect to what was possible in terms of the contours of the feminist judgment. We also tried to be attentive to the language which was used at the time; although the desire to create a *feminist* document perhaps made this challenging.

We also considered the suggestion that the judgment be written as a Separate Opinion, as this might have allowed us as a chamber greater flexibility, in the sense that a Separate Opinion would have permitted us to speak directly within the text to the existing judgment. In the same vein, the feminist judgment might also have been produced as a dissenting judgment. However there was consensus that using the feminist judgment as an alternative judgment – following the structure of the original judgment and envisaging the Court as one which was prepared to make foundational statements about the nature of international law but drawing on materials available at the time – was quite important in the sense that this was not an adjunct to the existing judgment but rather an alternative, different judgment.

An additional concern we had, driven by the nature of the Court, was that we could not make a Court Order because we did not find a breach of international law. In addition, we were not – at least in terms of outcomes – departing from what the original judgment actually concluded. However, we did still decide to make a Declaratory Order. Further, the original *Lotus* case is important for what was said *obiter.* So is our judgment. In addition, as a chamber we felt frustrated that we could only answer the question as given to the Court. This ultimately limited our response, although we did work creatively to draw on material available at the time to open apertures that were not components of the original judgment. Some aspects of this were easier than others, for example the idea of equality had already been considered by the PCIJ and expanding upon this seemed within the realm of the possible of a feminist chamber sitting in 1927. Nevertheless, were also were aware that the PCIJ was, in 1927, still a relatively new court that exercised caution in its judgments in part to secure its own future. All of these background issues run through and into the conversations that created the final feminist judgment and helped underline the situated nature of Courts and their judgments: temporally, historically and politically.

Can Law be Feminist?

As a chamber we also discussed how a judgment can be feminist within the limits of law. We concluded it can be feminist but it can only go so far, and to go beyond this maybe we would need to go beyond law to find satisfactory legal transformation. This reflects the types of concerns Rosemary Hunter addresses in her response to

Carol Smart's work[1] and the larger recognition within feminist writings on international law between resistance and compliance.[2] Connected then to the concerns expressed above, there remains a question of what role the function and working processes of an institution play in re-shaping and modelling external accounts to align with the expectations of the system. Feminist judgment projects take us to the line between the desire to resist co-optation and the desire to re-fashion institutions from within via the appearance of compliance. It seems unnecessary to attempt to resolve this persistent tension other than to say in writing a feminist judgment there was a somewhat satisfying insider/outsider space where the form and process of judgment-writing was used and yet our own methods (for example, writing collaboratively and drawing on specific feminist sources) resisted the expectations of the institution in subtle ways. This seems an excellent parallel to contemporary gender and feminist engagements with international institutions that we should not lose sight of.

Tensions Between a Female and a Feminist Project

As a chamber we also spoke about the distinction in the title of the project between a Feminist International Judgment Project and the (original) subtitle, ultimately not used for this publication, which focused on Women's Voices in International Law. We asked ourselves whether there was a distinction between a feminist project and a project centred on women's voices, definitely preferring the former and yet in many ways mobilising the latter.

From the outset the chamber felt there was a tension between the goal in the larger project of feminist judgments between finding women's voices within international law and the need for 'telling a story differently'.[3] We have preferred to think of writing this judgment as an exercise in telling a story differently – drawing on existing feminist texts and legal outcomes – rather than seeing it as a project centred on asserting women's voices in an assumed silence. At a practical level, and importantly, the composition of our chamber included a male judge, as such the chamber decided against aligning with a specific construction of gender representation, preferring to focus on what constituted a feminist judgment. A focus on the writing of a 'women's judgment', the chamber felt, risked an assumption, and a projection, of gender difference that raised further issues regarding essentialism. Nevertheless, we did actively seek to record and parallel the work of women at the time to understand what the contours of feminist thinking that might have

[1] R Hunter, 'The Power of Feminist Judgments?' (2012) 20(2) *Feminist Legal Studies* 135.

[2] S Kouvo and Z Pearson (eds), *Feminist Perspectives on Contemporary International Law, Between Resistance and Compliance?* (Oxford, Hart Publishing, 2011).

[3] See further, Hunter, above n 1, at 139.

influenced what the judgment would, or could, have been had feminists been invited to decide the *Bozkurt* case in 1927. This allowed us to appreciate the lively and entrenched transnational feminist networks that existed at the time. However, our commitment to creating a feminist intervention meant that we also paid attention to how feminist ideas had been absorbed by the States before the Court and this involved acknowledging work for its content rather than the gender of its author.

Collaborative Projects and 'Indicators' of Contemporary Academic Life

Before concluding, we feel it is important to make some final comments with regard to the collaborative nature of the project. In many ways a collaborative project challenges contemporary ideas within the academy with respect to researcher outputs which, in the UK at least, are increasingly individualised. The Research Excellence Framework – a regular, state-wide assessment of academic research outputs in the UK – requires established academics to put forward four publications for assessment approximately every seven years. Although joint authored pieces are accepted, academics are encouraged to focus (and often report) on their individual outputs and the scheme for measurability of outputs is both in terms of quantity and quality assessed for each academic. The collaborative process in this project, we found, changes understandings of ownership – ideas emerged in discussions from an individual and were rapidly commented upon, refined, altered etc by the group making it impossible to follow the evolution of all ideas; it was never clear therefore that there was specific ownership (nor was it desired) with respect to the final text. The question of whether a writing project such as this would be presentable for assessment became subordinated to the clear research gains that we all benefited from: working collaboratively in and of itself was productive of new forms of knowledge and ideas. However, not only was the project therefore less likely to be one that any of us might submit as for assessment under the next research assessment exercise, the time spent on the project highlighted to each of us the way through which processes such as the research assessment framework shapes academic time. As academics, the intellectual gains of participating in the chamber and in the feminist international judgments project, as well as the larger network of feminist judgment projects, were high and yet this is the kind of work that many of us might have chosen to leave behind given the dominance of the research excellence framework in contemporary UK academic spaces.

At the same time, the nature of collaboration, which was not just within the chamber but with colleagues working on critical legal histories, revealed to us that even within critical frameworks there is insufficient dialogue. Historical projects remain on one track while gender projects are on another. This is part of a wider pattern of compartmentalisation in international legal scholarship. For us, the bringing together of these diverse perspectives was personally rewarding and enhanced the richness of the project.

What does this say about the role of the university researcher more broadly where two parallel, and linked, developments around the requirement for individual research outputs and self-management of time that detracts from the potential to embark on collaborative projects? Given the history of collaborative and collective enterprises in feminist histories and that one of the first pieces of feminist publishing on international law was a jointly authored piece,[4] are there additional gendered dimensions of the turn to individualised research outputs that isolate researchers and produce an academic model that potentially values less the collaborative, communal writing space? As a chamber, we concluded that collaborative scholarship is important to how we think, exchange ideas and produce feminist writing, as well as how we maintain commitments to feminist processes and care for each other as researchers in an increasingly neoliberal higher education setting.

[4] H Charlesworth, C Chinkin and S Wright, 'Feminist Approaches to International Law' (1991) 85 *American Journal of International Law* 613.

International Court of Justice

3

Reservations to the Convention on the Prevention and Punishment of the Crime of Genocide

KASEY McCALL-SMITH, RHONA SMITH
AND EKATERINA YAHYAOUI KRIVENKO

Authors' Note

The International Court of Justice (ICJ), created in 1945,[1] is the primary judicial organ of the United Nations (UN) and, as outlined in the previous chapter, a successor to the League of Nations' Permanent Court of International Justice. Although it has both contentious and advisory jurisdiction, initially more advisory opinions were sought than contentious cases lodged.[2] Indeed, the *Reservations to the Convention on the Prevention and Punishment of the Crime of Genocide* advisory opinion was the sixth request for an advisory opinion submitted to the new court.[3] This particular opinion on which this chapter focuses has had a significant impact on the development of treaty law, marking the first international judicial foray into the nature and effect of reservations to multipartite treaties.

Reservations are a complex aspect of treaty law[4] whereby States seeking to accept a treaty effectively exclude the legal effect of certain provisions of that treaty. Such modifications of obligations are required to be made upon signature, ratification or accession. By 1948, practice concerning reservations to treaties varied from State to State and between regions, though most States considered the entering of

[1] Charter of the United Nations and Statute of the International Court of Justice (adopted entered into force) 1 UNTS XV.

[2] The first case lodged, however, was contentious: the *Corfu Channel Case* (*UK v Albania*) (Merits) [1949] ICJ Rep 4.

[3] Reservations to the Convention on the Prevention and Punishment of the Crime of Genocide, (Advisory Opinion) [1951] ICJ Reports 15.

[4] See, eg, A Aust, *Modern Treaty Law and Practice* 3rd edn (Cambridge, Cambridge University Press, 2013) ch 8; E Swaine, 'Reserving' (2006) 31 *Yale Journal of International Law* 307.

reservations to be a legitimate exercise of sovereignty.[5] The UN Secretary-General, as a new depository of multilateral treaty ratifications and reservations in the UN system, began by deploying the common practice utilised by the League of Nations; upon receipt of a purported reservation, all existing contracting States were contacted to enable each to determine whether to accept it.[6] Any objection to the reservation would trigger efforts at diplomatic settlement; however, failing an agreement, the reserving State would not be permitted to become party to the treaty whilst maintaining the reservation.[7]

Treaties are the principal building blocks of contemporary international law. They are the basis upon which States hold one another to account and the governing texts in the event of a dispute between States parties to these agreements. Written texts, with authenticated versions publicly available, prove what obligations states have accepted and which States have signed, ratified, acceded to or succeeded to any treaty.[8] With the establishment of the UN in 1945,[9] the number of global multilateral treaties increased. As the UN pursued decolonisation policies,[10] its membership increased.[11] So too did the numbers of States party to treaties.[12] Indeed, the international community embarked on a process somewhat akin to mass legislation[13] as ever more treaties were agreed, many under the auspices of the new UN. In 1946, the International Law Commission was tasked by the UN General Assembly with 'promotion of the progressive development of

[5] See, eg, discussions in M Hudson, 'Reservations to Multipartite International Instruments' (1938) 32 *American Journal of International Law* 330; W Sanders, 'Reservations to Multilateral Treaties made in Act of Ratification or Adherence' (1939) 33 *American Journal of International Law* 488; H Malkin, 'Reservations to Multilateral Conventions' (1926) 7 *British Yearbook of International Law* 141; J Peters, 'Reservations to Multilateral Treaties: How International Legal Doctrine Effects World Vision' (1982) *Faculty Scholarship Series*, Paper 2185. Available at: http://digitalcommons.law.yale.edu/fss_papers/2185.

[6] Arguably this system is a restricted version of the system under the auspices of the League of Nations by which even non-State parties could object to any reservation.

[7] For a discussion of early examples, see H Lauterpacht, 'Some Possible Solutions of the Problems of Reservations to Treaties' (1953) 39 *Transactions of the Grotius Society* 97.

[8] At the time of the opinion, this database was held by the Office of the Secretary General of the UN. Most Member States kept comprehensive lists of States party to the treaties they accepted. This information was available through Ministries of Foreign Affairs. Today it is easily and freely accessible online.

[9] Charter of the United Nations 1945, Statute of the International Court of Justice 1945, above n 1.

[10] General Assembly Declaration 1514 (XV) on the Granting of Independence to Colonial Countries and Peoples (14 December 1960) UN Doc A/RES/15/1514.

[11] From 51 in 1945 to 60 by 1951 then 193 by 2015 when this work was submitted.

[12] The steadily increasing number of UN Member States and potential Member States naturally leads to a larger number of parties to treaties as it is the primary way in which States define their relationships. For an overview of the increasing States in the international community, see J Crawford, *The Creation of States in International Law* (Oxford, Oxford University Press, 2006) Annex I.

[13] On international constitutionalism, see for example, J Klabbers, A Peters and G Ulfstein, *The Constitutionalization of International Law* (Oxford, Oxford University Press, 2009); J Dinoff and J Trachtman (eds), *Ruling the World? Constitutionalism, International Law, and Global Governance* (Cambridge, Cambridge University Press, 2009).

international law and its codification.'[14] As a result, codifying existing customary international law and general practices became common and new areas of treaty-based law emerged, including international human rights. The Commission's study on the law of treaties was expanded to include reservations in light of the advisory opinion request before the ICJ.

The International Law Commission eventually included in the 1969 Vienna Convention on the Law of Treaties the rule that the ICJ had established in the Genocide Convention advisory opinion.[15] Thus, the impact of the advisory opinion on the development of treaty law forever shaped the ability of States to unilaterally alter their treaty obligations once the text is adopted. Substantively, the advisory opinion concerned the legal effect of reservations to a treaty aimed at preventing and punishing genocide. Genocide, as a term, was very new, 'coined by [Polish jurist Raphael Lemkin] to denote an old practice in its modern development',[16] before finding legal expression in the Nuremberg International Military Tribunal[17] and thereafter in the Genocide Convention 1948.[18] Although international law remained firmly the domain of States, the status of individuals as the beneficiaries of human rights obligations, while still peripheral, was arguably entering the consciousness of international actors. The UN Charter and the Universal Declaration of Human Rights each clarified that the protection of individuals was a key feature of the new UN.[19] This precipitated a shift in the understanding of international legal personality from being solely attributable to States to an acknowledgement that individuals also had rights at the international level. Additionally, the work of the Nuremberg and Tokyo military tribunals focussed on holding individuals to account for atrocities committed during the Second World War, rather than States being held to account for atrocities committed in their name, thus further endowing individuals with international legal personality. Collectively, these efforts cemented the position of individuals in the international legal system.

Looking beyond genocide, there is evidence of the recognition of individuals in a range of practices contemporaneous to (or predating) the Genocide Convention. The Trusteeship Council of the United Nations emphasised 'good governance' practices, including consideration of individuals living under the

[14] Statute of the International Law Commission, adopted by the General Assembly in resolution 174 (II) of 21 November 1947, art 1.

[15] Vienna Convention on the Law of Treaties, (adopted 23 May 1969, entered into force 27 January 1980) (Vienna Convention), 1155 UNTS 331, art 19(c).

[16] R Lemkin, *Axis Rule in Occupied Europe* 2nd edn (New Jersey, The Lawbook Exchange, 2008) Ch IX, 79.

[17] Lemkin worked with the US prosecution team.

[18] Convention on the Prevention and Punishment of the Crime of Genocide, UNGA 260 (III) A, 9 December 1948. See also W Schabas, 'Introduction' to Lemkin, above n 16; and Lemkin, above n 16, 93–94.

[19] Universal Declaration on Human Rights, UNGA Res 217 A (III), 10 Dec 1948.

control of a foreign State.[20] To an extent, this followed the work of the League of Nations with its regime of minority guarantee clauses.[21] The Slavery Conventions were well established and slavery in the explicit ownership form (as opposed to modern forms) was proscribed and confirmed as contrary to customary as well as treaty law. A range of humanitarian focussed laws had also been adopted; *jus in bello*, these instruments sought to ameliorate the impact of armed conflict and protect civilian populations and non-combatants. The 1864 Geneva Convention on the amelioration of the condition of the wounded in armies in the field (and indeed the establishment of the International Committee of the Red Cross) was influenced by the bloody battle of Soferino.[22] The Hague Peace conferences of 1899 and 1907 followed some of the ethos of this by limiting armaments which essentially were indiscriminate in effect – chemical weapons, for example.[23] Of course, contemporaneous to the advisory opinion, the International Committee of the Red Cross was redrafting the Geneva Conventions. Following a conference convened in April 1948, the four Geneva Conventions were adopted in 1949.[24] The fourth was the most radical, extending protection to civilians, rather than simply those injured soldiers, sailors and airpersons recognised by the traditional protections. This closed a gap in protection and addressed the systemic failures which led to the abuse, maltreatment and death of so many civilians during the 1939–45 wars. Thus for the first time, women and children, in addition to men, were explicitly addressed by international law. Common article 3 demands humane treatment of those in enemy hands irrespective of their status, while multiple articles outline the extra precautions to be taken with women and children. This was subsequently developed in the optional protocols to take account of the impact of civil conflict.

At the time of the advisory opinion, there is thus evidence that the (negative) impact State policies and laws can have on the lives of individuals was being recognised. It is perhaps worth remembering that the Genocide Convention was adopted on 9 December 1948, the day before the General Assembly adopted the Universal Declaration of Human Rights. However, discourse on international law remained firmly predicated on the centrality of States within the international regime. Individuals were recognised only indirectly, States themselves being the primary obligees in terms of the treaties outlined above. Due to the male dominance in State leadership, prioritising women's issues was rarely, if ever, considered. Even in the context of the Nuremburg or Tokyo Tribunals, the specific impact

[20] The Trusteeship Council operated from 1945 to 1994 when Palau became independent, see www.un.org/en/mainbodies/trusteeship.

[21] P Azcarate and EE Brooke, *League of Nations and National Minorities: An Experiment* (Washington DC, Carnegie Foundation for International Peace, 1945).

[22] See H Dunant, *A Memory of Solferino* (Geneva, International Committee of the Red Cross/Crescent/Crystal, 1986, originally published 1862).

[23] Subsequent developments include the Biological Weapons Convention of 1972 and the 1993 Chemical Weapons Convention.

[24] With the subsequent protocols in 1977. See generally: www.icrc.org/en/war-and-law/treaties-customary-law/geneva-conventions.

on the female populations in terms of damage to reproductive capabilities in concentration camps or issues around comfort women in Japan were not raised. The Universal Declaration of Human Rights also failed to effectively acknowledge how human rights protection could specifically improve the lives of women, who generally suffer violations disproportionately when compared with men.[25]

The Convention on the Prevention and Punishment of the Crime of Genocide arguably sought to capture an emerging consensus on the need to protect peoples against extermination. The prohibition did not represent customary international law, or *ius cogens*, in 1948; thus, it was through this treaty that the prohibition against genocide would become binding on States.[26] In the UN, treaties deemed 'law-making' in this way were subjected to a more stringent regime and reservations were not permitted without unanimous acceptance by all States Parties – the common basis of the treaty 'integrity' position.[27] With 'genocide' articulated as an international crime for the first time in the Convention,[28] the UN Member States were seeking to lay the foundations for a new world order. Moreover, they were mindful of the evidence of mass slaughter emerging in the Tokyo and Nuremberg tribunals as well as the stated general objective of the UN to maintain international peace and security.

According to the dissenting opinion and documents filed with the Court, eight States had entered 18 reservations to the Genocide Convention by December 1950. The reservations related to Articles IV, VI, VII, IX and XII of the Convention. All eight States' reservations curtailed (to a greater or lesser extent) Article IX, which provides for the compulsory jurisdiction of the ICJ. Some of these reservations were objected to by other States. This raised the question of whether this rendered the Convention void for the States concerned. Moreover, there was disagreement on the effect of these reservations, as evidenced by debates in the General Assembly at the time.[29] It should be noted that in the same resolution that the General Assembly requested the advisory opinion, it also invited the International Law Commission to consider reservations in the process of its work on codifying the law of treaties. That plan of work resulted in the 1969 Vienna Convention on the Law of Treaties and later in the 2011 Guide to Practice on Reservations.[30]

[25] Art 1 notes that all humans are born free and equal in rights whilst Art 2 notes that the Declaration should be applied without distinction as to, inter alia, sex.

[26] For its evolution, see W Schabas, *Genocide in International Law: The Crime of Crimes* (Cambridge, Cambridge University Press, 2000).

[27] UN Secretary-General, UN Doc. A/1372 (1950), Annex I, para 2; Written Statement of the United Nations Secretary-General, *Genocide Opinion*, Pleadings, Oral Arguments, Documents, 28 May 1951, 77–180, 104. See also C Redgwell, 'Universality or Integrity? Some Reflections on Reservations to General Multilateral Treaties' (1993) 64 *British Yearbook of International Law* 245, 246.

[28] For an exposition, see R Lemkin, 'Genocide as a Crime in International Law' 41 (1947) *American Journal of International Law* 145.

[29] K McCall-Smith, 'Severing Reservations' (2014) 63 *International and Comparative Law Quarterly* 599, 603ff.

[30] *Report of the International Law Commission (Guide to Practice on Reservations with commentary)*, General Assembly, Official Records, Sixty-sixth Session, Supplement No 10, 2011, UN Doc A/66/10/Add.1.

The General Assembly of the UN sought the ICJ's advice concerning treaty reservations. The questions posed to the Court concerning reservations to the Genocide Convention were as follows:

I. Can the reserving State be regarded as being a party to Convention while still maintaining its reservation if the reservation is objected to by one or more of the parties to the Convention but not by others?
II. If the answer to Question I is in the affirmative, what is the effect of the reservation as between the reserving State and:
    a. The parties which object to the reservation?
    b. Those which accept it?
III. What would be the legal effect as regards the answer to Question I if an objection to a reservation is made:
    a. By a signatory which has not yet ratified?
    b. By a State entitled to sign or accede but which has not yet done so?

The Court's opinion was as follows: on question I, by seven votes to five, it held that such a State could only remain a party if the reservation was compatible with the object and purpose of the convention; on question II, that the objecting State can consider the reserving State with a reservation contrary to the object and purpose of the convention not a party to that treaty, though a State with a compatible reservation can be deemed to remain a party; and on question III, that objections to reservations only have legal effect upon ratification.[31]

At the time, there was little judicial guidance or written international agreement on treaty law. It was in 1969 that the International Law Commission concluded its work drafting the Vienna Convention on the Law of Treaties.[32] The Advisory Opinion was clearly influential in this process and the proposed draft advocated a flexible system of reservations.[33] The Vienna Convention rules outlining the impact of objections to reservations and the resulting legal effect draw directly on the ICJ's findings.[34] The 'object and purpose' test on the validity of reservations is embodied in the final articles of the Vienna Convention: Boerefijn notes that test is now crucial in determining the validity of reservations, noting its

[31] Reservations to the Convention on the Prevention and Punishment of the Crime of Genocide, (Advisory Opinion) [1951] ICJ Reports 15, 26ff.

[32] Vienna Convention on the Law of Treaties 1969, above n 15, drafted by successive British rapporteurs, final draft agreed by states at the 1968 and 1969 Vienna conferences. The treaty entered into force in 1980.

[33] C Redgwell, 'The Law of Reservations in Respect of Multilateral Conventions' in J Gardner (ed), *Human Rights as General Norms and a State's Right to Opt Out* (London, British Institute of International and Comparative Law, 1997) 6.

[34] McCall-Smith, above n 29; see also R Goodman, 'Human Rights Treaties, Invalid Reservations, And State Consent' (2002) 96 *American Journal of International Law* 531; R Moloney, 'Incompatible Reservations to Human Rights Treaties: Severability and the Problem of State Consent' (2004) *Melbourne Journal of International Law* 155.

origin in the Genocide Convention Advisory Opinion.[35] It is unlikely that either the judges in the advisory opinion or the drafters of the Vienna Convention could foresee the challenges that would arise with regard to the specific question of reservations to human rights treaties[36] and other treaties humanitarian in character. The Convention on the Elimination of Discrimination against Women and the Convention on the Rights of the Child, for example, have been subjected to more reservations than there are parties to either treaty.[37] The imprecise nature of the Vienna Convention's 'object and purpose' test and voluntary nature of the state-policing system set out in Article 20 enable states to make reservations to such an extent that treaties, such as the Convention on the Rights of the Child, are often stripped of any real opportunity for impact in the ratifying state. Due to the nature and volume of reservations submitted to some human rights treaties difficulties remain in determining the compatibility of reservations, the consequences of incompatible reservations and the effect of objections to claimed incompatible reservations.

The core of the concern in re-writing the advisory opinion was the need to overcome the State-centricity of the reservations regime. This was particularly difficult considering at the time it was delivered, there was little academic or practitioner opinion available and therefore the Court utilised a perfunctory style of opinion. Recall that this was one of the earliest advisory opinions issued by the Court and it held little similarity to more comprehensive and nuanced analytical approach found in contemporary ICJ opinions. We made the decision to remain true to this style in order to fully experience the difficulties that the Court encountered at the time.

From a feminist perspective, the presentation of the State as an abstract neutral entity operates to prevent us from questioning the bias – including gender bias – that the State embodies. Therefore, the feminist approach adopted in re-writing the advisory opinion focused on avoiding State-centricity as much as possible. The original advisory opinion simply presumes that States will have an interest in protecting humanitarian values or safeguarding the integrity of treaties directed at the protection of human beings. As the subsequent practice on reservations has demonstrated, this assumption was incorrect. Within the context of an area such as treaty law – which is by definition about States – avoiding State-centricity is a very challenging task. Two main mechanisms were adopted in the re-written opinion to address treaty law's State-centricity on the question of reservations: (1) the use of adjudicatory bodies and (2) a specific mechanism requiring States

[35] I Boerefijn, 'Impact on the Law on Treaty Reservations' in M Kamminga and M Scheinin (eds), *The Impact of Human Rights Law on General International Law* (Oxford, Oxford University Press, 2009) 68.

[36] K McCall-Smith, 'Reservations and the Determinative Function of the Human Rights Treaty Bodies' (2011) 54 *German Yearbook of International Law* 521.

[37] Convention on the Elimination of Discrimination against Women, 1249 UNTS 13 (adopted 18 December 1979, entered into force 3 September 1981); Convention on the Rights of the Child, 1577 UNTS 3 (adopted 20 November 1989, entered into force 2 September 1990). To review the reservations to either treaty, see the website: treaties.un.org.

to provide justifications for their reservations. These strategies are imperfect. For example, adjudicatory bodies suffer from their own gender bias and States, even if they must justify their reservations and objections, remain the primary focus of the reservations regime. However, we believe these strategies enable better oversight of States' reservations and create more opportunities to challenge reservations, rather than relying solely on the existing system. Finally, the re-written opinion attempts to avoid the 'object and purpose' test and return to the criteria of legal effects of reservations, thereby reducing the regime's ambiguity and increasing State accountability. Due to aforementioned limited literature or law specifically addressing women at the time, in our attempts to remain true to the era we have approached the re-written judgment as more of a reworking of the procedural tools in order to better accommodate the consideration of the impact of reservations on women that would follow many decades later.

On a few occasions in our re-written opinion we have remained true to the language of the original opinion. This is done with the purpose of demonstrating that even such an apparently conservative body as the ICJ writing in 1948 expresses opinions and uses a writing style that is not completely alien to feminist theory. Taking into account the enduring marginality of feminist approaches in international law, it is important to demonstrate the existing affinities between mainstream international law and the goals and approaches of feminist scholars working on international law issues.

JUDGMENT

RESERVATIONS TO THE CONVENTION ON THE PREVENTION AND PUNISHMENT OF THE CRIME OF GENOCIDE

International Court of Justice

Judges: Smith (President), McCall-Smith and Yahyaoui Krivenko

Advisory Opinion of May 28th, 1951

In so far as concerns the Convention on the Prevention and Punishment of the Crime of Genocide in the event of a State ratifying or acceding to the Convention subject to a reservation made either on ratification or on accession, or on signature followed by ratification:

I. Can the reserving State be regarded as being a party to the Convention while still maintaining its reservation if' the reservation is objected to by one or more of the parties to the Convention but not by others?

II. If the answer to Question I is in the affirmative, what is the effect of the reservation as between the reserving State and:
(a) The parties which object to the reservation?
(b) Those which accept it?

III. What would be the legal effect as regards the answer to Question I if an objection to a reservation is made:
(a) By a signatory which has not yet ratified?
(b) By a State entitled to sign or accede but which has not yet done so?

- -

Consideration of the law of treaties relating to reservations will follow some general observations on international law. Though the law of treaties is an amalgamation of customary rules and State or regional practices, several overarching principles can be discerned. That a State cannot be bound without its consent is a fundamental principle of international law. It therefore follows that a multilateral treaty represents the final agreement following consensual negotiations between States. Until recently, this fact of international treaty negotiation did not warrant reconsideration as the number of States participating in mutual treaties was small. However, in the decolonization era of this Twentieth Century the expansion in the number of nation-states demands that we recognize the reality that not all States are able to fully participate in the negotiation of every multilateral treaty. Treaty law must allow some flexibility for States to participate in the systems created through international codification. Reservations facilitate one dimension of such flexibility by allowing a State to subscribe to a treaty regime with some obligations being excluded that would otherwise be part and parcel of the State's treaty commitments.

Recognizing the importance of flexibility in treaty making, a second, long-accepted principle exists in international law, namely that Contracting Parties are not entitled to frustrate, impair or negate the objects and purposes of a treaty by means of a unilateral decision in the form of a reservation.[1] The fundamental integrity of a treaty must be upheld at all times. To allow a single State to degrade the integrity of a freely concluded agreement would be to cast off the solemn purposes with which States take up the task of good faith negotiation. At the same time, preventing a State from becoming a party to a treaty due to a good faith reservation firmly rooted in its national law ignores the role of the State as the outward embodiment of a particular people with distinct legal systems and social priorities.

The Court also observes that the three questions before it are purely abstract in character. They refer neither to those reservations which have, in fact, been made to the Genocide Convention by certain States, nor to the objections which have been made to such reservations by other States. They do not even refer to reservations that may in future be made in respect of any particular article; nor do they refer to the objections in response to reservations already made, despite the availability of specific documentation (Pleadings, Oral Arguments, Documents, Annexed Documents 1–22). However, it is not possible to provide an answer to the questions addressed to the Court without considering the existing practice of States, including the existing reservations and objections to the Genocide Convention. Therefore, while maintaining the framework of the questions as they are formulated in the General Assembly resolution (limited to the Genocide Convention and abstract or unrelated to any specific reservation or objection), the Court is bound to consider the broader rules regulating reservations and objections to multilateral international treaties as well as the nature and content of existing reservations and objections to the Genocide Convention.

In recent history, the League of Nations addressed the issue of reservations to a humanitarian convention, namely the Slavery Convention of 1926. Much like the Genocide Convention, the humanitarian reach of the Slavery Convention assigns no benefit to the States that become a party thereto: the sole beneficiaries are individual human beings and accordingly, reservations to the substantive provisions are not considered in the text, nor have any reservations been formulated. (League of Nations, Slavery Convention, 25 September 1926, entry into force 7 March 1927). The Slavery Convention does permit a State to exclude its application to certain of its territories with the option of subsequent, territory specific accession at a later date (Slavery Convention, article 9), however, this does not in any way impair the integrity of the Convention as applied to the territories that have

[1] HW Malkin, 'Reservations to Multilateral Treaties' (1926) 7 *British Yearbook of International Law* 141, 142.

ratified it. Furthermore, in connection with the adoption of the Convention on Opium and Drugs of 1925, the League Committee for the Progressive Codification of International Law outlined (League of Nations Document C.357.M.130.1927.V) that:

> In order that any reservation whatever may be validly made in regard to a clause of the treaty, it is essential that this reservation should be accepted by all the contracting parties, as would have been the case if it had been put forward in the course of the negotiations. If not, the reservation, like the signature to which it is attached, is null and void.

Though the Committee did not hold a law-making function, the debate within that group and its ultimate view on reservations reflected the consensus of the States therein. Subsequently, the Secretary-General continued the practice of unanimity (United Nations Secretary-General Report to the General Assembly, UN Doc. A/1372 (1950), Annex I), which, in turn, led to the consideration of the questions before the court today.

There is no doubt that the landscape in which multilateral treaties are developed has undergone substantial change in the last fifty years. The number of States in 1900, roughly 45, has almost doubled in a very short span of time. With this expansion, the corpus of international law is now faced with highly varied legal systems and societies that must be reconciled in pursuit of a common law of nations. As guardians of international law, it therefore has fallen upon this Court to consider whether this substantially changed international community of States must adhere strictly to those rules of law observed when the international community was markedly different in composition. How further expansion of this international community and potential treaty parties might be affected by our decision is also at the forefront of our deliberations.

Question I is framed in the following terms:

> Can the reserving State be regarded as being a party to the Convention while still maintaining its reservation if the reservation is objected to by one or more of the parties to the Convention but not by others?

The United Nations Sixth Committee considered the plausibility of permitting reservations during the preparation of the draft Genocide Convention. Although it ultimately decided not to insert a special article on reservations, comments were prepared by the Secretary-General on the draft note:

> … (1) It would seem that reservations of a general scope have no place in a convention of this kind which does not deal with the private interests of a State, but with the preservation of an element of international order …; (2) perhaps in the course of discussion in the General Assembly it will be possible to allow certain limited reservations (Document E/447, p. 55, in Written Statement of the Untied Nations, (14 December 1950), *Genocide Opinion*, Pleadings, Oral Arguments, Documents, 28 May 1951, p. 88).

The potential to make limited reservations to the Convention is confirmed both by comments made during the drafting process of the Convention (United Nations Sixth Committee, 1–2 December 1948), by the Secretary-General and also, implicitly, by the very terms of Question I. It is now for this Court to examine what kind of reservations may be made while preserving the ultimate purpose of the Convention. It necessarily follows that we must then determine what kind of objections may be made and with what legal effect.

In the post-war period, where the recollections of the many atrocities set against human kind continue to shape our collective thinking, the purpose behind humanitarian-focused treaties is to protect against future repetitions of the actions that led to such great human suffering. States discussed this context extensively during the drafting of the articles that were ultimately included in the Genocide Convention. Crucial to the preservation of the aims of the Convention is the opportunity to call a State to account when it is deemed to have breached a provision of the treaty. It follows that any reservation against the automatic jurisdiction of this Court to hear disputes, as outlined in Article IX of the Genocide Convention, would undermine the intention of the contracting States in including the automatic dispute resolution solution outlined in its text and are therefore not permitted. While the automatic dispute resolution mechanism ensures resolution of issues regarding treaty compliance, reservations regarding other non-essential aspects of the treaty may nonetheless be envisaged and are, indeed, acceptable.

If negotiating States elect to permit reservations, directions as to what reservations are permissible should in the first instance be set out under the terms of the treaty. The Pan-American Union has, by previous agreement, established an alternative reservations practice to that of the Secretary-General, which applies only to multilateral treaties adopted within that system:

> The Pan-American Union procedure permits a State to proceed with its ratification in spite of the fact that one or more of the signatory States may object to the reservation, *whereas the procedure followed by the Secretary-General of the United Nations has the effect of preventing the particular State from becoming a Party to the convention if any single State among those which have already ratified voices its disapproval of the proposed reservation.* (Written statement by the Organization of the American States (14 December 1950), *Genocide Opinion*, Pleadings, Oral Arguments, Documents, 28 May 1951, pp. 15–20, p. 19, *italics* ours, see also Organization of American States, Convention on Treaties, 20 February 1928, articles 6–7).

Yet another example is found in the recent European Convention for the Protection of Human Rights and Fundamental Freedoms of 1950:

> 1. Any State may, when signing this Convention or when depositing its instrument of ratification, make a reservation in respect of any particular provision

> of the Convention to the extent that any law then in force in its territory is not in conformity with the provision. Reservations of a general character shall not be permitted under this Article.
> 2. Any reservation made under this Article shall contain a brief statement of the law concerned.

These examples demonstrate that alternative reservations practices can and do exist as long as the negotiating States are willing to articulate practices that depart from the, apparently, broadly accepted unanimity practice exercised by the Secretary-General and his predecessor in the League of Nations. These examples are, however, different from the situation we are faced with in so far as those regimes have agreed in advance to permit certain reservations. We are faced with the fact that the drafting committee for the Genocide Convention did not intend to permit unilateral reservations, whether compatible with the objects and purposes of the Convention or not. During the preparation of the draft Genocide Convention, the Secretary-General highlighted in the commentary on draft Article XVII (Draft Convention of the Crime of Genocide, 26 June 1947) that no proposition had been put forward on reservations and elaborated as follows:

> *Comment.*
> At the present stage of the preparatory work, it is doubtful whether reservations ought to be permitted and whether an article relating to reservations ought to be included in the Convention.
> We shall restrict ourselves to the following remarks:
>
> (1) It would seem that reservations of a general scope have no place in a convention of this kind which does not deal with the private interests of a State, but with the preservation of an element of international order.
>
> For example, the convention will or will not protect this or that human group. It is unthinkable that in this respect the scope of the convention should vary according to the reservations possibly accompanying accession by certain States.
>
> (2) Perhaps in the course of discussion in the General Assembly it will be possible to allow certain limited reservations.
>
> These reservations might be of two kinds: either reservations which would be defined by the convention itself, and which all the States would have the option to express, or questions of detail which some States might wish to reserve and which the General Assembly might decide to allow.

Subsequent comments by States on the Ad Hoc Committee on Genocide underscored that there was 'no need for any reservations' (UN Document E/AC/25/10, p. 5). This position was adopted unanimously by the full Ad Hoc Committee on 27 April 1948 (UN Document E/AC/25/SR/23, p. 7). Subsequent discussions in the Sixth Committee revealed that some States did question whether reservations to one or another of the articles would be permissible and the response received by the rapporteur indicated that:

> … if a government made reservations regarding a convention, it could not be considered as a party to that convention unless the other contracting parties accepted those reservations, expressly or tacitly.

Thus, it seems from the discussions and decisions taken in the finalization of the text of the Genocide Convention that no reservation was deemed possible unless accepted unanimously by the other contracting parties. However, immediately preceding the adoption of the Convention, the Sixth Committee heard from several States which indicated that their governments would only sign the Convention subject to certain reservations (1st and 2nd December 1948). Thus the seemingly clear position on reservations to the Genocide Convention adopted in the Ad Hoc Committee on Genocide was thrown into question following the adoption of the text and subsequent opening for signature of the Convention.

A range of States commented on the issue of reservations in connection with this matter as raised before the Court. The United Kingdom, for example, firmly supports the practice of the Secretary-General, citing the law-making nature of the agreement (Written statement by the United Kingdom (Jan. 1951), *Genocide Opinion*, Pleadings, Oral Arguments, Documents, 28 May 1951, pp. 48–76 (UK Statement to the ICJ), p. 49). Furthermore, the United Kingdom pointed out that it was not necessarily the making of reservations to which it was opposed, but rather the fact that there was a 'failure to adopt the proper methods and procedures for doing so' in the Genocide Convention (UK Statement to the ICJ, p. 54, n. 1); therefore, the effect of unilateral reservations in the absence of a provision for such was an entirely different proposition than making a reservation when the process was specifically outlined in a convention. The United Kingdom was also concerned that unchecked reservations would impede the finality of the text as the negotiated terms would always be subject to variation in light of subsequently-made reservations.

An almost opposite approach advocated by the Union of Soviet Socialist Republics and a number of associated States is premised on the principle of absolute sovereignty. The position dictates that making reservations is the sovereign act of the State, a right which is absolute and necessary (UK Statement to the ICJ, p. 53; UNGA, 6th Sess., Official Records of the Sixth Committee, 273rd meeting, paras. 34 and 36).

The United States of America advanced the principle of consent as the essential element in determinations regarding treaties. The US reiterated that 'States entitled to ratify or accede may do so subject to reservations even if these are objected to by one or more other parties to the Convention' (US statement to the ICJ, p. 25).

The Court must consider the special characteristics of the Genocide Convention; it has several aspects which may distinguish it from traditional public international law treaties. The origins of the Convention show that the

United Nations intended to condemn and punish genocide as a crime under international law because it denies entire human groups the right to exist: such a denial shocks the conscience of mankind and results in great losses to humanity, and is contrary to moral law and to the spirit and aims of the United Nations (Resolution 96(I) of the General Assembly, 11th December 1946). The aims, effects and consequences of the Convention transcend the discrete will of states and their individual national interests. Rather, it was adopted for a humanitarian purpose; namely, the protection of individuals from a particular form of arbitrary exercise of power by States as international actors. The Convention's aims and objectives therefore extend beyond the sum of interests of States parties. They establish a common interest of the international community to eradicate one of the causes of injustice and suffering, placing the interests and well-being of individuals and groups other than the State at the center of international law's preoccupations.

In furtherance of these objectives, the Convention obliges States to undertake certain measures. If States could tailor their obligations or avoid them completely through reservations, the aims of the Convention may not be met. In a convention of this type, one cannot speak of individual advantages and disadvantages to States; rather, the high ideals which inspired the Convention provide, by virtue of the common will of the parties, the foundation and measure of all its provisions. This can present challenges to States as the aims and benefits of the Convention are not felt directly by States themselves, but by individuals within those States. This means that even without the Convention, States are bound by the prohibition of genocide. It would be strange to allow, through the use of reservations, States who are parties to the Convention to be bound by lesser obligations than States that are not parties to the Convention. As a consequence, States cannot enter any reservations they may wish. Only some reservations are permitted. If the reservation would affect obligations that States are bound to respect by virtue of customary law, such a reservation would not be permitted. Reservations that would otherwise jeopardize the fulfilment of the aims and objectives of the Convention cannot be permitted either. Therefore, the question of objections to such a reservation and its effects does not arise. There is a need for an independent and objective determination of the nature of proposed reservations.

Nevertheless, the Genocide Convention is not completely unique. It is an outcome of, and one of the stages in, the modern development of international law that places individuals at the forefront of international law. Preambular paragraphs of the Charter of the United Nations acknowledge the centrality of human beings to international law; paragraph two reaffirms the faith of States Parties in human rights, in the dignity and worth of the human person and in the equal rights of all men and women; paragraph four addresses social progress and better standards of life. The promotion of human rights is also mentioned among the purposes of the United Nations (art. 1(3) UN Charter). The Universal Declaration of Human Rights, adopted by the General Assembly one day after the Genocide Convention, represents a stepping-stone towards development of a broader and more detailed framework for protection of individual human beings as discussed both during the drafting of the Universal Declaration and afterwards.[2] The Genocide Convention itself aims 'to liberate mankind from such an odious scourge' (Preamble to the Convention). In short, the sole purpose of the Convention is to protect every man, woman and child from the crime of genocide. This purpose leaves no room for States to exercise any interest of their own, nor does the text suggest the acceptability of any interest that would deter or contradict the singular, common purpose, which is the raison d'être of the Genocide Convention.

This brings us to the nature of acceptable reservations. As far as minor reservations are concerned, given the unique nature of the Convention, it is inconceivable that States would have contemplated that a minor reservation prevents a State from becoming a party to the Convention. However, it is important to exercise caution and to consider why States would want to make reservations to the Genocide Convention. Taking into account the nature of the Convention, its aims and objectives as described above, it is possible to affirm that a reservation to the Genocide Convention will be considered minor in highly exceptional circumstances. To give an example of such circumstances, some States parties to the Convention disagreed with art. XII of the Convention that permits application of the Convention to be extended to non-self-governing territories through a notification addressed to the Secretary-General. Curtailment of art. XII through a reservation demonstrates the different desires of States for the Convention to be applicable to the entirety of territories of States parties (including non self-governing territories) without any notification. Since this type of reservation does not limit the application of the Convention, but actually purports to enlarge its scope, it will not endanger the object and purpose of the Convention.

At this stage, we need to return to the issue of determination of the nature of reservations and the most appropriate way to distinguish minor reservations from more far-reaching – and thus impermissible – reservations. As will be indicated below, the practice demonstrates that it is not possible to expect States to make systematic and appropriate evaluation of the nature of reservations. Therefore, this task should not be left to States alone. Although from a point of principle, the prevention of genocide has now been stated to be a common aim of the international community as a whole, it does not follow that individual States will always be sufficiently attentive when faced with reservations that appear to either represent only a distant and unspecified threat to the aims of the Convention or that offer no threat to their own populations.

It may, however, be asked whether the General Assembly of the United Nations, in approving the Genocide Convention, had in mind the practice according to which the Secretary-General, in exercising his functions as a depositary, did not regard a reservation as definitively accepted until it had been established that none of the other contracting States objected to it. If this were the case, it might

[2] See the summary of various developments and discussions provided in Chapter V of the Yearbook of the United Nations 1948–49.

be argued that the implied intention of the contracting parties was to make the effectiveness of any reservation to the Genocide Convention conditional on the consent of all the parties.

While the Court does not consider that this view corresponds to contemporary practice, it does recognize that the Secretary-General exercises the same administrative practice utilized by his League of Nations predecessor as depositary for a broad range of multilateral treaties. Representatives from across the several lines of opinion expressed in both the fifth session of the General Assembly and the Sixth Committee took part in the negotiation and adoption of the Genocide Convention, though none felt it incumbent to specify a particular reservations practice. The prevailing attitude of non-commitment to a particular or clear reservation regime within the Genocide Convention may reflect the reality that within the broad international system there is little practice with regards to reservations. It also may reflect the fact that this type of treaty, which generates no specific benefits for the contracting States, but instead directly benefits humankind, renders it necessary to re-evaluate the silences of States on international treaty practice concerning reservations.

Ideally, when drafting this type of convention States should envisage the appointment of a dispute settlement body or the establishment of independent expert bodies entrusted with the task of evaluating the permissibility of reservations. Since the Genocide Convention does not establish such a body, we need to identify other possible ways of evaluating the legal effect of reservations. The first step, would be to require all States to express their opinion on any proposed reservation. As indicated above, silence on the part of States cannot be interpreted as an indicator of the nature of the reservation. In case of disputes or disagreements, it appears that within the existing framework of the Genocide Convention, article IX establishing the competence of this Court for resolution of disputes 'relating to the interpretation, application or fulfillment' of the Convention opens a suitable avenue for resolving issues related to the determination of the nature of reservations. If a particular reservation is deemed impermissible by the agreed mechanism, the State remains party to the Convention without the benefit of the reservation. Such a reservation is thus void *ab initio*. Reaching the conclusion of impermissibility is, however, more complex than handing the determinative function to the Court in absolute – as indicated by a number of the proposed reservations to the Convention. A simple one-State determination of permissibility is equally implausible. Therefore, the process of determining the permissibility of a reservation must be considered further.

In the instance that an established Contracting Party objects to a reservation based on its legal effects, it must provide a concise statement of law with specific reference to the Convention as to why it finds the reservation impermissible/invalid. Reservations that are deemed impermissible by a State may be deemed valid on fuller explanation by the reserving State. Through an exchange of letters, objecting States may work with the reserving State to correct the impermissible reservation. This dialogue between the States recognizes that domestic law may prevent a State from subscribing to every obligation in an unfettered manner. During the time of dispute and up until the impermissibility is resolved, the reserving State will not be considered a Contracting Party. If after six months the reserving and objecting States are unable to resolve the matter of legality, a wider Conference of the Parties should be called to ascertain the view of all Contracting Parties. If a super-majority view on the legality of the reservation cannot then be determined, the reserving State and the original objecting State or States may then refer the matter to this Court, as the appointed dispute settlement body. Until a final determination on the permissibility of the reservation can be made the reserving State will not be deemed party to the Convention.

Upon a final determination that the reservation is impermissible, the reserving State will have the option to sever the reservation from its instrument of consent to be bound to the Genocide Convention. Upon removing the reservation, the State will then become a party to the treaty subject to the provisions set out in the Convention. If the State refuses to remove the impermissible reservation it will be unable to become a party to the Convention. If the State has previously signed the Convention, the illegality of the reservation will not invalidate the signature and a good faith obligation not to thwart the Convention will continue. However, a State Party may not enjoy full status until the offending reservation is removed or redrafted to correct the impermissibility.

It is prudent to maintain a mechanism for assessing systems within each individual treaty regime by allowing the Contracting States to adjudge the permissibility, or legality, of a proposed reservation. Though this has not been spelled out in the Genocide Convention, international practice acknowledges, as does this Court, that reservations cannot be avoided in light of the increasing number of States with inevitably varied legal systems and diverse societies.

In consideration of the profound divergence of views of the States that have registered an opinion on the subject, the answer to Question I mandates that flexibility underpin reservations practice to the Genocide Convention. This flexibility accommodates a practice which permits a State filing a reservation along with its instrument of consent to be bound to the Genocide Convention to become a contracting party even in the face of an objection to the reservation by one or more States where other contracting parties have accepted the reservation as long as the objection is not based on impermissibility. However, in light of the negotiating States opting not to adopt a specific rule on reservations in the development of the Convention, special attention must be given to delimiting the extent to which this flexibility may be exercised.

Because an element of politics necessarily lurks beneath the surface of all interstate relationships, the Court finds that both the circumstances under which the Genocide Convention was adopted and the coherence of international law demand a tool of assessment to determine the validity of a reservation that does not ultimately turn on the political inclinations of the State. In other words, there must be a litmus test to determine at what point the reservation can stand alone or fall outwith the determination by another contracting party.

The omission of a convention-specific facility addressing reservations suggests two possible realities: first, as suggested above, the community of States has not had a great deal of experience with multilateral agreements on the scale of the Genocide Convention; or, two, the natural self-interest and subjective nature of States prevented serious contemplation of how reservations might be employed by contracting parties. The established principles of international law are challenged by the introduction of the Genocide Convention due to the specific nature of the Convention as a norm-creating or standard-setting convention. Though an element of flexibility underpins the increasing number of multilateral treaties being generated through the United Nations, specific attention to the nature of this particular Convention, its objects, and the opportunity for wider participation, mandate careful consideration of how reservations will impact the Convention overall. For these reasons, the onus must remain on the reserving State to provide detailed reasoning as to why the reservation is necessary.

In response to Question I, the Court finds that the determination of whether a State can be considered a party to the treaty following a reservation which is objected to by some Contracting Parties and accepted by others must follow a two-fold enquiry. Initially, when a reservation is proposed in connection with a State's consent to be bound to the Genocide Convention, all existing Contracting Parties must deliver written notification of acceptance or objection to a purposed reservation within twelve months of the reservation being filed with the United Nations Secretary-General as the official depositary. The objecting State should clarify on what legal grounds the objection to the formulated reservation is based. Usually, an objection may be based on a general opposition – with a preference of maintaining maximum treaty integrity – or impermissibility. The former will not have any bearing on the ability of the reserving State to become a party to the treaty. The latter will instigate a resolution process focused on ensuring that the reservation upholds the integrity of the treaty as determined by the States Parties to the Genocide Convention. A State Party will be able to avoid a prolonged road to confirmed treaty relations by outlining both a clear legal purpose for any reservation lodged and any legal effects for the implementation of Convention obligations within its jurisdiction.

Contemporary international law does not prohibit reservations *per se*; it also does not prevent the situation that one State may object to a reservation based on the alteration of substantive obligation effected by the reservation (UN Secretary-General, UN Doc. A/1372 (1950), Annex I). An alteration in legal effect does not render a reservation illegal. Permissible reservations couched in legitimate domestic opposition to a particular treaty obligation are understood as the epitome of a reservation in theory. Such a situation is precisely that which was considered by both the General Assembly debates and the Sixth Committee discussions on reservations to the Genocide Convention, which underscored that some States could only subscribe to a multilateral treaty of its nature if reservations were permitted. Fellow States Parties are nonetheless not prohibited from lodging an objection to a reservation that is inherently permissible. As guardians of the treaty regime to which all States Parties have committed, diligent monitoring of both fellow States Parties and potential States Parties speaks to the good faith and high purposes that the Genocide Convention embodies. To achieve the ultimate purpose of the Convention it is both preferable and acceptable for States Parties to take a view on all reservations proposed, even where the reservation is permissible.

Permissible reservations will not prevent the reserving State from becoming a party to the treaty. It is incumbent upon the objecting State to elucidate the reasons behind the objection and, where those reasons are not based on the reservation's impermissibility, it will not prevent the reserving State from becoming party to the treaty. The effect of this situation between the parties concerned will be addressed in the Court's response to Question II. Objections based on the incompatibility of the reservation present a more difficult situation.

To maintain a focus on the ultimate purpose of the Convention, it is also prudent to limit the duration for which a reservation may be in effect. Contracting parties should review the need to maintain reservations submitted upon first subscription to the Convention at intervals established by them, but not greater than five years.

The context described above highlights the specificities of the Genocide Convention, but also reflects new developments in international law that bring the individual towards the centre of the discipline's preoccupations. From this perspective, we need to ask anew the question about the appropriate rules to govern reservations to this type of convention. Can reservations to such a convention be permitted? Taking into account the universal character of the Convention, the fact that without a broad participation of almost all states the aims of the Convention might be challenging to achieve, the answer to this question is in the affirmative. It would be difficult to imagine that participation in a convention of such a universal character would be impeded by a slight disagreement over minor aspects of the Convention. Shall any reservations to the Convention be permitted? This question is of fundamental importance. As we previously observed, the aims of the Convention demand that states are prevented from tailoring the obligations formulated in the Convention according to their individual desires.

It follows from the foregoing considerations that Question I, on account of its abstract character, cannot be given an absolute answer. The specific nature of the Convention requires individual consideration of purported reservations and objections thereto. This is specifically so when the objection concerns the incompatibility of the reservation at issue. However, it is clear that in other circumstances – that is, minor reservations – a reserving State can be a party to the Convention while still maintaining its reservation if the reservation is objected to by one of more of the parties to the Convention but not be others. Particularly in light of the purpose of the convention, it would be inconceivable that a single objection to a minor reservation would prevent a reserving State from becoming a party to the Convention.

- -

Having replied to Question I, the Court will now examine Question II which is framed as follows:

> If the answer to Question I is in the affirmative, what is the effect of the reservation as between the reserving State and:
>
> (a) the parties which object to the reservation?
>
> (b) those which accept it?

Therefore, the Court will now address the status of treaty relations between a reserving state and those States that accept the reservation and those that maintain an objection to a reservation following a full enquiry by a Conference of the Parties. The considerations which aided the formulation of the Court's response to Question I are equally, if not more, important in relation to Question II as the response speaks directly to the legal effect that will be generated by both objection and acceptance of a reservation. As previously outlined, the ability of each individual contracting State to the Genocide Convention to determine the validity of a reservation is accepted in international law. Though different practices are apparent across States, each practice, whether rigid or flexible, is grounded firmly in the principle of State sovereignty and the attendant principle that no State may be bound further it has consented. State sovereignty bestows upon both participants of the bilateral reservations dialogue the ability to determine the extent to which each State is willing to engage in relations with the other.

It is clear from the fifth session of the General Assembly and the Sixth Committee that State practice with regards to reservations accommodates a range of outcomes. The first prevents the reserving state from becoming a party to the Convention. This is the outcome where it is determined that a reservation is impermissible and the reserving State is unwilling to remove the reservation. The second and third practices permit the reserving State to become a contracting party to the Convention, but the relationship between it and the objecting State either will be modified or will not exist. The latter two practices necessitate an inquiry in to the nature of the objection because that underpins the extent to which the relationship is altered. Though not expressly stated, the crux of the issue is the permissibility of the reservation in the context of the wider Convention system: enjoying a flexible system cannot be at the cost of destroying the integrity of the treaty.

As previously stated, States are at liberty to object to reservations on purely political grounds or no grounds at all. In these instances, it is deemed that these objections are less concerned with the integrity of the treaty and more with the desire to avoid treaty relations with the reserving State. It is not the role of international law to pander to displays of political might. Therefore, the more accurate response to an objection that has no articulated legal basis is that, unless the establishment of treaty relations is expressly excluded in the language of the objection, treaty relations will have been established. This does not require comity between the reserving and objecting State; it merely supports both States as parties to the

Convention, pays homage to the purpose behind the obligations therein, and respects the objects of the Convention. The Organization of American States drew the Court's attention to the Havana Convention on Consular Agents. The Dominican Republic ratified the convention with several reservations. The United States objected on the ground that those reservations 'would deprive the convention of a large part of its value.' (Written Statement of the Organization of American States, ICJ, Pleadings, Oral Arguments, Documents, Reservations to the Convention on the Prevention and Punishment of the Crime of Genocide, Advisory Opinion of 28 May 1951, p. 19). No other State party objected. This can be attributed to at least one of two factors: either the reservation was not deemed by other States to be depriving the Convention of its value, or they simply did not exercise enough care in evaluating the consequences of the reservation. If the former is true, it signals the need to consider carefully the opinion of any State (albeit that States' statements about a reservation, and their reaction to it, is not necessarily determinative of the nature of that reservation). If the latter is true, no meaning can be attributed to the silence of States in so far as the evaluation of their position with regard to the reservation is concerned. In both cases, States are not always reliable defenders of the aims of a convention, even in such traditional fields of international law as consular relations. This statement holds even truer for a convention that aims to protect the lives of individuals.

The possibility of States having divergent views on the acceptability of a reservation to the Genocide Convention presents several hurdles. The status of a State that has filed a reservation to which there has been a firm objection presents the most challenging outcome concerning the resultant relationship between States Parties. Recalling the varied practices of States regarding the consequence resulting from a single State's objection to a reservation, the substantive consideration for determining the legal effect of an objection on the relationship between the reserving and objecting States is the basis of the objection to that reservation.

The exchange between the reserving state and objecting state establishes a unique and exclusive relationship that, in the first instance, is enjoyed only *inter se* and does not impact either State's relations with other contracting parties. If follows that the basis of the objection, as well as any statement on the legal effect of the objection on the relationship, will shape the relationship.

Objections based on impermissibility need not be considered further as the reserving State will not become a party to the treaty unless the reservation is ultimately deemed permissible following the review mechanisms outlined previously.

Good faith objections not based on impermissibility will not impair the establishment of treaty relations between the reserving and objecting States, unless this outcome is expressly stated in the objection. The relationship will, however, be modified in so far as the provision to which the reservation relates does not apply between the reserving and the objecting States to the extent of the reservation. By contrast, States accepting the reservation will be able to rely on the accepted doctrine of reciprocity and benefit from the accepted reservation in the same way as the reserving State. In the Genocide Convention, this is of little legal value to the objecting State Party as there are no benefits accruing to the States Parties by virtue of the nature of the Convention's obligations. However, in relation to some articles of the Convention, tangible difference in rights and obligations arising might arise between States who have accepted a reservation and those who have objected to it. Thus, if we recall the example of reservations to Art XII of the Convention, we can see that the Convention will apply to the non self-governing territories of States who do not object to it, without any need for notification. However, the Convention will not apply to the non self-governing territories of States objecting to the reservation, unless the objecting State decides so. While the requirement of notification as a legal obligation also disappears for the objecting State, the applicability of the Convention to non self-governing territories remains at the discretion of the objecting State.

The Court gives the following answers to the questions referred to it by the General Assembly:

> *On Question I*
>
> the specific nature of the Convention requires individual consideration of purported reservations and objections thereto, particularly when the objection concerns the incompatibility of the reservation at issue, but it would be inconceivable that a single objection to a minor reservation would prevent a reserving State from becoming a party to the Convention. A state can therefore remain a party to a treaty whilst maintaining its reservation.
>
> *On Question II*
>
> (a) if a party's reservation is considered impermissible, it will not become a party to the Convention; otherwise a good faith reservation will not impair the establishment of treaty relations between the reserving and objecting States unless otherwise outlined in the objection. The provision to which the reservation relates will not apply between the reserving and the objecting States to the extent of the reservation.
> (b) an objection to a reservation made by a State which is entitled to sign or accede to the treaty, but which has not yet done so, is without legal effect.

Reflections

The principal barrier encountered during the rewriting process was the need to keep the opinion true to the knowledge and writings of the time – ie almost 70 years ago. International law through the UN was very much in a formative period and internationally agreed human rights treaties were but an aspiration. As we mention in the authors' note, even the term 'genocide' itself was new and innovative, yet an absolutely necessary term given the evidence of atrocities emerging into popular knowledge through both the media and the work of the Nuremberg and Tokyo tribunals. Given that the UN itself was in its infancy, this posed some challenges, especially because from the outset it was clear to us that approaching this advisory opinion from a feminist perspective signified in the first place challenging the centrality of the State. However, it was difficult to come up with ideas on how to do so because the advisory opinion focuses on a field of international law that is *par excellence* about States and their will: treaty law. With a growing body of literature questioning the State-centricity of international law,[1] arguing for extending obligations (particularly in the field of human rights) to individuals, it would be easier to achieve this in the twenty-first century, particularly vis-a-vis parties to treaties. However, the issue of reservations and objections could arise with any (non-State) party under modern treaty law as is recognised by contemporary business and human rights discourse. Feminist approaches to international law have been articulated in the decades after this advisory opinion,[2] thus the need to keep the opinion contemporaneous inevitably tempered our approach. A particular difficulty stems from modern reflections on how this particular advisory opinion left the door wide-open for what has become substantial impairment of human rights treaty implementation due to wide-ranging reservations.[3] Combining the need for challenging the centrality of the state with the nature of the specific Convention that the advisory opinion deals with – namely a treaty

[1] See eg AC Cutler, 'Critical Reflections on the Westphalian Assumptions of International Law and Organization: A Crisis of Legitimacy' (2001) 27(2) *Review of International Studies* 133. For a more forceful argument on the role of individuals in international law and the ensuing challenge of state-centricity, see Ekaterina Yahyaoui Krivenko, *Rethinking Human Rights and Global Constitutionalism: From Inclusion to Belonging* (Cambridge, Cambridge University Press, 2017) 19.

[2] For an overview, see H Charlesworth, C Chinkin and S Wright, 'Feminist Approaches to International Law' (1991) 85(4) *American Journal of International Law* 613.

[3] KL McCall-Smith, 'Mind the Gaps: The ILC Guide to Practice and Reservations to Human Rights Treaties' (2014) 16 *International Community Law Review* 263; HB Schöpp-Schilling, 'Reservations to the Convention on the Elimination of All Forms of Discrimination Against Women: An Unresolved Issue or (No) New Developments' in I Ziemele (ed), *Reservations to Human Rights Treaties and the Vienna Convention Regime: Conflict, Harmony or Reconciliation* (Martinus Nijhoff, The Hague, 2004) 17–18; L Lijnzaad, *Reservations to UN Human Rights Traties: Ratify and Ruin?* (Martinus Nijhoff, The Hague, 1995); C Chinkin, 'Reservations and Objections to the Convention on the Elimination of Discrimination Against Women' in JP Gardner (ed), *Human Rights as General Norms and a State's Right to Opt Out: Reservations and Objections to Human Rights Conventions* (London, BIICL, 1997); B Clark, 'The Vienna Convention Reservations Regime and the Convention on Discrimination Against Women' (1991) 85 *American Journal of International Law* 281.

that is aimed at protecting human beings, not states and their interests – we felt that there was a strong need for a more active role for potentially affected persons within the treaty regime.

Ekaterina proposed that within the context of the reservations regime, this more active role of potentially affected persons (either as individuals or as groups of individuals) could be envisaged at the stage of determining the permissibility of a particular reservation. The mechanism she envisaged for this more active role was a referendum. Since States are not genuinely and systematically interested in upholding standards enshrined in these types of treaties, the determination of permissibility of reservations needs to be done by those who will be genuinely interested in the fulfilment of the aims of a particular treaty. In the case of the Genocide Convention and in the case of many human rights treaties, the genuinely interested and potentially affected parties are human beings themselves. Therefore, she suggested, by carefully organising referenda on each proposed reservation in order to determine the permissibility of the reservations, the voice of individuals could be introduced directly into the regime of treaty law. Of course, the organisation of referenda would be a very challenging process that needs to be supervised and conducted by an independent international institution. Notably, referenda would also carry a large economic cost and one that in the immediate aftermath of a devastating war, was undoubtedly not one that States would be eager to pursue as they faced the early stages of putting State infrastructure back together. Within this process, the determination of those who would be entitled to vote is of crucial importance because equating the voting population with the population of a particular State runs the danger of silencing minorities that especially within the context of the Genocide Convention would represent potentially the most affected population. Therefore, in some cases the circle of individuals entitled to vote has to be distinct from the population of a particular State. For instance, in relation to the Genocide Convention it might be necessary to compose groups based on the relevant criteria mentioned in the Convention itself: national, ethnical, racial or religious. Also, it could be envisaged that the population of several States constitutes the core of the potentially affected. Thus, a variety of technical details would need to be reflected upon in implementing this idea and these would, ultimately, exceed the competence of the ICJ. The Court is, as has been evidenced through its own experience, not able to direct states as to how to conduct their internal affairs, even if an international rule is a core feature of a particular action.[4]

Following extensive discussions, the chamber ultimately agreed that we could not pursue this idea within the re-written judgment. We arrived at a consensus that we wanted to produce a judgment that would be acceptable to the mainstream. Stretching the possibility of the law at the point in time in society and legal

[4] This has been demonstrated by cases such as *LaGrand* (Germany v US) [2001] ICJ Rep 466 and *Avena and other Mexican nationals* (*Mexico v US*) [2004] ICJ Rep 12 in terms of the enforcement of international law in the domestic legal system.

scholarship to create a clear recognition of women in international law would not, to us, benefit the overall project, which acknowledges that feminist theory was decidedly non-existent in international law at the time of the advisory opinion. We ultimately opted to tweak the mechanism that enables reservations in their modern form by increasing the oversight of States' reservations and demanding more stringent accountability for their use. We acknowledge that we could have been far more drastic, yet our tempered approach reflects impediments with the subject; we cannot rewrite history, but we can guard against these impediments in our work. Accordingly we acknowledged the need to introduce a degree of control over the nature of reservations through a less radical process, but one that would nevertheless ensure a more systematic and objective determination of the nature of reservations. Ultimately, we feel that our considered adjustments to the rule established by the ICJ could ultimately serve as an effective basis for examining reservations today and is not dissimilar to the approach adopted in the Istanbul Convention.[5]

The impact of the original advisory opinion has been especially marked in the field of human rights law. Article 19(c) of the Vienna Convention on the Law of Treaties draws on the advisory opinion, requiring reservations to be compatible with the object and purpose of the treaty. Today the practice of reserving and objecting can be more akin to a dialogue between States parties[6] as States exchange views on submitted reservations and declarations.[7] Reservations also are the focus of the dialogue that takes place between the reserving State and the treaty body, which is another mechanism and relationship that has grown out of the UN human rights system that was not anticipated at the time of the advisory opinion. In many ways, the evolution of the treaty bodies has lessened the burden on States to object to reservations as they address reservations in the context of their supervisory role.[8] This phenomenon contributed to the decision to be somewhat less radical in the redrafted opinion. However, there is debate as to whether restricting a substantive right or freedom can ever be in accordance with the object and purpose of a human rights treaty.[9] There is also debate as to which rights are, in fact, substantive considering the very broad range of obligations across the increasing number of human rights treaties. Nonetheless, the issue arises as evidenced by the number of

[5] Council of Europe Convention on Preventing and Combating Violence Against Women and Domestic Violence, CETS No 210 (adopted 11 May 2011, entered into force 1 August 2014) (Istanbul Convention).

[6] For an analysis of this with respect to CEDAW, see E Yahyaoui Krivenko, 'The Reservation Dialogue as a Constitution Making Process' (2013) 15 and (2014) 16(3) *International Community Law Review* 381 and 306, especially s 4.

[7] See C Redgwell, 'Universality or Integrity? Some Reflections on Reservations to General Multilateral Treaties' (1993) *British Yearbook of International Law* 245.

[8] K McCall-Smith, 'Reservations and the Determinative Function of the Human Rights Treaty Bodies' (2012) 54 *German Yearbook of International Law* 521.

[9] See, eg Human Rights Committee, General comment on issues relating to reservations made upon ratification or accession to the Covenant or the Optional Protocols thereto, or in relation to declarations under article 41 of the Covenant, UN Doc CCPR/C/21/Rev.1/Add.6 (1994).

declarations which purport to restrict the application of a treaty when such application is contrary to claimed religious or ideological values of the state party.[10] Such general 'reservations' are particularly common in human rights treaties.[11] The practice of producing very extensive and general reservations is particularly visible within the context of treaties that deal with issues of particular relevance to women. CEDAW is a paramount example of a treaty that, despite an almost universal record of ratifications (US, Iran and Sudan remaining notable exceptions), has attracted an impressive number of reservations that are not followed by a consistent pattern of objections.[12]

Perhaps a general lesson from our experience relates to the limitations inherent in this type of project. Revisiting one of the early advisory opinions of the ICJ, yet restricting interpretation to the sources available at time of that opinion was a major limitation as the law of treaties was still in the gestation phase and reservations, in particular, were only a marginal subject of study for long serving civil servants, all of whom were inevitably men. Whilst the benefit of hindsight demonstrates the impact of the opinion, it is hard to argue that the peace and stability focus of the UN in the post-Second World War context would have enabled any dramatically different opinion than that which was produced by the ICJ.

One important conclusion about the nature of international law that we drew from this experience is that the discipline of international law creates a series of internal pressures on those who self-identify as specialists of international law, thus limiting the range of available reform options. With regard to the nature of feminist approaches to international law, this exercise demonstrates the flexibility and diversity within feminist scholarship. To be a feminist does not necessarily mean any radical departure from the commonly accepted methods of international law. Feminism can be radical, challenging the very foundations of law, but it can also produce better outcomes within the existing framework.

[10] See, eg J Connors, 'The Women's Convention in the Muslim World' in JP Gardiner (ed), *Human Rights as General Norms and a State's Right to Opt Out: Reservations and Objections to Human Rights Conventions* (London, BIICL, 1997).

[11] On the Nordic approach, see J Klabbers, 'Accepting the Unacceptable? A New Nordic Approach to Reservations to Multilateral Treaties' (2000) 69 *Nordic Journal of International Law* 179.

[12] For an analysis of the inconsistent pattern of objections to reservations based on Islam, see E Yahyaoui Krivenko, *Women, Islam and International Law Within the Context of the Convention on the Elimination of All forms of Discrimination Against Women* (The Hague, Martinus Nijhoff, 2009).

4

The *Lockerbie Case* (*Libyan Arab Jamahiriya v United States of America*)

KATHRYN GREENMAN AND TROY LAVERS

Authors' Note

The Dead

Raafat al-Ghossain – or 'Fafo', as she was known to her father Bassam, mother Saniya and younger sister Kinda – was only 18 when she was killed on 15 April 1986. Her family home in Tripoli was destroyed by a bomb dropped during an American airstrike ordered by Ronald Reagan in response to the bombing of a Berlin nightclub earlier that same year, blamed on the Libyans, in which two American soldiers were killed. Raafat, in her first year at art college in London, was back in Libya visiting her family for the holidays. Just over two months before her death she had written in her diary: 'My life is changing. I'm slowly, at last, finding myself. It feels great at last to meet my real self. Freedom!!'[1]

***

On 21 December 1988, Frank Ciulla was travelling home to his wife, Mary Lou, and their three children in New Jersey for Christmas. As his flight, Pan Am 103, flew over the Scottish town of Lockerbie a bomb exploded on board the plane, killing all 259 passengers and crew and 11 people on the ground. His body was found eight miles from the main crash site on a farm belonging to Hugh and Mary Connell. The two families subsequently struck up a friendship, culminating

[1] R Fisk, 'Collateral Damage' *The Independent* (10 August 1996). Available at: www.independent.co.uk/artsentertainment/collateraldamage5604817.html.

in their meeting in Scotland in 1992. The following is an extract from a letter sent by the Connells to the Ciullas after their visit:

> I was so thankful that you made the effort to come and ask all of the questions you had always wanted to ask. You had at last found someone who could fill in those last hours, that piece that had always remained a mystery. It's the not knowing that can bring so much pain and bewilderment. We all have imaginations that can run riot in us and I'm sure your dear souls must have had untold agonies wondering and worrying. It was just wonderful to meet you face-to-face. We needed to talk to you all too. As you said, we will get to know Frank through you. He was never just another victim to us. For months we called him our boy. Then we found out his name, he was our Frank. Please believe me, we were deeply affected by his coming to us, we will never forget our feeling seeing him there, a whole bodied and handsome man, the life gone out of him in a twinkling.[2]

The Search for Justice

By the time of the International Court of Justice (ICJ)'s order in respect of provisional measures in the *Lockerbie Case*,[3] the relatives of the victims of the bombing of Pan Am 103 had endured nearly three years of frustrated searching for justice for their loved ones.[4] The Scottish investigators who initially led the inquiry, in collaboration with counterparts in the United States and Germany, quickly discovered that the bomb had been inside an unaccompanied suitcase, which had apparently come from Frankfurt and possibly originally from Malta.[5] The bomb was in a Toshiba cassette radio and links were immediately made to a cell of a Palestinian splinter group in Frankfurt, which had been found in possession of similar devices.[6] The Popular Front for the Liberation of Palestine – General Command (PFLP-GC) had a history of plane-bombings and was known to hire itself out to the governments of Iran and Syria (and previously Libya).[7] The Iranians had a motive – an Iranian commercial airliner had been shot down by the United States over the Gulf of Persia less than six months earlier – and it emerged that the leader of the PFLP-GC had offered his services.[8] There were media reports that alternatively placed suspicion on an unnamed Syrian group.[9]

[2] This letter was published in S Usher (ed), *Letters of Note* (Edinburgh, Canongate, 2013).

[3] *Questions of Interpretation and Application of the 1971 Montreal Convention arising from the Aerial Incident at Lockerbie (Libyan Arab Jamahiriya v United States of America)* (Provisional Measures) [1992] ICJ Rep 114 (*Lockerbie Case*).

[4] For full accounts, see R Wallis, *Lockerbie: The Inside Story* (Westport CT, Greenwood, 2000); P Foot, 'The Great Lockerbie Whitewash (1989–2001)' in John Pilger (ed), *Tell Me No Lies* (Galway, Vintage, 2004); G Peirce, 'The Framing of al-Megrahi' (2009) 31(18) *London Review of Books* 3.

[5] See Wallis, above n 4, 47; Peirce, above n 4.

[6] Wallis, above n 4, 47.

[7] Peirce, above n 4.

[8] Wallis, above n 4, 52; Peirce, above n 4.

[9] Wallis, above n 4, 145.

Arrests seemed imminent, but none came. The media reported that this was due to fear of prejudicing negotiations for the release of Western hostages held by Iranian- and Syrian-backed groups in Lebanon.[10] In both the United States and the United Kingdom, victims' families set up campaign groups and demanded inquiries.[11] In 1991, the investigation, now led by the CIA, changed tack. Libya was the country under suspicion. If this seems surprising, it has been suggested that the investigative/prosecutorial strategy reflected wider issues of Middle East politics more than the desire for justice for the victims. When Saddam Hussein invaded Kuwait in August 1990, the matrix of alliances in the Middle East took a sudden shift, necessitating détente with Iran and entente with Syria.[12] Libya defiantly backed Iraq. Under Ronald Reagan the United States government had adopted a covert policy to destabilise the Gaddafi regime as part of its new counter-terrorism foreign policy focus, which culminated in the 1986 bombing;[13] linking the Libyan regime with state-sponsored terrorism was nothing new. Eventually, in November 1991, two Libyans were indicted in both the United States and Scotland and their extradition to either country was sought. They were Libyan Airlines officials, said to be Libyan intelligence officers, Abdelbaset al-Megrahi and Al-Amin Khalifah Fhimah.[14]

Legal Context

The ICJ order that is the subject of this chapter concerned a request by Libya for provisional measures to prevent the United States, the United Kingdom and France from taking steps to force it to extradite the two Libyans suspected of having carried out the bombing of Pan Am 103 three years previously. Libya accused the United States and allies of illegally pressuring it to hand over the suspects by threatening economic, air and other (including military) sanctions and of obstructing its attempts to investigate the alleged offences. It contended that this was a violation of its sovereignty, territorial integrity and political independence, and of its rights under the Montreal Convention.[15] Libya argued that it had established jurisdiction over the alleged offences on the basis of Article 5(2) of the Convention, in light of the fact that the suspects had been present on Libyan

[10] Peirce, above n 4.

[11] Such as, for example, UK Families Flight 103.

[12] Peirce, above n 4.

[13] Peirce, above n 4; Francis A Boyle, *Destroying Libya and World Order: The Three-Decade U.S. Campaign to Terminate the Qaddafi Revolution* (Atlanta GA, Clarity Press, 2013); David C Wills, *The First War on Terrorism: Counter-Terrorism Policy during the Reagan Administration* (Lanham MD, Rowman & Littlefield, 2003).

[14] George Lardner Jr, '2 Libyans Indicted in Pan Am Blast' *Washington Post* (15 November 1991). Available at: https://www.washingtonpost.com/wp-srv/inatl/longterm/panam103/stories/libyans111591.htm.

[15] Convention for the Suppression of Unlawful Acts against the Safety of Civil Aviation (adopted 23 Sep 1971, came into force 26 Jan 1973) 974 UNTS 178 (Montreal Convention).

territory at the time of their indictment by the United States.[16] By the time the ICJ came to consider the request, sanctions had already been applied against Libya by the UN Security Council in its Resolution 748 acting under its Chapter VII powers.[17] Under Chapter VII of the UN Charter the Security Council can impose on all UN Member States binding measures necessary for the maintenance of international peace and security, as determined by the Security Council. According to Article 103 of the UN Charter, such measures take supremacy over all other international law obligations. Consequently, the fundamental legal issue facing the ICJ was the status of Libya's rights under the Montreal Convention in light of the Security Council resolution, which seemed to require UN Member States to act contrary to them: could the ICJ grant measures to protect Libya's right to exercise jurisdiction over the alleged offences under the Convention seemingly in defiance of the Security Council?

Aims and Contribution of the Re-Written Order

Contrasting the opening sections of this note reveals how a legal dispute before the ICJ takes a human tragedy, a bloody catastrophe, and sanitises it and reduces it to a (series of) formal legal question(s). In deciding to deny Libya's request for provisional measures, the ICJ's original order can be boiled down to the banal statement that 'whatever the situation previous to the adoption of [Security Council Resolution 748], the rights claimed by Libya under the Montreal Convention cannot now be regarded as appropriate for protection by the indication of provisional measures'.[18] In our re-written judgment, we thus wanted to redress a number of perceived shortcomings, from a feminist perspective, in the ICJ's original order.

The implication of the decision in the ICJ's original order is that it is for the Security Council to determine when a State is harbouring terrorists and what other States can do about it. Yet the ICJ failed to acknowledge, let alone engage with, the profound questions raised by the *Lockerbie Case* about the relationship between Security Council resolutions and other provisions of international law, and about the limits of the Security Council's powers, particularly relative to those of the ICJ. These questions go to the heart of how power is allocated in the international system. For our chamber, this issue of the allocation of power in the international

[16] Article 5(2) provides that: 'Each Contracting State shall … take such measures as may be necessary to establish its jurisdiction over the offences [against the safety of civil aviation covered by the Convention] in the case where the alleged offender is present in its territory and it does not extradite him … [The Convention] does not exclude any criminal jurisdiction exercised in accordance with national law.'

[17] UNSC Res 748 (31 March 1992) UN Doc S/RES/748. The measures in question included a flight ban, arms embargo and diplomatic sanctions.

[18] *Lockerbie Case* (Provisional Measures), above n 3, para 43.

system is an important determinant of whether international law operates for the emancipation of women and other historically marginalised groups or for their exclusion and exploitation. If power is concentrated in the hands of a white male Western elite and exercised arbitrarily at their whim, then the international legal order will offer much less potential for gender, racial and socio-economic justice than if power is shared amongst different interests and exercised accountably and in accordance with legal standards.

By re-writing the ICJ's order from an approach informed by feminist theory and using feminist methods,[19] we sought to expose the gendered and imperialist nature of the solution adopted by the ICJ and to show how questions about the allocation of power in the international system could have been answered differently. We wanted to offer an alternative vision of the international legal order, one which more closely reflects gender, racial and socio-economic justice. Our challenge was to write a judgment, answerable to the dead, to the victims of international violence – on all sides – rendered silent and invisible by the ICJ's approach in its original order.

Contextualisation was the feminist method central to our re-written order.[20] We wanted to put the *Lockerbie Case* and its facts in the wider context of US relations with the Gaddafi regime in Libya, in contrast to the ICJ's presentation of the bombing of Pan Am Flight 103 as a standalone event without antecedents.[21] We also wanted to try (within the limitations arising from the fact that we had to write as if it were 1992)[22] to make visible the actual effects of military strikes and sanctions on women's lived experiences.[23] Consideration of the effects of

[19] Regarding the aims of feminist judging and what might make it distinctively feminist, see D Majury, 'Introducing the Women's Court of Canada' (2006) 18 *Canadian Journal of Women and the Law* 1, 4; R Hunter, C McGlynn and E Rackley, 'Feminist Judgments: An Introduction' and R Hunter, 'An Account of Feminist Judging' in R Hunter, C McGlynn and E Rackley (eds), *Feminist Judgments: From Theory to Practice* (Oxford, Hart Publishing, 2010). For an introductory discussion of feminist theoretical perspectives and methods from an academic perspective, see, eg, H Charlesworth, C Chinkin and S Wright, 'Feminist Approaches to International Law' (1991) 85 *American Journal of International Law* 613; H Charlesworth, 'Feminist Methods in International Law' (1999) 93(2) *American Journal of International Law* 379; A Orford, 'Feminism, Imperialism and the Mission of International Law' (2002) 71 *Nordic Journal of International Law* 275.

[20] Regarding the introduction of contextual material as a key method in feminist judging, see Hunter, above n 19, 37–38.

[21] Regarding the importance of storytelling in judgment-writing in general and feminist judgment-writing in particular, see E Rackley, 'The Art and Craft of Writing Judgments: Notes on the Feminist Judgments Project' in Hunter, McGlynn and Rackley, above n 19.

[22] At which date neither of the two stories which begun this note had been published and the international exposure and denunciation of the devastating effect of sanctions in Iraq, and their disproportionate effect on women, was only just beginning.

[23] On the gendered impact of sanctions, see, eg, International Study Team on the Gulf Crisis, *Health and Welfare in Iraq after the Gulf Crisis: An In-Depth Assessment* (1991); B Bhatia, M Kawar and M Shahin, *Unheard Voices: Iraqi Women on War and Sanctions* (London, Change, 1992); S Zaidi, 'War, Sanctions, and Humanitarian Assistance: The Case of Iraq 1990–1993' (1994) 1(3) *Medicine & Global Survival* 147; L Buck, N Gallant and K Richard Nossal, 'Sanctions as a Gendered Instrument of Statecraft: The Case of Iraq' (1998) 24(1) *Review of International Studies* 69; Y Husein Al Jawaheri, *Women in Iraq: The Gender Impact of International Sanctions* (London, IB Tauris, 2008).

sanctions on women's lives reveals that for many women there is little difference, in terms of the violence they experience on a daily basis, between war and peace as understood by international law. This exposes the fallacy of the distinction which international law draws between terrorism (violence) on one hand and economic sanctions (law) on the other, exposing it to be neither stable nor self-evident. It challenges the separation assumed by the ICJ between the sphere of armed conflict and terrorism – the 'proper' domain of public international law – and the private sphere to which the effects of economic sanctions are largely restricted. Such separation renders sanctions' disproportionate impact on women invisible.[24] Through the introduction of wider contextual material, our re-written judgment seeks to broaden international law's current vision of prohibited violence so as to include more readily that which is typically suffered by women and other historically marginalised groups.

Highlighting the fact that the United States, as part of the Reagan regime's wider attempts to overthrow Gaddafi, had previously launched airstrikes against Libya in 1986 and shot down two Libyan aircraft in 1989, exposes the similarities between rogue and democratic States. Sanctions are supposedly justified by the international community's rejection of the idea of States being founded on violence and religious fundamentalism. However, our contextualisation of the *Lockerbie Case* shows how intervening States, purporting to act in the name of democracy and human rights, also ignore international law and exercise violence against those constructed as 'other' by reference to their gender, race and religion. While abstract international law concepts such as 'peace and security' and 'terrorism' are presented as neutral, when considered in the particular context of women's and other historically marginalised groups' experience of them, the gendered and imperialist nature of their operation becomes apparent.

International law – at least as conceived of by the ICJ in its original order – operates so as to prohibit certain types of violence, that exercised by terrorists and rogue States, while legitimising other sorts of militarism, that of the Security Council.[25] We envisage a more activist ICJ and a more accountable Security Council, an international legal order with checks and balances between its organs, where it is more difficult for a superpower State to appropriate international law for its own ends and where power is not entirely concentrated in the hands of a white male Western elite backed up by a monopoly over the legitimate use of force.[26] The Charter system set up after World War II conceived of the Security Council as the political/military means of resolving international conflicts and the ICJ as

[24] Regarding the feminist critique of the public/private distinction, see Charlesworth, Chinkin and Wright, above n 19, 625–28; C Chinkin, 'A Critique of the Public-Private Dimension' (1999) 10(2) *European Journal of International Law* 387; Hunter, McGlynn and Rackley, 'Feminist Judgments: An Introduction', above n 19, 23.

[25] A Orford, 'Contesting Globalization: A Feminist Perspective on the Future of Human Rights' (1998) 8 *Transnational Law and Contemporary Problems* 171, 192–94.

[26] Charlesworth, Chinkin and Wright, above n 19, 621–25.

that of legal dispute resolution. Feminist legal theory has sought to expose how in international discourse the former is coded as masculine and the latter, coded as feminine, is subsequently devalued.[27] This is a position that the ICJ's original order reinforced by deferring entirely to the Security Council.

Our re-written order seeks to challenge this devaluation of arbitration as passive and unmanly, and imagine a different type of international politics, in which violence and intervention are not the immediate responses to terrorist atrocities. Our re-written judgment, in rejecting Security Council intervention in Libya and demanding that the parties resolve their dispute in court, proposes a different way of responding to terrorism so as to break cycles of violence. As Judith Butler has written:

> One insight that injury affords is that there are others out there on whom my life depends, people I do not know and may never know. This fundamental dependency on anonymous others is not a condition that I can will away. No security measure will foreclose this dependency; no violent act of sovereignty will rid the world of this fact … To be injured means that one has the chance to reflect upon injury, to find out the mechanisms of its distribution, to find out who else suffers from permeable borders, unexpected violence, dispossession, and fear, and in what ways. … [T]he dislocation from First World privilege [safety], however temporary, offers a chance to start to imagine a world in which that violence might be minimized, in which an inevitable interdependency becomes acknowledged as the basis for global political community.[28]

Comparison of the Two Orders

The most obvious difference between the original and our re-written order is that, whereas in 1992 the ICJ denied Libya's request for provisional measures, we have granted them. Instead of absolutely deferring to the Security Council, in our re-written order we review the legality of its actions. In its original order, the ICJ assumed the supremacy of the Security Council's resolutions, following UN Charter Articles 25 ('[t]he Members of the United Nations agree to accept and carry out the decisions of the Security Council in accordance with the present Charter') and 103 ('[i]n the event of a conflict between the obligations of the Members of the United Nations under the present Charter and their obligations under any other international agreement, their obligations under the present Charter shall prevail').

In contrast, we found that the Security Council's 'primary responsibility for maintenance of international peace and security' was not necessarily an exclusive

[27] See, eg, C Cohn, 'War, Wimps and Women: Talking Gender and Thinking War' in M Cooke and A Woollacott (eds), *Gendering War Talk* (Princeton NJ, Princeton University Press, 1993); A Orford, *Reading Humanitarian Intervention: Human Rights and the Use of Force in International Law* (Cambridge, Cambridge University Press, 2003).

[28] J Butler, *Precarious Life: The Powers of Mourning and Violence* (London, Verso, 2004) xii–xiii.

responsibility, and that it was acceptable for the ICJ and the Security Council to be dealing with the same dispute at the same time, in accordance with the previous case law of the ICJ. In this case, however, unlike on those previous occasions, the proceedings before the Security Council had come into conflict with those before the ICJ. In our re-written order, we decided that the ICJ had the power to decide which organ's competence took priority since this was a matter of interpreting the Charter and since, under Article 36(6) of its Statute, the ICJ has the power to determine its own jurisdiction. Making such a decision required us to look at both the question of the limits on the Security Council's powers and whether there can be judicial review of the exercise of those powers.[29]

First, we found that the Security Council's powers could not be unlimited, something confirmed in the ICJ's previous case law, as this would be incompatible with the rule of law.[30] Our re-written judgment found that, as the Security Council's powers are conferred on it by the Charter, it must exercise those powers in accordance with the Charter. We interpreted the phrase 'in accordance with the present Charter' in Article 25 to mean that only *intra vires* decisions of the Security Council are binding. Second, we found that the ICJ had the power to review the exercise of the Security Council's powers for legality. Although there is nothing in the Charter explicitly providing for this, there is also nothing explicitly ruling it out. In light of this silence, we decided that the ICJ was competent to make such a review. Particularly, we argued that if a system is to be governed by the rule of law, power must not simply be limited but its exercise must entail accountability. We found that Resolution 748 exceeded the powers of the Security Council in several ways and, as a result, that the ICJ's jurisdiction to consider the request for provisional measures survived.

Two final points: first, we note that Libya also brought a case simultaneously against the United Kingdom, which the ICJ dealt with separately, accordingly, here we only address the dispute between Libya and the United States; and second, for ease of reading, we made the decision to depart from form by not beginning each paragraph with a 'whereas' as the ICJ did in its orders in 1992, but simply to begin the order with a single 'whereas' as the ICJ does today.

Afterword

As a poignant postscript, we know now that subsequent to the ICJ's order, the Security Council applied further economic sanctions on Libya,[31] which were not

[29] For an excellent discussion of these questions, particularly as they apply to sanctions, see A Tzanakopoulos, *Disobeying the Security Council: Countermeasures against Wrongful Sanctions* (Oxford, Oxford University Press, 2011).

[30] On the Security Council and the rule of law, see H Charlesworth and J Farrell (eds), *Strengthening the Rule of Law through the UN Security Council* (London, Routledge, 2016).

[31] These included an oil embargo and a freeze on Libyan funds in Member State territory. UNSC Res 883 (11 November 1993) UN Doc S/RES/883.

lifted until 2003.[32] Later, despite the ICJ holding in its preliminary objections judgment that it had jurisdiction and that Libya's claim was not inadmissible or without object,[33] the case was removed from the list at the request of the parties before the merits could be decided.[34] The two suspects, after years of diplomatic wrangling, were eventually tried between 2000 and 2001 by a Scottish court operating under Scots law at a disused United States air force base in the Netherlands.[35]

The result was the conviction of al-Megrahi, who was, however, later released from prison early due to ill health and died in 2012. Doubts about the conviction have been raised consistently,[36] and attempts in the Scottish courts to clear al-Megrahi's name are ongoing.[37] Conspiracy theories about the Lockerbie bombing continue to abound.[38] The Gaddafi regime was eventually overthrown in 2011 following military intervention by NATO with prior Security Council authorisation, in respect of which the United States voted in favour.[39] As we write this note, Libya remains mired in another devastating civil war and has once again endured foreign military intervention as part of the campaign against ISIS. At the same time, hundreds of refugees set out from Libya daily to make the treacherous crossing of the Mediterranean to reach Europe on a migrant trail through the state controlled by traffickers.[40] The challenge we faced in re-writing this order – to imagine an international legal order which promotes gender, racial and socio-economic justice and rejects militarism – thus remains as urgent today as it was in 1992.

[32] 'Security Council Lifts sanctions against Libya after Lockerbie bombing' *UN News Centre* (2 September 2003). Available at: www.un.org/apps/news/story.asp?newsid=8225&cr=libya#.WQQZCfmGOUk.

[33] *Questions of Interpretation and Application of the 1971 Montreal Convention arising from the Aerial Incident at Lockerbie (Libyan Arab Jamahiriya v United States of America)* (Preliminary Objections) [1998] ICJ Rep 115.

[34] *Questions of Interpretation and Application of the 1971 Montreal Convention arising from the Aerial Incident at Lockerbie (Libyan Arab Jamahiriya v United States of America)* (Order of 10 September 2003).

[35] Treaty for the Lockerbie Court: Treaty No 35699, treaty between United Kingdom of Great Britain and Northern Ireland and the Netherlands (adopted 18 September 1998, entered into force 8 January 1999) 2062 UNTS 81.

[36] In 2003, al-Megrahi's case was referred to the Scottish Criminal Cases Review Commission for review. Their final decision, which came in 2007, cast doubt on the original conviction in a number of respects. See M Townsend and D Smith, 'Evidence that casts doubt on who brought down Flight 103' *The Guardian* (17 June 2007). Available at: www.theguardian.com/uk/2007/jun/17/politics.lockerbie1.

[37] See, eg, Press Association, 'Lockerbie bomber's family pursues fresh bid to clear his name' *The Guardian* (5 June 2014). Available at: www.theguardian.com/world/2014/jun/05/lockerbie-bomber-megrahi-family-third-appeal-conviction; N Slawson, 'Abdelbaset al-Megrahi's family to appeal Lockerbie conviction' *The Guardian* (24 April 2017). Available at: www.theguardian.com/world/2017/apr/23/abdelbaset-al-megrahis-family-to-appeal-lockerbie-bombing-conviction-libyan.

[38] J Swire, 'Dr. Jim Swire: Lockerbie Seeking the Truth' *The Scotsman* (18 December 2013). Available at: www.scotsman.com/news/opinion/dr-jim-swire-lockerbie-seeking-the-truth-1-3237353; S Carrell, 'Lockerbie relatives urge inquiry into "suppressed evidence"' *The Guardian* (28 February 2012). Available at: www.theguardian.com/uk/2012/feb/27/lockerbie-relatives-urge-inquiry-evidence. See also: www.lockerbietruth.com.

[39] UNSC Res 1973 (17 March 2011) UN Doc S/RES/1973.

[40] Q Sommerville, 'Inside Zuwara, the heart of Libya's people-smuggling trade' *BBC News* (4 September 2015). Available at: www.bbc.co.uk/news/world-africa-34157123.

JUDGMENT

Case Concerning Questions of Interpretation and Application of the 1971 Montreal Convention Arising from the Aerial Incident at Lockerbie

LIBYAN ARAB JAMAHIRIYA v UNITED STATES OF AMERICA

Request for the Indication of Provisional Measures

International Court of Justice

Present: President Greenman and Judge Lavers.

14 April 1992

ORDER

Whereas:

Background to the Dispute, Outline of Events and Arguments of the Parties

1. Due to its geopolitically strategic position, and later its oil resources, Libya, as it has been known since the 1930s, has long been a target for overseas intervention. Libya was part of the Ottoman Empire before it was invaded by Italy in 1911 during the Italo-Turkish War. In 1943 it was occupied by the Allies, a situation which lasted until its declaration of independence on 24 December 1951. This was not, however, the end of foreign intervention, with both the United States and the United Kingdom retaining military bases and high troop numbers in the country post-independence, as well as significant economic influence.
2. The application which instituted the proceedings of which the Court is currently seized is the culmination of a long-running diplomatic and military confrontation between the United States and Libya. This dispute has its origins in the overthrow of the Senussi monarchy and the rise to power of Muammar Gaddafi in Libya in 1969, but has intensified dramatically since 1980 with the change of foreign policy that came with the Reagan administration. Relations between these two states were strained from the beginning of Gaddafi's rule, particularly thanks to his nationalisation of the oil reserves that removed the United States oil companies from Libya. The United States embassy staff was recalled when a group of demonstrators attacked the embassy in 1979, the year the United States designated Libya as a state that sponsors terrorism.
3. Relations worsened with the Gulf of Sidra incident of 1981, when two United States fighter aircraft engaged in combat with two Libyan fighters, downing

them both and killing one pilot, in the context of the United States carrying out naval manoeuvres in an area which Libya claimed were its territorial waters, a claim disputed by the United States. This incident led to economic sanctions being applied by the United States against Libya from 1982 to 1986. There were bans on imports of Libyan oil and a ban on exports from the United States to Libya. These bans were expanded to include commercial contracts, as well as the United States freezing all the assets of the Libyan government. Tensions over the Gulf of Sidra continued and in March 1986 there were further, more intense, skirmishes in which a number of Libyan servicemen were killed. Then in April of that same year, the United States carried out an aerial bombing campaign on two cities in Libya in retaliation for a bombing in a (then) West Berlin disco, which killed two United States servicemen, that was allegedly linked to Libya. One hundred people died in the airstrikes, including, according to news reports, Colonel Gaddafi's daughter. The Berlin disco bombing also provoked an intensifying of sanctions against Libya by the United States.

4. Then, on 21 December 1988, Pan Am Flight 103 exploded over the Scottish town of Lockerbie, killing 270 people, in what soon became clear was a terrorist attack. Three and a half years later, the families and friends of those killed that night are still waiting in anguish to find out the truth about what happened to their loved ones. The suspicions of the Scottish-led investigation team initially turned to Iran. The attack was a suspected retaliation for the shooting down of an Iranian airliner by a United States warship earlier that year. Connections were also made with Syria, Lebanon and Palestinian groups. Not until later did the investigation, now led by the CIA, turn to Colonel Gaddafi's Libya. This culminated on 14 November 1991 in the indictment by the United States of two Libyan nationals in a District Court for the bombing of Pan Am flight 103.
5. Four days later on 18 November 1991, there was a statement from Libya outlining that they had received the indictment documents and that a Libyan Supreme Court Justice had already been assigned to investigate the allegations against the two Libyan nationals. Libya released a statement confirming that Libyan judicial authorities were willing to cooperate with all legal authorities in the United States and the United Kingdom, and invited observers to watch any legal proceedings. At this time, the two Libyan suspects were arrested by the Libyan authorities. A joint declaration from the United States and United Kingdom followed later that month on 27 November, demanding the surrender of the two Libyan nationals and all evidence, as well as the payment of appropriate compensation by the Libyan government.
6. The following day, the Libyan authorities released a communiqué responding to the statement of the United States and the United Kingdom declaring that the investigation would be handled by competent authorities in Libya, with respect for international law and Libya's sovereignty, and with a balance for the victims and the accused. The Libyan investigating judge offered to travel

to the United States and the United Kingdom to review evidence in those territories. Since those offers were rejected or ignored, Libya sent follow up letters to both the United States and the United Kingdom stating that the three states are parties to the Convention for the Suppression of Unlawful Acts Against the Safety of Civil Aviation, signed at Montreal on 23 September 1971 (referred to hereinafter as the 'Montreal Convention'), and that as soon as the charges were laid against the two alleged Libyan defendants, Libya had exercised its jurisdiction according to Article 5(2) and (3) and Article 7 of the Montreal Convention:

> Article 5 … 2. Each Contracting State shall likewise take such measures as may be necessary to establish its jurisdiction over the offences mentioned in Article 1, paragraph 1 (a), (b) and (c), and in Article 1, paragraph 2, in so far as that paragraph relates to those offences, in the case where the alleged offender is present in its territory and it does not extradite him pursuant to Article 8 to any of the States mentioned in paragraph 1 of this Article. 3. This Convention does not exclude any criminal jurisdiction exercised in accordance with national law;

> Article 7. The Contracting State in the territory of which the alleged offender is found shall, if it does not extradite him, be obliged, without exception whatsoever and whether or not the offence was committed in its territory, to submit the case to its competent authorities for the purpose of prosecution. Those authorities shall take their decision in the same manner as in the case of any ordinary offence of a serious nature under the law of that State.

7. Article 8 provides that:

> 2. If a Contracting State which makes extradition conditional on the existence of a treaty receives a request for extradition from another Contracting State with which it has no extradition treaty, it may at its option consider this Convention as the legal basis for extradition in respect of the offences. Extradition shall be subject to the other conditions provided by the law of the requested State.

8. The letter from Libya to the United States and the United Kingdom dated 17 January 1992 reiterated that in accordance with Article 7 of the Montreal Convention, Libya had referred the matter to its judicial authorities which were investigating the offences; it noted, however, that Libya had received no cooperation from the United States and the United Kingdom authorities, which, they contended, breached Article 11(1) of the Convention. The letter also outlined the Libyan position agreeing to arbitration of the dispute in accordance with Article 14(1) of the Convention:

> Article 11. 1. Contracting States shall afford one another the greatest measure of assistance in connection with criminal proceedings brought in

> respect of the offences. The law of the State requested shall apply in all cases.
>
> …
>
> Article 14. 1. Any dispute between two or more Contracting States concerning the interpretation or application of this Convention which cannot be settled through negotiation, shall, at the request of one of them, be submitted to arbitration. If within six months from the date of the request for arbitration the Parties are unable to agree on the organization of the arbitration, any one of those Parties may refer the dispute to the International Court of Justice by request in conformity with the Statute of the Court.

9. Three days after the letters were sent to the United States and the United Kingdom, on 21 January 1992, United Nations Security Council Resolution 731 was passed:

> The Security Council … Deeply concerned over results of investigations which implicate officials of the Libyan Government and which are contained in Security Council documents that include the requests addressed to the Libyan authorities by France, the United Kingdom of Great Britain and Northern Ireland and the United States of America in connection with the legal procedures related to the attacks carried out against Pan Am flight 103 … (S/23306, S/23307, S/23308, S/23309, S/23317) … 2. Strongly deplores the fact that the Libyan Government has not yet responded effectively to the above requests to cooperate fully in establishing responsibility for the terrorist acts referred to above against Pan Am flight 103 …; 3. Urges the Libyan Government immediately to provide a full and effective response to those requests so as to contribute to the elimination of terrorism.

10. The application for provisional measures was filed by Libya with this Court on 3 March 1992. On 31 March 1992, the Security Council passed Resolution 748, this time under its Chapter VII powers, which stated that Libya would be subject to a set of sanctions until the Security Council was satisfied that it had complied with its demands for Libya to:

> 1. … comply without any further delay with paragraph 3 of resolution 731 (1992) regarding the requests contained in documents S/23306, S/23308 and S/23309;
> 2. … commit itself definitively to cease all forms of terrorist action and all assistance to terrorist groups and that it must promptly, by concrete actions, demonstrate its renunciation of terrorism.

11. Under these sanctions, the Security Council required member states, among other things, to:

> … [d]eny permission to any aircraft to take off from, land in or overfly their territory if it is destined to land in or has taken off from the territory

> of Libya, unless the particular flight has been approved on grounds of significant humanitarian need; [p]rohibit any provision to Libya by their nationals or from their territory of arms and related material of all types; [w]ithdraw any of their officials or agents present in Libya to advise the Libyan authorities on military matters; [s]ignificantly reduce the number and the level of the staff at Libyan diplomatic missions and consular posts and restrict or control the movement within their territory of all such staff who remain; [p]revent the operation of all Libyan Arab Airlines offices; and [t]ake all appropriate steps to deny entry to or expel Libyan nationals who have been denied entry to or expelled from other States because of their involvement in terrorist activities.

12. The sanctions set out in Security Council Resolution 748 were not only prescribed to every member state in accordance with Chapter VII, the Resolution also created a monitoring and review mechanism under a newly created Security Council committee. This committee is to review the implementation and effectiveness of the sanctions. Member states also have to report to the Secretary General on the measures they have taken so as to comply. In paragraph 13 of the Resolution, the Security Council established that every 120 days, or sooner if the situation should require it, there will be a review of Libya's compliance.
13. It is clear from the outline of events that the United States and the United Kingdom wish to force the handover of the two Libyan suspects. Libya relies on the Montreal Convention and wants the suspects to be tried in Libya. In its request for the indication of provisional measures Libya alleged that the United States was 'actively seeking to bypass the provisions of the Montreal Convention by threatening various actions against Libya in order to compel Libya, in violation of the Convention, to surrender its two accused nationals.' Libya remains concerned that the United States might 'impose economic or other sanctions against Libya.'
14. Libya, in its Application, considering that the Court's jurisdiction in the case is *prima facie* established under the Montreal Convention, submitted that there were no impediments to indicating provisional measures and asks the Court to adjudge and declare:

> (a) that Libya has fully complied with al1 of its obligations under the Montreal Convention; (b) that the United States has breached, and is continuing to breach, its legal obligations to Libya under Articles 5 (2), 5 (3), 7, 8 (2) and 11 of the Montreal Convention; and (c) that the United States is under a legal obligation immediately to cease and desist from such breaches and from the use of any and all force or threats against Libya, including the threat of force against Libya, and from al1 violations of the sovereignty, territorial integrity, and the political independence of Libya.

15. Libya asks the Court to indicate the following provisional measures:

    (a) to enjoin the United States from taking any action against Libya calculated to coerce or compel Libya to surrender the accused individuals to any jurisdiction outside of Libya; and (b) to ensure that no steps are taken that would prejudice in any way the rights of Libya with respect to the legal proceedings that are the subject of Libya's Application.

16. The United States contended that Libya had failed to show that it had *prima facie* jurisdiction under the Montreal Convention, on the basis that the six-month period stipulated by Article 14 had not yet expired and that Libya had not established that the United States had refused to arbitrate. The United States also contended that Libya had not demonstrated that provisional measures were necessary to protect rights at imminent risk of irreparable injury; that there was no proof that 'the United States was threatening Libya with economic sanctions and other actions, including the probability of recourse to the use of armed force', as alleged by Libya. The United States also argued that the requested measures did not relate to the rights claimed in the Application; that Libya had failed to establish the possible existence of the rights it claimed under the Montreal Convention; and that the requested measures would not preserve the rights of the United States. The United States also contended that the Security Council was actively seized of the situation which was the subject of the Application and that therefore the Court should not indicate provisional measures. The United States further contended that the requested provisional measures were improperly directed to restraining action in the Security Council.
17. In its observations on Security Council Resolution 748, the United States remarked that the Resolution was adopted under Chapter VII rather than Chapter VI of the Charter and was framed as a 'decision' and contended that, given the binding nature of that decision, no object would be served by provisional measures; that, irrespective of the rights claimed by Libya under the Montreal Convention, Libya has a Charter-based duty to accept and carry out the decisions in the Resolution, and other States have a Charter-based duty to seek Libya's compliance; that any indication of provisional measures would run a serious risk of conflicting with the work of the Security Council; that the Council had rejected (inter alia) Libya's contention that the matter should be addressed on the basis of the rights claimed by Libya under the Montreal Convention, which Libya asks the Court to protect through provisional measures; and that the Court should therefore decline the request.
18. From the foregoing outline of events and summary of the arguments of the parties it is clear to the Court that it is faced with a dispute between Libya and the US as to whether Libya is obliged to extradite the two suspects. Libya has sought to resolve the dispute before the Court and in accordance with the Montreal Convention, which, Libya argues, does not require extradition. The United States, on the other hand, has sought to resolve the dispute through

the Security Council, which, with its Resolution 748, has made a binding decision that Libya must hand over the suspects. Therefore, once the Court has established that it has jurisdiction to consider the request for provisional measures, and before deciding whether it is appropriate to grant them, it will have to decide what impact Resolution 748 has on its jurisdiction.

Reasoning for the Order

19. The Court would like to express its heartfelt sympathy to all those who are victims of the criminal bombing of Pan Am flight 103 – those who died on 21 December 1998 as well as their friends and families. The Court recognises that, as is often the case with legal disputes, the victims are overlooked in the arguments before the court. The Court is deeply concerned that those who lost loved ones at Lockerbie over three years ago are still waiting to find out what really happened on that night and acknowledges their right to the truth. However, the Court considers that justice and truth for the victims is best served by the perpetrators being brought to justice in accordance with the law. The Court would also like to express its outrage at the indiscriminate use of force against civilians in all its forms, whether that be through terrorist bombings or through the blanket application of sanctions by States.

(i) Prima facie *jurisdiction under Article 14 of the Montreal Convention*

20. Firstly, the Court turns to the question of its jurisdiction to hear the provisional measures application. As the Court stated in the *Nuclear Tests Case (Australia v France), Order of 22 June 1973, I.C.J Reports 1972,* p. 99, para. 13, and then reiterated in *Military and Paramilitary Activities in and against Nicaragua (Nicaragua v. United States of America), Provisional Measures, Order of 10 May 1984, I.C.J. Reports 1984,* p. 169, para. 24:

> Whereas on a request for provisional measures the Court need not, before deciding whether or not to indicate them, finally satisfy itself that it has jurisdiction on the merits of the case, or, as the case may be, that an objection taken to jurisdiction is well-founded, yet it ought not to indicate such measures unless the provisions invoked by the Applicant appear, prima facie, to afford a basis on which the jurisdiction of the Court might be founded.

21. The Court considers that its jurisdiction is *prima facie* established under the Montreal Convention. It is clear that there is a dispute within the meaning of Article 14(1) concerning the interpretation or application of the Montreal Convention.
22. The United States claims that the six-month period stipulated by Article 14(1) has not lapsed. Although it is true that six months have not passed since Libya's expression of willingness to arbitrate, the Court considers that, nevertheless, the actions of the United States in taking the matter to the Security Council demonstrate an incontrovertible intention to disregard Article 14 and a definitive refusal of arbitration, and that, in this light, Libya is absolved from having to wait for the six-month time limit before seizing this Court.

(ii) The relationship between the Security Council and the Court

23. The United States has argued that the Court should not consider the application for provisional measures because the Security Council is actively seized of the situation. However, there is nothing to prevent the consideration by this Court of an application for provisional measures while the same matter is also before the Security Council. In the past, several cases have appeared before the Court while being under consideration by the Security Council at the same time. These include *Aegean Sea Continental Shelf, Interim Protection, I.C.J. Reports 1976*, p. 3; *United States Diplomatic and Consular Staff in Tehran, Provisional Measures, I.C.J. Reports 1979*, p. 7; *Military and Paramilitary Activities in and against Nicaragua, Provisional Measures, I.C.J. Reports 1984*, p. 169. In the latter case, the Court stated that:

> The United States is … arguing that the matter was essentially one for the Security Council since it concerned a complaint by Nicaragua involving the use of force. However, having regard to the United States Diplomatic and Consular staff in Tehran case, the Court is of the view that the fact that matter is before the Security Council should not prevent it being dealt with by the Court and that both proceedings could be pursued pari passu. (*Jurisdiction and Admissibility, I.C.J. Reports 1984*, p. 392, para. 93)

24. In the *Tehran Hostages* case the Court held that:

> Whereas Article 12 of the Charter expressly forbids the General Assembly to make any recommendation with regard to a dispute or situation while the Security Council is exercising its functions in respect of that dispute or situation, no such restriction is placed on the functioning of the Court by any provision of either the Charter or the Statute of the Court. The reasons are clear. It is for the Court, the principal judicial organ of the United Nations, to resolve any legal questions that may be in issue between parties to a dispute; and the resolution of such legal questions by the Court may be an important, and sometimes decisive, factor in promoting the peaceful settlement of the dispute. (*Jurisdiction and Admissibility, I.C.J. Reports 1980*, p. 22, para. 40)

25. While the Security Council has the 'primary' responsibility for the maintenance of international peace and security under Article 24 of the UN Charter, this is not an exclusive responsibility. Professor Shabtai Rosenne, in his analysis of the relationship between the organs of the UN, observed that:

> … while the Court's task is limited to functions of a legal character, its power of action and decision is subject to no limitation deriving from the fact that the dispute before it might also be within the competence of some other organ. If the maintenance of international peace and security be regarded as the major function of the United Nations as a whole (including the Court), the Charter confers no exclusive competence upon any one principal organ. Even the fact that the Security Council has primary

responsibility for the maintenance of international peace and security under Article 24 of the Charter is not sufficient to give it exclusive competence over these matters.[1]

26. However, this situation is different to the previous occasions where the Court and Security Council were exercising their functions in a complementary manner. In each of the previous cases it was the same party to the dispute which seized both the Court and the Security Council. In this case, different parties have seized the Court and the Security Council, creating the possibility for conflict. With its binding decision that Libya shall comply with the requests to surrender its nationals, the Security Council has brought the proceedings before it into direct conflict with those before the Court. Parallel proceedings have become overlapping ones. In this case, the competence of one organ must take priority over the other. This is also the first such case to involve the exercise of the Security Council's Chapter VII powers, which further complicates matter since decisions taken under Chapter VII are binding on Member States above all other international obligations as per Articles 25 and 103 of the Charter.
27. The United States has contended that Libya's request to the Court for provisional measures is an improper attempt to restrain the Security Council. However, the Court considers that the opposite could equally be the case; the Security Council's decision that Libya must hand over the suspects could be an improper attempt to restrain the Court. Which view is correct depends upon one's understanding of the relationship between the Court and Security Council. Must the Court defer to the Security Council's decision given that it has been made using its binding Chapter VII powers, or can the Court's jurisdiction to grant provisional measures survive the Security Council's purported intervention? The Court considers that it is the appropriate body to answer this question since it is a matter of interpreting the Charter and since, under Article 36(6) of its Statute, the Court has the power to determine its own jurisdiction.
28. The Court has already noted above that the Security Council has primary responsibility for the maintenance of peace and security. It has the power, under Article 39, to 'determine the existence of any threat to the peace, breach of the peace, or act of aggression and shall make recommendations, or decide what measures shall be taken'. After 45 years of stalemate during the Cold War, the Security Council has only recently come to start making full use of these undoubtedly very broad powers, as it has done in this case. This raises new concerns about the limits on these powers and the accountability of their exercise. These are, however, two separate issues, which the Court shall address in turn. First, the question of the limits on the Security Council's

[1] S Rosenne, *The Law and Practice of the International Court of Justice* 2nd edn (Dordrecht, Martinus Nijhoff Publishers, 1985) 73.

powers and, second, whether there can be judicial review of the exercise of those powers.

(a) The limits on the Security Council's powers

29. In its Advisory Opinion of 20 July 1962 on *Certain Expenses of the United Nations (Article 17, paragraph 2, of the Charter) (1962)*, the Court held that:

> The primary place ascribed to international peace and security is natural, since the fulfilment of the other purposes will be dependent upon the attainment of that basic condition. These purposes are broad indeed, but neither they nor the powers conferred to effectuate them are unlimited. (*I.C.J. Reports 1962*, p. 168)

30. The Court considers that, in an international system which supposes itself to be rule-governed, it is inconceivable that the Security Council's powers can be unlimited. Any other result would be incompatible with the rule of law. Even the most basic idea of international justice requires that no actor can be above the law. The Court considers that, as the Security Council's powers are conferred on it by the Charter, it must exercise those powers in accordance with the Charter. In its Advisory Opinion of 28 May 1948 on the *Conditions of Admission of a State to Membership in the United Nations (Article 4 of the Charter) (1948)*, the Court confirmed that:

> The political character of an organ cannot release it from the observance of the treaty provisions established by the Charter when they constitute limitations on its powers or criteria for its judgment. To ascertain whether an organ has freedom of choice for its decisions, reference must be made to the terms of its constitution. (*I.C.J. Reports 1948*, p. 64)

31. It is thus for the Court to consider the limits on the Security Council's powers to be found in the Charter. First, Article 25 of the UN Charter provides that 'Members of the United Nations agree to accept and carry out the decisions of the Security Council *in accordance with the present Charter*'. The meaning of the phrase 'in accordance with the present Charter' is rather ambiguous. It is not clear whether it refers to the *carrying out* of the decisions or the decisions themselves. However, Professor Hans Kelsen has argued that:

> … in both cases the meaning of Article 25 is that the Members are obliged to carry out only those decisions which the Security Council has taken in accordance with the Charter … Consequently Article 25 may be interpreted to mean: the Members are obliged to carry out all resolutions of the Security Council which the Security Council is authorised by the Charter to issue with the intention to bind the Members at whom they are directed.[2]

[2] H Kelsen, *The Law of the United Nations: A Critical Analysis of its Fundamental Problems* (New York, Frederick A Praeger, 2000) 95.

32. This interpretation was implicitly confirmed by the Court in its Advisory Opinion of 21 June 1971 on the *Legal Consequences for States of the Continued Presence of South Africa in Namibia (South West Africa) notwithstanding Security Council Resolution 276 (1970)*:

> The Court has therefore reached the conclusion that the decisions made by the Security Council … were adopted in conformity with the purposes and principles of the Charter and in accordance with its Articles 24 and 25. The decisions are consequently binding on all States Members of the United Nations, which are thus under obligation to accept and carry them out. (*I.C.J. Reports 1971*, p. 16, para. 115)

33. The Court concludes that the implication of the words 'in accordance with the present Charter' is that only *intra vires* decisions of the Security Council are binding on Member States. This is the only interpretation consistent with the fact that Security Council resolutions receive their binding force from the Charter and are thus subordinate to it.
34. Article 24(2) of the Charter explicitly states that:

> In discharging these duties [under its responsibility for the maintenance of international peace and security] the Security Council shall act in accordance with the Purposes and Principles of the United Nations.

35. Furthermore, while it is for the Security Council to 'determine the existence of any threat to the peace, breach of the peace, or act of aggression', this discretion is afforded by law and as such cannot be unlimited; discretion without limit is simply arbitrariness. While it is clearly a very broadly conceived notion with much grey area at its edges, it cannot be that 'a threat or breach of the peace or act of aggression' is simply whatever the Security Council says it is, since this would render the phrase meaningless. The Security Council thus cannot stretch the meaning of 'a threat or breach of the peace or act of aggression' beyond all reasonable bounds; there are some things that are undisputedly not threats to the peace and the Security Council cannot determine otherwise.
36. While the Security Council can interpret the Charter widely, an organ cannot use the powers the Charter affords it so as to rewrite its constituent instrument. Thus, the Court considers that the Security Council cannot use a determination under Article 39 to rewrite the division of its powers between Chapters VI and VII. This division of the Security Council's competences under Chapters VI and VII reflects the Court's competence as the principal judicial organ of the UN and the primacy of pacific dispute settlement, and the Security Council cannot use a determination under Article 39 to infringe this division. Under Chapter VI on Pacific Settlement of Disputes, the Security Council can only make (non-binding) recommendations. There are a number of limits on its power to do so. In making recommendations under Chapter VI, Article 36(3) provides that the Security Council 'should also take

into consideration that legal disputes should as a general rule be referred by the parties to the International Court of Justice'. Article 27 provides that 'in decisions under Chapter VI … a party to a dispute shall abstain from voting'. Under Article 1(1), one of the purposes of the UN, which the Security Council is obliged to act in accordance with, is 'to bring about by peaceful means, and *in conformity with the principles of justice and international law*, adjustment or settlement of international disputes or situations which might lead to a breach of the peace' (emphasis added). The Security Council cannot use a determination under Article 39 simply for the purpose of improperly evading these limitations on its powers under Chapter VI. Under Article 37(2), if 'the Security Council deems that the continuance of the dispute is in fact likely to endanger the maintenance of international peace and security, it shall decide whether to take action under Article 36 or to recommend such terms of settlement as it may consider appropriate'. It thus should not use its Chapter VII powers.

37. Along similar lines, the Court considers that the Security Council also cannot use a determination under Article 39 to rewrite the distribution of competences between the UN's organs under the Charter. This division is of vital importance for a number of reasons. The Security Council's composition and procedures make it unsuited to decide legal disputes. It is dominated by its permanent five members, it is not independent and lacks a legal ethos. Since it does not work by judicial methods or adversarial process, the Security Council may take into account political factors which the Court would not, it may consider evidence inadmissible before the Court, and may not give each party to the dispute an equal opportunity to make its case. That priority is given to the Court in deciding legal disputes is important for the maintenance of peace, as the Court recognised in the *Tehran Hostages* case:

> It is for the Court, the principal judicial organ of the United Nations, to resolve any legal questions that may be in issue between parties to a dispute; and the resolution of such legal questions by the Court may be an important, and sometimes decisive, factor in promoting the peaceful settlement of the dispute. (op. cit., p. 22, para. 40)

38. It is also important for the administration of justice and the maintenance of respect for the principles of international law.

39. As well as there being limitations on the Security Council's power to make a determination under Article 39, the Court considers that there are also limits on the Security Council's power to decide what measures shall be taken in response. In its Advisory Opinion on *Certain Expenses of the United Nations*, the court held that:

> … when the Organization takes action which warrants the assertion that it was appropriate for the fulfilment of one of the stated purposes of the United Nations, the presumption is that such action is not ultra vires the Organization. (op. cit., p. 168)

40. The implication of this is that action inappropriate to achieve its intended goal potentially exceeds the Security Council's competence under the Charter. Given that the Security Council must act in accordance with the purposes of the UN, the measures it chooses must be linked to the objective of maintaining international peace and security and must reasonably be considered appropriate to achieve this end.

(b) The question of review

41. Having established the limits on the Security Council's powers provided for by the Charter, it now falls to the Court to consider whether it is able to review the exercise of those powers for legality. The Charter does not explicitly provide for any power of review over the Security Council's exercise of its functions either in the Court or any other body. However, there is also no article in the Charter which prevents the Court reviewing the legality of the Security Council's actions. Given this silence, the Court considers that such review is within its competence. Under Article 36 of its Statute the Court has jurisdiction over 'all cases which the parties refer to it' and the power to determine its own jurisdiction. In this case, the exercise of such jurisdiction requires a review of the legality of the Security Council's action and the Court thus considers itself authorised to carry out such a review.
42. If a system is to be governed by the rule of law, power must not simply be limited but its exercise must entail accountability. Otherwise such limits are meaningless. There is no other body in the international system which could fulfil this role, which the Court is well-placed to carry out. In the new world order, in which the activism of the Security Council looks likely to continue increasing, the legitimacy of the international order will depend on the existence of a system of checks and balances. While the Court may have been deferential in the past, the world is changing, and such deference is no longer appropriate. An increasingly activist Security Council requires an increasingly activist Court if the Council's extraordinarily wide powers are not to be abused. The Court considers that, if faith in international order and justice is to be maintained, it must defend its independence and its judicial function.
43. Thus, the Court considers that it is not bound to defer to the Security Council's decision in Resolution 748 regarding the extradition of the Lockerbie suspects. Rather, it can review the legality of the decision and, should it decide the decision to be *ultra vires*, the Court can go on to consider whether it should grant provisional measures in the case at hand.

(iii) Is Security Council Resolution 748 in accordance with the UN Charter?

44. Having established the limits on the action of the Security Council under the Charter and the Court's power to review the Security Council's exercise of its powers for legality, the Court will now move on to review Resolution 748. The Court finds that Resolution 748 exceeds the competences of the Security Council in a number of ways. First, the Court considers that Resolution 748

amounts to an improper incursion into the judicial function in contravention of the distribution of competences under the Charter and an improper use of the Security Council's Chapter VII powers to get around the limitations on its Chapter VI powers. Second, the measures which the Security Council has decided upon in Resolution 748 are not appropriate to the maintenance of international peace and security. Third, the Security Council has failed to act in accordance with the purposes and principles of the United Nations.

45. To take each of these issues in turn, it is clear that there is a legal dispute regarding the existence of an obligation on Libya to extradite the suspects, which is a matter of the interpretation of the Montreal Convention. Resolution 748 effectively decides the legal dispute in favour of the United States. It has done so without consideration of international law and without regard to due process. The Court considers that the danger of abuse to which the resolution of legal disputes by the Security Council potentially gives rise, has materialised here. In this case, the United States voted for the Resolution which decided the legal dispute in its favour. This dispute is properly to be decided by an independent court using judicial methods. We have already seen that relations between the parties have been poor for a while, with violence on both sides, and the Court thus considers that such legal resolution of the dispute by a neutral arbiter is essential for the maintenance of peace and security in this case. Resolution 748 effectively prevents the Court from deciding upon an application which it would otherwise have jurisdiction to decide. To this extent, the Court considers it to be an illegitimate incursion into the judicial function.

46. Furthermore, the Court considers that this is a dispute which should have been dealt with under Chapter VI. The Security Council, with Resolution 731, did not initially deal with this matter under Chapter VII. The Security Council cannot use its power under Article 39 simply to make an earlier non-binding resolution into a binding one. If the Security Council considered that the continuance of the dispute was likely to endanger the maintenance of international peace and security, it should, as per Article 37(2), have made recommendations under Article 36 or recommended such settlement as it felt appropriate, rather than making recourse to its binding Chapter VII powers. Doing so has allowed the Security Council to bypass the Charter requirements that it 'should take into consideration that legal disputes should as a general rule be referred by the parties to the International Court of Justice' (Article 36(3)), that disputes should be settled 'by peaceful means, and in conformity with the principles of justice and international law' (Article 1(1)), and that interested parties should not vote on decisions under Chapter VI (Article 27). The Court thus considers that Resolution 748 fails to respect the division of the Security Council's competences between Chapters VI and VII, a division which, furthermore, reflects the primacy of peaceful dispute settlement and the Court as the principal judicial organ, and is thus *ultra vires* on this basis.

47. To move on to the second issue, even if one does not accept the preceding arguments, the measures which the Security Council has decided upon in Resolution 748 are neither linked to their objective nor appropriate for its achievement. The Court does not consider that the imposition of sanctions in this case is aimed at furthering international peace and security. Rather, it is aimed at forcing Libya to extradite the suspects, in potential contravention of international law. It is therefore unsurprising that the Security Council's actions here have only heightened tensions and made the dispute more difficult to resolve. The Court is also concerned about the harmful and disproportionate impact of sanctions, particularly on women and children. The Court refers to the International Study team's report from 1991 on the 'Health and Welfare in Iraq after the Gulf Crisis: An In-depth Assessment', where the devastating effect of economic sanctions was highlighted:

> Economic sanctions have resulted in large price increases, massive unemployment, and a drastic reduction in real wages. Having utilized all their savings, 55% of the women interviewed report having had to sell their jewellery and other assets; 40% have incurred heavy debts. Some have even been driven to prostitution and begging. Vulnerable sections of the population including widows, abandoned, and divorced women have been worst affected. The sanctions, along with damage to the electricity, water and sanitation infrastructure caused by the Gulf Crisis, have had a damaging effect on child mortality and women's health. According to gynaecologists, the incidence of miscarriages and low birth-weight babies has significantly increased. Most women patients admitted to hospitals are severely anaemic. Due to physical and psychological hardship, 57% of the women reported suffering from health problems, including psychosomatic symptoms such as sleeplessness, weight loss and headaches. Shortages of electricity, fuel and water have meant that women must secure water and firewood for their families on a day-to-day basis. Shortages of food occur in almost every household, leading to malnutrition and further limiting women's ability to provide for the family. These added domestic burdens fill whatever little spare time women had prior to the conflict. While 74% of the women interviewed indicated that men's roles within the household had not changed, it became clear during the survey that women are not only responsible for nearly all household tasks, but also for providing stability to the family unit. A number of the women interviewed appeared to be suffering from depression, especially those who had lost family members during the crisis. The lives of Iraqi people now take the form of a daily struggle to satisfy basic needs, especially the need for food. Women fare the worst, and Iraqi families owe much to them for their survival. (p. 177)

48. While the sanctions applied against Libya by Resolution 748 may not be as wide-ranging as those applied against Iraq, the Court nonetheless considers that the impact of sanctions cannot be taken lightly. Furthermore, there is

a history of extensive sanctions being applied by the United States against Libya, which the Court considers must be taken into account here; in light of this history, the escalation of sanctions must be considered a real possibility. Given their disproportionate and discriminatory impact, the Court considers that the use of sanctions by the Security Council to try and resolve a legal dispute of this nature unnecessary and inappropriate and thus in excess of its competence under the Charter.

49. Finally, the Court considers that Resolution 748 contravenes the pacific settlement of disputes in accordance with justice and international law, which is both a principle and purpose of the UN under the Charter, as follows:

> Article 1.1. To maintain international peace and security, and to that end: to take effective collective measures for the prevention and removal of threats to the peace, and for the suppression of acts of aggression or other breaches of the peace, and to bring about by peaceful means, and in conformity with the principles of justice and international law, adjustment or settlement of international disputes or situations which might lead to a breach of the peace.
>
> …
>
> Article 2.1. All Members shall settle their international disputes by peaceful means in such a manner that international peace and security, and justice, are not endangered.

50. Since the Security Council is required to act in accordance with the principles and purposes of the UN, this renders Resolution 748 *ultra vires*.
51. The Court thus concludes that, for the reasons specified above, Resolution 748 is not in accordance with the Charter and not binding under Article 25, and therefore the Court's jurisdiction to consider the request for provisional measures survives. As a final important point, before moving on to consider the substance of the application for provisional measures, the Court would like to make it clear that it is only pronouncing upon the aspects of Resolution 748 which address the legal dispute about the extradition of the suspects. To the extent which Resolution 748 considers international terrorism more generally, the Court reserves any judgment since this is not relevant to the application before it.

(iv) Final reflections: Power in the international legal system

52. The importance of the power dynamic between the states involved in this dispute is a key element for the Court to consider. On one side, Libya is not a powerful state but it does have oil assets which are important to other states who wish to buy this precious resource. On the other hand, against Libya in this dispute are the United States and its allies, the United Kingdom and France. These states, the victors of World War II, were the key architects of the modern international system, which gave them essentially controlling power with a veto in the so called executive organ of the UN, the Security Council.

This veto power of the five permanent members allows them to have control over the Security Council, as is evident from this dispute. These states can use the Security Council to act in a way that will suit their own foreign policy goals, such as the handover of the suspects from Libya. While the Court addressed the issues raised by the parties in the earlier parts of the order, the Court has to recognise substantive aspects, or put simply, the reality of power and the patriarchal nature of the international legal system.

53. The United States in this instance is using its dominant position in the Security Council to force a desired result. The Court refers to an older decision of the Permanent Court of International Justice in the *Bozkurt case* of 1927: 'The Court notes with concern international law's history as one which persistently feminises weaker and primitive peoples, that is non-white non-Europeans, just as men, including white men from "civilised nations" have subordinated women and historically failed to give their sisters, mothers and wives full suffrage.' In the *Bozkurt case* the Permanent Court of International Justice commented that France had 'feminised Turkey' and indeed this Court is concerned that the United States is feminising Libya.
54. This subordination of Libya was apparent when the United States ignored the Montreal Convention, which is clearly in force between these two states in the dispute, and also when the United States avoided or ignored the main guiding principles of the UN Charter on the peaceful settlements of disputes mentioned above in order to maximise pressure through a UN body it controls with its allies, the Security Council. This pressure was made even more tangible with economic sanctions, and a monitoring mechanism for these sanctions has already begun with the two Security Council resolutions. The previous strained relationship between the United States and Libya has taken on a severely slanted power dynamic.
55. The Court wishes to point out that this order should in no way be taken to support terrorist acts around the world. The Libyan suspects should be investigated to determine if adequate evidence exists for a trial. That question is not for this Court. Evaluating the current dispute this Court sees the dominance of one state over another using the UN system and organs. The UN system does have a rich history of dominance through the use of trust territories in the past and the much discussed Security Council, as well as other organs. The UN system has been known to act in a patriarchal manner, however in this case the Court wishes to redress this past and acknowledge the skewed power dynamic and the attempt to subordinate Libya through the UN itself.

Concluding,

56. Having satisfied itself that *prima facie* jurisdiction has been established, and that such jurisdiction is not ousted by the Security Council's involvement in the dispute at hand, it now falls to the Court to consider the substance of Libya's request for provisional measures.

57. The right of the Court to indicate provisional measures as provided for in Article 41 of the Statute has as its object to preserve the respective rights of the Parties pending the decision of the Court, and presupposes that irreparable prejudice should not be caused to rights which are the subject of dispute in judicial proceedings (see *Fisheries Jurisdiction (United Kingdom v Iceland), Interim Protection, Order of 17 August 1972, I.C.J. Reports 1972*, p. 12, para. 21).
58. The Court is empowered to indicate provisional measures with a view to preventing the aggravation or extension of the dispute whenever it considers that circumstances so require (see *Frontier Dispute (Burkina Faso v Mali), Provisional Measures, Order of 10 January 1986, I.C.J. Reports 1986*, p. 3, para. 18). Furthermore:

> [W]hen two States jointly decide to have recourse to a chamber of the Court, the principal judicial organ of the United Nations, with a view to the peaceful settlement of a dispute in accordance with Article 2, paragraph 3, and Article 33 of the Charter of the United Nations, and incidents subsequently occur which not merely are likely to extend or aggravate the dispute but comprise a resort to force which is irreconcilable with the principle of the peaceful settlement of international disputes, there can be no doubt of the Chamber's power and duty to indicate, if need be, such provisional measures as may conduce to the due administration of justice. (op. cit., para. 19)

59. In light of the preceding considerations, the Court finds that there is reason to presuppose irreparable harm to Libya's rights under the Montreal Convention, as well as to its sovereignty and political independence (see *Military and Paramilitary Activities in and against Nicaragua (Nicaragua v United States of America), Provisional Measures, Order of 10 May 1984, I.C.J. Reports 1984*, p. 169, para. 41) should provisional measures not be indicated for their preservation in the present proceedings.
60. The United States argues that there is no urgent need to protect Libya through provisional measures and that no proof has been presented that there is a threat of the use of force or other measures that would adversely affect Libya. However, the Court considers, given the history of the application of economic sanctions and force against Libya by the United States, that Libya's fears of intervention are reasonable and well-founded. These fears have of course, to a certain extent, been borne out by the passing of Resolution 748 a mere twenty-seven days after Libya's application was filed with this Court.
61. The Court therefore considers that the requirements of urgency imposed by a request for the indication of provisional measures (see *Passage through the Great Belt (Finland v Denmark), Provisional Measures, Order of 29 July 1991, I.C.J. Reports 1991*, p. 12, para. 23) are fulfilled. Action prejudicial to Libya's rights has already been taken since the request for provisional measures was

made, and there is reason to suppose that further such action is likely before the final judgment is delivered. Such action is not only likely to aggravate the dispute, but, furthermore, is irreconcilable with the peaceful settlement of disputes. The Court therefore considers that the indication of provisional measures is required to ensure the due administration of justice in the present proceedings.

62. The decision given in the present proceedings in no way prejudges the question of the jurisdiction of the Court to deal with the merits of the case or any questions relating to the merits themselves, and leaves unaffected the right of the Governments of the United States of America and Libya to submit arguments in respect of such jurisdiction or such merits.

* * *

63. For these reasons,

THE COURT

Indicates, pending its final decision in the proceedings instituted on 3 March 1992 by Libya against the United States of America, the following provisional measures:

(1) Unanimously,

The United States should immediately cease and desist from any activities which are aimed at forcing Libya to relinquish its rights under the Montreal Convention prior to the resolution of the dispute regarding those rights in accordance with that Convention, particularly the threat or application of sanctions, whether directly or through its actions as a permanent member of the Security Council.

(2) Unanimously,

Libya's sovereignty and political independence should be fully respected and should not in any way be jeopardized by activities which are prohibited by the principles of international law, in particular the principle that States should refrain in their international relations from the threat or use of force against the territorial integrity or the political independence of any State, and the principle that States shall settle their international disputes by peaceful means in such a manner that international peace and security, and justice, are not endangered, principles embodied in the United Nations Charter Article 2(3) and (4).

(3) Unanimously,

The Government of Libya should ensure that all steps within its power are taken with a view to the proper prosecution of the offences arising as a result of the bombing of Pan Am flight 103 in accordance with its obligations under the Montreal Convention.

(4) Unanimously,

The Governments of the United States of America and Libya should each of them ensure that no action of any kind is taken which might aggravate or extend the dispute submitted to the Court.

(5) Unanimously,

The Governments of the United States of America and Libya should each of them ensure that no action is taken which might prejudice the rights of the other Party in respect of the carrying out of whatever decision the Court may render in the case.

Reflections

Collaborating

A characteristic typical of feminist approaches to international law is reflecting upon the practices and procedures through which they produce knowledge. In this case, this was a deliberately self-styled collaborative project. But this raised a number of questions. What exactly is collaboration? And were we doing it? Could we assume that collaboration meant the same thing to all of us? What if some of us thought we were collaborating while others disagreed? Feminist international law scholars have written about the potential of collaboration as method: how the production of ideas through conversation, interchange and engagement between members of a scholarly community, in different places and with different perspectives, challenges the fantasy of the sovereign and autonomous knowledge-creating individual and offers opportunities to 'de-centre' the doing of international law and destabilise its male First World hegemony; how, 'when you collaborate with another person, you cannot avoid the insight, which has long been primarily identified with feminist theory, that your own standpoint shapes your perspective'.[1]

Yet it feels like we ultimately experienced a rather 'thin' version of collaboration. Based at different times over the life of the project in the Netherlands, Australia and the United Kingdom respectively, we were only able to be in the same physical location twice during the life of the project. Neither time nor money allowed otherwise. Despite the possibilities offered by Skype, it seems that technology cannot yet entirely overcome geographical distance; nothing can quite replace corporeal togetherness; sitting down face-to-face is invaluable. In the end, such limitations led our working process to be more one of division of labour, with each of us taking on our individual parts of the overall output, rather than genuine collaboration. Working 'separately together' often described best what we were doing. While the conversations we had at the workshops, not just amongst ourselves but with members of other chambers, discussants and speakers, left us feeling inspired, it was often hard to keep hold of the momentum these generated once we were back to our everyday academic work and lives, with all the pressures and demands these involve. For all the enriching connections facilitated by our participation in the project, we are perhaps left with a sense of only having scratched the surface of the potential of collaboration it implied.

[1] R Buchanan and S Pahuja, 'Collaboration, Cosmopolitanism and Complicity' (2002) 71 *Nordic Journal of International Law* 297, 301–02.

Some Limitations

Like all the other chambers, we were restricted in writing our order to referring to sources that were available when the order was originally written in 1992. This meant that, frustratingly, references we wished to include had to be excluded. This includes the victims' stories with which we begin the authors' note, which would have been a powerful addition to the order, but were not published until later. There was also a lot of material regarding the harm of economic sanctions that post-dated 1992. For example, a UNICEF report published in 1999 listed the deaths of half a million children under the age of five as a direct result of the economic sanctions imposed on Iraq after its 1991 invasion of Kuwait.[2] Dennis Halliday, former Assistant Secretary-General of the UN, resigned over the sanctions. He stated that the 'very provisions of the Charter and the (Universal) Declaration of Human Rights have been set aside and we are waging a war through the UN'.[3]

There were also examples of other Security Council resolutions since 1992 that have potentially been considered to violate international law, fairness and due process principles. Take, for example, Resolution 1422 (2002), which gave immunity to Peacekeepers, and which the Security Council refused to renew in 2004.[4] To quote Nigel White, '[R]esolution 1422 is the clearest example of a decision that is extremely difficult if not impossible to reconcile with UN law … its demise is illustrative of a basic form of accountability to the member states'.[5] Other examples include the Security Council Al-Qaida and Taliban Sanctions Committee, which allows sanctions without trial or recourse to judicial remedy:[6] the only way to challenge a person's inclusion on the list is through domestic or regional courts. In several cases, domestic courts have found the actions of the Security Council here to be a breach of international law.[7] Finally, there is an excellent discussion of the limits on the Security Council's powers and whether there can be judicial review of the exercise of those powers in Antonios Tzanakopoulos's *Disobeying the Security Council: Countermeasures against Wrongful Sanctions*, to which we acknowledge

[2] See, eg, UNICEF, 'Questions and Answers for the Iraq Child Mortality Surveys' (16 August 1999). Available at: www.casi.org.uk/info/unicef/990816qa.html.

[3] Stated in the documentary J Pilger with A Lowery, *The War You Don't See* (Dartmouth Films, 2010). Also see D Rieff, 'Were Sanctions Right?' *New York Times* (27 July 2003). Available at: www.nytimes.com/2003/07/27/magazine/were-sanctions-right.html?pagewanted=all&src=pm.

[4] UNSC Res 1422 (12 July 2002) UN Doc S/RES/1422.

[5] N White, *Law of International Organisations* (Manchester, Manchester University Press, 2005) 194.

[6] See, eg, UNSC Res 1267 (15 October 1999) UN Doc S/RES/1267, para 4 (freezing the funds of the Taliban as well as closing Taliban operated property off to aircraft); UNSC Res 1333 (19 December 2000) UN Doc S/RES/1333, paras 5–8 (continuing to freeze funds of Taliban and close off Taliban controlled territory and offices); UNSC Res 1390 (16 January 2002) UN Doc S/RES/1390, para 2 (continuing restrictions on Taliban and Al-Qaida); UNSC Res 1455 (17 January 2003) UN Doc S/RES/1455, para 4 (requesting that all States provide information concerning Al-Qaida and the Taliban).

[7] See, eg, *Hay v HM Treasury* [2009] EWHC 1677; *A, K, M, Q and G v HM Treasury* [2010] UKSC 2; Commission Regulation 2199/2001 [2001] OJ L295/16; Case T-306/01 *Aden v Council* [2002] ECR II 2387; joined cases C-402/05P and C-4-14/05P *Kadi and Al Barakaat International Foundation v Council and Commission* [2008] ECR I 6351.

our debt.[8] However, we were in 1992 and thus, we were – to our frustration – unable to refer to these materials in our order.

Judging, or It's Hard in Here for a Feminist Judge

Judging posed innumerable challenges – methodological, political, legal and ethical – for us as feminists and international lawyers. Perhaps the most fundamental was the question of how to offer a more just vision of international law from within the formal confines of an ICJ judgment, using the procedures, structures and language that produced the very order we sought to critique. As academics, we are used to engaging with international law from a position (relatively) external to it, generally from an anti-formalist and pluralist perspective, exploring international law's complexity and indeterminacy, its contingency and situated-ness. As feminists, we have been committed to questioning international law's very premises and its positioning as an unequivocal force for emancipation, to exposing its complicity in injustice and oppression, and to analysing its contribution to the construction of international problems rather than proposing it as a solution to them. Now suddenly we were doing the opposite. We had to come to an answer, to sign up to a final, determinative decision, to speak from a supposedly singular and universal position; to do, in other words, precisely that which we understood to be impossible: to use the master's tools to dismantle the master's house. This made judging at times an unfamiliar and uncomfortable experience.

Initially, it seemed appealing to assert the objectivity of law and its institutions as a means to criticise the instrumentalisation of the Security Council by United States exceptionalism. Yet was it our best, or only, option to make strategic use of legal language and concepts for feminist ends? Did it make sense to ask the United States, the United Kingdom, France and the Security Council to respect international law and its institutions, despite our feminist scepticism about them? In proposing the ICJ as a check on the power of the Security Council, were we not assuming that the ICJ (only) speaks truth to power, thereby reinforcing law's supposed objectivity and autonomy from politics which feminists have spent so long trying to challenge? In proposing national sovereignty as a check on Western imperialism, were we not legitimising the violent Libyan regime and assuming the sovereignty of postcolonial States as an ally against patriarchal imperialism, while feminists have worked hard to expose the masculinist foundations of sovereignty and its service in the exclusion of women from international legal discourse?[9]

[8] A Tzanakopoulos, *Disobeying the Security Council: Countermeasures against Wrongful Sanctions* (Oxford, Oxford University Press, 2011).

[9] See, eg, K Knop, 'Re/Statements: Feminism and State Sovereignty in International Law' (1992) 3 *Transnational Law & Contemporary Problems* 283; H Charlesworth and C Chinkin, *The Boundaries of International Law: A Feminist Analysis* (Manchester, Manchester University Press, 2000); R Buchanan and R Johnson, 'The "Unforgiven" Sources of International Law: National-Building, Violence and

Our predicament called to mind that of those international lawyers who had publicly intervened to criticise the illegality of intervention in Iraq prior to the invasion by the United States and its allies in 2003:

> How was it that we were now international law's earnest champions? Had not some of us based our work on the effort to knock international law off its pedestal, and expose its darker dimensions? Had we not routinely criticized sovereignty as purely formal, frequently oppressive, and lacking explanatory power? Yet here we found ourselves invoking international law, and with it state sovereignty, in defence of Iraq. More than that, we found ourselves replicating in the process the same Manichean structure of argument we sought to challenge. They had hegemony; we had sovereignty. They had the axis of evil; we had the sovereign equality of states. They had politics; we had law … Why were we encouraging faith in international law as an agent of justice and peace when we know that it helps to legitimate oppression and justify violence, and we devote a considerable portion of our energies to showing how?[10]

Thus, we had to try and find a position which enabled us to oppose both US exceptionalism and Security Council militarism on one hand and traditional State sovereignty on the other within all the limitations of ICJ judgment writing, and to reflect on how the ICJ itself exercises power in writing its judgment and how its judgments may be instrumentalised by power. As critical scholars, we know that international law is not, of course, just one thing, and if it is a discourse of power, it is also a discourse of resistance; dominant currents always have their counter. For all our scepticism, we must on some level believe in the emancipatory potential of international law, or else we would not do international law at all, surely. Nevertheless, the experience of delivering a judgment forced us into direct confrontation with the challenges, not just of theorising about it, but of trying to make it real.

One way in which this dilemma played itself out was when it came to deciding whether to grant Libya provisional measures and, if so, how far we could go in doing so. We hardly felt we could let the sanctions applied against Libya stand. Yet would granting provisional measures offer political capital to the Gaddafi regime and effectively condone his non-cooperation with the investigation into the Lockerbie bombing and perpetuate impunity, or even amount to a failure to condemn the attack on Pan Am 103? And what would it mean to reserve for ourselves as the ICJ the power to judicially review the actions of the Security Council? Would we in so doing render the ICJ a utopian irrelevancy? Or conversely, who or what might we be sacrificing in such an act of self-empowerment? Of course, it is never possible to finally resolve such dilemmas, to definitively transcend international law's structural tensions. In the end, we could reach only a provisional resolution of the competing tensions we faced, an imperfect compromise. Perhaps our essential experience of judging was one of bearing the discomforts and dangers of doing international law as a feminist in a patriarchal world.

Gender in the West(ern)' in D Buss and AS Manji (eds), *International Law: Modern Feminist Approaches* (Oxford, Hart Publishing, 2005).

[10] M Craven, S Marks, G Simpson and R Wilde, 'We Are Teachers of International Law' (2004) 17 *Leiden Journal of International Law* 363, 366 and 371.

5

Germany v Italy

ZOI ALIOZI, BÉRÉNICE K. SCHRAMM
AND EKATERINA YAHYAOUI KRIVENKO

Authors' Note

Facts, Background and Legal Context

The sequence of events that led to the judgment of the International Court of Justice (ICJ) in the *Germany v Italy* case, also known as the *State Immunities* case,[1] originates in World War II. The fundamental issue at stake was the determination of the scope of, and possible limitations to, state immunities in civil suits brought before national courts as far as they relate to *acta jure imperii* only.[2]

During World War II, the conduct of German forces either as an occupying power or in the course of hostilities included a series of acts that even at the time of their commission constituted violations of the laws of war and other rules of public international law. After the surrender of Italy to the Allies in September 1943 and subsequent occupation of parts of Italian territory by Germany, Italian civilians were subjected to massacres, deportation and forced labour, treatment experienced by civilian populations in other parts of Europe. Many Italian prisoners of war were deported and subjected to forced labour.[3] While half of the forced labourers in Europe were women,[4] it appears that only Italian men were subjected to it while Italian women were left behind, with children and the elderly, and suffered injuries related to the occupying National Socialist (Nazi) forces.[5] Gender

[1] Jurisdictional Immunities of the State (Germany v Italy: Greece intervening) [2012] ICJ Reports 99 (Judgment).

[2] Since the case dealt with the conduct of military forces and other state organs in the course of war, both parties agreed that they constitute *acta jure imperii* despite their unlawfulness. See Judgment, para 60 in particular.

[3] See factual and historical background below, Judgment, above n 1, paras 20–36.

[4] JC Beyer and SA Schneider, *Forced Labor Under the Third Reich. Part I* (Study Paper, Nathan Associates, 1999) 10.

[5] See the Italo-German Historians' Commission Report: Rapporto della Commissione storica italo-tedesca insediata dai Ministri degli Affari Esteri della Repubblica Italiana e della Repubblica Federale di Germania il 28 marzo 2009 (luglio 2012) 32–33. Available at www.villavigoni.it/contents/files/Relazione_finale_in_italiano.pdf.

is therefore both a present and absent dimension of the present case: as a matter of fact, litigation relative to Italian forced labour reparations has been led by male claimants, probably as a result of the gendered nature of international legal frameworks available at the time and until now. To our knowledge, nothing has been done to repair indirect injury suffered by Italian women and their families as a result of the deportation of Italian men. This case is therefore, by the very facts at stake and by the operation of the law available then and now, a critical example of, on the one hand, the relevance of the public-private divide to better understand transitional justice, and of, on the other hand, the need to apply feminist theory across the memorial, historical and legal boards in order to ensure justice's inclusivity. Given the historical and judicial background of the case, the present re-written judgment will focus on the male claimants' injuries while acknowledging, when necessary, the direct and indirect prejudice suffered by others, in particular women. This will be made possible through a feminist re-articulation of war reparations in the context at stake.

After the end of World War II, Germany adopted a series of measures aimed at compensating victims of crimes perpetrated by the National Socialist Party, both within the context of World War II as well as outside of this context.[6] The network of measures established was quite dense and complex since each measure was focused on particular types of victims or suffering inflicted. The final result, as became apparent in the ICJ's judgment, was that some victims and their relatives were not covered by any measure and thus were denied any compensation or were awarded only derisory amounts. In particular, and in view of the fact that forced labour can be said to reside at the 'cutting edge' between war reparations and indemnities for persecution,[7] many male Italian citizens subjected, either as civilians or military, to deportation and forced labour found themselves unable to access any means of redress. As a result, those denied compensation commenced a lengthy litigation process before Italian[8] and

[6] With regards to indemnities for persecution, see: Art. 77 of the 1947 Peace Treaty signed between the Allied Powers and Italy; the German Federal Compensation Law concerning Victims of National Socialist Persecution adopted in 1953 by the Federal Republic of Germany and amended in 1965; Arts 1 and 2 of the Bonn Agreements signed in 1961 between the Federal Republic of Germany and Italy; s 11 and s 16 of the German 'Remembrance, Responsibility and Future' Federal law adopted in 2000. With regards to war reparations, see: the 1953 London Agreement on German External Debt signed between the Federal Republic of Germany and a number of State creditors; the 1990 Moscow Treaty on the Final Settlement with regard to Germany signed between the Federal Republic of Germany, the German Democratic Republic and the four Powers that occupied Germany at the end of World War II.

[7] A Gattini, 'War Crimes and State Immunity in the Ferrini Decision' (2005) 3 *Journal of International Criminal Justice* 225.

[8] Initiated at the Tribunal of Arezzo, followed by an appeal before the Court of Appeal of Florence. See Trib Arezzo 3 Novembre 2000 n 1403/98; App Firenze 14 gennaio 2002 n 41/02 (both unreported). See also, following this jurisprudence, Cass sez un 11 marzo 2004 n 5044/2004 (English translation in (2004) 128 *ILR* 661–75) and the 12 orders rendered by the Italian Court of Cassation on 29 May 2008 (Cass sez un 29 maggio 2008 n 14201-212) dealing with compensation claims submitted

German[9] courts, both to contest existing compensation measures that excluded them and to demand adequate compensation. Faced with a lack of success before the German courts, they turned to lodging complaints with the European Court of Human Rights, which were also unsuccessful.[10]

The stance taken by the Italian Court of Cassation towards these claims, however, was different. The main argument that allowed that Court to recognise the right to compensation of the claimant, Mr Ferrini, derived from a monist and systemic approach to international law and Italian law. Believing in the necessity of an uncompromising answer to the criminal acts at stake which violated fundamental human rights, the Italian judges relied on the operation of international law through its incorporation by the Italian Constitution to provide reparation to the claimants.[11] In other cases, the reasoning revolved around the creative and cross-referential (international-domestic) use of the general principles of law of respect for liberty and dignity as inherent values of every human person.[12] Witnessing the success of Italian claimants, a group of Greek victims also excluded from various German compensation measures was successful before Greek courts in getting a judgment in their favour;[13] however, crucially, they were unable to execute the judgment either in Greece or in Germany.[14] They thereafter turned to the Italian legal system. On the basis of the *Ferrini* jurisprudence mentioned above, the Italian

by other victims, including *Repubblica Federale di Germania v Presidenza del Consiglio dei Ministri and Maietta*, Cass Sez un 29 maggio 2008 n 14209 and *Repubblica Federale di Germania v Presidenza del Consiglio dei Ministri e Giovanni Mantelli*, Cass sez un 29 maggio 2008 n 14201, in addition to the criminal proceedings instituted against Josef Max Milde before military courts (Trib Mil Spezia 10 ottobre 2006 n 49; App Mil 18 dicembre 2007 n 72; Cass sez I penale, 21 ottobre 2008–13 January 2009 n 1072).

[9] The Italian claims were discussed by the German Federal Constitutional Court (Bundesverfassungsgericht) in BVerfG 28 June 2004 2BvR 1379/01 (15 February 2006).

[10] *Associazione Nazionale Reduci and 275 Others v Germany*, App no. 45563/07, ECtHR, 4 September 2007; (2008) 46 EHRR SE11. The European Court of Human Rights declared the claim inadmissible *rationae temporis* with regards to certain aspects of it, and *rationae materiae* with regards to others. Among the claimants were civilians such as Mr Ferrini, along with former prisoners of war.

[11] See Cass sez un 11 marzo 2004 n 5044/2004, par 5, 7.1, 7.2–7.4 and 9–9.2, above n 8.

[12] See in particular the *Milde* case, above n 8.

[13] *Prefecture of Voiotia v Federal Republic of Germany*, Case No 11/2000 (Hellenic Sup Ct 4 May 2000). This Supreme Court judgment and the trial court's judgment is discussed in M Gavouneli and E Bantekas, 'Case Report: Prefecture of Voiotia v. Federal Republic of Germany' (2001) 95 *American Journal of International Law* 198. Also see: Protodikeio/Regional Court of Livadia (1997), confirmed by the Areios Pagos/Court of Cassation (4 May 2000), in the *Distomo* case, which held the German State liable to compensate Greek nationals who were the victims of a massacre perpetrated at Distomo in Greece by German armed forces in 1944.

[14] Greek Code of Civil Procedure, Art 923 of the KpolD. The Minister of Justice, Mr Athanasiou, refused to allow the enforcement of the judgment for political reasons; as the majority of the media argued, this was due to the economic dependency on the German government that Greece had developed in recent years. Βασίλης Π. Τζεβελέκος, 'Η υπόθεση του Διστόμου στο Διεθνές Δικαστήριο', ΑΡΧΕΙΟ ΜΟΝΙΜΕΣ ΣΤΗΛΕΣ, Καθημερινή, 29 Sept 2011 (VP Tzevelekos, 'The Case of Distomo in the International Court' Permanent Collumns, Kathimerini, 29 Sept 2011). The following is the procedural history in Germany of the Greek claimants: LG Bonn, 23 June 1997, 1 O 358/95; OLG Köln, 27 August 1998, 7 U 167/97; BGH, 26 June 2003 III ZR 245/98; BVerfG, 15 February 2006, 2 BvR 1476/03.

courts declared the judgment executable,[15] and, in order to ensure the payment of compensation, even allowed for the seizure of German State property.[16] Faced with immediate suits and even seizure of state property, Germany initiated proceedings against Italy before the ICJ alleging violation of its jurisdictional immunities, a principle of international law that prevents suits in the courts of one State to be brought against another State without its consent.[17]

Issues at Stake

As a preliminary remark, it should be emphasised that the ICJ's decision in this case uses customary international law as its only source. The existing treaty law, the European Convention on State Immunity, was not applicable as Italy is not party to this convention.[18]

Germany argued that by allowing the proceedings before Italian courts against Germany to be initiated, by declaring the Greek judgment executable and by imposing measures of constraint, the Italian courts, and therefore Italy, violated Germany's jurisdictional immunity.[19] Italy's response to these claims did not question the existence of jurisdictional immunity for states in civil proceedings as such; its arguments focused, rather, on the extent of, and possible limitations to, such immunities. One argument was focused on the so-called territorial tort exception; namely, that 'a State is no longer entitled to immunity in respect of acts occasioning death, personal injury or damage to property on the territory of the forum State'.[20] This argument was dismissed.[21] The present re-written judgment does not address this argument both because of lack of space and because of the lesser significance of this argument in comparison with the second argument, which relies on the circumstances and subject matter of claims brought before the Italian courts. That argument is summarised by the ICJ as follows: 'Germany was not entitled to immunity because those acts involved the most serious violations

[15] See *Repubblica Federale di Germania c Autogestione prefettizia di Voiotia*, Cass sez un, 12 gennaio 2011 n 11163. Italy argued that the enforcement of the Distomo Massacre judgment was not a result of the Ferrini decision (See Cass sez un 11 marzo 2004 n 5044/2004, above n 8) and that there is no principle that decrees any foreign state immune from proceedings. Additionally, Italy argued that the Greek courts had not recognised immunity to Germany based on the same justifications and on similar circumstances as those of the *Ferrini* case, Italy had no duty to accord immunity to Germany. See ICJ, Verbatim Record, CR 2011/21, 28–9, paras 1–4.

[16] The Court of Cassation affirmed the decisions of the Court of Appeals in two judgments: Cass sez un, 12 gennaio 2011, n 11163; Cass sez un, 29 maggio 2008, n 14199, (2009) 92 *Rivista di diritto internazionale* 594.

[17] For a good recent overview see KE Bankas, The State Immunity Controversy in International Law: Private Suits against Sovereign States in Domestic Courts (Berlin and Heidelberg, Springer, 2005).

[18] Judgment, para 54.

[19] ibid, para 37.

[20] ibid, para 62.

[21] For the reasoning of the ICJ, see ibid, paras 62–79.

of rules of international law of a peremptory character for which no alternative means of redress was available.'[22] In its judgment, the ICJ deconstructs this argument into three elements and considers each element separately: the gravity of the violations;[23] the *jus cogens* character of norms violated;[24] the question of last resort, that is the absence of any other way to get compensation to victims.[25] Finally, the Court considers the combined effect of these arguments.[26] In all cases the Court found in favour of Germany. The Court's argument with regard to the declaration of the executability of Greek judgments and imposition of constraint measures against German property was in essence simply a repetition of what the Court had stated with regard to the Italian judgments. Since our re-written judgment focuses on the second Italian argument according to which, based on the circumstances and subject matter of claims brought to Italian Courts, immunity can be disregarded, the legal reasoning of the ICJ for rejecting this argument will be the object of further discussion below.

With regard to the part of the argument based on the gravity of violations, the Court briefly reviewed decisions of national courts as well as relevant conventions or draft conventions, concluding that there are uncertainties surrounding any possible rule postulating an exception to state immunities in the case of serious violations of international law. With regard to the relationship between the rules of *jus cogens* and the rule protecting state immunity, the ICJ affirmed that no conflict between those rules exists because the rule regarding State immunity is procedural while *jus cogens* is substantive in nature. The ICJ also referred to several decisions from national courts that rejected a similar argument about *jus cogens* rules displacing the rule on State immunity.

The ICJ's reasoning regarding the 'last resort' argument follows the same pattern as that adopted in relation to the *jus cogens* argument. Namely, the ICJ simply states that the rule on State immunity and the rule on reparations are distinct and apply to different issues, so there is no dependency between them. First, the Court associates the issue of reparations with substantive rules.[27] Then, it asserts that it 'can find no basis in the State practice from which customary international law is derived that international law makes the entitlement of a State to immunity dependent upon the existence of effective alternative means of securing redress'.[28] Thus, the Court affirms that rules on redress and rules on state immunity function in isolation from each other. Finally, as an additional argument, the ICJ mentions that any rule granting State immunity that would be conditional on effective redress would be difficult to apply.[29] In its final paragraph dedicated to

[22] ibid, para 61.
[23] ibid, paras 81–91.
[24] ibid, paras 92–97.
[25] ibid, paras 98–104.
[26] ibid, paras 105–06.
[27] ibid, para 100.
[28] ibid, para 101.
[29] ibid, para 102.

this argument[30] the ICJ mentions the possibility that the two States in this particular case might negotiate further redress and compensation measures. This stance of the Court – shifting from legal arguments (the absence of a rule), to effectiveness arguments (the practical difficulties in application), and then to possible political solutions – demonstrates the Court's uneasiness with its own stance. The Court recognises that a group of victims was left without any access to justice in a non-legal sense and entrusts their fate to the uncertainties of the political will of States.

How the Judgment Resonated in the Literature

The part of the judgment that attracted the most interest from scholars concerns the relationship between *jus cogens* rules and the granting of State immunity. Interestingly, although the ICJ had addressed this issue in one of its previous judgments,[31] the intensity of the reaction from scholars to the *Jurisdictional Immunities* case was significantly heightened.[32] This can be explained by the quite detailed reasoning of the Court in its judgment, as compared to its previous judgments. Perhaps subject matter played its role too. The distinction the Court established between substantive and procedural rules attracted the most criticism.[33] However, it should be noted that many scholars expressed a general support for the conclusion reached by the ICJ on this issue.[34]

Purposes of the Re-written Judgment

The re-written judgment focuses on only one of the arguments submitted by Italy: the impact of the context and subject matter of claims on the scope of State

[30] ibid, para 104.

[31] Arrest Warrant of 11 April 2000 (*Democratic Republic of Congo v Belgium*) Judgment [2002] ICJ Reports 3.

[32] A search on case comments with keywords 'human rights' and 'ICJ' in January 2014 provided 333 results. Among them only four dealt with the *Arrest Warrant* case and 16 with the *Jurisdictional Immunities* case. Interestingly, another ICJ case which introduced the procedure/substance distinction in relation to *jus cogens*, namely the case opposing the Democratic Republic of Congo to Rwanda (*Armed Activities on the Territory of the Congo (New Application: 2002) (Democratic Republic of the Congo v Rwanda)*, Jurisdiction and Admissibility Judgment [2006] ICJ Reports 6) did not attract a lot of attention either: only four instances in the above search.

[33] See eg KN Trapp and A Mills, 'Smooth Runs the Water Where the Brook is Deep: The Obscured Complexities of Germany v Italy' (2012) 1 *Cambridge Journal of International and Comparative Law* 153.

[34] A Gattini, 'The Dispute on Jurisdictional Immunities of the State before the ICJ: Is the Time Ripe for a Change of the Law?' (2011) 24 *Leiden Journal of International Law* 173; M McMenamin 'State Immunity before the International Court of Justice: Jurisdictional Immunities of the State (Germany v Italy)' (2013) 44 *Victoria University of Wellington Law Review* 189; S Shah, 'Jurisdictional Immunities of the State: Germany v Italy' (2012) 12 *Human Rights Law Review* 555; S Talmon, '*Jus Cogens* after Germany v. Italy: substantive and procedural rules distinguished' (2012) 25 *Leiden Journal of International Law* 979.

immunities. Within the original judgment the extent of State immunities was also addressed from the perspective of the territorial tort principle.[35] However, taking into account the approach adopted in the re-written judgment, it is not necessary to consider the territorial tort principle separately as the issue becomes resolved through an appropriate consideration of the relationship between the scope of State immunities and the context and subject matter of the claims. Therefore, despite this omission, the re-written judgment can be read as a stand-alone piece that successfully resolves the dispute between the parties.

Since feminist legal studies encompass a variety of approaches, one of the challenges was to identify and define what a feminist re-writing of an ICJ judgment meant to our chamber. This task was further complicated by the abstract and at first glance gender-neutral, nature of several important aspects of the judgment.

Ultimately, the following elements of feminist theorising became integral to our approach in re-writing the judgment:

- Context specific analysis. For the re-written judgment, this meant the chamber having as thorough as possible an understanding of facts beyond simplified and abstract description that dominated the original judgment.[36]
- Attention to the individual and his/her suffering. Despite the State-centred framework of international law and its approach to issues as State immunities, it is not possible to produce context-specific analysis and an adequate judgment without understanding the plight of the people who initiated cases in domestic courts.
- Intersectionality.[37] Intersectionality teaches that a deep understanding of an issue or situation involves looking at this issue or situation from a variety of perspectives simultaneously. In re-writing the judgment, particular care was taken not to isolate issues but keep them connected and not to partition judgment into too many pieces. Thus, a conscious decision was made not to follow the original judgment's division of the subject-matter argument.
- Deconstruction of binaries.[38] Attention to binaries is one of the fundamental elements of feminist scholarship, since many if not all binaries exemplify the basic male/female distinction. The original judgment is structured around a

[35] According to Italy's argument, the territorial tort principle as a part of customary international law postulates that 'a State is no longer entitled to immunity in respect of acts occasioning death, personal injury or damage to property on the territory of the forum State, even if the act in question was performed jure imperii' (judgment, para 62).

[36] For example, avoiding references to 'forced labour' or 'massacre of civilians' with no further details. For more details on the importance of context-specific analysis to feminist legal scholarship, see KT Bartlett, 'Feminist Legal Methods' (1990) 103 *Harvard Law Review* 829.

[37] On intersectional analysis, see K Crenshaw, 'Mapping the Margins: Intersectionality, Identity Politics, and Violence against Women of Color' (1991) 43 *Stanford Law Review* 1241.

[38] This is well articulated and applied in relation to human rights law in D Otto, 'International Human Rights Law: Towards Rethinking Sex/Gender Dualism,' in M Davies and V Munro (eds) *A Research Companion to Feminist Legal Theory* (Farnham, Ashgate, 2013) 197.

series of binaries that are presented as clear, self-evident and unproblematic: international/domestic, *acta jure imperii*/*acta jure gestionis*, substance/procedure, *jus cogens*/ordinary norm to name just a few. In our re-written judgment, effort was made to avoid these binaries to the extent possible. This was done by resorting to a more nuanced and teleological type of reasoning, ensuring that justice would be dispensed for the victims.

- Absence of hierarchies. Each binary implies an actual or potential hierarchy. Within gendered discourse, male is usually presented as superior to female. The goal of much feminist theorising is not to reverse this hierarchy, but rather to eliminate it altogether through the deconstruction of the binary. Thus, this point is closely connected to the previous one. Within the original judgment, the most important and clearly visible hierarchy was expressed through the use of the notion of *jus cogens*. Despite the many ideals and promises *jus cogens* carries within itself, it is fundamentally a hierarchical notion antithetical to the ideal of equality, or at least absence of oppression. One of the central goals in re-writing was to produce a judgment that does not require reliance on *jus cogens*. Therefore, the re-written judgment has no references to the concept of *jus cogens* in its arguments.[39]

In the authors' opinion, based on the above elements of feminist theorising, the following problematic aspects of the judgment needed to be addressed anew: the nature of events and the suffering of victims including the question of the identification of victims; binary oppositions that determine the outcome of the case; and the hierarchies that underlie the reasoning of the ICJ.

While the issue of the relationship between *jus cogens* and State immunities was identified from the outset as the most disturbing aspect of the judgment, the intention of the authors is not simply to reverse the hierarchy but to deconstruct the binary opposition itself in line with the fourth element of feminist theorising mentioned above. To what extent this endeavour is in fact realistic is a question to be asked when one realises that we continue to operate within a system that is fundamentally built on a binary logic. The authors nevertheless decided to attempt targeting this binary logic from within the framework of the existing international law scholarship and thinking. The resulting judgment therefore follows as much as possible the linguistic and argumentative style of the ICJ. The application of the above-mentioned feminist elements led, however, to a more detailed depiction of facts that relied on more extensive historical documentation.[40] It also led

[39] The notion of *jus cogens* is mentioned once in para 13 and again in para 21 of the re-written judgment. This is because in the former instance the argument based on *jus cogens* was brought up by one of the parties to the dispute and in the latter case the judgment that is used to support the argument utilises this notion. However, it is in no way relevant to the argument of the re-written judgment.

[40] The relevant documentation that helped establish facts of the case more vividly is based on the Italo-German Historians' Commission report issued in July 2012: *Rapporto della Commissione storica italo-tedesca insediata dai Ministri degli Affari Esteri della Repubblica Italiana e della Repubblica Federale di Germania il 28 Marzo 2009* (lulio 2012). Available at: www.villavigoni.it/contents/files/Relazione_finale_in_italiano.pdf.

to a holistic approach to the question addressed by the Court, so that there was no need to discuss separately the gravity of violations, *jus cogens*, and the last resort argument. Relatedly, as already mentioned above, in order to avoid maintenance of hierarchy, the judgment does not rely on the concept of *jus cogens* or for that matter of 'fundamental' or 'serious' human rights violations. As a consequence of this approach, the outcome is also different. The feminist judgment concludes that in this particular case Germany's State immunities were not violated.

Including excerpts of correspondences and various historical testimonies, the use of this report was also a way to bypass the structural absence of witness procedures at the Court. Obviously, this report was not available in its final form to the judges of the ICJ at the time of writing. However, the work of the Italo-German Historians' Commission started several years before the ICJ's judgment, in 2009. We consider that as a feminist court interested in the context of the case, the suffering of victims and precise details of the events, the ICJ could have easily become aware of the work of the Commission, request access to documentation and eventually to the draft report. A similar disclaimer applies to the use of the article by G Painter Renard, 'Thinking Past Rights: Towards Feminist Theories of Reparations' (2012) 30 *Windsor Yearbook of Access to Justice* 33. Although this article appeared in print after the delivery of the ICJ judgment, its author confirmed that the draft article was submitted already in 2011 and was previously presented at various conferences. Against the backdrop of imagined feminist orientation of the judges, we presume that they should have been aware of this most recent innovative scholarship and could have gained access to the draft version.

JUDGMENT

GERMANY v ITALY: GREECE intervening

International Court of Justice

E Yahyaoui Krivenko (President), Z Aliozi, BK Schramm (Judges)

3 February 2012

JURISDICTIONAL IMMUNITIES OF THE STATE

Facts

1. The case brought before the Court by Germany originates in a series of judgments rendered by Italian tribunals and courts regarding compensation claims submitted by Italian and Greek nationals in relation to grave violations of humanitarian law they, or their relatives, have been subjected to by the Nazi forces during World War II. While the Court is not asked to adjudicate upon the reality of the serious violations Italy refers to, it must emphasize that Germany does not contest any aspect of those, and the responsibility it bears as a result of its status as the successor to the responsibility for crimes committed by the Nazi regime. In light of such concordance of opinions and in view of the importance for victims to have their sufferings acknowledged, if not compensated for, in institutional fora, especially judicial ones, the Court finds it useful to start by recounting the horrific events amounting to war crimes and crimes against humanity (*Jurisdictional Immunities of the State (Germany v Italy), Counter-Claim, Order of 6 July 2010, I.C.J. Reports 2010*, p. 310, par. 8) leading the Italian and Greek claimants to initiate legal proceedings against Germany before Italian tribunals and courts, which detailed account the Court will then proceed to give.
2. As mentioned both by Germany and Italy in their written submissions, the claimants can be divided into four categories. A first group is constituted by Italian nationals, mostly young men at the time, who were arrested on Italian territory and sent to Germany to perform forced labour. A second group comprises members of the Italian armed forces who were taken prisoner by the German armed forces and were soon thereafter used as forced labourers as well. A third group is composed of relatives of victims of massacres perpetrated by German forces on Italian territory during the last months of World War II. A fourth group is made of Greek nationals, relatives of victims of a massacre committed by German military units during their withdrawal in 1944 from Greek territory. The Italian claimants' situation will be recalled first.

3. In June 1940, Italy entered World War II as an ally of the German Reich. On 8 September 1943, following the removal of Mussolini from power, Italy surrendered to the Allies and, the following month, declared war on Germany. German forces, however, occupied two thirds of Italian territory, mainly the central and northern parts of it – where on 23 September 1943 a fascist Italian Republic had been set up under the leadership of a fleeing Mussolini. Between October 1943 and the end of the War, German forces perpetrated many atrocities against the population of the occupied territory, including massacres of civilians and the deportation of large numbers of civilians for use as forced labour. In addition, German forces took prisoner, both inside Italy and elsewhere in Europe, several hundred thousand members of the Italian armed forces. As a result of the continuing alliance between the Nazi regime and the artificial fascist Italian Republic, most of these prisoners (hereinafter the 'Italian military internees') were denied the status of prisoner of war and deported to Germany and German-occupied territories for use as forced labour in the industrial complex created to sustain the patriarchal Nazi economy while German men were fighting the war and German women were looking after their homes.

4. The occupied territory was therefore the theatre of daily battles opposing the losing German forces assisted by fascist soldiers, the Italian resistance forces (also called partisans), and the civilian population. An example among others and the leading case in the Italian jurisprudence at stake before this Court, M. Luigi Ferrini, aged 18 at the time and resident of Talla, a small Tuscan village in the countryside of Florence, was captured on 4 August 1944 by the German forces during a raking operation in the area. He was immediately deported to the Kahla concentration camp (or *Lager*), in the Eastern part of Germany (Thuringia), where he was forced to work in two privately-owned underground industrial compounds where he contributed to the manufacturing of aeroplanes and weapons of war. It has been reported that women have also been captured and deported to work as maids for German officers at headquarters in Germany. Besides the trauma that being kidnapped and forcefully deported away from one's home country entails, Mr. Ferrini has described his life conditions in the camp as inhumane in light of the amount of work requested, the little food provided (one beetroot per day and one loaf of bread to share with five other labourers), the lack of hygiene, the discipline enforced, the recurring bombings and so on. Out of the seven persons deported from Talla, only him and another man survived this ordeal, including the attempted collective murder the German forces failed to carry out against all Kahla's forced labourers when the American forces arrived near the camp. Mr. Ferrini was freed in August 1945 and came back in a weak condition and with an open injury (*Ferrini judgment* (Court of Appeal of Florence, 2011)). He is now 86.

5. The 'Italian military internees' experienced similar, if not harsher conditions. After Italy surrendered, several hundreds of thousands of Italian soldiers turned

to the German forces fearing retaliation from them. Instead of being let free, they were right away deported to forced labour camps where, if they survived the hardship of the transfer, they usually suffered ill-treatment worse than civilians given the Germans' resentment going back to World War I events, and the lack of prisoner-of-war special treatment provided for by humanitarian laws. It is only when, in September 1944, their overseeing was transferred to civilian authorities in accordance with their lost prisoner-of-war status that their living conditions improved a little (*Italo-German Historians' Commission report unofficial draft*).
6. The following account of the transfer to the camps sheds some light on the harshness and inhumanity of the conditions experienced by the two groups of victims:

> During the journey, the wagon's windows remained totally sealed (…) We were like sardines in a can, without any air, any food or possibility to relieve ourselves: three dead bodies and myself with running fever and a very painful wound in the leg. (…) We didn't know whether it was day or night time. After some time, they opened the door. A man said in Italian "Don't move or I'll shoot you." I saw [a sign] where it was written "Monaco". They made us get off the train and gave us some black bread: the loaf was stamped with the date 1938 (…), I will never forget it. (*Italo-German Historians' Commission report unofficial draft*; translation by BK Schramm.)

7. At the same time, the Italian civilian population – which was mainly composed of women, children and elderly persons as the majority of men were away resisting or being deported – experienced rigorous conditions of life in occupied territories. While women took on the jobs those men had done in addition to performing their traditional roles of at-home caregivers, the families' farming products, food and any other useful belongings were frequently stolen, their houses looted and destroyed by German forces. They also suffered brutal and murderous attacks as retaliation for partisan activities. One such instance is the Civitella massacre that has been the object of the *Milde* case, part of the relevant Italian jurisprudence before the Court today: on 29 June 1944, four days after four German soldiers were assassinated by partisans, Sergeant Max Josef Milde, member of the Herman Göring division, led three squads into the territory of the Tuscan communes of Civitella, Cornia and San Pancrazio where a religious celebration was taking place and the population had gathered. 203 people, mostly elderly persons, women and children, were killed with cruelty and premeditation; women were raped before being murdered, and corpses were torn to pieces.
8. Although historical accounts are still very scant, some estimates of the number of Italian civilians (not including partisans) killed by the German forces amount to 10.000–15.000, and the number of Italian military internees to 600.000 (*Italo-German Historians' Commission report unofficial draft*), and the total number of deported Italian forced labourers to 1.800.000 (*Forced Labor under the Third Reich* – part I (1999, p. 6)). It is undeniable that the trauma left from these dreadful and months-long events was long lasting. The influence that the state of

war and the serious violations of humanitarian law brought along with it – sending men away, requiring women to perform even more tasks than traditionally, huge economic losses, brutal assaults and deaths – profoundly shaped the Italian population of the time and also that of subsequent generations, especially in the light of the lack of historical and commemorative work done in this regard. (*Italo-German Historians' Commission report of July 2012 unofficial draft*, recommendations at p. 163).

9. The trauma and suffering of civilian populations is further reflected in the fate of Greek citizens in the *Distomo* case that gave rise to the intervention by Greece before this Court. It should be noted that the *Distomo* case is only one instance in a series of systematic gruesome attacks on the Greek population. By 2001, the number of cases resulting from World War II events – reported and filed in the Greek justice system – exceeded 60,000.[1]

10. These cases were introduced by Greek citizens. In the case of Distomo (located in the Prefecture of Voiotia), the claimants had their relatives assassinated by Nazi forces in Nazi occupied Greece on June 10, 1944. A few days before, revolutionary freedom fighters of E.L.A.S. (Hellenic Public Liberating Army) had ambushed an SS unit, resulting in the killing of 40 Nazi soldiers. As a result, the Nazis directed a 'measure of atonement' and retaliations against the whole village of Distomo. Victims of these atrocities included twelve captured partisan fighters and 300 villagers – mainly non-resisting women, children and elderly who did not contribute to the armed conflict. The barbaric nature of the unjustified killings, which were in violation of humanitarian law, included: rape, slaughtering of pregnant women, beheadings, dismembering of infants and corpses, cutting off of female body parts such as breasts. This action ended with the complete destruction and burning of the village.

11. The report of the Red Cross that visited the village immediately after the massacre provides a glimpse into the suffering inflicted on civilians:

> From the edges of the road, vultures got up from low height, slowly and unwillingly, when they heard us approach. From every tree, along the road and for hundreds of metres, human bodies were hanging, stabilised with bayonets, some of whom were still alive. They were villagers who were punished in this way: they were suspected for helping the partisans of the area, who attacked an SS detachment. The smell was unbearable. Inside the village, the fire was still burning in the ashes of the houses. Hundreds of people, of all ages, from elders to newborns, were lying on the ground. They [the Nazis] had torn the uterus and removed the breasts of many women; others were lying strangled with their intestines still tied around their necks.[2]

[1] R Dolzer 'The Settlement of War Related Claims: Does International Law Recognize a Victim's Private Rights of Action? Lessons after 1945' (2002) 20 *Berkeley Journal of International Law* 2969–7.

[2] S Linnér, 'Min Odyssé' (1982), reprinted in P Antaios et al (eds), Η Μαύρη Βίβλος της Κατοχής (*The Black Book of Occupation*), 2nd edn (Athens, National Council for the Claim of Reparations Owed by Germany to Greece, 2006).

12. Despite all the efforts and lengthy proceedings through various domestic judicial systems, the victims at the origin of the present case have not been able to get an appropriate remedy. Even though Italian and Greek courts have in some cases recognised the right of these victims to a remedy, the actual realisation of any remedy was frustrated at the execution stage by arguments relying on the inviolability of state immunity.

Argument

13. Italy's argument is that the denial of state immunity is justified on account of the particular nature of the acts forming the subject-matter of the claims before the Italian courts and the circumstances in which those claims were made. There are three strands to this argument. Firstly, Italy contends that the acts that gave rise to the claims constituted serious violations of the principles of international law applicable to the conduct of armed conflict, amounting to war crimes and crimes against humanity. Secondly, Italy maintains that the rules of international law thus contravened were peremptory norms (*jus cogens*). Thirdly, Italy argues that the claimants having been denied all other forms of redress, the exercise of jurisdiction by the Italian courts was necessary as a matter of last resort.
14. In the oral proceedings, Italy also contended that its courts had been entitled to deny state immunity because of the combined effect of these three strands. The Court does not deem it necessary to consider each of the strands separately. This would result in an artificial dismembering of the situation and fate of victims. Rather, as Italy argued in the oral proceedings, the Court needs to approach the situation as a whole and decide whether under given circumstances of the particular case the denial of state immunity was warranted.
15. By an Order dated 6 July 2010, the Court dismissed Italy's counter-claim application regarding the alleged violation by Germany of its obligation to provide effective reparation to Italian victims of grave breaches of humanitarian law committed by the German forces during World War II (*Jurisdictional Immunities of the State (Germany v. Italy), Counter-Claim, Order of 6 July 2010, I.C.J. Reports 2010*, p. 310). However, it cannot be disputed that at the core of the dispute between the parties to this case is the question of reparations in light of state jurisdictional immunity. This is illustrated in Germany's and Italy's respective submissions, which adopt contrasting positions on this point. While Germany held at various occasions throughout the proceedings that 'reparations were made' through 'a comprehensive scheme for all countries concerned and covering all war damages' including lump-sum payments, Italy has maintained that '[a] very large number of victims remained uncovered' as the schemes mentioned did not provide an effective legal avenue for numerous Italian victims to obtain reparation. The only legal avenue left, according to Italy, was therefore for its domestic courts to waive jurisdictional immunity in order to entertain those pending claims. Germany contests the legality of such waivers under current international law. As a consequence, to resolve this specific and difficult controversy, the Court must examine

the relationship between remedies and reparations to victims of war crimes and the granting of State immunity.

16. In order to do so, the Court will first elaborate on the place and functions of remedies and reparation for victims of war crimes and serious violations of human rights law. Thereafter, the Court will examine the nature and underlying functions of State immunity in international law.

Reparations

17. As many legal regimes, war reparations is a complex and evolutive regime that intersects with different areas of international law: international humanitarian law, international human rights law and the law on state responsibility. It is useful to briefly go through the relevant dispositions pertaining to those areas. As for customary international humanitarian law, as reflected in Article 3 of the 1907 Fourth Hague Convention and Article 91 of the 1977 Additional Protocol and, for instance, by a number of military manuals (Canada, Côte d'Ivoire or the United States), it provides that a belligerent party responsible for a breach of the other provisions of the relevant texts is 'liable to pay compensation.' Establishing the International Criminal Court's mandate with regards to 'Reparations to Victims', Article 75 of the Rome Statute shall also be mentioned. As for customary State responsibility as codified by the International Law Commission, Article 31 of the Articles on State Responsibility provides that the state responsible for an international wrongful act is 'under an obligation to make full reparation for the injury' caused by this act. This echoes this Court's predecessor famous stance on the matter since 1928 (*Factory at Chorzów, Merits, Judgment No. 13, 1928, P.C.I.J., Series A, No. 17*, pp. 29 and 47–48). The Permanent Court also made the following clear: inasmuch as the obligation to provide reparation is governed by international law in all its aspects, the responsible state cannot invoke its own domestic law to evade its satisfaction (*Jurisdiction of the Courts of Danzig, Advisory Opinion, 1928, P.C.I.J., Series B, No. 15*, pp. 26–27; *Greco-Bulgarian 'Communities', Advisory Opinion, 1930, P.C.I.J., Series B, No. 17*, pp. 32 and 35; *Free Zones of Upper Savoy and the District of Gex, Judgment, 1932, P.C.I.J., Series A/B, No. 46*, p. 167; *Treatment of Polish Nationals and Other Persons of Polish Origin or Speech in the Danzig Territory, Advisory Opinion, 1932, P.C.I.J., Series A/B, No. 44*, p. 24). The afore-mentioned principles are found today in Article 34 and 32 of the Articles on State Responsibility. Article 33 stipulates that '[t]he obligations of the responsible State set out in this part may be owed to another State, to several States, or to the international community as a whole'; it however adds that the implementation of these obligations is without prejudice 'to any right, arising from the international responsibility of a State, which may accrue directly to any person or entity other than a State.' With regards to non-binding instruments, the United Nations Commission on Human Rights adopted in 2005 a resolution on the Basic Principles and Guidelines on the Right to a Remedy and Reparation for Victims of Gross Violations of International Human Rights Law and Serious Violations of International Humanitarian Law (Resolution 2005/35): its paragraph IX starts by

recalling that '[a]dequate, effective and prompt reparation is intended to promote justice by redressing gross violations of international human rights law or serious violations of international humanitarian law' and that, '[i]n accordance with its domestic laws and international legal obligations, a State shall provide reparation to victims' of these violations.

This catalogue therefore makes it quite clear *in abstracto* that a state responsible for grave violations of international humanitarian law is under an international obligation to provide reparation to the victims. In the present case, Germany has explained to the Court the various steps it has taken at the international and at the domestic levels since the end of World War II by way of providing adequate compensation to victims of the Nazi regime. Germany first of all invokes the waiver included in Article 77(4) of the 1947 Peace Treaty signed with the Allies. Said provision reads thus: 'Without prejudice to these and to any other dispositions in favour of Italy and Italian nationals by the Powers occupying Germany, Italy waives on its own behalf and on behalf of Italian nationals all claims against Germany and German nationals outstanding on May 8, 1945, except those arising out of contracts and other obligations entered into, and rights acquired, before September 1, 1939. This waiver shall be deemed to include debts, all intergovernmental claims in respect of arrangements entered into in the course of the war, and all claims for loss or damage arising during the war.' This article cannot however be deemed to have waived any rights of victims of serious breaches of international humanitarian law to claim reparation. As indicated above, the obligation to compensate for injury suffered from breaches of international humanitarian law is directly connected to those breaches. The humanitarian character of the norms thus violated prohibits any insuperable distinction made between the necessity to abide by said norms and the actual possibility of obtaining compensation for their violations. This would otherwise run contrary to the very fundamental values of humanitarianism. It would moreover lead to the protection of the protectors, namely the States, to the detriment of their protégées,[3] their nationals, engendering for the latter a second injury. After the moral, physical and economic injuries suffered as a result of the violation of humanitarian law, the victims would experience another powerful type of injury, a symbolic one, that of denial of justice. Letting the waiver stand as it is, in view of the current unrepaired situation of the remaining victims and their heirs, would enable a rigid, ossified and backward-looking view of international justice to prosper. This type of justice, which is limited to certain categories of victims, and to certain types of measurable and direct injustices objectified through the notion of rights or viewed through the lens of traditional patriarchal values, is a justice which once again operates often to the greatest detriment of women. This is not the type of justice this Court can satisfy itself with. Instead, reparations need to be thought out as a process

[3] H Charlesworth and C Chinkin, *The Boundaries of International Law: A Feminist Analysis* (Manchester, Manchester University Press, 2000) 49.

which is both backward and forward looking, allowing for an open and inclusive encompassing outcome.[4] Moreover, States should view individual and collective reparations as interrelated and mutually reinforcing when designing appropriate measures of reparation. However, in the remainder of this judgment the emphasis will be placed on individual reparations due to the nature of the case and the way it was brought to the attention of this Court.

18. Until the current century, none of the schemes set up by Germany did actually address compensation for grave violations of humanitarian law: only those pertaining to Nazi persecution entailed reparation, and then only with regards to victims residing in Germany or having a link with that country, or else having the status of refugee. Such schemes clearly left Italian and Greek claimants outside of their scope, without any reparation. The 2000 Foundation Law was enacted following the signing of an executive agreement between Germany and the United States specifically to cover categories of victims of forced labour not covered by previous mechanisms and who had started suing German companies before United States courts. However, Section 11 of the Foundation Law, which listed those eligible for compensation, explicitly excluded forced labourers with prisoner-of-war status (paragraph 3). This included all the Italian military internees: the German government invalidated their status' change, under the Nazi regime, from prisoner-of-war to civilian prisoners as its unilaterality violated international humanitarian law. As a consequence, a number of former Italian military internees commenced litigation before German courts and before the European Court of Human Rights, however to no avail. As an example of how the claims of civilian forced labourers' claims have fared, it appears that, in 1998, Mr. Ferrini was offered by Germany a minor symbolic lump-sum payment on the condition that he renounced his parallel claims before the Italian courts after all his attempts before German courts had failed. He refused the indemnity and pursued his litigation leading to the results we know today.

19. Furthermore, the war reparations regime goes hand in hand with the human right of access to justice,[5] understood broadly: one without the other renders justice lost. Germany insisted that, because its obligation to provide for war reparations derives from general international law, settlements should be dealt with at the interstate level only. It therefore opposed World War II victims submitting individual compensation claims before a domestic judge. The Court cannot share this view for two important reasons, both related to a dynamic idea of post-war justice, particularly when serious violations of international humanitarian law are at stake. While nothing short of a non-State-centered justice mechanism is explicitly mentioned in Article 3 of the 1907 Fourth Hague Convention or Article 91 of the 1977 Additional Protocol, this Court's predecessor held as early as 1928

[4] G Painter Renard, 'Thinking Past Rights: Towards Feminist Theories of Reparations', draft version on file, 33.

[5] F Francioni (ed), *Access to Justice as a Human Right* (Oxford, Oxford University Press, 2007).

that 'the very object of an international agreement (…) may be the adoption by the parties of some definite rules creating individual rights and obligations and enforceable by the national courts.' (*Jurisdiction of the Courts of Danzig, Advisory Opinion, 1928, P.C.I.J., Series B, No. 15*, pp. 17–18. This has also been the rationale used by this Court in two more recent cases: *LaGrand (Allemagne c Etats-Unis), arrêt, C.I.J. Recueil 2001*, p. 466; *Avena et autres ressortissants mexicains (Mexique c Etats-Unis d'Amérique), arrêt, C.I.J. Recueil 2004*, p. 12.) The second reason is related to the positive evolution of the individual on the international plane due to, preponderantly, the emergence and strengthening of international human rights law. Illustrative of such evolution is the 2010 Resolution adopted by the International Law Association with regard to Reparations for Victims of Armed Conflicts whose Article 6 provides that '[v]ictims of armed conflict have a right to reparation from the responsible parties.' In view of the failure both by Germany to initially provide remedies to the victims' grave sufferings and by Italy to thereafter succeed in its diplomatic protestations against Germany in that regard, the Court, as the principal judiciary organ of the United Nations, cannot remain itself silent and take part in the denial of justice Italian and Greek victims have been confronted with since they were first abused. While war and reparations for violations of its laws used to be framed mainly at the state level, times have changed and so have warfare and the regime for compensation of its abuse.

20. The present case's special circumstances must again be pressed when eventually turning to the issue of state jurisdictional immunity in light of the existing individual right to reparation as enabled by that of access to justice. The Court is not asked to devise a general framework about this type of immunity with regard to serious violations of international humanitarian law. It is rather required to determine whether in the case of those Italian and Greek claimants whose access to justice has been until now denied, Italian courts have in fact violated Germany's jurisdictional immunities by entertaining the claims submitted to them. To proceed with such determination, it is first important to acknowledge the domestic courts' widely recognised authority to review the underlying factors of the case in order to determine whether or not an exception to immunity applies (see, for example, *Comrades v United Kingdom* (1981), 65 *ILR* 205 (Hanover Labour Court); *Farouk Abdul Aziz v Yemen* (2005) the Court of Appeal (Civil Division) of England, [2005] EWCA civ 745, paras. 61–62; Supreme Court of Canada, *Kuwait Airways Corp. v Iraq*, 2010 SCC 40, [2010] 2 *SCR* 571, para. 33). In addition to this capacity of domestic courts, it is equally important to note the specificity of the Italian constitutional setting. Italian courts operate within the limits of the Italian Constitution. Its Article 10 requires the Italian legal system to conform to the generally recognised principles of international law, such as the human right of access to justice. This means that, both under international law and domestic law, this right finds protection against other general rules of international law from which it has been possible to derogate since the end of the XIXth century, namely the rules on state immunities. At the regional level, it is worth mentioning that while the majority in the European Court of Human Rights did not, when presented with a civil claim for

acts of torture constituting violations of *jus cogens*, lift immunity in the *Al-Adsani* case, it did mention the existence of limitations to it to the latter rule (*Al-Adsani v United Kingdom* [GC], application No. 35763/97, judgment of 21 November 2001, *ECHR Reports* 2001-XI, p. 101, para. 61; *ILR*, Vol. 123, p. 24; (2002) 34 EHRR 11). The Grand Chamber in the *McElhinney* case also noted the existence of 'a trend in international and comparative law towards limiting State immunity' although it is 'by no means universal' (*McElhinney v Ireland* [GC], application No. 31253/96, judgment of 21 November 2001, *ECHR Reports* 2001-XI, p. 39; *ILR*, Vol. 123, p. 73, para. 38; (2002) 34 EHRR 13) As to the *Kalogeropoulou and others v Greece* case which was brought by claimants in the present case, relatives of victims of the Distomo massacre, the ECHR's Chamber considered state immunity as one of the limitations inherent to fair trial although it stated that it did not 'preclude a development in customary international law in the future' (*Kalogeropoulou and Others v Greece and Germany*, application No. 59021/00, decision of 12 December 2002, *ECHR Reports* 2002-X, p. 9; *ILR*, Vol. 129, p. 537;).

21. General international law must be conceptualized and interpreted as a system with various sub-regimes that coexist, as the Court has recalled in its judgment on the merits in the *Ahmadou Sadio Diallo* case (*Ahmadou Sadio Diallo (Republic of Guinea v Democratic Republic of the Congo), Merits, Judgment, I.C.J. Reports 2010*, par. 66–67). It is therefore impossible to disconnect the current state of general international law from emerging trends in other legal regimes, be they international, regional or domestic ones. It is the interaction and reciprocation of these regimes that make up the international norms as they stand today. The present case is a cogent illustration of this. Italian military internees' lives and the various legal contexts they are inserted in are therefore to be assessed against the backdrop of the necessity for justice to be done where basic human rights have been grossly violated and no compensation offered whatsoever. As a result, the disputed Italian jurisprudence can only be welcomed as a new step on the path of the potential emergence of a new customary limitation to state jurisdictional immunities. Only such a limitation can ensure that reparation in case of serious violations of international humanitarian and human rights law is now made possible.

Immunities

22. State immunity from jurisdiction has a long history. However, the concept has evolved over time. While the development of the law on state immunity began with the notion of absolute immunity (*The Schooner Exchange v McFaddon*, US, 11 US (7 Cranch) 116 (1812)), which protected a sovereign state from the jurisdiction of any foreign domestic courts, it has progressively been replaced by the current trend of restrictive immunity, which offers certain exceptions to the rule. For instance, State immunity in civil law matters, which was originally absolute, has evolved to encompass a distinction between *acta jure imperii* and *acta jure gestionis*, whereby immunity is only attached to the former. The meaning of these two notions is not carved in stone: it is subject to a continuously changing interpretation that varies

with time, reflecting the changing priorities of society. Other exceptions to absolute immunity commonly recognised today include the tort exception or implied waivers. The evolution from unconditional to limited immunity is an irrevocable development. Accordingly, contemporary international law on state immunity comprises the rule of restrictive immunity, and the correlative sovereign right of states to claim an exception to the exercise by the forum state of its jurisdictional and administrative powers against one another. Further, rather than a discrete and rigid rule, State immunity is best understood as a principle of international law, legally binding yet amenable to adaptation.

23. Moreover, international State immunity does not historically originate in interstate legislation but is the product of intrastate practice, namely judicial activism by domestic courts. Its hybrid nature therefore reflects not only its specific coming into existence, but is also living proof of the complex nature of international law-making. It notably entails the balancing, by various actors of the international legal sphere, of incongruous fundamental principles, mirroring the interaction between international law sub-regimes as discussed in the previous paragraphs. As to the law on State immunity, it is thus a vivid example of the salience of domestic legal orders' take on the matter. Hence, while states agree on the general principles guiding the granting or denial of immunity, the legal structure of the notion of immunity is subject to constant variations regarding the conditions under which the domestic court is to grant or deny immunity to a defendant State.

24. By guiding state and individual behaviour, international legal norms embody, and hence protect, certain fundamental values while evading or suppressing others. In this regard, the principle of State immunity is no exception. In contemporary international law, the law of privileges and immunities, including State immunity from civil jurisdiction, retains its importance as a guarantee of the proper functioning of the network of mutual inter-State relations, which is of paramount importance for a well-ordered and harmonious international system. Essentially, State immunity aims at allowing a State to function without external interference, and to only be subjected to equal and fair third-party adjudication, both of which goals being potentially compromised where a State is called to defend itself before a court of foreign jurisdiction.

25. The concept of State immunity does not accordingly exist in a vacuum. It is part and parcel of an international system of rules, principles and regulations, all of which are aimed at achieving harmony in international relations. When deciding whether in any particular case waiving state immunity did violate rules and principles of international law, the Court needs to take into account all affected interests and see how best to ensure harmony in international relations in a particular case. Giving the variety of rules and principles that in any particular case need to be taken into account and balanced against the principle of State immunity, it might be impossible to formulate a universally applicable set of rules about exceptions to State immunity. The individual circumstances of each particular case will be crucial. In light of this, the Court will now proceed to examine

the particular circumstances of this case as they are known to the Court in order to find an appropriate solution.

The Situation in the Present Case

26. As discussed above, the present case raises the issue of how to achieve justice for victims of war crimes and serious violations of human rights where no other route is available but to disregard State immunities. The following aspects of the present case need to be highlighted in this regard. Neither party to the dispute contests the seriousness or the illegality of the acts committed by Germany. Germany even acknowledged it over the course of the proceedings. The facts of every individual case and circumstances surrounding them are also publicly available, although not always easily accessible. It is to be noted that historical work is far from having exhausted the archival and witnessing sources still available. With the time passing and many of the survivors, such as Mr Ferrini, or their relatives dying, much of this knowledge is being lost. Therefore, this judgment necessarily represents only a partial historical account of what happened. The judgment does not pretend to draw a full and exhaustive picture of this period but strives to achieve the fullest account possible for adjudication purposes, while encouraging the carrying out of further historical work by all affected parties. What is however indisputable is the fact that, as has been explained above (see para. 19), the victims at the origin of the present case fall between the cracks of existing reparations measures. Despite quite a dense network of reparation measures adopted by Germany, several specific groups of victims have not had access to any compensation.

27. In classical State-centred international law, the treaties concluded at the end of a war were a subject of political negotiations by States and constituted their final settlement. These treaties gave direct voice to, or addressed the needs of, individuals only marginally. This was perhaps a sustainable option a century or two ago. Notably, the Nuremberg trials embodied one of the first attempts to bring the individual into the picture of this State-negotiated and State-centred post-war settlement. However, such efforts met with limited success. In such an international system, this type of war settlement excluding individuals and as such, an imprint of the relevant power distribution, was still deemed a satisfactory solution conducive to an adequate level of harmony at the time. This is no longer the case today, when individuals and their human rights are at the heart of the international system. Leaving victims without any access to remedies or reparations in a system of international relations that puts human rights and individuals at its centre will only reinforce feelings of injustice and lead to further disputes and contestations.

28. Faced with the need to ensure a harmonious international system, this Court is of the opinion that, in the particular circumstances of the case, upholding State immunities at all price would be too formalistic a solution. Taking into account, on the one hand, that the illegality of the acts and the absence of any adequate reparation measures so far is acknowledged by Germany, and, on the other, that the facts of the cases are widely known, we conclude that there is consequently no

danger that the proceedings before Italian courts will in any way threaten German sovereignty or create undue impediments to the international relations between those States. The only aspect that needs to be dealt with care is the execution of judgments because the ultimate goal of the claimants is to re-establish justice and truth while securing adequate compensation. The execution of judgment shall not undermine these interrelated goals.

29. With regard to execution, all involved parties should proceed in the spirit of mutual cooperation and understanding. In particular, the seizure by Italian authorities of Villa Vigoni is of questionable usefulness in the present case. Villa Vigoni is a German-Italian Centre for European Excellence, whose aim is to foster the relationship between Italy and Germany in the fields of scientific research, higher education and culture. Villa Vigoni fosters Italian-German dialogue. The activities conducted in the Villa Vigoni also contribute to the fostering of harmony and cooperation between States and individuals, including remembering a common past. The seizure of Villa Vigoni, and especially the subsequent execution of that seizure, might endanger these valuable activities. Therefore, Italian authorities need to carefully consider the consequences of seizure and execution before proceeding further. On the other hand, Germany has to exhibit a degree of cooperation in complying with judgments of Italian courts and be ready to offer alternatives to the seizure of its property. The Court is ready to provide guidance to the parties in this matter if so required.

30. Last but not least, the Court feels strongly obliged to express its distress at the unacceptable amount of time and obstacles that have had to be overcome to achieve justice, albeit only symbolically in the form of the present judgment, for the Italian and Greek claimants in this case. Many of the surviving victims or their relatives are now dead; the psychological, sociological and structural consequences of the horrific crimes those victims and those around them then and now, in particular women as survivors of sexual crimes or accrued gender discrimination and violence have never been, and will never be, fully addressed. The least one could have expected from Germany and Italy likewise was the immediate creation of institutional activities providing for the gathering, protection and honouring of their memory. This has not been the case until very recently. In this regard, the Court finds some satisfaction in the work of the *ad hoc* Italo-German Historian Commission's final report, a draft of which was made available to the Court. This report is another important step on the way towards justice for all the forgotten victims of atrocities perpetrated by the Nazi regime during World War II.

31. In accordance with the foregoing, the Court will now make a final statement as to the nature of the measures of reparation expected to be provided to the victims and/or their relatives. While the Court did refer to its judgment in the *Chorzow Factory* case (see above, par. 17), the notion of 'integral reparation' (*restitutio in integrum*) must be understood nowadays in a broader manner, given the present circumstances and in the light of a recent international jurisprudential trend in this perspective (*Gonzàlez* et al *v Mexico ('Cotton Field'), Preliminary Objection, Merits, Reparations and Costs, Judgment*, Inter-American Court of Human Rights

(ser. C) 205, f113-136 (Nov. 16, 2009)). This entails, on the one hand, the re-establishment, when possible, of the previous situation and the elimination of the effects produced by the violation, as well as the payment of compensation for the damage caused, in addition to, on the other hand, allowing for a change in such an original situation. Integral restitution is therefore as much about restitution as it is about rectification. From this perspective, the contemplated reparations measures should (i) refer directly to the violations as found by the Court; (ii) repair the pecuniary and non-pecuniary damage proportionately; (iii) not make the beneficiaries richer or poorer; (iv) restore the victims to their situation prior to the violation insofar as possible, to the extent that this does not interfere with the obligation not to discriminate; (v) adopt a gendered perspective, bearing in mind the different yet correlative impact that violence has on men and on women, and (vi) take into account all the juridical acts and actions in the case which, according to the States, tend to repair the damage caused.

32. For the reasons outlined above,

THE COURT,

1. Unanimously
   Finds that Italy has not violated Germany's jurisdictional immunity by allowing civil claims brought against it, by taking measures of constraint against Villa Vigoni, by declaring decisions of Greek courts executable.
2. Unanimously
   Finds that Italy and Germany remain under an obligation to provide an adequate, and not simply symbolic, financial compensation to victims as a form of execution of relevant judgments.
3. Unanimously
   Finds that Italy and Germany remain under an obligation to actively set up and support institutional activities as well as create a framework for facilitating private initiatives allowing for the gathering, protection and honouring of the memory of victims.
4. Unanimously
   Finds that Italy and Germany are under an obligation to ensure wide publication and circulation of this judgment in order to acknowledge their international responsibility.

Reflections

Our reflection on the process is structured in the following way. First, a broad picture of our understanding of feminist approaches to the re-writing of the present judgment is drawn. In the second part of these reflections we focus on the four following questions: What was it like to work collaboratively? How was the process of delivering 'judgment' experienced? What did the experience reveal about the structures and norms of international law? Were the feminist methods and theory adopted able to transcend international law's biases effectively? Our answers to those questions are at times joint, and at other times individual. In this latter case, the name of the person expressing the opinion is clearly indicated. This patchwork approach to the reflective piece was adopted in order to provide space for expression of personal style and opinions that was suppressed in the process of the judgment re-writing.

Since feminist legal studies encompass a variety of approaches, one of the challenges in re-writing the *Germany v Italy* judgment was to identify and define what a feminist re-writing of an ICJ judgment meant to our chamber. As explained in the authors' note, five elements were identified and applied: context specific analysis; paying attention to the individual and his/her suffering; intersectionality; the deconstruction of binaries and the avoidance of hierarchies.

As challenging as the search for a feminist approach in re-writing this judgment might be, it was even more pressing because of the collective nature of our endeavour; we needed to accommodate three different perspectives on what a feminist approach to this particular judgment meant. Therefore, compromises were inevitable, as explained further in this note.

What was it Like to Work Collaboratively?

Collaborative projects such as the Feminist International Judgment Project are multidimensional spaces that enabled us to engage in self-reflective deconstruction of the methodological/scientific intersectionalities of the feminist project itself. While the participants were all drawn to it with a common label, that of 'doing feminist international law', the drafting work in itself and the collective workshops shed light on one of feminisms' fundamental truths, ie that there is not one single truth, or feminism. This therefore meant, within our chamber, that divergent postures had to be reconciled, and compromises found, along the lines of the following implicit questions: especially in light of the not explicitly gendered structure of the legal notions at stake, at times it was difficult to decide whether a particular position we adopted was sufficiently feminist. This led us to also question the boundaries usually drawn between method and substance, and the inevitable stumbling blocks we encountered along the way: it became clear that using feminist method does not always yield feminist results. Further, and this is something we only became conscious of during the collective workshops, feminist method is also about action, i.e. the politics of collaborative work: by contrast to other chambers, we divided the work among ourselves in a very individualistic and authorship-conscious way. While this made sense as we were not working in the same country, this proved problematic both throughout the process with regards to mutual expectations, and at a later stage with regards to harmonising the final piece. All in all, working collaboratively proved challenging, but so enriching. For instance, we had a long debate about whether we should openly quote individual or separate opinions within the text of our decision. While it made sense in terms of content and approaches as some of these opinions displayed arguments or references that supported a feminist understanding of the case or of the relevant jurisprudence and that feminist legal methodology supports the use of informal sources, the Court's Statute (in particular its famous Article 38 on the applicable law) do not mention these opinions nor does the Court's practice show an existing trend in this regard.[6] As the editors' instructions insisted on the moot character of this drafting exercise, that is the fact that the judgment should read as similar in style and form as the original ones, we settled the matter with a productive compromise: while we definitely made use of arguments and data collected in opinions, we refrained from directly quoting them, only referencing them in footnotes for purposes of scientific rigor and transparency (see also next subsection). These conflicting views, and the solution reached, shed light on the different schools of legal thought and training we still belonged to – namely European versus American legal traditions – in spite of our common feminist goal. It also revealed the hidden ways in which procedure actually shapes the content of a judgment and that what makes an 'authentic' ICJ judgment is more often than not its silences, confirming once again the importance of a feminist deconstruction of it/them.

[6] Since its establishment, the Court has only made reference to individual opinions of one of its judges in the three following instances: one direct reference to the declaration of several judges in the Order regarding Fiji's application to intervene in the *Nuclear Tests* case (*Continental Shelf (Tunisia v Libyan Arab Jamahiriya)*, Application for permission to intervene, Judgment, [1981] ICJ Reports 3); one mention of the consultation of some of the separate but concurring opinions of the *Aerial Incident of 27 July 1955* case in order to understand the majority's judgment in that case (*Barcelona Traction, Light and Power Company, Limited (Belgium v Spain)*, Preliminary Objections, Judgment [1964] ICJ Reports 29); and finally, a direct quotation of Judge Lauterpacht's separate opinion in the advisory opinion on the *Admissibility of Hearings of the Committee of South West Africa* (*Gabčikovo-Nagymaros (Hungary v Slovakia)*, Judgment, [1997] ICJ Reports 50). In any case, in a public statement issued in 1986, the Court asserted that 'the appended opinions elaborate or challenge the decision, but the reasoning of the decision itself, reviewed as it is finally is with knowledge of the opinions, cannot be fully appreciated in isolation from them. In short, the individual opinions are or may be essential to the full understanding of the Court's decision' (see 'Observation of the International Court of Justice on the Report of the Joint Inspection Unit (5 December 1986) UN Doc A/41/591/Add.1, Annex II, para 8). For an exhaustive doctrinal review of individual opinions at the ICJ, see GI Hernández, *The International Court of Justice and the Judicial Function* (Oxford, Oxford University Press, 2014) 95ff and in particular 96 and 113.

How was the Process of Delivering 'Judgment' Experienced?

Bérénice

Our non-collective writing method combined with our different legal expertise made, I believe, our respective experiences in delivering this judgment quite different. As an ICJ expert myself, I often experienced feeling torn between the feminist posture and a more traditional ICJ style. How far would be going too far in our feminist judgment, to be plausible and convincing? As Judith Butler very aptly once put it, parody is as much about desire as it is about ambivalence: the parody relies on the intimacy with the parodied while trying to create distantiation from, and discussion of, it.[7] This experience was therefore very profitable, as it illustrated the power of the traditional/conservative outlook on international law, as embodied by the ICJ, and the extent to which we allow ourselves to criticise it.

By way of anecdote, delivering this judgment led me to wonder whether Judge Cançado Trindade is a feminist lawyer without knowing because to my knowledge he never identified himself as such. His way of writing and questioning the usual dichotomies of international law, and emphasising the human being before everything else, echoed some aspects of the feminist legal methodology we used ourselves. This in turns explains why we relied in the re-written judgment on material found in the dissenting opinion of Judge Cançado Trindade (eg the ICRC report referred to in paragraph 11 of the judgment) and in that of Judge Yusuf.[8]

Zoi

To ask from three legal experts to assume the role of a judge, and become ourselves the medium where morality finds an expression in restoring justice, was a challenging but fruitful task. Despite our different feminisms, I believe that we shared a common goal, and that was to engage in an honest assessment of the judgment assigned to us, from a feminist perspective. In delivering the judgment, I was discouraged by the inevitability of compromising with and in a twisted way

[7] J Butler, 'Merely Cultural' (1997) 52 *Social Text* 265.

[8] The reader is strongly encouraged to take a look at their opinions. A Brazilian national, Judge Cançado Trindade was elected to the ICJ in 2009. A recent compilation of his individual opinions (which are also all available on the ICJ's website) has been published: AA Cançado Trindade, *Judge Antônio A Cançado Trindade. The Construction of a Humanized International Law: A Collection of Individual Opinions (1991–2013)* (Leiden, Brill Nijhoff, 2015). A Somalian national, Judge Abdulqawi Ahmed Yusuf was also elected in 2009, held the position of Vice President from 2015–18, and has been, since 2018, the Court's President. While his scholarship has often focused on international law in Africa, he has also written on human rights: A Yūsuf, 'The International Court of Justice (ICJ) and the Development of Human Rights Law: From Collective Rights to Individual Rights' in *La tutela dei diritti umani e il diritto internazionale: XVI Convegno, Catania, 23- 24 giugno 2011* (Napoli, Editoriale Scientifica, 2012) 573.

contributing in upholding the patriarchal morality. In other words, I felt frustrated by the necessity to use the same masculine legal tools that make sense only in an androcentric legal world. It seemed impossible to work outside these lines in certain parts of the case, and in my view this had a great impact on the process of delivering the final feminist judgment. Being a legal expert with moral philosophy in my core toolkit, my main priority when in doubt, is to focus on exposing the Truth, rather than to be formalistic and politically correct in my choice of language. Unfortunately, lawyers and legal academics alike, have been conditioned to use law as a 'sacred text'. In my view, the only way to improve law is to be critical about it, and expose its many inadequacies. I am convinced that the essence of feminist legal scholarship is self-explanatory, but it is the feminist legal scholar that mess up the picture by not knowing when and how to act.

Ekaterina

I subscribe to the views expressed by my colleagues. In addition, as a chair/president of the chamber I had to struggle with the task of negotiating a middle way between our three different and, at times, conflicting visions. Since we were guided by the same goal, the same motivation, we were able to reconcile our differences. However, I felt that it came at times at the expense of more radical solutions and possibilities, which was accompanied by frustration on the part of the chamber's member who had to abandon a more ambitious route. In my view, the abandonment of these more radical positions did not impact the substantive outcome: we were able to find a way to deliver a judgment that offers avenues for a more just solution than that offered by the original judgment in this case. However, feminist approaches are not only about substantive outcomes (the main, obvious result of the case), but also about the process and how the process and methodological choices made either re-enforce existing structures and hierarchies or challenge them. In this sense, the abandonment of some more radical approaches meant that some parts of the system were not challenged but re-enforced. For instance, we deliberately decided to maintain the language and style of ICJ judgments, thus precluding a more radical use of language that could have challenged hierarchies embedded in the linguistic structure of public international law. For a more radical re-writing, I would advocate for the opening to a more emotional use of language, including poetry. This would have challenged the linguistic structure of legal language but would run the danger of not been taken as seriously by the mainstream as the present outcome.

What did the Experience Reveal About the Structures and Norms of International Law?

Because of the facts at stake, re-writing this particular judgment revealed the ontological and political tensions existing between law and time. The law is still very much thought as a remote eternal, out of reach of the human finitude, as Mr Ferrini's death in July 2012, four months after the original judgment of the ICJ was issued, sadly reveals. Transcendental justice as allegedly embodied in the current structures and norms of international law is therefore far from being humanely just: this is where the feminist project shows its irresistible merit. It indeed helped us uncovering World War II's justice fallacy as epitomized by the Nuremberg trials myth, as we wondered whose justice and for whom? The question of reparation is therefore also one of appropriate juridicisation or judicialisation of history.

This in turn forced us to grasp another fundamental tension, of a scientific and political nature, existing between judging and doing historical work, and the challenges that doing the latter poses when in the former's seat. While the ICJ (and State counsels) are usually zealous historians with regards to territorial delimitation, their historical thoughtlessness in the *Germany v Italy* case is quite striking, if not appalling. In its modern and western form, law centres around texts as public meaningful territories to possess: victims' narratives are often still non-textual and/or deemed private and are therefore less amenable to the traditional legal historiography used by non-critical international lawyers and judges.

More generally, we all felt that the structures and norms of international law had quite a strong grasp on us, despite our resolutely feminist stance. We realised how much we internalised traditional methodologies, structures and norms of international law that we as specialists in various areas of international law also contribute albeit unwittingly to the perpetuation of norms and structures of the very international law we attempt to transcend.

The notion of *jus cogens* was very illustrative of this paradox. While, in theory and as expounded at the outset, we are well aware of the limitations of such a hierarchical concept, when faced with real facts, one realises that it is very difficult, if not impossible, to think in legal terms outside of any binary or value-ridden perspectives. We focused instead on the issue of reparations and on the correlative right to justice, only to realise at the end of the process, that it was perhaps just another way to bring in hierarchy again, although in a different way. Obviously, feminism is not a-ethical, but well on the contrary. However, doing away with patriarchal values and promote feminist ones within the structures and strictures of a rigid and conservative legal system, proved to sometimes be a rather utopian enterprise. But one that usefully – although, at times, overwhelmingly – reminds us of all that is left to do.

Were the Feminist Methods and Theory Adopted Able to Transcend International Law's Biases Effectively?

Bérénice

Feminist methodology allowed, if not required, us to genuinely engage with the tension generated by the activity of adjudicating a dispute originating in historical facts. Quite uniquely, law is as much a prospective as a retrospective analytical framework. By qualifying and drawing specific consequences from certain facts, judges posit a judicial truth which is often concomitant if not mirroring historical truth. This means that, in our case and as we actually performed historical work relative to the sufferings of the Italian prisoners of wars and their families, the re-writing process opened up, but did not give straightforward answers to, the following questions: how much of a historian can a judge actually be when official sources are lacking? What version of history should he or she side with? Finally, can the judge use new historiographical methodologies? Through the re-writing process, it also became apparent that feminist methodology can be antithetical to mass claims in courts: how can we reconcile judicial expediency and individual narratives? Were we successful in this endeavour in our own judgment? We questioned whether this was an exercise doomed to failure in light of the ICJ's judging style. The Court's judgments display a very impersonal and indirect style: the facts of the case are usually recounted without the use of direct quotations, mirroring the fact that expert reports can only be submitted in written form and that the Court does not allow for personal testimony during the oral proceedings. This thick and rigid lens through which the Court's narrative is constructed ensures that individual stories are, at worst, not told or, at best, amalgamated; that public and powerful voices speak over private and othered ones; that male voices, some more than others, speak over female ones. This means that judicial truth, as obtained in the Peace Palace, is more often than not the direct translation of official historical truth and the correlative silencing, once again, of all the other (his/her/us)tories.

Further, and going back to Butler's notion of parodic efficacy, I have wondered how convincing (read: legitimate) our arguments are – both regarding the relationship between the humanitarian character of the norms violated and the obligation to provide for reparation, and also that relating to the characterisation of the emergence of a new custom on the basis of 'soft' sources – to a non-feminist audience? I questioned the relationship between feminist methods and logics in the activity of judging. Is feminist judging only about soft logics, that is the use and the connection of 'soft' rather than 'hard' sources? One is therefore left both with a feeling of inadequacy (if not, powerlessness); the Master's house/Master's tools conundrum was unavoidable,[9] and an illegitimate desire emerged to perhaps end up writing feminist judgments as poems instead.

Zoi

My main concerns are of an epistemological nature, and I tried to translate these worries in the methodology employed. The underlying question that I kept reflecting on during my engagement with this project was how men can have knowledge of women's experiences. But most importantly, I wondered which

[9] A Lorde, 'The Master's Tools Will Never Dismantle the Master's House' in A Lorde, *Sister Outsider* (Berkeley CA, The Crossing Press, 1984).

feminist methods to use, and which traditional legal tools of analysis to include or to eliminate in our contribution.

I am confident that this project makes a real contribution by adding the woman into the ICJ's frame of reference, thereby tackling her invisibility in international law. Yet on the other hand, simply recognising women as subjects of global concern and of justice is not sufficient. It is not just the symptoms that we are called to treat, but the root and source of the problem. So in my view, what we need is a holistic and systematic analysis of law from a feminist perspective. I kept asking myself, should we produce more extreme feminist legal work? Or will this strategy generate more inequality in the opposite direction? Would that be a sacrifice we are willing to make, because the overall utility is for the best and serves restoring justice? Or should we be fair and respect equality in a deontological way, and follow the rules of fairness and the rule of law? Because in the first option one could argue that women are placed temporarily above the law, in a disrespect of the rule of law.

I am convinced that to uncritically follow the established international legal methodology is to silently accept centuries of oppressive and short-sighted masculine legal thought. There is great utility in identifying the legal tools and methodological schemes that are a clear product of masculine legal thought. Re-writing this judgment placed an obligation on me to expose this methodological insight.

Ekaterina

International law is a fundamentally masculine construction, as volumes of feminist writings demonstrate.[10] Using feminist tools to re-arrange or modify this construction can only bring partial results. Many of our difficulties and tensions in this re-writing are a direct consequence of the limited and partial improvements that using feminist tools can bring about in a masculine construction. Therefore, my answer is that feminist and, for that matter, any other critical approach to law is doomed to failure as long as it operates within this system/construction. Law as a system is self-reproducing and we as lawyers, even feminist lawyers, are part of this self-reproducing system. We change one part of the system, but the system balances this change by producing another mechanism or piece that outweighs our efforts: we deconstruct one binary, but another binary is produced instead. Therefore, only when 'humanity will play with law'[11] will we arrive at a conception and practice of justice independent of law, where 'the world appears as a good that absolutely cannot be appropriated or made juridical.'[12]

[10] It suffices to mention here a few most prominent examples: H Charlesworth and C Chinkin, *The Boundaries of International Law: A Feminist Analysis* (Manchester, Manchester University Press, 2000); D Buss and AS Manji (eds), *International Law: Modern Feminist Approaches* (Oxford, Hart Publishing, 2005); S Kouvo and Z Pearson (eds), *Feminist Perspectives on Contemporary International Law. Between Resistance and Compliance?* (Oxford, Hart Publishing, 2014).

[11] G Agamben, *State of Exception* (Chicago IL, University of Chicago Press, 2005) 64.

[12] ibid.

Court of Justice of the European Union

6

Gómez-Limón Sánchez-Camacho v Instituto Nacional de la Seguridad Social (INSS) and others

MARTA CARNEIRO, KIRSTEN KETSCHER
AND FREYA SEMANDA

Authors' Note

Gómez-Limón Sánchez-Camacho[1] was decided by the Court of Justice of the European Union (CJEU) on 16 July 2009, under preliminary ruling proceedings. The case concerned the application of the Parental Leave Directive[2] and the Social Security Directive,[3] and was brought in order to enable the referring court to assess the validity of Spanish statutory social security provisions on contributions to, and calculation of, a permanent invalidity pension in connection with periods of employment under parental leave in the form of reduced working time.

The section of the judgment that is most relevant to this project, and on which we have chosen to focus, concerns the fifth question referred by the Juzgado de lo Social No 30 de Madrid to the CJEU. It specifically pertains to the interpretation of Community law to assess the conformity of Spanish legislation with the principle of equal treatment between women and men, and the principle of non-discrimination on grounds of sex in matters of social security, as they apply within the EU.

The facts of the case can be summarised as follows. From 17 December 1986, Ms Gómez-Limón Sánchez-Camacho worked full-time as an administrative

[1] C-537/07 *Gómez-Limón Sánchez-Camacho v Instituto Nacional de la Seguridad Social (INSS) and others*, [2009] ECLI:EU 462.

[2] Council Directive 96/34/EC of 3 June 1996 on the framework agreement on parental leave concluded by UNICE, CEEP and the ETUC, OJ L 145, 19.6.1996, 4–9. The version in force at the relevant time was prior to Council Directive 2010/18/EU of 8 March 2010 implementing the revised Framework Agreement on parental leave concluded by BUSINESSEUROPE, UEAPME, CEEP and ETUC and repealing Directive 96/34/EC (Text with EEA relevance), OJ L 68, 18.3.2010, 13–20.

[3] Council Directive 79/7/EEC of 19 December 1978 on the progressive implementation of the principle of equal treatment for men and women in matters of social security, OJ L 6, 10.1.1979, 24–25.

assistant for Alcampo SA, a business in the superstore sector. As from 6 December 2001, Ms Gómez-Limón took parental leave in the form of reduced working hours, as provided for under Spanish legislation promoting balance between family life and professional life. On that basis, Ms Gómez-Limón's daily working time was reduced by a third in order to enable her to take care of her child. Remuneration was reduced in proportion. Since no special alternative agreement was made, the amount of her and the employer's contributions to the general social security scheme was likewise proportionately reduced. Subsequently, on 30 June 2004, the Spanish National Social Security Institute deemed Ms Gómez-Limón permanently disabled due to her pathological myopia and awarded her an invalidity pension of 55 per cent of a base amount of 920.33 euros per month. This was assessed with reference to contributions actually made between 1 November 1998 and November 2004, thus reflecting the reductions during her parental leave. Ms Gómez-Limón brought an action before the Juzgado de lo Social No 30 de Madrid. Her complaint was that the invalidity pension should have been calculated as if she had continued working without the reduction in working time under parental leave, and that failure to do so negated the effectiveness of an instrument (providing for parental leave) that aims to promote equality and non-discrimination on the grounds of sex.

As such, the re-writing exercise undertaken by this chamber focuses primarily on the matter of discrimination, as raised by the national court in the following question:

> In the specific circumstances of the case, does the reduction in the grant and accrual of social security entitlements during the period of parental leave constitute direct or indirect discrimination contrary to the provisions of Directive 79/7 … and is it contrary to the requirements of equality and non-discrimination between men and women, in accordance with the tradition common to all the Member States, to the extent that this principle must apply not only to conditions of employment but also to the public activity of social protection of workers?

In its judgment, the CJEU decided that the national rule determining the reduced grant and accrual during parental leave in the form of reduced working time did not breach the Community principle of equality and non-discrimination. In its reasoning, the Court started off, as it normally does, by defining discrimination as the equivalent of different rules being applied to comparable situations or the same rules being applied to different situations. Based on this equivalence, the CJEU dismissed the claim by concluding that workers taking parental leave in the form of reduced working time are in a specific situation that cannot be compared to that of a man or woman who works on a full-time basis. Thus, different rules should apply. Moreover, and equating said parental leave users to part-time workers, the CJEU went on to add that Community law does not preclude a retirement pension being calculated pro rata temporis in the case of part-time employment, thus allowing for the same rule to apply in this case.

As already indicated, our re-writing exercise focuses on the discrimination issue. It specifically concerns the practice and reasoning of the CJEU when reviewing indirect discrimination cases, and this case in particular. In this context, and as sometimes mentioned in EU anti-discrimination legal scholarship, the CJEU often adopts a stance that is strongly embedded in notions of sameness/difference.[4] This seems to derive from a legal understanding of discrimination that is shaped (almost to the point of exclusivity) by strict equal treatment analyses (the Aristotelian equality formula). More generally, an equal treatment model of discrimination has been the object of fierce critiques for failing to contest dominant norms against which *relevant differences* disappear/become something other than normal (by comparison with).[5] This model has been reflected in certain decisions of the Court, resulting in a legal analysis of discrimination that is limited by, and at times reduced to, testing issues of material comparability between variably – and often dubiously – chosen groups. This approach has delivered instances of legal adjudication that purportedly operate under a principle of non-discrimination but in fact fail to address the discrimination issue altogether.

Looking at the particular case at hand, the same, rarely challenged, premise led the Court to engage in a blind search for a comparator. The purpose of the Court's enquiry became solely to establish what treatment is equal and what is different for workers taking parental leave in the form of reduced working time. On this basis, the Court decided to compare such workers with full-time workers (asserting difference thereto) and with part-time workers (asserting similarity thereto). This prevented the Court from going beyond a substantively questionable search[6] in order to look at parental leave users as a unique group, with its own specificities. Their contractual situation is that of full-time workers who temporarily avail themselves of the possibility of reducing their working time to take care of children. This situation is particular to that group, and not necessarily equal to or different from that of other full-time or part-time workers. What is more, as

[4] JH Gerards, *Judicial Review in Equal Treatment Cases* (Leiden, Martinus Nijhoff Publishers, 1997); S Prechal, 'Equality of Treatment, Non-Discrimination and Social Policy: Achievements in Three Themes' (2004) 41 *Common Market Law Review* 533; C Tobler, *Indirect Discrimination: A Case Study into the Development of the Legal Concept of Indirect Discrimination under EC Law* (Antwerpen, Intersentia, 2005).

[5] C Barnard, 'The Principle of Equality in the Community Context: P, Grant, Kalanke and Marschall: Four Uneasy Bedfellows' (1998) 57 *The Cambridge Law Journal* 352; M Bell, 'Direct Discrimination' in D Schiek, L Waddington and M Bell (eds), *Cases, Materials and Texts on National, Supranational and International Nondiscrimination Law* (Oxford, Hart Publishing, 2007); J Conaghan, 'Pregnancy, Equality and the European Court of Justice: Interrogating Gillespie' (1998) 3(2) *International Journal of Discrimination and the Law* 115; S Fredman, 'European Community Discrimination Law: A Critique' (1992) 21(2) *Industrial Law Journal* 119; M Malik, 'Modernising Discrimination Law: Proposals for a Single Equality Act for Great Britain' (2007) 9 *International Journal of Discrimination and the Law* 73; CB Whitman, 'Law and Sex' (1987) 86(6) *Michigan Law Review* 1388.

[6] For example, one can reasonably claim that such parental leave users are, to all effects, full-time workers that decide to take up parental leave for a period of time. Therefore, comparison would be between full-time workers that take up parental leave and those who do not, which demonstrates that those who do, suffer a detriment. What this goes to show is that one rarely questions the legitimacy of the comparators and the underlying criteria on which they are based: why should the comparison be that one and not the other? In fact, given the nature of parental leave, it seems reasonable to argue that these parental leave users are contractually closer to full-timers than part-timers.

soon as we manage to bring ourselves back to the matter of discrimination, we immediately notice that the issue of disadvantage experienced by a group on the basis of their sex (= discrimination) has completely disappeared from the Court's analysis.

Therefore, the original *Gómez-Limón* judgment suffers from the above described analytical compression (the blind application of an equal treatment model of discrimination). That is to say, although the primary notion in indirect discrimination is that of a particular impact that occurs on the basis of a prohibited ground of discrimination, the CJEU reduced the analysis to points of material comparability (put simply: part-time and full-time workers are materially different, *therefore* there is no discrimination on grounds of sex of workers taking parental leave in the form of reduced working time). As it is already apparent, several aspects of discrimination were missed on that account and several others can be questioned on the grounds of their substantive irrelevance.

The central fact that more women than men generally take up parental leave and are, therefore, more likely to suffer a reduction in their invalidity pension, was accorded minimal consideration and side-lined as a marginal matter, mentioned only in passing.[7] As a result, the Court was unable to establish the presumption of indirect discrimination which derived directly from that uncontested fact, thereby failing to recognise the legal relevance of the underlying disadvantageous social position of women in family–work relations. Moreover, it thereby dismissed any debate at the level of objective justification, again trivialising or ignoring the social imbalances at play. Once a presumption of discrimination is established, the Court moves on to assess whether the measure at stake can be objectively justified. Therefore, the objective justification test is about testing the defendant's arguments against the claimant's arguments (that led to the presumption in the first place). As such, if this stage of analysis is foreclosed by comparator arguments (which generally pertain to the defendant's arguments), the disadvantage is never made relevant, the presumption of discrimination can never be established, and the claimant's point of view can never vindicate, because it is left invisible. On that account, social imbalances are always irrelevant to a determination of whether a measure is justified or not, whereas the need for the assessment is created by those very imbalances. It renders the whole exercise circular and pointless. Therefore, even looking at material comparability between parental leave users as against full-timers or part-timers, had the Court left it to the assessment carried out under the objective justification test, it would have produced a more balanced reasoning: one that, in fact, identifies the subordinated position of a group in society and measures the defendant's aims and means against it.

[7] In one very short paragraph of the original judgment (para 55): 'In that regard, it must be noted, as the national court has pointed out, that, in order to devote themselves to bringing up their children, women opt much more frequently than men for periods of reduced working time and a proportional reduction in salary, resulting in a reduction in social security entitlements derived from the employment relationship.'

In connection with this last point, the substantive objectives of parental leave as a legal and public policy instrument disappeared completely in the review of the discrimination question, arguably following from the Court's analytical selectivity. The fact that working time was reduced for the specific purpose of taking care of children became devoid of legal significance; caring for children was rendered nothing more than a private interest, seemingly irrelevant to the state and, therefore, underserving of protection. This, in and of itself, is a construction that is highly stereotypical and reproduces the same representations that anti-discrimination law aims to eliminate (care work as feminine and traditionally female, private and largely devoid of value to society). Consequently, the specific aim of parental leave – promoting balance between family life and work, thus enhancing equality between men and women – became ultimately frustrated by the unorthodoxy of an analysis (of that same parental leave) that did not comprise the crucial point of sex discrimination.

In light of the above, the re-writing of the feminist judgment as put forward by this chamber proposes to foreground the core notions that make up the concept of indirect discrimination. The aim is thereby to illustrate the legal possibility of an alternative reasoning that focuses on the substantive rationale of the principle of non-discrimination, particularly through the indirect discrimination tool, and re-empower parental leave to be the driver of change that it was intended to be. To achieve this, the re-written judgment focuses on the relevant group at stake, on its own, with no need for comparators: that is, workers taking up parental leave in the form of reduced working time, who are mostly women who are not in a de facto position to negotiate the burden and division of care work with the fathers. By highlighting the structural disadvantage of women, the presumption of indirect discrimination becomes evident and the objective justification test a necessity. Moreover, in this context, it is not simply the aim of the rule on reduced contributions that matters, but also the aim of parental leave itself and, specifically, that of balancing work and family life and promoting equality between women and men. The assessment can never be truly balanced if any of these elements is unaccounted for. These are the invisible elements that our Chamber endeavoured to render visible, thus delivering on the principle of indirect discrimination's promise; that is, to achieve substantive equality.

JUDGMENT

EVANGELINA GÓMEZ-LIMÓN SÁNCHEZ-CAMACHO
v
INSTITUTO NACIONAL DE LA SEGURIDAD SOCIAL (INSS),
TESORERÍA GENERAL DE LA SEGURIDAD SOCIAL (TGSS),
ALCAMPO SA

Case C-537/07,

The Court of Justice of the European Union composed of;
Judge Carneiro (President of the Chamber),
Judge Ketscher, and Judge Semanda

16 July 2009

1. This reference for a preliminary ruling relates to the interpretation of Clause 2(6) and (8) of the framework agreement on parental leave concluded on 14 December 1995, annexed to Council Directive 96/34/EC of 3 June 1996 on the framework agreement on parental leave concluded by UNICE, CEEP and the ETUC (OJ 1996 L 145, p. 4; 'the framework agreement on parental leave'), and of Council Directive 79/7/EEC of 19 December 1978 on the progressive implementation of the principle of equal treatment for men and women in matters of social security (OJ 1979 L 6, p. 24).
2. The reference has been made in proceedings between Ms Gómez-Limón Sánchez-Camacho and the Instituto Nacional de la Seguridad Social, the managing body for social security ('the INSS'), the Tesoreria General de la Seguridad Social, and her former employer, Alcampo SA, concerning entitlements to permanent invalidity pension acquired during parental leave.

LEGAL CONTEXT

Community legislation

3. Article 3(1) of Directive 79/7 provides:

   This Directive shall apply to:

   (a) statutory schemes which provide protection against the following risks:
       - invalidity,

...

4. Pursuant to Article 4(1) of Directive 79/7:

> The principle of equal treatment means that there shall be no discrimination whatsoever on ground of sex either directly, or indirectly by reference in particular to marital or family status, in particular as concerns:
>
> …
>
> - the obligation to contribute and the calculation of contributions,
> - the calculation of benefits, including increases due in respect of a spouse and for dependants and the conditions governing the duration and retention of entitlement to benefits.

5. Article 7 of Directive 79/7 provides:

> 1. This Directive shall be without prejudice to the right of Member States to exclude from its scope:
>
>   (a) …
>
>   (b) advantages in respect of old-age pension schemes granted to persons who have brought up children; the acquisition of benefit entitlements following periods of interruption of employment due to the bringing up of children; …

6. Directive 96/34 seeks to implement the framework agreement on parental leave annexed thereto which sets out minimum requirements on parental leave and time off from work on grounds of force majeure, as an important means of reconciling work and family life and promoting equal opportunities and treatment between men and women.

7. The recitals in the preamble to the framework agreement on parental leave state:

> …
>
> 8. Whereas men should be encouraged to assume an equal share of family responsibilities, for example they should be encouraged to take parental leave by means such as awareness programmes; …
>
> 10. Whereas Member States should provide for the maintenance of entitlements to benefits in kind under sickness insurance during the minimum period of parental leave;
>
> 11. Whereas Member States should also, where appropriate under national conditions and taking into account the budgetary situation, consider the maintenance of entitlements to relevant social security benefits as they stand during the minimum period of parental leave;
>
> …

8. Clause 1 of the framework agreement on parental leave provides:

> 1. This agreement lays down minimum requirements designed to facilitate the reconciliation of parental and professional responsibilities for working parents.
>
> …

9. Clause 2 of the framework agreement on parental leave provides:

   1. This agreement grants … men and women workers an individual right to parental leave on the grounds of the birth or adoption of a child to enable them to take care of that child, for at least three months, until a given age up to 8 years to be defined by Member States and/or management and labour.

   …

   3. The conditions of access and detailed rules for applying parental leave shall be defined by law and/or collective agreement in the Member States, as long as the minimum requirements of this agreement are respected.

   …

   6. Rights acquired or in the process of being acquired by the worker on the date on which parental leave starts shall be maintained as they stand until the end of parental leave. At the end of parental leave, these rights, including any changes arising from national law, collective agreements or practice, shall apply.
   7. Member States and/or management and labour shall define the status of the employment contract or employment relationship for the period of parental leave.
   8. All matters relating to social security in relation to this agreement are for consideration and determination by Member States according to national law, taking into account the importance of the continuity of the entitlements to social security cover under the different schemes, in particular health care.

United Nations Conventions

10. Article 5 of the Convention on the Elimination of All Forms of Discrimination against Women (CEDAW) provides:

    States Parties shall take all appropriate measures:

    (a) To modify the social and cultural patterns of conduct of men and women, with a view to achieving the elimination of prejudices and customary and all other practices which are based on the idea of the inferiority or the superiority of either of the sexes or on stereotyped roles for men and women;

    (b) To ensure that family education includes a proper understanding of maternity as a social function and the recognition of the common responsibility of men and women in the upbringing and development of their children, it being understood that the interest of the children is the primordial consideration in all cases.

Article 11 of CEDAW provides:

1. States Parties shall take all appropriate measures to eliminate discrimination against women in the field of employment in order to ensure, on a basis of equality of men and women, the same rights …
2. In order to prevent discrimination against women on the grounds of marriage or maternity and to ensure their effective right to work, States Parties shall take appropriate measures:

…

(c) To encourage the provision of the necessary supporting social services to enable parents to combine family obligations with work responsibilities and participation in public life, in particular through promoting the establishment and development of a network of child-care facilities

…'

Background to the dispute

11. The claimant Ms Gómez-Limón Sánchez-Camacho gave birth to a child in 2001 and, taking advantage of the EU framework agreement on parental leave, reduced what were her full-time working hours by one-third from 6 December 2001.
12. Ms Gómez-Limón Sánchez-Camacho thereafter worked two-thirds of a full-time contract and her social security was reduced accordingly. Until her parental leave she had worked for 14 years on a full-time contract as an administrative assistant for the enterprise Alcampo SA. During this period, she had paid full social security contributions.
13. During her period of reduced working time Ms Gómez-Limón Sánchez-Camacho was hit by an illness making her unable to continue working in her present job because of physical and functional difficulties. She was deemed totally unable to work in her usual occupation as result of invalidity by the Spanish social security court (INNS) in a decision of 30 June 2004.
14. Her invalidity pension was, according to Spanish law, calculated on the basis of her social security contributions paid during the preceding eight years. Ms Gómez-Limón Sánchez-Camacho has contested the grounds for this calculation, which she considers discriminatory for women and a violation of the principle of equality between men and women. This calculation means that her taking of parental leave has had a disadvantageous effect on her pension rights as she now, because of her reduced working hours, only qualifies for an invalidity pension of 55% instead of 100%.
15. Ms Gómez-Limón Sánchez-Camacho relies on both dir. 96/34 and the framework agreement annexed hereto and on dir. 79/7 on equal treatment in social security matters as it is an undisputed fact that significantly more women than men make use of the possibility to take parental leave. An accidental illness during a parental leave will therefore hit women much harder than men,

thereby making the goal of the framework agreement to reconcile work life and family life illusory.

16. Overall, Ms Gómez-Limón Sánchez-Camacho claims that this way of calculating her invalidity pension more generally violates the fundamental principle of equal rights between men and women, contrary to The Charter of Fundamental Rights art. 21 and art. 23. The grounds for this disadvantageous calculation of the invalidity benefit is the classification of her as a part-time worker. Spanish law relies on the assumption that the claimant would have reduced her working time permanently because she now has a child, which is the way that women usually reconcile work and family life.
17. However, Ms Gómez-Limón Sánchez-Camacho claims that she is a full-time worker who is taking advantage of the parental leave that is now an integral part of Union law. Treating her a part-time worker in this situation is also a violation of CEDAW convention article 5(a) and article 11 which forbids such stereotyping. The CEDAW Convention is a recognised basis for interpreting the EU equality principle. The result of this stereotyping is that she gets worse social protection because she, as a full-time worker, has decided to take parental leave. Ms Gómez-Limón Sánchez-Camacho wants to be considered a full-time worker and not reduced to being a part-time worker.
18. Recognising that significantly more women than men opt to take parental leave, the Juzgado de Io Social No 30 de Madrid has decided to stay the proceedings and refer the following question to the Court for a preliminary ruling:

    Considering that parental leave shall promote equality between women and men and make it possible to reconcile work and family, is it contrary to dir. 96/34 on parental leave with the annexed framework agreement, directive 79/7 on equality in social security and the general fundamental principle in EU law on equality between the sexes as made visible in the Charter of Fundamental Rights of the European Union as proclaimed on 7 December 2000:

    a) To assign the status of part-time worker to the claimant because she was hit by illness during her parental leave with reduced working hours?;
    b) To make it necessary to conclude a special agreement to preserve the same contribution base as before the reduction of work time because of parental leave, which is a possibility under the Spanish social security law of 30 July 1991 art. 14?

LEGAL QUESTION

19. On the basis of the arguments presented by Ms Gómez-Limón Sánchez-Camacho, the National Court wishes this Court to answer the question of

how far the general principle of equality between men and women in Union Law applies in a situation where an invalidity benefit is calculated on the basis of part-time work during a parental leave for a claimant who until taking that leave has been a full-time worker.

20. The wording of the national legislation concerning parental leave is neutral and therefore does not constitute direct discrimination. The task for this Court, consequently, is to examine the case in light of indirect discrimination. If a *prima facie* case of indirect discrimination is made out, the burden of proof rests on the member state to demonstrate that the reduction of the claimant's benefit is not discriminatory.
21. Indirect discrimination means that a national practice or legislation which affects a greater number of women than men must be explained independently of the worker's sex. The practice must correspond to a real need and be appropriate with a view to achieving the objectives pursued and necessary to that end (case 170/84 *Bilka – Kaufhaus GmbH v Karin Weber von Hartz* [1986] ECR 01607, paragraph 36).
22. Ms Gómez-Limón Sánchez-Camacho claims as an undisputed fact that women are much more likely than men to take parental leave and, in this way, benefit from this right now established in Union law by the framework agreement annexed to dir. 96/34. It is for the national court to examine this. If such a fact is verified, this case consequently must be treated as a *prima facie* case, entailing that such a practice must be justified. It is then a task for the national court to analyse possible justifications to establish that they do not violate the principle of equality between men and women.
23. EU law demands an explanation for the real need to treat women on parental leave as part-time workers, and why the means (that is, the reduction of invalidity benefit) are appropriate and necessary.
24. It is, then, necessary to ascertain whether this is a detriment that affects, or has the potential to affect, more women than men. This is ascertained by looking at women's particular position in society with regards to care work and employment.
25. In that regard, it must be noted that, due to still-prevalent stereotypical gender roles, as the national court and the claimant also have pointed out, women opt much more frequently than men for periods of reduced working time in order to take care of children, with a proportional reduction in salary and reduction in social security entitlements derived from employment.
26. It is widely recognised that gender representations limit women and men's participation and choices in the labour market and determine the unbalanced division of care work between them. Social representations in terms of women and men's capacities, skills, and competences dictate, early on, educational choices and, later on, opportunities and horizontal occupational segregation in the labour market, where typically male professions are more valued than female professions. Also on that account, women are confronted with barriers in accessing decision making and better paid positions; the gender

pay gap increases with education and qualification levels. Women are therefore confronted with a higher risk of poverty, particularly in old age.[1]

27. The perception of women as primary caregivers, the devaluing of those caring roles, and the different expectations of women in the labour market, lead women to be more likely than men to take up flexible work arrangements.
28. Working to reinforce that perception, the national rules *sub judice* equate parental leave in the form of reduced working time to part-time work through the reduction of contributions and benefits, and the possibility of concluding a special insurance agreement. In so doing, they assert that same stereotype by seemingly assuming that those taking up parental leave (mostly women) change their employment status and will continue as part-time workers after that leave is over.
29. These are the same social patterns, based on stereotyped roles for men and women, which Member States should eliminate according to article 5 of CEDAW, as the claimant points out.
30. In line with the above, and given that women are more likely to take up parental leave than men, it must consequently be concluded that more women than men are likely to suffer a particular disadvantage due to the detriment of reduced permanent invalidity pensions by reason of reduced contributions paid while on parental leave, in this case in the form of reduced working time. It follows that the national legislation at issue is presumed to be indirectly discriminatory on grounds of sex (similarly, in Case C-102/88 *Ruzius Wilbrink* [1989] ECR 4311, concerning Article 4(1) of Directive 79/7, the Court concluded that there was a presumption of indirect discrimination just by looking at the relevant group, 'where that measure affects a much larger number of women than of men' – paragraph 17).
31. It remains to be assessed whether the national measure can be objectively justified by a legitimate social policy objective that is pursued by means that are appropriate and necessary (see Case C-8/94 *Laperre* [1996] ECR I-273, paragraph 14 and the case-law cited: 'the Court has consistently held that Article 4(1) of the directive precludes the application of a national measure which, although formulated in neutral terms, works to the disadvantage of a much higher percentage of women than men, unless that measure is based on objective factors unrelated to any discrimination on grounds of sex. That is the case where the measures chosen reflect a legitimate social policy aim of the Member State whose legislation is at issue, are appropriate to achieve that aim and are necessary in order to do so').
32. It falls on the Member State, 'as the author of the allegedly discriminatory rule, to show that the said rule reflects a legitimate aim of its social policy, that that aim is unrelated to any discrimination based on sex, and that it

[1] Council Conclusions on Equal opportunities for women and men: active and dignified ageing, 2947th Employment, Social Policy, Health and Consumer Affairs Council meeting, Luxembourg, 8 June 2009. Available at: www.consilium.europa.eu/uedocs/cms_Data/docs/pressdata/en/lsa/108375.pdf.

could reasonably consider that the means chosen were suitable for attaining that aim' (Case C-167/97 *Seymour-Smith and Perez* [1999] ECR I-623, paragraph 77).

33. While it is ultimately for the national court, which has sole jurisdiction to assess the facts and interpret the national legislation, to determine whether and to what extent the legislative provision in question is justified by such an objective reason, 'the Court of Justice, which is called on to provide answers of use to the national court [in the context of a reference for a preliminary ruling], may provide guidance based on the documents in the file and on the written and oral observations which have been submitted to it, in order to enable the national court to give judgment' (Case C-167/97 *Seymour-Smith and Perez*, paragraphs 67 and 68 and the case-law cited).

34. As a preliminary issue, it should be noted that the exception provided in article 7(1)(b) of Directive 79/7 is not applicable *in casu*. On the one hand, the national measure does not seem to make use of that derogation with a view to temporarily maintaining a more advantageous treatment of women which is the derogation's underpinning *rationale* (see, *mutatis mutandis*, Case C-9/91 *The Queen v Secretary of State for Social Security, ex parte the Equal Opportunities Commission* [1992] I-04297, paragraph 15: '[a]lthough the preamble to the Directive does not state the reasons for the derogations which it lays down, it can be deduced from the nature of the exceptions contained in Article 7(1) of the Directive that the Community legislature intended to allow Member States to maintain temporarily the advantages accorded to women with respect to retirement in order to enable them progressively to adapt their pension systems in this respect without disrupting the complex financial equilibrium of those systems, the importance of which could not be ignored'). Looking at the national measure: where it directs the applicable regime to the general part-time regime, this has no connection to the purpose of the directive's derogation as pertaining to the protection of women who, *in casu*, are the ones most often availing themselves of work arrangements to take care of children. In fact, it neglects that link by simply equalising it with part-time employment.

35. On the other hand, the exception covers the acquisition of benefit entitlements following periods of *interruption* of employment due to the bringing up of children. It is clear from settled case-law that, 'given the fundamental importance of the principle of equal treatment, the exception to the prohibition of discrimination on grounds of sex … must be interpreted strictly' (on article 7(1)(a) of Directive 79/7, see Case C-207/04 *Paolo Vergani v Agenzia delle Entrate, Ufficio di Arona* [2005] ECR I-07453, paragraph 33, and Case C-356/09 *Pensionsversicherungsanstalt v Christine Kleist* [2010] ECR I-11939, paragraph 39). As it is apparent from the facts, Ms Gómez-Limón Sánchez-Camacho has not interrupted, or even suspended, her employment relationship; on the contrary, she has, in fact, endeavoured to maintain that relationship by way of reducing her working hours.

36. On this basis, it must be concluded that the exception provided in article 7(1)(b) of Directive 79/7 does not apply, and therefore it is relevant to continue the assessment under the principle of equal treatment and non-discrimination on grounds of sex.
37. Concerning the objective justification specifically, it is true that the Court has already held that 'Community law does not preclude a retirement pension being calculated *pro rata temporis* in the case of part-time employment' (see, regarding officials, Joined Cases C-4/02 and C-5/02 *Schönheit and Becker* [2003] ECR I-12575, paragraphs 90 and 91: '[t]he fact that, in addition to the number of years spent working in the civil service, an official's actual period of service during those years, as compared with the actual period of service of an official who has worked on a full-time basis throughout his career, is also taken into account is an objective criterion unrelated to any discrimination on grounds of sex, allowing his pension entitlement to be reduced proportionately'). This should be tested as to whether it applies, *mutatis mutandis*, to the calculation of a permanent invalidity pension when referring to periods of reduced working time under a parental leave.
38. In this context, legitimacy of aim and appropriateness and necessity of means can only be assessed if viewed in connection with the purposes of the relevant legal framework; otherwise, the exercise of assessing justification would be opaque and risk becoming irrelevant both to the facts of the case and the wider legal system. A rule that is a consequence and instrumental to another (calculation of entitlements) can only be understood when placed within the system to which it pertains (parental leave). It has no independent existence.
39. As such, a blind application of the pro rata rule to the present circumstances, without any further consideration, fails to account for this case's specificities. In this context, reduced working time is a particular modality of parental leave taken within a full-time employment contract, a possibility that is directly provided for by national legislation; therefore, it cannot be presumed outright that the case pertains simply to part-time employment. More specifically, the reduction in working time was due to the taking up of parental leave, i.e. to the need to take care of a minor, and this must be duly weighed when considering the merits of the case. Failing to do so leads to a reasoning that has no bearing on the case by ignoring the interests at stake and the objectives of the broader public policy in question.
40. In this connection, parental leave under the Framework Agreement aims to achieve substantive equality between women and men by way of reconciling occupational and family obligations and, hence, of promoting equality.
41. As such, in view of the presumption of indirect discrimination, and, as the applicant pointed out, the national rules applied to her are liable, in practice, to negate the effectiveness of a measure intended to eliminate discrimination on grounds of sex, if they cannot be objectively justified; and what is more,

with the risk of reproducing the stereotype that those same rules seem to deem 'the norm' (women as part-time workers due to their caregiving role). This is a discriminatory anachronism. Contrary to how the Court reasoned in Case 163/82 *Commission v Italy* [1983] ECR 03273 (that entitling only adoptive mothers, and not adoptive fathers, to a leave in the first three months after the entry of the child into the family was justified 'to assimilate as far as possible the conditions of entry of the child into the adoptive family to those of the arrival of a newborn child in the family during the very delicate initial period' – paragraph 16), these type of considerations can no longer be accepted.

42. Moreover, the Court cannot accept the argument that an assumed different nature between military service that is performed mainly by men and parental leave that is more often taken by women is capable of justifying the disadvantage, a point where the Court disagrees with Advocate General Sharpston's opinion (paragraph 49: '[i]n so holding, the Court pointed out that while performance of national service corresponds to a civic obligation laid down by law and not governed by the individual interests of the worker, parental leave is taken voluntarily by a worker in order to bring up a child').

43. Only a limited and socially disconnected understanding of parental leave interprets it as being solely in the interest of the individual worker. This construction ultimately rejects the undeniable benefits of parental leave to society as a whole, by protecting the child and promoting fertility rates, and by fighting the structural barriers that uphold a gendered caretaker–breadwinner model which result in a very unbalanced division of care work and ensuing participation of women and men in the labour market, to the serious disadvantage of women, as explained above.

44. What is more, such understanding allows the State to refuse to undertake a responsibility that it has, in fact, taken upon itself (as soon as it decided to regulate parental leave) and derives from Community law. Community law establishes a basis for Member States' duty to protect those who assume family responsibilities to ensure equal opportunities between women and men, as reflected in the framework agreement on parental leave (just as it creates a legal basis also for the employers to take into account their employees' choice to reconcile work and family responsibilities, thus contrasting with the conclusion in Case 170/84 *Bilka – Kaufhaus GmbH v Karin Weber von Hartz* [1986] ECR 01607 that 'the imposition of [such] an obligation … goes beyond the scope of Article 119 and has no other basis in Community law as it now stands' – paragraph 42).

45. Similarly, CEDAW stresses the social value of parenthood and treats the upbringing and development of children as a shared responsibility between women and men (article 5). What is more, pursuant to its article 11(2)(c), States should take appropriate measures to ensure parents have a genuine opportunity to balance work and family responsibilities.

46. Therefore, any social policy aim that is put forward by the Member State to justify the national measure can only be accepted after a rigorous balance is struck that takes due account of the disadvantageous impact on women, together with the specific aims of parental leave.
47. This is to say, once indirect discrimination is presumed, the proportionality assessment to be undertaken by the national court in considering the necessity and appropriateness of the national rule, must duly balance the national pro rata rule at stake against: (i) the particular disadvantage suffered by women from the automatic application of that rule in cases of parental leave in the form of reduced working time, (ii) the gender stereotypes and structural sex discrimination that underlies that disadvantage, (iii) the purposes and benefits of parental leave.
48. In this context, it is questionable that a strict proportionality rule as between contributions and cover in the case of parental leave in the form of reduced working time is the most appropriate or, indeed, the only possible way of pursuing a balance between that rule and the purposes of creating equality between men and women through family–work arrangements. Such a solution adds weight to one side of the scale only. Once the State addresses both sides, it must structure the applicable social protection scheme accordingly.
49. Finally, and in line with previous case-law, it should be noted that failure to ponder any type of protection carries the risk of deterring workers from taking parental leave due to its impact on social security benefits, negatively affecting parents/carers, their children, and the prospects of future parents/carers and those wishing to become parents/carers. Similar to *Tele-Danmark*, where failure to protect pregnant fixed-term workers against dismissal was a risk to their mental and physical health, 'including the particularly serious risk that they may be encouraged to have abortions,' (Case C-109/00 *Tele Danmark A/S v Handels- og Kontorfunktionærernes Forbund i Danmark* [2001] ECR I- 06993, paragraph 26), these consequences frustrate the aims of parental leave and the underlying rules must therefore be scrutinised through a balanced exercise that is able to include all relevant considerations.
50. The goal of dir. 96/34 is to reconcile family life and work life. The Spanish legislation which grants workers the right to work less for a certain period because of parental leave does not reconcile or promote a more equal division of family responsibility. On the contrary, it perpetuates a classical situation where women shoulder the risk for taking care of children by having to accept diminished social security. The Court cannot accept a mechanical interpretation where after the bare fact that a woman is working on reduced time *per se* means that she must be classified as a part-time worker. It is for the national court to take all circumstances into consideration, i.e. both the work pattern of the woman in the concrete case and the dynamic change in women's work pattern generally.

On those grounds, the Court hereby rules on the question regarding interpretation of the fundamental principle in EU law on equality between men and women in dir. 96/34 on parental leave and dir. 79/7 equality between men and women in social security matters in a situation where an invalidity benefit is calculated on the basis of part-time work during a parental leave for a claimant who until this leave has been a full-time worker:

1) **The goal of dir. 96/34 is to reconcile family life and work life. The Spanish legislation which grants workers the right to work less for a certain period because of parental leave is not reconciling or promoting a more equal division of family responsibility. On the contrary it perpetuates a classical situation where women shoulder the financial risk of taking care of children by having to accept a diminished social security. The Court cannot accept a mechanical interpretation where after the bare fact that a woman is working on reduced time per se means that she must be classified as a part-time worker. It is for the national court to take all circumstances into consideration i.e. both the working pattern of the woman in the concrete case and the dynamic change in women's work pattern generally.**
2) **Dir. 79/7 on the progressive implementation of equal treatment for men and women in matters of social security states in art. 4:**

> **'The principle of equal treatment means that there shall be no discrimination whatsoever on ground of sex either directly or indirectly … in particular as concerns:**
>
> - **…**
> - **the obligation to contribute and the calculation of contributions …'**

The option for workers on parental leave to insure themselves against the risk of invalidity essentially means that women on parental leave must pay more for their insurance than men. Consequently, it is contrary to the principle of equality between women and men to make it necessary to conclude a special agreement to preserve the same contribution base as before the reduction of work time because of parental leave. So this possibility in the Spanish social security law of 30 July 1991 art. 14 violates the equality principle in dir. 79/7 based on an interpretation of the fundamental principle of equality between men and women in the EU-charter art. 21 and 23 and the underlying principles from the CEDAW Convention articles 5 and 11.

Reflections

The collaborative work of this chamber developed with great ease. The chamber consisted of three judges, Kirsten Ketscher, Freya Semanda and Marta Carneiro, who, at the time of re-writing the judgment, were all researchers at the Centre for Legal Studies in Welfare and Market Integration (WELMA), Law Faculty of the University of Copenhagen. The choice of *Gómez-Limón Sánchez-Camacho* as the judgment to re-write was inspired by an earlier research piece by Marta Carneiro (2011),[1] president of the chamber, which denounced some of the omissions in the reasoning of the Court of Justice of the European Union (CJEU).

The working process very much resembled that of the Court, whereby one of the judges prepares a draft decision which is then the basis for the chamber's discussion and deliberation. Similarly, all drafts of the project's outputs (authors' note, judgment and reflections) were prepared by Marta Carneiro, circulated by email to the other judges, and later discussed in chamber. This way of working was naturally facilitated by the shared workplace of all three members (Law Faculty, University of Copenhagen) which allowed the chamber to replicate an actual deliberating environment. The three members were present at all meetings.

The chamber presented its preliminary ideas at the project's first workshop and its final findings at the project's second workshop, both of which were held in London. In both instances, very helpful input was received from the other project participants and integrated into the chamber's discussions. After the workshops, an internal seminar was organised at the research centre WELMA, Law Faculty, University of Copenhagen, where the chamber gave a general presentation on the project and, more specifically, on its role and work in re-writing the judgment. This elicited extremely insightful feedback for further chamber discussions and revealed a surprising interest for wider dissemination, application and use of the judgment re-writing method.

As for the experience of delivering judgment, the project's method established that each chamber had to comply with the same procedural rules and should try to simulate the same constraints as imposed on the original court. In the case of a chamber of the CJEU, this meant, among other things, that it was not possible to have dissenting opinions. In this way, chamber members experienced the reality of having to produce a decision that was able to accommodate the range of views of the judges. Also, the chamber had to be creative as the project's rules dictated that the re-written judgment should only be based on the law and the facts as they were at the time of the original judgment (the re-written decision, we were instructed, must be one that could have been written by the relevant tribunal at the time). This was challenging in light of developments that followed *Gómez-Limón*. To give

[1] M Carneiro, 'Work-life Balance: Is There a Genuine Choice? A Case of Indirect Sex Discrimination' in S Poulsen and S Jørgensen (eds), *Frit Valg. Velfærd i den Europæiske Union* (Copenhagen, Jurist- og Økonomforbundets Forlag, 2011).

one example, in *Meerts*,[2] which was decided shortly after, the Court concluded that workers under parental leave in the form of reduced working time are in a situation similar to that of full-time workers as regards their initial employment agreement; therefore, they should enjoy the same rules (at stake was the calculation of compensation in lieu of notice prior to dismissal). Although the Court's reasoning still insisted on the comparator-based model, referring to it in this context would have contributed to denouncing the randomness of comparisons (even if to the benefit of the claimant) and, at the same time, to emphasising the particularity of parental leave users. Parental leave accommodates a reality (raising a child) that is unique and should not depend on comparisons in order to merit substantive analysis; it is also uniquely characterised by an endeavour to retain a connection to the labour market while pursuing an activity that is ultimately beneficial for the labour market itself and society as a whole. The continued inability to value this endeavour provides support to public policies that fail to give working parents a genuine choice to reconcile work and caring responsibilities. In addition, the parental leave directive at stake (Council Directive 96/34/EC of 3 June 1996) has been altered in the meantime[3] and further changes are being discussed as we write.[4]

Furthermore, the chamber was mindful of the need to respect the division of functions between the national courts and the CJEU, which is an essential feature of the preliminary ruling procedure. One could even argue that to a greater extent than the original judgment itself, the re-written judgment succeeds in providing more comprehensive and balanced guidance to the national court without encroaching on its competence to decide the underlying dispute. As outlined in the authors' note, the re-written judgment places the substantive notion of equality that underlies the concept of indirect discrimination firmly at its centre. That is to say, indirect discrimination elicits an analysis that, by definition, cannot be anything other than contextual; therefore, it is irreconcilable with formalistic notions of equality that fail to look at the particular situation of the groups at stake. For this purpose, the aim was to give voice to Ms Gómez-Limón and, through her, to women who are structurally disadvantaged in the labour market. Comparing the original and the re-written versions of the judgment clearly shows how that voice is invisible in the former and visible in the latter, and how this unquestionably shapes the Court's reasoning by removing or adding more substantive layers. Without determining the final outcome (which is ultimately for the national court to do), this exercise demonstrates how, *just* by giving law back its substantive

[2] NV C-116/08 *Christel Meerts v Proost* [2009] ECLI:EU:645.

[3] Council Directive 2010/18/EU of 8 March 2010 implementing the revised Framework Agreement on parental leave concluded by BUSINESSEUROPE, UEAPME, CEEP and ETUC and repealing Directive 96/34/EC (Text with EEA relevance), OJ L 68, 18.3.2010, 13–20.

[4] Proposal for a Directive of the European Parliament and of the Council on work-life balance for parents and carers and repealing Council Directive 2010/18/EU, COM(2017) 253 final, http://eur-lex.europa.eu/legal-content/EN/TXT/HTML/?uri=CELEX:52017PC0253&from=HR.

purpose and role, the reasoning becomes more responsive, more legitimate, more humane. By doing this, the re-written judgment more fully empowers the national court to give a balanced decision, discharges the CJEU's task of providing guidance, and fulfils the principle of non-discrimination.

Finally, worthy of mention is the undeniable weight that comes with dealing with a real case decided by a real court, as if somehow that reality became more *real* through this method than through traditional academic analysis. The weight of the responsibility immediately kicks in. The search for context in law is in no way instantaneous; the work of filling law with reality is never-ending and never straightforward. Once we turn abstract exercises of conceptual materialisation into concrete decision-making in real life cases, an awareness of the implications of the task becomes much more acute and the search for intellectual justification more urgent. Curiously, this process unveiled the need to really dig deep into lived experiences (and a certain frustration at not being able to do so). It revealed how determinant choices at this level give room to a particular perspective that really impacts upon the extent to which law becomes aware of, and responsive to, individuals. Indeed, the task of judges is no easy one.

This experience was particularly revealing of the way legal structures do not necessarily carry an exclusive voice. Naturally, the exercise entailed working within a clearly defined legal structure supplemented by a strong judicial practice; these necessarily delimitate what one can do (for example, the closed list of discrimination grounds in the directives[5]). However, what the re-writing exercise proved was that, even using the same structures and norms, and following the same analytical exercises and canons as the CJEU in discrimination cases, there is a great deal of space left for choice, a choice as to what is made visible, a choice as to what is left invisible. Therefore, re-writing in this manner creates a space that allows us to question how intentional those *choices* are and what meaning they carry. The re-written judgment demonstrates how that space could be filled alternatively in a way that, we argue, actually accords more fully with the purposes of the EU legal antidiscrimination framework and, more specifically, with the legal concept of indirect discrimination. In fact, *Gómez-Limón* offered a perfect fit with the proposed method. It allowed the chamber to make actual use of the law and thereby to emphasise law's potential to be more inclusive, to be more alive, and highlighted the need for it to be more engaged with. Ultimately, this was a very enlightening and rewarding experience.

This said, we can only conclude that this challenge was an eye-opening exercise that played with our own way of understanding the work of judges and the potential of the law. A number of promising convergences unfold. Not only does feminist theory open up the analysis for what is left out, so do the antidiscrimination structure and norms automatically claim substantive authenticity through

[5] We are not considering here the impact of the EU Charter of Fundamental Rights, which gained the same legal status as the Treaties following the Lisbon Treaty.

that inclusion. Not only do antidiscrimination norms reconquer relevance within feminist narratives, so does the theory regain awareness of their potential. This actually revealed itself to be a freeing exercise; to become aware of possibilities and of the hope that comes with that awareness. It only makes agency more urgent.

However, the opening of possibilities carries with it an expression of the closures that continue to dominate and to silence the dominated. In this sense, this exercise was also an illustration of the paradoxical parallel between a formal legal protection that has witnessed major developments and a blindness to the structural and the systemic that perseveres and continues to produce great harm, thus rendering that protection empty. This is a confirmation of the absence of context, a confirmation of the insufficient effort towards context. Therefore, progress must be pursued always and this project, together with its predecessors, proved itself a powerful contribution.

PART III

Human Rights

European Court of Human Rights

7

Christine Goodwin v the United Kingdom

SARA BENGTSON, DAMIAN GONZALEZ-SALZBERG,
LOVEDAY HODSON AND PAUL JOHNSON

Authors' Note

Introduction

When the Grand Chamber of the European Court of Human Rights ('ECtHR' or 'the Court') delivered its judgment in the case of *Christine Goodwin v the United Kingdom*,[1] it was celebrated by many as a progressive development for trans' rights.[2] After a number of failed attempts in Strasbourg to challenge the lack of legal recognition of transsexuals'[3] gender reassignment and to obtain redress for the resultant difficulties trans individuals face, including in terms of marriage,[4] such non-recognition was acknowledged as a breach of rights under the

[1] *Christine Goodwin v the United Kingdom* [GC], no 28957/95, ECHR 2002-VI, (2002) 35 EHRR 18.

[2] 'Transsexuals win historic rights ruling in the European Court', the organization Liberty, which had appeared before the Court as a third-party intervener, declared (*Liberty*, 11 July 2012). See www.liberty-human-rights.org.uk/news/press-releases/transsexuals-win-historic-rights-ruling-european-court.

[3] Making use of the terminology proposed by Stephen Whittle, we use *trans* as an umbrella concept, to refer to every person who does not perceive their gender identity as the same as the one they were socially expected to fulfil as a result of their sex designation at birth. The term *transgender* is used to refer to those individuals who live, or desire to live, a part of their life performing a gender role that does not follow the socially expected one that is allegedly correlative to the sex assigned to them at birth. Lastly, the term *transsexual* is specifically reserved to refer to those individuals who intend to undergo, are undergoing, or have undergone a sex-reassignment process. S Whittle, *Respect and Equality: Transsexual and Transgender Rights* (Abingdon, Routledge, 2002) xxii–xxiii.

[4] The *Rees v the United Kingdom*, judgment of 17 October 1986, Series A no 106, (1987) 9 EHRR 56; the *Cossey v the United Kingdom* judgment, 27 September 1990, § 42, Series A no 184, (1991) 13 EHRR 622; the *X, Y and Z v the United Kingdom*, judgment of 22 April 1997, Reports of Judgments and Decisions 1997-II, (1997) 24 EHRR 143; and the *Sheffield and Horsham v the United Kingdom*, judgment of 30 July 1998, Reports of Judgments and Decisions 1998-V, (1999) 27 EHRR 163.

Convention for the Protection of Human Rights and Fundamental Freedoms (ECHR or the Convention) in *Goodwin*. The judgment was consequently a significant step in the Court's jurisprudence and a trans rights victory, and as such it perhaps seems a somewhat odd choice to re-write. Nevertheless, as a feminist chamber, we found the victory to be bittersweet because, while the original judgment was unquestionably progressive, it was based on similar presuppositions about the nature of gender that underpinned previous cases. Moreover, according to our chamber, the victory was accompanied by a number of failures and silences. In our re-written judgment, we have worked at redressing these problems through both substantial and methodological means, playing within the limits set by the Convention. Methodologically, we have made use of procedural possibilities available to the Court and, sitting as a progressive feminist bench, have used these creatively. As such, we often invoke dissenting opinions as legal authorities, and we also use the principle *jura novit curia* to engage with issues under articles not explicitly relied on by the applicant, contrary to the Court's usual practice. Substantially, above all, in our judgment we question the real Court's understanding of sex and gender.

Legal-historical Context

In England and Wales, every child is registered at birth. On the birth certificate – which is an authenticated copy of the entry into the register – the child's sex is indicated.[5] The birth certificate, in its turn, is the source of information for various administrative purposes. Until 2004, opportunities for amending the register were very restricted.[6] For instance, errors could be amended, but only if the error in question occurred at the time when the birth was registered. In short, a birth certificate presented the facts as they stood at the time of the child's birth. At the relevant time, the law of England and Wales treated gender as both innate and binary. For legal purposes, the test for determining a person's legal sex was set out in *Corbett v Corbett*:[7] sex, it was held, depends on the congruence between chromosomes, gonads and genitals; and since sex was therefore considered innate, operative 'sex change' interventions had no impact for the purposes of a person's legal sex.[8]

[5] Births and Deaths Registration Act 1953.

[6] In 2004, the Gender Recognition Act was enacted as a response to the Court's judgment in *Goodwin*.

[7] *Corbett v Corbett (otherwise Ashley) (No 1)*, [1971] P 83; [1970] 2 WLR 1306.

[8] The *Corbett* definition of sex became the leading authority for the determination of sex in various legal fields in the United Kingdom. See, inter alia, *Regina v Tan and Others* 1983, [1983] 2 All England Law Reports 12, in which a male-to-female transsexual was regarded as a man for the purposes of s 30 of the Sexual Offences Act 1956 and s 5 of the Sexual Offences Act 1967. In the cases R (P) 1 and R (P) 2 (in the 1980 vol of National Insurance Commissioner Decisions), two male-to-female transsexuals were treated as men for the purposes of retirement age.

Although the law of England and Wales as it stood might be seen as merely an administrative matter that did not stop trans persons from living their day-to-day lives in their chosen gender, in practice the problems and distress it caused were considerable. That the law was also an expression of a particular understanding of the innateness of gender, which oppressed the applicant in the current case and her predecessors, was for the first time acknowledged in *Goodwin*. As we will go on to explore, however, we believe that the problems bound up with the legal regulation of gender are broader than this.

Christine Goodwin, as we already indicated, followed a line of applicants who challenged in Strasbourg the incongruence between their legal sex and lived reality. *Rees v United Kingdom*, saw the first such challenge before the ECtHR in the mid 1980s.[9] In *Rees*, the facts of which were similar to those in *Goodwin*, the Court observed that the issue in question was the existence and scope of a positive obligation under the Convention.[10] As there was little common ground among the State parties to the Convention regarding the recognition of gender transition, the state was accorded a wide margin of appreciation. Despite acknowledging 'the seriousness of the problems affecting transsexuals and of their distress',[11] the Court held that finding for the applicant would impose significant administrative requirements and new duties on the rest of the population.[12] The applicant's situation could thus not give rise to any obligation under the Convention. The Court did not find the fact that the UK had cooperated in the applicant's medical treatment towards transitioning to be a persuasive argument for imposing such a positive obligation on the State.[13] Nevertheless, the Court held that 'the need for appropriate legal measures should be kept under review having regard particularly to scientific and societal developments'.[14]

Despite its stated awareness of the problems facing transsexuals, the ECtHR adopted the same approach four years later in *Cossey v the United Kingdom*. Granting considerable deference to scientific understandings of sex, the Court held that no significant scientific developments had occurred in the intervening period since the *Rees* judgment. Maintaining a binary view of sex, the Court said it remained the case that 'gender reassignment surgery does not result in the full acquisition of all the biological characteristics of the opposite sex'.[15] Furthermore, it held, among the Member States there was 'the same diversity of practice as obtained at

[9] *Rees*, above n 4.
[10] ibid, para 35.
[11] ibid, para 47.
[12] ibid, para 42.
[13] In contrast, the European Commission of Human Rights and the applicant had argued that the failure to legally recognise the applicant's new sexual identity, whilst on the other hand cooperating in his medical treatment, 'had the effect that the applicant was treated as an ambiguous being'. ibid para 41.
[14] ibid, para 47.
[15] *Cossey*, above n 4.

the time of the Rees judgment', entailing that the margin of appreciation remained wide.[16] Eight years later still, in the case of *Sheffield and Horsham v the United Kingdom*,[17] it was clear that time was beginning to run out for the UK government, which had not taken steps to address the harm experienced by trans individuals. Although the Court remained unpersuaded that the evidence presented demonstrated such scientific and legal development as to affect the UK's broad margin of appreciation,[18] it went on to say:

> Even if there have been no significant scientific developments since the date of the Cossey judgment which make it possible to reach a firm conclusion on the aetiology of transsexualism, it is nevertheless the case that there is an increased social acceptance of transsexualism and an increased recognition of the problems which post-operative transsexuals encounter. Even if it finds no breach of Article 8 in this case, the Court reiterates that this area needs to be kept under review by Contracting States.

The tide seemed to be turning against tolerating the State's intransigence.

The *Goodwin* Case

Christine Goodwin, a trans woman who had undergone gender reassignment surgery, applied to the Court in 1995. Although the assignment was provided and paid for by the National Health Service, her reassignment was not recognised in law, her birth certificate remained unchanged and she was denied a new national insurance number. The incongruence between her legal and lived gender meant the applicant faced a number of significant difficulties in her daily life. On starting a new job, for example, her national insurance number revealed to her employer her birth-assigned gender, which led her to experience harassment and discrimination at work. Her attempts to pursue a case of sexual harassment against colleagues were unsuccessful because, in law, she was deemed to be a man. Further, she was ineligible for a state pension at the age of entitlement for women in the UK; she remained obliged to pay the higher motor insurance premiums applicable to men at the time; and she had continuously to choose between revealing her assigned sex and foregoing those benefits that were conditional upon her producing her birth certificate.

Before the Court, the applicant complained of a violation of Article 12 (right to marry), relating to her inability to marry a man, and Article 8 (right to respect for private and family life) in respect of the humiliation and discrimination she had experienced as a result of the non-recognition of her gender in law. The Court, in unanimously finding a violation of Article 8, relied on the existence of a 'continuing international trend in favour … of legal recognition of the new sexual

[16] ibid.
[17] *Sheffield and Horsham*, above n 4.
[18] ibid, paras 56–58.

identity of post-operative transsexuals'.[19] Similarly, the Court unanimously found the applicant's argument under Article 12 to be persuasive: '… the Court finds no justification for barring the transsexual from enjoying the right to marry under any circumstances'.[20] It found that there was no separate issue of discrimination to consider under Article 14 (prohibition of discrimination) and no violation of Article 13 (right to an effective remedy).

The Re-written Judgment

We turn now to consider the specific issues that inspired our feminist chamber to re-write this undoubtedly progressive judgment. Before the Court, Christine Goodwin argued under Article 8 that the lack of recognition of her gender reassignment led to humiliating experiences in her daily life, which resulted in violations of her right to private life. In the original judgment, the Court reasoned that the case raised the question of whether the state had failed to comply with a positive obligation under Article 8.[21] As a chamber, we questioned that approach. Christine Goodwin was in law considered to be the sex she did not identify with, as were those applicants who preceded her. In our judgment we identified the State's creation of a rigid legal and administrative system that led to non-recognition as an interference with her rights (rather than as a failure to fulfil a positive obligation). By treating gender reassignment recognition as a positive obligation for the State, the real Court has subscribed to an understanding in which a 'true' sex exists, from which people who have transitioned depart. Our re-written judgment frames this as a question of negative duties: specifically, is the State obliged to refrain from imposing a legal sex onto someone who does not identify with that sex? Whether a State's obligation under the Convention is conceived of as negative or positive may have considerable practical and legal relevance. The burden on the applicant is heavier as regards positive rights, since she must show that what she has suffered weighs heavier than the public interest. Conversely, as regards negative rights, she only needs to establish that an interference has occurred. Thereafter, it falls on the State to prove the lawfulness of the interference, the legitimacy of its aim and that it is necessary in a democratic society.[22]

Underpinning the Court's analysis of the State's obligations under Article 8 was an implicit acceptance of binary genders: Ms Goodwin was successful because – as a result of the surgery she underwent – she had, in the eyes of the Court, transitioned and 'become' a woman. The entrenchment of rigid gender binaries was something that we saw as potentially damaging, a view confirmed in more recent

[19] *Goodwin*, above n 1, para 84.
[20] ibid, para 103.
[21] cp *Rees*, above n 4, para 35; *Cossey*, above n 4, para 36; and *Sheffield and Horsham*, above n 4, para 51.
[22] This is the case in respect of the 'qualified rights' contained in Arts 8–11 of the Convention.

case-law before the Court that has challenged various criteria that States have used to identify the point of transition from one gender to another (which include the requirement of divorce,[23] sterilisation,[24] and other forms of medical intervention). As a group of scholars with an established commitment to LGBT rights, we were also attuned to the possibility that homophobia might underpin the Court's approach to trans cases, resulting in a failure or refusal to acknowledge the complexity of gender and sexuality.[25] Consequently, in the re-written judgment, influenced by different streams of feminist theory, from the radical feminism of Monique Wittig to the post-modern feminism/queer theory of writers such as Judith Butler,[26] we have attempted to avoid the actual Court's assumptions about the binary nature of gender. This affected our analysis of Article 12 too. The original Court's finding of a violation of this article was conditional upon an understanding that the applicant would be entering into an opposite-sex marriage. That many people have been excluded from marriage rights as a result of this approach – not least, for instance, those trans people who have been required to divorce or undergo sterilisation before having their transition recognised – was a key issue that we were compelled to re-think.

Another issue we perceived to be problematic with the original judgment was the ongoing medicalisation of trans bodies and pathologisation of trans people.[27] Although the original judgment found there had been a violation of Article 8, in reaching this conclusion the Court followed its earlier cases regarding recognition of gender reassignment, in which it held that the State's margin of appreciation depended on the state of medical science and the law and practice of Member States. Regarding the state of medical science, the Court partly accepted what it had earlier established: gender reassignment surgery did still not result in the full acquisition of all the biological characteristics of the opposite sex.[28] However, the Court held, 'with increasingly sophisticated surgery and types of hormonal treatments, the principal unchanging biological aspect of gender identity is the chromosomal element.'[29] Nevertheless, it was 'not apparent to the Court that the chromosomal element, amongst all the others, must inevitably take on decisive significance for the purposes of legal attribution of gender identity for transsexuals.'[30] In approaching Article 8 in our feminist judgment, we wanted to

[23] *Hämäläinen v Finland*, [GC] Application no 37359/09, 16 July 2014.

[24] *A P, Garcon, and Nicot v France*, Application nos 79885/12, 52471/13 & 52596/13, judgment, 6 April 2017.

[25] DA Gonzalez-Salzberg, 'Confirming (the Illusion of) Heterosexual Marriage: Hämäläinen v Finland' (2015) 2 *Journal of International and Comparative Law* 173, 186.

[26] M Wittig, *The Straight Mind and Other Essays* (Boston MA, Beacon Press, 1992); J Butler, *Gender Trouble* (New York NY, Routledge, 1990).

[27] DA Gonzalez-Salzberg, 'The Accepted Transsexual and the Absent Transgender: A Queer Reading of the Regulation of Sex/Gender by the European Court of Human Rights' (2014) 29 *American University Law Review* 797, 812.

[28] cp *Cossey*, above n 4, para 40.

[29] *Goodwin*, above n 1, para 82.

[30] ibid, para 82.

question the authority accorded to medical science when determining sex as a legal category. Consequently, we completely disregard examination of the current state of medical science. Since the regulation of sex is a matter of law rather than medicine, we argue, the legal recognition of gender identity should not depend on the opinion of medical science.

In our re-written judgment we were anxious to address the considerable harm experienced by the applicant as result of the lengthy discrimination and marginalisation she experienced prior to legal recognition of her gender. Thus, it became apparent to us that it was important that we, as a chamber, initiate an Article 3 (prohibition of torture and inhuman and degrading treatment) complaint on the applicant's behalf. This was necessary to highlight and give due consideration to the very real harm and distress that trans people experience as a result of the law's failure to recognise their gender. It was also an indication of our belief that the Court's case law under Article 3 has not been sufficiently developed in relation to harms that result from entrenched structural beliefs about gender.

Like the applicants in the earlier cases, Christine Goodwin also complained of a violation of Article 14 (in conjunction with Article 8), which prohibits discrimination in the enjoyment of the rights under the Convention. She argued that the lack of legal recognition of her gender transition was the cause of numerous discriminatory experiences. Unlike the real Court, which seldom examines Article 14 after finding a violation of any of the substantive articles, our chamber wanted to emphasise the discriminatory character of the experiences Christine Goodwin had gone through. To us, the institutionalised structural discrimination of trans people is at the heart of this case and we wanted to address the different ways in which the law treats people who identify with their assigned sex and those who do not. Accordingly, we make progressive use of the non-exhaustive list of non-discrimination grounds in Article 14 in order to find that the applicant had suffered discrimination, contrary to the Convention, in respect of the incongruous relationship between her experienced and legally assigned gender.

JUDGMENT

CHRISTINE GOODWIN v THE UNITED KINGDOM

(Application no. 28957/95)

A Chamber of the European Court of Human Rights consisting of:

Paul Johnson (President), Sara Bengtson, Damian Gonzalez-Salzberg, Loveday Hodson

11 July 2002

THE FACTS

1. The applicant is a citizen of the United Kingdom, born in 1937 and is a transsexual who has undergone male to female gender reassignment.
2. The applicant was 'diagnosed' as a transsexual in the mid-1960s and, though she married a woman and they had four children, her conviction was always that her 'brain sex' did not fit her body. Until 1984 the applicant dressed in a way that might be recognised as signalling a male identity for work but, at other times, she dressed in a way that expressed her female identity and, in 1985, she began treatment at the Gender Identity Clinic at the Charing Cross Hospital, which included consultations with a psychiatrist as well as a psychologist. The applicant was prescribed hormone therapy, began attending grooming classes and voice training, and began to live fully as a woman. In 1986, she underwent surgery to shorten her vocal chords and, in 1987, she was accepted on the waiting list for gender re-assignment surgery. The applicant's gender transition was completed in 1990 when she underwent National Health Service funded gender re-assignment surgery at a National Health Service hospital.
3. The applicant became divorced from her former wife but continued to enjoy the love and support of her children.
4. The applicant claims that between 1990 and 1992 she was sexually harassed by colleagues at work and attempted to pursue a case of sexual harassment in the Industrial Tribunal. She claims her case was unsuccessful because she was considered in law to be a man. She was subsequently dismissed from her employment for reasons said to be connected with her health, but alleges that reason for the dismissal was that she was a transsexual.
5. In 1996, when the applicant started work with a new employer she was required to provide her National Insurance (NI) number. Because she was concerned that the new employer would be in a position to use the NI number to find details about her past, the applicant requested the allocation of a new NI number from the Department of Social Security (DSS) but this was rejected. The applicant claims

that the new employer has ascertained details of her identity using the NI number because she began experiencing problems at work, such as colleagues stopping speaking to her and talking about her.

6. The DSS Contributions Agency informed the applicant that she would be ineligible for a State pension at the age of 60 (the age of entitlement for women in the United Kingdom) and that her pension contributions would have to be continued until the date at which she reached the age of 65 (being the age of entitlement for men).

7. The applicant's files at the DSS were marked 'sensitive' to ensure that only an employee of a particular grade had access to her files. This meant that the applicant had to make special appointments with the DSS to deal with the most trivial matters and could not deal directly with the local office or deal with queries over the telephone.

8. In a number of instances, the applicant stated that she has had to choose between revealing her birth certificate and foregoing certain advantages which depended upon her producing her birth certificate. In particular, she has not followed through a loan conditional upon life insurance, a re-mortgage offer and an entitlement to winter fuel allowance from the DSS. The applicant also remains obliged to pay the higher motor insurance premiums applicable to men. The applicant did not feel able to report a theft of 200 pounds sterling to the police, for fear that the investigation would require her to reveal her identity.

ALLEGED VIOLATION OF ARTICLE 8 OF THE CONVENTION

9. The applicant, who lives as a woman and desires to be recognised as such under the law, claims a violation of Article 8 of the Convention, the relevant part of which provides as follows:

> 1. Everyone has the right to respect for his private … life …
> 2. There shall be no interference by a public authority with the exercise of this right except such as is in accordance with the law and is necessary in a democratic society in the interests of national security, public safety or the economic wellbeing of the country, for the prevention of disorder or crime, for the protection of health or morals, or for the protection of the rights and freedoms of others.

The Court's assessment

1. Preliminary considerations

10. In the past, the Court has made use of the terms 'sex' and 'gender' as if they were identical concepts (see *Rees v the United Kingdom*, 17 October 1986, Series A no. 106, (1987) 9 EHRR 56; *Sheffield and Horsham v the United Kingdom*, 30 July 1998, *Reports of Judgments and Decisions 1998-V*, (1999) 27 EHRR 163), which might lead to a lack of clarity in cases, such as the present one, brought by applicants who identify themselves as transsexuals (see paragraph 1 above).

11. In order to avoid confusion, the Court will adopt the following criterion in this case. It will use the term 'legal sex' to refer to the attribution by the State of a sex category to every newborn, based on observed anatomical criteria. Similarly, it will use the term 'gender identity' to refer to an individual's identification with the sex category of either male or female. In addition, the Court will reserve the term 'trans' to refer to individuals, such as the applicant, who feel that the 'legal sex' attributed to them at birth is incongruent with their own 'gender identity'.
12. In previous cases the Court has held that a refusal by a Contracting State to alter an entry on the birth register, which records an individual's legal sex at the time of their birth, at the request of an adult transsexual whose gender identity is incongruous with the birth register did not amount to a violation of Article 8 of the Convention (*Rees v the United Kingdom*, cited above; *Cossey v the United Kingdom*, 27 September 1990, § 42, Series A no. 184, (1991) 13 EHRR 622). However, the Court is persuaded by the seriousness of the issues raised in the present complaint to revisit its approach.
13. It is clear that the decision to attribute a legal sex to every person at birth, and to register that legal sex, interferes with the private life of the individual. As a consequence, it is also clear that an interference takes place when a Government refuses to alter the registration of an attributed legal sex at the request of a person who no longer identifies with it.
14. It is evident that the interference in question 'is in accordance with the law'. However, it is less clear whether the interference pursues an aim specified in paragraph 2 of Article 8. The respondent Government have submitted that the refusal to alter the applicant's entry on the birth register strikes a fair balance between the rights of the individual and the 'general interest of the community'. However, such an objective is not one of the aims set out in paragraph 2 of Article 8. Nevertheless, the Court agrees with the opinion of Judge Van Dijk that the refusal to alter the applicant's entry on the birth register is based on the view that legal certainty and consistency in a society is required for the protection of the rights of others (*Sheffield and Horsham v the United Kingdom*, cited above, Dissenting opinion of Judge Van Dijk, § 6) and, this being an aim specified in paragraph 2 of Article 8, is prepared to accept that the interference in question pursues a legitimate aim.
15. As a consequence, the main issue that remains to be decided by the Court is whether it is 'necessary in a democratic society' to refuse, at the request of a transsexual, to change a record of legal sex entered on the birth register. In considering this issue, the Court notes that Contracting States enjoy a margin of appreciation when striking a balance between the general interest of the community and the interests of the individual, the search for which balance is inherent in the whole of the Convention (*Cossey*, cited above, § 37).

2. The applicant's situation as a transsexual

16. The Court observes that the applicant, registered at birth as male, has undergone a gender transition process and has lived as a woman since 1985.

Nonetheless, she continues to be treated as a man for many legal purposes. For instance, while she has been allowed to adopt a female name that is registered in her passport and driving license, she is treated as a man for other legal purposes, such as in the area of pensions and retirement age.

17. Serious interferences with private life can arise when domestic law conflicts with an important aspect of personal identity (see, mutatis mutandis, *Dudgeon v the United Kingdom*, judgment of 22 October 1981, § 41, Series A no. 45, (1982) 4 EHRR 149). The stress and alienation arising from discordance between actually being a woman and the status imposed by a legal regime that refuses to recognise gender transition, cannot be regarded as a minor inconvenience arising from a formality. A conflict between reality and law arises, which places transsexual individuals in an anomalous position, in which they experience feelings of vulnerability, humiliation and anxiety.

18. In previous similar cases, the Court has examined the countervailing arguments put forward by the respondent Government, which were of a public interest nature, and accepted these as justifying the continuation of the present situation. It observes that in previous cases weight was given to medical and scientific considerations, as well as to the state of any European and international consensus. The Court feels that these aspects require reconsideration.

3. Medical and scientific considerations

19. The Court notes that medical science continues to pathologise transsexuality. Transsexuality has wide international recognition as a medical condition for which treatment is provided in order to afford relief (for example, the *Diagnostic and Statistical Manual*, fourth edition (DSM-IV) replaced the diagnosis of transsexualism with 'gender identity disorder'; see also the *International Classification of Diseases*, tenth edition (ICD-10)). The United Kingdom's National Health Service, in common with the vast majority of Contracting States, supports the understanding of transsexuality as a medical condition and provides treatment, including irreversible surgery.

20. In the past, the Court has made explicit reference to transsexuality as a pathological condition. In the *Sheffield and Horsham* judgment (cited above), one of the reasons for refusing the applicants' claims was that '[i]n the view of the Court, the applicants have not shown that since the date of adoption of its Cossey judgment in 1990 there have been any findings in the area of medical science which settle conclusively the doubts concerning the causes of the condition of transsexualism' (*Sheffield and Horsham*, cited above, § 56). However, in the present case, the Court is prepared to reconsider such a view.

21. While it is not the role of the Court to tell medical science how to understand transsexuality, neither is it for the Court to allow medical science to determine the scope of the fundamental rights and freedoms guaranteed by the Convention. Consequently, the on-going scientific and medical debate as to the causes of transsexuality is of diminished importance for this case.

22. In light of this, the Court must re-examine its previous conclusion that transsexual individuals have no right under the Convention to have their gender identity recognised by the State because they cannot acquire all of the 'biological characteristics' of their acquired sex (*Sheffield and Horsham*, cited above, § 56). The Court notes that such a view was never unanimously accepted. As Judge Van Dijk stated in his dissenting opinion in *Sheffield and Horsham*: 'I cannot see any reason why legal recognition of reassignment of sex requires that biologically there has also been a (complete) reassignment; the law can give an autonomous meaning to the concept of "sex", as it does to concepts like "person", "family", "home", "property", etc.' (ibid., Dissenting opinion of Judge Van Dijk, § 8). The Court now adopts the view that the relevant 'cause' of the lack of congruence between the gender identity of the applicant and her legal sex is the attribution of her legal sex by the State at the time of her birth. While this unrequested attribution of legal sex might be irrelevant for most individuals, who develop a gender identity congruent to the sex attributed to them at birth, it is of fundamental relevance for a transsexual person. As such, the Court is now persuaded that the requirements for belonging to a particular legal sex must be 'legal' rather than 'biological' requirements and, therefore, that the legal recognition of sex cannot be dependent on medical opinion. Since the regulation of sex is a matter of law, rather than medicine, the legal recognition of gender identity should not depend on the opinion of medical science either. In this respect, the Court notes that the role of the medical community – and of domestic legislation – should be to make the gender transition process as simple and painless as possible.

23. In addition, in this case, as in many others, the applicant's gender re-assignment was carried out by the State-operated National Health Service, a situation that deserves further consideration. While the Court does not consider that any specific treatment or medical procedure should be made a pre-requisite to granting an individual's request to change the legal sex attributed to them, the fact that the United Kingdom provided the applicant with her gender transition process is an element that carries a certain weight. The Court must therefore examine the coherence of the administrative and legal practices within the domestic system. In this respect, the Court considers that when a Contracting State has authorised and financed a gender transition process, it appears illogical – and even cruel – to refuse to address the legal implications which result from the process.

4. European consensus and striking a fair balance

24. The Court observes that in the case of *Rees* in 1986 it noted that little common ground existed between Contracting States, some of which did permit gender reassignment and some of which did not, and that, generally speaking, the law seemed to be in a state of transition (cited above, § 37). In the more recent case of *Sheffield and Horsham* (cited above, § 57), the Court emphasised the absence of a common European approach to the legal repercussions of altering a record of legal sex in areas such as marriage, filiation, privacy or data protection.

While this would appear to remain the case, the Court regards the lack of a common approach among Contracting States, with their widely diverse legal systems and traditions, as unsurprising.
25. The issue at stake in the present case refers to an individual's gender identity, which is an essential and intimate element of private life (see, mutatis mutandis, *Pretty v the United Kingdom*, no. 2346/02, § 71, ECHR 2002-III, (2002) 35 EHRR 1). While it is not for the Court to validate the legal binary based on sex that is a fundamental aspect of the legal order of all Contracting States, it is mindful of the importance to the applicant of being legally recognised as a woman. The fact that there is no European consensus on the matter should be balanced against the fundamental value of the right at stake.
26. In this respect, the Court recalls that the very essence of the Convention is respect for human dignity and human freedom. Under Article 8 in particular, where the notion of personal autonomy is an important principle underlying the interpretation of its guarantees, protection is given to the personal sphere of each individual, including the right to establish details of their identity as individual human beings (see, inter alia, *Pretty v the United Kingdom*, cited above, § 61; and *Mikulić v Croatia*, no. 53176/99, § 53, ECHR 2002-I).
27. As it has done on multiple occasions, the Court must determine an appropriate interpretation and application of the Convention 'in the light of present-day conditions' (see *Tyrer v the United Kingdom*, 25 April 1978, § 31, Series A no. 26, (1979–80) 2 EHRR 1, and subsequent case-law). In the twenty-first Century, the right of transsexuals to personal development and to physical and moral security, in the full sense as enjoyed by others in society, cannot be regarded as a matter of controversy requiring a further lapse of time to cast clearer light on the issues involved. In short, the unsatisfactory situation in which transsexuals cannot obtain full legal recognition of their acquired sex is no longer sustainable.
28. The Court does not underestimate the difficulties posed by this issue nor the important repercussions which any major change in the legal system will inevitably have, not only in the field of birth registration, but also in the areas of access to records, family law, affiliation, inheritance, criminal justice, employment, social security and insurance. However, these problems are far from insuperable. No concrete or substantial hardship or detriment to the public interest has been demonstrated as likely to flow from any change to the legal sex of transsexuals and, in regard to other possible consequences, the Court considers that society may reasonably be expected to tolerate a certain inconvenience to enable individuals to live in dignity and in accordance with their gender identity.
29. In fact, tolerance might not be the right value that is expected from individuals in a democratic society. In a democratic society, diversity in areas such as gender identity should be celebrated rather than merely tolerated. This is consistent with the Convention, which guarantees fundamental rights and freedoms to every human being irrespective of their personal characteristics.
30. Having regard to the above considerations, the Court finds that the respondent Government cannot claim that the matter falls within its margin of appreciation.

Since there are no significant factors of public interest to weigh against the interests of the applicant in obtaining legal recognition of her acquired sex, the Court reaches the conclusion that the fair balance that is inherent in the analysis of Article 8 tilts decisively in favour of the applicant. There has, accordingly, been a failure to respect the applicant's right to respect for private life amounting to a violation of Article 8 of the Convention.

ALLEGED VIOLATION OF ARTICLE 14 OF THE CONVENTION

31. The applicant also claimed a violation of Article 14 of the Convention, which provides as follows:

> The enjoyment of the rights and freedoms set forth in this Convention shall be secured without discrimination on any ground such as sex, race, colour, language, religion, political or other opinion, national or social origin, association with a national minority, property, birth or other status.

1. Preliminary considerations

32. The Government submitted that no issues arose under Article 14 of the Convention which were different from those addressed under Article 8 and that the complaints failed to disclose any discrimination contrary to the above provision.
33. On various previous occasions the Court has held that an examination of a complaint under Article 14 is not generally required when it has found a violation of another Article taken alone. However, the Court has also held that '[t]he position is otherwise if a clear inequality of treatment in the enjoyment of the right in question is a fundamental aspect of the case' (*Airey v Ireland*, 9 October 1979, § 30, Series A no. 32, (1979–80 EHRR 305; *X and Y v the Netherlands*, 26 March 1985, § 32, Series A no. 91, (1986) 8 EHRR 235). As such, the Court has proceeded to examine a complaint under Article 14 in conjunction with another Article when it has already found a violation of a substantive right (*Marckx v Belgium*, 13 June 1979, §§ 32–65, Series A no. 31, (1979–80 2 EHRR 330; see also *Chassagnou and Others v France* [GC], nos. 25088/94, 28331/95 and 28443/95, § 89, ECHR 1999-III, (2000) 29 EHRR 615).
34. Consideration of the merits of an Article 14 complaint, subsequent to finding a violation of a substantive right, is a means by which the Court can examine the potential discriminatory character of the violation in question. Furthermore, such an examination provides the Court with the opportunity to assess the wider implications of discrimination in a Contracting State for the individual or group in question. In this respect, the Court reiterates that its judgments serve not only to decide those cases brought before it but, more generally, to elucidate, safeguard and develop the rules instituted by the Convention, thereby contributing to the observance by the States of the engagements undertaken by them as Contracting Parties (*Ireland v the United Kingdom*, 18 January 1978, § 154, Series A no. 25, (1979–80) 2 EHRR 25).

35. In light of this, the Court cannot simply dismiss the applicant's claim that she has suffered discrimination contrary to Article 14 solely on the basis that it has already found a violation of Article 8 alone. It first has to establish whether a clear inequality of treatment in the enjoyment of the right in question is a fundamental aspect of the case.

36. In this respect, the Court notes that the core issue of the applicant's complaint is the refusal of the domestic authorities to grant her request to change the registration of her legal sex. Since this core issue exists solely because of the applicant's status as a transsexual person, a status that differentiates her from non-transsexual persons, the Court cannot but conclude that a clear inequality of treatment is a fundamental aspect of the case.

2. Applicable principles

37. The Court recalls that Article 14 has no independent existence, since it has effect solely in relation to the rights and freedoms safeguarded by the other substantive provisions of the Convention and its Protocols. However, the application of Article 14 does not presuppose a breach of one or more of such provisions and to this extent it is autonomous. For Article 14 to become applicable it suffices that the facts of a case fall within the ambit of another substantive provision of the Convention or its Protocols (*Thlimmenos v Greece* [GC], no. 34369/97, § 40, ECHR 2000-IV, (2001) 31 EHRR 15).

38. The Court further recalls that according to its established case-law a difference in treatment is discriminatory if persons in a relevantly similar situation are treated differently (*Fredin v Sweden (no. 1)*, 18 February 1991, § 60, Series A no. 192, (1991) 13 EHRR 784) and the difference in treatment has no objective and reasonable justification, that is; it does not pursue a legitimate aim or there is not a reasonable relationship of proportionality between the means employed and the aim sought to be realised. Moreover, the Contracting States enjoy a certain margin of appreciation in assessing whether and to what extent differences in otherwise similar situations justify a different treatment (*Larkos v Cyprus* [GC], no. 29515/95, § 29, ECHR 1999-I, (2000) 30 EHRR 597).

3. Application of the principles to the present case

39. The Court notes that it has already determined that the facts of the complaint fall within the scope of Article 8 and, to this extent, Article 14 is applicable. The Court will therefore consider the complaint under Article 14 taken in conjunction with Article 8.

40. The Court notes that 'gender identity', which is intrinsically linked to 'sex', is a concept that is undoubtedly covered by Article 14. In this respect, the Court reiterates that the list of grounds enumerated in Article 14 is illustrative and not exhaustive, as is shown by the words 'any ground such as' (in French, '*notamment*') (*Engel and Others v the Netherlands*, 8 June 1976, § 72, Series A no. 22, (1979–80) 1 EHRR 647).

41. The Court further notes that a person whose gender identity corresponded to the legal sex assigned to her or him at birth would not have found herself or himself in the legal position of the applicant and, consequently, would not have encountered the social and legal difficulties experienced by the applicant. The Court therefore concludes that the applicant can be regarded, for the purposes of Article 14, to have been treated differently to persons in a relevantly similar situation.
42. It remains for the Court to determine whether the difference in treatment complained of has an objective and reasonable justification. In this respect, the Court notes that the Government submitted that, the case being examined under Article 8, no separate issue arose under Article 14. In relation to the complaint under Article 8, the Government submitted that there was no generally accepted approach among the Contracting States in respect of transsexuality and that the States were accorded a wide margin of appreciation in this area. The Court has already established under Article 8 that the absence or existence of a European consensus cannot be the basis for granting a State a margin of appreciation in respect of a fundamental human right relating to a core aspect of person's identity (see paragraph 28 above). The obligation which Article 1 of the Convention places on the Contracting State to secure to everyone within their jurisdiction the rights and freedoms contained in the Convention would be seriously undermined by such an approach.
43. In the absence of the Government providing an objective and reasonable justification for the difference in treatment complained of by the applicant, the Court concludes that there has been a violation of Article 14 taken in conjunction with Article 8 of the Convention.

ALLEGED VIOLATION OF ARTICLE 12 OF THE CONVENTION

44. The applicant also claimed a violation of Article 12 of the Convention, which provides as follows:

> Men and women of marriageable age have the right to marry and to found a family, according to the national laws governing the exercise of this right.

1. Preliminary considerations

45. The Court would initially observe that marriage is, for many people, one of the most important milestones of their lives. The love, companionship and security that marriage offers individuals may be fundamental to their current happiness or to their future aspirations. Despite the changes that marriage has undergone since the Convention first entered into force, the desire for marriage remains remarkably undiminished. The precise meaning of a wedding day to the people entering into a marriage will differ, but recognition of its symbolic, familial and spiritual significance is almost universal.
46. The Court is also mindful of the considerable practical advantages that flow from entering into a legally recognised marriage. While marriage can be understood

as a personal commitment made between individuals, the State, through its laws, plays a central part in shaping and bolstering the institution by conferring advantages to married persons in a great number of areas. These include, but are not restricted to, parental responsibility, property rights, welfare benefits, as well as fiscal and other administrative privileges.

2. Applicable principles

47. Article 12 secures the fundamental right of men and women to marry and to found a family. Exercise of the right to marry enshrined in Article 12 is subject to the national laws of the State. In all of the Contracting States, limitations imposed on the right to marry appear as conditions and are embodied in procedural or substantive rules. The former relate mainly to publicity and the solemnisation of marriage, while the latter relate primarily to capacity, consent and certain impediments. However, any limitation on the right to enter into a marriage must be proportionate to meeting a legitimate aim (*F v Switzerland*, 18 December 1987, §§ 36–40, Series A no. 128, (1988) 10 EHRR 411) and 'must not restrict or reduce the right in such a way or to such an extent that the very essence of the right is impaired' (*Rees*, cited above, § 50). Under the Convention, therefore, considerable importance is attached to ensuring that consenting adults can freely enter into marriage with a partner of their choice. The fact that the Court has heard very few complaints under Article 12 indicates that individual autonomy with respect to marriage is a shared European value. In short, as a rule, adults in Europe face very few restrictions when choosing to enter into a legally recognised union.

3. Application of the principles to the present case

48. The Court must begin by considering whether Article 12 is applicable to the applicant's complaint. Article 12 refers to the right of 'men and women of marriageable age' to marry. In previous cases, the Court has taken the view that 'the right to marry … refers to the traditional marriage between persons of opposite biological sex' (*Rees*, cited above, § 49; *Sheffield and Horsham*, cited above, § 66). In this respect, the Court has held that Article 12 is applicable only to marriage between a 'man' and a 'woman', each defined by their fixed biological sex. Consequently, the applicants' Article 12 complaints in *Rees*, *Sheffield and Horsham* and *Cossey* (cited above) were dismissed. If the Court were to maintain its established approach, the applicant, as a transsexual woman, would not meet this strict biologically-determined criterion for womanhood and therefore have no recognised right to marry a man. To argue that, at least in theory, the applicant still enjoys the right to marry a woman clearly holds no comfort for her and, furthermore, renders the right to marry, for her and others similarly situated, theoretical or illusory rather than practical and effective (*United Communist Party of Turkey and Others v Turkey* [GC], 30 January 1998, § 33, Reports of Judgments and Decisions 1998-I, (1998) 26 EHRR 121).

49. In considering whether to maintain its previously adopted approach, the Court notes with interest that a more nuanced understanding of sex and gender has recently been developed in the domestic courts of the respondent State which has challenged the idea of biological fixity. Indeed, the Court of Appeal of England and Wales has recently held that '[the] words "sex" and "gender" are sometimes used interchangeably, but today more frequently denote a difference … It would seem … that it would be impossible to identify gender at the moment of the birth of a child' (*Bellinger v Bellinger*, [2002] Fam. 150, § 23).
50. In light of this development, and reiterating that the Convention is a 'living instrument' (*Marckx v Belgium*, cited above, § 58), the Court considers that its previous interpretation of the words 'men and women' in Article 12 must be seen to reflect a certain temporal understanding of sex and gender. In respect of whether to evolve its interpretation, the Court noted in its *Cossey* judgment that a departure from previous case-law can be justified 'in order to ensure that the interpretation of the Convention reflects societal changes and remains in line with present-day conditions' (cited above, § 35). Furthermore, on more than one occasion, the Court has pointed out that its supervisory functions oblige it to pay the utmost attention to the principles of pluralism, tolerance and broadmindedness, which are the hallmarks of a democratic society (*Handyside v the United Kingdom*, 7 December 1976, § 49, Series A no.24, (1979–80) 1 EHRR 737; *Lingens v Austria*, 8 July 1986, § 41, Series A no. 103, (1986) 8 EHRR 407). Finally, in approaching the task of interpreting the word 'men and women' in Article 12, the Court is particularly mindful of the fact that Article 9 of the Charter of Fundamental Rights of the European Union has omitted, no doubt deliberately, these words from the right to marry.
51. The Court considers that an attempt to fix all persons into one of two sexes is, as this case amply demonstrates, a thankless and, ultimately, fruitless task. Therefore, the Court is of the opinion that to interpret the wording of Article 12 as imposing on adults wishing to marry a requirement to possess particular biological characteristics in respect of sex amounts to an erroneous and unnecessarily restrictive reading of that Article. The words 'men and women' should be understood as an expression, at the time of the drafting of the Convention, of a particular conception of the binary nature of both sex and gender that has since changed. Consequently, the Court can no longer agree that an attachment to 'the traditional concept of marriage' (*Sheffield and Horsham*, cited above, § 67) must underpin its interpretation of Article 12 and concludes that this Article is applicable to the applicant's complaint.
52. The key question that the Court must address is whether or not allowing the applicant to marry a person of her choice falls within the State's margin of appreciation. In this respect, the Court notes that whilst the 'nuclear family' – a married opposite-sex couple and their offspring – is an ideal type that retains considerable influence in framing laws and policies affecting personal relationships including marriage across Contracting States, the concepts of 'marriage' and 'the family' are

neither static nor unitary. Consequently, neither the concepts, or the ideal of the nuclear family they give rise to, can blind the Court to the increasingly diverse relationships that are at the core of many people's lives, as this and similar previous complaints demonstrate. Because marriage as an institution is not static and the legal consequences of marriage across States are not always identical, the Court's approach to marriage and to the family must be a flexible one.

53. The respondent Government has put forward no justification for affording it a broad margin of appreciation under Article 12 to maintain inflexible marriage laws that do not accommodate the fluidity of sex and gender experienced by many in its society. However, even if the respondent Government had submitted reasons for maintaining the current legal regime, the Court considers that there can no longer be any acceptable justification for depriving an individual of the right to marry solely on the basis of their sex. Consequently, there is no reason to regard the restriction imposed on the applicant as a proportionate response to meeting a legitimate aim. The Court therefore concludes that national laws that prevent the exercise of the right to marry solely on the basis of an individual's sex restrict or reduce the right to such an extent that the very essence of the right is impaired. There has, therefore, been a violation of Article 12.

ARTICLE 3 OF THE CONVENTION

54. The applicant submitted that she has suffered numerous humiliating experiences in her everyday life as a result of her inability to change to her legal sex. Although the applicant did not invoke Article 3 of the Convention in her application, the Court considers that Article to be relevant to her complaint because of the centrality and extent of the claims about humiliation. When taken together, the facts submitted by the applicant – in particular, the alleged discrimination at work; the problems at work arising from the link between her previous sex and her National Insurance number; the difficulties created in dealing with the DSS; the inability to access certain advantages in goods and services because of the requirement to produce a birth certificate; and a fear of reporting a crime to the police – suggest that the issue of humiliation is fundamental to every aspect of the applicant's complaint about her inability to reconcile her gender identity with her legal sex. Therefore, the Court considers it appropriate to consider the applicant's complaint under Article 3 of the Convention, which provides as follows:

> No one shall be subjected to torture or to inhuman or degrading treatment or punishment.

1. Preliminary considerations

55. Complaints about humiliation by transsexuals living in similar circumstances to the applicant have previously been raised in several complaints considered by

the Court. In *Rees*, for example, the applicant stated that the 'discrepancy between his apparent and his legal sex [...] caused him embarrassment and humiliation' (cited above, § 34). In his Dissenting Opinion in *Cossey*, Judge Martens stated that the situation in the United Kingdom placed transsexuals in a position whereby revealing the legal 'truth' of their sex meant that they faced 'at least the possibility of very humiliating or even hostile reactions' (cited above, § 3.4). Furthermore, in their Joint Partly Dissenting Opinion in *Sheffield and Horsham*, Judges Bernhardt, Thór Vilhjálmsson, Spielmann, Palm, Wildhaber, Makarczyk and Voicu considered that the legal arrangements in the United Kingdom exposed transsexuals 'to the likelihood of recurring distress and humiliation' (cited above). The Court considers that, like in previous similar complaints, the issue of humiliation is a core aspect of the present complaint.

56. In respect of the applicant's Article 8 complaint, the Court has recognised that the stress and alienation arising from discordance between the gender identity of a transsexual and the status imposed by law, which refuses to recognise gender transition, cannot be regarded as a minor inconvenience arising from a formality. The Court has further recognised that a conflict between social reality and law places a transsexual in an anomalous position, in which he or she may experience feelings of vulnerability, humiliation and anxiety (see paragraph 17 above). However, the Court does not consider that this experience of vulnerability, humiliation and anxiety falls solely within the ambit of the right to respect for private life guaranteed by Article 8. The Court considers that the claims of humiliation raised by the applicant necessitate a consideration under Article 3.

57. In this respect, the Court reiterates that, according to Article 32 of the Convention, its jurisdiction extends 'to all matters concerning the interpretation and application of the Convention'. It further reiterates that it is master of the characterisation to be given in law to the facts of the case and is not bound by the characterisation given by the applicant. By virtue of the *jura novit curia* principle the Court has, for example, considered of its own motion complaints under Articles not relied on by those appearing before it. A complaint is characterised by the facts alleged in it and not merely by the legal grounds or arguments relied on (see *Guerra and Others v Italy*, 19 February 1998, § 44, *Reports of Judgments and Decisions* 1998-I, (1998) 26 EHRR 357).

58. The Court has full jurisdiction only within the scope of the case before it, which is determined by the decision on the admissibility of the application. Within the compass thus delimited, the Court may take cognisance of every question of law arising in the course of the proceedings and concerning the facts submitted (see *Philis v Greece (no. 1)*, 27 August 1991, § 56, Series A no. 209, (1991) 13 EHRR 741). The Court notes that the European Commission of Human Rights (the Commission) unanimously declared the complaint admissible under Articles 8, 12, 13 and 14 of the Convention. The Commission's admissibility decision was taken in light of the presented facts in which the applicant claimed that, as a result of her lack of legal status as a woman, she was 'constantly

facing […] humiliating situations' (Commission decision, 1 December 1997). The Court sees no reason why the scope of the case, determined by the decision on admissibility by the Commission, should preclude a consideration of the applicant's alleged humiliation under Article 3.

2. Applicable general principles

59. As the Court has stated on many occasions, Article 3 enshrines one of the most fundamental values of a democratic society. It prohibits in absolute terms torture or inhuman or degrading treatment or punishment (*Labita v Italy* [GC], no. 26772/95, § 119, ECHR 2000-IV, (2008) 46 EHRR 50).

60. For ill-treatment to fall within the scope of Article 3, it must attain a minimum level of severity. The assessment of this minimum is relative; it depends on all the circumstances of the case, such as the duration of the treatment, its physical and mental effects and, in some cases, the sex, age and state of health of the victim (*İlhan v* Turkey [GC], no. 22277/93, § 84, ECHR 2000-VII, (2002) 34 EHRR 36).

61. The Court has defined torture for the purposes of Article 3 as 'deliberate inhuman treatment causing very serious and cruel suffering' (*Ireland v the United Kingdom*, cited above, § 101). The Court has established that treatment is inhuman if it causes 'either actual bodily injury or intense physical or mental suffering', and degrading if it is such as to 'arouse in the victims feelings of fear, anguish and inferiority capable of humiliating and debasing them' (*Kudła v Poland* [GC], no. 30210/96, § 92, ECHR 2000-XI, (2002) 35 EHRR 11).

62. Although the question of whether the purpose of any treatment was to humiliate or debase the victim is a factor to be taken into account, the absence of any such purpose cannot conclusively rule out finding a violation of Article 3 (see, among other authorities, *V v the United Kingdom* [GC], no. 24888/94, § 71, ECHR 1999-IX).

63. The Court has established that Article 3 creates positive obligations for Contracting States. Specifically relevant to the present complaint is the obligation imposed upon Contracting States by Article 1 of the Convention to secure to everyone within their jurisdiction the rights and freedoms defined in the Convention which, taken together with Article 3, requires States to take measures to ensure that individuals within their jurisdiction are not subjected to torture or inhuman or degrading treatment, including such ill-treatment administered by private individuals (*A v the United Kingdom*, 23 September 1998, § 22, *Reports of Judgments and Decisions* 1998-VI). State responsibility may therefore be engaged where the framework of law fails to provide adequate protection (ibid., § 24) or where the authorities fail to take reasonable steps to avoid a risk of ill-treatment about which they knew or ought to have known (*Osman v the United Kingdom*, 28 October 1998, §§ 115–116, Reports of Judgments and Decisions 1998-VIII, (2000) 29 EHRR 245).

3. Application of general principles

64. The Court considers that it is most appropriate to consider the applicant's complaint under Article 3 in the context of the prohibition of degrading treatment.
65. In this respect, the Court reiterates that for any treatment to fall within the scope of Article 3 it must attain a minimum level of severity. Treatment will be deemed to reach this minimum if it 'humiliates or debases an individual, showing a lack of respect for, or diminishing, his or her human dignity, or arouses feelings of fear, anguish or inferiority capable of breaking an individual's moral and physical resistance' (*Pretty*, cited above, § 52).
66. The Court notes at the outset that the Commission previously expressed the opinion that treatment of an individual in similar circumstances to the applicant's did not amount to degrading treatment under Article 3 (*B v France*, no. 13343/87, Commission report of 6 September 1990, §§ 86–87). However, the Court also notes that, because the Convention is a 'living instrument', the classification of treatment under Article 3 inevitably changes over time (*Selmouni v France* [GC], no. 25803/94, § 101, ECHR 1999-V, (2000) 29 EHRR 403).
67. The chief issues before the Court, therefore, are whether the circumstances of the case – which include, inter alia, the duration of any ill-treatment, its physical or mental effects upon the applicant, and any factors relating to the sex, age and state of health of the applicant – disclose ill-treatment that meets the minimum level of severity required by Article 3 and, if so, whether the Contracting State was under a positive obligation to prevent or protect the applicant from such treatment.
68. With regard to the treatment alleged by the applicant to be humiliating, the Court considers a number of principles to be important. First, the duration of the treatment complaint of by the applicant, if this is calculated from the point that she underwent gender re-assignment surgery in 1990, extended over a period of 12 years. Second, and relatedly, the mental effects resulting from the numerous humiliating experiences complained of by the applicant have been suffered over an extended period of time. And third, the treatment complained of during this period related to the applicant's gender identity, which, as the Court has already established, is an important aspect of personal identity (see paragraph 17 above) and an intimate element of private life (see paragraph 25 above).
69. It is clear, therefore, that over an extensive period of time the applicant has been required to endure a fundamental discordance between her gender identity and the status of sex imposed by law. This has resulted, across numerous contexts and situations, in the applicant repeatedly feeling fearful each time that she has been confronted with the danger of her previous sex being exposed. The Court finds it highly regrettable that knowledge of a transsexual's previous sex can constitute a basis for their ill-treatment and in no way condones either the need to hide or deny information about sex in light of the potential of such ill-treatment. However, the Court cannot but recognise the social reality of the hostility often directed at transsexual persons. In the case of the applicant, it was the continual danger posed by such hostility that underpinned her attempt to mitigate against exposure of her

previous sex by, inter alia, seeking to prevent her colleagues and employer gaining knowledge of her past, forgoing a range of private and public benefits, and deciding not to seek the protection of the police when she was the victim of a crime. For the past 12 years the applicant has therefore endured the mental effect of fear that is the direct outcome of her anomalous position in society.

70. When taken in total, the Court considers that the facts of the case demonstrate that the applicant has been required to live in a legal context for an extended period of time that has repeatedly aroused in her feelings of fear, anguish and inferiority that have been humiliating and debasing to the extent of compromising her moral resistance. The Court therefore concludes that the treatment of the applicant meets the minimum level of severity required by Article 3.

71. In determining whether the ill-treatment of the applicant amounts to a violation of Article 3, the Court regards as decisive the question of whether the Contracting State was under a positive obligation to prevent such treatment. In this respect, the Court notes that the State was, in large part, responsible for the treatment of the applicant. The State has long been aware that sustaining the rigidity of a legal framework that denies transsexuals recognition of their acquired sex results in experiences reported to be humiliating (*Rees*, cited above). The Court considers that an awareness of such humiliation placed an obligation on the State to create a framework of law that provided transsexuals with adequate protection from forms of ill-treatment. The Court cannot but conclude that the State has made no significant legal changes to ensure this framework of protection. Accordingly, there has been a violation of Article 3.

FOR THESE REASONS, THE COURT

1. *Holds* unanimously that there has been a violation of Article 8 of the Convention;
2. *Holds* unanimously that there has been a violation of Article 14 taken in conjunction with Article 8 of the Convention;
3. *Holds* unanimously that there has been a violation of Article 12 of the Convention;
4. *Holds* unanimously that there has been a violation of Article 3 of the Convention.

Reflections

What Would the Consequences of Our Judgment Be?

In re-drafting the *Goodwin* judgment we experienced a heady mix of hope and humility. To stand as a convincing account of what a feminist European Court of Human Rights chamber might have achieved in this case, we were careful to follow the Court's methodological and analytical approaches, and what we have written is, we believe, recognisable as a judgment from that court. However, the cost of adopting this, perhaps, conservative approach to our task is apparent and, ultimately, we sense that what we have achieved is rather more modest than we initially envisaged. Nevertheless, our judgment indicates what a progressive Court might achieve. At the very least, our judgment provides an opportunity to consider the Court's approach to sex and gender identity, which has often been characterised by a refusal to challenge dominant social norms.

Our first achievement was to directly challenge the legally-constructed, rigid binary gender system that was the cause of Ms Goodwin's painful experiences.[1] As Anthony has argued: 'If rights were not allocated on the basis of sex, then deciding who qualifies as a "man" and a "woman" would become more of an academic exercise'.[2] The language of gender and sex proved to be highly contested in the drafting of our judgment. The process of writing demonstrated just how imprecisely these words are used in the Court's judgments. We attempted to ameliorate this linguistic looseness, but in its place we recognise that we may have introduced some linguistic knots. Nevertheless, our judgment challenges the binary approach to gender that is engrained in the Court's case law and relies on a richer and more fluid approach to gender in which the trans applicant is no longer seen to have the task of demonstrating that they have satisfactorily met the criteria for transitioning from one sex to another. In practical term, this addresses the strain placed on applicants following the real *Goodwin* judgment to demonstrate the 'truth' of their transition; to demonstrate, often through their bodies, that they belong in their new gender. The Court's binary approach has had particular negative consequences for bodily autonomy (which feminists have long fought for): trans men and women have borne the burden of sterilisation requirements[3] and gender reassignment surgery,[4] which the Court is just now beginning to address.

[1] For a fuller critique of mandatory, binary gender system, see DA Gonzalez-Salzberg, 'The Accepted Transsexual and the Absent Transgender: A Queer Reading of the Regulation of Sex/Gender by the European Court of Human Rights' (2014) 29 *American University Law Review* 797.

[2] DJ Anthony, 'Caught in the Middle: Transsexual Marriage and the Disconnect Between Sex and Legal Sex' (2012) 21 *Texas Journal of Women and the Law* 153.

[3] *Y Y v Turkey*, no 14793/08, ECHR 2015 (extracts).

[4] *A P, Garcon, and Nicot v France*, Application nos 79885/12, 52471/13 & 52596/13, 6 April 2017 (extracts).

In the words of Gonzalez-Salzberg, '[m]edical and legal discourses constructed the truth towards which the transsexual's expectations have crashed'.[5] However, the approach that we take to gender in our judgment is not uncontroversial. For many trans people, a binary understanding of gender is appropriate: their demand is simply to have the truth of their gender recognised. How satisfied can we be, then, with our feminist intervention that ultimately may be seen to exclude trans women and men having their truth recognised? Further, we were acutely aware both of certain feminist critiques of the expansion of the category of woman[6] and of the central importance that some feminists attach to that category.[7] These were not issues that could be dismissed lightly, and indeed we spent several hours debating them, both as a chamber and among the wider project participants.

A key outcome of our judgment is that under Article 12, marriage would be open to any two adults, regardless of their sex or gender. In its *Cossey* judgment, the Court held that 'attachment to the traditional concept of marriage provides sufficient reason for the continued adoption of biological criteria'.[8] The Court has since loosened its belief in the innateness of gender, but not its belief in the essentially heterosexual character of marriage. Consequently, our judgment makes an important contribution to the debate about extending marriage rights to same-sex couples, which the Court, in spite of the considerable steps it has taken in recent years towards the recognition of same sex relationships, has not yet achieved. Were our judgment adopted by the actual Court, trans applicants married in their assigned gender to an opposite-sex partner would no longer face the need to obtain a divorce before having their new gender recognised.[9]

Finding the UK government in violation of Article 3 in our judgment for the treatment that Christine Goodwin experienced probably felt like the most fantastic aspect of our judgment, in terms of how far it expanded the scope of the Court's current jurisprudence; and yet, within our chamber considering the applicant's case under this article was a source of little disagreement. We all felt compelled to insist upon acknowledging the harm that non-recognition, and the resulting stigma and discrimination, does to trans people. Law plays a key role in the stigmatisation of minority groups. The Court has failed to pay sufficient attention to the harm that results: pathologisation; exclusion; pressure to have corrective surgery; denial of desired corrective surgery; financial hardship; lack of support

[5] n 1 above, 809.

[6] R Riley-Cooper, 'Why Self-Identification Shouldn't be the Only Thing that Defines our Gender' *The Conversation* (13 May 2016). Available at: www.theconversation.com/why-self-identification-shouldnt-be-the-only-thing-that-defines-our-gender-57924.

[7] G Greer, *The Whole Woman* (London, Black Swan, 2007); J Raymond, *Transsexual Empire: The Making of the She-male* (London, The Women's Press, 1980); S Jeffreys, *Gender Hurts: A Feminist Analysis of the Politics of Transgenderism* (Abingdon, Routledge, 2014).

[8] *Cossey v the United Kingdom*, 27 September 1990, Series A no 184, para 46, (1991) 13 EHRR 622.

[9] cf *Hämäläinen v Finland*, [GC] Application no 37359/09, 16 July 2014.

for relationships. If our approach were adopted by the Court, it would open the door to further attention to be paid to the connection between the State's positive obligations and this seldom-used article.

Finally, we demonstrated how the Court might avoid falling back on consensus analysis. The furthering of LGBT rights claims before the Court has frequently depended upon the Court following the social and legal developments in member states. While this might make jurisprudential developments in Strasbourg more palatable, those developments also become stripped of ideological and ethical content.[10] The alternative is a more activist Court that seeks to take a clear stance on questions perceived to be sensitive, and to outline and defend its understanding of the principles upon which the Convention is founded.

What Did the Experience Reveal About the Structures and Norms of International Law?

We found international law, as a manifestation of legal normativity, to be an essentially anti-queer tool.[11] The art of judging was, in fact, the art of demarcation. A feminist method was a potentially useful tool to challenge the structural biases of international law,[12] but it was clear to us that those tools are rather blunt. In so far as progressing feminist aims are concerned, the outcome of our judgment is perhaps questionable. We were left with an abiding sense that the Court is a rather limited tool for (trans) women. Perhaps this was something of a failure of imagination on our part. It may also be the case that law is not the appropriate field for achieving radical changes.

How Was the Process of Delivering 'Judgment' Experienced?

Delivering judgment brought into sharp focus the conflicting commitments that we juggled as 'judges', and the process was experienced by our chamber as deeply political and driven primarily by ideological concerns. In terms of ideological commitments, the feminist, trans rights, queer and LGBT rights agendas that, to varying degrees, informed our individual approaches to the judgment were in conflict. To judge was to choose between positions that we would ordinarily – by preference and instinct – adopt a more nuanced position in relation to. We are

[10] For a critical discussion of consensus analysis, see M D'Amico and C Nardocci, 'LGBT Rights and the Way Forward: The Evolution of the Case Law of the ECTHR in Relation to Transgender Individuals' Identity' (2016) 17 *ERA Forum* 191.

[11] CF Stychin, *Law's Desire: Sexuality and the Limits of Justice* (Chicago IL, Routledge, 1995) 156.

[12] D Otto, 'Lost in Translation: Re-scripting the Sexed Subjects of International Human Rights Law' in Anne Orford (ed), *International Law and its Others* (Cambridge, Cambridge University Press, 2006) 356.

acutely aware, for instance, that some members of the trans community would find our judgment a disappointment. We are also aware that some feminists would have hoped for a clearer engagement with questions of womanhood.

Finally, our thoughts turn to Christine Goodwin herself. In the ideological and legal territory on which our discussions took place, the applicant herself was, in truth, a rather distant and shadowy figure in our discussions. The formalities of legal discourse served to create a distance between our discussions and the applicant, the real person at the heart of the case. Christine Goodwin actually passed away in December 2014, just as this project began. Her case before the Court stands as testimony to her bravery in challenging legal norms, striking a path to Strasbourg, using her own name – insisting that 'she had nothing to be ashamed of'.[13] It is, however, worth recalling the personal costs to applicants of taking a case to the European Court of Human Rights. In a touching eulogy, Christine Goodwin's daughter wrote that after her success in Strasbourg, her dad 'was broke, the road to recognition had taken their toll physically, mentally and financially'.[14]

[13] 'Trans rights trail blazer Christine Goodwin passed away' *Transgender Europe* (8 January 2015). Available at: tgeu.org/trans-rights-trail-blazer-christine-goodwin-passed-away/.

[14] C Allington, 'Christine Goodwin – Trans Pioneer but Also My Daddy' *Huffpost Lifestyle* (10 February 2015). Available at: www.huffingtonpost.co.uk/clare-allington/christine-goodwin_b_6629108.html.

8

Leyla Şahin v Turkey

AMEL ALGHRANI, AMAL ALI AND JILL MARSHALL

Authors' Note

Judgment in *Leyla Şahin v Turkey*,[1] a case concerning a Muslim woman's freedom of religious expression, was initially delivered in June 2004 by the Chamber of the European Court of Human Rights (ECtHR); the case was subsequently referred to the Grand Chamber (GC) who heard it in May 2005 and delivered its judgment on 10 November 2005. The Court considered Article 9 (1) on the right to freedom of religious expression and Article 2 of Protocol 1 on the right to education to be engaged. With little analysis as to the reason for its decision, the majority of the Court found that there had been no violations of these provisions. The reasoning rests on whether the legal restriction preventing the applicant wearing her Islamic headscarf at a university in Turkey was necessary in a democratic society. At the relevant time, university students were not permitted to wear the Islamic headscarf on campus due to the government's secularist policy. The majority of the Court agreed that the restrictions were necessary in a democratic society, placing emphasis on Turkey's margin of appreciation and its ideas of secularism and gender equality. The Belgian judge, Judge Tulkens, dissented. She said that gender equality needed to be reconciled with the concept of personal autonomy as developed by the Court in its interpretation of Article 8's right to respect for our private life. As we discuss further in the 'Reflection' section later in this chapter, we came to the Judgment sympathetic to this position. Marshall had written a case note criticising the Judgment shortly after its publication.[2] She had written further on the 'headscarf cases' at the European Court of Human Rights and on the development of 'respect for one's private life' into a right to autonomy, identity and integrity more generally.[3]

[1] *Leyla Şahin v Turkey*, no 44774/98, ECHR 2005-XI, (2007) 44 EHRR 5.

[2] J Marshall, 'Case Review: Freedom of Religious Expression and Gender Equality: Sahin v Turkey' (2006) 69 *Modern Law Review* 452.

[3] J Marshall, 'Conditions for Freedom? European Human Rights Law and the Islamic Headscarf Debate' (2008) 30 *Human Rights Quarterly* 631; J Marshall, 'Women's Right to Autonomy and Identity in European Human Rights Law: Manifesting One's Religion' (2008) 14 *Res Publica* 177;

When the GC's original Judgment was delivered in 2005, the Court turned to its previous case law. The most pertinent perhaps was *Dahlab v Switzerland*.[4] That case, unlike *Şahin*, involved a workplace employment situation with a primary school teacher wearing a hijab when teaching five-year-old pupils at a state school. The relevant Swiss ban on schoolteachers wearing religious symbols was found not to violate the Convention. The Court had highlighted what they referred to as the potential proselytising effect of the Islamic headscarf. They found that wearing it 'was hard to square with'[5] tolerance and pluralism. At the time, we found this language to be astonishing, and it does not reflect the current European Court of Human Rights position.[6] The *Şahin* Judgment, unlike *Dahlab*, came after the 9/11 attacks in New York. In the summer of 2005, there had been attacks on the London transport system with the death of 52 people and the injury of hundreds in the 7/7 bombings. There was a heightened atmosphere of disquiet in many quarters over the effects of the wars in Afghanistan and Iraq, an ever-rumbling tension in the Middle East, and increasing numbers of refugees, asylum seekers and migrants into Europe. This heightened atmosphere of disquiet included riots with fires burning in Strasbourg when the Judgment was delivered. Is this context relevant, and was it relevant to the Judgment delivered by the majority of the Court?

In our view, to some extent echoing the observations of the *Bozkurt* chamber in this collection, the most relevant factor was that this was a case against Turkey. Turkey has an overwhelming population of Muslims – about 99 per cent of the population. Since the creation of the republic, it has sought to strictly separate public life from religion and has a Constitution seeking to uphold equality between men and women and the secular nature of the Turkish state. Turkey has changed in many ways since 2005, including allowing the wearing of the Islamic headscarf on university campuses.[7] However, the world we live in today is even more dangerous and difficult in terms of European responses to the conflicts which are now much more widespread within the Middle East and North Africa. In the current political climate, where there is any perceived link to Islamic fundamentalism, Convention rights that are invoked are likely to be interpreted narrowly.

A look at the national context is insightful here. Turkey has one of the lowest numbers of women in the workforce in comparison with mainland Europe, with only 25 per cent of women in employment as of 2006. 49 per cent of these women

J Marshall, *Personal Freedom Through Human Rights Law?: Autonomy, Identity and Integrity under the European Convention on Human Rights* (Leiden, Martinus Nijhoff, 2009).

[4] *Dahlab v Switzerland* (dec), no 42393/98, ECHR 2001-V.

[5] ibid, 13.

[6] See *S A S v France* [GC], no 43835/11, ECHR 2014 (extracts). See J Marshall, '*S.A.S. v France: Burqa* Bans and the Control or Empowerment of Identities' (2015) 15 *Human Rights Law Review* 377.

[7] Efforts had been made in the late 1980s to permit the headscarf on campus but this had been declared unconstitutional by the Turkish Constitutional Court. Since the *Şahin* judgment, in 2008 an amendment was made to the Constitution to permit them. However, this was annulled by the Turkish Constitutional Court. Now though almost all universities have abandoned the official prohibition on headscarves.

work in agriculture in rural areas, 37.1 per cent work in the service sector and 15 per cent work in industry.[8] Many of these jobs are part-time, temporary or seasonal and include no access to state benefits.[9] Certain claims have been made that the reason for such a low composition of women in the workforce is as a result of the cultural structure of Turkey and, more specifically, as a result of household and childcare duties, but research on a national scale has proven this to be incorrect.[10] Instead, it seems one of the reasons is the headscarf ban in employment. Between 1998 and 2002, 5000 female civil servants were dismissed for wearing a headscarf to work without any offer of alternative employment. This has spread to the private sector.[11]

Ali noted during her PhD research how in the *Şahin* Judgment the Turkish government argued they took gender equality seriously, yet the lack of research documenting the incidence and prevalence of violence against women and girls in Turkish society limits the response of the Turkish government. Her analysis of the available research demonstrates that social tolerance for violence in police stations, public prosecution offices, courts and healthcare facilities is widespread.[12] Specific violent acts towards women in Turkey can include 'virginity controls' and 'honour killings', both of which occur in the private sphere as a method of controlling social ethics and the women's behaviour in the name of 'honour'.[13] The legal rights of women are routinely not adequately enforced, and both women and girls are exposed to cultural, sexual and psychological harassment.[14] Furthermore, women's experience of violence and any power dynamics in their relationships with men affect their behaviour in decision-making in the family. It is significant that religious, cultural and sociological doctrine has been used to legitimate the subordination of women. However, restricting the right to education of Muslim women is not, in our view, a useful response to the situation. It is important to note that at the core of these studies, it was emphasised that women with lower levels of education were more likely to be dependent on male relatives.[15] As will be highlighted in the judgment, education is central in order to promote the social mobility of women.

It is therefore important that the Court re-conceptualises and re-contextualises the problems that occur through limiting the right to manifest a religious belief of women who wear the headscarf. The jurisprudence of the Court and the way

[8] JB White, *Islamist Mobilisation in Turkey: A Study in Vernacular Politics* (Seattle WA, University of Washington Press, 2002) 29.

[9] ibid.

[10] ibid.

[11] ibid.

[12] While participating in this project Amal was completing a PhD at the University of Sheffield in which she examined the intersection of law, gender and religion.

[13] B Erci, 'Women's Efficiency in Decision Making and their Perception of their Status in the Family' (2003) 20(1) *Public Health Nurse* 6.

[14] ibid.

[15] ibid.

in which plurality is managed has left women at the margins by limiting their ability to access tertiary education and the workforce in a misguided attempt to protect gender equality. In our re-writing of the judgment, we sought to bring our individual views on feminist legal methods and scholarship. We saw the potential in reinterpreting notions of autonomy and freedom of expression to see these not in conflict with gender equality but as holistically in harmony with it. That is, we aim to interpret women's freedom or autonomy taking into account the social construction of choices in an unequal world; but the starting point must not be to ban women's behaviours on the basis that they stem from 'false consciousness'. Such a reaction penalises women and fails to take them seriously as persons in their own right with a capacity and ability to plan their own lives. As such, it is patronising and against liberal principles of equality, freedom, rights and the rule of law. Instead we need an empowering, inclusive, notion of equality that starts by acknowledging the existing choices made by women to wear that which they say they want to wear.

In writing this judgment, we addressed our disappointment in the original *Şahin* judgment, which upheld the Turkish government's ban on women in universities wearing the headscarf. The effect of the original judgment is that Muslim women who chose to wear the garment are denied access to Higher Education, or placed in the invidious position of going through higher education dressed in a manner that offends their conscience. We depart from the original judgment which we believe was overly deferential to the Turkish government. That original judgment was, in our view, wrong in holding that the headscarf ban was justified to protect the rights and freedoms of others by ensuring that female students who wear the headscarf do not coerce those who do not (just by wearing it), and thus protects the rights of women within a largely Muslim context and encourages pluralism. Further, the original judgment was wrong in deciding that the ban was necessary in order to protect the principle of secularism which guarantees democratic values; and lastly it was also wrong in its interpretation that there are differing restrictions on this type of religious dress for university students within Europe. Instead we argue there was an unjustified violation with the applicant's fundamental human rights under Articles 8, 9 and 10 and Article 2 of Protocol 1. The reasoning that women who wear a headscarf may be a threat to public order, or to women who do not wear it, is unsupported, unfounded and rather tenuous. To uphold the Turkish ban compromises the right to education and democracy by forcing those wishing to practise their religious beliefs, such as Ms Şahin, out of education. Ultimately women (and men) should not be discriminated or excluded from education on the grounds of their dress or manifesting their religious beliefs.

In interpreting the relevant provisions of the Convention in this way, our judgment is one which leads to Ms Şahin, and others like her, being free to wear what she wants as an adult. In this way, our Judgment differs from the majority in the actual *Şahin* judgment. It shares common ground with Judge Tulkens, the dissenting Judge in the real case, in her emphasis on personal autonomy, but tries to develop and expand the logic behind these issues and seeks to cover more ground. To represent a spectrum of feminist thought, in our chamber we decided to write a 'devil's advocate' dissenting judgment by an imaginary additional chamber member. This character is entirely fictitious and is described in our Judgment as *ad hoc* judge, Dost Düşman Ayirt Etmek. That dissent makes clear that there are feminists who take the view that the headscarf is a sign of inequality, even oppression, and as such women need protection from such patriarchal religious and cultural practices: in the vein of Jean-Jacques Rousseau, they will be 'forced to be free'. We are opposed to this approach and this is reflected in that part of the judgment dealing with adults' personal choices.

JUDGMENT

LEYLA ŞAHIN v TURKEY

(Application no. 44774/98)

The Grand Chamber of the European Court of Human Rights consisting of:

Jill Marshall (President of Chamber), Amel Alghrani and Amal Ali.
Joined by *ad hoc* judge, Dost Düşman Ayirt Etmek.

10 November 2005

THE FACTS

1. Leyla Şahin is a practising Muslim. She wears the Islamic headscarf, covering her head but not her face. In February 1998 she was in her fifth year as a Medical student at the University of Istanbul. Due to the University's Vice-Chancellor's actions regulating students' admission to the university campus on the basis of religious clothing, including the Islamic headscarf, names and numbers of 'offending' students were not to be added to the lists of registered students, and procedures were set out for non-compliance. Within a few months, the applicant had been denied access to a written examination, refused enrolment onto a course, refused admission to a lecture and refused entrance to a further written examination. She lodged an application for an order to set aside this circular on human rights grounds. The Istanbul Administrative Court dismissed her application in March 1999 on the basis that the relevant statute empowered the Vice-Chancellor to regulate students' dress to maintain order. The Supreme Administrative Court dismissed her appeal in April 2001. Ms Şahin suffered as a result. In September 1999, she felt she had to leave her own country to complete her education while being true to herself, her identity and her beliefs. She enrolled at the University of Vienna where there were no restrictions on the wearing of the Islamic headscarf.
2. The events leading to the Vice-Chancellor's circular of 1998 started in the early 1980s when the relevant Higher-Education Authority's circulars banning headscarves in lecture theatres were held lawful by the Supreme Administrative Court in December 1984. A further transitional provision of 1988 made modern dress compulsory inside higher-education institutions but the wearing of a veil or headscarf permissible for religious reasons. However, the Turkish Constitutional Court (TCC) declared this provision unconstitutional in March 1989. It was seen as being contrary to Articles of the Turkish Constitution ensuring secularism, equality before the law, freedom of religion, and the principle of sexual equality. The TCC stressed that outside the private sphere of individual

conscience, freedom to manifest one's religion could be restricted on public order grounds to defend the principle of secularism. A further transitional provision came into force which was noted by the TCC in July 1991 to not allow headscarves to be worn in higher-education institutions. At the University of Istanbul, campaigns by female students wishing to have the freedom to wear the headscarf led to the Vice-Chancellor issuing memoranda, culminating in the circular of February 1998. The Vice-Chancellor's powers emanated from section 13 of the Higher Education Act.

3. The applicant wears the headscarf out of her desire to comply strictly with her Islamic faith duties as she sees them. She submitted that the ban on wearing the Islamic headscarf in institutions of higher education constituted an unjustified interference with her rights under Article 9 (the right to freedom of religion and particularly in this instance the right to manifest that religion), Article 8 (the right to a private and family life), Article 10 (the right to freedom of expression), Article 14 (the prohibition of discrimination) and Article 2 of Protocol 1 (the right to education).

4. The Chamber Judgment found that the regulations interfered with the applicant's right to manifest her religion. It then found the interference to be prescribed by law and pursued a legitimate aim under Article 9 (2). It was justified in principle and proportionate to the aims pursued and could therefore be regarded as having been 'necessary in a democratic society' (*Leyla Şahin v Turkey*, no. 44774/98, § 66-116, 29 June 2004, (2005) 41 EHRR 8.).

5. The Court must consider whether the applicant's rights under these provisions were interfered with and, if any were, whether the interference was 'prescribed by law', pursued a legitimate aim and was 'necessary in a democratic society' within the meaning of subparagraph two of each of the relevant parts of the Convention.

THE COURT'S ASSESSMENT

6. This Court usually proceeds on the basis that, insofar as the law is criticised by individuals like the applicant because it prevents adherence to required religious practice, the issues call to be analysed mainly with regard to the freedom to manifest one's religion or beliefs pursuant to Article 9 (see, for example, *Kokkinakis v Greece*, 25 May 1993, Series A no. 260-A, (1994) 17 EHRR 397). Whilst this is important, we consider the provisions the applicant alleges to be violated to be of equal importance. We consider it necessary, as well as more coherent, to examine and interpret these together as a whole. That is, in a way that interprets the provisions together so they do not conflict with each other. We therefore take the view that, rather than examining each provision in turn, we primarily examine this application from the perspective of the concepts or values that need to be protected.

7. The underlying purpose of the human rights set forth in the Convention is respect for human dignity and individual freedom. We aim to interpret the

applicant's complaints in the light of these principles, and, in doing so, this Court considers that secularism, equality and liberty should be harmonised and not weighed against one another.

8. The Court is of the view that personal choices as to an individual's desired appearance, whether in public or in private places, relate to the expression of his or her personality and thus fall within the notion of private life. It considers, like the European Commission on Human Rights (see in particular the decisions of *McFeeley and Others v the United Kingdom* no. 8317/78, 15 May 1980, § 83, (1981) 3 EHRR 161; and *Kara v the United Kingdom*, no. 36528/97, 22 October 1998, (1999) 27 EHRR CD 272), that choice of clothing is covered by Article 8. A measure emanating from a public authority, which restricts a choice of this kind, will therefore in principle constitute an interference with the exercise of the right to respect for private life within the meaning of Article 8 of the Convention. Consequently, a restriction on wearing clothing designed to cover the head falls under Article 8 of the Convention.

9. Since the 1970s and early 1980s, this Court has expressed respect for private life as comprising the right to establish and to develop relationships with other human beings, especially in the emotional field, for the development and fulfilment of one's own personality (*X v Iceland*, no. 6825/74, Commission decision of 18 May 1976, Decisions and Reports 5, p. 86; *Brüggemann and Scheuten v Germany*, no. 6959/75, Commission decision of 19 May 1976, Decisions and Reports 5, p. 103). Limiting the notion of private life to an 'inner circle' in which the individual may live his own personal life as he chooses and excluding entirely the outside world not encompassed within that circle, has been held to be too restrictive (see *Niemietz v Germany*, 16 December 1992, Series A no. 251-B, (1993) 16 EHRR 97.

10. In *Pretty v the United Kingdom* (no. 2346/02, § 71, ECHR 2002-III, (2002) 35 EHRR 1), the Court described the notion of personal autonomy as an important principle underlying the interpretation of its guarantees. Private life clearly encompasses a person's physical and psychological integrity and is stated to be primarily intended to ensure the development, without outside interference, of the personality of each individual in his or her relations with other human beings (*Von Hannover v Germany*, no. 59320/00, ECHR 2004-VI, (2005) 40 EHRR 1). This right to autonomy and personality includes doing so in relation to others and to be free to live the life of our own choosing (*Christine Goodwin v the United Kingdom* [GC], no. 28957/95, ECHR 2002-VI, (2002) 35 EHRR 18).

11. Therefore, paternalism runs counter to the case law of this Court, which has developed a real right to personal autonomy on the basis of Article 8. This personal autonomy, in line with the preamble of the Convention, is consistent with respecting human dignity and individual freedom in the sense that we respect the individual applicant's own subjective view of the good life as she herself sees it, and not as a government or as a Court finds it. As she is an adult woman of sound mind, we start from the position that she is deemed to be capable of making these decisions for herself.

12. The applicant herself maintains that wearing the headscarf is a choice she freely makes as an adult. For the reasons set out above, we consider Article 8(1) to be engaged. She also maintains that she wears the headscarf as a matter of religious obedience and 'recognised practice' and that she has been prevented from attending the educational establishment of her choice and has had to leave it because of restrictions placed on her freedoms by the university. In wearing the headscarf, she is obeying a religious precept and manifesting her desire to comply with the duties imposed on her by the Islamic faith. This decision may therefore be regarded as motivated or inspired by a religion or belief and thus any restrictions constitute an interference with the applicant's right to manifest her religion under Article 9 (1). As she was prevented from attending lectures and examinations and from the university itself, her right to education is rendered ineffective and therefore we consider Article 2 of Protocol 1 to be engaged. With regard to Article 14, we note that the applicant did not provide detailed particulars in her pleadings before us. It is the Court's view that Articles 8 and 9 and Article 2 of Protocol 1 are engaged and that there has been an interference with these. We now have to examine whether such interference is prescribed by law, follows a legitimate aim and is necessary in a democratic society.

(a) *'Prescribed by Law'*

13. Having considered the submissions, the Court reiterates its settled case law that the impugned measure should have a basis in domestic law, that it should be accessible to the persons concerned and formulated with sufficient precision to enable them to foresee the consequences which a given action may entail and to regulate their conduct (see *Gorzelik and Others v Poland* [GC], no. 44158/98, § 64 ECHR 2004-I, (2005) 40 EHRR 4). The Court finds that there was a legal basis in Turkish law for the interference, that it was accessible, and that it can be considered to be sufficiently precise to satisfy the requirement of foreseeability. It would have been clear to the applicant from the moment she entered Istanbul University that there were restrictions on wearing the Islamic headscarf and that, from 23 February 1998, she was liable to be refused access to lectures and examinations if she continued to do so.

(b) *Legitimate aim*

14. The Court is able to accept that the interference primarily pursued the legitimate aim of protecting the rights and freedoms of others and of protecting public order, a point that is not in issue between the parties.

(c) *'Necessary in a democratic society'*

15. Prior to this case, European human rights institutions have found that bans on the Islamic headscarf were compatible with individual rights under the Convention. In *Karaduman v Turkey* (no. 16278/90, Commission decision of 3 May 1993,

Decisions and Reports 74, p. 93), the applicant, like Ms Şahin, had been a university student in Turkey. Having completed her education, she wished to graduate and obtain her degree certificate. However, as she wore the Islamic headscarf, she was denied her degree certificate unless and until she submitted a photograph of herself with her head uncovered as required by university disciplinary regulations. She refused to remove her headscarf and submit such a photograph. The European Commission agreed with the TCC's decision to uphold the ban in public institutions and found no violation of Ms Karaduman's rights.

16. In *Dahlab v Switzerland* ((dec.), no. 42393/98, ECHR 2001-V), Ms Dahlab also wore a headscarf. She was a convert to Islam and a state primary school teacher. She was prohibited from wearing the headscarf in her employment. She taught infants in the age range of 4–8 years old. She had been wearing the headscarf for six years before this prohibition came into effect, during which time there were no complaints made, including from pupils or parents. In the domestic litigation, her claims were dismissed with the courts placing emphasis on the neutrality of teachers as state school employees and the incursion into the public sphere of her private religious beliefs. This applicant brought her claims under Article 9 and 14 of the Convention. Her Article 14 claim was based on arguments that a Muslim man would not be prohibited from teaching in the way that she had been.

17. Having regard to the circumstances of the case and the terms of the relevant authorities' decisions, the Court found that the relevant Swiss provisions were prescribed by law and pursued a legitimate aim under Article 9(2): namely the protection of the rights and freedoms of others, and the maintenance of public safety and public order. In finding such interference necessary in a democratic society, the margin of appreciation was emphasised and the question asked whether the restriction was justified in principle: is it relevant and sufficient and proportionate to the legitimate aim pursued? The Court held that in determining whether an appropriate balance has been struck, it is necessary to take into account the rights and freedoms of others. In the Court's view in *Dahlab:*

> It cannot be denied outright that the wearing of a headscarf might have some kind of proselytising effect, seeing that is appears to be imposed on women by the precept which is laid down in the Koran and which, as the Federal Court [in Switzerland] noted, is hard to square with the principle of gender equality. It therefore appears difficult to reconcile the wearing of an Islamic headscarf with the message of tolerance, respect for others, and above all, equality and non-discrimination that all teachers in a democratic society must convey to their pupils. (cited above, p.13)

18. In *Dahlab*, the Court expressly noted that teachers are important role models especially when, as in the applicant's case, the pupils were very young children attending compulsory primary school. In this case the Court upheld the Swiss decision to prohibit a primary school teacher from wearing a headscarf in the classroom. In their analysis, the Government stated that the measure prohibiting

the applicant from wearing a headscarf in her capacity as a teacher at a State school did not amount to interference with her right to freedom of religion. Further that it was compulsory in state schools to observe the principle of denominational neutrality and there was need to preserve such pluralism, particularly when the pupils came from different cultural backgrounds. The Court balanced the applicant's right to manifest her religious belief, against the small children's right to neutrality in the classroom. The Court found, after taking into consideration the ages of the schoolchildren that Switzerland had not exceeded its margin of appreciation. While certain restrictions may potentially be justified for teachers of small children (although this Court does not necessarily agree on this), primary school teachers are in a distinctly different position to teachers of older children and university students. This court is of the view that teachers of small children wearing clothing of certain kinds including the Islamic headscarf should be free to wear those clothes. We do not find any contradiction between wearing the headscarf and conveying equality and non-discrimination to young children. We are of the view that diversity in cultures and beliefs should be celebrated in the classroom as it shows that different religious groups are free to manifest their religious beliefs equally. The Court finds that *Dahlab* significantly differs from the present case where the applicant is a University Student. No other state has a ban on wearing religious symbols by adult students in university education.

ADULTS' PERSONAL CHOICES

19. The Court acknowledges the impact that social conditions have on the formation of who we are, on our personalities. The ability of one's personality to flourish in tune with the identity one chooses for oneself, including living in accordance with one's religion and community values, is a right that needs to be safeguarded by this Court.

20. It seems inappropriate to this Court for European democracies to espouse the idea that the Islamic headscarf is not a free choice for adult women. Some argue that these are 'adaptive preferences', meaning that they are shaped by a patriarchal religion and the fathers and brothers related to the women involved. As such, wearing the garment is seen as a result of oppression. This Court takes the view that the existence of social conditions enabling free informed choices to be made is part of the goal of justice and gender equality. It is part of the positive obligations on States to have such conditions. However, these goals will not be met by legal bans and restrictions on clothing which adult women say they freely choose to wear themselves. People become who they are through and in communities and relationships, including chosen religious affiliations. The choice of such affiliations does not depend upon approval by the majority. This interpretation involves a reconciliation and harmonisation of gender equality with notions of identity and autonomy.

21. A personality is not developed through being left alone, but is developed in ways that allow for the free formation of informed choices when persons are treated

as equals; entitled to equal respect and equal concern;[1] and given the necessary prerequisites to live their own lives, a life of meaning and value to them.[2] Choices are made in contexts, but are still made by the particular people concerned. The choices made by individuals may be unpalatable to other people but it is not the place of human rights law to prevent them from being made. Feminist work on autonomy and choice shows the importance of understanding that autonomy is a capacity that is built through the maintenance of supportive and interdependent relationships and a strengthening of self-esteem.[3] As Emily Jackson says:

> … our choices are, of course, shaped by multiple external influences, but they are the only choices we have, and they are therefore of critical importance to our sense of self … our sense of being the author of our own actions is profoundly valuable to us.[4]

Ms Şahin, like many other women like her, says she freely wishes to wear the Islamic headscarf as part of her own sense of self and it is not the role of a Court of law to judge the validity of these choices other than to respect and uphold them when they are made by adult women.

22. This is also in line with other Council of Europe organs that stress the importance of personal autonomy as a human rights principle. For example, in a Recommendation of the Committee of Ministers on a coherent policy for people with disabilities, provision is sought to be made for the disabled, inter alia, '[i]n order to avoid or at least alleviate difficult situations … and to develop personal autonomy.' (see Committee of Ministers Recommendation No R (92) 6, adopted 9 April 1992).

23. In viewing these provisions holistically, we consider it important that women, particularly university students, are permitted to experiment with different ways of looking and appearing in public in ways that encourage their own sense of identity, of who they are, to come into being. This interconnects Articles 8, 9 and 10 through a right to personality and identity. Considering the issue this way ensures that women are listened to, taken seriously, acknowledged as persons in their own right to be accorded respect in the European democracies in which we live. Young women need to be encouraged to think for themselves and to develop their critical self-awareness, self-confidence and self-esteem. This applicant is an adult. She says she freely makes this choice to wear the Islamic headscarf and that no one forces her or tells her to wear it.

24. Further, we disagree with the remarks made by the court in *Dahlab*. Wearing the veil has many meanings. It is not our role to say if it is proselytising or if it

[1] R Dworkin, *Taking Rights Seriously* (Cambridge MA, Harvard University Press, 1977).

[2] R Norman, 'Does Equality Destroy Liberty?' in K Graham (ed), *Contemporary Political Philosophy: Radical Studies* (Cambridge, Cambridge University Press, 1982).

[3] See J Nedelsky, 'Reconceiving Autonomy' (1989) 1 *Yale Journal of Law and Feminism* 7.

[4] E Jackson, *Regulating Reproduction: Law, Technology and Autonomy* (Oxford, Hart Publishing, 2001), especially 3–8.

is a sign of humiliation, subordination or oppression by a patriarchal religion or community.
25. Whilst we have still to attain a gender equal world, the starting place is to listen and respect the choices of adult women including those choices with which not everyone will personally agree. We remain strongly of the view that it is not the role of a human rights court to tell women or any adult how to dress.

EDUCATION

26. The first sentence of Article 2 of Protocol No 1 provides that no one shall be denied the right to education. Although the provision makes no mention of higher education, there is nothing to suggest that it does not apply to all levels of education, including higher education.
27. Preventing access to education may pose a greater threat to democracy. Ironically, extremism is more likely to be caused by a lack of education and isolation, non-integration with other faiths, and by staying outside of mainstream education. It is also important to note that the applicant wore the headscarf while studying medicine for four years at university, without being seen as disruptive. We are told that the applicant comes from a traditional family of practising Muslims and considers it her duty to wear the Islamic headscarf. She did not promote Islam, nor did she coerce other women to wear the headscarf. She stated throughout the case that she had no intention to protest, pressure, provoke or proselytize other university students into wearing the headscarf and in fact supports secularism. There is no evidence she was ostentatious, aggressive, exerted pressure to provoke a reaction, proselytised, spread propaganda, or undermined the personal convictions of others. Indeed, the Turkish Government did not argue that this was the case, and there was no evidence before the Court to suggest that the applicant had any such intention. Further, it has not been demonstrated that there was any disruption in teaching or in everyday life at the university, or any disorderly conduct, as a result of the applicant's decision to wear the headscarf.
28. We do not want to compromise the right to education and democracy by forcing women who wish to practise their religious beliefs, such as the applicant, out of education. Not all may be able to afford to relocate abroad to complete their studies as she did.
29. The court should not be misguided into making false assumptions regarding women who wear the headscarf. It is incorrect to assume that the prohibition on wearing the Islamic headscarf obliged students to choose between education and religion and discriminated between believers and non-believers. A headscarf alone does not determine whether one is a believer or not. The applicant is only stating that whilst some students in various attires could get an education, only those wearing the headscarf were discriminated against. It is important to note that while Article 9 does not protect every act motivated by religion or belief, the Court accepts that the wearing of the headscarf is intimately linked to the religion or belief of the applicant. The applicant has adequately illustrated in her

submission the difficulties of not being able to manifest her religious belief and pursue her degree. This ban essentially obliged her and other Muslim women who veil to choose between their religious convictions and continuing their education. It is unclear to the Court how such a ban is 'necessary in a democratic society'.

30. Reasoning that women who wear a headscarf may be a threat to public order or to women who do not wear it is unsupported, unfounded and rather tenuous. To uphold the decision of Turkey compromises the right to education and democracy by forcing those wishing to practise their religious beliefs, such as Ms Şahin, out of education. Ultimately women (or men) should not be discriminated against or excluded from education on the grounds of their dress or manifesting their religious beliefs.

FUNDAMENTALISM

31. The tenuous linking of the headscarf with extremism and fundamentalism is offensive to many (not just those women who wear the scarf). Merely wearing the headscarf cannot be associated with fundamentalism, and there is nothing before this Court that suggests the applicant held fundamentalist views. The Quranic term *hijab* relates to the Islamic dress code in general and is applicable to both men and women. Quranic commentators have noted that the early Muslims did not take hijab to mean what it is commonly understood to be, namely a way of concealing women.[5] The majority of Muslim scholars who write about hijab will examine themes such as modesty, privacy and the lowering of the gaze; the actual clothes which women wear (the Arabic term for which is *khimaar*) are in fact to some scholars a secondary notion.

32. It is erroneous to regard the wearing of the Islamic headscarf as irreconcilable with tolerance, respect for others, equality and non-discrimination. While we respect Member States' need to take steps to prevent radical Islamism, merely wearing the headscarf cannot itself be associated with fundamentalism: it is vital to distinguish those who wear the headscarf through choice, from 'extremist' men who seek to impose the headscarf on women. The applicant is a young adult and a university student, living in a democracy and whom might reasonably be expected to have a heightened capacity to resist pressure. The applicant's education and both her personal and religious autonomy cannot be sacrificed and subjugated to the public interest in fighting extremism. It is established that it is not justified for institutions of higher education to regulate the manifestation of the rites and symbols of a religion by imposing restrictions as to the place and manner of such manifestation, under the masquerade that it is necessary to ensure the peaceful coexistence between students of various faiths.

33. Extremism is more likely to be caused by a lack of education and isolation and non-integration with other faiths. For individuals like the applicant, wearing the

[5] SS Alvi, H Hoodfar and S McDonough (eds), *The Muslim Veil in North America: Issues and Debates* (Toronto ON, Women's Press, 2003) 184.

headscarf is merely a form of dress prescribed by one's religion, which must be protected by Article 9 and religious freedom. Fear, suspicion and prejudice must not take over at the cost of universally held values and justice.

SECULARISM: A PLURALISTIC AND INCLUSIVE VERSION

34. The Court acknowledges that pluralism, tolerance and broadmindedness are hallmarks of a democratic society. This Court has to be a neutral and impartial arbitrator and therefore must not adopt stereotypes of what a Muslim woman is like, being particularly aware of the need to avoid adopting a stereotypical victim/perpetrator paradigm within its judgments.

35. Secularism is undoubtedly one of the fundamental principles of the Turkish State. The definition of secularism adopted by the TCC is that of 'the guarantee of democratic values, the principle that freedom of religion is inviolable … and … is the meeting point of liberty and equality'. The TCC argued that allowing women to wear headscarves within the university would equate to granting preferential treatment to one religion and thus undermine the neutrality of the State. The applicant sought only to pursue her education, as she had done for the previous four years. Prohibiting her from sitting her exam and attending her lectures infringed Article 2 Protocol 1 as the banning of the headscarf was disproportionate to the aims pursued. Little attention was given to how allowing the applicant to wear her headscarf could have actually respected secularism in positively respecting individuals' personal and religious autonomy, as protected in democratic States.

36. Although individual interests must on occasion be subordinated to those of a group, democracy does not simply mean that the views of a majority must always prevail: a balance must be achieved which ensures the fair and proper treatment of people from minorities and avoids any abuse of a dominant position (see, *mutatis mutandis*, *Young, James and Webster v the United Kingdom*, 13 August 1981, § 63, Series A no. 44, and *Chassagnou and Others v France* [GC], nos. 25088/94, 28331/95 and 28443/95, § 89, ECHR 1999-III, (2000) 29 EHRR 615). Pluralism and democracy must also be based on dialogue and a spirit of compromise, which necessarily entails various concessions on the part of individuals or groups of individuals that are justified in order to maintain and promote the ideals and values of a democratic society (see, mutatis mutandis, the *United Communist Party of Turkey and Others v Turkey* [GC], 30 January 1998, § 45, Reports of Judgments and Decisions 1998-I, (1998) 26 EHRR 121; and *Refah Partisi (the Welfare Party) and Others v Turkey* [GC], nos. 41340/98 and 3 others, § 99, ECHR 2003-II, (2003) 37 EHRR 1). It is precisely this constant search for a balance between the fundamental rights of each individual that constitutes the foundation of a 'democratic society' (see *Chassagnou and Others*, cited above, § 113).

37. Furthermore, in order to establish that the ban on wearing the headscarf is necessary in a democratic society, there needs to be evidence of a 'pressing social need'. This case differs from cases the Court has previously heard in that Islam

is the majority religion in Turkey. There is tension between secular-oriented and Islamist individuals as outlined in the Turkish Government's submission. It has been argued that secular-oriented Turkish citizens consider themselves to be liberal, progressive and individualistic and view Islamists as 'traditional, authoritarian, patriarchal, religiously fanatic and collectivist'.[6] The difference between the two is that secularists view Islam as a religion to be practised solely in the private sphere, whereas Islamists view Islam as a religion and a lifestyle to be practised in all aspects of their lives. While it is perfectly legitimate to take into account the specific situation in Turkey, especially the strong and unifying tradition of secularism, it nonetheless remains the task of the Court to protect minorities against disproportionate interference with their rights. Women like the applicant are in the minority as they do not fit either political category and require protection. She argues that secularism and her right to wear an Islamic headscarf are not mutually exclusive. Furthermore, Turkey did not submit sufficient evidence to suggest that there is in fact a sufficient "pressing social need" that would justify the ban on wearing the Islamic headscarf.

38. We also need to point out the consequences of this ban on women's lives. It prevents women from going to university.[7] It could lead to an increasingly isolated, marginalised, ostracised and potentially indignant and enraged Muslim community. It could lead to even greater isolation of women and girls within that community who choose to wear the headscarf.

39. Such a ban means imposing one set of standards across the board, and denies women like the applicant the freedom they are entitled to under the Convention. In the increasingly diverse and pluralist societies of Europe, a more complex understanding of equality needs to be acknowledged and investigated. Taking into account the statistics cited above, it is evident that when Turkish Muslim women are forced to choose between manifesting religious beliefs and remaining in the public sphere, thousands of women may prioritise their religious duties and become disconnected from public life. This is not the hallmark of a truly pluralistic and equal society.

40. Finally, the fact that other universities have not implemented a similar ban is evidence that order can be maintained without such a ban.

MARGIN OF APPRECIATION

41. In order to determine the scope of the margin of appreciation that states enjoy when regulating students' dress in an educational setting there must be due

[6] See, for example, JB White, *Islamist Mobilisation in Turkey: A Study in Vernacular Politics* (Seattle WA, University of Washington Press, 2002) 29.

[7] See, for instance, Human Rights Watch, *Memorandum to the Turkish Government on Human Rights Watch's Concerns with Regard to Academic Freedom in Higher Education, and Access to Higher Education for Women Who Wear the Headscarf* (Human Rights Watch, 29 June 2004) at www.hrw.org/legacy/backgrounder/eca/turkey/2004/headscarf_memo.pdf.

consideration of the right's importance and the 'nature' and 'aim' of the restricted activity. The extent to which this Court should defer to the national authorities has been considered one of the crucial questions that arise when examining the regulation of religious pluralism across Europe.

42. The applicant submitted that the Contracting States should not be given a wide margin of appreciation to regulate students' dress since no European State prohibits its students from wearing the Islamic headscarf at university. She added that there have been no signs of tension in institutions of higher education that would justify such a radical measure.

43. In many areas, especially those that might be considered sensitive, national authorities possess a margin of appreciation that reflects, inter alia, the notion that they are 'better placed' to decide how best to discharge their Convention obligations. It is noted that the doctrine of the margin of appreciation should not in any circumstances exempt the Court from the duty to exercise the function conferred on it under Article 19 of the Convention, which is to ensure the observance of the engagements undertaken by the High Contracting Parties in the Convention and the Protocols thereto. The Court's jurisdiction is, of course, subsidiary and its role is not to impose uniform solutions, especially 'with regard to establishment of the delicate relations between the Churches and the State' (see *Cha'are Shalom Ve Tsedek v France* [GC], no. 27417/95, § 84, ECHR 2000-VII) even if, in certain other judgments concerning conflicts between religious communities, the Court has not always shown the same judicial restraint (see *Serif v Greece*, no. 38178/97, ECHR 1999-IX, and *Metropolitan Church of Bessarabia and Others v Moldova*, no. 45701/99, ECHR 2001-XII). Thus the Court must seek to reconcile universality and diversity and it is not its role to express an opinion on any religious model.

44. The rationale for the margin of appreciation was first articulated in *Handyside v the United Kingdom* (7 December 1976, § 49, Series A no.24, (1979–80) 1 EHRR 737). The Court acknowledged that national authorities are better placed to assess the content of any limitations on Convention rights based on contextual considerations, as well as the necessary extent of those limitations. The Court has affirmed that 'the scope of this margin of appreciation is not identical in each case but will vary according to the context … Relevant factors include the nature of the Convention right in issue, its importance for the individual and the nature of the activities concerned' (*Buckley v the United Kingdom*, 25 September 1996, § 74, Reports of Judgments and Decisions 1996-IV, (1997) 23 EHRR 101).

45. This margin of appreciation goes hand in hand with European supervision embracing both the law and the decisions applying it. The Court's task is to determine whether the measures taken at the national level were both justified in principle and proportionate (see *Manoussakis and Others v Greece*, 26 September 1996, § 44, Reports of Judgments and Decisions 1996-IV, (1997) 23 EHRR 387). In delimiting the extent of the margin of appreciation in the present case, the Court must have regard to what is at stake, namely the need to protect the rights and

freedoms of individuals to practise their religion without being discriminated against and excluded from higher education. This is necessary if true religious pluralism is to respected, which is vital to the survival of a democratic society.

46. The margin of appreciation is of limited application for a further two reasons. Firstly, there is a lack of European consensus on the question of wearing religious symbols in higher education. In the vast majority of the member States, this is not specifically regulated and there are generally no restrictions on religious dress worn by university students. Secondly, the issue raised by this application, namely the scope of religious freedoms guaranteed by the Convention, is not merely a 'local' issue, but one that is of importance to all the Member States. European supervision of this fundamental human right should not be escaped simply by invoking the margin of appreciation.

47. Consequently, the Court concludes in the present case that Members States should not be given a wide margin of appreciation to regulate students' dress in higher education. The Court's duty is to ensure the observance of the engagements undertaken by the parties to the Convention and the Protocols thereto, which in this instance the Court deems to have been violated.

INTERSECTIONAL DISCRIMINATION

48. A number of jurisdictions, including Canada and the United States, acknowledge in their jurisprudence that discrimination can occur at the intersections of identity categories. Both jurisdictions have allowed claimants to pursue claims on the basis of multidimensional discrimination in a number of cases. The recognition of intersectional discrimination highlights the reality for individuals who face discrimination as a result of the interaction of multiple identities and experience exclusion and subordination as a result of this.[8]

49. In the case of a number of U.S. Courts, this was usually done in order to protect women who were discriminated against on the basis of gender and race. These courts have recognised within their case law that the use of the comparator could be a hindrance to gender equality as for example, black women experience a different type of discrimination than black men and white women. In the case of *Hicks v Gates Rubber Co.,* the claimant who identified as a black woman, accused her employer of discrimination on the grounds of sex and race (see *Marguerite Hicks v The Gates Rubber Company*. No. 84-1232. United States Court of Appeals, Tenth Circuit. Nov. 25, 1987). The Court held that the racial slurs used against the claimant were not frequent enough to warrant a racial discrimination claim and there was not enough evidence to prove a case in sexual harassment. However, the Court found that the combination of the two would allow for a hostile work environment claim under Title VII of the Civil Rights Act 1964.

[8] See the scholarly work of K Crenshaw, 'Mapping the Margins: Intersectionality, Identity Politics, and Violence against Women of Color' (1991) 43 *Stanford Law Review* 1241.

50. The Canadian courts have notably developed their human rights jurisprudence in order to tackle intersectional discrimination (see the Ontario Human Rights Commission, 'An Intersectional Approach to Discrimination: Addressing Multiple Grounds in Human Rights Claim' (2001)). Just under a decade ago, the Supreme Court of Canada in *Egan v Canada* ([1995] 2 S.C.R. 513 at 551-2) held that:

> We will never address the problem of discrimination completely, or ferret it out in all its forms, if we continue to focus on abstract categories and generalizations rather than specific effects. By looking at the grounds for the distinction instead of at the impact of the distinction … we risk undertaking an analysis that is distanced and desensitised from real people's experiences … More often than not, disadvantage arises from the way in which society treats particular individuals, rather than from any characteristics inherent in those individuals.

51. Over the ten years that followed, the Canadian courts have focussed on a contextualised approach when tackling anti-discrimination claims, which places less emphasis on the protected characteristic of the individual and instead focuses on the context in which the discrimination took place. We consider this to be the correct approach to take in this case.

52. In considering gender equality as a legitimate justification for limiting the manifestation of religious beliefs, we need to define this gender equality, making it clear what we mean and in connection with that we have to consider the intersectional identities of women. We need to move away from single protected identity and instead focus on the context in which the discrimination took place. The 'Islamic headscarf' is an obviously intersectional issue: the very term, used by this Court, suggests that the garment in question is religious in nature. It is also clearly gender-specific, as only Muslim *women* adopt the practice of wearing it, thus the debate on the headscarf is intersectional as it involves at the very least gender and religion.

53. Equality and non-discrimination are subjective rights, which must remain under the control of those who are entitled to benefit from them. As we have said above, the headscarf can have multiple meanings to a woman. Women's voices need to be included in the debate regarding the symbolism behind the headscarf. Wearing the headscarf has no single meaning. There are those who maintain that, in certain cases, it can even be a means of emancipating women. What is lacking in this debate is the opinion of women, both those who choose to wear the headscarf and those who choose not to. We wish in any future cases to hear the voices of these actual women, which Turkey should have submitted if they wanted the Court to consider their claim that the Islamic headscarf runs counter to equality and non-discrimination.

54. Article 14 of the Convention not only requires that persons in a similar situation be treated in an equal manner, but also requires that persons whose situations are significantly different must be treated differently' (see *Thlimmenos v Greece* [GC], no. 34369/97, § 47, ECHR 2000-IV, (2001) 31 EHRR 15). The Court takes the view

that Turkey's approach to gender equality is paternalistic and runs counter to the female applicant's intersectional identity. The banning of the Islamic headscarf in Turkish universities is an intersectional issue in that it only affects Muslim women who veil. It is not sufficient for a State to argue that a measure applies equally to all of its inhabitants. The ban has a disproportionate effect on Muslim women and the Court has held in the past that where there is evidence of discrimination to a group, the State has a positive duty to address this. The Court strengthened the protection of minority groups such as women and ethnic minorities, when Article 14 has been invoked, by examining the instances where they are disproportionately affected. In this case, we use a similar approach, when using gender equality as a reason for limiting a woman's Article 9(2) rights, as this would have a disproportionate effect on women.

55. Gender equality is a constitutional right under the Turkish Constitution. It is one of the key principles underlying the Convention and a goal to be achieved by member states of the Council of Europe. Consideration must be given to the context of this case, brought against a country in which the majority of the population are Muslim, and the considerable potential impact on other women of allowing the headscarf to be worn. It is understandable why some feel strongly about the restriction on Muslim clothing in public institutions, particularly given Turkey's Kemalist, secularist roots. Turkey puts forward the view that a secularist view of gender equality in a country with a majority Muslim population is needed to strengthen the values of pluralism and the equality of women and men. However, this view of gender equality as sameness and uniformity can tend to 'essentialism', treating all women as the same, and can coerce women into ways of being and living which are out of tune with a harmonisation of the relevant provisions of the Convention.

56. There is a relationship between gender, race, ethnicity and religion that combines into a communal identity. Those who argue that multiculturalism and the acceptance of religious practices are contrary to the aims of advancing gender equality fail to adequately take into account the voices of women in Europe who are disenfranchised and who straddle the public and private spheres. It is important that inequality is seen in its multiple dimensions in order to tackle it successfully. This Court encourages Member States to recognise and tackle the disadvantage faced by women who may be at the margins as a result of their multiple identities.

57. It is important to highlight that, like feminism, religious discourse often uses a different language to that of the law. This Court does not want women to be doubly discriminated against on the basis of gender and faith. Europe is becoming increasingly more multicultural, which brings with it a multiplicity of different cultures and different faiths. As has been highlighted earlier, the manifestation of religious belief lies at the heart of Article 9, which the Court has held to be a precious asset.

58. It is therefore important for the Court to mediate between the interests of the individual to manifest their religious beliefs and the interests of wider society.

For the Court to continue to instil public confidence in our maintenance of the rule of law, and our ability to adjudicate fairly, we must be seen to do so. Having considered of all of these issues, we find that the interference is not justified under subparagraph two of the relevant Articles: it is not 'necessary in a democratic society.'

For these reasons the Court:

1. Holds by three votes to one that there has been a violation of Article 8, 9 and 10 and Article 2 of Protocol 1.
2. That there is insufficient pleading regarding Article 14.

DISSENTING JUDGMENT OF JUDGE DOST DÜŞMAN AYIRT ETMEK

1. I respectfully disagree with the majority Judgment in this application. Banning the Islamic headscarf at Turkish universities serves legitimate aims pursuant to Articles 8 to 10 of the Convention: by protecting the 'rights and freedoms of others' and the 'maintenance of public order' in an overwhelmingly Muslim, but secularly governed, country. When examining the question of the Islamic headscarf in the Turkish context, the impact of wearing such a symbol must be borne in mind, which is presented or perceived as a compulsory religious duty, on those who choose *not* to wear it. The headscarf is a powerful external symbol and I fear in the Turkish context that it may have a potential proselytizing, or peer pressure, effect on other university students who may not already wear the Islamic headscarf. Therefore, it may infringe on the rights and freedoms of others. In a country in which the majority of the population, while professing a strong attachment to the rights of women and a secular way of life, adhere to the Islamic faith, it may be necessary to impose such limitations on freedom in this sphere to serve the cause of gender equality.

2. The legitimate aim of gender equality, which is proclaimed to be one of the key underlying principles of the Convention, and indeed has *jus cogens* status in International law, needs to be ensured. For many, the Islamic headscarf is a sign of women's inferiority and subservience to men, implying that women have to dress modestly to avoid the attention of men. We live in the Twenty First Century. There is supposed to be gender equality, or at least it is a value to which our institutions are supposed to aspire. Unequal standards cannot apply to the clothing of men and women: women should not wear clothing that signals their inequality, oppression and patriarchal subjugation. It is important to preserve pluralism in a university space in a way that is consistent with gender equality for all women, and for many the headscarf disempowers women. Therefore, a ban on wearing the headscarf is compatible with the Convention.

3. This religious symbol has taken on political significance in Turkey in recent years and has been linked with Islamic fundamentalism. I have not lost sight of the fact that there are extremist political movements in Turkey that seek to impose on society as a whole their interpretation of Islam, including their understanding

of religious symbols and attitudes to women, and conception of a society founded on religious precepts. I am mindful of these facts in deciding that Articles 8, 9 and 10 are engaged, and that there are violations of the provisions based on the rights and freedoms of others and the maintenance of public order qualifications in paragraph 2.

4. It also seems convincing that the ban to wear the headscarf can be justified on the legitimate grounds of secularism. Turkey has been a secular (*laik*) state since 1923, which is reflected in Article 2 of the Turkish constitution. Since 1923 there have been a number of reforms in order to ensure the separation of religion and state which includes abolishing the caliphate, closing down religious schools and restricting religious dress in order to ensure neutrality and secularism. The restrictions on religious manifestations are not limited to the wearing of a headscarf, albeit this is the most visible, and in allowing the applicant to continue to wear it would privilege one manifestation over another. This would lead to inequality. We should not underestimate the unique position Turkey holds, in that it is the only Muslim majority country that has adopted a liberal democracy.

5. The Court has recognised both secularism and neutrality to be a legitimate ground for such prohibitions in a number of analogous cases (such as *Karaduman v Turkey*, cited above). There should also be a distinction between situations where the majority religion is curtailed for the principle of secularism and neutrality and the instances where minorities are disproportionately affected. As highlighted above, the fact that there are extremist political movements at play in Turkey is an important factor. Istanbul University has had a number of violent clashes between opposing radical groups and there have been a number of complaints from students about pressures from Islamic fundamentalists. It is therefore not unreasonable for Turkey to draw the line at religious manifestations, precisely because it can amount to a form of pressure on those who do not practise Islam (see *Dahlab v Switzerland*, cited above). This could potentially open the floodgates to other aspects of religious practice that would threaten both the neutrality and secularism of the state, such as, but not limited to, some of the severe aspects of shariah law and the subjugation of women.

6. The wearing of religious symbols in public spaces/public educational institutions is clearly a contentious issue. Religious freedom may be restricted by the requirements of secularism, which is an important and underlying element of democracy. In light of the diversity of Member States of the Council of Europe it is expected that states should enjoy a wide margin of appreciation in determining the balance to be struck between individuals right to manifest their religion (Article 9) and the need to protect the rights and freedoms of others. States have a legitimate interest in implementing measures to ensure educational institutions remain places of education rather than indoctrination. To this end the restrictions placed on manifestations of religious dress at University can be deemed necessary in order to uphold the secular nature of the institution and in pursuit of the legitimate aims of public safety, health, order or the protection of the rights and freedoms

of others. A wide margin of appreciation can be justified since in a democratic society, opinions as to the relations between religion and state may vary widely amongst member states. There is no clear consensus on the regulation of wearing religious dress and thus such decisions are best decided at a local level.

7. Thus, the interference is one which can be deemed necessary in a democratic society; the limitation placed on the applicant's Article 9 right is proportionate to the legitimate aims sought to be protected, namely the need to protect the rights and freedoms of others, to preserve public order and to secure civil peace and true religious pluralism, which is vital to the survival of a democratic society.

Reflections

Jill Marshall

Knowing of the initial English Feminist Judgments Project edited by Rosemary Hunter et al,[1] this new international project presented an opportunity to re-write a judgment that fitted with my research on women's freedom and human rights. I had a particular interest in the *Şahin* case since the first Chamber's judgment was delivered, so the decision to choose this judgment to re-write was easy. I remember first reading the Judgment and being appalled that we were living as women in the twenty-first century but were seen as not capable of making our own decisions on the wearing of a piece of clothing. I found this particularly patronising as a woman, and potentially racist and discriminatory in its portrayal of Muslim women, even though I am not one, including those who choose to wear a hijab or similar. In my opinion, it is not the role of any law to tell me, or any woman, what to wear. I grew up in Northern Ireland at the height of 'the Troubles' in the 1970s and 1980s. As I see it, this experience contributed to a strong belief in the fundamental importance of individual freedom, including self-worth, respect for others, choice and freedom of expression. I was always encouraged to hear, listen, see and take into account different points of view, including those from people who lived geographically close to me but who had the completely opposite view from me on certain issues. In turn, I expected my views and expressions to be listened to and taken into account. Then as grown up adults, we would all agree to disagree if necessary, or agree on a commonly held viewpoint. It was also fundamentally important that this would happen without any violence so we could all live in peace.

At the first workshop of the project, we briefly presented on the case and our initial thoughts on some potential direction for our re-writing. That day was very informative with talks, including from Rosemary Hunter and Erika Rackley who had been involved in the English project, and lots of discussions with others participating in this project. It was a good day as it gave us all an opportunity to meet each other and to hear about our different judgments. It was encouraging to see so many scholars interested in feminist methods in law. After this meeting, Amal became involved. We emailed and I met her at a separate conference. We agreed to focus on different aspects of the Judgment to reflect our expertise.

As Chamber 'President', I would aim to lead in terms of moving things forward; in terms of writing, I would focus on explaining the facts of the case, freedom of choice, expression, autonomy, identity and a holistic conception of

[1] R Hunter, C McGlynn and E Rackley (eds), *Feminist Judgments: From Theory to Practice* (Oxford, Hart Publishing, 2010).

gender equality, that is, one that does not conflict with women's freedom. This was in line with my previous publications on women's freedom in general and on women's freedom and the Islamic headscarf, especially a piece I had published in the *Human Rights Quarterly* in 2008. Our communications were mainly by email. After an early productive meeting we had a list of work allocation to apply to the then very rough version, with the first full draft Judgment being produced in advance of the workshop at SOAS, London. This was ready for circulation to the attendees and to the discussant, Samia Bano. I first met Amel at the June workshop where we all presented on our parts of the draft Judgment and heard Samia's insightful reflections and comments. We agreed to revise our parts of the judgment. Also, I had written a very rough draft 'devil's advocate' dissent and I agreed to develop it based on alternative (to our viewpoint) feminist arguments that religious head covering is oppressive to women.

It was a challenging and rewarding learning experience working together with other colleagues in different institutions and in different geographical parts of the country. We had a variety of viewpoints on feminist interpretations of the judgment as we mention in our authors' note. To a certain extent, it is probably evident to readers that we wrote different parts of the judgment as we all agreed on the end goal of deciding in favour of Ms Şahin, but with certain differences in our reasoning as to why. We think this is totally to be expected and compatible with the broad church that we see feminist legal theory to be. This is the version we produced and we hope you enjoyed reading it.

Amel Alghrani

The case appealed to me on a personal level. Originally, as part of the feminist international judgments project I had agreed to a re-write a different judgment and was placed in a different chamber – one that fell within my research area as a medical lawyer and that was concerned with foetal rights and abortion. When I read the *Şahin* judgment, I was so interested that I swapped with a colleague who had originally been assigned to this Chamber. Having come to the end of the re-write, I am very happy I did make that swap. Despite not being familiar with this area of law, my excellent colleagues on this judgment, Jill and Amal, steered the way. It has been a steep, but very enjoyable learning curve.

The methodology and how we divided the tasks worked well. With regards to the facts of the case, I was of the view the margin of appreciation was interpreted too widely and to that end, I was grateful I got to focus on this in the re-writing of the judgment on that aspect. I felt quite strongly on the issue that states should not prevent students from attending higher education because they may choose to express their faith through their dress. Whether it is a student of the Jewish faith wearing a skull cap, a Sikh student wearing a turban, or a Muslim woman wearing a headscarf, one cannot infer a student dressing as such is 'fundamental', and a threat to society or social order and that they will promote extremism merely based on the fact they choose to wear an item of clothing to express their beliefs.

I found the case interesting as a Muslim western woman myself. Whilst I do not wear a headscarf, I was interested in how subjective notions of such things as dress and religion could be reconciled within supposedly objective judicial principles. The judgment linked Islam with fundamentalism and extremism, terms that are highly politicised and not value free. The case highlighted the challenges and concerns for the impartiality of judges. This case was decided in 2005, four years after the 9/11 atrocities in the USA. Those terrorist attacks agitated negative public and political sentiments against Islam and a widespread fear of potential links between the religion and 'extremism'. In reading the judgment and undertaking the re-write I questioned whether the outcome would have been different if the female student covering her hair was not a Muslim, but, for instance, an orthodox Greek woman, orthodox Jewish woman, or a nun, who may also cover their hair as part of their religious beliefs. As a Western Muslim woman, in undertaking the re-write it was difficult to get away from a core belief that the way one dresses is an intimate matter of one's personal autonomy and is a private choice. Excluding people from public spaces, such as universities, and depriving them from an education because of their dress sets a dangerous precedent that will serve only to erode an individual's fundamental liberty to dress in a manner they choose. The court in the *Şahin* case subtly promoted the Western assumption that a woman that veils is one who has been coerced into submission; that they have been oppressed by religion or men to veil and that this runs counter to the idea of gender equality.[2] Yet true gender equality would be to accept that a woman might independently choose to veil, that such a woman's choice should still be accepted, respected and accommodated in public spaces; that whether a woman veils or not, should not bar her from receiving equal rights to higher education and subsequently fruitful employment.

The context in which the case was decided cannot be ignored but was difficult to cover in the judgment re-write as I wanted to avoid doing the very thing I had criticised the judgment for; namely, linking Islam to fundamentalism and being influenced by the political landscape and the global 'war on terror'.

I also learnt how difficult being objective and impartial is when doing the re-write. As a Muslim and a woman, I found the references to Islam and fundamentalism offensive and whilst doing the re-write I had to keep that at bay. In this context, re-writing the judgment was difficult, clearly my thoughts are influenced by my beliefs. Writing a truly objective judgment is no easy feat, by the very nature of the complex matrix that make up human agency, it is difficult to isolate decisions and opinions from one's belief system that at some subconscious

[2] H Elver, *The Headscarf Controversy: Secularism and Freedom of Religion* (New York NY, Oxford University Press, 2012) 199.

level influence one's thought processes. Often as an academic lawyer reading judgments with a rather critical eye, one can tend to take for granted that the judiciary are mere humans and they too may be influenced by broader factors; in this case there were clear undertones throughout the judgment of the wider global political climate and the growing fear of Islam as a religion liked to fundamentalism. Whilst the judiciary endeavour to be impartial and objective in their judgments, this project developed a greater awareness of how difficult a task this is in practice.

Lastly the project gave me an enhanced appreciation of the difficult task that faces the judiciary when writing judgments. Participating in this project makes me read judgments differently, with a much greater appreciation of how difficult a task the judiciary have in having to reconcile and balance conflicting rights, especially at an international level.

Amal Ali

I chose to take part in re-writing *Leyla Şahin v Turkey*, primarily because the intersections of human rights law, religion and gender fell within the topic of my PhD research. When I first read this case it seemed counter-intuitive to me that the language of human rights and gender equality were being used in a way that undermines them. It is difficult as a feminist, an academic and a Muslim woman who veils to separate my knowledge from my work; the *Şahin* judgment itself undermined my confidence in both human rights law and feminism. This prompted my interest in my PhD research and this feminist judgment and is the reason why reflexivity was central in my approach to writing the judgment and this reflection.

In this judgment we tried to conceptually shift the focus of international law in order to take all the identities of the individual into account. We tried to approach the judgment in two ways. Firstly, we explored the gendered public/private dichotomy aspect of the judgment. The original judgment did not take into consideration the way in which the Court interprets Article 9(2) to create a public/private dichotomy, where women are relegated to the private sphere. Leyla Şahin may have been able to afford to finish her medical education at another institution, but many women found that they could not afford to do so and were forced to either unveil, something which caused them deep personal stress or stop their tertiary education altogether.[3] Secondly, we felt that it was important to contextualise the problem, which is why we divided the judgment in terms of themes instead of Articles of the Convention.

It was difficult to write an intersectional judgment, due to the lack of information about the applicant. We also found that there were quite a few methodological

[3] FN Seggie, *Religion and the State in Turkish Universities: The Headscarf Ban* (Basingstoke, Palgrave Macmillan, 2011) 38.

constraints in our judgment writing. Other than the fact that Leyla Şahin was 25 years old, a medical student, female and a headscarf wearing Muslim, we couldn't really explore all the intersecting aspects of her identity that it had been suggested we explore during the workshops. One of the issues that had been raised was a risk of essentialising Muslim women, which we actively tried to avoid. This is a problem for all judges, as explained by Justice L'Heureux-Dube, who recognises 'that women's diverse experience have been sadly lacking in many areas of law and I have continually emphasized the necessity of incorporating them in our judicial decisions'.[4]

By initially highlighting that we were trying to incorporate a Muslim voice into the debate, we failed to identify what Muslim voice that would be, other than that of the applicant. This is difficult to reconcile with feminist judging which requires that feminist critiques are taken into consideration and much of the feminist critique in the *Şahin* case is around essentialism. Upon further reflection, all we can do as feminist judges is to ensure that the applicant's voice and perspectives are considered.

It became quite obvious that, as lawyers, in our methods we utilised the usual black letter tools of legal interpretation, but at the same time recognised and highlighted when these tools perpetuated gendered norms. It is interesting that the Court has used a more holistic approach to gender equality in its Article 14 jurisprudence, as outlined by Judge Tulkens and in its Article 8 jurisprudence.

Interestingly, I did feel a power dynamic when writing the judgment. When I took on the voice of a judge, armed with both legal reasoning and professional, political clout I found it easier to write the judgment. I started off referencing in my judgment writing in order to write a more convincing argument supported by the authority of others, but did so less and less, until the final draft only contained references to other jurisdictions, critical texts and empirical studies to evidence my normative claims. Writing this reflective note in fact proved to be the hardest part of the judgment writing process, precisely because I stopped writing as a judge and was writing once again in my own voice.

I enjoyed writing the judgment and working with both Jill and Amel, whose academic work, work ethic and ability to manage a stressful workload I admire. Both have taken on a mentor role during the judgment-writing period, which I am grateful for as the least qualified and most junior judge. I also enjoyed writing a judgment that I believe to be wholly intersectional as opposed to the one-dimensional form of feminism demonstrated in the devil's advocate judgment. Our backgrounds, viewpoints and critiques fit together seamlessly, in most part thanks to Jill who edited the final judgment.

[4] C L'Heureux-Dube, 'Making a Difference: The Pursuit of a Compassionate Justice' (1997) 31 *University of British Columbia Law Review* 1, 6.

9

Burden v the United Kingdom

NICOLA BARKER

Author's Note

Introduction: The Legal Context and Facts of the Case

The case of *Burden v the United Kingdom*, heard in both the Chamber[1] and the Grand Chamber[2] of the European Court of Human Rights (ECtHR), was brought by elderly sisters who had lived together all of their lives, neither sister having married or had children. Their claim was that they were being discriminated against under Article 14 of the European Convention on Human Rights (in conjunction with Article 1 of Protocol 1, the protection of property) through their exclusion from the inheritance tax exemptions that are available to spouses and civil partners. The sisters had reportedly written to every Chancellor of the Exchequer since 1976 to request the inheritance tax exemption to be extended to them as cohabiting siblings[3] but it appears that it was the recent introduction of civil partnerships for same-sex couples in 2005 that had provided the impetus for their claim in the ECtHR: '"We just want to be treated the same as lesbians and homosexuals" says Sybil. "If we pay the same taxes, then we should have the same rights," adds Joy.'[4]

Although they limited their claim to access to the tax exemption and did not argue in the case for access to civil partnership status, it is not surprising that the creation of civil partnerships was referenced by the sisters: the plight of 'spinster sisters' had been prominent in the debates and media surrounding the passage

[1] *Burden and Burden v the United Kingdom*, no 13378/05, 12 December 2006, (2007) 44 EHRR 51.

[2] *Burden v the United Kingdom* [GC], no 13378/05, (2008) 47 EHRR 38.

[3] BBC News, 'Sisters Lose European Tax Battle' (29 April 2008). http://news.bbc.co.uk/1/hi/england/wiltshire/7372555.stm.

[4] Sybil and Joyce Burden, interviewed in R Hardman, 'What about our rights? If they'd been gay, there would have been no problem. But this week, two sisters who risk losing their home challenged Britain's crazy inheritance laws in court. Here, this very English pair tell their extraordinary and touching story …' *Daily Mail* (16 September 2006) 36.

of the Civil Partnership Act 2004, with the supposed lack of rights for sisters and other 'deserving' family members juxtaposed with (presumably undeserving) same-sex partners.[5] In fact, several opponents of the Bill had attempted to attach a wrecking amendment that would have allowed siblings and other family members to become civil partners, arguing that they also ought to be able to enjoy the tax advantages that same-sex couples would now have access to.[6] These arguments appeared to influence the sisters' submissions to the Chamber and Grand Chamber that they were in an analogous situation to spouses and civil partners because they 'had chosen to live together in a loving, committed and stable relationship for several decades, sharing their only home, to the exclusion of other partners'.[7] Indeed, the sisters stated in their submission that 'they would have entered into a civil partnership had that route been open to them'.[8] Furthermore, while they accepted that it was not for the Court to dictate potential remedies, the sisters noted that the proposed amendments to the Civil Partnership Bill, passed by the House of Lords but removed by the House of Commons, 'showed that it would be possible to construct a statutory scheme whereby two siblings or other close relations who had cohabited for a fixed number of years … could obtain certain fiscal rights or advantages'.[9]

The Burden sisters also argued that the exclusion of cohabiting adult siblings from the tax exemption serves no legitimate aim: 'only a small minority of adult siblings were likely to share the type of relationship enjoyed by the applicants, involving prolonged mutual support, commitment and cohabitation'.[10] Furthermore, extending the exemption to siblings and other cohabiting family members would 'serve the policy interest … [of] the promotion of stable, committed family relationships among adults', and thus excluding them did not serve a legitimate aim and was not proportionate.[11] They also argued that any lost revenue 'would have to be offset by the potential gains, for example, those flowing from an increased tendency, encouraged by the exemption, of close relations to care for disabled or elderly relatives, thus avoiding the need for state funded care'.[12]

[5] This was a recurring trope in the Parliamentary debates, for which Lord Higgins coined the term 'the spinster sister problem': Civil Partnership Bill HL Deb 22 April 2004 vol 660 cc387–433, 429. During the Marriage (Same Sex Couples) Bill debates, Baroness Deech and O'Cathain co-signed an amendment to require a review of civil partnerships to consider extending access to civil partnerships to unpaid carers and family members who have cohabited for five years after the age of 18. In introducing this amendment, Baroness Deech referred directly to the Burden sisters and argued that: 'The state should not prefer sexual relationships, which may be short-lived and serial, over blood relationships that have proved to have endured decades.': HL Deb 24 June 2013 vol 746 c527.

[6] For an overview of these arguments, see N Barker, 'Why Care? "Deserving Family Members" and the Conservative Movement for Broader Family Recognition' in J Wallbank and J Herring (eds), *Vulnerabilities, Care and Family Law* (London, Routledge, 2014).

[7] *Burden*, above n 1, para 50.

[8] *Burden*, above n 2, para 53.

[9] *Burden*, above n 1, para 52.

[10] ibid, para 51.

[11] ibid, para 52.

[12] ibid, para 52.

The Chamber and Grand Chamber Judgments

It is striking that while the Chamber and Grand Chamber ultimately both ruled against the Burden sisters, they did so for very different reasons.[13] The Chamber does not consider in any detail whether or not siblings are similarly situated to spouses, this being generally the first question in a discrimination case under Article 14. Instead, it glosses over this question and its focus turns quickly to the (usual) second question of justification. The majority accepted the Government's submission that the inheritance tax exemption for spouses and civil partners pursues the legitimate aim of promoting stable, committed, relationships: 'The State cannot be criticised for pursuing, through its taxation system, policies designed to promote marriage; nor can it be criticised for making available the fiscal advantages attendant on marriage to committed homosexual couples'.[14]

Furthermore, they held that, bearing in mind both the legitimate policy aims of the exemption and the wide margin of appreciation in relation to taxation, it is inevitable that any taxation scheme will create 'marginal situations and individual cases of apparent hardship or injustice' but it is primarily for the state to determine how to strike the appropriate balance.[15] In this case, the UK did not exceed the margin of appreciation and the difference in treatment between siblings and spouses or civil partners would be reasonably and objectively justified, even if they were similarly situated. Therefore, the Chamber concludes that there was no violation of Article 14, read in conjunction with Article 1 of Protocol 1.

In contrast to the Chamber's approach, the Grand Chamber begins with the question of whether siblings are similarly situated to spouses and, finding that they are not, finds no reason to move on to the question of whether differences in treatment are justified or proportionate. Sibling relationships, they hold, are 'qualitatively of a different nature' to spouses and civil partners:

> The very essence of the connection between siblings is consanguinity, whereas one of the defining characteristics of a marriage or Civil Partnership Act union is that it is forbidden to close family members. The fact that the applicants have chosen to live together all their adult lives, as do many married and Civil Partnership Act couples, does not alter this essential difference between the two types of relationship.[16]

The Grand Chamber also reiterated the 'special status' of marriage and reaffirmed the Court's previous judgment in *Shackell v the United Kingdom*[17] that married and unmarried heterosexual couples are not analogous because of that special status.[18]

[13] Although in the Grand Chamber, Judge Bratza, who was also a member of the Chamber's majority in this decision (sitting in both cases as the UK's judge on the Court) and Judge Björgvinsson both gave separate concurring opinions suggesting that they preferred the reasoning of the Chamber.

[14] *Burden*, above n 1, para 59.

[15] ibid, para 60.

[16] *Burden*, above n 2, para 62.

[17] *Shackell v the United Kingdom*, no 45851/99, 27 April 2000.

[18] *Burden*, above n 2, para 63.

They also extended this special status to civil partners because the legal consequences of this status, which are expressly and deliberately entered into by the couple, 'set these types of relationship apart from other forms of cohabitation'.[19] It is the existence of a public undertaking, not the length or supportive nature of the relationship, that is determinative: just as with unmarried cohabiting couples, 'the absence of such a legally binding agreement between the applicants renders their relationship of cohabitation, despite its long duration, fundamentally different to that of a married or civil partnership couple'.[20] As such, the applicants cannot be compared to spouses or civil partners and there is therefore no violation of Article 14.

The Dissenting Opinions

Two of the dissenting judgments (both of those in the Chamber) appeared to have been at least partly persuaded by the sisters' claim of potentially having to sell their home. Judge Pavolvschi appeared to be particularly moved by this prospect, placing the majority judgment in the category of 'legal, but unfair' based on the sisters' emotional connection to the family home, though interestingly he stated that had the property been purchased during their cohabitation (rather than inherited from their parents) he would have 'readily agreed' that it ought to be taxable property:

> This house is not simply a piece of property – this house is something with which they have a special emotional bond: this house is their home. It strikes me as absolutely awful that, once one of the two sisters dies, the surviving sister's sufferings on account of her closest relative's death should be multiplied by the risk of losing her family home because she cannot afford to pay inheritance tax in respect of the deceased sister's share of it.[21]

However, most of the dissenting judges took the view that if the tax exemption had remained exclusive to spouses the policy could have been justified by reference to Article 12 (the right to marry and found a family) but that once it was extended to civil partners, 'the problem left the specific sphere of Article 12' and now has to 'satisfy general standards of reasonableness and non-arbitrariness resulting from Article 14'.[22] In other words, now that civil partners also have the tax exemption, the Government must be able to justify why 'it has been offered to some unions while continuing to be denied to others'.[23] They also emphasise the similarity between the sisters and spouses, for example Judges Bonello and Garlicki noted that a cohabiting sibling relationship is 'not entirely different from

[19] ibid, para 65.
[20] ibid, para 65.
[21] *Burden*, above n 1, para O-II8-9.
[22] Joint dissenting opinion of Judges Bonello and Garlicki *Burden*, above n 1, para O-I2.
[23] ibid; see also Judge Zupančič, *Burden*, above n 2, para O-III12-13.

the situation of other unions, particularly as regards old or very old people. The bonds of mutual affection form the ethical basis for such unions and the bonds of mutual dependency form the social basis for them'.[24] As such, the siblings should also be protected from 'financial disaster' on the death of one cohabitant.[25] Although they accept that the Government may 'establish a very high threshold' for sibling relationships to be recognised, they reject the idea that they can 'simply ignore that such unions also exist'.[26] Similarly, Judge Zupančič questions whether the siblings' exclusion is 'rationally related to a legitimate governmental interest':[27]

> I ask myself, at this point, why would consanguinity be any less important than the relationship between married and civil partners? Of course, the quality of consanguinity is different from sexual relationships but this has no inherent bearing on the proximity of the persons in question … So what does the qualitative difference [between spouses/civil partners and siblings] come to? Is it having sex with one another that provides the rational relationship to a legitimate government interest?[28]

He concludes, referencing *Stec v the United Kingdom*,[29] that the state is not required to create extra-marital tax exemptions [for civil partners], but once it does, it should 'employ at least a minimum level of reasonableness while deciding not to apply the benefit to other groups of people in relationships of similar or closer proximity'.[30] Judge Borrego Borrego agrees, suggesting that the majority have 'disregarded' the precedent of *Stec* in their judgment[31] and have not addressed the question of whether continuing to exclude sisters from the tax exemption in light of the inclusion of civil partners 'is a measure proportionate to the legitimate aim pursued'.[32]

Responses to the Judgments

These cases can be read very differently depending on one's perspective. For the claimants, the central issue is an unfair tax system, which privileges couples (though as noted above, it was specifically the extension of this to *same-sex* couples that appeared to be the impetus for this case) whilst penalising cohabiting and

[24] *Burden*, above n 1, para O-I3.
[25] ibid.
[26] ibid.
[27] *Burden*, above n 2, para O-III13.
[28] ibid, para O-III16.
[29] *Stec and Others v the United Kingdom*, [GC], nos 65731/01 and 65900/01, § 53, ECHR 2006-VI, (2006) 43 EHRR 47.
[30] *Burden*, above n 2, para O-III19.
[31] ibid, para O-IV10.
[32] ibid, para O-IV9.

mutually dependent siblings who cannot claim the same tax exemptions despite arguably similar circumstances to spouses. Interestingly the language used by the sisters is similar to that of advocates for same-sex marriage: 'We are looked down upon for being single. We just want to be treated as equal citizens and given the rights we deserve.'[33]

For others, the facts of the case are read in the context of their mirroring a hypothetical scenario used to try to derail the passage of the Civil Partnership Bill in 2004 and thereby seek to undermine the recognition of same-sex relationships, known as the 'spinster sisters' wrecking amendment, proposed by Baroness O'Cathain and Lord Tebbit.[34] As a result, the focus for these commentators is on praising the courts' resistance of this homophobic agenda and the extension of the 'special status' of marriage to civil partnerships.[35] However, as some commentators noted, the extension of the inheritance tax exemption to same-sex couples through the Civil Partnership Act seemed to be a distraction in the *Burden* case,[36] which was not really about civil partnerships at all: 'It was a case about tax; about spousal privilege (and the extension of that privilege to gays and lesbians who register their partnerships); and about old age and vulnerability'.[37] It is these themes that I seek to address in my judgment.

While the commentaries generally reveal a certain amount of sympathy for the sisters, and some criticism of the Courts' reasoning in both cases, few argue that the ultimate finding of no violation in this case was incorrect. For example, Brian Sloan argued following the Chamber decision, that: 'This decision is as deferential as its result is tragic'.[38] He suggests that the inheritance tax system should be reformed to accommodate the situation of the Burden sisters, with a system oriented towards '*actual* economic interdependence' rather than formal relationship status able to produce fairer results, though this is 'likely to be considered unworkable in a system so dependent on categorisation'.[39] However, he agrees with the Chamber's decision not to find the Civil Partnership Act's exclusion of siblings to be in violation of Article 14 and that extension of civil partnerships to siblings would have undermined the purpose of the 2004 Act. Instead, reform should,

[33] Sybil Burden, interviewed in J Bale, 'Sisters Begin Battle Over Inheritance Tax Rights' *The Times* (4 September 2006) 11.

[34] For further details on this see Barker, above n 6, and N Barker, 'After the Wedding, What Next? Conservatism and Conjugality' in N Barker and D Monk (eds), *From Civil Partnership to Same-Sex Marriage: Interdisciplinary Reflections* (London, Routledge, 2015).

[35] See for example, European Human Rights Law Review 'Case Comment' (2008) 4 *European Human Rights Law Review* 556.

[36] See for example P Baker, 'Case Comment: Burden v Burden' (2008) 4 *British Tax Review* 329, 331.

[37] R Auchmuty, 'Beyond Couples: Burden v United Kingdom' (2009) 17(2) *Feminist Legal Studies* 205, 211.

[38] B Sloan, 'The Burden of Inheritance Tax (2007) 3(1) *Cambridge Student Law Review* 114, 114.

[39] ibid, 116, emphasis in original.

he suggests, 'be limited to the tax system'.[40] Similarly, the short commentary of the Chamber decision in the *European Human Rights Law Review* is sympathetic to the dissenting judgment of Judges Bonello and Garlicki in its dissatisfaction with the Court's 'over-reliance on the margin of appreciation as justification for the treatment of the applicants' and suggests that Parliament should address the situation that the Burden sisters found themselves in through separate legislation to the Civil Partnership Act.[41]

The reasoning of the Grand Chamber fared even less well than that of the Chamber. Several commentators found the rationale that sisters could not be analogous to spouses/civil partners because they are prohibited from entering a marriage/civil partnership by virtue of being sisters to be circular and unconvincing.[42] The question of whether or not the sisters' relationship was sufficiently analogous to a spousal relationship should have been established based on the nature of their relationship, rather than the fact that they were excluded from spousal status. This type of reasoning, I would suggest, is indicative of a more general criticism of the European Court of Human Rights: that it is far too deferential to what it describes as the 'special status' of marriage. This is another theme that I focus on in my feminist judgment.

One commentator who argued that there should have been a violation found in this case is Aeyal Gross in the course of his alternative judgment in the case.[43] Though he draws on the work of a number of feminist scholars, he comes to this conclusion on the basis of a more traditionally liberal, rather than feminist, view that the Court should enforce respect for the diversity of relationship types (including those of single people as well as those in non-conjugal and polyamorous relationships) and dismisses concern expressed by some feminists[44] of the 'hijacking' of a potentially progressive recognition of non-conjugal relationships by conservatives for their own purposes:

> The fact that conservative forces may want the same for their own reasons does not change my position that extending rights to various forms of relationships, and not discriminating against single persons, is a worthwhile project from the perspective of equality and diversity.[45]

[40] ibid, 117.

[41] European Human Rights Law Review, 'Case Comment. Taxation: Prospective Liability of Elderly, Cohabiting Sisters to Inheritance Tax – Difference in Treatment as Compared with Married Couples or Those in Civil Partnerships' (2007) 2 *European Human Rights Law Review* 199, 202.

[42] See Baker, above n 36, 332; B Sloan, 'The Benefits of Conjugality and the Burdens of Consanguinity' (2008) 67(3) *Cambridge Law Journal* 484, 485; A Gross, 'The *Burden* of Conjugality' in E Brems (ed), *Diversity and European Human Rights: Rewriting Judgments of the ECHR* (Cambridge, Cambridge University Press, 2013), 278; Barker, above n 6, 66.

[43] Gross, ibid.

[44] See for example: R Graycar and J Millbank, 'From Functional Family to Spinster Sisters: Australia's Distinctive Path to Relationship Recognition' (2007) 24 *Washington Journal of Law and Policy* 121; and Barker, above n 6.

[45] Gross, above n 42, 287–88.

Gross appears to prefer a functional approach, and the basis of his alternative judgment is that the sisters' relationship was functionally similar to that of spouses/civil partners, but he is not particularly tied to this as his priority is the recognition of non-conjugal relationships: if the State could achieve this through expanding opt-in relationship recognition, effectively to any two people, this would appear to be an equally acceptable remedy for him in this case. Alternatively, the third option offered to the UK in his judgment is to remedy the discrimination by abolishing inheritance tax exemptions altogether. Each of these potential solutions would have radically different implications for UK taxation policy, and it may well be appropriate for the Strasbourg court to leave the question of which to choose to the UK government. However, Gross makes the finding of discrimination in this case based only on the functional similarities between the Burden sisters and spouses/civil partners. The next stage of the Article 14 test is whether the discrimination between those who are similarly situated can be objectively justified, (including whether it is within the UK's margin of appreciation). These issues are not considered in his judgment and the result is that it does not particularly challenge the notion of the special status of marriage any more than the Chamber or Grand Chamber did. It simply requires more (potentially an infinite number of) people to have access to it.

In contrast, Rosemary Auchmuty provides a feminist reading of the case, putting it in the context not only of the taxation of the sisters' relative wealth and the privileging of spouses at the expense of everyone else, but also old age and vulnerability. Noting that 'single women and old people … have a long history of being overlooked and disregarded in the handing out of privileges', Auchmuty suggests that the way to resolve this case is, 'not to extend the definition of couples eligible to form a civil partnership, nor to abolish inheritance tax, but to *get rid of the spousal exemption*'.[46] I would suggest that it is Auchmuty's feminist approach that led her in a different direction to the other commentators, who for the most part came to the opposite conclusion: that the exemption should be extended in some way but not through allowing siblings access to civil partnerships. Sharing this feminist approach, I have come to a similar conclusion based not only on a different reading of the relevant ECHR provisions, which I set out in my judgment, but also a different reading of the facts of this case and through taking into account the broader social, economic and political context in which the inheritance tax rules operate. I outline this below (see Reflections), alongside a consideration of the arguments relating to conjugality and care, which have been made by several feminists as well as the commentators on this case.

My aim in writing this feminist judgment, in the form of a sole-authored separate concurring opinion, was to demonstrate that there is a way to challenge the privileged legal status accorded to spouses (and extended to civil partners) over

[46] Auchmuty, above n 37, 216. Emphasis in original.

and above that of single people, non-conjugal and other non-traditional relationships, whilst also avoiding both the trap of simply extending this privilege a little further (rather than abolishing it) and of creating a tax avoidance mechanism for carers and other non-conjugal cohabitants that benefits only the wealthy. As a result, my judgment differs from both the majority and dissenting judgments in the Chamber and Grand Chamber in two key ways. First, I seek to challenge the existing Convention jurisprudence on the 'special status' of marriage, which unquestioningly accepts that spouses ought to be treated more favourably in law than others and as such undermines the protection that Article 14 should provide from marital status discrimination.[47] Second, I take into account both the relative wealth of the sisters and the broader social context. Therefore, while I agree with the ultimate conclusion of the Chamber and Grand Chamber that the Court should find against the sisters, I do so for very different reasons. Taking a socialist feminist approach to deciding this case means being mindful of the broader, gendered, economic and social conditions in which the sisters' claim is situated. In particular, it means recognising the problematic and sometimes discriminatory nature of spousal benefits and the ways in which they operate to sustain and perpetuate privilege.

[47] See for example *Gas and Dubois v France*, no 25951/07, ECHR 2012, (2014) 59 EHRR 22. Though this case could not be included in my judgment as it occurred after *Burden*, I alluded to it using a 'hypothetical' scenario of cohabiting same-sex couples who are prevented from marrying and therefore have no possibility of accessing spousal privileges in many High Contracting Parties, though this had obviously been rectified in England and Wales through the Civil Partnership Act 2004 at the time of this case.

JUDGMENT

BURDEN v THE UNITED KINGDOM

(Application no. 13378/05)

The Grand Chamber of the European Court of Human Rights

Concurring Opinion of Judge Barker

28 April 2008

O-V1 The applicants' claim is that their exclusion from the spousal inheritance tax exemption under the Inheritance Tax Act 1984, s18(1), constitutes a violation of Article 14 in conjunction with Article 1 of Protocol 1 (A1P1). The applicants are sisters who have lived together all their lives, the last thirty years of which was in a four-bedroom house built in 1965 at a cost of £7000 on land inherited from their parents. During the subsequent 40 years, the home and its 30 acres of farmland have increased in value to £550,000. It is noteworthy that each applicant's share of the home would be below the current inheritance tax threshold of £300,000 but for the fact that they also own other property, with their total property holdings listed as worth £875,000, in addition to another £300,000 in investments and other assets. They own all their assets jointly and have each written a will leaving her share to the surviving sister, who would have to pay tax at 40% of any amount over that threshold. Their claim was that the survivor 'might have to sell the house in order to pay the tax' (*Burden and Burden v the United Kingdom* (2007) 44 EHRR 51, at para. 11). However, based on the assets listed in the Chamber judgment, I have calculated the survivor's tax bill as £115,000,[1] which, though a large sum, could be paid by selling the deceased sister's additional portfolio of investments and property, which would leave the survivor with a post-tax inheritance of £35,000 plus the deceased's share of the house. Therefore, while this case has been framed by some as being about a vulnerable pensioner who may lose her home when her sister dies, it is important to not lose sight of the fact that these applicants are very wealthy and appear to have sufficient assets to comfortably meet the tax bill without the sale of their home.

O-V2 The majority judgment explains why the complaint falls within the ambit of A1P1 and I concur with that analysis. My disagreement is in relation only to their

[1] In these figures the home and surrounding land is worth £875,000 at the time of the hearing, with each sister owning an additional portfolio of investments and other property worth £150,000, taking the total value of each sister's estate to £587,500. The first £300,000 would not be liable for inheritance tax, so the tax bill would be 40% of £287,500, or £115,000.

application of Article 14, though my ultimate conclusion on the facts of this case concurs with the majority. Article 14 provides that:

> The enjoyment of the rights and freedoms set forth in this Convention shall be secured without discrimination on any ground such as sex, race, colour, language, religion, political or other opinion, national or social origin, association with a national minority, property, birth or other status.

It is well established that 'other status' covers a range of personal characteristics, including marital status (*Sahin v Germany* [GC], no. 30943/96, ECHR 2003-VIII).

O-V3 As the majority correctly note, not every difference in treatment will constitute a violation of Article 14. The difference in treatment must first of all be between those who are in relevantly similar situations (*D H and Others v Czech Republic* [GC], no. 57325/00, ECHR 2007-IV, (2008) 47 EHRR 3). It is at this point that the majority consider the applicants to have failed because they can be distinguished from spouses/civil partners on the basis that 'the very essence of the connection between siblings is consanguinity, whereas one of the defining characteristics of a marriage [or civil partnership] is that it is forbidden to close family members' (§ 62). Furthermore, they find that marriage confers a special status, which gives rise to social, personal and legal consequences, and is protected under Article 12. Similarly, the 'legal consequences of civil partnership … which couples expressly and deliberately decide to incur, set these types of relationship apart from other forms of cohabitation' (§ 65). As such, it is not the length and nature of the relationship that is determinative, but rather the absence of a legally binding agreement between the applicants renders it 'fundamentally different' to that of spouses or civil partners (§ 65).

O-V4 In my view, the majority have erred in their analysis on this point and have been led in that direction by erroneous case law on the 'special status' of marriage in previous decisions in which unmarried couples have been treated less favourably than married couples (*Shackell v the United Kingdom*, no. 45851/99, 27 April 2000), even when the law prevents them from marrying as in the case of same-sex couples in many States. It is illogical and circular to distinguish a relationship between those who are legally prohibited from making the sort of legally binding public undertaking that spouses and civil partners make, on the basis that they have not done so. Indeed, making a distinction on this basis renders the prohibition of marital status discrimination under Article 14 completely ineffective in any case that seeks to compare the treatment of married and unmarried couples.

O-V5 There is, perhaps, an arguable case to be made that in a situation where a couple have chosen not to marry, despite it being available to them, that they have declined the various protections and privileges that spousal status brings and therefore any difference in treatment could be justified. However, this is not the set of facts under consideration in this case and in any event this would speak to the second part of the test, as a question of justification of differential treatment and proportionality rather than as an indication that they are not similarly situated to spouses for the purposes of the first part of the Article 14 test.

O-V6 In a situation such as this one, where siblings are not permitted to marry or become civil partners, or a situation where same-sex couples are not permitted to marry or become civil partners, it is unjust to effectively punish them (by not providing them access to even the first stage of Article 14 protection) for the decision of the State to prevent them from undertaking a legally-binding agreement. This is not to suggest that the State must allow any type of relationship access to spousal status, nor is it to suggest that they cannot necessarily treat spouses differently to non-spouses, but these points need to be dealt with in the second and third stages of the Article 14 test. Therefore, for the first part of the Article 14 test we must consider the *substantive* aspects of the relationship, rather than the (absent) formalities.

O-V7 Perhaps the reason why this Court has turned to the legal form in the past is because the characteristics of spousal relationships are so difficult to determine, as they can be widely diverse between different relationships. However, some jurisdictions have recognized unmarried relationships for different purposes and in doing so have compiled general lists of characteristics that should be met in order to qualify. For example, the Property (Relationships) Act 1984 of New South Wales, Australia, seeks evidence of a set of criteria that is clearly based on assumptions about marriage, such as: a long-term, cohabiting, sexual relationship; financial dependence or interdependence; mutual commitment to a shared life; and the reputation and public aspects of the relationship (s4(2)). However, none of these factors is required except cohabitation and 'a court determining whether such a relationship exists is entitled to have regard to such matters, and to attach such weight to any matter, as may seem appropriate to the court in the circumstances of the case' (s4(3)).

O-V8 Whilst this Act is not binding on the UK or this Court, its existence demonstrates that it is not outside the ability of this Court to construct a similar list of spousal characteristics to test whether a non-marital relationship could be relevantly similar to spouses. If we compare the facts of the applicants' relationship to this list as an example, there are few potential difficulties in coming to the conclusion that they are in fact similarly situated to spouses/civil partners. There is little doubt that they have a long-term, cohabiting relationship, financial interdependence, and mutual commitment to a shared life. They do not meet the sexual relationship aspect and the 'reputation and public aspects of the relationship' are unlikely to be that they are in a spousal relationship but the question is what weight should be attached to these matters in the context of the inheritance tax exemption in question. Is the sexual nature of the relationship really the most important determining factor for a tax exemption? I would suggest not. Rather, the most weight should be placed on financial interdependence and, given the family home is claimed to be at stake in this case, cohabitation.

O-V9 According to the Government's submission, the purpose of the tax exemption for spouses is to 'provide the survivor with a measure of financial security, and thus promote marriage' [50]. Leaving aside the issue of promoting marriage, which I return to later, it is difficult to believe that this measure of financial security is really due only to those who are in a sexual relationship. Financial interdependence and sexual relations are quite separate issues. Though they are often found in the same relationship, the applicants provide an example of where the former can exist without the latter. It is also worth noting that, while civil partnerships were intended to provide a marriage-like relationship for same-sex couples and extend the tax exemption to them, they do not, technically, require sexual relations at any point during the relationship, as there is no mention of consummation in the Civil Partnership Act 2004. Similarly, it is incredibly rare that a marriage is nullified for non-consummation in the UK; in fact, non-consummation on its own is not a ground for nullity. Rather, there must have been an inability or wilful refusal to consummate on the part of the respondent to a petition (Matrimonial Causes Act 1973, s.12(a) and (b)). Spouses may quite legitimately agree that it is not to be a sexual relationship without invalidating their lawful marriage. On this basis, rather less weight should be attached to the sexual nature of the relationship in any circumstances.

O-V10 It is worth noting that the applicants are not seeking access to marriage or civil partnership. They seek only a remedy to their tax liability, which in their view is discriminatory because others in similar relationships are exempt, namely spouses and civil partners. Though it was mentioned in their submission that they would have entered into a civil partnership had it been possible, I hope that on reflection the sisters would have realised that this marriage-like institution is not suitable for siblings, regardless of the length of their cohabitation or their financial interdependence, due to the legal structure imposed on the recognition of spousal relationships that are not necessarily relevant in the taxation context. The legal institutions of marriage and civil partnership are designed to recognise an exclusive relationship between two people, voluntarily entered into, and, although it is intended to be for life, there is a mechanism for the legal dissolution of this relationship. It may be that the applicants would be willing to forgo other potential spousal relationships after they had registered their civil partnership, but if one sister did subsequently form a romantic relationship she would have to demonstrate the 'irretrievable breakdown' of her relationship with her sister in order to marry or get a civil partnership with this partner. Similarly, if there had been a third surviving Burden sibling who also cohabited with the applicants, or if they were brother and sister rather than sisters, they would find themselves excluded once again, or in the former case facing a difficult decision about which two siblings would enter the civil partnership. The amendment to the Civil Partnership Bill that was introduced in the UK Parliament was merely a wrecking amendment and would not have been a workable solution to the problem of marital status discrimination in this case.

O-V11 Marital status discrimination does not occur as a result of exclusion from the institution of marriage *per* se. It is well within a State's margin of appreciation to set the terms of who may marry, as acknowledged in the wording of Article 12, that 'men and women of marriageable age have the right to marry and found a family, *according to the national laws governing the exercise of this right*' (my emphasis). It is instead the legal and economic privileging of this spousal relationship over and above other similarly situated relationships for the purpose of promoting marriage above other family forms that results in what is in my view unlawful marital status discrimination. As a result, the focus must be on the individual spousal privilege and whether or not there is a justification for continuing with this particular privilege and, if so, continuing to exclude similarly situated non-marital relationships from it. In this, I am assisted by the persuasive recommendations of the Law Commission of Canada's (2001) report, *Beyond Conjugality: Recognizing and Supporting Close Personal Adult Relationships*.

O-V12 Therefore, looking at the totality of the circumstances of the applicants' lives and the fact that they meet what are arguably the most significant indicators of a spousal relationship *in this context* of tax liability (that is, long-term cohabitation, mutual support and commitment to a shared life, and most importantly financial interdependence), I would conclude that they are sufficiently similarly situated, in a relevant way according to the context of the claim (being tax-related), to be analogous to spouses or civil partners.

O-V13 The next part of the Article 14 test is whether the difference in treatment is objectively and reasonably justified. In other words, it must pursue a legitimate aim and 'there must be a reasonable relationship of proportionality between the means employed and the aim sought to be realised' (*Stec and Others v the United Kingdom*, [GC], nos. 65731/01 and 65900/01,§ 51, ECHR 2006-VI, (2006) 43 EHRR 47). While the majority in this Court did not find it necessary to go on to consider this, having already found that the applicants were not analogous to spouses, the Chamber did consider this part of the test. The claimants failed before the Chamber as it accepted the UK Government's submission that the inheritance tax exemption for spouses and civil partners pursues the legitimate aim of promoting stable, committed relationships: 'The State cannot be criticized for pursuing, through its taxation system, policies designed to promote marriage …' [59].

O-V14 However, I would answer the question of whether that is a legitimate aim in the negative. The UK Government's claim that the difference in treatment is designed to promote marriage is not compatible with the prohibition on marital status discrimination under Article 14. The promotion of marriage above other forms of family is also not justified by Article 12.

O-V15 There appears to be an assumption in the previous case law that because the right to marry is protected separately under Article 12 then it must follow that special legal privileges for those who are married are justifiable (see for example *Shackell v United Kingdom*, cited above). I disagree with this interpretation.

Article 12 provides not only for a right to marry but also to found a family, and States have been offered a wide margin of appreciation by virtue of the additional phrase 'according to national laws governing the exercise of this right'.[2] States should not, by virtue of Article 12, impede the right to marry and found a family but this is not the same as a requirement to actively promote marriage above other forms of family. I would also suggest that it does not in itself give States *permission* to actively prefer the marital family to other forms of family in its laws and fiscal policies.

O-V16 Analogy on this point may be made to the protection for freedom of religion in Article 9. There is no suggestion that States must actively promote a religion, or give additional benefits to citizens who have religious beliefs over those given to those who do not. To do so would be contrary to the Convention as a fundamental aspect of Article 9 is the right to freedom from religion, the right to have no religious belief (*Buscarini v San Marino* [GC], no. 24645/94, ECHR 1999-I, (1999) 30 EHRR 208). Just as States should not prefer one religious organization or belief over other (or none) under Article 9, they also should not prefer one method of founding a family over another under Article 12. Even if the majority in this Court would not go so far as to agree that there should also be freedom *from* marriage under Article 12, the prohibition of marital status discrimination under Article 14 at a minimum supports the proposition that spouses (and now civil partners) should not be treated more favourably than similarly situated unmarried adults who have formed families in other ways than through marriage, or who have not formed families at all.

O-V17 Giving spouses a 'special status' above that of other forms of family and relationship treats everyone else as having less value than spouses and on that basis cannot be justified under the Convention. In the words of Lady Hale:

> Treating some as automatically having less value than others not only causes pain and distress to that person but also violates his or her dignity as a human being … such treatment is damaging to society as a whole. (*Ghaidan v Godin-Mendoza* [2004] UKHL 30, per Lady Hale, para 132)

Although this decision is not binding on this Court it is highly persuasive as it is a decision from a national superior court interpreting the Convention in line with national law. Having therefore concluded that promoting marriage is not a legitimate aim there is no need to consider whether it is proportionate.

O-V18 In theory, the State could overcome this problem by extending the spousal privileges to other forms of family but this would almost inevitably shift the

[2] See for example the patience demonstrated by the Court in the line of cases brought by trans people seeking access to marriage prior to *Christine Goodwin v the United Kingdom* [GC], no. 28957/95, ECHR 2002-VI, (2002) 35 EHRR 18, and the cases brought by same-sex couples: *Rees v United Kingdom*, 17 October 1986, Series A no. 106, (1987) 9 EHRR 56, *Cossey v United Kingdom*, 27 September 1990, Series A no. 184, (1991) 13 EHRR 622; *Sheffield and Horsham v the United* Kingdom, judgment of 30 July 1998, Reports of Judgments and Decisions 1998-V, (1999) 27 EHRR 163.

discrimination onto single people and, in the context of this case, have a disastrous impact on tax revenue. Therefore, the next question is whether the best way to remedy this marital status discrimination is to abolish the tax exemption altogether. The UK claims that the other purpose of the tax exemption is to provide financial security on the death of a spouse. As I have concluded that others, such as the applicants, could be similarly situated to spouses, and it must be the case that some people would be wealthy enough to continue to enjoy financial security on the death of their spouse despite paying inheritance tax, it would be more rational to distribute this particular privilege on the basis of financial need rather than marital status. In general, I would recommend that privileges associated with marriage should be abolished and where they are valuable for a purpose other than merely promoting marriage should be allocated on a different, non-discriminatory, basis, such as financial need rather than a preferred family status. The way this is to be achieved is, of course, a matter of policy for each government, but the need to eliminate discrimination on the basis of marital status is a matter of law.

O-V19 The final part of the Article 14 test is whether the Government is within its margin of appreciation in treating the applicants less favourably than spouses or civil partners. There is a margin of appreciation for the state in 'assessing whether and to what extent differences in otherwise similar situations justify differences in treatment' (*Stec v United Kingdom*, cited above, § 51). The margin of appreciation is wide in relation to taxation matters but this does not give the Government a complete exemption from abiding by Article 14 where they have created hardship or injustice. It is also wider where there is a lack of agreement between the laws of member states. On this issue, there has been a series of case law that has allowed governments to discriminate on the basis of marital status and I hope this judgment marks the beginning of the end for that line of reasoning. There is a wide margin of appreciation but states must now be on notice that it will no longer be acceptable to discriminate on the basis of marital status by privileging marriage through the tax system and in other ways. The right to marry does not include a right to extra privileges or more advantageous treatment on the basis of that marriage because the state should not favour one form of family life over another.

O-V20 However, in the circumstances of this particular case, I find that these applicants have failed to demonstrate hardship sufficient to overcome the UK's margin of appreciation. Their assets, as reported to this Court, are more than adequate to cover their tax liability without them having to sell the family home and on that basis they will not suffer a particular hardship that suggests a tax exemption ought to be extended to them. Nevertheless, this Court has been far too deferential to both the institution of marriage and the States' margin of appreciation in respect of marriage's supposed 'special status' at the expense of properly enforcing the non-discrimination provision of Article 14. There is no legitimate reason to give spouses privileges over and above other family forms but extending this privilege to siblings (particularly in this context where there is no evidence of significant financial hardship for the applicants) would merely exacerbate the problem. As such, I reluctantly concur with the majority's conclusion, albeit for different reasons.

O-V21 In sum, I find that the sisters' relationship is similarly situated to that of spouses for the purposes of Article 14. They meet all the usual expectations of spouses (including financial interdependence, arguably the most significant for taxation purposes) other than the existence or possibility of a sexual relationship between them. While a sexual relationship may be significant in relation to some spousal benefits, it has little relevance to inheritance tax. The financial security that the UK government seeks to provide to spouses through this tax exemption is just as applicable to financially interdependent cohabiting siblings. I also find that there is no legitimate justification for the difference in treatment between these similarly situated groups. While the UK may wish to promote marriage, it must recognise that this is not the only form of a stable and socially beneficial relationship. The legal and economic privileging of marriage cannot be justified by the fact of an existence of a right to marry under Article 12: a right to marry is different from a right to or justification of special privileges by virtue of being married. However, I reach the same conclusion as the majority on the basis of the final part of the discrimination test: these sisters have not suffered hardship through the discriminatory treatment such as to overcome the UK's wide margin of appreciation on taxation issues. Nevertheless, I would strongly recommend that the UK consider ways to withdraw its existing spousal privileges and redistribute them (where necessary) on a more rational basis than merely promoting marriage.

Reflections

This judgment takes the form of a sole-authored opinion because it was originally written for a workshop, *Radically Rethinking Marriage*, that I co-organised with Professor Suzanne Lenon at the International Institute for the Sociology of Law in Oñati, Spain.[1] I chose this case as a vehicle to 'radically rethink' marriage because it has the potential to give life to a proposal that has been put forward by several progressive scholars (including myself) in various forms, that we ought to de-centre the institution of marriage,[2] and yet the facts of this case also demonstrate how such proposals could be co-opted to further an agenda of private wealth transmission rather than to collectivise social responsibility for care. The process of drafting this judgment was informed in two key ways by my socialist feminist perspective as I sought to take a different approach to the interpretation of Article 14.

First, the Grand Chamber heard this case in 2008, the year of the financial crash that led to this subsequent decade (and counting) of austerity. Though it was not appropriate to explicitly bring this into the judgment within the context of the jurisprudence of the European Court of Human Rights, the impact of state austerity (particularly the way in which it has impacted hardest on children while pensioners, and particularly wealthy pensioners, have been largely protected) was prominent in my mind while I wrote the judgment. In particular, I could not help but consider the privilege of the Burden sisters, who were seeking to retain the entirety of their (inherited) wealth, compared to the struggles faced by the younger generation who are widely reported to be giving up on the idea of home ownership as a result partly of house price inflation and a shortage of affordable housing.[3] Though the trope of the vulnerable and poor pensioner was drawn upon by the Burden sisters in this case, in general the pattern of poverty in the UK has changed dramatically over the last 20 years, when 'pensioner poverty has fallen sharply, while child poverty has fallen slowly and unevenly and working-age poverty has

[1] For the papers from this workshop, which includes an earlier version of the of the *Burden* judgment rewritten by me, see: www.iisj.net/en/about-iisj/news/osls-vol-6-no-6-2016-radically-rethinking-marriage.

[2] MA Fineman, *The Neutered Mother, The Sexual Family and other Twentieth Century Tragedies* (New York NY, Routledge, 1995); MA Fineman, *The Autonomy Myth: A Theory of Dependency* (London, The New Press, 2004); Law Commission of Canada, *Beyond Conjugality: Recognizing and Supporting Close Personal Adult Relationships* (2001); J Herring, 'Making Family Law More Careful' in J Wallbank and J Herring (eds), *Vulnerabilities, Care and Family Law* (London, Routledge, 2014); N Barker, 'After the Wedding, What Next? Conservatism and Conjugality' in N Barker and D Monk (eds), *From Civil Partnership to Same-Sex Marriage: Interdisciplinary Reflections* (London, Routledge, 2015).

[3] See for example: P Inman, 'Young People in UK Increasingly Giving up on Owning a Home – Halifax Survey' (*The Guardian*, 7 April 2015). Available at: www.theguardian.com/money/2015/apr/07/young-people-uk-increasingly-giving-up-owning-home-halifax-survey.
The rise of campaign group *Generation Rent*, which 'campaigns for professionally managed, secure, decent and affordable private rented homes in sustainable communities' is also indicative of the shift from home ownership to private renting: www.generationrent.org.

risen, particularly in the last decade'.[4] As such, I would argue that it is not horizontal transmission of wealth between siblings that should be the primary concern of tax policy but rather addressing poverty, which at the moment is statistically much more likely to impact the younger generation, with 34 per cent of 16–19 year olds and 29 per cent of 20–24 year olds in poverty in the UK, a six point increase from a decade earlier.[5] It is not at all clear how this would be addressed by reducing or eliminating inheritance tax for the wealthiest few estates in recognition of care that has been provided, even where that care is inter-generational and at the expense of the carer's paid employment rather than the more mutual support and interdependence of the Burden sisters' case.

Furthermore, in considering the surviving Burden sister's dilemma of choosing between downsizing from a four-bedroom home to a smaller property or selling some of her other investments to pay the tax bill, I was also mindful of the plight of the poorest people in the UK who receive housing benefit and have recently had their benefits cut as part of the notorious 'bedroom tax', or under-occupancy penalty, which was introduced in April 2013.[6] Under these regulations, housing benefit has been reduced by 14 per cent for those who are deemed to have a 'spare' bedroom in their home, or by 25 per cent for those who are deemed to have two or more spare bedrooms, despite a shortage of affordable smaller one-bedroom properties for people to transfer into. The tenants, often already living in poverty, then need to pay the additional cost, usually to a private landlord due to the shortage of public housing. The bedroom tax does not apply to those who are over 65 years old and there are exemptions for people with certain disabilities who require a room for overnight carers but there are multiple reports of disabled people having to pay this tax and not receiving help with it, despite local authorities being given a fund to make 'discretionary housing payments' to cover the difference in such cases.[7] In this economic and social policy context it is difficult to have sympathy for the Burden sisters, whose total wealth places them in the top 4.8 per cent of estates, which are those liable for inheritance tax (Office for Budget Responsibility 2014).

However, second, and being mindful of the adage that hard cases make bad law, the question remains of whether there might nevertheless be principled reasons to recognise interdependence between non-spouses, particularly as a way

[4] T MacInnes et al, *Monitoring Poverty and Social Exclusion 2014* (New Policy Institute and Joseph Rowntree Foundation, 2014). Available at: www.jrf.org.uk/sites/default/files/jrf/migrated/files/MPSE-2014-FULL.pdf.

[5] ibid, 28.

[6] Housing Benefit (Amendment) Regulations 2012.

[7] Cases where the bedroom tax has been challenged by people with disabilities include: *Burnip v Birmingham City Council and Secretary of State for Work and Pensions*, *Trengrove v Walsall Metropolitan Council and Secretary of State for Work and Pensions*, and *Gorry v Wiltshire Council and Secretary of State for Work and Pensions* [2012] EWCA Civ 629; *R (on the application of MA and Others) v Secretary of State for Work and Pensions* [2014] EWCA Civ 13; and *Rutherford v Secretary of State for Work and Pensions and Pembrokeshire County Council* [2014] EWHC 1631.

of addressing vulnerability within both the elderly population and their carers.[8] With an aging population needing care, and this care increasingly provided within the family or friendship network, as a feminist judge I had to consider whether it is really justifiable to continue to limit legal and economic privileges of marriage to spouses and civil partners. In other words, should the inheritance tax exemption remain, but be based on demonstrating a relationship of care and dependency, rather than a spousal relationship? Some family lawyers have made arguments along these lines, though more broadly than just in relation to the inheritance tax claim at issue in this case. For example, Martha Fineman argues that the whole system of spousal privileges ought to be reoriented away from the sexual relationship between adults, with marriage abolished as a legal institution, and the state should focus its attention on encouraging and supporting caretaker-dependent relationship.[9] Similarly, Jonathan Herring draws on Fineman's work (amongst others) in making his argument that family law in the UK should be more focused on care, rather than sex.[10] He argues that for each of the three functions of family law (as identified by John Eekelaar:[11] namely protective, adjustive and supportive), the existence of a sexual relationship is irrelevant and not necessarily a good indicator of commitment or intimacy. Instead a caring relationship is what creates the vulnerability that the law ought to address and it is these relationships that benefit the state, particularly where the care would otherwise have to be provided by the state and as such they should receive the support of the state.[12]

Moving away from privileging sexual relationships through the marriage model is an attractive proposition, and it is one that I sought to advance in my feminist judgment through rejecting the earlier line of jurisprudence that uses Article 12 to justify discrimination in favour of spouses above other types of relationships. However, my concern about both Fineman's and Herring's approaches is that by recognising and privileging care, there becomes an expectation that care will be provided within the family and a resulting withdrawal of state services.[13] There is also the important question of what happens when the recipient of care does not have the resources to adequately compensate the carer's financial disadvantage through property redistribution. It seems they would be in the same position as many wives find themselves on divorce: having to rely on state welfare and

[8] For example, one of the ways in which people seek to avoid inheritance tax, by transferring assets to family while they are alive, can increase the vulnerability of elderly people.

[9] Fineman 1995, 2004, above n 2.

[10] Herring, above n 2.

[11] J Eekelaar, *Family Law and Social Policy* (London, Weidenfeld & Nicolson, 1984) 24–26.

[12] Herring, above n 2, 55.

[13] See also SB Boyd (ed), *Challenging the Public/Private Divide: Feminism, Law and Public Policy* (Toronto, University of Toronto Press, 1997) 14; SB Boyd, 'Family, Law and Sexuality: Feminist Engagements' (1999) 8(3) *Social and Legal Studies* 369, 377; and CFL Young, 'What's Sex Got to Do With It? Tax and the "Family" in Canada' (2006) 2(1) *Journal of the Australasian Tax Teachers Association* 16, 22.

stigmatised as a result. While collective responsibility for care is hidden behind incentives for privatised responsibility, these rewards for care in the form of legal recognition and privileges render both the carer and the cared for vulnerable to changing family circumstances, even in families that initially did have sufficient resources. It should also not be assumed that legal recognition will result in financial benefits for all those in caretaking relationships: as Claire Young has found in relation to the recognition of same-sex couples in Canada's tax laws, while some benefited from inclusion others, usually those least able to afford the additional cost, have actually acquired an increased tax burden.[14] She demonstrates the ways in which many of these relationship tax breaks, including those focused on dependency, are 'inequitable and discriminate without good reason against those couples with low incomes and in favour of those with high incomes', as arguably would be the case with the expansion of the inheritance tax exemption sought by the Burden sisters.[15] Therefore, in writing my judgment I was cognisant of the ways in which reorienting legal recognition and privilege in this way can serve the interests of the privatising, neo-liberal state and work against poorer carers and non-carers.

On the basis of her analysis of the Canadian tax system, Claire Young argues in favour of enacting the recommendations of the Law Commission of Canada (LCC).[16] They rejected any relationship-based approach to legal privileges as far as possible, focusing instead on the objective of the individual provision. This means that if we were to apply that methodology in the case of the Burden sisters, the question would be not about how deserving or otherwise the sisters are of recognition but rather about what the objective of the inheritance tax exemption is, and whether the sisters' relationship fulfils that objective-based criterion. However, the LCC methodology could not be used in an international law context (and would be a radical step even for a national Supreme Court), being more suited to a policy process than a judicial one. The 'discipline' of a feminist judgment is to show how a feminist judge could have decided a case on existing legal principles and within the court's norms,[17] so I was confined to a rather more traditional approach, asking the familiar Article 14 questions: are the sisters similarly situated to spouses? If so, is the difference in treatment justified? Is the UK within its margin of appreciation? Nevertheless, this approach allowed me to go some way towards reconciling my own internal conflict between on the one hand wanting to move away from conjugality as the privileged relationship form to the detriment of others, and

[14] CFL Young, 'Taxing Times for Lesbians and Gay Men: Twenty Years Later' in R Leckey (ed), *After Legal Equality: Family, Sex, Kinship* (Abingdon, Routledge, 2015) 134.

[15] Young, above n 13, 17.

[16] Law Commission of Canada, above n 2.

[17] R Hunter, C McGlynn, and E Rackley, 'Feminist Judgments: An Introduction' in R Hunter, C McGlynn, and E Rackley (eds), *Feminist Judgments: From Theory to Practice* (Oxford, Hart Publishing, 2010) 3.

on the other hand seeking to avoid further entrenchment of economic privilege through expansion of tax exemptions for wealthy carers/carees at the expense of poorer families. It was the margin of appreciation, the final question that neither the Chamber nor the Grand Chamber needed to make in their judgments, that allows me to avoid extending the tax exemption, finding that there was no particular hardship in this case that serves to overcome the wide margin of appreciation that States have in relation to taxation issues. Yet, in some respects I remain uneasy, not least because had the facts been slightly different it would have been much more difficult (perhaps impossible) to avoid finding in favour of the sisters and thus extending the tax exemption and, for these hypothetical applicants that would have been the right outcome. For example, had the sisters had no other assets besides their shared home, which had dramatically appreciated in value such that the tax bill did exceed their savings and other income (and assuming the absence of measures such as a capacity to defer the tax payments until after the death of the surviving sister), I would have had to find that this was hardship such as to overcome the UK's margin of appreciation, even though in property-value terms the sisters would have remained amongst the UK's wealthiest households. This perhaps represents the limitations of international courts, being bound by the principle of subsidiarity and not being able to enter into a dialogue with national legislatures about the broader policy issues at stake.

10

Opuz v Turkey

SHAZIA CHOUDHRY AND JONATHAN HERRING

Authors' Note

The facts of *Opuz v Turkey*[1] were at the same time shocking but depressingly familiar. A tragic story, reminiscent of countless others across the decades and around the globe. A man and woman meet and fall in love. They move in together, and then the abuse starts; apparently minor at first, but gradually increasing in severity. Help is sought from the police and state authorities but there is no intervention or that which is done is ineffective. The woman is told to try and make things up with her husband. The abuse is dismissed as simply a family matter. It is just her word against his. It is not serious enough for the police. The abuse escalates until there is serious violence that leads to death.

Of course, for Nahide Opuz this was not simply 'another story of domestic abuse'. Her experience was of abuse throughout the marriage. She was stabbed with a knife by her husband seven times, suffering life-threatening wounds; she and her mother were run down by a car; and finally her mother was shot dead by her husband. Her repeated calls for help to the authorities, went largely unheeded.

This judgment might be seen as a somewhat anomalous addition to this collection as it has been viewed as generally positive in feminist circles, mainly because of its ground-breaking recognition that domestic violence falls within the scope and ambit of the European Convention on Human Rights (ECHR).[2] The European Court of Human Rights (the Court or ECtHR) held that domestic abuse cannot be dismissed as simply a private matter. The State has positive obligations to protect women from domestic abuse. A victim of domestic abuse's human rights are breached even if the abuse comes from an individual actor, rather than the State. In other words, the State is both required not to commit torture or use inhuman or degrading treatment and to take positive steps to ensure that individuals

[1] *Opuz v Turkey*, no 33401/02, ECHR 2009, (2010) 50 EHRR 28.

[2] eg P Londono, 'Developing Human Rights Principles in Cases of Gender-based Violence: Opuz v Turkey in the European Court of Human Rights' (2000) 9 *Human Rights Law Review* 697.

do not torture or degrade one another. This straightforward, but key, argument was at the heart of the reasoning in this case. It enabled the Court to find a breach of Article 2 in relation to the killing of Ms Opuz's mother and Article 3 in relation to the abuse of Ms Opuz by her husband. The State was aware of Mr Opuz's abuse of his wife and the threats he made to both her and his mother-in-law. The State could have taken steps to protect them, but did not. The Court found that the State had therefore breached the victims' convention rights. Significantly, the Court also found a breach of Article 14 because the failure to protect victims of domestic abuse in Turkey impacted particularly on women and so amounted to discrimination on the grounds of sex.

In this sense, *Opuz* is not a judgment that springs to mind in terms of requiring a feminist re-write. However, when we revisited the judgment, some seven years later, it became clear that there were some elements of the judgment that could have been improved and some elements that were even troubling.

First, the judgment made no attempt to provide a definition of domestic violence. This is a significant omission not only in terms of the need for clarity concerning the range of behaviours that the term encompasses, but also in terms of how well the Court has engaged with the valuable research which has been undertaken to understand domestic violence.[3] Thus, in our re-written judgment we have included a wide-ranging definition of domestic violence. In particular, we have discussed Evan Stark's concept of coercive control, which he had written about well before this judgment was given. This allowed us to develop our discussion of the applicability of Article 3 in order to view domestic violence as part of a continued spectrum of events rather than as a series of individual incidents of harm/violence.

Second, in the original judgment there was no acknowledgement of the feminist explanation of domestic violence: that it exists as part of patriarchal social structures, constituting an intentional pattern of behaviour utilised to establish and maintain power and control over a female partner or ex-partner.[4] This is important, not just because it acknowledges the significant role that was, and continues to be, played by grass roots feminism in bringing domestic violence to the attention of law and policy makers, but also because an acknowledgement of the structural nature of domestic violence will necessarily have implications for the type of response needed from the courts as one element of the societal response to the issue. As a result, we refer to the gendered nature of domestic violence throughout our judgment, making clear that it is an issue that disproportionately affects women and therefore centralises the fact that domestic abuse is discrimination against women. Although this may seem a rather basic point to those who work in this field, we felt that we needed to explicitly lay this point down

[3] For a discussion of the terminology and definition of domestic abuse, see M Madden Dempsey, *Prosecuting Domestic Violence* (Oxford, Oxford University Press, 2009) ch 6.

[4] See Madden Dempsey, ibid, ch 8; E Stark, *Coercive Control* (Oxford, Oxford University Press, 2009).

as a 'marker', given the rather worrying increasing tendency to discuss domestic violence within law and policy circles in gender neutral terms.[5] Highlighting domestic violence as a form of discrimination against women also added to our analysis on the applicability of Article 14.

Third, we wished to address the lack of intersectional analysis and the implied 'othering' of Turkey in the original judgment. Although general statements were made in the original judgment concerning the 'phenomenon' of domestic violence, we were struck by the lack of explicit acknowledgement that this is a global – and culture-free – issue. The focus on the experience of women in Turkey, we felt, implied that this was an issue that disproportionately affected Turkey, rather than an issue which is widely acknowledged to be a worldwide epidemic.[6] Introducing an intersectional understanding of domestic violence informed the drafting of the part of our judgment which dealt with the development of positive obligations in this area. We included a number of examples of steps that could be taken, drawn from the Istanbul Convention,[7] which meet and recognise the diverse needs of victims of domestic violence.

Fourth, the original judgment lacked a specific discussion on, or acknowledgement of, the prevalence of domestic violence. We remedied this in our judgment by adding in a number of references to research and data demonstrating the prevalence of domestic violence, widely available at the time the original judgment was written, including Europe-wide research conducted by the Council of Europe and research from the UN. Providing this data had the added benefit of placing the concerns about Turkey within the overall context of the worldwide prevalence of domestic violence.

Finally, the absence of any reference to the rights of the children involved in the case, given the judgment was delivered in 2009, is particularly striking. Although the ECHR does not explicitly provide for the rights of children, the protection of children's rights by the ECtHR has, nonetheless, been steadily developed, not least due to the influence of the UN Convention on the Rights of the Child, reference to which has often been made by the Court.[8] However, no reference to the rights of the children involved in the case was made in the original judgment. The original court were therefore limited in terms of what we could include, given that no specific claim had been made in respect of the rights of the children in the case, as indeed we were in our judgment. However, we felt it important to include a paragraph explicitly setting out how the rights of the children could potentially be breached in any future cases concerning domestic violence in order to further increase the scope of the Convention with regards to the issue.

[5] See eg J Herring, 'The Istanbul Convention: Is Domestic Abuse Violence Against Women?' in G Douglas, M Murch and V Stephens (eds), *International and National Perspectives on Child and Family Law: Essays in Honour of Nigel Lowe* (Cambridge, Intersentia, 2017).

[6] World Health Organisation, *Violence Against Women* (Geneva, WHO, 2017).

[7] Council of Europe, Convention on Preventing and Combating Violence Against Women and Domestic Violence (The Istanbul Convention) (Council of European, 2011).

[8] eg *Ipek and Others v Turkey*, nos 17019/02 and 30070/02, 3 February 2009.

JUDGMENT

OPUZ v TURKEY

(Application no. 33401/02)

A Chamber of the European Court of Human Rights consisting of:

Shazia Choudhry (President) and Jonathan Herring

9 June 2009

THE FACTS

I. THE CIRCUMSTANCES OF THE CASE

1. The facts of this case are horrific and disturbing. Yet, they are also far too common. If ever this court had the power to make a judgment that will impact on the reality of the many individuals in the signatory states, this is it. Domestic abuse is and has been the reality of life for many women. The time has come to make the clearest possible statement: States must ensure that they comply with their obligations to protect victims from abuse.
2. Nahide Opuz and her step-brother (HO) started their relationship in 1990, when Ms Opuz was about 18 years old. They had three children together born in 1993, 1994 and 1996. They married in 1995. From the very start of this relationship, Ms Opuz suffered abuse at the hands of her partner.
3. Although we have been presented with a set of agreed facts by the parties detailing incidents of abuse, it is likely there are many more incidents for which there is no documentary proof and even incidents that Ms Opuz did not, at least at the time, perceive as abuse.
4. The accepted incidents were as follows:

   (i) On 10 April 1995, Ms Opuz and her mother filed a complaint with the Diyarbakir Public Prosecutor's Office, alleging that HO and his father had been threatening to kill them and demanding money from them. HO and his father also wanted to bring other men into the house, which could be seen as an implied sexual threat. Their complaint was evidenced by significant injuries including bruises, scratches and injuries. These were sufficiently severe to lead both Ms Opuz and her mother to have to take five days off work. Although proceedings were commenced against HO and his father, they were dismissed following the withdrawal of the complaints by Ms Opuz and her mother.

   (ii) On 11 April 1996, HO severely assaulted Ms Opuz to such an extent the medical report made on that occasion concluded her injuries were such as to endanger life. Again, criminal proceedings were started. HO was initially detained but was released during the proceedings and shortly after his release Ms Opuz withdrew her complaint and was recorded as saying that she and her husband had 'made their peace'.

(iii) On 5 February 1998, HO assaulted Ms Opuz, her mother, and her sister. He produced a knife and inflicted injuries. Ms Opuz could not work for seven days as a result. The prosecuting authority decided not to bring proceedings as there was insufficient evidence.

(iv) On 4 March 1998, HO drove into Ms Opuz and her mother, which resulted in life threatening injuries. He stated to the police that both women had thrown themselves in front of his car. He spent 25 days in prison in relation to that incident. Charges for issuing death threats were dismissed after the complainants withdrew their applications.

(v) On 29 October 2001, Ms Opuz was stabbed by her husband in front of the children after an argument over the meal she had prepared for him. She was treated in hospital for seven stab wounds, each up to 5cm in length. He was convicted and ordered to pay a fine of 839,957,040 Turkish liras, payable in eight instalments.

(vi) On 14 November 2001, a complaint from Ms Opuz that she had been mistreated by her husband was lodged, but no action was taken.

(vii) On 19 November 2001, further complaints of threats were made, specifically alleging that HO has said 'I am going to kill you, your children and all your family!' She complained he carried knives and guns around the home. Investigations were carried out, and on 22 February she complained of further threats, fearing her life was in immediate danger and requesting police help. The police made some enquiries of Ms Opuz's telephone company, but no further steps were taken.

(viii) On 11 March 2002, Ms Opuz's mother drove to her house to take her away from her husband. Shortly after they left, Mr Opuz stopped the van they were in and shot Ms Opuz's mother dead. In the subsequent criminal proceedings Mr Opuz claimed his wife was living an immoral life and her mother was taking 'his wife and children away from him'. He was convicted of murder in March 2008 and sentenced to life imprisonment, but the sentence with mitigated due to the provocation by the wife and his good conduct during the trial, so that he was fined 180 new Turkish liras. As he had spent time in pre-trial detention, the court decided he should be immediately released.

(ix) On his release, HO threatened Ms Opuz's new partner with violence unless he revealed where she was, as Ms Opuz had gone into hiding. He managed to discover her new identity and threats were made against her. The police circulated pictures of Mr Opuz to police forces in the region so he could be arrested if he approached the applicant's new home.

II. THE NATURE OF DOMESTIC VIOLENCE

5. Although this case concerns Turkey, the court recognises that violence against women is not confined to a specific culture, region or country, nor to particular groups of women within a society. The roots of violence against women lie in historically unequal power relations between men and women, and persistent discrimination against women.
6. 'Violence against women' must therefore be understood as a violation of human rights and a form of discrimination against women and shall include all acts of gender-based violence that result in, or are likely to result in, physical, sexual, psychological or economic harm or suffering to women, including threats of such acts, coercion or arbitrary deprivation of liberty, whether occurring in public or in private life.
7. The court also recognises that women and girls are often exposed to serious forms of violence such as domestic violence, sexual harassment, rape, forced marriage, crimes committed in the name of so-called 'honour' and genital mutilation, which constitute a serious violation of the human rights of women and girls and are a major obstacle to the achievement of equality between women and men.
8. We pause at this point to emphasise that the facts described in this case feature many of the hallmarks of the cycle of domestic violence. Domestic violence is the form of violence against women we are examining here. The cycle involves acts of abuse, followed by a desire for a reconciliation, followed by an escalation of violence. We see too the inability of the victim to exercise her autonomous choice to instigate criminal investigations against her former husband in the light of her continued vulnerability; the continued coercion she experienced from the perpetrator; and the failure of the various authorities to provide her with proper support and to take action.
9. The experiences of victims demonstrate that domestic abuse should not be understood as simply a series of discrete violent or abusive acts, but rather a continuum of violence and abuse which has at its heart a pattern of control. A number of terms have been suggested to encapsulate this point, but 'coercive control' stands out in particular.[1] The 'coercive control' model of domestic violence argues that understanding the impact of domestic abuse requires an appreciation of its controlling intent and impact and can only be understood by looking at the relationship between the parties as a whole. Thus, although a set of discrete abusive incidents can typically be identified within an abusive relationship, an understanding of the dynamic of power and control within an intimate relationship goes beyond these discrete incidents. To negate the impact of the time period between discrete episodes of serious violence – a time period during which the woman may never know

[1] E Stark, *Coercive Control* (Oxford, Oxford University Press, 2009).

when the next incident will occur, and may continue to live with on-going psychological abuse – is to fail to recognise what some battered women experience as a continuing 'state of siege'.[2]

10. The whole aim of the behaviour of the abuser is to dominate the victim and diminish her sense of self-worth. This is done by restricting the victim's access to work; isolating her from friends; manipulating the victim emotionally; and using physical attacks. Physical violence, then, is but one tool used in the relationship to keep one party inferior.[3] From this perspective, it is intimidation, isolation and control which should be the hallmarks of domestic violence rather than the means to achieve them, which may, or may not, involve violence.[4]
11. Viewing domestic abuse as coercive control has important implications. It means that an assessment of whether there is domestic violence must look at the whole relationship between the parties, rather than assessing the severity of individual attacks. Incidents which might appear trivial can be seen as having a significant impact when placed in their broader context. Coercive control abuse may involve physical attacks, and often does, but the abuser may not need to resort to those. The abuser seeks to intimidate, to isolate and to control. These effects, rather than physical violence, should be seen as the hallmarks of domestic violence. They also highlight the need for providing the victim with appropriate support from the authorities to enable her to exercise true agency and autonomy in reporting the actions of the perpetrator and seeking protection from the authorities.

III. THE INCIDENCE AND EFFECTS OF DOMESTIC VIOLENCE

12. Violence against women is a significant public problem, as well as a fundamental violation of women's human rights. Recent data from the UN (United Nations Division for the Advancement of Women, Factsheet DPI/2498 2008) confirms that: (1) the most common form of violence experienced by women globally is physical violence inflicted by an intimate partner; (2) On average, at least one in three women is beaten, coerced into sex or otherwise abused by an intimate; (3) Several global surveys suggest that half of all women who die from homicide are killed by their current or former husbands or partners; (4) Many women face multiple forms of discrimination and increased risk of violence. Indigenous women in Canada are five times more likely than other women of the same age to die as the result of violence. In Europe, North America and Australia, over half of women with disabilities have experienced physical abuse, compared to one-third of non-disabled women.

[2] M Dutton, 'Understanding Women's Response to Domestic Violence' (2003) 21 *Hofstra Law Review* 1191, 1204.

[3] ibid.

[4] N Jacobson and J Gottman, *When Men Batter Women: New Insights into Ending Abusive Relationships* (New York NY, Simon & Schuster, 2007).

13. An overview of prevalence studies in Europe suggests that across the various countries, one-fifth to one-quarter of all women have experienced physical violence at least once during their adult lives and more than one-tenth have suffered sexual violence involving the use of force. Figures for all forms of violence, including stalking, are as high as 45%. About 12%–15% of all women. have been in a relationship of domestic abuse after the age of 16, and many more continue to suffer physical and sexual violence once they are separated from the perpetrator (*Stocktaking study on the measures and actions taken in Council of Europe member States to combat violence against women*, Council of Europe, Strasbourg, 2006, CDEG (2006) 3, p.8).
14. Of course, domestic abuse primarily involves harm to the victim. However, the costs to society as a whole are extremely high. They include the direct costs of services to treat and support abused women and their children and to bring perpetrators to justice. The indirect costs include lost employment and productivity, and the costs in human pain and suffering.

IV. RELEVANT LAW AND PRACTICE

A. Domestic law and practice

15. The Turkish criminal law has the kinds of offences of violence which are typical in most criminal law systems. No complaint is made concerning the definition of those offences so we do not need to discuss those further here. Similarly, in the Family Protection Act (Law no. 4320, 14 January 1998) Turkish law allows a court in civil proceedings to make orders inter alia prohibiting violent or aggressive behaviour or removing someone from their home. Again, no particular complaint is raised about the substance of these provisions and we do not need to explain their details.

B. Relevant international and comparative law material

16. Historically, domestic abuse has been seen in many jurisdictions as simply a 'private matter' and best left to the individuals themselves. If rights were at all significant, it was the right to privacy and family life which were key and operated to deter any state intervention. The law has moved on considerably since then. As a result, the Court recognises that domestic abuse is a major infringement of the rights of the victim, for reasons we will explore further later.
17. Domestic abuse is also recognised as a major impediment to achieving gender equality, and for that purpose is a rights issue too. That is recognised in the Convention on the Elimination of All Forms of Discrimination against Women (CEDAW), which was adopted in 1979 by the UN General Assembly and ratified by Turkey on 19 January 1986. The Committee on the Elimination of All Forms of Discrimination Against Women states 'gender-based violence is a form of discrimination that seriously inhibits women's ability to

enjoy rights and freedoms on a basis of equality with men' and is thus prohibited under Article 1 of CEDAW. It explicitly recognises domestic abuse as a form of discrimination (see, CEDAW/C/TUR/4-5 and Corr.1, 15 February 2005, § 28).

18. In 1992, the CEDAW Committee adopted General Recommendation No. 19 on Violence against women, and in doing so provided a clear explanation of gender-based violence against women as a form of discrimination against women falling under the CEDAW definition of discrimination against women. General Recommendation No. 19 states: 'Gender-based violence, which impairs or nullifies the enjoyment by women of human rights and fundamental freedoms under general international law or under human rights conventions, is discrimination within the meaning of Article 1 of the Convention.' (paragraph 7)

19. The Recommendation further clarifies: 'The Convention in Article 1 defines discrimination against women. The definition of discrimination includes gender-based violence, that is, violence that is directed against a woman because she is a woman or that affects women disproportionately. It includes acts that inflict physical, mental or sexual harm or suffering, threats of such acts, coercion and other deprivations of liberty. Gender-based violence may breach specific provisions of the Convention, regardless of whether those provisions expressly mention violence.' (paragraph 6)

20. The CEDAW Committee also explained the responsibility of States with respect to State actors and non-State actors: 'The Convention applies to violence perpetrated by public authorities. Such acts of violence may breach that State's obligations under general international human rights law and under other conventions, in addition to breaching this Convention.' Further it explained that discrimination under the Convention is not restricted to actions by or on behalf of Governments and recalled that under Article 2 (e) of the Convention 'States may also be responsible for private acts if they fail to act with due diligence to prevent violation of rights or to investigate or to punish such acts of violence, and for providing compensation that obliges States Parties to prevent and prosecute violence against women by private persons.' (paragraph 9)

21. This interpretation of the 'due diligence' standard was developed in the *Velásquez Rodrígez* case (*Velásquez Rodríguez v Honduras*, Judgment of July 29,1988, Inter-Am.Ct.H.R. (Ser. C) No.4 (1988)). The case centred on the extent of State responsibility for human rights violation of non-state actors and its application to violence against women committed by private persons and further elaborated the link between human rights obligations and acts of private persons. The CEDAW Committee clarified that full implementation of the Convention requires States to apply the 'due diligence' standard and to take positive measures to prevent or eliminate violence against women, including domestic and sexual violence. In providing an understanding of violence against women committed by a private person as a human rights

violation this 'due diligence' standard was later incorporated in the 1993 UN Declaration on the Elimination of Violence against Women and 1994 Inter-American Convention on Prevention, Punishment and Eradication of Violence against Women (The Convention of Belem do Para).

22. In its first case on domestic violence, *A T v Hungary* (Communication No. 2/2003, 26 January 2005, CEDAW/C/32/D/2/2003), the CEDAW Committee recalled its general recommendation No. 19 and explained that the failure to sufficiently respond to gender base violence may breach specific provisions of the Convention (paragraph 9.2). It established that the State party failed in its duty to provide the claimant with effective protection from the serious risk to her physical integrity, physical and mental health and her life from her former common law husband (paragraph 9.2). For four years, the author of that communication was beaten by her former common law husband and was not able to request a restraining or protection order since neither option existed at that time. She was also unable to flee to a shelter because none were equipped to accept her together with her children, one of whom is seriously disabled. In its reasoning the Committee stressed: 'Women's human rights to life and to physical and mental integrity cannot be superseded by other rights, including the right to property and the right to privacy' (paragraph 9.4). It also recommended: 'immediate and effective measures to guarantee the physical and mental integrity of A. T. and her family'.

In two other domestic violence cases against Austria – *Şahide Goekce (deceased) v Austria* (Communication No. 5/2005, 6 August 2007, CEDAW/C/39/D/5/2005) and *Fatma Yildirim (deceased) v Austria* (Communication No. 6/2005, 1 October 2007, CEDAW/C/39/D/6/2005) – the Committee found violations of the rights to life and physical and mental integrity under Article 2 (a) and (c) through (f), and Article 3 of the Convention read in conjunction with Article 1 of the Convention and General Recommendation No. 19 on violence against women. The Committee held Austria accountable for failing to exercise 'due diligence' to protect the two victims from domestic violence. In both cases, the Committee expressed a view that: 'the perpetrator's rights cannot supersede women's human rights to life and to physical and mental integrity'. In the case *V K v Bulgaria* (Communication No. 20/2008, 17 August 2011, CEDAW/C/49/D/20/2008) the Committee found that the State party failed to provide the claimant with an effective protection order and to protect her against domestic violence. It also found that the unavailability of shelters where she and her children could have stayed constituted a violation of the State party's obligation under Article 2 (c) and (e) of the Convention to provide for the immediate protection of women from violence, including domestic violence.

The United Nations Special Rapporteur on Violence against Women, its Causes and Consequences has elaborated on the due diligence standard to provide governments with guidance on what it entails in relation to preventing and combating violence against women. In her 2003 report *Integration of the Human Rights of Women and the Gender Perspective: Violence Against Women* (E/CN.4/2004/66), the Special Rapporteur recommended that State accountability is embedded in the standard of due diligence to protect women's bodily integrity: to prevent, investigate and punish private or State violence against women in accordance with human rights law. In so doing, the State and its agents must undertake gender analysis in order to accurately assess how, why, and under what circumstances specific forms of violence are perpetrated.

23. In addition, the United Nations Special Rapporteur on Torture and other Cruel, Inhuman or Degrading Treatment or Punishment has further emphasised that domestic (intimate partner) violence against women can engage a State's responsibility for torture if they fail to act with due diligence in the response to it. (Report of the United Nations Special Rapporteur on Torture and Other Cruel, Inhuman or Degrading Treatment or Punishment, Manfred Nowak, *Promotion and protection of all human rights, civil, political, economic, social and cultural rights, including the right to development*, A/HRC/7/3, 2008).

C. The Council of Europe

24. Recognising violence against women as a human rights violation forms a cornerstone of the Council of Europe's approach to combating this scourge. Recommendation Rec (2002) 5 on the protection of women against violence places states under an obligation to exercise due diligence to prevent, investigate and punish all acts of violence, whether those acts are perpetrated by the state or by private individuals, and provide protection to victims. The Council of Europe Campaign to Combat Violence against Women, including Domestic Violence, encouraged member states to recognise violence against women as a human rights violation that needs to be responded to accordingly. (Campaign Outline Paper, Council of Europe, Strasbourg, 2008, EG-VAW-FP (2008)2 rev).

25. In signing and ratifying the Convention for the Protection of Human Rights and Fundamental Freedoms, all member states of the Council of Europe have agreed to secure a significant range of fundamental rights and freedoms to everyone in their jurisdiction. Of these, the right to life (Art. 2), the prohibition of torture (Art. 3), the right to liberty and security (Art. 5), the right to respect for private and family life (Art. 8) and the prohibition of discrimination (Art. 14) are particularly relevant to domestic abuse. Taken together, these rights and freedoms make it clear that Council of Europe member states have a responsibility to prevent violence, protect women and punish perpetrators of violence against women.

D. Reports concerning domestic violence and the situation of women in Turkey

26. Sadly, we have received evidence that in Turkey the legal procedures designed to protect victims of domestic abuse are not operating effectively. The report prepared by Purple Roof Women's Shelter Foundation (Mor Çatı Kadın Sığınağı Vakfı) demonstrates significant delays in proceeding for victims facing civil orders. The report indicates of 900 women who have sought protection from state authorities only 120 have succeeded. Reports of the police not taking complaints seriously, siding with the male or seeking to act as arbitrator abound.
27. The Research Report prepared by the Women's Rights Information and Implementation Centre of the Diyarbakır Bar Association (KA-MER) on the Implementation of Law no. 4320, dated 25 November 2005 finds violence against women is widespread and tolerated in many cases. The laws designed to protect victims of domestic abuse are rarely used and when they are rarely successful. Amnesty International's 2004 Report entitled *Turkey: Women Confronting Family Violence* (1 June 2004, EUR 44/013/2004), found that there is a culture of domestic violence, where domestic violence crimes are not taken seriously and legal protections are in effect not accessible. The attitudes of the general community and officials is one of tolerance towards domestic abuse.
28. The recent report of the UN Special Rapporteur on Violence against Women, Yakin Ertuk, following her Mission to Turkey (A/HRC/4/34/Add.2, 5 January 2007) also paints a bleak picture of women inhabiting the Eastern regions. She notes that:

    > … while from a gender perspective the penal law framework is now overall adequate, significant problems persist in its implementation. Many politicians and administrators still regard domestic violence and forced marriages as internal family matters in which the State should not intervene. In the few cases reported to the law enforcement authorities, officials often try to broker an agreement between parties of inherently unequal power instead of protecting the victims and prosecuting the perpetrators. Particularly in the context of the volatile political situation in the region, some officials are also prone to tacitly subordinate State law to customary forms of conflict resolution in order not to upset relations with local power structures. (paragraph 59)

    She goes on to note the lack of an effective institutional framework to protect women facing violence. The Law on Municipalities, adopted in July 2004, requires all municipalities with more than 50,000 inhabitants to provide a shelter for women victims of violence but by and large this law has not been implemented: 'In Turkey, a country of over 70 million people, there are only

28 institutions that provide services for women subjected to violence according to information provided by the Government'. (paragraph 67)

V. ADMISSIBILITY

29. Given the severity of the issues at hand, we were surprised and disappointed to find the government raising some technical arguments that the application was not admissible. We might have hope that the government would be keen to demonstrate its determination to protect the rights of victims of domestic violence and compensate those it failed, rather than seeking to avoid its responsibility through procedural issues. It was argued that the applicant had failed to observe the time limit of six months (article 31§ 1 of the Convention) in respect of indices between 1995 and 2001. It was also claimed the applicant had failed to exhaust her domestic remedies. Neither of these claims has any merit. The true extent of the State's failure to protect Ms Opuz arose when her mother was killed and she brought the proceedings within six months of that event. As to the argument the domestic remedies were not exhausted, the whole complaint is about the effectiveness of the remedies available. Having found the remedies available were inadequate it does not matter that the applicant did not exhaust them.

VI. ALLEGED VIOLATION OF ARTICLE 2 OF THE CONVENTION

30. Ms Opuz has complained that her mother's rights under Article 2 of the Convention have been breached. Article 2 states:

    1. Everyone's right to life shall be protected by law. No one shall be deprived of his life intentionally save in the execution of a sentence of a court following his conviction of a crime for which this penalty is provided by law …

    She has described her experiences of domestic abuse and the response of the police and the courts. It is clear from her story that the Turkish authorities tolerated the violence and the perpetrators were immune from legal sanctions. She had made numerous reports of domestic violence and the state authorities had provided no effective protection of her life, the life or her mother or the life of her partner.

31. This court has made it clear in a series of cases that Article 2 requires not only that the State does not intentionally take the life of a citizen, it also has a responsibility to ensure protection from the rights of third party (*Osman v the United Kingdom*, 28 October 1998, § 115, Reports of Judgments and Decisions 1998-VIII, (2000) 29 EHRR 245). That said, while every intentional killing is a breach of a person's fundamental human rights, it may not be reasonable to hold the state to account in every case. The state must in general put in place legal provisions to protect life. Where a state knows or ought to know

that there is a real risk to the Article 2 rights it must take reasonable steps to protect that citizen (see *Osman v the United Kingdom*, cited above, § 115). What counts as reasonable, will depend on the competing claims on state resources; the level of awareness of the situation of the victim; and the ability of the victim to protect themselves.

32. However, we emphasise that the breach of an Article 2 is the most serious breach of human rights, and thus threats to the protection of life must be given the highest priority. We note, furthermore, the increased awareness, research and information regarding the particular situation of domestic violence that is now in the public domain since the *Osman* decision and recent developments internationally. These developments have contributed to a general consensus concerning the applicability to the right to life to domestic abuse and the positive obligation upon state authorities to organise their response in a way that allows the relevant authorities diligently to prevent, investigate, punish and provide reparation for such acts. This will include the obligation to devise and implement policies, which would comprise a multitude of measures to be taken by different actors and agencies and which, taken as a whole, offer a holistic response to violence against women. States must therefore ensure that the adopted policies are implemented by way of effective multi-agency co-operation. Good practice examples in some member states show that results are enhanced when law enforcement agencies, the judiciary, women's non-governmental organisations, child protection agencies and other relevant partners join forces on a particular case, for example to carry out an accurate risk assessment or devise a safety plan.
33. Preventive measures must also specifically address and take into account the needs of vulnerable persons. Perpetrators often choose to target such persons because they know that they are less likely to be able to defend themselves, or seek prosecution of the perpetrator and other forms of reparation, because of their situation. Persons made vulnerable by particular circumstances include: pregnant women and women with young children; persons with disabilities, including those with mental or cognitive impairments; persons living in rural or remote areas; substance abusers; prostituted people; persons of national or ethnic minority background; migrants – including undocumented migrants and refugees; gay men, lesbian women bi-sexual, intersex and transgender persons; HIV-positive persons; homeless people; children; and the elderly.
34. In summary, we consider that in cases of domestic violence, the obligation upon the State to intervene is particularly strong due to the particular vulnerability of the victim who may have suffered abuse over a long period of time and been subject to a high degree of coercion and control. We note also that state authorities may have been in contact with the victim on more than one occasion regarding the abuse and that victims often refuse or withdraw their co-operation to investigations and/or proceedings. However, this must not be seen as a reason to discontinue or abort investigations and/or proceedings

in itself. In circumstances such as these, state authorities must consider the feasibility of a continued investigation and/or prosecution in the interests of the wider public and society and particularly where certain aggravating factors are present such as serious violence, the presence of a particular vulnerability and the presence of children. Indeed, the fact the victim has withdrawn co-operation could be evidence that they have been subject to further domestic abuse. State authorities should also demonstrate an awareness of the pattern of abuse and that an individual risk assessment has taken place when making operational decisions regarding the safety of the victim. Any inaction must therefore be justified.

35. Applying these principles to Ms Opuz's case, it is manifestly clear that the state authorities failed in their obligations to protect the Article 2 rights of Ms Opuz's mother. The relationship between Ms Opuz and her husband bore many of the hallmarks of a relationship marked by domestic abuse. First, the experience of violence, followed by reconciliation, followed by further violence. Second, Mr Opuz when questioned by the State authorities blamed Ms Opuz for the violence he did to her, and there is evidence that this was taken into account by the State authorities. However, blame by abusers of victims for their injuries is a hallmark of abuse and should be seen as an aggravating, rather than mitigating, factor. Third, Mr Opuz used his violence in an attempt to prevent Ms Opuz having access to work or family, by injuring her so she had to take time off and threatening her family. Finally, the applicant made complaints to the police which were subsequently withdrawn, in circumstances in which it seems likely there had been a threat of violence.

36. The authorities were repeatedly informed of the threats to her life and the violence against Ms Opuz's mother. They were aware this was a domestic violence case and that the attacks were of increasing severity. They also knew children of the family had witnessed the continued abuse of their mother and grandmother and had been undoubtedly affected by this experience.

Despite this, there is no evidence that any kind of risk assessment took place of the danger that the applicant and her mother were placed in or that adequate support measures were put in place to protect her from further harm. A number of agencies were made aware of their situation yet there appeared to be no co-ordinated effort to properly investigate and appreciate the real threat to the applicant and her family.

37. The government has argued that any further interference in the private life of the family would have constituted a breach of their Article 8 rights. However, if there is any breach under Article 8 then it would be justified under the second paragraph of that Article and by virtue of the obligations on the state under Article 2 to protect the interests of Ms Opuz and her children (see, *K A and A D v Belgium*, no. 42758/98 and 45558/99, § 81, 17 February 2005).

It has been claimed by the government that criminal prosecutions and investigations require the co-operation of the victim. We do not consider this to be true, and nor is it true as a matter of practice in a number of Member States. Research by Louise Ellison[5] has demonstrated that victimless prosecution is feasible. It may require the use of imaginative policing, including the use of technology and imaginative prosecution. But these must be used to ensure compliance with Convention obligations.

VII. ALLEGED VIOLATION OF ARTICLE 3 OF THE CONVENTION

38. Ms Opuz has also claimed that she has been subject to breaches of her rights under article 3: 'No one shall be subjected to torture or to inhuman or degrading treatment or punishment.'

A. Applicable Principles

39. According to the Court's previously established principles, torture involves the intentional infliction of severe mental or physical pain or suffering for the pursuit of a specific purpose (such as obtaining information or gaining control over another). 'Inhuman or Degrading treatment' includes conduct which humiliates or debases an individual; or shows a lack of respect for, or diminishes, human dignity. It also includes conduct which arouses feelings of fear, anguish or inferiority capable of breaking an individual's moral and physical resistance (*Wieser v Austria*, no. 2293/03, § 36, 22 February 2007, (2007) 45 EHRR 44)

40. Domestic abuse clearly falls within this definition. Depression, learned helplessness, post-traumatic stress disorder, guilt and denial have been cited as resulting from abusive relationship. This suggests that an on-going relationship in which the victim is subject to a series of incidents, which seen individually might appear minor, but which create an atmosphere of coercive control, could amount to a breach of article 3. A lack of respect of a person's humanity can be included (*Albert and Le Compte v Belgium*, 10 February 1983, § 22, Series A no. 58, (1983) 5 EHRR 533). In serious cases, persistent infantilisation and emotional abuse could, therefore, fall within article 3, even if physical violence has not taken place. As the Parliamentary Assembly, Council of Europe, Committee on Equal Opportunities for Women and Men (*Domestic Violence* (2002), para. 12) put it:

> It has been demonstrated that violence in the home is like a form of torture. The victims are injured physically and psychologically and humiliated in body and soul. Like torture, conjugal violence is something that goes on and on.

[5] L Ellison, 'Prosecuting Domestic Violence without Victim Participation' (1993) 65 *Modern Law Review* 834.

The severity of the abuse can only be understood when put in the context of the model of coercive control outlined above.

41. As explained earlier, this model claims that the behaviour of the abuser is designed to dominate the victim and diminish her sense of self-worth, restrict access to employment and isolate her from friends. Not only does the abuse itself enforce control, it reduces self-esteem and ensures future compliance. In one study of men arrested for domestic violence, 38% admitted preventing partners freely coming and going in their daily route and 59% had denied partners access to money or resources.[6]
42. The abuse of trust within an intimate relationship causes an especial harm. Intimate relationships are central to our identity and sense of self. Within our intimate relationships we can be truly ourselves, free of pretence. Through them, we can there explore and discover ourselves. Domestic abuse strikes at the very conception of the self for the victim.[7] These features all demonstrate how a coercive controlling relationship can cross the threshold to breach Article 3.
43. The research on domestic abuse as coercive control also explains why if a victim appears to consent to the abusive relationship, the apparent consent can be questioned. In any event, Article 3 is drafted in absolute terms. This means that once the conduct is classified as torture or inhuman or degrading treatment the question of consent is irrelevant. Consequently, the Turkish government's argument that the withdrawal of the complaint by Ms Opuz in justifying the failure to act is firmly rejected.
44. The Court has also previously established in its case law, and in line with the reasoning used above in relation to Article 2, that the State could be held responsible, under Article 3, for the ill-treatment inflicted on persons by non-state actors and that Member States are obliged to take measures to ensure that individuals within their jurisdiction are not subjected to treatment that comes within the scope of Article 3 (see, *mutatis mutandis*, *H L R v France*, 29 April 1997, § 40, *Reports of Judgments and Decisions* 1997 III, (1998) 26 EHRR 29). It has also noted that children and other vulnerable individuals are in particular entitled to enhanced State protection in the form of effective deterrence against such treatment (see *A v the United Kingdom*, 23 September 1998, § 22, *Reports of Judgments and Decisions* 1998-VI). Having regard to the wealth of research evidence available it is clear that victims of domestic violence are capable of falling within the categorisation of vulnerable individuals that require an enhanced level of protection (see, *A v the United Kingdom*, cited above, § 22).

[6] ES Buzawa, GT Hotaling, A Klein and J Byrne, *Response to Domestic Violence in a Pro-Active Court Setting. Final Report Submitted to the National Institute of Justice* (Lowell MA, University of Massachusetts–Lowell, 1999).

[7] O Rachmilovitz, 'Bringing Down the Bedroom Walls: Emphasizing Substance over Form in Personalized Abuse' (2007) 14 *William & Mary Journal of Women and the Law* 495.

45. Where, therefore, the State authorities are aware the relationship is marked by domestic abuse such that Article 3 is breached, there is an obligation upon Member States to exercise due diligence to prevent, investigate, punish and provide reparation for acts of violence. These will include the need to take the necessary legislative or other measures to provide or arrange for, in an adequate geographical distribution, immediate, short- and long-term specialist support services to any victim subjected to any of the acts of violence covered by the scope of Article 3. This will also include the provision of appropriate, easily accessible shelters in sufficient numbers to provide safe accommodation where necessary; round-the-clock (24/7) telephone helplines, free of charge, to provide advice to callers; and the need to ensure that victims have access to health care and social services, and that services are adequately resourced and professionals are trained to assist victims and refer them to the appropriate services.

    These measures should be taken in a manner that responds to the needs of particularly vulnerable victims of domestic violence and their specific needs. Furthermore, any measures should not be dependent upon the co-operation of the victim.

46. In this case, Ms Opuz suffered sufficiently serious physical abuse to amount to a breach of Article 3. The court is also satisfied that the emotional abuse she suffered was sufficient to amount to breach of Article 3. She was subject to repeated threats and controlling behaviour. Mr Opuz blamed her for the injuries he inflicted.

47. We are surprised that no one has raised the rights of the children in this case. There is ample evidence that domestic violence harms children.[8] We will not pursue this further as it is clear that a consideration of the rights of the children would only strengthen the arguments made in this judgment, particularly bearing in mind the provisions of the United Nations Convention on the Rights of the Child. Future cases, where appropriate, might draw the courts' attention to the particular rights of children in this context, in terms of the effect on their right to family and private life and their right to live a life free from inhuman and degrading treatment. In some cases, where their lives have indeed been extinguished by the perpetrator, their right to life will also be engaged. These issues should undoubtedly be taken into account by the authorities when considering applications by the perpetrator for contact under Article 8 and it may be the case that if there is sufficient evidence that the perpetrators actions represent a risk of harm to such children, that the denial or restriction of contact between them would be a proportionate response to the legitimate aim of the protection of their rights and interests and that of the wider society.

[8] The research is summarised in J Kelly and M Johnson, 'Differentiation among Types of Intimate Partner Violence' (2008) 46 *Family Court Review* 467.

48. It is clear, then, that the Turkish authorities were aware that Ms Opuz and her children were suffering from a breach of their Article 3 rights and a State, reasonably alert to the problem of domestic abuse, would have been aware of that and so had a duty to protect her and the children from further violence.

While in the case at hand the authorities did undertake some investigations and undertook medical examinations, and there was a short detention of Mr Opuz; however, we do not accept that these steps were sufficient to comply with the obligation to protect them from continued breaches of Article 3.

Furthermore, the woeful provision of shelters for victims of domestic abuse in Turkey and the lack of co-ordinated and effective support services available to victims of domestic violence undoubtedly contributed to the increase in risk to the applicant, her mother and her children of further treatment within the scope of Article 3.

49. The local authorities in this case manifestly failed to act in response to the threats faced by Ms Opuz. There was a failure to properly investigate her complaints; to prosecute the offences when they could have been; to sentence appropriately following the conviction; to offer Ms Opuz and her children safe housing or alternative accommodation; or to enable Ms Opuz to access civil remedies.

VIII. ALLEGED VIOLATION OF ARTICLE 14 READ IN CONJUNCTION WITH ARTICLES 2 AND 3 OF THE CONVENTION

50. Article 14 of the Convention provides:

> The enjoyment of the rights and freedoms set forth in [the] Convention shall be secured without discrimination on any ground such as sex, race, colour, language, religion, political or other opinion, national or social origin, association with a national minority, property, birth or other status.

The applicant complains that under Article 14, in conjunction with Articles 2 and 3 of the Convention, she and her mother have been discriminated against on the basis of their gender.

This court finds that domestic violence is an offence that has a very particular impact on women and upon children. A failure to adequately protect victims of domestic abuse constitutes sex discrimination per se. The United Nations Commission on Human Rights expressly recognised in resolution 2003/45 that 'all forms of violence against women occur within the context of *de jure* and *de facto* discrimination against women and the lower status accorded to women in society and are exacerbated by the obstacles women often face in seeking remedies from the State.' We agree.

51. In 2005, a World Health Organization study found rates of woman suffering physical or sexual violence at the hands of an intimate partner at some

point in her life varying across countries between 15% and 71%; with most countries falling between 29% and 62% (World Health Organisation, *Multi-country Study on Women's Health and Domestic Violence against Women* (WHO, 2005). The European Parliamentary Assembly found that for women between 16 and 44 years of age, domestic violence is thought to be the major cause of death and invalidity, ahead of cancer, road accidents and even war' (European Parliamentary Assembly Recommendation 1582, *Domestic Violence Against Women* (2002), para 2).

52. Domestic violence not only relies on existing inequalities within society, it reinforces them. For example, the attempts by the male perpetrators of abuse to prevent their female partners entering the workplace or public arena and but imitations of broader attempts to restrict women's access to the workplace. Professor Michelle Madden Dempsey explains the link in these ways:

> … the patriarchal character of individual relationships cannot subsist without those relationships being situated within a broader patriarchal social structure. Patriarchy is, by its nature, a social structure – and thus, any particular instance of patriarchy takes its substance and meaning from that social context. If patriarchy were entirely eliminated from society, then patriarchy would not exist in domestic arrangements and thus domestic violence in its strong sense would not exist … Moreover, if patriarchy were lessened in society generally then *ceteris paribus* patriarchy would be lessened in domestic relationship as well, thereby directly contributing to the project of ending domestic violence in its strong sense.[9]

We agree, and accept that the gendered aspect of domestic abuse if crucial to a proper understanding of its nature.

53. The failure of the Turkish State to give practical effect to its measures designed to protect victims of domestic violence breaches Article 14. We note that the failure is in changing the attitude of public authorities and staff. That is a matter of education, training and supervision of employment, but these can all be reasonably be expected of a government which is seeking to combat domestic abuse. We note also the importance of appreciating how particular discrimination can arise when individuals belong to two or more groups protected by Article 14 and the disadvantages combine to create unique categories of disadvantage (so called intersectionality). Although not argued before us, there can be cases where it will necessary to explore the particular position of, for example, women from a particular ethnic or religious group, or older women, or disabled women.

[9] M Madden Dempsey, 'Towards a Feminist State: What does "Effective" Prosecution of Domestic Violence Mean?' (2007) 70 *Modern Law Review* 908, 938.

54. We note the government has not sought to challenge the statistical evidence concerning the failure to prosecute domestic violence. We think it likely this is because the Government has no statistics on the rates and prosecution of domestic violence. This itself is indicative of the failure of the State to make serious efforts to combat this problem. It cannot be claimed that the government is unaware of the problems of domestic violence. It is aware of the problem but has deliberately turned a blind eye to it. The court finds an intentional discrimination against women and children in the failure to ensure that the rights of victims of domestic abuse under Articles 2 and 3 in a way which is discriminatory on the basis of both age and sex.

IX. APPLICATION OF ARTICLE 41 OF THE CONVENTION

Article 41 of the Convention states:

> If the Court finds that there has been a violation of the Convention or the Protocols thereto, and if the internal law of the High Contracting Party concerned allows only partial reparation to be made, the Court shall, if necessary, afford just satisfaction to the injured party.

The applicant claimed 70,000 Turkish liras (TRL) (approximately 35,000 euros (EUR)) in respect of pecuniary damage resulting from the death of her mother and TRL 250,000 (approximately EUR 125,000) for non-pecuniary damage. Given the severity of the impact upon Ms Opus of Domestic abuse and the intentional nature of the discrimination, we believe this sum inadequate and award EUR 300 000 in respect of the damage sustained by her as a result of violations of Articles 2, 3 and 14 of the Convention. We also award her EUR 7,750 for the costs and expense incurred by the court.

FOR THESE REASONS, THE COURT UNANIMOUSLY

1. *Dismisses* the Government's procedural objects to the applications and declares it admissible.
2. *Holds* that there has been a violation of Article 2 of the Convention in respect of the death of Ms Opuz's mother;
3. *Holds* that there has been a violation of Article 3 of the Convention in respect of the authorities' failure to protect Ms Opuz and her children against domestic violence perpetrated by her former husband;
4. *Holds* that there has been a violation of Article 14 read in conjunction with Articles 2 and 3 of the Convention;
5. *Holds*

   (a) that the respondent State is to pay the applicant, within three months from the date on which the judgment becomes final in accordance with

Article 44 § 2 of the Convention, the following amounts, to be converted into Turkish liras at the rate applicable at the date of settlement:

(i) a total sum of EUR 300,000 plus any tax that may be chargeable, in respect of non-pecuniary damage;

(ii) EUR 6,500 (six thousand five hundred euros), plus any tax that may be chargeable to the applicants, for costs and expenses;

(b) that from the expiry of the above-mentioned three months until settlement simple interest shall be payable on the above amounts at a rate equal to the marginal lending rate of the European Central Bank during the default period plus three percentage points.

Reflections

The collaboration process went relatively smoothly. Although the authors are at different institutions, we have worked together previously and have an established working relationship. Unfortunately, as we were appointed late in the project we were not able to attend or contribute to the workshop on the ECHR judgments, but were able to attend the workshop session on the general international law judgments held at the School of Oriental and African Studies, London. We found this to be very helpful in terms of understanding how to approach the re-writing project and the different positions that could be taken in our judgment.

In addition to the above, there were a number of general issues that were of concern in terms of how we approached and crafted the judgment itself. We were guided very much by Rosemary Hunter and Ericka Rackley's chapters in *Feminist Judgments: From Theory to Practice.*[1] Attending the workshop at SOAS for this project produced some novel and innovative views on how to approach the writing of the judgments, including the use of satire and poetry. However, we quickly realised that we preferred a more realistic approach, one that was as close to 'real' judgment-writing as possible but with an unashamedly feminist perspective.

One of the reasons for that is that we both have a particular interest in formulating feminist arguments in a way that would be accepted by courts or doctrinal lawyers. While the traditional forms of law can constrain feminist thought, by restricting it to established categories and doctrines, subverting these to feminist ends has merit for two reasons. First, until the feminist revolution (!) we are stuck with patriarchal legal systems and short term gains can be made by using these tools to make gains. Second, it may be possible to find allies or potential allies who are convinced by the arguments couched in traditional legal terms, even if they are not (yet) convinced by the larger scale feminist project. We were keen, therefore, to keep this judgment strictly in line with the kinds of arguments and to avoid more general theorising.

To that end, we tried to ensure that we achieved a number of objectives in our drafting. We sought to ask and answer the 'woman question',[2] and we included women both in terms of their 'lived' experiences but also to understand these in terms of the broader social and political context. In terms of the remedies proposed, by way of the development of the positive obligations in the case, we sought to advance substantive equality by suggesting concrete steps that Member States should be taking to comply with their duties of due diligence in this regard.

[1] R Hunter, 'An Account of Feminist Judging' and E Rackley, 'The Art and Craft of Writing Judgments: Notes on the Feminist Judgments Project', both in R Hunter, C McGlynn and E Rackley (eds), *Feminist Judgments: From Theory to Practice* (Oxford, Hart Publishing, 2010).

[2] By this we mean looking at the question specifically in terms of its impact on women.

Furthermore, we drew on feminist scholarship throughout the judgment to contextualise the situation of victims of violence. Finally, we tried to employ an anti-essentialist and intersectional approach throughout the judgment by highlighting the diverse experiences of victims and their diverse needs.

This last point has proved particularly contentious in recent work on domestic abuse and is something that we struggled with in writing this judgment.[3] On the one hand, a key aspect of domestic violence is its gendered nature and the role it plays in sustaining, and being sustained by patriarchy.[4] On the other hand, there are two real dangers in seeing domestic abuse in terms *simply* of gender. The first is that one overlooks the intersecting social inequalities that, for example, render a poor black woman's experience of domestic violence to be very different from that of a rich white woman. Religion, culture, class, sexuality and age can all impact significantly on the experience of domestic abuse. In the *Opuz* case, gender eclipsed the other sources of disadvantage at play because the legal argument was most clearly presented in terms of Article 14 on the basis of sex. Other intersecting factors could have been relevant here: however, religion, class and ethnicity, for instance, were not raised in the judgment because consideration of them was not necessary for the case itself, and Article 14 does not readily lend itself to a sophisticated intersectional analysis. We did try to at least raise this issue in our judgment, but were limited in the extent we were able to do so. The second danger is that seeing domestic violence as primarily a matter of sex discrimination can lead to inadequate responses to cases of domestic abuse in same-sex relationships, or the very rare cases of female on male domestic abuse.[5] The danger is that highlighting sex discrimination through Article 14 may lead to a weaker level of protection outside the context of violence in a heterosexual relationship. This danger need not materialise. A victim of domestic abuse who cannot rely on sex discrimination under Article 14[6] can still rely on a straightforward breach of Article 3 or 8, or indeed another head of discrimination in Article 14. As a legal judgment inevitably focuses on the case at hand, there was not space in our judgment to fully explore this issue.

A final issue that must be addressed in writing a judgment in this context is the place of reason and emotion. It is hard for those who have experienced or been impacted by domestic abuse to put emotions aside. Even those judges who

[3] S Choudhry, 'Towards a Transformative Conceptualisation of Violence Against Women – A Critical Frame Analysis of Council of Europe Discourse on Violence Against Women' (2016) 79 *Modern Law Review* 604.

[4] M Madden Dempsey, *Prosecuting Domestic Violence* (Oxford, Oxford University Press, 2009).

[5] For a further discussion, see J Herring, 'The Istanbul Convention: Is Domestic Abuse Violence Against Women?' in G Douglas, M Murch and V Stephens (eds), *International and National Perspectives on Child and Family Law: Essays in Honour of Nigel Lowe* (Cambridge, Intersentia, 2017).

[6] Arguments could be made that even in non-heterosexual relationship domestic abuse can be seen as sustaining patriarchy: see M Madden Dempsey, 'Response to Commentators' (2014) 8 *Criminal Law and Philosophy* 557.

have not must deal with the inevitable feelings of compassion for the victim. Traditionally, the quality most sought for a judge is rationality, neutrality and objectivity. Susan Bandes writes that:

> … the notion of compassion seems anathema to the rule of law. If the rule of law safeguards against arbitrary decisions, promotes predictability and elevates the supremacy of law above the whims of individuals, then compassion may threaten all these ideals. It may pull law in unforeseen, arbitrary directions based on surges of fellow-feeling or other unpredictable emotions.[7]

She then goes on to critique that conception of judging and promotes the use of compassion. Not all judges would agree with the view that judging should be compassion-free. Former Justice of the California Supreme Court, Joyce Kennard, argued that compassion 'can create a space within which the voices of the persons affected by the decision can be heard, their humanity acknowledged, their sufferings understood and properly taken into account'.[8] There is no doubt that law-making in the area of domestic abuse is complex. Compassion for the victim, together with the judges' emotions connected to personal experiences of domestic abuse, will potentially be raised by the case. At the same time, the judgment must be one that demands respect within the legal community and the wider world. We would nonetheless suggest that emotions such as empathy and compassion are central to an effective legal response. Unless an attempt is made to come alongside the victim of domestic abuse, unless the judge can draw on her own experience, it is not possible to appreciate or fully understand what has happened. How can one begin to make the legal assessment of whether there has been inhuman or degrading treatment without coming alongside the victim and drawing on one's own experiences? This tension between using emotional knowledge and formatting that into legal language was something we were acutely aware of in writing this judgment.

We started this judgment slightly concerned that we would have nothing to contribute, given that it seemed to be a positive judgment for women. However, we soon realised that we had a lot to say and as it turned out, a lot to add. This was undoubtedly due to the application of a clear feminist methodology as outlined above and our insistence on keeping in mind the most important question of all throughout the redrafting process: the 'woman question'. In doing so, we uncovered a number of issues that had not been dealt with by the original judgment and, hopefully, in the process made the judgment a truly feminist one.

[7] S Bandes, 'Compassion and the Rule of Law' (2017) 13 *International Journal of Law in Context* 184. Citations removed.

[8] Justice Kennard, 'Why Justice Is More than Law' (1997) 83(4) *Women Lawyers Journal* 10–11. See also C L'Heureux Dubé, 'Making a Difference: The Pursuit of a Compassionate Justice' (1997) 31 *University of British Columbia Law Review* 1.

11

A, B and C v Ireland

HELEN FENWICK, WENDY GUNS
AND BEN WARWICK

Authors' Note

The *A, B and C v Ireland* case is an important one both in the history of the European Court of Human Rights (ECtHR), and in the history of the Irish law's engagement with abortion. It involved three women, all in different circumstances, who were unable to obtain an abortion in Ireland in early 2005 (or at least were significantly restricted in their attempts to seek one). Applicant A had a range of existing family issues and had children in care. She felt that a pregnancy and newborn child would be detrimental to her family and its future. Applicant B felt unable to care for a child on her own in her current situation. Applicant C sought an abortion as she felt uncertain about the risks to her own health and life as she recovered from cancer. She sought an assurance that she could access an abortion in the face of a possibility that the cancer might recur, requiring chemotherapy. All of the women travelled to England to obtain an abortion. All applicants experienced some form of after-effect or complication upon their return to Ireland and all avoided medical professionals or felt that the medical treatment provided in Ireland was inadequate. Applicants A and B were additionally under financial strain, with A turning to a money lender (or 'loan shark').

The Irish law was, and remains, grounded in article 40.3.3 of the country's Constitution. This subsection of the Constitution is more commonly known as the Eighth Amendment, as the Constitution was amended following a referendum in 1983. The amendment recognised, for the first time, 'the right to life of the unborn' and brought with it a significant number of knock-on effects.[1] Irish abortion law had previously been subject to high-profile scrutiny by the ECtHR. In the *Open Door* case, the availability of certain information to women choosing whether to travel abroad for an abortion was discussed.[2]

[1] F de Londras, 'Constitutionalizing Fetal Rights: A Salutary Tale from Ireland' (2015) 22(2) *Michigan Journal of Gender and the Law* 243.

[2] *Open Door and Dublin Well Woman v Ireland*, 29 October 1992, Series A no 246-A, (1992) 14 EHRR CD131.

The *ABC* case was contested by all three applicants on the grounds of a violation of articles 3, 8, 13 and 14 (rights to be free from torture, to a private and family life, to an effective remedy and to non-discrimination). In addition, applicant C contested the case on the ground of article 2 (the right to life), as the lack of legislation effectively implementing article 40.3.3 meant that she was in effect unable to avail herself of its provision for the 'equal right to life of the mother'.

Although the Court in the original judgment found in favour of applicant C in relation to her article 8 claim, it dismissed the remainder of her claims and all of the claims of applicants A and B. In addition to this outcome, we felt that the way in which the Court dismissed the women's claims warranted a feminist re-write. For example, the Court dismissed as inadmissible the applicants' claim under article 3. We explore in our re-written judgment how, rather than being 'manifestly ill-founded', this claim can be reasoned to be justified and a violation found. Elsewhere, the original judgment rejects (by 11 votes to six) any violation of article 8 as regards the first and second applicants. However, as is explored in the re-written judgment, this finding can be challenged by a more contextualised reading of the situation and the right. Finally, the original Court found that there were no separate issues arising under article 14 of the Convention. Revisiting the judgment from our feminist standpoint, we differed, feeling that a detailed assessment of the discriminations arising from the legal framework was entirely germane to the conclusion of the case.

The time period in which the judgment re-writing occurred has proved to be a significant one in Ireland's protracted history of abortion activism. Ongoing attention to the cases of Mrs Y and Savita Halappanavar,[3] the campaign to 'Repeal the 8th' amendment of the Irish Constitution that culminated in a landslide referendum vote to amend the Constitution in May 2018,[4] and an array of creative pro-choice campaigns, have all occurred since the writing process was begun.[5] More recently, the High Court across the border in Northern Ireland found that elements of the restrictive abortion regime in that jurisdiction constituted a breach of article 8 of the Convention.[6]

These events provide an important context for the re-writing of this judgment. They also provide a reminder of the implications of the *ABC* case to activism today, and situate the original case within the context of activist efforts. We felt

[3] P Cullen and K Holland, 'Husband's action over death of Savita Halappanavar settled' *Irish Times* (2016), at www.irishtimes.com/news/crime-and-law/courts/high-court/husband-s-action-over-death-of-savita-halappanavar-settled-1.2566536. K Holland, 'Timeline of Ms Y case' *Irish Times* (2014), at www.irishtimes.com/news/social-affairs/timeline-of-ms-y-case-1.1951699.

[4] For some feminist reflections on the campaign see M. Enright, 'Watching Women's History in the Irish Pro-Choice Referendum' (2018) at http://criticallegalthinking.com/2018/05/04/watching-womens-history-in-the-irish-pro-choice-referendum/.

[5] See, for example, 'Speaking of Imelda' (Facebook, 2017), at www.facebook.com/SpeakingofIMELDA/.

[6] *The Northern Ireland Human Rights Commission's Application* [2015] NIQB 96.

an attempt at such a connection created important recognition of the *ABC* case as the outcome of activist efforts. Moreover, acknowledging the pro-choice activist context is, we suggest, an important, if partial, rebalancing away from the concentrated (and male) power of the European Court of Human Rights.

The efforts by those seeking reform of Irish abortion laws may be contrasted with the limited response of an international Court, the ECtHR, which attempted in its judgment to provide a narrow measure of rights protection while respecting national sovereignty via an over-reliance on the margin of appreciation doctrine and consensus analysis. Contemporary events also demonstrate the ongoing need for an alternative – feminist – reasoning in abortion cases under the ECHR. One of the features of the original judgment was the manner in which it downplayed a range of contextual factors, and failed to account properly for the particular manner in which these combined to give rise to particularly severe circumstances. One aspect of our feminist re-writing aimed to redress this omission and to deliberately delve into the detail of the women's predicaments. In particular, our discussion reframes the issues that the women's cases raised under article 3 (prohibition of torture) and also article 8 (right to respect for private and family life) in conjunction with article 14 (prohibition of discrimination). It does this in order to take proper account of the harm done to women by exceptionally restrictive laws and practices in this area. The intention in relation to article 14 was to ensure that it was pivotal to the re-written judgment, to frame the harm created by restrictive abortion laws and culture as a particularly gendered one with its roots in discrimination. This, we felt, would redress the weak treatment of that article in the original judgment.

Contemporary events serve as an unpleasant reminder of the dangers of casting law as a set of discrete events and isolated developments. While a landmark judgment (albeit limited and cautious) might create a passing (popular) interest, the effects of an unfortunate judgment and poor law are not short-lived, abstract or remote. Rather, judg(e)ment is experienced and *lived* by individuals (in this case women), and on a continuing basis. This longevity and continuity serves only to underscore the importance of judgment-writing.

While our primary concern has been the judgment of the ECtHR in the *ABC* case, we have in re-writing it also been conscious of the legal and political lead-up to that case.[7] It was seen as a landmark case, and followed what might be described as a perpetual debate of the 'abortion issue' in the Irish Republic. The country had seen three referenda over a period of nearly 20 years and the restrictive ruling in the *X* case.[8] In this context, taking a case to the ECtHR might be seen as an ultimately strategic move on the part of some activist communities. However, the

[7] See, for a summary of the legal position in the jurisdiction, M Enright et al, 'General Scheme of Access to Abortion Bill 2015' (2015) 5(1) *feminists@law* 1.

[8] *Attorney General v X*, [1992] IESCI 1; [1992] 1 IR 1.

diverse backgrounds of the women – A, B and C – are a firm rebuttal to such claims, and each represents a 'normal' Irish life. While this clearly made the task of the Court in the original judgment more difficult, and was also a challenge in our re-writing, the diversity of the women's situations, combined with the failure of the Court to fully respond to that diversity, provides a powerful illustration of the varying realities created by the exceptionally restrictive regime in Ireland.

JUDGMENT

A, B and C v IRELAND

(Application no. 25579/05)

The Grand Chamber of the European Court of Human Rights consisting of:

Helen Fenwick (President of Chamber), Wendy Guns and Ben Warwick

16 December 2010

THE APPLICANTS' SUBMISSIONS

1. The first two applicants complained under Articles 3, 8, 13 and 14 of the Convention about the prohibition of abortion in Ireland on health and well-being grounds. The third applicant complained under Articles 2, 3, 8, 13 and 14 of the Convention about the absence of legislative implementation of Article 40.3.3 of the Constitution which, she argued, meant that she had no appropriate means of establishing her right to a lawful abortion in Ireland on the grounds of a risk to her life.

ALLEGED VIOLATION OF ARTICLE 8 OF THE CONVENTION

2. The first and second applicants complained under Article 8 about the restrictions on lawful abortion in Ireland which meant that they could not obtain an abortion for health and/or well-being reasons in Ireland, and the third applicant complained under the same Article about the absence of any legislative implementation of Article 40.3.3 of the Constitution.

Whether Article 8 applied to the applicants' complaints

3. Article 8 of the Convention is a broad concept which has relevance in the context of access to abortion (see the judgment in *Tysiąc v Poland*, no. 5410/03, ECHR 2007-I, (2007) 45 EHRR 42, § 107). The Court also points out that the issue of abortion-seeking represents a particularly intimate aspect of a woman's private life, such that Article 8 can be interpreted as meaning that pregnancy and its termination pertain uniquely to the woman's private life, given that becoming pregnant has immense consequences for a woman's psychological and physical well-being, and also has consequences for a range of other aspects of her life. The experience of becoming pregnant must be contextualised within the particular experiences of the woman in question. Departing from the judgments in *Tysiąc*, § 106, and adopting an evolutive method of interpretation of Article 8 (taking account of measures allowing access to abortion in certain circumstances within virtually all the member states), it is therefore found that Article 8 can, accordingly, be interpreted as conferring a right of access to abortion.

Positive obligations under Article 8 of the Convention

4. Positive obligations are inherent in effective respect for private life, and obviously pertain to the right of access to abortion under Article 8 which the Court has found to be apparent. The Court considers it appropriate to analyse the first and second applicants' complaints as concerning positive obligations; their core argument can be conceptualised as being that the prohibition in Ireland of abortion where sought for health and/or well-being reasons failed to respect that aspect of their right to respect for their private lives. Recognition of a right of access to abortion under Article 8 does not imply that member states may place no restrictions on such access (*Brüggemann and Scheuten v Germany*, no. 6959/75, Commission decision of 19 May 1976, Decisions and Reports 5, p. 103). Nevertheless, having regard to the broad concept of private life within the meaning of Article 8, including the right to personal autonomy and to physical and psychological integrity, the Court finds that the prohibition of the termination of the first and second applicants' pregnancies sought for reasons of health and/or well-being amounted to an interference with their right to respect for their private lives. The essential question which must be determined is whether the particular prohibition in Ireland constitutes an unjustified failure to honour a positive obligation to respect their rights under Article 8 of the Convention.
5. The Court notes that the prohibition of which the first two applicants complained comprised sections 58 and 59 of the 1861 Offences Against the Person Act (it being an offence to procure or attempt to procure an abortion, to administer an abortion or to assist in an abortion by supplying any noxious thing or instrument, punishable by penal servitude for life) as qualified by Article 40.3.3 of the Constitution as interpreted by the Supreme Court in the *X* case (see also Articles 40.3.1 and 50 of the Constitution).
6. To determine whether this interference entailed a violation of Article 8, the Court must examine whether or not it was justified under the second paragraph of that Article namely, whether the interference was 'in accordance with the law' and 'necessary in a democratic society' for one of the 'legitimate aims' specified in Article 8(2) of the Convention.

Was the interference 'in accordance with the law'?

7. The applicants accepted that the restriction was in accordance with the law. We agree with this assessment and make no further comment.

Did the interference pursue a legitimate aim?

8. The Court points out that, in the above-cited *Open Door* case, it found that the protection afforded under Irish law to the right to life of the unborn pursued the legitimate aim of the protection of morals of which the protection in Ireland of the right to life of the unborn was deemed to be one aspect. We are persuaded that now it is time to take a different approach to this question.

9. The first and second applicants maintain that the will of the Irish people had changed and, they argue, so should our approach to this question. The moral position the Irish Government rests its arguments on is an historic one. Since 1983, the population of Ireland has not been requested to vote in a referendum proposing any broader abortion rights in Ireland. In fact, in 1992 and 2002 the Irish people refused in referenda to restrict the existing grounds for lawful abortion in Ireland, on the one hand, and accorded in those referenda the right to travel abroad for an abortion and to have information about that option, on the other.
10. In light of the above, the Court finds that the opinion polls on which the first and second applicants relied are indicative of a change in the views of the Irish people concerning the grounds for lawful abortion in Ireland, so as to displace the State's opinion to the Court on the exact content of the requirements of morals in Ireland. The Court also notes that it is now possible to find in the legal and social orders of the Contracting States a uniform European conception of morals on the question of when life begins, given the acceptance of access to abortion in the laws of the vast majority of member states (see the discussion of the European consensus on this issue, below). The member states may therefore be found to have determined – in the vast majority of cases – that the protection of morals does not require that the idea that life begins at conception should be reflected in law.
11. Accordingly, the Court finds that the impugned restrictions in the present case were not based on moral values concerning the nature of life accepted in the majority of member states, or clearly reflected in the *current* stance of the majority of the Irish people.
12. The Court concludes that the impugned restriction therefore did not pursue the legitimate aim of the protection of morals of which the protection in Ireland of the right to life of the unborn was one aspect. So finding does not preclude a finding in future that certain restrictions on abortion, e.g. as to the upper limits for the timing of an abortion, could fall within one or more legitimate aims within Article 8(2).

Was the interference 'necessary in a democratic society'?

13. Given the above findings as to the legitimate aim, it is clear that a breach of Article 8 has arisen in respect of all three applicants. Nevertheless, for clarity and to provide guidance for future cases, the Court will examine whether there existed a pressing social need for the measure in question and, in particular, whether, had a legitimate aim been found to be present, the interference would have been proportionate to that aim.
14. The Court points out that a number of factors must be taken into account when determining the breadth of the margin of appreciation to be enjoyed by the State when determining any case under Article 8 of the Convention, in which intimate personal interests are weighed against moral and ethical concerns. There can be no doubt as to the acute sensitivity of the question of abortion as an aspect of the private lives of women, or as to the profound implications in terms of dignity

and autonomy for women of continuing or not continuing a pregnancy. In this context, the Court is required to consider whether a margin of appreciation should be extended to the State (and if so, its breadth) in the light of the consensus that has been reached on the question of abortion.

15. A European consensus has been reached on how to negotiate the balance between the health and well-being of the mother and the protection of rights of others (the foetus at a certain stage of development). In the majority of European States, the health and autonomy of the female is prioritised over the protection of the foetus (see also argument below as to Article 14 read with 8). Most Contracting Parties have in their legislation resolved the conflicting rights and interests in favour of greater legal access to abortion. Given the evolutive interpretation of the Convention (*Tyrer v United Kingdom*, 25 April 1978, Series A no 26, (1979–80) 2 EHRR 1), this consensus must be a decisive factor in the Court's examination of whether the impugned prohibition on abortion in Ireland for health and well-being reasons struck a fair balance between the conflicting rights and interests.

16. The Court, therefore, is convinced that this consensus decisively narrows the margin of appreciation of the State in this case.

17. Although applicants A and B do not fall under the 'real and substantial risk' exception outlined in Article 40.3.3, and confirmed in the *X case*, their claim is that the prohibition in prohibiting abortion even when health and well-being is threatened disproportionately affects their right to private life. The Court has conceptualised the claim as one involving a failure to respect the positive obligation under Article 8 to provide access to abortion (within certain limits as reflected in the majority of the laws of the member states), and must consider whether such access would cover the situations of A and B. While C could fall within the 'real and substantial risk' exception due to the possibility that her cancer could recur, a finding as to the positive obligation in question, as applied to her situation, would create greater certainty in terms of the response which the state should have taken to that situation.

18. In this case, in order to protect the private life of the applicants and, in particular, to safeguard their health and well-being, the margin of appreciation must, therefore, be narrow. A prohibition of abortion to protect unborn life at all stages of foetal development is not justified under the Convention on the basis of unqualified deference to the protection of morals, an aspect of which concerns – the Government argues – the protection of pre-natal life. Nor is a prohibition justified on the basis that the expectant mother's right to respect for her private life is of a lesser stature. The regulation of abortion rights is not solely a matter for the Contracting States, as the Government maintained, relying on certain international declarations. Rather, the Court must decide on the compatibility with Article 8 of the Convention of the Irish State's prohibition of abortion on health and well-being grounds on the basis of the above-described positive obligation to which – in the light of the European consensus on the matter – a narrow margin of appreciation is applicable.

19. From the lengthy, complex and sensitive debate in Ireland as regards the content of its abortion laws, a choice has emerged. Irish law prohibits abortion in Ireland for health and well-being reasons but allows women, in the first and second applicants' position who wish to have an abortion for those reasons, the option of lawfully travelling to another State to do so, which has a greater impact on women in poverty. Irish law placed C in an uncertain position, given that she could not obtain clear advice from doctors as to whether she came within the 'real and substantial risk' exception, meaning that she also travelled to England for an abortion on health and well-being grounds.
20. The Court notes at this point that the option to travel abroad to procure an abortion calls into question the pressing social need identified by the Government in the protection of morals, a central aspect of which – in this case – is the assumed majoritarian stance against abortion. It is difficult to envisage how the Government's argument that it protects morals and upholds foetal life by restricting abortion whilst accepting that women do travel abroad can succeed. The Court cannot simply ignore the implications for the private life of the woman inherent in the choice between accepting restrictive prohibition and travel to another country.
21. The restrictive prohibition on abortion in Ireland rests, according to the applicants, on the assumption that those who require an abortion have the choice to travel abroad. However, as all three applicants have shown, the restrictive prohibition on abortion in Ireland places pregnant women in a sometimes impossible scenario whereby they must choose between their health and well-being or travelling abroad for the purposes of procuring an abortion, with the attendant consequences for their health and well-being. The Court considers that the State can only be afforded a narrow margin of appreciation in balancing the private life of the applicants against a potential majoritarian interest in restrictive abortion, given the European consensus on this matter. Moreover, the Court does not consider that *the choice* of travelling abroad which is afforded to pregnant women is demonstrative of the State's interest in the protection of morals, an aspect of which is the protection of foetal life. As in the above-cited *Open Door* case, the restrictive prohibition on abortion is at any rate ineffective to protect the right to life because women travel abroad anyway. At issue in this case is the extent to which they do so at risk to their health and well-being and, thus, by the creation of detriment to their private life.
22. The right to travel abroad lawfully for an abortion with access to appropriate information and medical care in Ireland is not a substitute for the positive protection of the rights of the applicants within their own jurisdiction. The Court, therefore, considers that the prohibition in Ireland of abortion for health and well-being reasons, even if it were to be found to be based on the profound moral views of the Irish people as to the nature of life (see above) and as to the consequent protection to be accorded to the right to life of the unborn, exceeds the margin of appreciation accorded in that respect to the Irish State.
23. The Court finds that this implicit obligation to travel for an abortion imposes a disproportionate interference on the private life of the individual concerned,

creating a violation of the positive obligation identified. Allowing travel for abortion cannot, for the reasons given, be viewed as satisfying that obligation. Given that Ireland barred abortion on any grounds except that of a risk to the life of the mother – and even in respect of that ground, it did not appear that in practice there was clarity as to whether an abortion could be obtained, as Applicant C argued, the Court has no doubt that the positive obligation in question was breached, and does not need to consider further grounds of abortion which a State would have to put in place in order to avoid breaching that obligation.
24. The Court considers that the restrictive prohibition on abortion disproportionately interferes with the right to private life of the three applicants and it, therefore, concludes that there has been a violation of Article 8 of the Convention as regards the three applicants.

ALLEGED VIOLATION OF ARTICLE 14 OF THE CONVENTION TAKEN IN CONJUNCTION WITH ARTICLE 8

Applicability of Article 14

25. Despite having already found a breach of Article 8, it is important to consider also the application of Article 14, in order to examine the discriminatory aspects of the virtual bar on abortion in Ireland. As the Court has consistently held, Article 14 complements the other substantive provisions of the Convention and its Protocols. It has no independent existence since it has effect solely in relation to 'the enjoyment of the rights and freedoms' safeguarded by those provisions. Although the application of Article 14 does not presuppose a breach of those provisions – and to this extent it is autonomous – there can be no room for its application unless the facts at issue fall within the ambit of one or more of the latter (see, e.g., *Karlheinz Schmidt v. Germany*, judgment of 18 July 1994, Series A no. 291-B, p. 32, § 22; *Petrovic v Austria* 6/1996/775/976, 125).
26. The Court has said on many occasions that Article 14 comes into play whenever 'the subject-matter of the disadvantage … constitutes one of the modalities of the exercise of a right guaranteed' (see *National Union of Belgian Police v Belgium*, judgment of 27 October 1975, Series A no. 19, p. 20, § 45, (1979–80) 1 EHRR 578), or the measures complained of are 'linked to the exercise of a right guaranteed' (see *Schmidt and Dahlström v Sweden*, judgment of 6 February 1976, Series A no. 21, p. 17, § 39, (1979–80) 1 EHRR 632).
27. The Court has already determined that the facts of the present case come within the scope of Article 8 and, consequently, of Article 14 of the Convention.

Preferential treatment of persons in an analogous position

28. The Court has held that not every difference in treatment will amount to a violation of Article 14. It must be established that other persons in an analogous or relevantly similar situation enjoy preferential treatment and that this distinction is discriminatory (see *Ünal Tekeli v Turkey*, no. 29865/96, § 49, ECHR 2004-X, (2006) 42 EHRR 53).

29. In the applicants' submission, different treatment of women and men with respect to gaining access to medical services in Ireland was present, and women and men were in relevantly similar situations. They submitted that women more than men are disadvantaged in Ireland since only women can be pregnant and a pregnant woman may face obstruction in obtaining access to ordinary domestic medical services, and to information regarding the availability of those services, such as to chemotherapy treatment for cancer (in the case of C) or as to medical services in general, domestically (in the case of all three applicants) which a man seeking such information or services would not face. They submit in support of this contention that the Court in *Tysiąc v Poland* (cited above) referred to the efficacy of medical procedures in respect of a woman who was a potential abortion-seeker rather than to access to abortion. Both men and women in Ireland seek to access medical procedures, but only women experience difficulty in so doing, if pregnant, and are in that sense disadvantaged, in comparison to men seeking access to such procedures. The applicants argue that the discriminatory treatment consisted of the creation of obstacles to access to medical services or information as to possible steps to accessing an abortion, where a man would not have found difficulty in obtaining analogous services or relevant analogous information.

30. It was not disputed that that amounted to a difference in treatment in terms of accessing medical services and information as to their availability on grounds of gender on the basis of an inherent characteristic of the generality of women (but not men) – to be pregnant.

31. Ability to access medical services and information as to their availability is primarily intended to safeguard the health of persons within a state. While aware of the differences which may exist between women and men in terms of the ability of women but not men to become pregnant, the Court starts from the premise that the state of being pregnant is not viewed as one in Europe in general that would create a foundation for denying access to health services. In so far as access to such services is concerned, both men and women are 'similarly placed'.

32. It follows from the above that for the purposes of access to medical services, the applicants were in an analogous situation to men seeking to access such services but were treated differently.

An objective and reasonable justification?

33. A difference of treatment for the purposes of Article 14 is discriminatory if it has no objective and reasonable justification; in other words, if it does not pursue a legitimate aim or if there is not a reasonable relationship of proportionality between the means employed and the aim sought to be realised (see *Stec and Others v the United Kingdom*, [GC], nos. 65731/01 and 65900/01, § 51, ECHR 2006-VI, (2006) 43 EHRR 47); see also the *Karlheinz Schmidt* judgment, 18 July 1994, § 24, Series A no. 291-B). In *Karner v Austria* (no. 40016/98, ECHR 2003-IX, (2004) 38 EHRR 24) the aim put forward was that of protecting traditional, heterosexual family life. The Court held: 'where there is a difference in treatment based on sex or sexual orientation, the principle of proportionality does not merely require that

the measure chosen is in principle suitable for realising the aim sought. It must also be shown that it was necessary …' (§ 41).

34. The Contracting States enjoy a certain margin of appreciation in assessing whether and to what extent differences in otherwise similar situations justify a difference in treatment (see *Gaygusuz v Austria*, 16 September 1996, § 42, Reports 1996-IV, (1997) 23 EHRR 364). The scope of the margin of appreciation will vary according to the circumstances, the subject matter and its background (see *Rasmussen v Denmark*, 28 November 1984, § 40, Series A no. 87, (1985) 7 EHRR 371), but the final decision as to the observance of the Convention's requirements rests with the Court. The Convention is first and foremost a system for the protection of human rights; the Court must, however, have regard to the changing conditions in Contracting States and respond, for example, to any emerging consensus as to the standards to be achieved (see *Weller v Hungary*, no. 44399/05, § 28, 31 March 2009; *Stec and Others*, cited above, §§ 63 and 64; *Ünal Tekeli*, cited above, § 54; *Stafford v the United Kingdom* [GC], no. 46295/99, § 68, ECHR 2002-IV, (2002) 35 EHRR 32).

35. The Court further reiterates that the advancement of gender equality is today a major goal in the member States of the Council of Europe, and internationally, and very weighty reasons would have to be put forward before such a difference of treatment could be regarded as compatible with the Convention (see *Burghartz v Switzerland*, 22 February 1994, § 27, Series A no. 280-B, (1994) 18 EHRR 101, and *Schuler-Zgraggen v Switzerland*, 24 June 1993, § 67, Series A no. 263, (1996) 21 EHRR 404).In particular, references to traditions, general assumptions or prevailing social attitudes in a particular country are insufficient justification for a difference in treatment on grounds of sex. For example, States are prevented from imposing traditions that derive from the man's primordial role and the woman's secondary role in the family (see *Ünal Tekeli*, cited above, § 63).

36. However, the Contracting States enjoy a certain margin of appreciation in assessing whether and to what extent differences in otherwise similar situations justify a different treatment in law. The scope of the margin of appreciation will vary according to the circumstances, the subject matter and its background; in this respect, one of the relevant factors will tend to be the existence or non-existence of common ground between the laws of the Contracting States – a 'European consensus' (see, among other authorities, *Rasmussen v Denmark*, cited above, § 40; *Rees v the United Kingdom*, 17 October 1986, Series A no. 106, (1987) 9 EHRR 56, [37]; *Cossey v the United Kingdom*, 27 September 1990, Series A no. 184, (1991) 13 EHRR 622; *Evans v the United Kingdom*, no.6339/05, 7 March 2006, (2006) 43 EHRR 21). See also the discussion of the impact of finding such a consensus above.

37. The Government submitted that the fact that there was no common European standard in the matter of protection for unborn life meant that the Irish government's stance based on the protection for unborn life recognised under the Irish Constitution, according to which foetal life should be accorded equal status with maternal life, fell within the margin of appreciation left to the Contracting States in respect of determinations as to the protection of foetal life. Furthermore, the

government contended that the position in question reflected the outlook of Irish society in general.

38. The Court does not find, contrary to the Government's submission, that there is a lack of a common standard with regard to the protection for unborn life in the member States. The Court conducted a comparative study of the legislation in respect of abortion of thirty-three member States of the Council of Europe (Albania, Armenia, Austria, Azerbaijan, Belgium, Bosnia and Herzegovina, Bulgaria, Croatia, Cyprus, the Czech Republic, Estonia, Finland, the 'Former Yugoslav Republic of Macedonia', France, Georgia, Germany, Greece, Italy, Latvia, Lithuania, Luxembourg, Malta, Moldova, the Netherlands, Poland, Portugal, Romania, Serbia, Spain, Sweden, Switzerland, Turkey and the United Kingdom). The comparative study suggests that abortion is available in virtually all the member states on certain fundamental grounds, including that of a serious risk to a woman's health. That indicates that there is a consensus as to the lack of parity between foetal life and maternal life, in contrast to the position in Ireland (see also the discussion of the consensus under Article 8 taken alone, above). The Irish position is reflected in three micro-states: in Malta, San Marino, and Monaco it is not clear that abortion is available to save the life of the mother.

39. But in the rest of Europe that is not the case. For example, Poland operates a restrictive abortion regime compared to the majority of States in Europe, but provides three exceptions within which lawful abortion in permitted (see Polish Law on Family Planning (protection of the human foetus and conditions permitting pregnancy termination) Statute Book 93.17.78: abortion is permitted before 12 weeks where conception was a result of rape, the foetus is severely disabled, or where continuing the pregnancy would pose a serious threat to the health of the woman. In the case of a serious threat to health, this must be attested to by two medical specialists: s4(a) of the 1993 Act, and s2 Ordinance issued by the Minister of Health on 22 January 1997). Thus, in relation to comparable States, Ireland operates the most restrictive abortion regime in Europe, and is therefore out of step with the common standard (see *Petrovic v Austria*, 27 March 1998, *Reports of Judgments and Decisions* 1998-II, (2001) 33 EHRR 14). It is clear that at the material time, that is at the end of the 1990s, there was a common standard in this field, since at that time the majority of the Contracting States provided for abortion in the circumstances described.

40. If the implied consensus on the protection for unborn life in Europe is taken to indicate that there is no general acceptance of parity between foetal life and maternal life, where there is a serious threat to the health of the woman, that would mean that the margin of appreciation accorded to Ireland in respect of its treatment of C would be narrow since C faced a serious threat to her life if she was unable to access chemotherapy (due to her continued pregnancy) if her cancer returned, which would have posed a serious threat to her health and possibly her life. But the Court finds that it would also be narrow in respect of A and B since the evidence demonstrated that both had to travel to England to obtain an abortion,

creating stress, and preventing them from accessing abortion aftercare immediately post-abortion, due to the prohibition in Ireland (which meant that A and B were reluctant to seek such care in Ireland), and the necessity of returning immediately to Ireland due to the stigmatisation they might have faced had the fact that they had travelled for an abortion become more generally known on their return to Ireland. These factors also apply to C. Thus the margin of appreciation accorded to Ireland in respect of its treatment of all three applicants is narrow, and weighty reasons are necessary to justify the difference in treatment in terms of accessing medical services, between men and women.

41. It remains to be ascertained whether the difference in treatment between men and women in this respect was objectively and reasonably justified under Article 14, according a narrow margin of appreciation to the State.

42. The Court does not lose sight of the special context of the present case, in Ireland, given the Constitutional position. But, in respect of restrictions on the family and private life of women due to the *de facto* requirement to travel abroad for an abortion, the relevant restrictions concern 'a most intimate part of an individual's private life', so there must exist 'particularly serious reasons' before such interferences can satisfy the requirements of Article 8 § 2 of the Convention. In particular, there must be a reasonable relationship of proportionality between the restrictions imposed and the (potential) legitimate aim of protecting foetal life. Such restrictions are acceptable only where there is a real threat to the furtherance of that aim. Assertions as to that threat must be 'substantiated by specific examples' (see *Smith and Grady v the United Kingdom*, nos 33985/96 and 33986/96, ECHR 1999-VI, (1999) 29 EHRR 493, [89], [94]). The Court notes the lack of a rational connection with creating such protection by imposing a requirement, in effect, to travel for abortion. Ireland has not demonstrated that the imposition of the prohibition combined with the fact that a large number of women travel from Ireland for an abortion every year, furthers the aim in question.

43. Turning now to the circumstances of the present case, the Court notes that the Government advanced several arguments to justify the difference in treatment between men and women as regards accessing medical services. The Court will examine them in turn.

44. As regards the argument relating to the special status of women as child-bearers, the Government firstly argues that men and women are not in analogous positions as regards access to medical services since men cannot become pregnant, and secondly if they are deemed to be in analogous positions, there is a sound basis for treating pregnant women differently on the basis that the unborn child must also be equally protected, a consideration that is irrelevant in respect of men. The Court observes that the approach of the Irish government to that status reflects a determination to take an essentialised view of women as child-bearers, which in effect accords them a diminished status in comparison with men as users of health services. An objective and reasonable basis for differentiating between women and men cannot itself be tainted by discrimination. Thus this reason does not provide the necessary reasonable and objective justification.

45. Secondly, the Government argues that there is no causal relationship between the differentiation in question as to access to medical services and gender since pregnant women and men are in general in a similar position as regards such access. Most medical services accessed by men and by pregnant women are similarly available, without differentiation. The difference arises due to a woman's decision to seek an abortion; thus the causal relation in question is due to that decision, rather than to a general policy of differentiating between women and men in relation to access to medical services. The Court observes, however, that very compelling reasons may arise, placing women in the position of seeking an abortion, which erodes the choice in question. Such reasons arose in the case of C, since the reason for seeking an abortion (the possibility that her cancer might re-emerge) was not within her control. In general, the Court observes that the presence of the criminal prohibition on abortion in Ireland creates a coercive climate in relation to access to certain significant medical services affecting women but not men, meaning that a causal relationship between barriers to such access and gender is created by the State rather than by the woman's decision to seek an abortion.
46. In view of the foregoing, the Court considers that the placement of pregnant women in a position where their access to medical services or to information as to such services is impaired, while it is not so impaired in relation to men, cannot be said to be reasonably or objectively justified. The Court concludes that this difference in treatment, of which the three applicants were victims, amounted to discrimination on grounds of sex.
47. There has therefore been a violation of Article 14 taken in conjunction with Article 8 on the ground of gender in respect of all three applicants. In view of that finding, the Court will not consider whether the fact that the first applicant would have been adversely affected by virtue of her financial status would be sufficient to ground a complaint under Article 14 of the Convention.

ALLEGED VIOLATION OF ARTICLE 3 OF THE CONVENTION

48. The applicants allege a violation of Article 3 of the Convention, submitting that the actions and inactions of the Contracting State in the circumstances amounted to cruel, degrading or inhuman treatment, or torture. The Irish government in its submissions, dismisses this argument on three levels; that the applicants have failed to adequately explain how 'taboo and stigma' prevented them from accessing appropriate advice and aftercare; that in any case, the State did not cause such stigma to arise; and, in the round, that the women's experiences do not amount to ill-treatment severe enough to fall within Article 3.

Relevant Facts

49. It is worth reiterating the turmoil that was brought upon these women, A, B, and C, by an unfortunate amalgam of the Irish restrictions on access to abortion, the associated socio-cultural atmosphere, an unexpected pregnancy, and personal circumstances. 'Personal circumstances', while sounding so contained,

masks the huge personal strain and upset that is obviously caused to any one by poverty, unemployment, having one's children taken into care, alcohol dependency, depression, the fear of an ectopic pregnancy, cancer or chemotherapy. Yet for the applicants these very serious and challenging issues were only part of a larger story.

50. The extant legislative and socio-cultural situation of Ireland brought further difficulties for the women. It is clear from the arguments heard by the Court that reproductive rights in Ireland are surrounded by a high-level quasi-controversy that filters into the everyday lives of women. Much argument was heard as to the multiple legal provisions of the State, referenda, landmark case law, guidance of professional and statutory bodies, international agreements and scrutiny, Committees and Groups. It is, of course, important for the purposes of fulfilling its obligations under the present Convention that the Contracting State pursue these legal questions, yet it is also clear that the determination of legal questions is not sufficient to ensure protection at the individual level. The letter of the regulatory framework was only one factor in the distressing experience of the applicants. Also significant was the fear of being 'found out' and the uncertainty as to the legal position that was also present.

51. It is often said that Irish women seeking an abortion must 'travel' abroad to receive one. Again, the notion of 'travel' (and its associated excitement and exploration) hardly does justice to the experiences of these women. For A, travel meant delay, careful planning to avoid affecting her life with her children, secrecy, debt, and emergency treatment as she began bleeding on the last leg of her journey. For B, travel meant an anxious Christmas holiday period as she awaited advice, secrecy (to the extent that B did not to have a next of kin listed), expense, and two nights alone in London. For C, travel also entailed uncertainty, with severe delays as a result of her having difficulties in sourcing her preferred medical treatment abroad.

52. It should be cause for serious reflection that these women's difficult personal situations have been aggravated unnecessarily. Yet Article 3 protections entail more than protection for those in difficult, challenging or vulnerable situations. The essence of a prohibition on cruel, inhuman, and degrading ill-treatment goes further, and promotes personal autonomy and human dignity. Article 3 is closely connected to the Convention's *raison d'etre* as expressed in the preambular provision; Contracting States 'have a common heritage of … political traditions, ideals, freedom and the rule of law'. This emphasis upon 'freedom' (also present in the title of the Convention itself), is pertinent to a full understanding of Article 3. More than merely protecting women in the positions of A, B and C, the purpose of the Article can be interpreted as prohibiting ill-treatment for the purpose of enabling an individual's full expression of personal choice and freedom of action.

53. This Court's previous determinations on the question of the severity threshold for an Article 3 violation have been numerous. It is necessary to note the Court's previous finding that Article 3 questions need not be determined in *abstracto* and that the severity of ill-treatment is relative to the individual circumstances

(*Chember v Russia*, no.7188/03, § 52, ECHR 2008). This enables the Court to have regard to the sex, age, and state of health of the victim etc. The duration of the ill-treatment has also been noted as relevant to the determination of severity (*Ireland v the United Kingdom*, Series A no. 25 (1978) 2 EHHR 25, p. 65, para 162). The Court reiterates these findings here and notes that Article 3 determinations in respect of the applicants are deeply connected to their circumstances and do not necessarily imply a more general ill-treatment.

54. The case of *T v the United Kingd*om ([GC], no. 24724/94, § 69, 16 December 1999, (2000) 30 EHRR 121) is instructive on the question of the threshold of severity: treatment has been held by the Court to be 'inhuman' because, inter alia, it was premeditated, was applied for hours at a stretch and caused either actual bodily injury or intense physical and mental suffering, and also 'degrading' because it was such as to arouse in its victims feelings of fear, anguish and inferiority capable of humiliating and debasing them. In order for a punishment or treatment associated with it to be 'inhuman' or 'degrading', the suffering or humiliation involved must in any event go beyond that inevitable element of suffering or humiliation connected with a given form of legitimate treatment or punishment.' (*Soering v the United Kingdom*, 7 July 1989, Series A no. 161, 11 EHHR 439, p. 39, para 100).

55. The Court finds that all three applicants were subject to treatment of a severity adequate to cross the threshold into inhuman and degrading treatment under Article 3. The treatment of the women was clearly beyond the level to be expected in the 'legitimate' treatment of everyday life. The ill-treatment was physical in that they were subjected to the whole-body pressures that a pregnancy causes, and insofar as the applicants suffered additional complications, pain and bleeding as a result of the restrictive reproductive regulations and accompanying culture in the Contracting State. The general effect of the experience upon the women's physical health cannot be known. More significantly for these women was the range of mental ill-treatment. Brought on by the dominant anti-abortion sentiment in Ireland, the applicants suffered from fear of legal or social sanction, the mental stress of keeping secrets from one's close family and friends, anxiety and perhaps also a sense of shame. The severity of this mental suffering, when combined with the physical aspects of the applicants' ill-treatment, and the extended period of suffering, is sufficient for a finding of inhuman and degrading treatment.

56. Whether such ill-treatment is attributable to the Contracting State has not yet been discussed. It is clear that the Irish State did not directly inflict the ill-treatment. As such, it falls to be determined whether it was incumbent upon the State to ensure positive measures to avoid such inhuman and degrading treatment, and if so whether adequate positive measures were taken.

57. It has previously been found by this Court that the Convention entails positive obligations to ensure practical measures are taken to ensure certain Convention rights (See *Chember v Russia*, § 50, cited above, and *Öneryildiz v Turkey* [GC], no. 48939/99, ECHR 2004-XII, (2005) 41 EHHR 20, para 332). The Court has gone further to distinguish the level of positive duty incumbent upon a State in relation to different Convention rights. Thus it was noted in *Budayeva v Russia*,

that 'the fundamental importance of the right to life requires that the scope of the positive obligations under Article 2 includes a duty to do everything within the authorities' power' (*Budayeva v Russia*, nos. 15339/02 and 4 others, § 175, ECHR 2008 (extracts), para 175). On the current issue of the positive obligations inherent in Article 3 (when taken in light of Article 1), the Court finds that there are strong positive obligations upon the State to do everything that is reasonably practicable in the circumstances to prevent torture, inhuman or degrading treatment or punishment. This obligation remains subject to the qualification of the Court that positive 'obligations [must not] be interpreted in such a way as to impose an impossible or disproportionate burden' (*Ilaşcu and Others v Moldova and Russia* [GC], no. 48787/99, § 332, ECHR 2004-VII, (2005) 40 EHRR 46).

58. In relation to the positive obligations under Article 3, the State's provision of a number of abortion counselling services, and its distribution of advisory leaflets in England and Ireland, is commendable. While it is not for the Court to specify the exact measures that should be undertaken by the Contracting State, it is empowered to find that the existing measures are inadequate. There was a much more comprehensive range of actions that might have been supported by the State, which would have avoided the suffering of the applicants, and which would fall well within the bounds of possibility and proportionality. As such the Contracting State fell short of fulfilling its obligations under Article 3 of the Convention.

ALLEGED VIOLATION OF ARTICLE 14 IN CONJUNCTION WITH ARTICLE 3 OF THE CONVENTION

59. The applicants have complained that there is a violation of Article 14 of the Convention taken in conjunction with Article 3 of this treaty. This provision prohibits discrimination on the basis (inter alia) of an individual's gender. This should be interpreted as prohibiting differential treatment of individuals in the same situation unless there is a reasonable and objective justification. It additionally prohibits equal treatment of individuals in significantly different situations when there is no reasonable and objective justification (See *Belgian Linguistic Case*, 23 July 1968, Series A no. 6, (1979–80) 1 EHHR 252). Article 14 of the Convention also prohibits indirect discrimination (See *Zarb Adami v Malta*, no. 17209/02, ECHR 2006-VII, (2007) 44 EHRR 3).

60. The Court has noted that where a policy or a measure has a disproportionate impact on a group of people, it may be considered discriminatory even if it is not specifically aimed at that group. A Contracting State must provide very weighty reasons to justify such a difference in treatment on the basis of gender, in order to avoid breaching the Convention.

61. The Court considers that all the applicants had to travel abroad to undergo an abortion. As a result of the female biology, this experience is unique to women. Men do not get pregnant or have to experience the distress caused by having to travel abroad to undergo a medical procedure. Of course, men can be affected by an abortion of their partner but they themselves are not primarily affected.

Considering that a majority of the Irish women wishing to have an abortion make the arrangements and travel to the UK or elsewhere in secret, the policy first and foremost affects them. As such, it can be demonstrated that these applicants were treated differently from men on the basis of their female biology.

62. The abortion policies of the Irish government impose a significant burden on women. Official statistics of the United Kingdom demonstrate that 4422 women travelled to that jurisdiction to obtain an abortion in 2009 (Department of Health, *Statistical Bulletin: Abortion Statistics, England and Wales 2009*, table 12a). The cost of this procedure – abortion – in the UK can be as much as 2000 euros, a figure that excludes travel and accommodation costs. This places a significant financial burden on women, and for some of them it will lead to debt. Debt can have a negative impact on one's health. Research has found poor mental health to be both a cause and a consequence of experiencing financial difficulty for people living in debt. They will exhibit measurably higher levels of stress, anxiety and depression than those who are financial secure. There is also evidence to suggest that women are particularly at risk of suffering ill health because of poverty. Debt is cited as one of the causes of their ill health. There is a strong link between maternal depression and worries about debt.[1]

63. Travelling abroad to obtain an abortion imposes not only a financial burden upon women but also an emotional one. As noted above, the stigma attached to abortion in Ireland means that women often travel in secret and do not tell their family and friends that they are going abroad to obtain this procedure. The financial pressures and isolation from health services and from the closeness of their friends and families have a negative impact on the health and the well-being of the women involved. They are alone or have to travel at a time when they tend to need physical rest and emotional support, partly because they do not have easy access to abortion and have to make an extra effort to plan and arrange the procedure. As a consequence, almost a third of the abortions for Irish women are carried out at ten weeks or later into the pregnancy. Delaying access to abortion services means that women are facing an increased risk of complications and exposes women to additional risks to their health.

64. A prima facie case of a breach of Article 14 is established, as differential treatment is present. In establishing if a reasonable and objective justification exists for differential treatment, the two factors that play an important role in determining the Court's decision are the lack of consensus and the subject matter at issue (*Rasmussen v Denmark*, cited above). In reviewing whether Irish abortion policies and legislation constitute a violation of Article 8 of the Convention in conjunction with Article 14, the Court has already established that there is a common standard on abortion within the member states. It has concluded that Ireland is one of the few Contracting States that employs such a restrictive approach to abortion

[1] R Reading and S Reynolds, 'Debt, Social Disadvantage and Maternal Depression' (2001) 53 *Social Science & Medicine* 441.

legislation and that the majority of Contracting States allow women to obtain an abortion in their home country, within certain limits.

65. The Court is aware of Ireland's legal positions and its grounds for restricting abortion. The Irish government disputes the claims of the applicants and states that they are based on subjective and general assertions, which were unproven and not tested. It does not accept that the health and the well-being of the applicants are affected because of abortion policies and legislation. The Irish government also pointed out that there is adequate post-abortion care available and that 95% of Irish doctors do provide medical care after this procedure. The Court notes that these arguments are not sufficient to ground a claim of reasonable and objective justification for the differential treatment that men and women face due to this legislation. The Court finds therefore that there has been a breach of Article 14 when taken in conjunction with Article 3 of the Convention.

Reflections

Re-writing this judgment entailed two particular challenges. Firstly, the question arose as to how the substance of the judgment should be altered to address feminist concerns more effectively and offer – in a hypothetical sense – a more feminist type of justice. The other challenge was one of form. This latter challenge meant considering which lines of argument are open to judges (generally, as well as in this particular case), and how even arguments constrained by existing jurisprudence can be better expressed to acknowledge the judges' dilemmas.

In developing our thoughts on these challenges, the workshop session was informative and constructive. The atmosphere was encouraging, and had a collective spirit. There was room for debate and feedback was given in the friendliest way possible. This was probably due to the nature of the project, and the fact that everyone was really committed to it and wanted the project to succeed. The discussant, Keina Yoshida, was involved with the original case and provided constructive feedback. She mentioned that the issue of poverty was dominant in the original submission and felt, together with the other participants present, that that could be addressed in greater detail throughout the feminist judgment. Poverty as a feminist issue was investigated in this judgment, but only applied to the Article 3 section. There was a tension in bringing this issue into the judgment: while it was clearly justified by the women's context and by an intersectional reading of feminism, the ECtHR is not renowned for its credentials in this respect. Its inclusion therefore risked stretching the judgment into another substantive area and perhaps beyond the realms of credibility.

The first version of our judgment included references to the relationship between overseas travel to obtain an abortion and issues related to economic deprivation. In the section addressing Article 8 read in conjunction with 14, it was concluded that the difference in treatment related to biological differences between men and women; this nevertheless did not preclude a finding that they were in analogous positions as regards accessing medical services such as chemotherapy. Men do not have to travel overseas to access medical services in the majority of Member States in order to maintain their health and well-being. In contrast, in Ireland women cannot, even where their health might be at risk, maintain their health and well-being by accessing abortion services domestically. An additional approach for our judgment would have been to examine under Article 14 the inequality that exists between women who do have the money to travel overseas and those who cannot afford to do so at all or cannot access loans. Due to the length of the judgment and the constraints of the word count, that additional approach was not pursued under Article 8 in conjunction with 14, but was pursued instead under Article 3.

There is a question of the purpose and significance of the process of judgment re-writing, and the broader project of feminist judging. Of course, there is some inherent value in critiquing and rethinking the approach of any institution that impacts upon people's lives in the way that the ECtHR does. But beyond these general virtues of scholarship, what additional *feminist* motivation is there for re-writing this case? One could think of the re-written judgment as having at least some impact in terms of righting an injustice for the women concerned. Conceivably, the judgment is a written recognition of the different choices that might have been made and consequently of the Court's complicity in the harm to the women A, B and C and those that continue to follow them. At least the re-written judgment clearly demonstrates an appreciation of the injustice in which the Court is complicit. But, obviously, making alternative choices in a fictional judgment without the authority to give them legal effect cannot claim to make much difference to past injustices.

If we accept this limitation on the judgment's impact on the past, what future value does the re-written judgment seek to have? Several of us have oscillated between 'innovative' and 'realistic' approaches to our 'judicial' reasoning. The judgment as presented represents a thoroughly mixed approach in this regard, and we see this approach as coherently 'feminist'. On the one hand, the urge to innovate fits neatly with Peters' discussion of the (international) scholarly role as one which shapes and orders the law.[1] Conversely, the more conservative impulse to produce a believable line of reasoning (ie one which the Court itself might have taken), perhaps better fits with Feichtner's view of the practitioner (including judges and legal counsel) as being less free to pursue her politics than scholars are.[2] In this respect the re-written judgment provides a model which inter alia could possibly influence practitioner approaches and judicial reasoning within or outside the ECtHR in this context in future.

It is possible that the value of the re-written judgment lies at this point of disjuncture. Its purpose was to show that a different – a better, more feminist – way of adjudicating this case was possible. At least some of this potential value was realised. Yet, perhaps with a more explicit rejection of the constraints under which the Court usually operates, even greater gains could have been made here. However, in the process of showing that a feminist approach was possible, the judgment also concretely demonstrated that there was not a single feminist approach, but rather a multitude of feminist – and non-feminist – approaches that can be taken to judgment-writing.

In relation to the argument under Article 8, European consensus analysis was relied on to an extent in order to find a breach in respect of all three claimants. It might appear counter-intuitive to rely on consensus analysis as a tool for furthering feminist aims. Reliance on finding such a consensus in socially sensitive contexts can merely lead to acceptance of detrimental treatment of women traditionally vulnerable to discrimination. Such reliance creates the danger that the Strasbourg jurisprudence will be influenced by national choices arising from

[1] A Peters, 'Realising Utopia as a Scholarly Endeavour' (2013) 24 *European Journal of International Law* 533, 538.

[2] I Feichtner, 'Realizing Utopia through the Practice of International Law' (2012) 23 *European Journal of International Law* 1143, 1151–52.

prevailing discriminatory attitudes towards women in certain member states. The use of consensus analysis by the Court in the original *A, B and C v Ireland* itself provides a telling example. However, the re-envisaged judgment indicates that the Court misused consensus analysis in *ABC*. Used correctly, it revealed that there *is* a consensus in Member States as to protection of foetal life; impliedly, the majority of Member States, via their abortion laws, accept that such protection is potentially severely limited, at early stages of gestation, by the need to protect the mother's health from, for example, being jeopardised in various ways due to the pregnancy. Once a consensus is identified, the margin of appreciation accorded to a state that is out of line with the rest – as is the case in respect of Ireland in this instance – narrows, rendering it more likely that a breach will be found. Thus, reliance on consensus analysis can, in a crude fashion, advance feminist goals.[3]

However, in other contexts, the use of consensus analysis could tend to retard feminist progress since any advances that are confined to a minority of States would not be part of a European consensus; States would probably still tend to enjoy a wide margin of appreciation, and would probably not therefore be pressured by adverse Court judgments to come into line with Member States at the forefront of furthering feminist goals. Therefore, our judgment takes the stance that where a particularly intimate aspect of private life is at stake, as in the instance of abortion (but this would obviously have broader application), an emerging trend or minority consensus should be sufficient to deny a Member State a wide margin of appreciation in relation to the claim.

With regards to Article 3 of the Convention (read alone and in conjunction with Article 14), one of the issues we had to decide upon while writing the judgment was whether to focus on torture, inhuman treatment or degrading treatment. Article 3 prohibits three distinct categories of conduct. Torture was never considered because the criteria for this breach of human rights would never be met. This meant we had to agree as to whether to concentrate on inhuman treatment or degrading treatment. Inhuman treatment is associated with 'premeditation; long duration; intense physical and mental suffering and acute psychiatric distress', whereas degrading treatment can include feelings of fear, anguish and inferiority, humiliation and being debased.[4] There is some overlap between these terms, but it is argued that degrading treatment allows more room to focus on the emotional injury rather the physical pain.[5] Initially, we made different choices. We agreed that based on the facts presented in the case, a violation of the inhuman treatment aspect would be the easiest to argue. A reason for this was that the applicants could have provided more evidence of the connection between their suffering and the Irish abortion policies. For example, applicant A stated that she had to borrow a

[3] See also *Konstantin Markin v Russia* [GC], no 30078/06, ECHR 2012 (extracts), (2013) 56 EHRR 8.

[4] MW Janis, RS Kay and AW Bradley, *European Human Rights Law: Text and Materials* (Oxford, Oxford University Press, 2008) 181.

[5] ibid.

significant amount of money at a high interest from a money-lender and that she suffered from depression. The applicant failed to point out that those two circumstances may have been related. One could argue that this would have made her case stronger. Despite this, we decided to focus on degrading treatment because of the nature of the women's experience as presented in the case. We also felt that a feminist approach would provide us with a more flexible interpretation of what constitutes degrading treatment within the context of this provision, and finally a progressive explanation of degrading treatment would allow us more room to explore the socio-economic aspects of the case.

It is clear to us from our own judgment-writing, and in watching others within the project undertake the same exercise, that the process of judging is (or at least, can be) a compromising experience. The multitude of shapes that this judgment might have taken is challenge enough in itself. When combined with a chamber of judges each with their own feminist perspective, the diversity increases still further. Perhaps, then, the achievement of a (or at least, this) re-written judgment lies in its ability to pursue a roughly shared goal through compromise, collective effort and feminist debate.

12

Ruusunen v Finland

MERRIS AMOS, MARIBEL CANTO-LOPEZ
AND NANI JANSEN REVENTLOW

Authors' Note

Facts and Background

The judgment of the European Court of Human Rights (ECtHR) in *Ruusunen v Finland*[1] concerned the 2009 criminal conviction under Finnish national law of Ms Susan Ruusunen for disclosing information about the private life of the former Prime Minister of Finland, Matti Vanhanen. Ms Ruusunen disclosed the information as part of an autobiographical book she wrote about her nine-month relationship with Vanhanen while he was in office. At the time of the relationship, Vanhanen was a divorced father of two children and Ruusunen was a divorced mother of three children. The couple met via an online dating service. Vanhanen was aware that the book was being written, had consented to the use of a photograph of the couple for the cover of the book, and did not try to prevent its publication.

Publication of the book in 2007 generated considerable interest in the Finnish media and much public comment. More than 45,000 people signed an internet petition objecting to the book as they found its contents in poor taste. Some bookshops refused to stock it. However, it was widely reported in the Finnish media that the book actually helped Vanhanen's Centre Party to its narrow victory in the 2007 general election. Vanhanen was said to be 'riding on a wave of unprecedented popularity' which produced a rather unexpected result for his Centre Party and enabled it to maintain its position as the largest party with 23.1 per cent of the vote.[2] It was reported in *The Sunday Times* that Vanhanen was 'transformed from a colourless politician into a national sex symbol'.[3]

[1] *Ruusunen v Finland*, no 73579/10, 14 January 2014.

[2] T Raunio, *European Parties Elections and Referendums Network Election Briefing No.32: Europe and the Finnish Parliamentary Elections of March 2007*. Available at: www.sussex.ac.uk/webteam/gateway/file.php?name=epern-election-briefing-no-32.pdf&site=266.

[3] M Oscarsson, Steamy Exposé Boosts Finnish PM's Standing' *The Sunday Times* (London, 9 March 2008).

Legal Context

Criminal charges were brought against Ruusunen, her publishing company and a representative of the publishing company under the Finnish Penal Code for having disclosed information about the private life of the Prime Minister.[4] However, Vanhanen himself did not originally pursue any charges or compensation claims. The lower court dismissed the charges against Ruusunen and the public prosecutor appealed. Although Vanhanen had not been a party to the proceedings in the lower court, he also appealed as Finnish law granted him the power to do so as an injured party. The Appeal Court convicted Ruusunen for the dissemination of information violating personal privacy.[5] She was sentenced to 20 day-fines, in total 300 euros, and the proceeds of the crime of 4,270 euros were ordered forfeit to the State. The Supreme Court later quashed the conviction in part, but upheld it in relation to the passages in the book addressing the couple's sex life. It upheld the sanction imposed by the Court of Appeal.

The right to freedom of expression and the right to private life are protected by the Finnish Constitution and had been applied by the Finnish courts.[6] The conclusion of the national courts was that, in this instance, the right to freedom of expression of Ruusunen was outweighed by the right to private life of Vanhanen. Seven parts of the book were found to deal with core areas of private life, and it was held by the Finnish Supreme Court that publication of this information caused Vanhanen suffering and brought contempt upon him. In her application to the ECtHR, Ruusunen alleged that her right to freedom of expression had been violated by her conviction.

The ECtHR agreed with the applicant that the conviction and fines imposed upon her constituted an interference with her right to freedom of expression as guaranteed by Article 10 of the European Convention on Human Rights (ECHR). The interference, therefore, had to be justified in accordance with Article 10(2), meaning it had to be both 'prescribed by law' and 'necessary in a democratic society … for the protection of the reputation or rights of others'. Referring to its conclusion in an earlier judgment concerning this part of the Finnish Penal Code,[7] the Court held that there was no ambiguity in the law and that the restriction was consequently prescribed by law.[8] It also concluded that the interference pursued the legitimate aim of 'protecting the reputation or rights of others'.[9]

[4] Ch 24, Section 8 (1) of the Penal Code provides that 'a person who unlawfully … disseminates private information … of the private life of another person, so that the act is conducive to causing that person damage or suffering, or subjecting that person to contempt, shall be sentenced for dissemination of information violating personal privacy to a fine or to imprisonment for at most two years.'

[5] Ch 24, Section 8, Finnish Penal Code.

[6] Art 10 of the Constitution of Finland guarantees the right to private life; Art 12 guarantees the right to freedom of expression.

[7] *Eerikäinen v Finland*, ECtHR, no 3514/02, 10 February 2009.

[8] ibid at [36].

[9] ibid at [34].

In assessing the necessity of the interference, the Court held that Finland enjoyed a margin of appreciation and that its own task was not to take the place of the national authorities but rather to review the decisions they had taken in the light of Article 10. The Court's role therefore was to determine whether the interference was proportionate to the aims pursued and whether the reasons adduced by the national authorities to justify it were relevant and sufficient. Taking into consideration previous Grand Chamber judgments in *Von Hannover v Germany*[10] and *Axel Springer v Germany*,[11] the Court listed six factors to be taken into account when assessing the proportionality of a restriction on free speech. However, in its judgment the Court did not give consideration to all of these factors.

The Court concluded that the interference with the applicant's Article 10 rights was proportionate. It noted that Vanhanen was a public figure, and was therefore expected to tolerate a greater degree of public scrutiny, and it further noted that the book contained elements of public interest. However, in relation to the information in the book about Vanhanen's sex life and intimate events between the couple, it agreed with the Finnish Supreme Court that the interference with the applicant's freedom of expression was proportionate:

> … such information and hints and their unauthorised publication was conducive of causing the Prime Minister suffering and contempt. According to the Supreme Court, it was thus necessary to restrict the applicant's freedom of expression in this respect in order to protect the former Prime Minister's private life … The Court finds this reasoning acceptable.[12]

Legal and Social Responses to the Original Judgment and its Consequences

The judgment was well received in Finland, where the overwhelming view in the print media was that Ruusunen had behaved badly and should be punished.[13] Päivi Tiilikka, Professor of Media Law at Helsinki University, interpreted the judgment of the ECtHR as supporting her view that even people in the highest positions of power have some degree of protection of their right to private life.[14] Following the judgment, Finnish news website Uutiset quoted Vanhanen's statement that he felt the court had made 'a good ruling on right to privacy issues' and that 'people in

[10] *Von Hannover v Germany (no 2)* [GC], nos 40660/08 and 60641/08, ECHR 2012, (2012) 55 EHRR 15.

[11] *Axel Springer v Germany* [GC], no 39954/08, 7 February 2012, (2012) 55 EHRR 6.

[12] ibid at [51]–[52].

[13] See further, M Oscarsson, 'Steamy Exposé Boosts Finnish PM's Standing' *The Sunday Times* (London, 9 March 2008).

[14] N Rolander, 'European Court Upholds Finnish Ruling' *The Wall Street Journal* (14 January 2014). Available at www.wsj.com/articles/SB10001424052702304049704579320622874808390.

positions of power have the right to the protection of privacy'. He also described the judgment of the Court as having wider significance:

> The possibilities for people to obtain information about other people and abuse them have become more common. It's important that people start to respect the right to privacy and remember that according to the Constitution, everyone's right to private life is guaranteed. But it's not something that you can take for granted, you need to fight for it.[15]

Ruusunen, meanwhile, continued to insist that she was not guilty of any wrongdoing as the book contained no senseless exposés.[16]

Academic commentary on the judgment has been very limited. Those who have commented are generally supportive of the ECtHR's approach. For example, Crossley agreed with the judgment observing that there is a 'line in the sand beyond which a publisher cannot go' and that 'intimate accounts of sexual encounters will need a compelling public interest to justify publication'. In his view, simply because the subject is the Head of State will not be enough to justify publication in public interest.[17] Agate observed that the judgment was not surprising:

> In a kiss and tell scenario, the participants in a relationship have the right to tell their story, but this will generally extend to the bare facts of a relationship and will not extend to the right to discuss intimate details or cause damage and distress to others involved, particularly children. Predictably, in the current case it was the specific details of the couple's sex life which were found to be in breach of the Prime Minister's right to privacy.[18]

Some observed that the judgment could have implications for other world leaders who have relationships, either extra-marital or otherwise, whilst holding public office. Dr Riitta Ollila, from Jyvaskyla University, observed that the judgment could have implications for *Closer* magazine's revelations concerning French President Hollande's affair as 'even prime ministers have some private sphere if there is no public interest reasoning'.[19] In short, apart from Ruusunen's comments immediately following the judgment, there was no real criticism of the judgment or appreciation that the Court had applied the same standards to Ruusunen, the female author of an autobiographical work, as it applied to publishing companies.

[15] 'Former PM: Protection of privacy is a right worth fighting for' (*Uutiset*, 15 January 2014) https://yle.fi/uutiset/osasto/news/former_pm_protection_of_privacy_is_a_right_worth_fighting_for/7031797.

[16] S Reinboth, 'Fine handed to Vanhanen's ex-girlfriend does not infringe freedom of speech, ECHR rules' *Helsinki Times* (15 January 2014). Available at www.helsinkitimes.fi/finland/finland-news/domestic/8964-fine-handed-to-vanhanen-s-ex-girlfriend-does-not-infringe-freedom-of-speech-echr-rules.html.

[17] D Crossley, 'The Private Life of a Prime Minister' (*Inform's Blog*, 20 January 2014) at https://inforrm.wordpress.com/2014/01/20/case-law-strasbourg-ruusunen-v-finland-the-private-of-life-of-a-prime-minister-dominic-crossley/.

[18] J Agate, 'Privacy in the Public Eye' (2014) 25 *Entertainment Law Review* 156.

[19] D Ponsford, 'European Court says prime minister had right to privacy over affair with single mother' *Press Gazette* (15 January 2014). Available at www.pressgazette.co.uk/european-court-says-prime-minister-had-right-privacy-over-affair-single-mother.

There was also little discussion of the fact that Vanhanen might have actually benefited from the publication of the book.

Despite the lack of criticism the *Ruusunen* judgment received, recently the ECtHR has adopted a change in approach. We have not applied these new principles in our re-written judgment as it was necessary for us to write the judgment utilising the facts and case law available at the time of the original judgment. However, given that this later judgment reflects many of the points we make in our re-written judgment, it is important to briefly consider it in this note.

On 10 November 2015 the Grand Chamber of the ECtHR delivered its judgment in *Couderc and Hachette Filipacchi Associés v France*.[20] The application concerned an article in a French magazine concerning the 'secret son' of Prince Albert of Monaco which contained photographs and an interview with the child's mother. A French court had held that the publication interfered with the Prince's private life and protection of his own image and awarded him EUR 50,000 in non-pecuniary damages. The ECtHR concluded that the publication contributed to a debate of public interest and that the Prince was a public figure and, most importantly, that the Prince's private life was not the sole subject of the article. The article in question also concerned the private life of the mother and her son:

> These were elements relating to Ms Coste's private life, in respect of which she was certainly not bound to silence and was free to communicate. In this regard, the Court cannot ignore the fact that the disputed article was a means of expression for the interviewee and her son.[21]

It concluded that the combination of elements relating to the mother's private life and to that of the Prince had to be taken into account in assessing the protection due to him. Furthermore, in relation to the method of obtaining the information and its veracity, the Court held that the photographs of the Prince with his son did not present him in a 'light which might undermine his public standing from the reader's perspective'. The Court continued: 'Nor did they present a distorted image of him, and above all they lent support to the content of the interview, illustrating the veracity of the information contained in it.'[22]

With respect to the content, form and consequences of the impugned article, it held that the photographs, showing the Prince holding the child, were private, but their publication could be justified by the fact that they added credibility to the account of events. In relation to the mother, it noted that 'she had at her disposal no other evidence which would have enabled her to substantiate her account and enable the applicants to forgo publication of the photographs.'[23]

> In consequence, although publication of these photographs had the effect of exposing the Prince's private life to the public, the Court considers that they supported the

[20] *Couderc and Hachette Filipacchi Associés v France* [GC], no 40454/07, ECHR 2015.
[21] ibid at [127].
[22] ibid at [135].
[23] ibid at [148].

> account given in the article, which has already been found to have contributed to a debate of public interest.[24]

It concluded that there had been a violation of Article 10. As Voorhoof has noted, importantly in this judgment the ECtHR recognised and protected a woman's right 'to tell the story of a relationship as a matter of personal identity'.[25]

Aims and Contribution of Re-written Judgment

The judgment has been re-written to achieve a variety of objectives. Overall, we have attempted not to perpetuate, and further entrench, inequality for traditionally disadvantaged groups,[26] such as single women in economic need. The approach to gender equality taken by our chamber recognises the current distribution of power in society, with men usually having more power than women. In the judgment we have considered the applicant as an author telling her story and not as someone seeking to make money from having had a relationship with a powerful public figure.

In our decision-making we also took into account the fact that freedom of expression is often restricted when women of lower status attempt to tell their story about a relationship with a powerful male public figure. We have attempted to reverse the ECtHR's tacit acceptance that women are excluded from telling their stories if their accounts involve sexual encounters with powerful men and must be marginalised as wrong-doers and criminally prosecuted. In essence, the re-written judgment reflects the interest of a woman in also having her story heard.[27] Most importantly, by contrast to the original judgment, we have concluded that the passages in the book concerning the sex life of Ruusunen and Vanhanen gave veracity to the book as a whole and that it was not for the ECtHR to exercise editorial control or be a moral arbiter. Many male authors of autobiographies include sex where women are inconsequential.[28] In Ruusunen's biography, sex was included as a part of a healthy and loving relationship and illustrated her pleasure rather than any harm it had caused her. We were conscious that often the demand

[24] ibid at [148].

[25] D Voorhoof, 'Grand Chamber challenges male-oriented view on keeping silence over mistress and lovechild in pivotal privacy case' (Strasbourg Observers, 12 November 2015) at http://strasbourgobservers.com/2015/11/12/grand-chamber-rules-in-pivotal-privacy-case-and-challenges-male-orientated-view-on-keeping-silence-over-mistress-and-lovechild/#more-3037.

[26] I Radacic, 'Gender Equality Jurisprudence of the European Court of Human Rights' (2008) 19(4) *European Journal of International Law* 841.

[27] R Greenslade, 'Human rights judges back magazine for revealing Prince Albert's secret child' *The Guardian* (12 June 2014) at www.theguardian.com/media/greenslade/2014/jun/12/european-court-of-human-rights-privacy.

[28] See, for example, the biography of Tino Best where he claimed to have slept with between 500 and 650 women: J Wilson, A Flintoff and T Best, *Mind the Windows: Tino Best – My Story* (London, John Blake Publishing Ltd, 2016); and the biography of Michael Douglas in which his struggles with sexual addiction are portrayed in J Parker, *Michael Douglas: Acting on Instinct* (London, Headline, 2013).

is for women to narrate stories detailing sexual encounters where they have been harmed, rather than those where they have enjoyed pleasure.[29]

To re-write this judgment from a feminist perspective, we have done a number of things. Firstly, we have included more detail in the facts regarding how the couple met, the nature of their relationship and the intimate details revealed in the book. Whilst the particular passages in the book which resulted in the conviction were never extracted in the original judgment, and the book is no longer available for sale, from Finnish newspaper sources, in English, it has been possible to find a little more detail. Secondly, we have deliberately not referred to Vanhanen throughout the judgment as 'the former Prime Minister' as the original court did. It was clear from the outset that this was his status, but to refer to him consistently in this way gives the impression that he deserves special treatment from the Court. Thirdly, the margin of appreciation in the re-written judgment is much narrower than that afforded in the original judgment. We have been careful to ensure that the strong feelings against the actions of the applicant, as reflected in the Finnish media, have not influenced the conclusion of the ECtHR. Furthermore, a narrow margin of appreciation would be the usual approach of the ECtHR in an application concerning a criminal punishment imposed on a form of expression. Why it was so broad in the original judgment could be because the national media, and other institutions, including the Supreme Court, had decided against the applicant on a gendered basis.

Fourthly, a much fuller consideration has been given to each of the factors, set out in the ECtHR's earlier judgments in *Von Hannover* and *Axel Springer*, which must be taken into account when Article 8 is balanced against Article 10. Whilst these were mentioned in the original *Ruusunen* judgment, the Court did not give each factor rigorous consideration. Little consideration was also given in the original judgment to the Article 8 rights of Ruusunen whose interest was in narrating a personal experience in a manner of her choosing. We also added an additional factor to be taken into account when the Court was balancing Article 8 against Article 10, namely the nature or seriousness of the alleged harm that had been caused by the publication. In our view, this was particularly important here as a more detailed exposition of the facts revealed that publication of the book could have been instrumental in Vanhanen's political party securing a narrow victory in a general election. This was not appreciated at all in the original judgment. It is apparent from the facts that Vanhanen only joined the prosecution against Ruusunen when it became politically expedient to do so. The re-written judgment, particularly the separate opinion of Merris Amos, reflects the difficulties faced by a single mother with limited financial resources in negotiating the complex legal world of criminal penalties for invasion of personal privacy. Our judgment reflects our understanding that, whilst the Finnish laws interfering with freedom of

[29] See, for example D McConnell, *I Own You* (Basingstoke, Pan, 2017); M Thomas, *You Can't Run* (London, Ebury Press, 2015).

expression may be clear and accessible to a publishing company which can afford detailed legal advice, the same principles should not be applied to an author who is unable to afford such specialist advice.

Taking into account all of these factors, in contrast to the original judgment we concluded unanimously that the interference with the applicant's freedom of expression was not based on sufficient reasons to show that the interference complained of was necessary in a democratic society for the protection of the reputation and rights of others and consequently that there had been a violation of Article 10 of the Convention. In response to comments made on our re-written judgment, we have also concluded that if the positions were reversed and a man had written about this relationship with a female Prime Minister, we would find in his favour as well.

JUDGMENT

RUUSUNEN v FINLAND

(Application no. 73579/10)

A Chamber of the European Court of Human Rights consisting of:

Maribel Canto-Lopez (President of Chamber),
Merris Amos and Nani Jansen Reventlow

14 January 2014

THE FACTS

1. The applicant, Ms Susan Ruusunen, was born in 1970 and lives in Helsinki where she runs her own catering business, and has also worked as a part-time actor and writer. She is divorced and is the mother of three children. In 2006, the applicant had a nine-month relationship with the then Prime Minister of Finland, Matti Vanhanen, who was born in 1955, is divorced and has two children. The applicant and Vanhanen, who divorced his former wife in 2005, met via an Internet dating service and, according to the applicant, Vanhanen ended their relationship by sending her a text message. Vanhanen held office as Prime Minister from June 2003 to June 2010. During his relationship with the applicant she accompanied him once in public to a summer festival. Their relationship was the subject of considerable media interest.
2. On 19 February 2007, the applicant published a book *Pääministerin morsian* (*The Prime Minister's Bride*), which was an autobiographical book about her relationship with Vanhanen based on her personal diary and messages exchanged between them during the relationship. The photograph on the front cover showed the couple smiling and sitting side by side on a sofa, with Vanhanen's arm around the applicant. Vanhanen had consented to the use of this photograph for the cover and did not try to prevent publication of the book. Intimate details of their relationship were included in the book, including how Vanhanen once compared the applicant to an oven baked potato, how he liked to take a sauna before sex and enjoy his favourite meal of beef and baked potatoes afterwards.
3. Publication of the book generated considerable interest in the Finnish media and was the subject of much public comment and debate. While several thousand copies of the book were sold, more than 45,000 people signed an internet petition objecting to the book and some bookshops refused to stock it. In the 2007 general election, Vanhanen's Centre Party won a narrow victory,

gaining one more seat in Parliament than the National Coalition Party. Prior to the election, polls revealed that 49 percent of voters favoured him as Prime Minister. His nearest rival, the Social Democrat Eero Heinaluoma, had 11 percent support. A further poll for Finnish television showed that 72 percent of voters believed that Vanhanen's credibility was intact and only 19 percent thought he had lost ground because of the publication of the book.

4. On 5 October 2007, the public prosecutor brought charges under Chapter 24, section 8, of the Penal Code against the applicant, the publishing company and the representative of the publishing company for having disclosed information about the private life of the Prime Minister (*yksityiselämää loukkaavan tiedon levittäminen, spridande av information som kränker privatlivet*).
5. On 5 March 2008, the Helsinki District Court dismissed the charges against the applicant. By letter dated 18 April 2008 the public prosecutor appealed to the Helsinki Appeal Court. Vanhanen also appealed. On 10 February 2009, the Helsinki Appeal Court convicted the applicant for dissemination of information violating personal privacy and sentenced her to 20 day-fines totalling €300, with the proceeds of the crime (€4,270) ordered forfeit to the State. The court found that the passages in the book concerning Vanhanen's intimate dating life and his children's feelings and behaviour violated the core areas of his private life and he had not disclosed these details earlier in the media. In the court's opinion, he had not waived his right to protection of his private life and the book had no relevance to his political functions or assessment of his personal qualities. The applicant appealed to the Supreme Court (*korkein oikeus, högsta domstolen*) by letter dated 14 April 2009.
6. On 16 June 2010, the Supreme Court upheld the Appeal Court's conviction but quashed the forfeiture to the State. It gave a narrower scope to Vanhanen's private life than the Appeal Court, holding that the only references in the book that illegally disclosed information about Vanhanen's private life were those containing information and hints about their sexual relationship. The court found that such information and intimations fell within the core area of private life and their unauthorised publication was capable of causing Vanhanen suffering and bringing contempt upon him.

THE COURT'S ASSESSMENT

7. The applicant filed a complaint with the Court, arguing that the judgment of the Finnish Supreme Court violated her freedom of expression. The Court agrees that the applicant's conviction and the fines imposed on her constituted an interference with her right to freedom of expression, as guaranteed by Article 10 § 1 of the Convention. The Court furthermore notes that these measures had a basis in Finnish law, namely Chapter 24, section 8 of the Penal Code, and that the interference complained of had a legitimate aim, namely the protection of the private life and reputation of others.

Having concluded that there was an interference with the applicant's right to freedom of expression which was in accordance with the law and was in the pursuit of a legitimate aim, the Court will now assess if the interference was necessary in a democratic society.

8. The test of 'necessity in a democratic society' requires that the Court determine whether the interference complained of corresponded to a 'pressing social need'. The Contracting States have a certain margin of appreciation in assessing whether such a need exists, which goes hand in hand with European supervision. The Court is therefore empowered to give the final ruling on whether a 'restriction' is reconcilable with freedom of expression as protected by Article 10. (See, among many other authorities, *Perna v Italy* [GC], no. 48898/99, ECHR 2003-V, (2004) 39 EHRR 28; *Association Ekin v France*, no. 39288/98, ECHR 2001-VIII, (2002) 35 EHRR 35; and *Pedersen and Baadsgaard v Denmark* [GC], no. 49017/99, ECHR 2004-XI, (2006) 42 EHRR 24).

9. However, the Court's task is not to take the place of the domestic courts, but rather to review under Article 10 the decision they have taken. This does not mean that the supervision is limited to ascertaining whether the respondent State exercised its discretion reasonably, carefully or in good faith. The Court has to look at the interference complained of in the light of the case as a whole, including the particular content of the book held against the applicant and the context in which this information was included in the book.

10. The Court must determine whether the interference in issue was 'proportionate to the legitimate aims pursued' and whether the reasons adduced by the national authorities to justify it were 'relevant and sufficient' (see *Sunday Times v the United Kingdom (no. 1)*, 26 April 1979, Series A no. 30, (1979–80) 2 EHRR 245; *Lingens v Austria*, 8 July 1986, Series A no. 103, (1986) 8 EHRR 407; *Barfod v Denmark*, 22 February 1989, Series A no. 149; *Janowski v Poland* [GC], no. 25716/94, ECHR 1999-I, (2000) 29 EHRR 705; and *News Verlags GmbH & Co.KG v Austria*, no. 31457/96, ECHR 2000-I, (2001) 31 EHRR 8). In assessing the relevance and sufficiency of the national courts' findings, the Court, in accordance with the principle of subsidiarity, thus takes into account the extent to which the former balanced the conflicting rights implicated in the case, in the light of the Court's established case law in this area. If the reasoning of the national court demonstrates a lack of sufficient engagement with the general principles of the Court under Article 10 of the Convention, the degree of the margin of appreciation afforded to the authorities will necessarily be narrower.

11. In *Von Hannover v Germany (no. 2)* ([GC], nos. 40660/08 and 60641/08, ECHR 2012, (2012) 55 EHRR 15), and *Axel Springer v Germany* ([GC], no. 39954/08, 7 February 2012, (2012) 55 EHRR 6) the Court defined the Contracting States' margin of appreciation and its own role in balancing these

two conflicting interests. The Court went on to identify a number of criteria as being relevant where the right of freedom of expression is being balanced against the right to respect for private life, namely:

1. The extent to which a contribution is made to a debate of general interest;
2. How well-known the person concerned is, and the subject of the report;
3. The prior conduct of the person concerned;
4. The method of obtaining the information and its veracity;
5. The content, form and consequences of the publication; and
6. The severity of the sanction imposed.

12. Turning to the facts of the present case, the Court notes that a number of these criteria were not given due regard by the Supreme Court of Finland in balancing the applicant's right to freedom of expression against the right to respect for private life.

Contribution to a debate of general interest

13. The impugned book described a period of nine months in the applicant's life when she, as a single mother, had a relationship with Vanhanen who was, at the time, divorced from his wife.
14. The Court considers that even though the emphasis of the book was on Vanhanen's private life, it contained elements of public interest. We agree with the Supreme Court that the information about how and when Vanhanen had met the applicant and how quickly their relationship had developed had relevance to general public discussion. The Court also agrees with the Supreme Court that the information concerning the great differences in the standard of living between the applicant and Vanhanen, his lifestyle, the data protection concerns and the protection of the highest political authorities in general had relevance for a general public discussion. It is clear from the above that the narrative of the autobiography contributed to a debate of general interest.
15. The Court considers that the information contained in the autobiography referring to their sex life and intimate events are necessarily interconnected with the narrative of the book. It is not possible to separate the parts of the book describing the sex life of the applicant and Vanhanen and the intimate encounters between them from the rest of the book as recounting these moments gave the book much of its veracity and thereby formed part of a debate of general interest. Moreover, these parts of the book supported the applicant's description of her time with Vanhanen and without them, the book would have been disembodied. However, while the public at large could be considered to have the right to receive information about a Prime Minister's nine-month relationship with a single mother, recounted by her from her viewpoint, the Court cannot in light of this conclude that all

intimate details provided on a public figure's relationships constitute a contribution to a debate of public interest. While the existence, including its start and subsequent development, of the relationship between the applicant and Vanhanen can be considered a matter of public interest, as established above, this does not lead to the automatic conclusion that every detail of the relationship falls within this category. In this context, the Court notes that the passages containing details of the applicant's and Vanhanen's sex life, while perhaps arguably connected with the overall narrative, do not constitute essential elements of the narrative that should be the subject of public debate, even when considering Vanhanen's position as the former Prime Minister.

How well-known is the person concerned and what is the subject of the report

16. The impugned book discusses the private life of both the applicant and Mr Vanhanen, the former Prime Minister of Finland. As Prime Minister of Finland, Mr Vanhanen was the holder of public office and therefore a public figure.
17. The book describes a situation in which two different realities of present day Finnish society were brought together: the Prime Minister and a single mother. The book also described the sex life and intimate moments between the applicant and Vanhanen when they were dating. While the majority of the information concerning Vanhanen's private life disclosed in the book had already been widely published and was of general public knowledge, the information about the former Prime Minister's sex life and intimate events and his children's feelings and behaviour had not been disclosed to the public before. The Supreme Court concluded that only the references to the sex life and intimate events between the applicant and Vanhanen were published unlawfully.
18. This Court recalls its consistent finding that the limits of permissible criticism are wider as regards a politician than as regards a private individual. Unlike the latter, the former inevitably and knowingly lay themselves open to close scrutiny of their words and deeds by journalists and the public at large, and they must consequently display a greater degree of tolerance (see, for example, *Lingens v Austria,* cited above; *Incal v Turkey*, 9 June 1998, *Reports of Judgments and Decisions* 1998-IV, (2000) 29 EHRR 449; *Castells v Spain*, 23 April 1992, Series A no. 236). Therefore, as a public figure, the Prime Minister must display a greater tolerance to a general public interest in his private life than if he were an ordinary individual. The Court also considers that the right to freedom of expression is applicable not only to 'information' or 'ideas' that are favourably received or regarded as inoffensive or as a matter of indifference, but also to those that offend, shock or disturb.
19. The applicant had simply written her account of her relationship with Vanhanen. This is something she was entitled to do as a participant in the relationship, and the account depicts all aspects of a normal and healthy

relationship, including their sexual relationship, which could hardly be construed as an intolerably detailed description of Vanhanen's intimate life. If one were to imagine the course of events without the above-mentioned parts of the book, the public would have made the same assumption about the nature of their relationship. The Court therefore considers the subject of the book not to go beyond the scope of the level of privacy someone like Vanhanen could have expected when entering into his relationship with the applicant while he was still in office as Prime Minister.

Prior conduct of the person concerned

20. In the present case, the applicant's autobiography disclosed information about Vanhanen's private life. However, it was known that he had already widely disclosed information about his family and habits, as well as about his relationship with the applicant. Vanhanen had published an autobiography in 2005, had given several interviews, ran a personal blog and even permitted photographs to be taken at his home. He had therefore disclosed many aspects of his personal life. The conduct of the person prior to publication and whether related information has already appeared in an earlier publication are factors to be taken into consideration (*Von Hannover v Germany (no. 2)* [GC], cited above; *Sapan v Turkey*, no. 44102/04, 8 June 2010), and having had previously revealed details about his private life in a number of interviews, it was clear that Vanhanen had actively sought out publicity. This has the effect of reducing his legitimate expectation that his private life would be effectively protected. (*Axel Springer v Germany* [GC], cited above). While the mere fact of having cooperated with the press on previous occasions cannot serve to deprive the party concerned of all protection against publication (*Von Hannover v Germany (no. 2)* [GC], cited above; *Axel Springer v Germany* [GC], cited above; *Egeland and Hanseid v Norway*, nos. 34438/04, 16 April 2009, (2010) 50 EHRR 2), under the circumstances, the Court could not come to the conclusion that the Prime Minister had made efforts to keep his private life out of the press (*Von Hannover v Germany (No. 3)*, no. 8772/10, 19 September 2013).
21. In the present case, Vanhanen consented to the use of his photograph on the cover of what he knew to be an autobiography written by the applicant. The fact that he had not tried to prevent the publication of the book does not mean that he had given tacit consent to publish the information presented in the book. Nonetheless, the fact that no steps were taken to prevent publication of the autobiography (*Fuentes Bobo v Spain*, no. 197/2006) and that Vanhanen consented to use of his photograph are important factors to be considered in weighing the protection of private life against freedom of expression.

Method of obtaining the information and its veracity

22. The way in which the information in question has been obtained and its veracity are important factors to be considered by the Court. In cases

concerning the media, the Court has frequently held that exercising the right to freedom of expression carries with it 'duties and responsibilities', including a duty to act in good faith, and on an accurate factual basis, and to provide reliable and precise information in accordance with the ethics of journalism (*Axel Springer v Germany* [GC], cited above; *Fressoz and Roire v France* [GC], no. 29183/95, ECHR 1999-I, (2001) 31 EHRR 2; *Pedersen and Baadsgaard v Denmark*, cited above; *Stoll v Switzerland* [GC], no. 69698/01, ECHR 2007-V, (2008) 47 EHRR 59). However, the applicant is not a journalist, but a private individual who authored an autobiography. The applicant maintains that she disclosed information about her private life and, by doing so, had also revealed information about her then partner's private life. Therefore, a different standard applies to her than to members of the press.

23. The applicant acted in good faith and told the truth based on her experience of dating Vanhanen for nine months. The Court notes that the facts set out in the book in issue were not in dispute, even before the domestic courts. In fact, the District Court observed that it was never suggested that the facts disclosed were not true.

24. The Court must look at the context in which information about Vanhanen's sex life was obtained. There is no suggestion that details of the book or the photograph of Vanhanen were obtained by subterfuge or other illicit means (compare *Von Hannover v Germany (no. 2)* [GC], cited above; *Flinkkilä and Others v Finland*, no. 25576/04, 6 April 2010). On the contrary, the applicant obtained the former Prime Minister's consent to use his photograph on the cover of her autobiography (*Von Hannover v Germany (no. 2)* [GC], cited above; *Gurguenidze v Georgia*, no. 71678/01, 17 October 2006; *Reklos and Davourlis v Greece*, no. 1234/05, 15 January 2009). The information in the book was obtained legitimately over the course of a nine-month relationship between the applicant and Vanhanen. The Court notes that the veracity and truth of the statements have not been disputed by Vanhanen.

Content, form and consequences of the publication

25. The Court observes that the impugned book describes a period of nine months in the applicant's life when she, as a single mother, dated the Prime Minister of the time, who had divorced his wife. The book described the dating couple's life and made reference to their intimate interactions. Even if the emphasis of the book was on describing the private life of the applicant, the book also described, as noted by the District Court, a situation in which two different realities of present day Finnish society met: a wealthy party leader and Prime Minister on the one hand, and a single mother on the other hand.

26. The Court notes that the facts in the book were presented in a compassionate manner and the style was not provocative or exaggerated. There is no evidence, or indeed any allegation, of factual misrepresentation or bad faith on the part of the applicant (see, in this connection, *Flinkkilä and Others v Finland*, cited above; *Jokitaipale and Others v Finland*, no. 43349/05,

6 April 2010; *Axel Springer v Germany* [GC], cited above), nor was the account given in the book sensationalist in nature (*Ungváry and Iradalom Kft v Hungary*, no. 64520/10, 3 December 2013).

27. The Court observes that in their analysis the domestic courts attached importance both to the applicant's right to freedom of expression as well as Vanhanen's right to respect for his private life. The domestic courts examined the case in conformity with principles embodied in Article 10 and the criteria laid down in the Court's recent case-law. All domestic courts, and especially the Supreme Court, balanced in their reasoning the applicant's right to freedom of expression against Vanhanen's right to reputation, by considering if restricting the applicant's right to freedom of expression for the sake of Vanhanen's right to reputation served a 'pressing social need' and was proportionate. The Supreme Court also narrowed down the number of passages in the book it considered problematic. It enumerated only certain parts of the book which it considered to contain information falling within the core area of the private life of Vanhanen, most notably those regarding the applicant's and Vanhanen's sex life. The Supreme Court found that such information and their unauthorised publication caused Vanhanen suffering. According to the Supreme Court, it was thus necessary to restrict the applicant's freedom of expression in this respect in order to protect Vanhanen's private life.

28. The Court finds this reasoning only partly acceptable. The Supreme Court properly assessed the restrictions to the exercise of the applicant's freedom of expression, taking into account the Court's case-law, when considering the majority of the applicant's book. However, in considering those passages of the book addressing the applicant's and Vanhanen's sex life as falling within the scope of permissible restrictions, the Supreme Court failed to demonstrate why these passages should be assessed differently from the rest of the publication. The Court takes particular note in this context of the fact that this case does not only concern the applicant as a transmitter of information concerning a public figure that is potentially of public interest, but that the book in question is an autobiography; in her autobiography, the applicant narrates her personal experience of being in a relationship with Vanhanen. The applicant has a personal interest in narrating her own experience in the manner of her choosing. The applicant used the style of an autobiography, which is a different form of expression than news media. In expressing herself through this means, the applicant is entitled to a great degree of artistic freedom, and considerations need to be made towards the effect of disproportionate control on this genre as a means of expression.

29. As set out above, the book concerns the applicant's account of her relationship with Vanhanen. As is evident from the publication, sex was an integral part of the relationship. It is therefore a subject that the applicant, as a participant in the relationship, had an equal right to discuss in public. The Court notes in this context that, in relation to the couple's sex life, as with the other passages, no defamatory allegations were made. Nor has the veracity of the

account been contested by Vanhanen (see *Ojala and Etukeno Oy v Finland*, no. 69939/10, 14 January 2014). The Court would also like to establish that, generally, it deals with the penalisation at the national level of defamatory acts or the publication of intimate details of someone's private life which cast a person in a negative light. This case concerns the contrary, the impugned parts of this publication do not cast Vanhanen in a negative light, but detail a loving and fulfilling relationship between the applicant and Vanhanen, told by the applicant, who obviously had very deep feelings for Vanhanen. The harm done when women are stereotyped as victims requires this Court to ensure that women are free to tell their stories when relationships or events are consensual, not just when the story to tell is one of harm.

30. Finally, there has been no assertion or evidence otherwise of any negative repercussions Vanhanen may have suffered from the publication of these details (*Print Zeitungsverlag GmbH v Austria*, no. 26547/07, 10 October 2013). In fact, it was reported in both Finnish and UK national media that the book actually increased the personal popularity of Vanhanen. Having regard to the foregoing considerations, the Court finds that the Supreme Court, by disregarding the above elements, did not establish convincingly a proper balance between the applicant's Article 10 rights and the Article 8 rights of a public figure when taking into account the content, form and consequence of the applicant's book.

Severity of the sanction imposed

31. Finally, in order to assess whether the 'necessity' of the restriction on the exercise of the freedom of expression has been established convincingly, the Court must examine the issue from the standpoint of the relevance and sufficiency of the reasons given by the domestic courts for convicting the applicant and imposing a fine. The Court must determine whether her conviction and the criminal sanction imposed on her struck a fair balance between the public, Vanhanen's, and the applicant's interests, and whether the standards applied were in conformity with the principles embodied in Article 10 (*Von Hannover v Germany (no. 2)* [GC], cited above, *Axel Springer AG v Germany* [GC], cited above). The Court has taken into account the severity of the sanctions imposed on the applicant. The applicant was convicted under criminal law and was ordered to pay a fine of 300 euros. No other sanctions or financial consequences were imposed; the book had already been withdrawn from sale by the publisher on 15 February 2008. The Court also notes that, in accordance with the domestic law, no entry of the conviction was made on the applicant's criminal record as the sanction imposed only concerned a fine. Copies of the book on sale and ready for distribution were destroyed.

32. The Court finds that, although lenient, these sanctions can be deemed capable of having a chilling effect on other partners of public figures wanting

to exercise their Article 10 rights (compare *Axel Springer v Germany* [GC], cited above). To criminalise the inclusion of such details in autobiographical literature has a chilling effect on this genre, resulting in self-censorship and the publication of sanitised versions of the lives of politicians and other public figures. Moreover, it stifles the exercise of the author's right to give her or his own account of events that happened to them personally, and which they want to share with the world in the style they see fit, and with the level of detail they deem appropriate. If this were to be criminally sanctioned, it would be impossible to write an autobiography containing remarks about intimate life with anybody.

33. The Court also takes special note of the applicant's economic position as a single mother undergoing financial hardship. It is established case-law of this Court that the effect that the payment of a fine has on the applicant should be assessed at the individual level and taken into account when assessing the proportionality of an interference with an applicant's Article 10 rights (*Steel and Morris v the United Kingdom*, no. 68416/01, ECHR 2005-II, (2005) 41 EHRR 22). In this case, what may seem like a modest fine is in fact a significant burden for someone in the applicant's economic position and the interference with her Article 10 rights must therefore be deemed disproportionate.

Conclusion

34. In light of the above considerations, and notwithstanding the national authorities' margin of appreciation, the Court finds that the interference with the applicant's freedom of expression was not necessary in a democratic society for the protection of the rights and reputation of others.
35. There has therefore been a violation of Article 10 of the Convention.

APPLICATION OF ARTICLE 41 OF THE CONVENTION

36. Article 41 of the Convention provides:

> If the Court finds that there has been a violation of the Convention or the Protocols thereto, and if the internal law of the High Contracting Party concerned allows only partial reparation to be made, the Court shall, if necessary, afford just satisfaction to the injured party.

Pecuniary Damage

37. The applicant claimed EUR 4,000 in respect of pecuniary damage. This amount corresponds to the fine she was obliged to pay (EUR 300), and the amount she did not receive as a result of the book being withdrawn from sale.
38. The Government did not object to the reimbursement of the above amounts.
39. The Court considers that the applicant suffered pecuniary losses on account of the amount she was ordered to pay as a fine and the lost profits from the sale of her book. It awards the claimant EUR 1,800.

Non-pecuniary Damage

40. The applicant also claimed EUR 10,000 in respect of non-pecuniary damage she suffered as a result of the violation of the Convention entailed by the Supreme Court's judgment. The proceedings against her had subjected her to a heavy burden as a single mother living on a modest income. She had been referred to as a 'criminal' and her honour and reputation had suffered. Moreover, the matter had caused her and her family emotional and psychological pain and suffering.
41. The Government contested this claim considering that a finding of violation by the Court would constitute adequate just satisfaction.
42. The Court accepts that the applicant must have suffered some non-pecuniary damage as a result of the domestic court's judgments in respect of her book which were incompatible with Convention principles. This damage cannot be sufficiently compensated for by a finding of violation. Taking into account the circumstances of the case and having regard to its case law, the Court awards the applicant EUR 7,500 on the basis of equity.

Costs and expenses

43. The applicant also claimed EUR 9,000 for the legal fees incurred before the Court. This figure corresponds to 40 hours of legal work billed by her lawyer.
44. The Government disputed this claim.
45. According to the Court's case law, an applicant is entitled to the reimbursement of costs and expenses only in so far as it has been shown that these have been actually and necessarily incurred and are reasonable as to quantum. In the present case, regard being had to the information in its possession and the above criteria, the Court awards EUR 7,000 to the applicant

FOR THESE REASONS, THE COURT, UNANIMOUSLY,

1. *Declares* the application admissible;

2. *Holds* that there has been a violation of Article 10 of the Convention.

Done in English, and notified in writing on 15 December 2015, pursuant to Rule 77 §§ 2 and 3 of the Rules of Court.

CONCURRING OPINION OF JUDGE MERRIS AMOS

I have voted with the majority in favour of finding a violation of Article 10. However, I have found a violation of Article 10 for a different reason to the majority as I do not believe that the interference with the applicant's right to freedom of expression, as guaranteed by Article 10(1) of the Convention, is prescribed by law as required by Article 10(2).

According to the Government, the impugned measures had a basis in Finnish law, namely in Chapter 24, section 8, of the Penal Code. Moreover, the interference complained of had a legitimate aim, namely the protection of the private life and reputation of others. The applicant agreed but contended that Chapter 24, section 8, of the Penal Code failed to meet the standards of the Court's case law. She submitted that Chapter 24, section 8 which made it an offence to disseminate private information conducive to causing that person damage or suffering, or subjecting that person to contempt, was not clear in its application to her book. Furthermore, she submitted that the exception contained in Chapter 24, section 8 relating to persons in politics where the information 'may affect the evaluation of that person's activities in the position in question' and the information was 'necessary for purposes of dealing with a matter with importance to society' was also unclear. She pointed out that the Helsinki District Court dismissed the charges against her, illustrating that the same law might have had different consequences depending upon which court were to apply it to the facts. She also submitted that she was not in a financial position which would have enabled her to seek comprehensive legal advice on how Chapter 24, section 8 might apply to her book, and relied upon her publisher for this information and advice. The applicant with publisher had consulted a lawyer before publication. Her publisher and a representative of the publishing company were also convicted under Chapter 24, section 8.

The Government observed that the conviction had been based upon Chapter 24, section 8 of the Penal Code which had been published in full and there had been a number of high profile prosecutions under Chapter 24, section 8. The applicant could have foreseen that publication of the parts of her book concerning her sex life and other intimate events with the former Prime Minister would not fall within the exception contained in the law and that she would be liable to criminal penalty. It submitted that Chapter 24, section 8 of the Penal Code was formulated with sufficient precision.

The expression 'prescribed by law' not only requires that the impugned measure should have a legal basis in domestic law, but also refers to the quality of the law in question, which should be accessible to the person concerned and foreseeable as to its effects. See, among other authorities, *Verein gegen Tierfabriken (VgT) v Switzerland (no. 2)*, no. 32772/02, ECHR 2009, (2011) 52 EHRR 8.

One of the requirements flowing from the expression 'prescribed by law' is foreseeability. Thus, a norm cannot be regarded as a 'law' unless it is formulated with sufficient precision to enable citizens to regulate their conduct. They must be able to foresee, to a degree that is reasonable in the circumstances, the consequences which a given action may entail. Such consequences need not be foreseeable with absolute certainty: experience shows this to be unattainable. Again, whilst certainty is highly desirable, it may bring in its train excessive rigidity, and the law must be able to keep pace with changing circumstances. Accordingly, many laws are inevitably couched in terms which, to a greater or lesser extent, are vague and whose interpretation and application are questions of practice.

The level of precision required of domestic legislation depends to a considerable degree on the content of the law in question, the field it is designed to cover and the number and status of those to whom it is addressed. In previous judgments, such as *Perinçek v Switzerland* (no. 27510/08, 17 December 2013, (2016) 63 EHRR 6), and *Delfi AS v Estonia* (no. 64569/09, 10 October 2013, (2014) 58 EHRR 29), the Court has held that the requirement of foreseeability can be satisfied if the citizen affected can only understand the impact of the law in question with appropriate legal advice. The Court has held that this is particularly true in relation to persons carrying on a professional activity who are used to having proceed with a high degree of caution when pursuing their occupation. However, seeking, and paying for legal advice is not appropriate where the law in question is a criminal law, the sanctions imposed for breach of the law are criminal in nature and the publisher of the information who will be prosecuted is a private individual rather than a professional journalist, media company or publishing company. In such instances, the law must be formulated with sufficient precision to enable a citizen to regulate their conduct without legal advice.

The Court has already found in *Eerikäinen v Finland* (no. 3514/02, 10 February 2009) in which the earlier provision of the Finnish Penal Code was at stake, and in *Reinboth v Finland* (no. 30865/08, 25 January 2011, (2013) 57 EHRR 34) that it did not discern any ambiguity as to its contents. The exception in the second sentence of the provision concerning persons holding a public office or function, or involved in professional life, a political activity or another comparable activity was also held to be clearly worded in *Flinkkilä v Finland*, cited above, in respect of the earlier provision. However, in *Eerikäinen* the applicants were a journalist, editor and publishing company. In *Reinboth* the applicants were journalists and a newspaper company. And in *Flinkkilä* the applicants were magazine editors and a journalist. In *Reinboth* the Court held that had the applicants had doubts about the exact scope of the provision in question they should have either sought advice about its content or refrained from disclosing the identity of the person. It was also held that as the applicants were professional journalists, they could not claim to be ignorant of the content of the Penal Code 'since the Guidelines for Journalists and the practice of the Council for Mass Media, although not binding, provide even more strict rules that the Penal Code provision in question'. A similar conclusion had been made in the earlier judgment, *Flinkkilä*.

Here the applicant was not a professional writer, journalist, editor or media company. She was a single mother who had had a relationship with the former Prime Minister and had published a book about it. Whilst she was convicted on the basis of an instrument which was accessible, Chapter 24, Section 8 of the Penal Code does not satisfy the Court's requirements as to precision and foreseeability taking into account the requirement that the criminal law as imposed on a private individual must be precise and foreseeable to enable a citizen to regulate their conduct without seeking legal advice. It is not clear, on the face of the law that the prohibition would apply to the information at issue which formed a small part of the book. It is not foreseeable that these parts of the book would cause 'damage or suffering' or subject that person to 'contempt'. It is also not clear why the exception would not apply to the applicant. The information in question could clearly 'affect the evaluation of that person's activities' and it could be considered 'necessary for the purposes of dealing with a matter with importance to society'. The applicant was a single mother writing about her relationship with the Prime Minister, a public figure, who had consented to the use of his photograph on the cover and had not sought to stop publication of the book. She had no reason to suspect that she might face criminal penalties as a result of the publication of some of the content of the book. She primarily relied on her professional publisher for advice and is not reasonable to expect that she would be able to interpret the application of this law to certain parts of her book for herself.

For these reasons, I conclude that the interference with the applicant's freedom of expression as protected by Article 10(1) was not prescribed by law as required by Article 10(2) and accordingly there has been a violation of Article 10.

Reflections

The Impact of the Feminist Judgments Project and our Re-written Judgment

The judgments of courts are an important source of law and can act as a catalyst for change, particularly in common law legal systems. One judgment can alter society and greatly enhance women's equality. For example, the recent judgment of the UK's Supreme Court in *Brewster*,[1] that it was unlawful discrimination to exclude a woman unmarried to her partner from a survivor's pension, was a significant victory for the rights of unmarried women. The judgments of international courts can also play an important role in directly shaping law and also acting as a catalyst for change in national legal systems. Sometimes progress is not possible at the national level without the input of an international court. As Karen Alter notes:

> [International courts (ICs)] are new political actors on the domestic and international stage. Their international nature allows ICs to circumvent domestic legal and political barriers and to create legal change across borders. Their legal nature allows ICs to provoke political change through legal reinterpretation and to tap into diffuse support for the rule of law and pressure governments. Their legal and international nature allows litigants to harness multilateral resources and to knit together broader constituencies of support.[2]

Of all of the international courts, the ECtHR is the most prolific and has the greatest impact on the development of human rights jurisprudence globally, regionally and nationally.[3] It is therefore crucially important that its judgments are subject to academic critique to expose issues such as lack of rigour, inconsistency and, as this collection has done, inherent bias against women.[4]

In our re written judgment in *Ruusunen v Finland*, we have determined the application afresh, utilising the same facts, but removing the stereotypes and assumptions prevalent in the original judgment. Once we did this, by contrast to the original judgment, we decided the application in favour of the applicant concluding unanimously that the interference with the applicant's freedom of

[1] *In the Matter of an Application by Brewster for Judicial Review* [2017] UKSC 8.

[2] K Alter, *The New Terrain of International Law* (Princeton NJ, Princeton University Press, 2014) 5.

[3] Christopher Greenwood notes, 'Compulsory jurisdiction of human rights courts, in the strong sense as a condition of membership remains limited to the ECHR'. C Greenwood, 'Remarks' in C Cerna, C Greenwood, H Hannum and T Farer, 'Bombing for Peace: Collateral Damage and Human Rights' (2002) 96 *Proceedings of the Annual Meeting (American Society of International Law)* 95, 99; A Orakhelashvili, 'The Idea of European International Law' (2006) 17 *European Journal of International Law* 315; B Cali, 'The Purposes of the European Human Rights System: One or Many?' (2008) 3 *European Human Rights Law Review* 301.

[4] J Resnik, 'On the Bias: Reconsideration of the Aspirations for our Judges' (1988) 61 *Southern California Law Review* 1877; S Palmer, 'Critical Perspectives on Women's Rights: The European Convention on Human Rights and Fundamental Freedoms' in A Bootmely (ed), *Feminist Perspectives on the Foundational Subjects of Law* (London, Cavendish Press, 1996); E Grabham and R Hunter, 'Special issue – Encountering Human Rights: Gender/Sexuality, activists and the Promise of Law: Editorial Introduction' (2008) 16 *Feminist Legal Studies* 1.

expression was in violation of Article 10 (freedom of expression) of the European Convention on Human Rights (ECHR). We hope our re-written judgment will highlight the unconscious bias which can influence the judgments of courts, equip lawyers and applicants before the Court to argue against this, and alert those who utilise the jurisprudence of the ECtHR that it is important to approach its decision making with a critical eye. A clear vision without preconceptions is needed; listening to women's perspectives on their stories and contextualising those stories helps to break those preconceptions.[5]

Shortly after the initial drafting of our judgment, the ECtHR held in *Couderc and Hachette Filipacchi Associés v France*[6] that a similar finding of invasion of privacy by a French court concerning the secret son of Prince Albert of Monaco was in breach of Article 10. In this judgment, the ECtHR gave far more attention to the rights and interests of the mother of the child whilst still balancing the right to respect for private life of the Prince.

The case concerned the publication of an article disclosing the identity of the illegitimate child of Prince Albert of Monaco and 'Ms C'. The article contained an interview with Ms C and photographs of the mother, father and child. These were published in the French tabloid *Paris Match* and a similar German magazine called *Bunte*. The Prince sued both publications, in spite of acknowledging later that the child was indeed his. The story bore a number of similarities to the *Ruusunen* case. Both concerned the description of a relationship between an 'ordinary person' and a public figure; in both cases the story was told by the woman involved in the relationship; and both accounts included photographs of the men, who had consented to these pictures being taken.[7]

In *Couderc* as we advocated in our judgment, Strasbourg utilises a clearer balance between Article 8 ECHR and Article 10 ECHR. The rights of Ruusunen and Ms C to share their stories with the public was weighted as carefully as the rights to private life of public powerful figures, such as Vanhanen and Albert (prince of Monaco). The Court in *Couderc* did recognise that while there was a need to protect Prince Albert's private life, this could not be at the expense of Ms C right to communicate her story as a contribution to 'a debate of public interest'.[8] This is definitely a step in the direction we have advocated, and a new perspective on how these two rights must be balanced in this type of situation.[9]

[5] S Palmer, 'Feminism and the Promise of Human Rights: Possibilities and Paradoxes' in S James and S Pamer (eds), *Visible Women: Essays on Feminist Legal Theory and Political Philosophy* (Oxford, Hart Publishing, 2002).

[6] *Couderc and Hachette Filipacchi Associés v France* [GC], no 40454/07, ECHR 2015.

[7] N Jansen 'The Prince, his mistress and his lovechild – a feminist perspective on the Couderc and Hachette Filipacchi Associés v. France Grand Chamber referral' (*Intlawgrrls*, 17 February 2015), https://ilg2.org/2015/02/17/the-prince-his-mistress-and-his-lovechild-a-feminist-perspective-on-the-couderc-and-hachette-filipacchi-associes-v-france-grand-chamber-referral/ accessed 10/02/17.

[8] *Couderc and Hachette Filipacchi Associés v France* [GC], no 40454/07, ECHR 2015.

[9] E Kingdom, *What's Wrong with Rights? Problems for Feminist Politics of Law* (Edinburgh, Edinburgh University Press, 1992); A McColgan, *Women Under the Law: The False Promise of Human Rights* (Harlow, Longman, 2000).

The Process of 'Re-writing' a Judgment Collaboratively and the Experience of Collaboration

All members of the chamber are busy professionals, and while we met in person during the project's two workshops, geographical limitations hindered our communication somewhat, with two of us based in London and one in Leicester. One member of the chamber is a practising human rights lawyer who temporarily moved to the United States during the course of the project, preferring to connect via Skype in addition to exchanging drafts, especially in the latter stages of the project. The other two members of the chamber are academics and more used to corresponding via email, or meeting in person and working on drafts, exchanged via email, collaboratively. With everyone's busy schedules, discussing our different approaches proved to be difficult, so we reverted to conversation via emails in order to discuss the outstanding issues before revising the final re-write. On reflection, would it be better if the members of the chamber were geographically closer and in the same line of work? Despite the challenges we faced, our answer is 'no'. There was dedication from the chamber to start to learn from each other's point of view, and that collaboration has enriched our judgment's perspective.

With respect to the process of re-writing the judgment, Merris started with a very clear perspective on what she wanted the re-written judgment to achieve. Maribel changed her position over time as she learned more about the applicant, Susan Ruusunen, and gained a greater appreciation of the assumptions and stereotypes that lay beneath the surface of the original judgment. Nani valued the feedback provided in the workshopping process and in particular how many of the points raised pushed us to consider some of the issues more carefully, such as whether or not the contested parts of the book were a matter of 'public interest' and how we had portrayed the applicant in the re-written judgment. We debated the merits of our different approaches and learnt from each other's positions. Working out our different perspectives through shared debates and negotiations made us reconsider our own feminist approaches.[10]

Although we were not able to discuss the judgment in more detail in person, we did all have equal input into re-writing the judgment and composing the authors' note. One member of the team would usually take the lead and the others would make revisions. We had very few serious disagreements as to which direction the judgment should take. Both Merris and Maribel were more willing to depart from the discourse informing the judgment in *Ruusunen v Finland* and start with a clean slate. It was valuable that we had different perspectives, it would have been a fruitless collaborative exercise otherwise. We reached a compromise in the end, which we imagine is how the ECtHR often arrives at its judgments. We believe that the

[10] R Hunter, 'Introduction: Feminist Judgments as Teaching Resources' (2012) 46:3 *The Law Teacher* 214.

experience of three different people with different outlooks on this case has in the end enriched our decision, a judgment which reflects now our evolving values.[11]

Decisions Which were Difficult to Convincingly Reach

The main point of disagreement between us was whether or not the passages in the book addressing the couple's sex life were a matter of public interest. As these passages were not extracted in the judgment, and the book has been withdrawn from sale, we were never able to determine how explicit these were. Based on the current jurisprudence of the Court, it is not possible to describe these passages as a matter of public interest. Whilst both academics were eager to elevate these passages to the status of public interest, along with the rest of the book, we maintained that this would detract from the authority of our re-written judgment. It was therefore necessary to determine whether or not other factors tipped the balance in favour of a judgment finding a violation of Article 10.

Avoiding this issue altogether, Merris gave a separate opinion finding that there was a violation of Article 10 as the interference with freedom of expression stemming from Finnish law was not 'prescribed by law' as required by Article 10. It was therefore not necessary to determine the necessity of the interference. However, Nani and Maribel did address this in the judgment, finding that whilst these passages were not matters of public interest, they lent veracity to the book as a whole, had done no harm to Vanhanen and recognised the right of a woman to tell her story as well. By reconsidering the factors important in balancing Article 10 against Article 8 (respect for private life) it was possible to convincingly determine that there had been a violation of Article 10.

What we have Learned About the Dominant Values of International Human Rights Law

Whilst the three authors are all very familiar with the judgments of the ECtHR, and were aware that these judgments often display a bias towards the interests of States through the use of the margin of appreciation, none of us had previously had the opportunity to consider whether particular judgments could be subject to feminist critique and emerge lacking. This project has illustrated that dominant paradigms also make their way into the judgments made by courts. It is not surprising that such systemic bias can also be evident in the judgments of international courts such as the ECtHR. Whilst in some instances the ECtHR has been an important champion for the rights of women, its judgment in *Ruusunen v Finland*

[11] MC Belleau and R Johnson, 'Judging Gender: Difference and Dissent at the Supreme Court of Canada' (2008) 15 *International Journal of the Legal Profession* 57.

illustrates that it must also take care not to reflect societal norms even where the application does not obviously concern a stereotypical women's issue such as abortion, rape as a means of torture or domestic violence.[12] Nevertheless, as the Court's recent judgment in *Couderc and Hachette Filipacchi Associés v France*[13] illustrates, in response to the right kind of argument, it can change its approach on important issues and produce a judgment more reflective of the female perspective. In our re-written judgment, we have transcended this inherent bias by focussing more on the applicant, her circumstances and her rights and interests.[14] We looked at Ruusunen not judging her for the choices she made, but we contextualised her case. We constructed the space on our judgment so a different perspective could be welcomed.[15] This is not a single mum behaving badly, but a woman with a right to tell her story as a matter of identity and autonomy.[16]

By utilising the same tools as the original judges, we have produced a feminist judgment which would not be out of place in the jurisprudence of the Court itself. One final note, we authors are all now considering established and new ECtHR jurisprudence in a new light, aware that international courts are just as vulnerable as national courts and institutions to both conscious and unconscious bias against women.

Limitations of Judgment-writing as a Methodology for Advancing Feminist Critique

Re-writing judgments collaboratively in this way is an important means for advancing feminist critique. However, there are limitations. Judgments can be long and boring, full of facts and law and reasoning. If the author wants to make a point about inherent bias against women in the judgment, it may be simpler and more

[12] C Backhouse, 'The Chilly Climate for Women Judges: reflections on the backlash from the Ewanchuk case' (2003) 15 *Canadian Journal of Women and the Law* 192; R Hunter, 'Can Feminist Judges Make a Difference?' (2008) 15 *International Journal of the Legal Profession* 1; T Etherton, 'Liberty, the Archetype and Diversity: a philosophy of judging' (2010) *Public Law* 739.

[13] *Couderc and Hachette Filipacchi Associés v France* [GC], no 40454/07, ECHR 2015.

[14] R Hunter, 'Analysing Judgments from a Feminist Perspective' (2015) 15 *Legal Information Management* 10.

[15] S Palmer, 'Feminism and the Promise of Human Rights: Possibilities and Paradoxes' in S James and S Palmer (eds), *Visible Women: Essays on Feminist Legal Theory and Political Philosophy* (Oxford, Hart Publishing, 2002); I Radacic, 'Gender Equality Jurisprudence of the European Court of Human Rights' (2008) 19 *European Journal of International Law* 841.

[16] J Nedelsky, 'Reconceiving Autonomy' (1989) 1 *Yale Journal of Law and Feminism* 7; J Nedelsky, 'Law, Boundaries and the Bounded Self' (1990) 30 *Representations* 162; MA Fineman, *The Autonomy Myth: A Theory of Dependency* (New York NY, New Press, 2004); R Hunter, C McGlynn and E Rackley, 'Feminist Judgments: An Introduction, in R Hunter, C McGlynn and E Rackley (eds), *Feminist Judgments: From Theory to Practice* (Oxford, Hart Publishing, 2010) 3, 5–6, 13–15; R Hunter, 'An Account of Feminist Judging' in R Hunter, C McGlynn and E Rackley (eds), *Feminist Judgments: From Theory to Practice* (Oxford, Hart Publishing, 2010) 30.

effective to write an article setting out the objectionable parts of the judgment and providing a detailed feminist critique. However, this will not illustrate to the Court itself how it could have possibly done things differently, or those parts of the judgment which might surprisingly enforce traditional gender roles such as, in *Ruusunen v Finland*, the tendency of the ECtHR to refer to Vanhanen throughout the judgment as 'the former Prime Minister' rather than by his name. Furthermore, the uniqueness of re-writing judgments in this way can capture attention of a larger audience, better than 'just another' academic article. Attention must be focussed on all parts of the judgment including the amount of damages awarded, the language used throughout; and the way the facts are described, as they set the stage for the subsequent reasoning and frame the way in which the Court looks at the case.

Committee on the Elimination of Discrimination against Women

13

Cecilia Kell v Canada

LOLITA BUCKNER INNISS, JESSIE HOHMANN
AND ENZAMARIA TRAMONTANA

Authors' Note

Introduction

In 2008, Cecilia Kell, an indigenous woman from the Behchokǫ̀ community[1] in Canada's Northwest Territories (NWT), submitted a complaint to the Committee on the Elimination of Discrimination against Women ('CEDAW Committee'). Over a decade earlier, Kell had been living in a common-law relationship with her partner, William Senych. Together, they had lived in housing specially set aside for indigenous people, allocated by the Northwest Territories Housing Corporation. Senych himself was not indigenous. Senych was abusive, and Kell was forced from their home on multiple occasions. On one occasion, she returned to find the locks changed, and to discover that Senych, who was a member of the Community's housing board, had exploited his position on the board to have her name removed from the title to the property.[2]

Over the next 11 years, Kell struggled to regain her home. In multiple engagements with the Canadian legal system, many of them mediated through state-provided legal aid lawyers, Kell found the law deaf to her claims. As a marginalised person seeking to be audible to the law, her struggles reveal the almost Kafkaesque nature of legal engagements for marginalised actors. Her legal aid lawyers advised her not to contest her forced removal from the home. They pursued compensation while she sought restitution of the home itself. They acted contrary to her instructions. The lack of independent funds to pursue her case hampered her. Her claims were dismissed without written reasons. Throughout, however, she remained committed to one aim: regaining her home.

[1] The Community's website includes information on the Community's governance, history, culture, geography and other matters. See: www.tlicho.ca/communities/behchoko-k.

[2] The facts are set out in *Kell v Canada*, Communication No 19/2008, 28 February 2012, CEDAW/C/51/D/19/2008, paras 2.1–2.13.

Although the CEDAW Committee found in Kell's favour, our re-written decision is motivated by a number of issues that we perceive to be problematic with the CEDAW views in this case from a feminist perspective.

Notably, the CEDAW Committee's decision hints at, but fails to fully expose, the multiple ways in which the law marginalised and silenced Cecilia Kell. The decision reveals a failure to grasp the intersectional nature of the discrimination that Kell experienced, and its impact on her ability to pursue her legal claims. More particularly, we were unsatisfied with the construction and application of some of the CEDAW provisions, notably on the right to housing, the right to independently conclude a contract, and on women's property ownership. We were also surprised that the Committee did not pay more attention to Kell's indigeneity and the fact that the loss of her housing had resulted from abuse suffered in the home.

The Kell case is representative of the problems that face marginalised women when they seek to assert their rights both in domestic legal contexts, and indeed under CEDAW. As such, we have re-written this decision to make evident the ways in which the law can silence or render the claims of women invisible. But also to demonstrate how the law – and specifically CEDAW – can, using alternative (and importantly, feminist) methodologies, hear and see them. Our work here is informed by insights from film theory, particularly the concept of the 'space off', representations of women in the law, critiques of the public/private distinction and its operation in the law, and the concept of intersectionality.

Facts, Background and Legal Context

The facts of Cecilia Kell's case are complex, lengthy and deeply entangled in the procedural history of her struggle for recognition before, and a hearing in, the Canadian judicial system. The complexities are such that it is difficult to provide a brief summary of either the facts or procedural history of the complaint she ultimately communicated to the CEDAW Committee in 2008. At a fundamental level, however, Kell's complaint was a straightforward one, and reflects the all too common experience of women who attempt to assert their independent legal status, their rights to housing, and to other forms of property. Women's struggles in such matters are particularly acute in instances where they are subjected to violence by their male partners.

Cecilia Kell is a member of the indigenous Behchokǫ̀ community in Canada's Northwest Territories. After a period away from the community, during which she attended college, she sought to return, and to be provided with housing for herself and her children. Having experienced some difficulties being approved as a single applicant for housing prioritised for indigenous people in the community, she was advised by the Community's Housing Board to apply as a family with her common law spouse, William Senych. As a non-indigenous person, Senych himself was not entitled to housing under the scheme, although he was a director of the Housing Board. Kell and Senych were successful in their application for housing, and their names were entered jointly on the assignment of lease.

Senych repeatedly subjected Kell to violence and abuse, and on several occasions, she was forced to leave her home for her safety. During one such absence, Senych changed the locks on the house, excluding Kell. At this point, it emerged that Senych, without authorisation, and through abuse of his position on the Housing Board, had had Kell's name removed from the housing deed, leaving himself with sole legal rights to the property.

Over a period of 11 years, Kell engaged in a continuous struggle with the Canadian legal system to regain her right to her home. It is clear from the views adopted by the CEDAW Committee that her claims before the Canadian courts had pursued this sole aim. It is equally clear that the Canadian legal system was, in myriad ways, unable to hear this claim. Her legal aid lawyers advised her not to pursue her claims, or acted contrary to her instructions, treating her in many respects as though she were a child, rather than an independent person before the law. Kell's intersecting marginality (as woman, indigenous person, indigenous woman, mother, victim of violent abuse, marginalised financial actor) seemed to render her both invisible and inaudible to the law.

It is important to point out that the facts, the procedural aspects of the matter *and* their entanglement, are central to the outcome of the case. This aspect of the decision posed problems for the CEDAW Committee. The difficulties the CEDAW Committee clearly had in dealing with this entangled factual and procedural situation raised feminist issues for analysis, which we deal with below.

Issues at Stake

Kell asserted that she had been the victim of multiple violations of the rights recognised under CEDAW. First, she asserted a violation of Articles 1 and 2(d) because the State party had failed to ensure that its agents refrain, respectively, from discrimination against her on the basis of her sex, marital status and cultural heritage, as a women applicant for housing, and from engaging in any act or practice of discrimination against women, when they removed her name from the lease without her consent. Second, she asserted that the fact that the State Party did not take any action to remedy the situation when it was brought to its attention violated article 2(e) of the Convention. Third, she claimed that the State Party had violated article 14(2)(h), by failing to ensure that its agents took all appropriate measures to eliminate discrimination against women in rural areas, particularly with respect to housing. Fourth, she submitted that the State party had contravened Article 15(1) and (2), as it failed to ensure that its agents recognised her equal rights to conclude a legal contract, in particular a leasehold, independently of her partner, and to administer property independently and equally in all stages and procedures in court. Fifth, she argued that the State Party had contravened Article 15(3) and (4), as it had failed to ensure that its agents respect the Agreement for Purchase and Sale; had failed to rectify the fraudulent act of her partner; and had failed to ensure that the new assignment of lease, on which the author's name was not included, was declared null and void.

Finally, she submitted that the State Party had contravened Article 16(1)(h), as it had failed to ensure that its agents afforded the same rights to her in comparison to her partner's rights in respect of ownership, acquisition, management, administration and enjoyment of property.

The CEDAW Committee found in favour of Kell, although it did not accept that Canada had violated all of the CEDAW rights Kell alleged. Its view was that Canada had violated Articles 2(d) and (e), and 16(1)(h), read in conjunction with Article 1 of the Convention.

The Committee's recommendations included both individual remedies, as well as structural reparations. As to the former, it recommended Canada provide Cecilia Kell with housing commensurate in quality, location and size to the house that she had been deprived of; it further called upon the State to provide appropriate monetary compensation for material and moral damages commensurate with the gravity of the violation of her rights. As to the latter, it recommended the State recruit and train more Aboriginal women to provide legal aid to women from their communities, including on domestic violence and property rights; and that it review its legal aid system to ensure that Aboriginal women who are victims of domestic violence have effective access to justice.

There was one dissent, from Committee Member Patricia Schulz, arguing that the communication should be considered inadmissible on the ground of failure to exhaust domestic remedies and that, if considered on the merits, the communication should be rejected on the ground that the author had failed to advance evidence to support her allegations.

Reception of the Original Judgment in Scholarship and Practice

The *Kell* decision has not achieved fame, or even notoriety. There was some domestic media coverage in the immediate aftermath of the decision, particularly from local media sources in the Northwest Territories. Much of the media attention focused on the fact that this was Canada's first censure in a contentious case by the CEDAW Committee.[3] Some of the attention also focussed on the legal aid reforms the Committee had called for in its recommendations.[4] The case has, further, served as a (small) plank in the broader framework of civil society and union activism within Canada,[5] and in domestic efforts for legal aid reform.[6]

[3] See eg, L Herman 'UN Determines NWT woman was discriminated against' *Northern News Service Online* (7 May 2012) www.nnsl.com/frames/newspapers/2012-05/may7_12hr.html.

[4] See L Track, 'Women's Rights Still Imperfect' *Vancouver Sun* (17 October 2012) www.vancouversun.com/life/Women+rights+still+imperfect/7406312/story.html.

[5] See eg, Public Service Alliance of Canada/Alliance de la Fonction Publique du Canada: 'International Women's Day 2013: Women are ALL affected by the Conservative Government' (Public Service Alliance of Canada, February 2013) 6.

[6] L Leslie, *The Right to Legal Aid: How British Columbia's Legal Aid System Fails to Meet International Human Rights Obligations* (Lawyers' Rights Watch Canada, 2014) 55; Canadian Feminist Alliance

It is also important to note the reception of the decision by Kell herself. While we found the CEDAW views problematic in a number of ways, Kell herself has expressed satisfaction with the decision, and a representative of Kell was quoted in the local media stating: 'They covered it all … We were ecstatic over the victory.'[7]

Scholars, too, have engaged with the *Kell* case only to a limited extent. Some scholars have pointed to the *Kell* decision as an example of the CEDAW Committee's successful movement towards recognising and challenging intersectional discrimination[8] (although we ourselves found it lacking in this respect). Others have noted that the *Kell* case is important because it counters the general trend wherein the CEDAW Committee has not, in general, upheld claims based on economic, civil or political matters, while cases concerning violence against women have met with a warmer reception.[9] Of course it is important to note the ties between domestic violence and the political, economic and civil matters in the *Kell* case. Jessie Hohmann has considered *Kell* in the context of the right to housing, and as an expression of the complex and profound attachments women may have to home, even when their experience of and in the home has been deeply marked by violence and violation.[10] A few other scholars have considered *Kell* as a contribution to the debate on women and the right to housing,[11] but in general, the decision has not been analysed in any sustained way. In sum, there has been little attention by scholars and academics to the *Kell* case either domestically or internationally. The decision has not been treated to the in-depth analysis that it deserves. In our re-writing of this judgment, we hope to remedy this void.

for International Action, *Submission to the UNHRC on the Occasion of the Second Universal Periodic Review of Canada* (October 2012) paras 59–60, available at www.womensdirectorate.gov.yk.ca/pdf/fafiaupr_submission_2012.pdf.

[7] A Hache, representative spokesperson for Kell, quoted in Northern News Service online, above n 3. See the interview with Kell herself, 'Group Says Canada Failing Aboriginal Women who Face Violence' *CBC News North* (22 November 2012), available at www.cbc.ca/news/canada/north/group-says-canada-failing-aboriginal-women-who-face-violence-1.1270515.

[8] See A Nguyen, 'Through the Eyes of Women? The Jurisprudence of the CEDAW Committee' (2014) 30 *Outskirts Online Journal*, available at www.outskirts.arts.uwa.edu.au/volumes/volume-30/athena-nguyen; L Hodson, 'Women's Rights and the Periphery: CEDAW's Optional Protocol' (2014) 25 *European Journal of International Law* 561, 578.

[9] See S Cusak and L Pusey, 'CEDAW and the Rights to Non-Discrimination and Equality' (2013) 14 *Melbourne Journal of International Law* 54, 77.

[10] J Hohmann, *The Right to Housing: Law, Concepts, Possibilities* (Oxford, Hart Publishing, 2013) 39–41.

[11] See eg, F Banda, 'Gender Discrimination and the Right to Family Life' in J Eekelaar and R George (eds), *Routledge Handbook of Family Law and Policy* (Abingdon, Routledge, 2014) 313. Banda observes of the *Kell* decision that state provided housing for domestic violence victims is not by itself a remedy for women dispossessed from housing and may in some cases exacerbate the problems of such women. Banda notes that Cecilia Kell's residency in a women's shelter enabled her partner to exclude her from their shared home.

Purposes of the Re-written Judgment

Despite the lack of attention to, and analysis of, the *Kell* decision, and despite Cecilia Kell's own apparent satisfaction, the decision raises issues of particular significance from a feminist perspective. Our concerns included the following.

First, we were unsatisfied with the approach of the Committee to some of the CEDAW provisions. Notably, this was the first time that the Committee had considered Article 14(2)(h) on the (limited) right to housing for rural women, and we felt that the Committee had not interpreted the provision correctly in general, or applied it correctly to Kell's case.

Second, we were concerned with the approach of the Committee to Kell as an independent legal subject, rights holder and economic actor. We felt that her independent right to property had not been given full expression. In many ways, the decision reveals that the Canadian legal system had not treated Kell as a subject of rights and as having full capacity as a legal actor, but rather as though she were a child, in a position of legal dependency, particularly in her interactions with her legal aid lawyers. The CEDAW Committee decision did not acknowledge and address this wrong.

Third, and in contrast to some of the scholarship above, we found the Committee's failure to address what is clearly intersectional discrimination in this case problematic. Why, for instance, did the Committee make so little of Kell's status as an indigenous woman, even using the European name Rae-Edzo rather than the indigenous Behchokǫ̀ to identify her community and its geographic location?[12] In 2005, the name of the community was officially changed to Behchokǫ̀, but well before this change, the community had always been known as and referred to as Behchokǫ̀ in the Aboriginal language of the local people, Tłı̨chǫ. Indigeneity was clearly central to the factual basis of her claim; only Kell, as an indigenous woman, not Senych, had access to housing under the scheme through which he eventually managed to claim sole right to the home.

The marginality of indigenous women the world over is also a deplorable fact the Committee has clearly been made aware of over the years, yet this marginality is not acknowledged in the Committee's views. This is all the more puzzling when we reflect on the fact that the CEDAW Committee was at the time of the judgment working on a significant report on the profoundly shocking harms that indigenous women currently experience in Canadian society and in their interactions with the justice system.[13]

Finally, and perhaps most significantly, were two background issues that seemed to us to pervade the Committee's views. The first was the issue that the Canadian legal system had appeared largely deaf to Cecilia Kell's claims and silent in response to them, even when it acknowledged hearing any aspects of Kell's claims.

[12] *Kell*, above n 2, para 2.1.

[13] CEDAW, *Report of the Inquiry Concerning Canada* CEDAW/C/OP.8/CAN/1 (30 March 2015).

The system – and, notably, its procedures – had seemed unable to comprehend what Kell was asking for and to give any redress. The result, while not completely Kafkaesque, at least calls to mind the scene in Dickens' *Bleak House* where legal claims are reduced to a cacophony of which 'the law' takes no notice whatsoever.[14]

Legal silences about women's lives are not unusual. This is largely because many general accounts of law record events from a male-centric perspective.[15] The presence of a male-centric perspective remains even though the general nature of legal endeavour has been typically framed as objective, broadly inclusive, autonomous and unbiased. Such accounts of the legal enterprise are typically premised upon fixed understandings with singular goals.[16] However, the absence of women, as well as the racially and sexually marginalised, from the purview of law points up the problem with this sovereign notion of law. Law's freedom from many external influences, or at least its failure to acknowledge them, means that there are few opportunities for outsiders to advocate for change even while law internally transforms itself. Law has thus sometimes operated as an unrestrained meta-doctrine that constantly re-invents itself, 'manufacturing the conditions of its own existence'.[17] The CEDAW Committee strained to overcome this deafness, and to speak where there had been silence, but the Committee was in turn constrained by its own limits. One limit in particular is the rule on the exhaustion of domestic remedies, which, we would argue, results in the peculiar and intractable way in which the procedural history and the merits claims in this case are entwined.

Relatedly, but deserving of separate analysis, was the fact that so much that underlies the views of the CEDAW Committee is unstated and remains opaque, but can be felt pulling at the reader's consciousness like a deep undertow. This in particular, once again, is flagged up in the way that the Committee deals with the issue of lack of merits hearing at the domestic level. It is not clear in the original CEDAW views that Cecilia Kell ever succeeded in having the merits of her claim (the details of her matter and the ways in which those details support her claims) heard in full by the Canadian courts, despite her multiple engagements with the

[14] In Dickens' *Bleak House*, readers are introduced to a dark, dank English Court of Chancery in which cases are interminable and complex, relief is rarely forthcoming, and where parties compete for the attention of the Lord Chancellor who is frequently deaf to their entreaties. One character, a financially ruined suitor without legal representation, has appeared for years seeking vainly to have his matter heard by the Lord Chancellor. The man keeps an eye on the judge at all times, ready to call out 'My lord!' if an opportunity for address presents itself. However, this is unlikely ever to occur since the Chancellor is 'legally ignorant' of the man's existence. C Dickens, *Bleak House* (Ware, Wordsworths Classics, reprinted 1993).

[15] See B Welke, 'Willard Hurst and the Archipelago of American Legal Historiography' (2000) 18 *Law and History Review* 197.

[16] Consider, for example, the words of Owen Fiss: 'Law is an autonomous sphere of human activity that serves no master other than justice. We value law for that very reason and celebrate it by proclaiming that all must bow to the rule of law.' O Fiss, 'The Autonomy of Law', (2001) 26 *Yale Journal of International Law* 517, 517.

[17] R Van Krieken, 'Law's Autonomy in Action: Anthropology and History in Court' (2006) 15 *Social and Legal Studies* 574, 574.

Canadian legal system over a period of 11 years. It was obvious that the Committee was not willing to say that Kell had not exhausted domestic remedies – her claim was accepted as admissible even though it was equally obvious that she had never received a full merits hearing before the Canadian courts.

The *Kell* case (domestically and before the CEDAW Committee) exemplifies the limits of the law with respect to women's claims, demonstrating both that the law is not equally open to all women, or to all types of claims, and that even CEDAW, which is explicitly designed to redress the violation of women's rights, struggles to make visible within the legal frame the harms women experience.

Theoretical Underpinnings of the Re-written Judgment

The concept of the 'space-off' helpfully framed our thinking about the unstated undercurrents of the decision. The 'space off', a term borrowed from film theory, describes the imperceptible margins and background, very real and very present, but by their very nature not within the frame, and thus not at the visible forefront of 'represented space.'[18]

Kell's claim goes well beyond addressing her own personal grievance with the State's actions and omissions. It is about broader notions of space, identity and home. It also foregrounds issues of women's legal subjectivity, personhood and rights which are central to CEDAW. Kell's claim exposes to public view and hearing a group of persons who are largely unseen and unheard: Aboriginal women who, as a result of domestic violence and economic marginality, combined with the State's control of marital relations and private property (not to mention its sovereign control of the territory that is now settler-colonial Canada), face homelessness and dispossession.

It has been long understood that space and identity are frequently reciprocally produced.[19] The spaces that people occupy – such as home – help to shape identities, and those spaces in turn are formed and reformed by the people who occupy them.[20] In Kell's case, the search for home is at the foundation of her claim, and home in this case, and in others like it, is more than a physical structure. Home is also a powerful embodiment of figurative sanctuary, nurture, autonomy and freedom. 'Home' is a heavily charged word that calls forth a number of images.[21]

[18] For a fuller discussion of the concepts of space off and represented space in the context of women's rights, especially in the context of seeking home, see L Buckner Inniss, 'From Space-Off to Represented Space: A Review of Reimagining Equality' (2013) 28 *Berkeley Journal of Gender Law and Justice* 138, 147–49. See also T De Lauretis, *Technologies of Gender: Essays on Theory, Film, and Fiction* (Bloomington IN, Indiana University Press, 1987) 26.

[19] Buckner Inniss, ibid, 147. See also Hohmann, above n 10, chs 7 (identity) and 8 (space); S Razack, 'When Place Become Race' in S Razack (ed), *Race, Space, and the Law: Unmapping a White Settler Society* (Toronto, Between the Lines Press, 2002).

[20] Buckner-Inniss, above n 18. Hohmann, above n 10, 164, 169–70 and 193–94.

[21] See L Buckner Inniss, 'It's the Hard Luck Life: Women's Moral Luck and Eucatastrophe in Child Custody Allocation' (2011) 32 *Rutgers Women's Rights Law Reporter* 56, 74. See also R Marangoly

Home as a word also has wider meaning as the geographic space or place where one belongs: country, city, village and community.[22] Perhaps most ironic for Kell's claim, home is often construed as a 'woman's place', her natural environment.[23] An added trenchant irony is that Kell is an Aboriginal woman deprived of a home provided to her as part of a State sponsored scheme to address historic State dispossession in the process of colonisation. The spatial dynamics of Kell's struggle to regain her home re-enact those seen in the relation between dominant imperial power and the subordinate colonial subject.[24] The particular dynamics at work when race, gender and space come together, as in Kell's case, help to create and maintain sharp legal and spatial divisions between indigenous and white populations.[25] The construct of spatiality is all the more important given the ways in which home expresses an intensely personal relationship to an actual physical place.[26] The notion of home also articulates a shared understanding of inclusion and community.[27] The latter is especially significant for many Aboriginal persons like Kell for whom community is the source of personal satisfaction, economic well-being and political self-definition.[28]

Kell's situation is one that often remains away from the 'represented space' of legal scrutiny and within the raced and gendered 'space-off' that dwells 'at home' in the Aboriginal community. Borrowing from film theory, one scholar describes the 'represented space' of gender as ideological male-centred points of view made visible within a frame.[29] Represented space is contrasted with 'space-off', spaces not visible within the frame and which are only inferable from represented spaces and sometimes even erased or contained in the represented space by cinematic rules of narrative. Feminist concerns, practices or themes are often confined or erased in the margins of the space-off.[30] Thus, in constructing our decision we took particular efforts to address the ways that the actions or inactions of key figures in Kell's case failed to account for how she would be affected as a woman and a particular type of woman. In our work we sought to bring feminism into the mainframe.

George, *The Politics of Home: Postcolonial Relocations and Twentieth-Century Fiction* (Berkeley CA, University of California Press, 1999) 1–2; L Fox O'Mahoney, *Conceptualising Home: Theories, Laws and Policies* (Oxford, Hart Publishing, 2006).

[22] Buckner Inniss, above n 18, 147. Hohmann, above n 10, 195–96.

[23] Buckner Inniss, above n 21, 74 citing E Janeway, *Man's World, Woman's Place: A Study in Social Mythology* (New York NY, Delacorte Press, 1971) 15.

[24] EW Said, *Culture and Imperialism* (London, Vintage, 1993) 93.

[25] Razack, above n 19, 1, 6.

[26] C Holohan, 'Between a Rock and No Place: Ursula Meier's Home' in B Richardson (ed), *Spatiality and Symbolic Expression: On the Links between Place and Culture* (New York, Palgrave Macmillan, 2015) 177, 178.

[27] ibid.

[28] J Carens, *Culture, Citizenship, and Community: A Contextual Exploration of Justice as Evenhandedness* (Oxford, Oxford University Press, 2000) 189.

[29] Buckner Inniss, above n 18, 147–49.

[30] ibid.

Our purpose in re-writing the Kell decision was explicitly motivated by a desire to represent these invisible spaces, and to make them seen. Part of our project to render these spaces visible was to fill informational voids regarding Kell's culture and her community, so as to make clear how her particular characteristics shaped her own experiences and the way that others interact with her, particularly in having her claims heard.

VIEWS OF THE COMMITTEE

Submitted by: Cecilia Kell (not represented by counsel)

Alleged victim: The Author

State party: Canada

Communication No. 19/2008

The Committee on the Elimination of Discrimination against Women consisting of:

L Buckner Inniss, J Hohmann and E Tramontana

Date of communication: 24 June 2008 (initial submission)

Date of adoption of decision: 28 February 2012

Views under Article 7, Paragraph 3, of the Optional Protocol

1. The author of the communication, dated 24 June 2008, is Cecilia Kell, an Aboriginal woman living in the Northwest Territories (NWT) of Canada. She claims violations by Canada of her rights under Articles 1, 2(d) and (e), 14(2)(h), 15(1)–(4), and 16(1)(h), of the Convention on the Elimination of All Forms of Discrimination against Women (CEDAW). The author is acting on her own behalf and is not represented by counsel. The Convention and its Optional Protocol entered into force for Canada on 10 December 1981, and 18 January 2003, respectively.

The Approach of the CEDAW Committee

2.1. CEDAW specifically aims to eliminate *all forms* of discrimination against women. The Committee is elected to oversee State Parties' progress in this regard, and, for those State Parties who have ratified the Optional Protocol, to ensure the rights of individuals are protected when they are violated. It is therefore incumbent upon the Committee to understand discrimination as it relates to women's actual experiences, particularly taking account of and capturing those aspects of women's lives which law has, in the past, often remained blind to.

2.2. It is a strange paradox that women's bodies have long borne the work of depicting justice, yet as a whole, women have not experienced justice on the basis of equality with men. Well before the Roman Justicia, whose ideally feminised figure stands to deliver justice in courtrooms throughout the world, justice was portrayed as a woman.[1] Through history, many have noticed the irony behind Justicia's womanly persona and the frequent denial of legal personality and capacity to women in fact.[2] Yet the female form of Justicia is linked to the denial of women's participation in legal and political orders: Justice remained an abstraction, rather than a real woman, and could thus bear impassively her allegorical symbols of neutrality, authority, and impartiality in the process of adjudication.[3]

2.3. The irony of justice's typically feminine form is deepened by a second feature of justice's common portrayal: that of justice as blind. Blind justice has come to stand for neutrality and the rule of law. Yet these attributes represent only one reading of justice's blindfold, and justice's blindness remains a contested metaphor for the operations of the law.[4] Blindness can represent a turning away from the truth on the part of the judge;[5] blindness can represent the failure of the law to see the harms experienced by another person as wrongs in the law.[6] It is these readings of Justicia's blindness which speak to women's experience of the law.

2.4. CEDAW is premised on the need for a body of law, and a body – we the Committee – which will make women's experience of the world and the law central. The Convention turns explicitly towards women's experience of the law and of human rights violations, and seeks to see those harms that law has so often remained blind to. If, as we believe, the CEDAW Committee must see the violations of women's human rights, we must accept a greater role for the Committee in creating a feminist, not just feminine, justice. We, the Committee, must personify feminist justice.

Factual Background and Procedural History

3.1. The author Cecilia Kell is an Aboriginal woman who belongs to the Behchokǫ̀ indigenous community in Canada's Northwest Territories. Behchokǫ̀, known until 2005 as Rae-Edzo, has a population of approximately 43,000 people, more than half of whom are Aboriginal. The Tłicho Government is the governing authority within Tłicho lands, including the Behchokǫ̀ community, and exercises a large measure of self-government. The most recent Canadian census data shows that though today many residents are employed in Tłicho companies, in local government or private businesses, more than a third of the total population engages in traditional activities of hunting, trapping, and the production of traditional arts and crafts; half of all households rely on foods produced or harvested from the

[1] J Resnick and D Curtis, *Representing Justice: Invention, Controversy, and Rights in City States and Democratic Courtrooms* (New Haven CT, Yale University Press, 2011) 18–21.

[2] O De Gouges, *Declaration on the Rights of Women* (Reston VA, Pythia Press, 1989); M Wollstonecraft, *A Vindication of the Rights of Women: With Strictures on Political and Moral Subjects* (Boston MA, Peter Edes, 1792).

[3] Resnick and Curtis, above n 1, 95.

[4] See Resnick and Curtis, ibid, chs 3, 4 and 6.

[5] ibid 62.

[6] ibid 132.

land for at least 50% of their subsistence needs; and almost 40% of people speak an Aboriginal language.

3.2. The facts of the case, set out in detail below, demonstrate that Canadian law and the legal system failed to protect Kell's legal and human rights. Her partner, William Senych, abused Kell both physically and psychologically, silencing her, preventing her from accessing her legal rights. The Canadian legal system was unable to offer adequate assistance to her either to remedy her physical and psychological abuse, or to protect her legal rights to property, home and contract.

3.3. Kell left Behchokǫ̀ to attend college. She later returned to seek housing for herself and her two children. Kell thereafter began a common law relationship with William Senych, in 1989. This relationship came to be characterised by Senych's violence and abusive behaviour towards the author.

3.4. When housing became available in the Behchokǫ̀ community under a program for members of the local indigenous community, the author informed Senych that she wanted to apply for housing in order to bring her children, at the time living with relatives outside the community, home. Senych, on his own initiative and without telling Kell, applied for housing from the Behchokǫ̀ community in his own name. In November 1990 the Housing Authority board declined Senych's application because, as a non-indigenous person, he was not a member of the Behchokǫ̀ community and because he applied as a single man.

3.5. Senych told Kell that she had been turned down for housing. Because of Senych's violence and abuse towards her, Kell did not feel able to ask Senych any questions as to why she had been refused housing when she herself had not made an application. However, the Tenant Relations officer at Behchokǫ̀ informed Kell that her partner Senych could not apply for himself because he was not a member of the Behchokǫ̀ community. Authorities in the community advised Kell to apply for housing and to list Senych as her spouse. She complied with this advice. In October 1991 the Northwest Territories Housing Corporation (NWTHC), an agency of the NWT Government, issued an Agreement for Purchase and Sale to William Senych and Cecilia Kell as co-owners of the house into which the couple moved.

3.6. During the three-year period following Kell's move into the co-owned house, Kell obtained employment and became financially independent. Her increased autonomy heightened Senych's abuse. Senych controlled Kell's finances and movements. He threatened Kell, barred her from contact with her family, and physically assaulted her on numerous occasions. Senych attempted to prevent Kell from working and took actions that resulted in her losing jobs. As a result of Senych's actions, on occasions Kell sought and was admitted to a shelter for abused women in Yellowknife.

3.7. In 1992, at Senych's request and without Kell's knowledge or authorisation, the Rae-Edzo Housing Authority wrote to the NWTHC stating that Senych wanted Kell's name removed from the document that certified co-ownership of the home.

Senych was a board member of the Rae-Edzo Housing Authority at the time, and in 1993, the NWTHC complied with his request.

3.8. In early 1995, Kell took employment. In retaliation, Senych had the locks changed on the home and denied the author access. This expulsion left Kell homeless for several days. In February 1995, Senych allowed Kell to enter the house to retrieve a few of her belongings. At that time, Senych presented her with a letter from his lawyer requesting that she vacate the shared house. The letter further indicated that if the author did not, Senych would use all legal remedies available to him to compel her departure. Kell submits that Senych sought to remove her because she had left their shared house to escape the abusive relationship and because she sought refuge in an abused women's shelter.

3.9. In May 1995, Kell resolved to file the first court action against her partner before the Supreme Court of the NWT. Kell sought compensation for claims arising from assault, battery, sexual assault, intimidation, trespass to chattels, loss of use of her home and consequential payment of rent and related expenses. Kell also filed a declaration asserting that Senych had obtained the house through fraud, aided by the NWT Government. Kell applied for state-provided legal aid and was assigned a lawyer. The legal aid lawyer advised her to comply with the removal letter and not to return to her home, in order to avoid being charged.

3.10. Shortly after the first lawsuit was filed, Senych became ill with cancer. Due to his illness, Kell's lawyer recommended that the court action be delayed. Senych died in November 1995. In March 1996, Kell's lawyer initiated a second court action against Senych's estate (the Estate), the NWTHC and William Pourier, who was at the time residing in the house. Kell's subsequently appointed counsel amended her claim on 9 July 1998 to include a claim for damages for assault and intimidation.

3.11. In May 1999, the Estate and the NWTHC made a formal offer to settle in the amount of Can $15,000. Kell's lawyer focused his efforts on negotiating a settlement of Can $20,000. Kell maintained an express desire to regain her own home, rather than accept a monetary settlement.

3.12. No further steps were taken in respect of the author's outstanding legal actions. Thereafter, Kell's file was reassigned twice to different lawyers because one relocated to Alberta, and the other ceased employment with the Legal Services Board.

3.13. In November 1999, Kell was assigned a fourth lawyer, who insisted that she accept a monetary settlement, in contravention of her express wish to regain her own home. Because Kell's lawyer was unwilling to act according to Kell's wishes, she chose not to accept his advice. Thus rebuffed, Kell's fourth lawyer ceased acting on her behalf in June 2002. Kell was then denied another legal aid lawyer. She appealed her denial of legal aid to the Legal Services Board, which allowed her appeal and assigned her a fifth lawyer.

3.14. On 3 June 2003, the Estate filed a notice of motion to set aside Kell's statement of claims for want of prosecution. Such an order may be granted where it is clearly established that the litigant has inexcusably delayed advancing the litigation and that defendants are likely to be seriously prejudiced by the delay. The grounds of the motion were that Kell, as the party who initiated a legal action, had not diligently acted to pursue her claim. On 10 June 2003, the NWTHC also brought a motion to dismiss Kell's action.

3.15. Kell offered no opposition when the application for dismissal of the first action was heard in October 2003 in the NWT Supreme Court. Thus, Kell's first action was dismissed without appeal to the Court of Appeal for the NWT. However, Kell argued against the dismissal of the second action, on the ground that the Court should have reviewed all the actions in the two cases in its assessment of whether there had been a material delay in prosecution. Kell was actively responsive to the first action that was linked to the second case, hence she considered it unjust that the Court deemed that she had taken no action or had unreasonably delayed the prosecution. The NWT Supreme Court dismissed Kell's second action on 3 November 2003. Costs were imposed, which were later assessed at Can $5,800. Kell appealed against this decision in the NWT Court of Appeal. The appeal was dismissed without written explanation. Kell did not appeal any of these matters to the Canadian Supreme Court.

3.16. On 16 November 2004, the author initiated a new (third) action solely addressing the issue of her interest in and right to the property. In January 2005, a lawyer for the Estate brought a motion seeking summary judgment, alleging no genuine issue for trial. The Estate also in its motion asked for security costs in the alternative. The Estate had sold the property in question to third-party purchasers and a transfer of lease had been given to them in early November 2004. Kell's position was that the Estate still held her legal title and equitable interest, which she had acquired prior to the purchasers in question.

3.17. On 21 July 2005, the NWT Supreme Court, while hearing the application for summary dismissal in the third court action, held that since the third action sought essentially the same relief as the previous two actions, the author had to pay the amount of the taxed bill of costs in court with respect to the previous court actions as well as post security for the respondent's costs in this third action before continuing with the case. Kell could not pay the costs and security within the time period established, and the NWT Supreme Court accordingly dismissed the case on 26 April 2006.

The Complaint

4.1. Kell asserts that she was the victim of violations of the following Articles of CEDAW.

4.1.1. *Article 1*

Kell asserts a violation of Article 1 because the State Party allowed its agents – the NWTHC and the Behchokǫ̀ (then, Rae-Edzo) Housing Authority – to discriminate against her on the basis of her sex, marital status and cultural heritage, in that it failed to ensure that its agents provide equal treatment to women applicants for housing.

4.1.2. *Article 2(d) and (e)*

Kell claims a violation of Article 2(d), on the basis that the State failed to ensure that its agents refrain from engaging in any act or practice of discrimination against women, when they removed her name from the lease without her consent. She further contends that the fact that the State Party did not take any action to remedy the situation when it was brought to its attention is a violation of Article 2(e) of the Convention.

4.1.3. *Article 14(2)(h)*

Kell claims the State Party has contravened Article 14(2)(h) by failing to ensure that its agents take all appropriate measures to eliminate discrimination against women in rural areas. She alleges that the State party failed to ensure that its agents apply its policies and procedures with regard to the allocation of housing and the provision of adequate living conditions fairly and equally for men and women.

4.1.4. *Article 15*

Kell submits the State Party has contravened Article 15(1) and (2), as it failed to ensure that its agents recognise her equal rights to conclude a legal contract, in particular a leasehold, independently of her partner, and to administer property independently and equally in all stages and procedures in court and before the Housing Corporation. The author also submits that the State Party has contravened Article 15(3) and (4), as it failed to ensure that its agents respect the Agreement for Purchase and Sale, failed to rectify the fraudulent act of her partner and failed to ensure that the new Assignment of Lease, on which the author's name was not included, was declared null and void.

4.1.5. *Article 16*

Kell submits that the State Party has contravened Article 16(1)(h), as it failed to ensure that its agents afford the same rights to her partner in respect of ownership, acquisition, management, administration and enjoyment of property.

Admissibility

5.1. The State Party has raised a number of admissibility issues. First, that the communication does not reveal any discriminatory law, policy or government action, and as such the communication is insufficiently substantiated; that the CEDAW Optional Protocol was not in force for Canada at the date that Kell's name was removed from the Assignment of Lease, and as such the communication is inadmissible *ratione temporis*; and that the author did not exhaust domestic remedies. These grounds have been contested by the author.

5.2. The Committee finds that Kell has sufficiently substantiated a *prima facie* complaint of violations under CEDAW. She has raised issues under Articles 1, 2, 14, 15 and 16. It is proper for the Committee to proceed to hear the arguments on the merits, particularly as this communication alleges violations of CEDAW that the Committee has not previously considered. In addition, the author is unrepresented, and the Committee must take due account of the need to ensure those individuals who come before the law are not silenced by the technical procedures it imposes.

5.3. In addition, we do not agree that the alleged violation hangs on a 'relevant fact': that of the removal of Kell's name from the Assignment of Lease on her home. Rather Kell's claim is characterised by a confluence of numerous violations and harms, resulting in a pervasive situation of discrimination. This discrimination was not based only on the individual facts of Kell's case, but is revealed in the discriminatory effect of the Canadian legal process with respect to Kell's ability to have her claim heard at all. It is characterised by an overall failure of the Canadian legal system to adequately hear, and thus respond, to Kell's circumstances.

5.4. On exhaustion of domestic remedies, from her first contact with the legal aid system, when her assigned legal aid counsel advised her to comply with her removal notice, to the point at which her counsel pushed her to accept monetary compensation rather than the restitution of her own home, to the moment when a settlement was negotiated without, Kell submits, her consent, her claims have been diminished rather than regarded with any seriousness. In sum, the Canadian justice system has been both deaf and blind to Kell's claims, and it is the Committee's view that the application of further domestic remedies would be unlikely to bring effective relief to her.

5.5. Cecilia Kell's case forces us to make a decision as to how CEDAW will respond to women's experiences of injustice. The Canadian court system could neither see nor hear the violation of Kell's rights. For Kell, the Canadian justice system was both deaf and blind. We, the CEDAW Committee, hear and see Kell's experience of violation. We find her complaint admissible.

MERITS CONSIDERATION

Violation of States' General Obligations in Articles 2(d) and 2(e) and 15, paras. 1–4.

6.1. CEDAW defines discrimination against women in Article 1 as:

> … any distinction, exclusion or restriction made on the basis of sex which has the effect or purpose of impairing or nullifying the recognition, enjoyment or exercise by women, irrespective of their marital status, on a basis of equality of men and women, of human rights and fundamental freedoms in the political, economic, social, cultural, civil or any other field.

Under Article 2, sections (d) and (e), States undertake:

> (d) To refrain from engaging in any act or practice of discrimination against women and to ensure that public authorities and institutions shall act in conformity with this obligation;
> (e) To take all appropriate measures to eliminate discrimination against women by any person, organization or enterprise;

Article 15, paragraphs 1–4 of CEDAW provides:

> 1. States Parties shall accord to women equality with men before the law.
>
> 2. States Parties shall accord to women, in civil matters, a legal capacity identical to that of men and the same opportunities to exercise that capacity. In particular, they shall give women equal rights to conclude contracts and to administer property and shall treat them equally in all stages of procedure in courts and tribunals.
>
> 3. States Parties agree that all contracts and all other private instruments of any kind with a legal effect which is directed at restricting the legal capacity of women shall be deemed null and void.
>
> 4. States Parties shall accord to men and women the same rights with regard to the law relating to the movement of persons and the freedom to choose their residence and domicile.

6.2. By accepting these provisions of CEDAW, States commit themselves to undertake a series of measures to end discrimination against women in all forms, and, correspondingly, by all methods, including where such discrimination is not as a result of one attribute but of many, and where those plural attributes are intersectional in nature.

6.3. Race and sex have often been discussed in the context of 'intersectional analysis' – engaging in a multifaceted analysis that addresses the ways in which various socially or culturally-constructed identity categories interact.[7] Such intersectional attributes may, however, go well beyond race and gender. In the instant case, an intersectional analysis enriches our decision, as it allows us to be sensitive to the multiple forms of harm that Kell experienced as a woman and as an Aboriginal person.

6.4. We conclude that the discrimination experienced by the author is intersectional in nature. Kell was a victim of numerous forms of discrimination. Racism, sexism and poverty contributed to a State sanctioned or State enacted pattern of behaviour that was abusive and bullying. Domestic violence, unemployment,

[7] For a brief discussion of the nature and history of intersectionality and related concepts, see L Buckner Inniss, 'A Review of Mayeri's Reasoning from Race' (2001) 1 *Texas Law Review Dicta* 2; see also L Buckner Inniss, '"Other Spaces" in Legal Pedagogy' (2012) 8 *Harvard Journal of Racial and Ethnic Justice* 67.

dislocation and homelessness resulting from the seisure of Kell's home also played a role in her dispossession. We further conclude that the State Party's actions and its failure to refrain from and provide effective remedies to address discrimination constituted a violation of Canada's general obligations in Articles 2(d) and 2(e) of CEDAW. The State's actions and failures also violated Articles 15, 1–4. Our reasoning on these aspects, and their intersecting implications, follows.

6.5. The author is a member of the Behchokǫ̀ community. Although the people of Behchokǫ̀ have their own, independent, Aboriginal way of life, there are a number of non-Aboriginal persons in the area who are also permanent residents. Some, like Kell's partner Senych, intermarry with Aboriginal people.[8] Despite such intermixing, there is sometimes cultural conflict between Aboriginal and non-Aboriginal people, with non-Aboriginal people wielding greater power. For example, Aboriginal people in Canada have been shown to suffer widespread discrimination in their interactions with the Canadian legal system.

6.6. One of the clearest markers of what the Canadian Supreme Court has described as a crisis, is Aboriginal overrepresentation in the criminal justice system.[9] Aboriginal people in Canada also suffer poorer health than non-Aboriginal people, and this is often due to the adverse psychological, spiritual, cultural, economic, historical, sociological, and environmental factors they face in interacting with mainstream Canadian society.[10] Aboriginal women in Canada also face gender discrimination combined with racial discrimination.[11] This 'double-burden' exacerbates all the other ills faced by Aboriginal people and places Aboriginal women in a particularly precarious position.

6.7. The author's status as an Aboriginal parent made her especially vulnerable to the denial of her housing rights. Kell noted that a principal reason for obtaining housing was to be able to bring her children back to the community. Although this was a personal goal for Kell, it also reflects the interdependency between Aboriginal families and their broader communities. Aboriginal community resiliency has been shown to be deeply connected with the conditions of individual Aboriginal families and children and the extent to which they are able to attain economic and social stability within the community.[12] Community membership is a source of economic and social support for many Aboriginal people, and this support

[8] MO Dickerson, *Whose North?: Political Change, Political Development, and Self-government in the Northwest Territories* (Vancouver, University of British Columbia Press, 1992) 26–27.

[9] J Rudin, *Aboriginal Peoples and the Criminal Justice System*, Paper prepared for the Ipperwash Inquiry (2006). Available at www.attorneygeneral.jus.gov.on.ca/inquiries/ipperwash/policy_part/research/pdf/Rudin.pdf.

[10] J Burgess Waldram, A Herring, T Kue Young, *Aboriginal Health in Canada: Historical, Cultural, and Epidemiological Perspectives* 2nd edn (Toronto, University of Toronto Press, 2006) 3.

[11] M Gorelick, 'Discrimination of Aboriginals on Native Lands: A Comprehensive Crisis' (September 2007) 44(3) *UN Chronicle* 50–52. Available online at https://unchronicle.un.org/article/discrimination-aboriginals-native-lands-canadag.

[12] ibid.

may be greatly diminished by residency in areas outside of traditional Aboriginal communities.[13]

6.8. Paradoxically, Kell was in an especially difficult position with regard to making a claim for discrimination in the administration of Aboriginal housing: under Canadian legal provisions, persons who object to actions taken by their own tribal government or some aspect of that government are limited in the extent to which they may redress those claims under State-wide anti-discrimination norms.[14]

6.9. Kell was also a victim of gender bias in the form of a bias against the independent rights of a married or formerly married woman and as a victim of domestic violence. As a woman in a common-law marriage, she was treated as if she had no independent legal identity or rights.

6.10. Kell was told by authority figures in the community that she must apply with her partner Senych in order to obtain housing in her Aboriginal community. She was thereby denied her independent right to contract. In like fashion, when Kell's name was removed from the Assignment of Lease the document that certified co-ownership of the home, she also suffered gender discrimination related to her independent rights as a woman.

6.11. Much of this de jure discrimination against Aboriginal women was eliminated in recent decades.[15] Nonetheless, many governing entities, both Aboriginal and non-Aboriginal, impose patriarchal norms and frameworks that continue to subject some Aboriginal women to unfair and unjust treatment, often without legal foundation.[16] Kell, like so many other women, was subject to such biased treatment.

6.12. Kell's partner attempted to prevent her from working. His violence and threats of violence, along with other actions he took, resulted in her losing her job and in her being admitted a few times to a shelter for battered women in Yellowknife. This violence, and the State's failure to offer meaningful protection from it, also infringed Kell's right to contract with an employer.

6.13. Moreover, the failure to reach a settlement regarding Kell's housing claim was also a direct result of biased actions or lack of action on the part of her legal

[13] R Todd, 'Aboriginal People in the City' in DM Collins, R Todd and M Thornton (eds), *Aboriginal People and Other Canadians: Shaping New Relationships* (Ottawa, University of Ottawa Press, 2001) 98–99.

[14] S 67 of the Canadian Human Rights Act exempts persons living and working in communities operating under the Indian Act from filing complaints of discrimination arising from actions taken under the Indian Act. See R Dupuis, R Chodos and S Joanis, *Justice for Canada's Aboriginal Peoples* (Toronto, James Lorimer and Company, 2001) 61–65.

[15] PJ Blair, *Rights of Aboriginal Women On- and Off-Reserve* (Vancouver, The Scow Institute, 2005).

[16] National Aboriginal Women's Summit, *Strong Women, Strong Communities: Summary Report* (January 2008). Available at www.womensdirectorate.gov.yk.ca/pdf/naws1_2008_summary_report.pdf.

aid lawyers. Most of the lawyers would not hear her instructions, but instead gave Kell instructions and threatened to quit if she disputed their position; some lawyers acted on her behalf without her knowledge or consent.

6.14. In addition, Kell was a victim of gender bias in that the State Party's actions tended to force or coerce the marriage and/or cohabitation of the author with her partner. In February 1992, at the partner's request and without Kell's knowledge or consent, the Housing Authority wrote to the NWTHC stating that the partner wanted Kell's name removed from the Assignment of Lease. The partner was a member of the Housing Authority Board. In June 1993 the Northwest Territories Housing Corporation complied with the partner's request.

6.15. In May 1995 the author filed the first court action against her partner before the Supreme Court of the Northwest Territories. She sought compensation for assault, battery, sexual assault, intimidation, trespass to chattels, loss of use of her home and consequential payment of rent and attendant expenses. The author also filed a declaration that her partner had obtained the house through fraudulent methods, and that the partner was aided and abetted in taking the house by the government of the Northwest Territories.

6.16. The author applied for legal aid and was assigned a lawyer. Her lawyer advised the author to comply with the removal letter and not to return to her home. The lawyer indicated that the author would be charged if she returned home.

6.17. Shortly after the first court action was filed, the author's partner became ill with cancer. The author's lawyer suggested that the court action be delayed. The partner died in November 1995. In March 1996 the author's lawyer initiated a second court action against the estate of the partner, and the NWTHC. The court action was also filed against William Pourier, a man who was alleged to have been residing at the house with the author's partner at the time of the author's death, and who continued to reside there.

6.18. In sum, as a result of a continuous pattern and practice of discrimination, the legally unsupported desires of Kell's non-Aboriginal male partner were at all times prioritised over Kell's legally founded rights as an Aboriginal woman.

Article 14(2)(h) Right to Housing

The Purpose of Article 14

7.1. Article 14 is premised on the need for states to take particular account of the problems faced by rural women, and, moreover, to take measures to eliminate discrimination they face in rural areas, to ensure their equality with men, and to guarantee their equal benefit from rural development. As such, states are required to 'ensure to such [rural] women the right':

> (h) To enjoy adequate living conditions, particularly in relation to housing, sanitation, electricity and water supply, transport and communications.

Article 14 should not be narrowly construed. Its purpose is to overcome specific forms of discrimination experienced by rural women, who are subject to discrimination in multiple spheres of life.[17] The Committee has observed that across the world, women in rural areas experience greater problems in accessing education, health care, and access to resources and opportunities.[18] Women in rural areas are at particular risk of gender-based violence, especially where attitudes to the subordinate role of women are entrenched.[19] They also face particular discrimination in relation to rights to ownership, and transfer of land and property.[20] As such, Article 14(2)(h) responds to the specific problems with access to land and property *in and to the home*, which are experienced by rural women. We accept that 14(2)(h) is 'inextricably linked' to land and property rights, access to financing, and the rights to equality of treatment in Article 15 and 16,[21] (addressed further below) as well as rights to equality and non-discrimination which form part of customary international law.[22]

The Committee's Approach to Article 14(2)(h) and the right to housing

7.2. This communication is the first in which the Committee considers Article 14(2)(h). As such, it is necessary for the Committee to give careful consideration to interpreting the provision.

7.3. Article 14(2)(h) must, 'be articulated and implemented in ways that recognize the specific constraints and vulnerabilities of women.'[23] Women are the primary users of housing, and thus, are the most affected by it.[24] This is partly because of childbearing and childrearing responsibilities, and in many instances because of cultural mores that place women in and of the home.[25] Moreover, women have been systemically and historically denied rights to the home and property.[26] Thus housing remains of central importance in the lives of many women, yet women have often experienced great difficulty in accessing housing and asserting legal rights to it.

[17] CEDAW, *General Statement of the Committee on the Elimination of Discrimination Against Women on Rural Women* (Adopted 19 October 2011 during the 50th Session) 2. Available at www.ohchr.org/documents/HRBodies/CEDAW/Statements/StatementRuralWomen.pdf.

[18] ibid.

[19] ibid, 1.

[20] ibid, 2.

[21] UN Commission on Human Rights (UNHRC), *Women and Adequate Housing* (26 March 2003) E/CN.4/2003/55 para 12.

[22] ibid, para 13; Committee on Economic, Social and Cultural Rights, *General Comment No. 16* (2005), CESCR E/C.12/2005/4.

[23] UNHRC, above n 21, para 21.

[24] See for example, UNHRC, above n 21, paras 20, 25; L Farha, 'Women and Housing' in D Askin and DM Koenig (eds), *Women and International Human Rights Law: Vol 1* (Ardsley NY, Transnational Publishers, 1999) 486.

[25] UNHRC, 'Economic, Social and Cultural Rights: Women and Adequate Housing' E/CN.4/2005/43 paras 53–58.

[26] UNHRC, above n 21, paras 42, 45–48. See UNHRC, above n 25, paras 53–58.

7.4. Accordingly, the Committee understands that the realisation of the right to housing is an issue of special significance for women. We recognised this in our 2011 General Statement on Rural Women,[27] where we called on States to ensure rural women's equal access to basic social services such as housing, and to use and ownership of land and property.[28] In this Statement, we noted that indigenous women living in rural areas often face added layers of vulnerability, and can suffer from 'a severe lack of basic resources for subsistence, income security, access to health care, information on and enjoyment of their entitlements and rights.'[29] Indigenous women's right to adequate housing is also threatened by historical patterns of forcible land dispossession and decimation of the cultures of their Peoples, continuing violent conflict, large-scale development projects, and the contemporary failure to recognise land and self-determination rights.[30] The role of these underlying conditions is evident in Cecilia Kell's case.

7.5. CEDAW protects women's right to housing only in Article 14(2)(h), thus the right to housing in the Convention is necessarily linked to the human rights of rural women. Nevertheless, we adopt the approach of the Committee on Economic, Social and Cultural Rights (CESCR) to the right to housing as an element of the right to a broader adequate standard of living under Article 11 of the International Covenant on Economic, Social and Cultural Rights (ICESCR).[31] Housing is not an isolated material asset, but an inherent element of that larger right. This is reflected not only in the ICESCR, but also in Article 25 of the Universal Declaration of Human Rights (UDHR), where an adequate standard of living is based on the enjoyment of adequate housing, but also 'food, clothing, housing and medical care and necessary social services, and the right to security in the event of unemployment, sickness, disability, widowhood, old age or other lack of livelihood in circumstances beyond his control'. It should go without saying that CEDAW interprets this provision as applying to women, despite the gendered language.

7.6. The CESCR has interpreted the right to housing under ICESCR as requiring the presence of at the very least, the minimum core of each of seven elements. These are: (i) legal security of tenure; (ii) availability of services, materials, facilities and

[27] CEDAW Committee Statement on Rural Women, above n 17.
[28] ibid, 4.
[29] ibid.
[30] See UNHCR, above n 25, para 65.
[31] ICESCR Article 11(1):

> The States Parties to the Present Covenant recognize the right of everyone to an adequate standard of living for himself and his family, including adequate food, clothing and housing, and to the continuous improvement of living conditions. The States Parties will take appropriate steps to ensure the realization of this right, recognizing to this effect the essential importance of international co-operation based on free consent.

The CESCR's interpretations of the right to housing are contained primarily in UNCESCR, The Right to Adequate Housing (Article 11(1)): CESCR General Comment No. 4 (1991) E/1992/23 and UNCESC, The Right to Adequate Housing: Forced Evictions (Article 11(1)) CESCR General Comment No. 7 (1997) E/1998/22 Annex IV.

infrastructure; (iii) affordability; (iv) habitability; (v) accessibility; (vi) location; and (vii) cultural adequacy.[32]

7.7. These legal standards, and the expression of the right to housing as encompassing seven elements, are an authoritative approach to the right to housing in international human rights law, and should guide the CEDAW Committee, as much as and insofar as they are applicable to rural women. The CEDAW Committee is well placed to apply these standards, and to foreground the centrality of housing to women and their concurrent difficulties in realising their right to it, though its interpretation of Article 14(2)(h).

7.8. It should also be noted that although the ICESCR imposes a standard of progressive realisation in Article 2(1), CEDAW 14(2)(h) is not couched in those terms, and, moreover, the obligation on States to eliminate gender discrimination is one of immediate effect.[33]

The Right to Housing in Situations of Domestic Violence

7.9. Gender-based violence is 'a central thread in the fabric of human rights violations faced by women.'[34] More specifically, violence in the home – domestic violence – is a key cause of women's homelessness, the violation of the right to security of the person, and security of tenure.[35] The relationship between the experience of domestic violence and inadequate housing is reciprocal, as a lack of adequate housing makes women vulnerable to violence, and violence experienced in the home leads to a violation of housing rights.

7.10. Women subject to domestic violence are living in housing that is unsafe for their habitation. They are subject to both psychological and physical harm. Their security of tenure is compromised, and they are often rendered homeless when forced to flee violence. Women who live in situations where they are subjected to domestic violence are, de facto, living in inadequate housing. Thus, domestic violence is a breach of the right to adequate housing.

7.11. Domestic violence amounts to forced eviction when an individual is forced to flee her home.[36] A meaningful right to security of tenure and to be free from forced eviction should take *as the norm* the required removal of the perpetrator of domestic violence from the home, rather than the forced eviction of the victim of violence. This Committee has previously held in *A T v Hungary* that women victims of domestic violence should be provided with a safe home, through immediate and effective measures preventing the perpetrator from entering the woman's home, and/or through provision of an alternate, safe home.[37]

[32] UNCESCR General Comment 4, ibid.

[33] Common Article 3 ICESCR/ICCPR. See further CESCR General Comment No 16 (n 22).

[34] UNHCR, above n 25, Summary.

[35] UNHCR, above n 21, para 27.

[36] G Pagilione, 'Domestic Violence and Housing Rights: A Reinterpretation of the Right to Housing' (2006) 28 *Human Rights Quarterly* 120, 139.

[37] *A T v Hungary*, Communication No 2/2003, 26 January 2005, CEDAW/C/32/D/2/2003.

14(2)(h) in the instant case

7.12. Cecilia Kell is an Aboriginal woman living in a remote region of Canada. As noted above, the Behchokǫ̀ community is a rural indigenous community, located in Canada's far north. Many members rely on traditional subsistence activities such as hunting, trapping and fishing. As such, the Community as a whole can be considered rural for the purposes of falling within the protection of Article 14. Given that Aboriginal communities in Canada remain in a state of under-development in comparison with the euro-Canadian population, Article 14 is of particular relevance here.

7.13. The fact that the author of the complaint has spent time in urban centres does not prevent her from accessing relief under Article 14, provided that the violation, or its on-going effects, are tied to particular harms she experienced as a women in a rural location.

7.14. Housing is central to Cecilia Kell's claim. As is true for many women, Kell's relationship with her home and housing was not always positive. Nonetheless, throughout the domestic legal process she specifically asserted a claim for the restitution of her home. Her desire to make her home in the Behchokǫ̀ community was motivated by her desire to bring her children home. The author further asserted that a home in the Behchokǫ̀ community would fulfil her Aboriginal treaty rights, and is thus tied to cultural identity and belonging.

7.15. The Committee is of the opinion that the following elements of Cecilia Kell's Article 14(2)(h) right were violated.

Legal Security of Tenure and Forced Eviction

7.16. Security of tenure is the cornerstone of the right to housing. It protects against forced or arbitrary evictions or removals and provides crucial security and stability. When housing can be seized at will, or when one is subject to arbitrary or forced eviction, one does not enjoy the right to housing but resides at another's pleasure.

7.17. The CESCR defines forced evictions as occurring where there is 'permanent or temporary removal against their will of individuals … from the homes and/or land which they occupy, without the provision of, and access to, appropriate forms of legal or other protection.'[38] This duty extends to a state obligation to protect individuals from the actions of private persons.[39] The legal prohibition of forced evictions in international law would thus apply to the forced removal of Kell from her home in this case.

7.18. Canada owed an obligation of due diligence to protect Cecilia Kell from the forced eviction she experienced. The failure to provide a safe space is one of the

[38] CESCR General Comment 7, above n 31, para 3.
[39] CESCR General Comment 4, above n 31, para 9.

ways in which violence against Aboriginal women in contemporary Canadian society has become normalised,[40] accordingly the Committee regards Canada's due diligence obligations as heightened when indigenous women's safety in their homes is at stake.

7.19. First, Canada owed a duty to Kell to protect her from the experience of domestic violence, itself a violation of the right to adequate housing. Here, Kell was forced to flee her home and take refuge in a woman's shelter, despite her legal interest in the home and her right to benefit from housing under the specific housing scheme. The Committee reiterates that States should provide, as the de-facto position, that the perpetrator is removed from housing, rather than the victim of domestic violence is forced to flee the home. Second, Kell's right to housing was breached in respect of the right to security of tenure when the state failed to protect her or remedy the illegal removal of her name from the property lease. This aspect of rights violation is also considered further below.

Habitability

7.20. The requirement of habitability, as defined by the CESCR, ensures that housing is physically safe for its occupants.[41] Domestic violence can violate the habitability aspect of the right to housing, rendering the home unsafe for the dwellers.[42] As noted above, the State Party had an obligation of due diligence to ensure that Kell's housing rights were not violated by private parties. The failure to protect her from domestic violence was a violation of her right to housing. In addition, the failure of the State to provide alternative housing of adequate size and quality to house Kell and her family breaches this aspect of the right to housing.

Accessibility

7.21. Housing must be made accessible for disadvantaged groups. 14(2)(h) of CEDAW explicitly recognizes that rural women experience greater burdens of discrimination. Rural women should thus be accorded some degree of priority in access to housing. Aboriginal women are often among the most marginalized and disadvantaged of all groups. Thus, they fall directly within the priority groups contemplated by the CESCR in its goal of ensuring access to housing.

7.22. Likewise, the CESCR includes children in its list of disadvantaged groups for whom priority access should be ensured. Kell sought housing in the Behchokǫ̀ community specifically to bring her children home to live with her. As such,

[40] S Razack, 'Gendered Racial Violence and Spatialized Justice: The Murder of Pamela George' (2000) 15(2) *Canadian Journal of Law and Society* 91.

[41] CESCR General Comment 4, above n 31, para 8(c) and (d).

[42] L Farha, 'Is there a Woman in the House?: Re/conceiving the Right to Housing' (2002) 14 *Canadian Journal of Women and the Law* 118, 129.

her right to housing is intertwined with the rights of another vulnerable group – her children. In addition, it is to be noted that international standards such as the Universal Declaration of Human Rights Article 24(2), protect motherhood and childhood, as areas of special vulnerability and thus concern. These standards should inform the interpretation of CEDAW's Article 14(2)(h) and the right to housing under it.

7.23. In Kell's case, there was a specific housing scheme that was designed to give priority in family housing to indigenous people. Kell was initially able to access housing through this scheme, though ultimately only as a shared claimant with her non-indigenous male partner. The state failed to take steps to protect and ensure Kell's legal right to her home as an indigenous woman and mother, and her ability to access that home in practice. The accessibility element of her right to housing was, therefore, breached in this case.

Article 16(1)(h)

8.1. Under article 16(1)(h), States Parties shall take all appropriate measures to eliminate discrimination against women in all matters relating to marriage and family relations, and in particular shall ensure the same rights for both spouses in respect of the ownership, acquisition, management, administration, enjoyment and disposition of property.

8.2. The Committee is of the view that inequality within the family is one of the most serious forms of inequality experienced by women, affecting their most intimate relationships. Especially regarding matters related to property, the Committee reiterates, in accordance with its General Recommendation No. 21 on Equality in Marriage and Family Relations, that the right to own, manage, and dispose of property is crucial to a woman's right to enjoy financial independence.[43] This access to property is also vital to a woman's ability to earn a livelihood and provide adequate housing and nutrition for herself and for her children. Unequal access to property frequently has a deep impact on women's position within their families, leading in many cases to their being in subordinate positions with respect to their husbands or male partners. Such unequal access to property may also considerably affect women's life choices, especially but not exclusively their decision to freely enter into or leave marriage. Accordingly, the Committee considers that any discrimination in the assignment of property that rests on unacceptable gender biases should be strongly condemned and that States should take all necessary measures to protect women from property rights discrimination by institutions and by private individuals.

8.3. As to the merit of the case, the Committee takes note of the State party's submission that the author has not pointed out any property laws or customs that

[43] CEDAW General Recommendation 21: Equality in marriage and family relations, UN Doc A/49/38, 04/02/94.

discriminate against women in respect of the ownership, acquisition, management, administration, enjoyment and disposition of property; or any discriminatory laws that interfered with her ownership, acquisition, management, administration or enjoyment of the Behchokǫ̀ property in particular. However, the Committee has consistently stated that CEDAW's aim is the elimination of all forms of discrimination against women both *de jure* and *de facto*; and that while the recognition of formal legal equality is crucial to prevent women from being discriminated against because of their gender, States parties' commitment to equality must also encompass the adoption of all necessary measures to combat gender-based discriminatory conduct and attitudes that women experience *in practice*, resulting from the activities or omissions on the part of States parties, their agents, or committed by any persons or organisations in all fields of life.

8.4. Considering the facts at hand, the Committee is of the view that Kell's property rights have been prejudiced due to the removal of her name from the Assignment of Lease certifying co-ownership without her consent, and that she has been discriminated against as a woman since she has been treated by the authorities as *not having equal rights* to her partner Senych. Accordingly, the Committee concludes that the State party has violated Article 16(1)(h) as it failed to eliminate discrimination against women in all matters relating to marriage and, in particular, to ensure that its agents afforded Kell the same rights in comparison to those of her partner Senych in respect of ownership, acquisition, management, administration and enjoyment of the property.

Article 16(1)(g)

9.1. The Committee notes that from 1991 Kell was the victim of serious spousal abuse and that such violence worsened when she obtained a job and became financially independent. Her partner Senych controlled her finances, tried repeatedly to prevent her from working and took actions that resulted in her losing more than one job. In early 1995, it was as a consequence of Kell's decision to take employment without Senych's consent that the latter changed the locks on the family home and denied the author access, thereby leaving her with no place to live for several days and denying her access to her property and home.

9.2. Even if Kell has not expressly alleged a violation of Article 16(1)(g) of the Convention, the Committee is of the view that the principle of *pro homine*, which informs the interpretation and application of the CEDAW, provides it with the opportunity to rule on a matter not raised by the author, whenever functional to the achievement of a comprehensive protection of human rights and fundamental freedoms.

9.3. Accordingly, the Committee recalls that under Article 16(1)(g) States Parties shall take all appropriate measures to eliminate discrimination against women in all matters relating to marriage, and in particular ensure men and women the same personal rights as husband and wife, including the right to choose a profession and an occupation. Further, General Recommendation No. 21 on Equality in marriage and family relations states that '[a] stable family is one which is based on principles of equity, justice and individual fulfilment for each member', and refers to the duty of states to ensure the right of each partner to choose a profession or employment that is best suited to his or her abilities, qualifications and aspirations.[44]

9.4. In this regard, and considering the facts at hand, the Committee takes the occasion to stress that discrimination within the family affects women's economic well-being no less than labour market practices and laws. The Committee also notes that gender-based domestic violence manifests itself in myriad different ways, including oppressive practices aimed at preventing women from working outside the home. At the same time, it is relevant to consider that employment is central not only to women's right to enjoy financial independence, and to provide for her and her children's basic needs on her own, but also, and relatedly, to freely take life decisions, including the choice (as in the case under review) of leaving an abusive and violent husband.

9.5. The Committee recalls that Article 2(e) requires States Parties to take all appropriate measures to eliminate discrimination against women 'by any person, organization or enterprise', thus creating redress for violations of the Convention perpetrated by private actors, including those committed within the family.

9.6. At the same time, General Recommendation 19 on Violence against Women provides that States Parties should take appropriate and effective measures to overcome all forms of gender-based violence, that is 'violence that is directed against a woman because she is a woman or that affects women disproportionately'; and it specifies that States may be responsible not only for acts of violence perpetrated by public authorities, but also for private acts, if they fail to act with due diligence (i.e. with appropriate effort and effectiveness), to prevent or to investigate and punish their commission.[45]

9.7. In the light of these considerations, the Committee observes that, as a consequence of the State's failure to act with due diligence to prevent and stop spousal abuse against her, the author has been deprived of the opportunity to freely choose an occupation and lead an independent economic life on equal terms with her partner.

Intersectional Harms to the Author

10.1. The harm to the Author from all sources, and under all Articles cited herein, is not as a result of one or an accumulation of the claims alleged by Author, but also as a result of the intersection of the harms to the author.

[44] ibid.

[45] CEDAW General Recommendation n 19 on Violence against Women, UN Doc A/47/38 (1993). See C Chinkin, 'Violence against Women' in MA Freeman, C Chinkin and B Rudolf (eds), *The UN Convention on the Elimination of All Forms of Discrimination against Women: A Commentary* (Oxford, Oxford University Press, 2012) 443 ff. See also C Benninger-Budel (ed), *Due Diligence and Its Application to Protect Women from Violence* (The Hague, Martinus Nijhoff, 2008).

10.2. There has been in Canadian and other national legal literature some discussion in courts about intersectional oppression and about the extent to which, or whether, an intersectional approach can yield results in eradicating certain forms of discrimination.[46] The influence of intersectionality has extended beyond domestic social and legal spheres to international human rights discourses. For example, thematic reports to the United Nations (UN) have discussed the importance of intersectional forms of discrimination and how such discrimination exacerbates harm to women.[47] These recent discussions of intersectionality in international law build upon earlier work in this regard.[48] Because intersectionality has frequently relied on a relatively narrow definition of 'women' that fails to address identity markers such as race or class, explicit attention to these and other factors in the international arena represents significant progress for the world's women.

10.3. Throughout this Committee's opinions regarding State violations of Articles 1, 2(d) and (e), 14(2)(h), 15(1)–(4), and 16(1)(h), it is readily apparent that the intersection of Kell's status as an Aboriginal woman experiencing domestic abuse, poverty, and property dispossession has caused harm. These harms have served to deprive the author of her individual rights and agency. The harms also, however, contribute to broad structural inequalities faced by all women across states and cultures.

10.4. Accordingly, the Committee is of the view that the rights of the author under article 16(1)(g), of the Convention have been violated.

Recommendations:

11.1. Acting under article 7, paragraph 3, of the Optional Protocol to the Convention, and in the light of all the above considerations, the Committee is of the view that the State Party has failed to fulfil its obligations and has thereby violated the rights of the author under Articles 2(d) and (e), 15 and 16(1)(h), and 14(2)(h) read

[46] See K Crenshaw, 'Demarginalizing the Intersection of Race and Sex: A Black Feminist Critique of Antidiscrimination Doctrine, Feminist Theory and Antiracist Politics' (1989) 1 *University of Chicago Legal Forum* 139, 140 and 149. See further, K Crenshaw, 'Mapping the Margins: Intersectionality, Identity Politics, and Violence Against Women of Color' (1991) 43 *Stanford Law Review* 1241, 1242–44; G Valentine, 'Theorizing and Researching Intersectionality: A Challenge for Feminist Geography' (2007) 59(1) *The Professional Geographer* 10; RJF Day, *Multiculturalism and the History of Canadian Diversity* (Toronto, University of Toronto Press, 2002); D Khayatt, 'Boundaries of Identity at the Intersection of Race, Class and Gender' (1994) 14(2) *Canadian Woman Studies: Racism And Gender* 6; J Siltanen and A Doucet, *Gender Relations in Canada: Intersectionalities and Social Change* (New York NY, Oxford University Press, 2008).

[47] AN Davis, 'Intersectionality and International Law: Recognizing Complex Identities on the Global Stage' (2015) 28 *Harvard Human Rights Journal* 205; JE Bond, 'International Intersectionality: A Theoretical and Pragmatic Exploration of Women's International Human Rights Violations' (2003) 52 *Emory Law Journal*, 71.

[48] R Coomaraswamy, *Special Rapporteur on Violence against Women: Report to the Commission on Human Rights* (6 January 2003), UN Doc. E/CN.4/2003/75.

in conjunction with Article 1 of the Convention, and makes the following recommendations to the State party:

(a) Concerning the Author of the communication
- Provide housing commensurate in quality, location and size to the one that she was deprived of;
- Provide appropriate monetary compensation for material and moral damages commensurate with the gravity of the violations of her rights;
- Ensure that the Author is consulted and able to participate in the process of remedying her rights violations.

(b) General
- Ensure that appropriate protective and support services for victims of violence – including transportation to safe accommodation, healthcare, legal, psychological and employment counselling, social and financial support – are accessible to rural women and provided to isolated communities.
- Provide through law and policy the presumption that the perpetrator of domestic violence is removed from the shared home, rather than that the victim if forced to flee.
- Recruit and train more Aboriginal women to provide assistance to women from their communities who are victims of violence and other forms of gender-based discrimination.
- Review its legal aid system to ensure that women facing multiple discrimination, especially rural women, and women victims of violence, have effective access to justice and, in particular, establish adequate gender-sensitive training of judicial and law enforcement officials.
- Design and implement public policies and institutional programs to overcome existing stereotypes of the role of women in rural communities and promote the elimination of discriminatory socio-cultural patterns that prevent women from fully enjoying their human rights and attaining equality.
- Encourage the compilation of statistics and research on the extent, causes and effects of violence, and on the effectiveness of measures to prevent and deal with violence, especially violence against rural women.

11.2. With regard to general recommendations, the Committee takes the occasion to underline that when women's rights are violated it is crucial to award reparations from a gender perspective, and that adopting such perspective should influence the definition of both the beneficiaries and the content of reparatory measures. In particular, this requires us to supplement individual with general, structural forms of reparation directed to the society as a whole (rather than to the rights holder alone). These structural forms of reparation have the transformative potential to address – and progressively contribute to eradicate – widespread patterns of gender-based discrimination and violence forming the backdrop of individual violations.

11.3. In accordance with Article 7(4), of the Optional Protocol, the State Party shall give due consideration to the views of the Committee, together with its recommendations, and shall submit to the Committee, within six months, a written response, including any information on any action taken in the light of the views and recommendations of the Committee. The State Party is also requested to publish the Committee's views and recommendations and to have them widely disseminated in order to reach all relevant sectors of society.

Reflections

In the course of writing our judgment, we encountered several recurring issues that deserve attention here and that shine a light on the challenges of feminist judgment writing, but also some of its pleasures.

Aren't CEDAW Decisions Already Feminist?

First, as noted above, the three of us set out to write a decision that would be a significant, even radical, departure, from the existing CEDAW views. We wanted to make visible and audible the way law operates over women, and the silencing of women that often occurs, as here, through the domestic judicial process and even in international fora designed to rectify domestic failures. Why was this necessary? We might assume that the CEDAW Committee is by its very nature a feminist body, and that its decisions would therefore be feminist decisions, in which women's experience of human rights and their violation would be revealed in full force. The *Kell* decision is evidence that the application of CEDAW by the CEDAW Committee does not, by and of itself, make women's experience of the law fully visible. This is perhaps not surprising, as feminists have long known that simply applying law to facts does not result in 'the answer' being divinely revealed by the process, notwithstanding ancient notions of a female Justicia as the goddess of justice. As such, we found ourselves in the position of imposing a feminist judgment on the Committee of the Women's Convention.

One of our goals was thus to centre women's legal stories as specific topics and to deploy a feminist legal method more generally. By telling women's stories we refer to the exploration of their roles in legal events. We use feminist legal methods to describe a perspectivist approach to law that involves re-reading law from a feminist viewpoint or co-reading traditional male-centred legal stories along with legal stories that foreground women's perspectives. Related to this is what has been described as feminist legal realism, a feminist-focused legal movement whose goal is to deconstruct legal norms and engage in emancipatory or revisionist efforts to re-shape legal norms to include women.[1] We began with the issue of intersectionality.

Intersectionality

In our use of feminist methodologies, we sought to make intersectionality truly central to the decision. Gender and racial intersectionality is a paradigm that has

[1] See M Quinn, 'Feminist Legal Realism' (2013) 35 *Harvard Journal of Law and Gender* 1, 2–5.

long informed a number of legal discussions, although its use in international law is more recent.[2] However, problems often arise in deploying it to its greatest utility. These problems are often the result of the numerous complexities involved in crafting multifaceted theories. Such theories posit explanations for the way in which socially constructed categories of difference combine to create a social hierarchy. Because of these complexities, many efforts at addressing intersectionality begin and end by doing little more than noting the marginalisation of victims of intersecting (or perhaps interlocking) sources of oppression to victims and empowerment to oppressors. We were acutely aware of these issues, and sought to overcome them.

To our surprise and consternation – but also to our profound illumination – we discovered that the issue of intersectionality remained elusive and continually seemed to be marginalised in our CEDAW views. The very *form* of a legal decision constrained our ability to write about harms intersectionally. The fact that legal opinions – including CEDAW views – are organised on an issue-by-issue analysis, that proceeds sequentially through the violation of each individual article of the relevant law, meant that the ability to write about the totalising effect of the operation of the law over an indigenous single woman subject to violence in the home, and unable to assert her legal rights before the courts, kept slipping from our grasp. We found, as Hunter, McGlynn and Rackley identified, that judgments, even when broadly interpreted and loosely constrained as is the case with CEDAW views, are both constrained and constraining, 'and writing a judgment imposes certain expectations and constraints on the writer that inevitably affect – even infect – her theoretical purposes.'[3] At the same time, our own disciplinary training continually, almost subconsciously, and certainly against our stated intentions and wills, seemed to subvert our ability to think and write beyond the standard form. Even with our explicit attention turned towards intersectionality – both the intersectional power of Senych and the intersectional disempowerment of Cecilia Kell – we found it very difficult to include a meaningful picture of the intersectional nature of the human rights violations in this case.

Nevertheless, by specifically engaging intersectionality in Kell's case, we attempt to take up the baton of intersectionality and move it forward in a way that is both individually useful in assessing the facts of Kell's case and also more broadly serviceable in cases involving women (and men) whose multiple identities require address.

[2] A Nicole Davis, 'Intersectionality and International Law: Recognizing Complex Identities on the Global Stage' (2015) 28 *Harvard Human Rights Journal* 205; L Crooms, 'Indivisible Rights and Intersectional Identities or, "What Do Women's Human Rights Have to Do with the Race Convention?"' (1997) 40 *Howard Law Journal* 619. Another example is H Lewis, 'Global Intersections: Critical Race Feminist Human Rights and Inter/National Black Women' (1998) 50 *Maine Law Review* 309; LL Green, 'Gender Hate Propaganda and Sexual Violence in the Rwandan Genocide: An Argument for Intersectionality in International Law' (2002) 33 *Columbia Human Rights Law Review* 733, 735.

[3] R Hunter, C McGlynn and E Rackley, 'Feminist Judgments: An Introduction' in R Hunter, C McGlynn and E Rackley (eds), *Feminist Judgments: From Theory to Practice* (Oxford, Hart Publishing, 2010) 5.

Use of the CESCR's Approach to the Right to Housing

The CESCR's General Comments on the right to housing are some of the most advanced, explicit and authoritative available at the international level. As such, we felt it was appropriate for the CEDAW Committee to adopt them here as the international standard. However, we did this with some reserve, as it is not clear that the CESCR has, to date, itself adopted a particularly feminist understanding of the right to housing. As such, we also drew on the significant work of the UN Special Rapporteurs on the right to adequate housing, who have taken an explicitly feminist and gender sensitive approach to the right.[4] We also drew on a richer conception of the relationship between domestic violence and the right to housing than the CESCR has embraced to date, partly drawing on the work of UN Special Rapporteurs, but also academic sources.[5]

The Feminist 'Reveal', and What Sort of Feminist is Revealed?

We also wondered whether we should reveal ourselves as feminists, and the potential implications of doing so as judges (or at least Committee members), a question that has already been raised in various feminist judgment projects.[6] Taking as an assumed starting point that the CEDAW Committee should be a feminist body, we declared early on in our decision that the Committee would take on the mantle not just of feminine, but of feminist justice. We were alert to the political implications of this move, and it was a move that we as the Committee as a whole felt some discomfort with. We questioned whether this move was 'realistic' in light of the CEDAW Committee's actual composition, appointments process, and its views and other work. In the end, we decided that an ideal CEDAW Committee would make this commitment, and we would demonstrate how it could be done.

A further question arises: what sort of feminists might we be? Feminism is far more fluid than is sometimes acknowledged. However, it is important to point out that we can evaluate our work here, and the original CEDAW views, using schools of feminist thought which provide a useful analytical frame. For example, in our views we attempt to go well beyond the liberal legal subject, the 'atomised, self-interested, competitive being',[7] of liberal feminism which might be considered as

[4] See further J Hohmann, 'Principle, Politics & Practice: The Role of UN Special Rapporteurs in the Development of the Right to Housing in International Law' in A Nolan, R Freedman and T Murphy (eds), *The UN Special Procedures* (Leiden, Brill, 2017).

[5] Particularly in J Hohmann, *The Right to Housing: Law, Concepts, Possibilities* (Oxford, Hart Publishing, 2013), and see G Pagilione, 'Domestic Violence and Housing Rights: A Reinterpretation of the Right to Housing' (2006) 28 *Human Rights Quarterly* 120; L Farha, 'Is there a Woman in the House?: Re/conceiving the Right to Housing' (2002) 14 *Canadian Journal of Women and the Law* 118.

[6] See Hunter, McGlynn and Rackly, above n 3, particularly chs 2 and 3; H Douglas, F Bartlett, T Luker and R Hunter, 'Reflections on Rewriting the Law' in H Douglas, F Bartlett, T Luker and R Hunter (eds), *Australian Feminist Judgments: Rights and Rewriting Law* (Oxford, Hart Publishing, 2014).

[7] Hunter, McGlynn and Rackley, above n 3, 21.

the least confrontational or radical expression of feminism and which we might expect as the bare minimum level of feminism we would see from the CEDAW Committee.

However, in certain aspects of the *Kell* views, we found that the CEDAW Committee would have done well to treat Kell as an 'atomised individual.' Particularly in recognising her independent right to property and her autonomy as a full subject of rights and status in law, we as the CEDAW Committee stood firmly behind her formal rights to equality in law, a stance not strongly enough adopted in the original decision. In other areas, we felt that only a feminist stance that explicitly acknowledged the structural, historical, and relational aspects of women's marginalisation and the denial of rights and status in law could give effect to the claims Cecilia Kell made with such deep commitment and compelling steadfastness. We have noted above our efforts to write a judgment that took real account of, and responded to, intersectional discrimination, and our struggles to succeed in this respect.

In the end, we did not subscribe to any one 'feminism' in our decision. Our decision rather draws on a range of feminist insights, from critical and radical feminist and queer theory insights into represented space, to liberal feminist insistence on formal equality, to structural concerns about the historical and relational aspects of power and patriarchy. Our judgment demonstrates that 'feminisms' do not necessarily compete, and may rather complement our understanding of women's experience of the law. In addition, our work could be thought of in the view of what some scholars have labelled 'meta-feminism': that is, where feminism is self-reflective and explicitly struggles to define itself all while applying the label outside of itself.[8]

We conclude by observing that the very notion of engaging in this writing as a collaborative enterprise has been both feminist and self-reflexive in nature. We have, in short, produced feminist work while querying and shaping the nature of how we, as feminists, work together. It is difficult for academics working in any context to produce work that is non-traditional, broadly generative and explicitly ameliorative. It is all the more difficult to do so as a collaborative enterprise. Each of us has felt at various times in this project that it would certainly be easier to render a single-authored chapter. While we are all three legal scholars, we are also, in true intersectional fashion, women who represent a range of differences including nationality, ethnicity, race, professional and personal experiences, approaches to research and writing styles. We have had to bridge these differences in order to do our work, and we have developed methods of collaboration. In the process we have forged a new narrative identity that unites the merits of our individual voices into what we hope is one sonorous, highly enriched stereo-voice. Thus while feminism is notoriously difficult to define, we three authors have, implicitly if not explicitly, embraced shared notions of what it means to do feminist work.

[8] MJ Matthews Green, *Women and Narrative Identity: Rewriting the Quebec National Text* (Montreal, McGill-Queen's Press, 2001) 104.

PART IV

International Criminal Law

Special Court for Sierra Leone

14

AFRC Trial Judgment (*Prosecutor v Brima, Kamara and Kanu*)

OLGA JURASZ, SHERI LABENSKI, SOLANGE MOUTHAAN AND DAWN SEDMAN

Authors' Note

Due to the specific nature of international judgments, a project of (re-)writing a judgment of an international criminal tribunal is not without its difficulties. For one, the length of the judgment is an obstacle to producing a text that makes sense without knowledge of the original judgment. The particular judgment that our chamber was responsible for was decided by the Special Court for Sierra Leone (SCSL) against Alex Tamba Brima, Brima Bazzy Kamara and Santigie Borbor Kanu (the *AFRC* Trial Judgment) and is 630 pages long.[1] In structural terms, it follows a now well-established pattern which enables the judges to introduce in turn the specific case against the defendants (I); address challenges against the indictment and evidence (II and III); present the general context in which the alleged crimes took place and how this relates to the defendants (IV–VIII). Only then does the judgment assess the applicable law (IX) to the facts and arrive at the findings (X). In addition, the indictment against the three defenders included 14 separate counts, which the judgment addresses in turn. Therefore, our chamber decided to identify three main areas to which we wished to contribute and to focus on (re-)writing the applicable law and findings sections for each of the three crimes: rape, child soldiers and forced marriage. Finally, the rigid structure and dry language of judgments is not conducive to engaging with crimes that, due to their heinous nature, require a degree of emotional response. In terms of a feminist approach, Charlesworth writes 'feminist methods emphasise conversations and dialogue rather than the production of a single, triumphant truth'.[2] This neatly

[1] *Prosecutor v Brima, Kamara, Kanu* (Judgment) SCSL-04-16-T (20 June 2007, as revised 19 July 2007).

[2] H Charlesworth, 'Feminist Methods in International Law' (2004) 93 *American Society of International Law* 379, 379.

shows the tension between approaching international judgments from a feminist perspective and from a perspective that aims to discover one truthful narrative. In short, feminism emphasises the importance of diverse voices on a Bench.[3]

Before we assess the contributions of the *AFRC* Trial Judgment and expose the way in which we decided to address these issues in our (re-)write, it is necessary to present the general context of the case.

The *AFRC* Trial Judgment

The SCSL was established by an agreement between the Government of Sierra Leone and the United Nations on 16 January 2002 with jurisdiction over crimes committed in Sierra Leone since 30 November 1996.

Since Sierra Leone gained independence in 1961, numerous military coups and ensuing economic hardship were endured. The judgment focuses more specifically on the civil war that ravaged Sierra Leone between 1991 and 2002. Initially, this was a conflict initiated by the Revolutionary United Front (RUF) under the leadership of Foday Saybana Sankoh attempting to overthrow the Sierra Leonean Government. The Government was supported by the Sierra Leone Army (SLA) and a grouping of militias known as the Civil Defence Forces (CDF). By 1995, the RUF controlled large parts of Sierra Leone, especially in the north.

In May 1997, dissatisfied members of the Sierra Leonean army overthrew President Kabbah's newly elected government in a successful military coup. The RUF was invited to join the new military regime, which led to the establishment of the Armed Forces Revolutionary Council (AFRC). However, in February 1998 the AFRC government was overthrown and reinstated the government led by President Kabbah. Nonetheless, the AFRC forces continued to control parts of Sierra Leone until the Lomé Peace Agreement (July 1999) was brokered and the conflict formally ended in 2002.

Brima, Kamara and Kanu occupied senior positions in the AFRC, both as members of the AFRC Council and also as military commanders in the affiliated fighting forces. Whereas Brima and Kamara played an influential role in the running or policy-making of the AFRC government as Principal Liaison Officers, this was not proven to be the case for Kanu. Kamara and Kanu were both 'Honourables', a term given to members of a group of 17 who played a major role in the 25 May 1997 military coup.

In 2003, the three men were indicted by the SCSL on 14 counts of war crimes and crimes against humanity ranging from acts of terrorism to murder.

[3] On the topic of gender on the international bench see generally: GQUAL campaign www.gqualcampaign.org/home/; N Grossman, 'Sex Representation on the Bench and the Legitimacy of International Criminal Courts' (2011) 11 *International Criminal Law Review* 643; J Jarpa Dawuni and A Kuenyehia (eds), *International Courts and the African Woman Judge: Unveiled Narratives* (New York NY and London, Routledge, 2018).

Of particular interest to us in our feminist analysis and reimagining of the judgment are the indictments of sexual violence, including rapes and forced marriage, and also the indictments concerning child soldiers. Due to temporal constraints on jurisdiction, the crimes under scrutiny are limited to those committed between May 1997 and January 2000 throughout the territory of Sierra Leone. In 2007, Trial Chamber II composed of Presiding Judge Julia Sebutinde of Uganda, Judge Richard Lussick of Samoa and Judge Teresa Doherty of Northern Ireland found the three accused responsible for a number of crimes committed by the AFRC forces, including the crime of recruitment and use of child soldiers; it sentenced Brima and Kanu to 50 years' imprisonment and Kamara to 45 years' imprisonment.

Responses to the *AFRC* Trial Judgment

By bringing in multiple charges, the SCSL attempted to provide a record of the multiple harms suffered by the civilian population, in particular women and girls. In doing so, the original *AFRC* Trial Judgment raised awareness of the crimes of sexual slavery and forced marriage. Nonetheless, the tribunal did not enter any convictions for these crimes. It concluded that whilst there exists no bar to cumulative convictions in this case, the society's disapproval of the practice of forced marriage is already reflected sufficiently in the Court's recognition of such conduct as criminal and constitutes a crime against humanity.[4] Although the SCSL did enter a conviction for the crime of recruitment and use of child soldiers, it failed to recognise the particular gendered consequences of these crimes for girls. The conviction (or lack thereof) demonstrates a failure to interpret the crimes from a female perspective by ignoring either the complex nature of gender-based crimes, such as forced marriage and rape, or the gendered elements of the crime of using children in armed conflict. In both cases, the Court did not succeed in interpreting this set of crimes in a way that paid attention to the distinct experiences of women and girls during armed conflict. As a result, the Court's approach 'reflects male priorities'[5] and does not necessarily align with female perspectives and priorities. It reinforces gender biases, which hinders a more accurate understanding of gender issues in international law and undermines the legitimacy of the court's decision.[6]

[4] *Prosecutor v Brima, Kamara & Kanu* (Appeals Judgment) SCSL 2004-16-A (22 February 2008) para 202; V Oosterveld, 'The Gender Jurisprudence of the Special Court for Sierra Leone: Progress in the Revolutionary Front Judgments' (2011) *44 Cornell International Law Journal* 49, 51.

[5] H Charlesworth, C Chinkin and S Wright, 'Feminist Approaches to International Law' (1991) 85 *American Journal of International Law* 619.

[6] J Gruhl, C Spohn and S Welch, 'Woman as Policymakers: The Case of Trial Judges' (1981) 25 *American Journal of Political Science* 308, 309; N Grossman, 'Sex Representation on the Bench and the Legitimacy of International Criminal Courts' (2011) 11 *International Criminal Law Review* 643, 647.

The SCSL had the ability to expand the definition of rape, building upon the work of previous Trial Chambers; instead, it chose to reaffirm past understandings of rape without adding clarification. The fact that rape happens to both women and men during armed conflict needed to be stated definitively. Highlighting this would have disrupted the assumption that women are only victims in armed conflict.[7] The Trial Chamber also needed to address the areas of consent and penetration, specifically when involving a victim's mouth. The original judgment did not refer to rape as penetration of the mouth by any other object; our judgment includes this addition, which reinforces the nuances of sexual assault. The definition of rape in our judgment also recognises the influence and role of third parties in the commission of rape. This is especially relevant in armed conflict when sexual assault is encouraged or directed by individuals in positions of authority. Adding this element to our judgment addresses a particularity of rape within armed conflict. Our re-written judgment highlights the crime of rape, in order to emphasise the need for international legal institutions to recognise the multitude of experiences of sexual violence in armed conflict. While this expansion would have been useful in the context of this case in general, it would also have been beneficial for future trials. The discussion of consent in our re-written judgment highlights the presence of consensual sexual relations in armed conflict, which further illuminates the nuances of women and men's experience in armed conflict.

The SCSL was the first international criminal tribunal to charge and prosecute forced marriage. The indictment charged acts of forced marriage under two separate counts: Count 7 (sexual slavery) and Count 8 (other inhumane acts – forced marriage). The SCSL Trial Chamber in *AFRC* held that acts of forced marriage that occurred during the conflict in Sierra Leone were to be subsumed under the count of 'sexual slavery'. In adopting this approach, the SCSL failed to recognise the complexity of the phenomenon of forced marriage, especially in relation to non-sexual aspects of this crime, such as forced labour. However, the Trial Chamber also dismissed Count 7 (sexual slavery) for 'bad duplicity', resulting in the Judges applying evidence adduced on sexual offences to Count 9 (outrages upon personal dignity) and on non-sexual crimes to Count 11 (other inhumane acts).[8]

With regard to child soldiers, this judgment was the first to convict for this war crime. However, scholarly critique is generally limited to discussing the conduct elements of conscription, enlistment and using children to actively participate in hostilities, leaving aside the gendered experiences and consequences of the crimes.[9]

[7] R Kapur, *Erotic Justice: Law and the New Politics of Postcolonialism* (London, The Glass House Press, 2005) 101–05, 113, 127, 134.

[8] *AFRC* Trial Judgment, above n 1.

[9] V Oosterveld and A Marlowe, 'Special Court for Sierra Leone' (2007) 101 *American Journal of International Law* 848; V Oosterveld, 'The Special Court for Sierra Leone, Child Soldiers, and Forced Marriage: Providing Clarity of Confusion' (2008) 45 *Canadian Yearbook of International Law* 131; S Sivakumaran, 'War Crimes before the Special Court for Sierra Leone: Child Soldiers, Hostages, Peacekeepers and Collective Punishment' (2010) 8 *Journal of International Criminal Justice* 1009.

Similarly to the *AFRC* Trial Judgment, little attention is devoted in these critiques to the gendered aspects of this crime and the underlying question of whether rape, sexual slavery and forced marriage can be properly included in the scope of the crimes of recruiting and using child soldiers. This is particularly highlighted by the testimony of witness TF1-085:

> She testified she was abducted in Freetown in January 1999. She was then forced into a 'marriage' with her captor. She spent 'months' in Port Loko District where she endured a series of sexual crimes. After an attempt to escape, this witness too was shuttled back and forth between Port Loko and Makeni Districts where she was forced to undergo military training. Following a long, but imprecise, period of sexual enslavement, she was sent to participate in an attack on Kono.[10]

Interpreted from a gender-neutral perspective, the SCSL did little to develop the gendered aspects of crimes related to child soldiers and thereby silenced the gender-based violence suffered by girls. The AFRC Trial Judgment failed to recognise the plight of girl child soldiers within its definition of the elements that constitute the crime of recruitment and use of child soldiers. We aimed to rectify this.

The Contribution of the Re-written Judgment

The *AFRC* judgment is fertile ground for a feminist re-writing project, not least because it did not do justice to the gendered consequences of the particular conflict. Unlike the International Criminal Court's (ICC) *Lubanga* judgment, the subject of the next chapter in this collection, which only focused on the prosecution of the crimes of recruiting children and using children to actively participate in hostilities, the SCSL brought separate charges against the three accused for the crime of recruiting and using children to actively participate in armed conflict, the crime of rape and the crime of forced marriage (and/or sexual slavery) against women and girls. Consequently, the *AFRC* Trial Judgment allows us to scrutinise these three crimes through a feminist lens and highlight the points of connection between them.

The most important connection is the contribution by the SCSL to developing the contours of the crime of forced marriage. However, the judgment of Trial Chamber II missed an opportunity to conceptualise the elements of the offence of forced marriage and to clarify its legal status in international criminal law. Furthermore, the reasoning in the judgment of Trial Chamber II presented a limited understanding of the complex nature of forced marriage, leading to false labelling of this offence as an act subsumed in the category of 'sexual slavery'.

With regard to rape, although the SCSL in its *AFRC* Trial Judgment provides a historical record of the extent to which the bodies of women, men and children

[10] *AFRC* Trial Judgment, above n 1, para 1260.

became the theatre of war, the judgment failed to recognise that rape is perpetrated against all genders as gender neutral language in international judgments can imply a female victim. It is undoubtedly true that children need to be protected from the effects of war, and that this must be at the forefront of judicial decision-making. From a feminist perspective, the Court, in its interpretation of the crime and its elements, should be mindful not to limit its understanding of the experiences of children to the horrific experiences of boys as participants in hostilities whilst ignoring the equally horrific experiences of girls sexually abused by their commanders. The re-writing of the judgment thus provides an opportunity to reflect on children affected by conflict and explore the dominant gendered view of child soldiers' experiences – that leads to a focus on the experiences of boy soldiers – and to give broader recognition to the full spectrum of gendered experiences.

Finally, we have aimed in our judgment to address the interrelatedness of international crimes. The original judgment limits the ways in which gender is understood. Because the prosecutor diminished the role of females as former combatants or child soldiers and the Trial Chamber did not question the prosecutor's actions, there was a missed opportunity to establish the link between child soldiers and forced marriage. From the experience of the International Criminal Tribunal for the former Yugoslavia and International Criminal Tribunal for Rwanda, scholars have pointed to the importance of tribunals addressing sexual violence in their judgments, even where no charges relating to sexual violence have been included in the indictment.[11] However, in the *AFRC* Trial Judgment the judges did not take the initiative to do so.

In short, the SCSL did little to challenge gender stereotypes and present a more sensitive and complete account of the experience of boys and girls involved in conflict. Our judgment offers an alternative reading of the AFRC case by placing gender at the centre of the analysis as well as interrogating the context in which crimes took place. The definition of rape, which appeared in the original judgment, missed an opportunity to highlight the complexity of sexual violence in armed conflict. Implicitly stating that both females and males can be both perpetrators and victims of rape would have enhanced this and future understandings of sexual violence. The fact that male child soldiers might also be involved in forced marriages was also ignored by both the prosecutor and the Trial Chamber. Females were limited to roles of victim: acknowledging their active involvement in the hostilities, whether or not it was coerced, could have enhanced our understanding of victimhood and offered a more complete understanding of their involvement. Men were primarily seen as perpetrators and male child soldiers as victims of this particular crime, maintaining gendered

[11] K Askin, 'Gender Crimes Jurisprudence in the ICTR' (2005) 3 *Journal of International Criminal Justice* 1007, 1013.

understandings and preventing, in particular, further exploration of the nature and extent of the crimes of conscription of child soldiers and forced marriage. Our judgment attempts to emphasise the silences concerning the gendered reality of child soldiering soldiers, but it also engages with the customary traditions of marriage in pre-conflict Sierra Leone in order to subvert the notion that the crime of 'forced marriage' was in any way akin to 'marriage' as understood in customary and local (West African) context.

JUDGMENT

PROSECUTOR v ALEX TAMBA BRIMA, BRIMAN BAZZY KAMARA, SANGTIE BORBOR KANU

Case no: SCSL-04-16-T

Special Court for Sierra Leone

Before: *Justice Olga Jurasz, Justice Sheri Labenski, Justice Solange Mouthaan, and Justice Dawn Sedman*

20 June 2007

…

RAPE

1. In Count 6, the Prosecution charges the Accused with rape, a crime against humanity, punishable under Article 2(g) of the Statute.

Applicable Law

2. The Trial Chamber takes this opportunity to acknowledge that rape is committed during times of peace, as well as during armed conflict. Rape is not gender specific; it can be committed against both men and women and perpetrated by men and women. Gender, race, culture, socioeconomic status, and religion all intersect and shape the instances of sexual violence in armed conflict. The Tokyo Tribunal, the International Criminal Tribunal for the former Yugoslavia (ICTY), the International Criminal Tribunal for Rwanda (ICTR) and the International Criminal Court (ICC) have all established rape as a crime in international law.[1]

[1] F Lieber, *Laws of War: Instructions for the Government of Armies of the United States in the Field*, General Orders No. 100, Adjutant General's Office, 24 April 1863; *Convention (IV) respecting the Laws and Customs of War on Land and its annex: Regulation concerning the Laws and Customs of War on Land*, 3 Martens Nouveau Receuil (ser. 3) 461, 187 Consol. T.S. 227, entered into force 26 January, 1910; Article 27 of *Geneva Convention IV, 1949, Geneva Convention relative to the Protection of Civilian Persons in Time of War, 75 U.N.T.S. 287*, entered into force 21 October 1950; Article 76(1) of Additional Protocol I, *Protocol Additional to the Geneva Conventions of 12 August 1949, and Relating to the Protection of Victims of International Armed Conflicts*, 1125 U.N.T.S. 3, entered into force 7 December 1978; Article 4(2)(e) of Additional Protocol II, *Protocol Additional to the Geneva Conventions of 12 August 1949; Relating to the Protection of Victims of Non-International Armed Conflicts*, 1125 U.N.T.S. 609, entered into force 7 December 1978; ICTY Statute, Article 5(g); ICTR Statute, Article 3(g); Rome Statute, Article 7(1)(g); Article 18(j) of the Draft Code of Crimes Against the Peace and Security of Mankind, adopted by the International Law Commission (ILC|) at its 48th session, 1996, submitted to the General Assembly as part of ILC Report covering the work of that session.

Whilst the above courts and tribunals have prosecuted crimes of sexual violence, although predominately identifying women as the victims of rape, they have also demonstrated the existence of female perpetrators,[2] as well as male victims of sexual violence.[3] Recognising a broader range of individual experiences in armed conflict promotes a more inclusive understanding of sexual violence and gendered roles in armed conflict. The Trial Chamber believes that in order to prosecute crimes of rape, the definition and elements of the crime needs to include the multitude of situations that may occur in armed conflict. This process then moves international criminal law towards expanding the crime of rape into its own category of crime, thereby increasing prosecution and creating a historical record of the full range of sexual violence that exists in armed conflict. This Court further recognises that without an understanding of the extent of sexual violence in all of its varying forms during an armed conflict, it will not be possible to have an accurate picture of the armed conflict itself.

3. In addition to the chapeau requirements of crimes against humanity pursuant to Article 2 of the Statute, the Trial Chamber adopts the following elements of the crime of rape:

1. The non-consensual penetration, however slight, of the vagina, anus or any other orifice of the victim either by the penis of the perpetrator or by any other object used by the perpetrator or at the instigation of the perpetrator; and
2. The intent to effect this sexual penetration, and the knowledge that it occurs without the consent of the victim.[4]

4. In reference to element 1 of the definition of rape, the Trial Chamber recognises that the previous definition of rape, established by the ICTR, did not account for third party involvement. The actions of an individual who incites rape, but is not directly perpetrating sexual violence while carrying a leadership role, was absent from the first definition of rape. The presence of a third party was highlighted particularly, but not solely, during the prosecution of rape committed against men.[5] The perpetrator does not always play an active physical role, but rather coerces two victims to engage in sexual acts with each other or instructs a person under their command to rape. As a consequence, the perpetrator can be

[2] *Prosecutor v Plavšić* (Judgment) IT-00-39 & 40/1 (27 February 2003); *Prosecutor v Nyiramasuhuko et al* (Amended Indictment) ICTR-97-21-I (1 March 2001).

[3] *Prosecutor v Mučić et al* (Judgment) IT-96-21-T (16 November 1998); *Prosecutor v Tadić* (Judgment), IT-94-1 (26 January 2000); *Prosecutor v Češić* (Judgment) IT-95-10/1 (11 March 2004); *Prosecutor v Todorović* (Judgment) IT-95-9/1 (31 July 2001); *Prosecutor v Simić* (Judgment) IT-95-9/2 (17 October 2002).

[4] Rule 98 Decision, para. 106, referring to *Kunarac* Appeal Judgment, para. 127.

[5] *Prosecutor v Mučić et al.* (Judgment) IT-96-21-T (16 November 1998); *Prosecutor v Tadić* (Judgment) IT-94-1 (26 January 2000); *Prosecutor v Češić* (Judgment) IT-95-10/1 (11 March 2004); *Prosecutor v Todorović* (Judgment), IT-95-9/1, ICTY, 31 July 2001; *Prosecutor v Simić* (Judgment) IT-95-9/2 (17 October 2002).

either a person who physically perpetrates rape or a person in a position of authority who orders the commission of rape.

5. In addition, the Court adopts an inclusive strategy in which all instances of conflict-related rape are equally pertinent and within its purview. Therefore, the gender of perpetrators and victims of conflict-related rape should not be presumed to avoid the marginalisation of other categories. Previous international criminal case law demonstrates that all genders can be perpetrators and victims of rape.[6] In short, women and girls are not the only victims of sexual violence. Stating this fact does not overlook the reality that rape can be perpetrated against women specifically, as a result of societal gender-based practices and assumptions.[7] Moreover, the Court recognises that the definitions of 'man' and 'woman' are inherently limiting and that gender should be interpreted based on the chosen identity of those individuals involved in the crime, both victim and perpetrator. The Chamber will be considerate of the nuances and the decisions of those involved in the trials in relation to their identity. Furthermore, gender should not become a reason to avoid prosecuting in cases where the gender of the victim may be tied to the motive for the crime or where the gender of an individual is undefinable by Court personnel. Situations that intersect crimes of persecution based on a person's chosen identity with sexual violence, for example, should be treated with the same gravity and respect as other crimes of rape and sexual violence.

6. Lack of consent is an important element of rape in a substantial number of national legal systems. However, where there is evidence of a particularly coercive and oppressive context – such as the use of violence or force, threat, coercion, detention, mental manipulation and other coercive behaviors – non-consent is presumed.[8] 'Continuous resistance' by the victim, and physical force, or even threat of force by the perpetrator are not required to establish coercion.[9] However, the Trial Chamber acknowledges that consensual sexual acts occur during armed conflict. The Chamber does recognise that Children below the age of 16, however, cannot give valid consent to such acts.[10]

[6] *Prosecutor v Akayesu* (Judgment) ICTR-96-4-T (2 September 1998); *Prosecutor v Mučić et al* (Judgment) IT-96-21-T (16 November 1998); *Prosecutor v Furundžija* (Judgment) IT-95-17/1-T (10 December 1998); *Prosecutor v Musema* (Judgment and Sentence) ICTR-96-13-T (27 January 2000); *Prosecutor v Kunarac et al* (Judgment) IT-96-23-T & IT-96-23/1-T (22 February 2001); *Prosecutor v Semanza* (Judgment and Sentence) ICTR-97-20-T (15 May 2003).

[7] *Prosecutor v Akayesu* (Judgment), ICTR-96-4-T (2 September 1998); *Prosecutor v Muhimana* (Judgment) ICTR-95-1B-A (21 May 2007); *Prosecutor v Gacumbitsi* (Judgment) ICTR-2001-64-A (7 July 2006).

[8] *Kunarac* Appeal Judgment, paras 127 & 129–130.

[9] *Kunarac* Appeal Judgment, paras 128–130, 133; GJ McDougall, *Systematic Rape, Sexual Slavery and Slavery-like Practices During Armed Conflict*, Final Report submitted to the Commission on Human Rights Sub-commission on Prevention of Discrimination and Protection of minorities, 50th session, UN Doc. E/CN.4/Sub.2/1998/13, 22 June 1998, para. 25.

[10] Article 5.a. of the Statute, which provides that '[t]he Special Court shall have the power to prosecute persons who have committed the following crimes under Sierra Leonean law: a. Offences relating to the abuse of girls under the Protection of Women and Act, 1960 (Cap. 30): Intercourse with a girl under the age of 16 is considered statutory rape'.

7. The Trial Chamber acknowledges that during large scale conflict-related violence, there may be elements of social stigma that prevent proper evidence from being collected. In such cases, while circumstantial evidence can be used to demonstrate the *actus reus* of rape.[11] However, the Trial Chamber does not assume that social stigma exists in all conflicts.

FORCED MARRIAGE

8. The next matter before this Court is to determine whether acts of 'forced marriage', which took place during armed conflict in Sierra Leone, constitute crimes against humanity under Article 2(i) of the SCSL Statute ('other inhumane acts').
9. Count 8 of the Indictment[12] charges the accused with allegedly committing acts of forced marriage as an 'other inhumane act' within the meaning of Article 2(i) of the SCSL Statute.

Applicable Law

10. 'Other inhumane acts' is a residual category under Article 2 of the SCSL Statute. It was designed in order to enable the Court to charge and prosecute crimes that satisfy the threshold of this provision but are not otherwise provided for elsewhere in Article 2. An historical example of the use of 'other inhumane acts' can be found in art 6(c) of the Nuremberg Tribunal's Charter.[13] International Humanitarian Law may offer parameters to the use of the category of inhumane acts: Common Article 3 of the Geneva Conventions obliges 'humane treatment' during armed conflict and lists acts contrary to this including – relevant here – 'violence to life and person' and 'outrages on personal dignity'.[14]
11. In order to satisfy the threshold of Article 2(i) an alleged act must fulfil:

a. The chapeau requirements for crimes against humanity; and,
b. Elements of the crime of 'other inhumane acts' as defined under International Criminal Law.

In order to satisfy the chapeau requirements for crimes against humanity, an alleged act must be committed as a part of widespread or systematic attack directed against the civilian population. With regard to the latter criterion, the Chamber will rely on the statutory definition of this crime stipulated in Article 7(1)(k) of the Elements of Crimes of the Rome Statute of the International

[11] *Prosecutor v Muhimana* (Judgment) ICTR-95-1B-A (21 May 2007); *Prosecutor v Gacumbitsi* (Judgment) ICTR-2001-64-A (7 July 2006).
[12] *The Prosecutor v Brima, Kamara and Kanu* (Amended Consolidated Indictment) 2004-16-PT (13 May 2004).
[13] This was echoed in Art 2(1)(c) Control Council Law No. 10.
[14] Art 3(1)(a) and (c), Geneva Conventions 1949.

Criminal Court 1998.[15] Accordingly, it must be shown that the perpetrator inflicted great suffering, or serious injury to body or to mental or physical health, by means of an inhumane act; that the act was of a character similar to any other act referred to in this Court's Statute; and that the perpetrator was aware of the factual circumstances that established the gravity of the act.[16]

12. The gravity of the particular act needs to be assessed on a case-by-case basis. Indeed, jurisprudence of the ad hoc international criminal tribunals has shown that a range of various acts has in the past satisfied the threshold of 'other inhumane acts'.[17] These included acts of both a sexual and non-sexual nature.[18] For the purposes of determining the gravity of an act or omission, the scale, nature, manner, and impact of what took place are the key indicators. It is crucial that such assessment takes into account the following factors: the age and gender of the victim; the context in which the act was committed; the impact on physical and mental wellbeing of the victim; and the impact of the act on the victim's societal position and relations within it. Given the post-conflict context of the situation in Sierra Leone, it is also important to consider the long-term effect of the act on the life of the victim in the post-conflict society. Nonetheless, this factor shall not preclude the consideration of the direct and harmful effect of the act (or omission) on the victim at the very time when the act was committed.

13. The current case put before this Court marks the first time where an international criminal court or tribunal considers the issue of forced marriage as a crime against humanity. As such, there exists no statutory or common-law definition of the alleged crime. In light of this, the Chamber feels compelled to arrive at such definition by analysis of the facts of the current case, the submitted evidence, and other relevant materials addressing the issue of forced marriage.

[15] Elements of Crimes:

1. The perpetrator inflicted great suffering, or serious injury to body or to mental or physical health, by means of an inhumane act.
2. Such an act was of a character similar to another act referred to in Article 7, paragraph 1, of the Statute.
3. The perpetrator was aware of the factual circumstances that established the character of the act.
4. The conduct was committed as part of a widespread or systematic attack directed against a civilian population.
5. The perpetrator knew that the conduct was part of or intended the conduct to be part of a widespread or systematic attack directed against a civilian population.

[16] *Ibid.*

[17] *Prosecutor v Akayesu* (Judgment) ICTR-96-4-T (2 September 1998) para.697 (forced nudity); *Prosecutor v Kupreškić* (Judgment) IT-95-16-T (14 January 2000) paras.565–566 (forced prostitution); *Prosecutor v Niyitegeka* (Judgment) ICTR-96-14-T (16 May 2003) paras.462–465 (castration); *Prosecutor v Kajelijeli* (Trial Judgment) ICTR-98-44A-T (1 December 2003) paras.677–678 (acts of sexual violence to dead women's bodies).

[18] *Prosecutor v Krstić* (Judgment) IT-98-33-T (2 August 2001) paras.523, 532 (forcible transfer).

Marriage in Sierra Leone

14. Sierra Leone is a multi-ethnic and multi-faith West African country, which operates a pluralistic legal system. It comprises of general law (the Constitution, statutory law, common law), customary law and Islamic law.[19] This diversity is reflected in the family law sphere, in particular with reference to marriage. Under the general law, marriage is regulated by the Christian Marriage Act 1960, the Civil Marriage Act 1960, and the Matrimonial Causes Act 1960. Section Two of the Matrimonial Causes Act 1960 defines marriage as 'the union of one man and one woman for life to the exclusion of all others'. Under Islamic Law, marriage, divorce, and inheritance are governed by the Muslim Marriage Act.

15. Unlike under general law, there is no definition of customary law marriage. The rules and procedures attributed to customary law marriage vary amongst different ethnic groups across the country. Professor Harrell-Bond notes that 'a valid customary marriage results in the transference of the rights to the domestic, sexual and procreative services of a woman form her family to her husband and his family, with the consent of the male members of the both families concerned. A requirement of a valid marriage is that dowry is presented to the wife's family by the husband's family'.[20] Mostly, in contrast to general law, customary law marriage is polygamous and bears the requirement of payment of a marriage consideration. Professor Joko-Smart describes it as a 'transaction beginning with betrothal or a friendship arrangement culminating in the obtaining of the consent of the family of the wife to the marriage, the latter being, the most important essential without which a customary law marriage is non-existent, and finally ending with the wife taking her place in the husband's household.'[21]

16. The Expert Witness for the Prosecution, Mrs. Bangura also highlighted these elements in her report. Mrs. Bangura further explained that while there is no minimum age for marriage in Sierra Leone, in the context of customary law, the appropriate age of the bride is determined by the fact that she reached puberty and was initiated to the women's society, the Bondo.[22] However, it ought to be noted that the Committee on the Elimination of Discrimination against Women noted in its Concluding Observations on Sierra Leone a concern that legislation and customary laws that discriminate against women still remain in force, including laws concerning adoption, marriage, divorce, burial, or devolution of property on death.[23]

17. All of the above types of marriage in Sierra Leone have their own distinctive elements, which are a reflection of the faith or customs to which the spouses

[19] The Constitution of Sierra Leone 1991, Article 170.

[20] B Harrell-Bond, *Family Law in Sierra Leone: A Research Report* (Leiden, Afrikastudie-Centrum, 1971) 13.

[21] HM Joko Smart, *Sierra Leone Customary Family Law* (Atlantic Printers, 1983).

[22] Bangura Report, 10.

[23] Committee on Elimination of Discrimination Against Women, Concluding Observations (Sierra Leone), CEDAW/C/SLE/CO/5, 11 June 2007, paras.10, 12.

subscribe. Nonetheless, there are some common elements between them. These are: the element of consent (in general law and in Islamic law[24] it is the consent of the spouses, whilst in customary law it is the consent of bride's father or family); a form of ceremony in which marriage is concluded; and, finally, a form of redress available to spouses. Furthermore, it is also evident that marriage, whether secular, religious or customary, is not defined only by sexual relationship between the spouses but extends to other, non-sexual aspects of life together.

18. In addition, Sierra Leone is a party to several international law treaties that are concerned with various aspects of marriage.[25] This body of human rights law is clear and consistent in how a marriage is recognised under both international and regional human rights laws. Essentially predicated on principles of equality and dignity – themselves principles that underpin human rights generally – the recognition highlights full and free consent, equity between partners, equal responsibility for children and marital property and formal legal protection under national laws.

19. For example, the *Convention on the Elimination of All Forms of Discrimination against Women*, in force since September 1981, has specific provision detailing marriage and iterating the importance of equality.[26] These provisions have

[24] Bangura Report, 12.

[25] ICCPR (since 23 August 1996), CEDAW (since 11 November 1988), African Charter on Human and People's Rights (Banjul Charter) 1981 (since 21 September 1983).

[26] Article 16

> 1. States Parties shall take all appropriate measures to eliminate discrimination against women in all matters relating to marriage and family relations and in particular shall ensure, on a basis of equality of men and women:
>
> (a) The same right to enter into marriage;
> (b) The same right freely to choose a spouse and to enter into marriage only with their free and full consent;
> (c) The same rights and responsibilities during marriage and at its dissolution;
> (d) The same rights and responsibilities as parents, irrespective of their marital status, in matters relating to their children; in all cases the interests of the children shall be paramount;
> (e) The same rights to decide freely and responsibly on the number and spacing of their children and to have access to the information, education and means to enable them to exercise these rights;
> (f) The same rights and responsibilities with regard to guardianship, wardship, trusteeship and adoption of children, or similar institutions where these concepts exist in national legislation; in all cases the interests of the children shall be paramount;
> (g) The same personal rights as husband and wife, including the right to choose a family name, a profession and an occupation;
> (h) The same rights for both spouses in respect of the ownership, acquisition, management, administration, enjoyment and disposition of property, whether free of charge or for a valuable consideration.
>
> 2. The betrothal and the marriage of a child shall have no legal effect, and all necessary action, including legislation, shall be taken to specify a minimum age for marriage and to make the registration of marriages in an official registry compulsory.

been expanded on by its Committee in its 1994 *General Recommendation 21*.[27] Whilst there is no explicit protection from forced marriage in the UN General Assembly's *Declaration on the Protection of Women and Children in Emergency and Armed Conflict*,[28] it does seek to protect against violence and collective punishment during armed conflict; two decades later, the same body affirmed the *Declaration on the Elimination of Violence against Women*,[29] to protect against gender-based violence in peace-time, which includes (but is not limited to) examples of marriage-related violence such as marital rape and dowry-related violence.[30] The *Supplementary Convention on the Abolition of Slavery, the Slave Trade, and Institutions and Practices Similar to Slavery* also offers further protection against forced marriage and coercive practices.[31]

20. At the relevant regional level, the *Protocol to the Banjul Charter on the Rights of Women in Africa*, which entered into force in November 2005, contains an express provision on marriage, safeguarding equality and consent.[32] There are also

[27] UN Committee for the Elimination of All Forms of Discrimination against Women, 'General Recommendation No 21: *Equality in Marriage and Family Relations*' adopted at the Thirteenth Session of the Committee in 1994 (contained in UN Doc A/49/38).

[28] UNGA Resolution 3318, A/RES/29/3318 (14 December 1974).

[29] UNGA Resolution 48/104, A/RES/48/104 (20 December 1993).

[30] This affirmation was iterated in Beijing Action Point no. 29 two years later: United Nations, Report of the Fourth World Conference on Women, A/CONF.177/20 (17 October 1995) para.29.

[31] Supplementary Convention on the Abolition of Slavery, the Slave Trade, and Institutions and Practices Similar to Slavery (adopted 7 September 1956, entered into force 30 April 1957) 266 UNTS 3. Sierra Leone has been a party since 1962.

[32] African Union, *Protocol to the African Charter on Human and People's Rights on the Rights of Women in Africa*, 11 July 2003, available at: www.refworld.org/docid/3f4b139d4.html.

Article 6 – Marriage:

> States Parties shall ensure that women and men enjoy equal rights and are regarded as equal partners in marriage. They shall enact appropriate national legislative measures to guarantee that:
>
> (a) no marriage shall take place without the free and full consent of both parties;
> (b) the minimum age of marriage for women shall be 18 years;
> (c) monogamy is encouraged as the preferred form of marriage and that the rights of women in marriage and family, including in polygamous marital relationships are promoted and protected;
> (d) every marriage shall be recorded in writing and registered in accordance with national laws, in order to be legally recognised;
> (e) the husband and wife shall, by mutual agreement, choose their matrimonial regime and place of residence;
> (f) a married woman shall have the right to retain her maiden name, to use it as she pleases, jointly or separately with her husband's surname;
> (g) a woman shall have the right to retain her nationality or to acquire the nationality of her husband;
> (h) a woman and a man shall have equal rights, with respect to the nationality of their children except where this is contrary to a provision in national legislation or is contrary to national security interests;
> (i) a woman and a man shall jointly contribute to safeguarding the interests of the family, protecting and educating their children;
> (j) during her marriage, a woman shall have the right to acquire her own property and to administer and manage it freely.

related rights that are engaged in the event of a forced marriage.[33] Sierra Leone has been a signatory to this treaty since December 2003.

21. The international obligations arising from these treaties include the principle of equality of rights and responsibilities between spouses, the right to marry, obligation to set minimum age for marriage and the requirement to register marriages, the right to freely choose the spouse and – of particular relevance here – to enter into marriage with free and full consent.[34]

Forced Marriage in Sierra Leone

22. The practice of 'forced marriage' became a phenomenon in the context of the civil war in Sierra Leone. During the conflict, many girls were abducted and forced to become 'bush wives' (or 'rebel wives'): they were forcefully 'married' to the rebels and forced to live with them as husband and wife. As testified by witnesses TF1-209, TF1-334 and TF1-033, their duties as a 'wife' involved taking care of their 'husband's' belongings, carrying them, cooking, cleaning, doing laundry, taking care of the household, as well as being forced to have sex on demand. As a result, many women became pregnant and gave birth to children fathered by their 'husbands'. Some women also suffered physical injuries, miscarriages and long-term damage to their sexual health resulting from forced sexual intercourse.

23. Women and girls who were 'married' to the rebels were considered their property. As witness TF1-334 testified, the ownership rights that rebels exercised over their 'wives' included physical and mental ownership as well as exclusivity of sexual relations with the wife. To that end, the 'husbands' possessed complete control over their 'wives'' sexuality, taking away those women's ability to choose a sexual partner freely. This may be seen as a mechanism of protection from rape and sexual abuse by other rebels, and one to which the women concerned voluntarily adhered (and therefore a form of agency or strategisation by women as suggests by Dr Thorsen).[35] However, the coercive circumstances surrounding the situation of forced marriage would suggest that such 'choice' was motivated by survival rather than indicating real, unvitiated consent. This extends to witnesses TF1-085 and TF1-282 who testified to undergoing a ceremony to recognise their 'marriage'.

24. Given the unique character of forced marriage, it is essential to deconstruct the language used in circumstances where this phenomenon was taking place.

[33] Article 3 (right to dignity); Article 4 (rights to life, integrity and security of person); Article 5 (elimination of harmful practices); Article 8 (access to justice and equal protection before the law); Article 10 (right to peace); Article 11 (protection of women in armed conflicts) and Article 14 (health and reproductive rights).

[34] ICCPR 1966 (Article 23), CEDAW 1979 (Article 16), African Charter on Human and People's Rights (Banjul Charter) 1981 (Articles 2, 3, 18), Maputo Protocol 2003 (Article 6; Sierra Leone is signatory only).

[35] Thorsen Report, 16.

The use of the terms 'husband', 'wife' and 'marriage' by the rebels was strategic. In particular, the words 'husband' and 'wife' indicate a level of belonging to one another, as well as exclusivity. By calling a woman their 'wife', a rebel attached the notion of ownership and 'protective control' over woman's physicality, mentality and sexuality. The Bangura Report illustrates this relationship: for instance, the 'wife' was forbidden to have sex with any other person and the rape of a 'wife' was punishable by death.[36] Nonetheless, the conjugal relationship was not characterized exclusively by sexual relations between the 'husband' and 'wife'.

25. Witnesses who were called in this case by both Prosecution and Defence gave evidence based on their experience of being 'bush wives'. Witness TF1-094 gave evidence that 'Andrew', who subsequently forced her to be his wife, abducted her from her village.[37] Witnesses DAB-156, TF1-085 and TF1-282 also testified that they were forcefully abducted before being taken as wives.[38] The witness evidence further demonstrates that the majority of women were detained against their will and threatened with death when they attempted to escape from their captors.[39]

26. The witness evidence shows that the experience of being a bush wife was not uniform. Whilst the elements of abduction and forced conjugal relationship appear to apply to all cases of forced marriage, witness testimonies demonstrate subtle differences related to the treatment received by bush wives from their husbands. Evidence presented before this court indicates that some of the women were not forced to carry out any work. For instance, Witness TF1-023 clarified in her testimony that as a bush wife of the commander she was not forced to do any work, such as cleaning or cooking. She further asserted that due to her 'marriage' with the commander, people in lower ranks called her 'De Mammy' which reflected the status attributed to the Colonel.[40] Prosecution witness TF1-085, who was taken as a wife of 'Colonel Z', also stated that she was not expected to carry out work.[41] Witness TF1-094 stated that when she became pregnant, her 'husband' ('Andrew') asked her not to terminate the pregnancy and offered to legally marry her.[42]

27. Testimonies of witnesses TF1-023, TF1-085 and TF1-094 (above) indicate that the nature of duties of a 'bush wife' varied amongst some women. In particular, the experiences of women who became 'bush wives' of commanders varied from experiences of many women who 'married' rebels of lower ranks. The Chamber is of the view that whilst this is a clear indication that the day-to-day experiences of some women varied from the common descriptions of the duties

[36] Bangura report, 15–16.

[37] Witness TF1-094, Transcript 14 July 2005, 37.

[38] Witness DAB-156, Transcript 29 September 2006, 74; Witness TF1-085, Transcript 7 April 2005, 68, 96; Witness TF1-282, Transcript 13 April 2005, 9.

[39] Witness TF1-282, Transcript 13 April 2005, 18; Witness TF1-085, Transcript 7 April 2005, 43.

[40] Witness TF1-023, Transcripts 9 March 2005, 57.

[41] Witness TF1-085, Transcript 7 April 2005, 37.

[42] Witness TF1-094, Transcript 14 July 2005, 38.

of 'bush wives', this aspect does not diminish the very nature or gravity of the acts committed against all of these women. Similarly, the subsequent will of the 'husband' to formalise the relationship (which initially was forced upon the 'wife') should not in any manner take away from the seriousness of the acts involved in forced marriage in first place. Finally, neither of these should retroactively repudiate the original criminality of the act of forced marriage.

28. Forced marriage, then, is marriage that does not contain the core elements of marriage recognised under international human rights law; the presence of coercion in particular makes 'free and full consent' impossible. Due to the varied acts performed by those forced into a conjugal association (for example, child-rearing, household chores, sex) this offence encompasses more than an offence of sexual slavery or rape.[43] In addition, the impact – both societal and psychological, contemporaneously and post-conflict – of being a combatant's 'wife' further distinguishes the offence.[44]

Gravity of the Offence: The impact of forced marriage on victims

29. In order to determine what underlying offence would meet the threshold of an 'other inhumane act' (that is, one not explicitly listed already under art 2), the underlying offence must be of sufficient gravity; that is, it will have consequences equally serious to those acts explicitly listed under Article 2. How would that be determined? An approach employed by international jurisprudence – the ejusdem generis method – would be to look at the other crimes listed under art 2 in order to obtain a sense of the types of offences that are deemed sufficiently grave: murder, extermination, enslavement, deportation, imprisonment, torture, rape, sexual slavery, enforced prostitution, forced pregnancy and other forms of sexual violence, and persecution on a political, racial, ethnic or religious ground.[45]

30. In determining the relative gravity of forced marriage, the impact of the crime on the victim should be a paramount consideration. The gender-specific aspect of this crime or sexual elements of it should not in any way raise the threshold required by international law in order for an act to fall under the category of 'other inhumane acts'. In the past, ad hoc international criminal tribunals found that various acts (both of sexual and non-sexual nature) fell under the category of 'other inhumane acts' as crimes against humanity. The range of 'other inhumane acts' depended largely on the context in which the acts were committed as well

[43] Following the definition of rape as identified in the *Akayesu* Trial Judgment before the Rwandan Tribunal (2 September 1998, ICTR-96-4-T, para.688) and of sexual slavery in the McDougall *Contemporary Forms of Slavery UN* Report, presented to the Sub-Commission on Prevention of Discrimination and Protection of Minorities (UN Doc E/CN.4/Sub.2/1998/13) in June 1998.

[44] Bangura's Expert Report (section 2.2).

[45] This was the approach used in *Prosecutor v Kupreskic et al.* (Judgment) IT-95-16-T (14 January 2000).

as the impact upon victims. These included: forced nudity,[46] forcing victims to perform exercises naked,[47] sexual and physical violence perpetrated upon dead human bodies,[48] forcible transfer,[49] forced disappearance, psychological abuse, beatings, torture, confinement in inhumane conditions.[50]

31. The Kanu Defence submit that forcing a woman to enter a marital type relationship is not of a gravity similar to any other act referred to in Article 2(a) to (h) of the SCSL Statute and that a 'more nuanced and complicated relation' exists between 'husband' and 'wife' in this context, as suggested by Dr. Thorsen's report.

32. The evidence shows that women and girls who fell victims to forced marriage suffered both immediate and long-term consequences. Immediately, they were stigmatized as 'rebel wives' or 'bush wives'. This stigma has a particular bearing on the lives of these women in post-conflict circumstances. Many former 'wives' have continued to be stigmatized by their communities because of their experience of forced marriage.[51] In some cases, this included the refusal of entry into their native village communities or even their family homes, which had an effect on the ability of women to re-integrate into their communities after the war. This mental and moral aspect of victims' suffering, which continues many years after the war, contributes to the gravity of the crime of forced marriage.

33. Furthermore, being forced into marriage with the rebels causes women to suffer both physical and mental harm. The young age of some victims was a factor that exacerbated their vulnerability. The 'wives' were forced to provide sex to their 'husbands' whenever it was desired. As a result, some women became pregnant and gave birth to children fathered by the rebel husband. Many women suffered miscarriages (often as a result of forced sexual intercourse) and some suffered from sexually transmitted diseases, including HIV.

34. The Chamber takes the view that acts of forced marriage have a wide-ranging effect on the victims, including physical, mental, sexual and moral harm. The harm suffered had a long-lasting adverse effect on the lives of the victims, which had a personal, social and moral dimension. Based on the evidence heard, the Chamber agrees that the experience of being forced into a conjugal relationship is a grave act that results in great suffering which has a long-term effect on the victim.

[46] *Akayesu* (Judgment) para.697.

[47] Ibid.

[48] *Kajelijeli* (Trial Judgment), para.936; *Niyitegeka* (Trial Judgment), para. 465.

[49] *Prosecutor v Stakić* (Judgment) IT-97-24-T (31 July 2003) para.317; *Prosecutor v Blagojević* (Judgment) IT-02-60-T (17 January 2005) para.629.

[50] *Prosecutor v Kvocka et al.* (Judgment) IT-98-30/1-T (2 November 2001) paras. 206–209.

[51] Testimony, Expert Witness Zainab Bangura, 3 October 2005. This stigma effected from sexual abuse during conflict was recognised a decade earlier in the Preliminary Report submitted by the Special Rapporteur on violence against women, its causes and consequences, Ms. Radhika Coomaraswamy, in accordance with Commission on Human Rights resolution 1994/45 (UN Doc. E/CN.4/1995/42, 22 November 1994), para.281.

35. The Chamber recognises that prior to the current trial, the crime of forced marriage has not been defined or prosecuted in international criminal law, and neither has it been recognised in customary international law. Furthermore, in the human rights context, the term 'forced marriage' is commonly used (both at national and international level) to describe a marriage which is entered into without the consent of at least one of the parties and often involves pressure from family or community members. The term 'forced marriage' as understood in the context of the current case, has not been codified in any international treaties or in national legislation. Therefore, the Chamber is of the opinion that the categorisation of forced marriage as an inhumane act under Article 2(i) would violate the principle of legality which underpins international criminal law and the right to a fair trial.
36. Whilst the Chamber concludes that forced marriage does not amount to a crime against humanity under Article 2(i), it is of the opinion that the acts compromising this offence are akin to enslavement, which is an established crime successfully prosecuted before other international courts and prohibited under Article 2(c) of the Statute.

Enslavement

37. The evidence presented before this Court demonstrates the complex nature of the acts of forced marriage committed during the Sierra Leone conflict. Despite the nomenclature, those forced marriages lacked essential procedural elements of marriage: they were carried out without the consent of the 'wife' (or such consent was effectively vitiated by surrounding coercive circumstances), no formal ceremony took place and, finally, the parties involved had no means of access to remedy. In their testimonies, witnesses highlighted multiple formative elements of forced marriage. These included abduction by force, the act of being 'married off' to the rebel, forced sexual relations, forced labour, physical and mental control over the victim, the relationship of exclusivity, reference to the victim as 'wife'. Whilst some of these elements might be missing in cases of some victims, the unifying factor in all cases of forced marriage is the imposition (by threat or force or threat of force) of a conjugal relationship upon the victim by the perpetrator.
38. The nature of ownership which is indicated by these elements may suggest that the victim was held in sexual slavery. However, to describe the situation of forced marriage as sexual slavery would not only be wrong, but would also constitute a flawed reflection of the complexity of forced marriage as a phenomenon. The ICTY Trial Chamber in *Kunarac* held that 'indications of enslavement include elements of control and ownership; the restriction or control of an individual's autonomy, freedom of choice or freedom of movement; and, often, the accruing of some gain to the perpetrator. (…) Further indications (…) include exploitation; the exaction of forced or compulsory labour or service, often without remuneration and often, though not necessarily, involving physical hardship; sex;

prostitution; and human trafficking'.[52] Article 7(1)(g)(2) of the ICC Elements of Crimes defines sexual slavery as the act in which:

a. The perpetrator exercised any or all of the powers attaching to the right of ownership over one or more persons, such as by purchasing, selling, lending or bartering such a person or persons, or by imposing on them a similar deprivation of liberty.
b. The perpetrator caused such person or persons to engage in one or more acts of a sexual nature.

39. Whilst the above definitions contain some elements of forced marriage, their scope is much narrower. Both definitions focus on the crime of enslavement, with the latter definition addressing a specific form of it: sexual slavery. As such they are rooted in the concept of exercising powers of ownership over a person (physical or mental), an act of enslavement.

Findings

40. There can be little doubt that the effect of being forcibly entered into a conjugal association is a grave act that would result in great suffering. This has been shown through the testimony and expert reports of the witnesses before the Court. However, the crime against humanity of 'forced marriage' is without precedent: there has been no prior codification or jurisprudence that has recognised this crime. Whilst International Human Rights Law provides a positive definition of what marriage should involve (equality, consent, dignity) this does not automatically translate into a *criminal* offence should one or more of those elements be missing. If the recognition of marriage is underpinned by the elemental principles of IHRL – dignity and equality – then these same principles must underpin the practice of this Court: the principle of legality, precision and respect for fair trial must be fundamental to a Court that observes human rights standards, as protected under Article 17 of our Statute.

41. There is precedence for the underlying offence of enslavement, which has been defined as 'control of someone's movement, control of physical environment, psychological control, measures taken to prevent or deter escape, force, threat of force or coercion, duration, assertion of exclusivity, subjection to cruel treatment and abuse, control of sexuality and forced labour'.[53] This is the offence that was committed by the defendants. To categorise these acts as 'forced marriage' would be to adopt the defendants' own terminology and to legitimise it: adopting the terms 'bush wife' and 'forced marriage' in this context serves to coat with a civilizing veneer practices that are in reality abhorrent. The victims were

[52] *Prosecutor v Kunarac et al.* (Judgment) IT-96-23-T & IT-96-23-T/1-T (22 February 2001) para. 542.

[53] ibid para. 543.

repeatedly raped, endured threats of and actual violence, undertook forced labour, and suffered physically and mentally both contemporaneously and continuing to this day. It is unwise to use the term 'marriage'; there was no marriage here in either a *de jure* or *de facto* sense. The relationship was enslavement.

COUNT 12: CRIMES RELATING TO CHILD SOLDIERS (ARTICLE 4(C) OF THE STATUTE

42. Count 12 alleges the crime of conscripting, enlisting and/or using children under the age of 15 to participate in active hostilities. The indictment asserts that the AFRC/RUF routinely conscripted, enlisted and/or used boys and girls under that age to actively participate in hostilities. Thus the Accused are charged with this crime which is punishable under Article 4 (c) of the Statute.

Applicable Law

43. Article 4 of the Statute is entitled 'Other Serious Violations of International Humanitarian Law' and provides as follows:

> The Special Court shall have the power to prosecute persons who committed the following serious violations of international humanitarian law:
>
> …
>
> c. Conscripting or enlisting children under the age of fifteen years into armed forces or groups or using them to participate actively in hostilities.

44. The recruitment and use of child soldiers is an international crime and a human rights violation. In an earlier decision, the Appeals Chamber determined that by November 1996, customary international law recognised that this crime, regardless of whether it was committed as part of an international or non-international conflict, was a violation of the international law of armed conflict.[54] Additional Protocols I and II of the Geneva Conventions afford special protection and aid to children during armed conflict.[55] Furthermore, both explicitly state that 'children who have not attained the age of fifteen years shall neither be recruited in the armed forces or groups nor allowed to take part in hostilities'.[56] The Trial Chamber further notes that Sierra Leone has ratified the Convention on the Rights of the Child (CRC), thus expressing its commitment to protect children from all forms of violence and to take 'all feasible measures' to ensure that children under the age of fifteen are not recruited into armed forces or forced to

[54] *Prosecutor v Norman* (Decision on Preliminary Motion based on Lack of Jurisdiction (Child Recruitment)) SCSL 04-14-131 (31 May 2004).

[55] AP I, Article 77(1) and AP II, Article 4(3).

[56] AP I, Article 77(2) and AP II, Article 4(3)(c).

participate in armed conflict.[57] Article 38 of the CRC states that children under the age of 15 years should not be recruited or forced to take part in armed conflict.[58] Moreover, Article 19 of the CRC requires State Parties to take all appropriate measures to protect children from all forms of physical or mental violence, injury or abuse, neglect or negligent treatment, maltreatment or exploitation, including sexual abuse. These legal provisions should serve as a guide in determining the interpretation of the crime, in particular that human right and humanitarian obligations are complimentary and mutually reinforcing.

45. As a consequence, the above-mentioned Appeals Chamber held that:

> '... [c]hild recruitment was criminalised before it was explicitly set out as a criminal prohibition in treaty law and certainly by November 1996, the starting point of the time frame relevant to the indictments. As set out above, the principle of legality and the principle of specificity are both upheld'.[59] In addition, it found that 'States clearly consider themselves to be under a legal obligation not to practice child recruitment'.[60]

46. In order to satisfy the threshold of Article (c) an alleged act must fulfil:

a. The chapeau requirements; and,
b. The elements of the crime.

The Chapeau Requirements

47. The crimes listed in Article 4 of the Statute possess the same chapeau requirements as those in Article 3 entitled 'Violations of Article 3 Common to the Geneva Conventions and of Additional Protocol II', namely:

a. There must have been and armed conflict whether non-international or international in character at the time the offences were allegedly committed,
b. There must be a nexus between the armed conflict and the alleged offence;
c. The victims were not directly taking part in the hostilities at the time of the alleged violation.

48. As for Article 3 of the SCSL Statute, the Trial Chamber found that at all times relevant to the Indictment, there was an armed conflict in Sierra Leone and that the crimes were closely related to this conflict. Unless indicated otherwise in

[57] Sierra Leone ratified the CRC in June 1990, United Nations Treaty Collection: Multilateral Treaties Deposited with the Secretary-General, Convention on the Rights of the Child, available at: http:// untreaty.un.org/ENGLISH/bible/englishinternetbible/partI/chapterIV/ treaty19.asp.

[58] Convention on the Rights of the Child, 20 November 1989, 1577 UNTS 3, (adopted by GA Res. 44/25, UN GAOR, Annex, UN Doc. A/Res/44/25 (1989), entered into force 2 September 1990).

[59] *Prosecutor* v *Norman* (Decision on Preliminary Motion Based on Lack of Jurisdiction (Child Recruitment) SCSL 04-14-131 (31 May 2004) para.10-24.

[60] ibid at para.51.

its Factual Findings, the Trial Chamber is also satisfied that all victims were not directly taking part in the hostilities at the time the crimes occurred.

Elements of the Crime

49. The Rome Statute which guides this Court in interpreting this crime adopts the following elements of the crime of conscripting or enlisting children under the age of 15 years into armed forces or groups, or using them to participate actively in hostilities:[61]

a. The perpetrator conscripted or enlisted one or more persons into an armed force or group or used one or more persons to participate actively in hostilities;
b. Such person or persons were under the age of 15 years;
c. The perpetrator knew or should have known that such person or persons were under the age of 15 years;
d. The conduct took place in the context of, and was associated with, an armed conflict;
e. The perpetrator was aware of factual circumstances that established the existence of an armed conflict.[62]

50. Similarly, Article 4(c) of the SCSL Statute differentiates between three separate, alternative and independent conducts within the crime: 'conscripting' or 'enlisting' of children under the age of 15 into armed forces, or 'using' them to participate actively in hostilities.

51. The use of children to participate actively in hostilities is not limited to direct participation in combat, but also includes any activities connected to hostilities such as labour or logistical support that gives effect to, or helps maintain operation in a conflict. 'Conscription' and 'enlistment' are two alternative forms of recruitment. It should be noted that, due to the changing nature of armed conflicts from primarily inter-State conflicts to intra-State conflicts, 'conscription' and 'enlistment' may operate independently of a State and instead be imposed by an armed group. Article 4(c) acknowledges this by including 'conscription', 'enlistment' and 'use' not only by the armed forces of a State, but also armed groups. However, the Trial Chamber questions the validity of these two alternative forms of recruitment and instead proposes one single mode of 'recruitment into armed forces and groups' that dispenses of the need to explore the 'voluntary' nature or not of joining an armed force or group, but instead highlights the horrendous nature of the subsequent experience of children involved in an armed force or group.

52. Indeed, 'enlistment' indicates the child's voluntary enrolment into an armed force or group. Traditionally, enlistment requires a formal act identifying the

[61] Rome Statute of the International Criminal Court 1998, Article 8(2)(b)(xxvi) and 8(2)(e)(vii).

[62] Elements of crimes in the Rome Statute of the International Criminal Court, Articles 8(2)(b)(xxxvi) and 8(2)(e)(vii).

moment at which an individual is integrated as a soldier. In Sierra Leone, children joined or parents offered their children to the CDF, who fought on behalf of the government. Apart from an initiation process, no specific formal procedure for enlisting existed.[63] Identifying a specific act that furthers the child's enrolment within armed groups is difficult and risks being conflated with using a child to participate actively in hostilities, as the 'use' made of a child indicates their acceptance within the armed force or group. Therefore, a formal act of enlistment does not reflect the context of recruitment by government affiliated armed forces in Sierra Leone. In addition, this Trial Chamber doubts that criminalisation of enlistment without an act of force or pressure conforms to the principle of legality.[64]

53. 'Conscription' denotes an involuntary enrolment into an armed force or group. Traditionally, compulsory enlistment is reserved to government policies requiring citizens to serve in the armed forces. In Sierra Leone, evidence suggests that the RUF and AFRC abducted children into their fighting forces and established 'Small Boy Units' and 'Small Girls Units'.[65] Witness TF1-157 testified that he was abducted at the age of 13 and, on his journey towards Freetown, witnessed the commission of numerous crimes by his abductors, was subjected to forceful use of narcotics and was systematically exploited and abused and forced to undergo military training.[66] Within the context of child soldiering, compulsion does not encapsulate sufficiently the experiences of children who have been forcefully recruited or abducted into armed forces or groups. Therefore, the additional element of coercion enables a more accurate understanding reflecting experiences of children involuntarily and forcefully recruited into armed forces and/or groups.

54. Both 'enlistment' and 'conscription' of a child soldier occur at the moment a child under the age of 15 years joins an armed force or group. The prohibition on recruiting and using children under the age of 15 to actively participate in armed conflict is independent of whether that child's recruitment was voluntary or involuntary. Instead 'enlistment' and 'conscription' simply refers to different forms of recruitment. Thus the Trial Chamber believes the distinction between conscription and enlistment to be legally irrelevant and bereft of practical significance. The distinction does not serve any further purpose than unnecessarily requiring the evidence of an administrative act of putting a child's name on a list. Instead, the Trial Chamber emphasises that the main aim of the crime is to give vulnerable children full protection from the adverse consequences of

[63] Truth and Reconciliation Commission, Sierra Leone, *Witness to Truth: Final Report of the Sierra Leone Truth and Reconciliation Commission* (5 October 2004). Available at: www.sierraleonetrc.org/index.php/view-the-final-report/download-table-of-contents.

[64] *Prosecutor v Norman* (Decision on Preliminary Motion based on Lack of Jurisdiction (Child Recruitment) SCSL-2004-14-AR72(E) (31 May 2004) Dissenting opinion of Justice Robertson, para.4.

[65] Witness to Truth: Report of the Sierra Leone Truth and Reconciliation Commission, 5 October 2004.

[66] TF1-158, Transcript 26 July 2005, 39–41.

belonging to an armed force or group regardless of whether a child joined the armed group 'voluntarily' or not.[67] In addition, the 1977 Additional Protocols I and II and the CRC refer to recruitment without explicit reference to either conscription or enlistment. Graça Machel highlights the effects of armed conflict on children in her Report: 'While young people may appear to choose military service, the choice is not exercised freely. They may be driven by any of several forces, including cultural, social, economic or political pressures'.[68] In addition, it is never in the best interest of the child to be part of an armed group. Particularly in times of conflict, once the child has joined, whether voluntarily or not, he or she will be subject to violence, horrendous living and working conditions and abuse which will be detrimental to both his or her childhood and adulthood. As a consequence, children should be protected from the consequences of recruitment and related harms, including those perpetrated by the armed group the children belong to. Hence, it is important to approach this distinction with caution and should not be determinative to finding that the crime has occurred.

55. Accordingly, the Trial Chamber is of the view that the legal distinction between enlistment and conscription should be discarded in order to afford children the highest level of protection. Children under the age of 15 cannot consent to their own abuse and exploitation. The forcible or voluntary nature of their recruitment is not an element of the crime under Article 4 of the SCSL Statute and is merely a description of the methods of recruitment for indictment purposes. Recruitment should be prohibited based on the primacy of the child's right to survival and good development and freedom from violence over his or her participation rights.[69] The AFRC spread terror amongst civilians and routinely abused children in their own group from which they should be protected as fully as possible. Consequently, in line with all the relevant international legal instruments,[70] Article 4(c) encompasses two separate and distinct crimes. Firstly, the recruitment, regardless of whether this was on a voluntary or involuntary basis, of children under the age of 15 years for whatever purpose. Secondly the recruitment to use of children under the age of 15 years to participate actively in hostilities. The Trial Chamber will return to this distinction in its findings.

Facts and Findings

56. The Indictment in paragraph 65 alleges that '[a]t all times relevant to this Indictment, throughout the Republic of Sierra Leone, the AFRC/RUF routinely

[67] In line with the overall objectives of the CRC.

[68] UN Doc. A/51/306, *Impact of Armed Conflict on Children, Report of the Expert of the Secretary-General Ms Graça Machel*, submitted pursuant to GA resolution 48/157 (26 August 1996), para.38.

[69] Articles 6 and 19, CRC.

[70] In particular, the 1977 Additional Protocols, the 1989 CRC and its 2000 Second Options Protocol on the Involvement of Children in Armed Conflict and the 1999 ILO Convention n. 192 Concerning the Prohibition and Immediate Action for the Elimination of the Worst Forms of Child Labour.

conscripted, enlisted and/or used boys and girls under the age of 15 to participate in active hostilities. Many of these children were first abducted, then trained in AFRC/RUF camps in various locations throughout the country, and thereafter used as fighters'.[71]

57. The Trial Chamber read expert reports and heard evidence from Experts both for the Prosecution and for the Defence on the recruitment of child soldiers and their use as combatants.[72] The Trial Chamber heard evidence from witnesses, including the testimony of witnesses TF1-157[73] and TF1-158[74] providing reliable and credible information regarding their experiences as former child soldiers. From the evidence, the Trial Chamber was able to gain an understanding of the particular child soldiering experience and living conditions. Specifically, AFRC fighting forces abducted children coercively from their families or legal guardians to exploit and train them militarily to fight on the frontlines. In addition, child soldiers were subjected to horrendous living and working conditions; were subjected to beatings; forced to watch the commission of crimes against family members; given drugs to inhibit their fears; coerced to commit crimes, including rape, murder, amputation and abduction; used as human shields; and threatened with death if they tried to escape or refused to obey orders. Thus, the experience of children under the age of 15 recruited and used by the AFRC contravenes the objective of the CRC to secure children's rights to survival, dignity, wellbeing, health, development, participation and non-discrimination and violates the prohibition of all forms of violence against children.[75]

58. The Trial Chamber is satisfied that during the conflict, all factions, including the AFRC, commonly and systematically recruited persons under the age of 15 to participate actively in armed conflict during the period covered by the Indictment. In addition, the Trial Chamber has heard credible evidence that children recruited by the AFRC experienced appalling living and working conditions.

59. However, the Trial Chamber regrets that it was unable to confirm the full extent of the crime of recruiting and/or using children under the age of 15 to participate in active hostilities. The prosecution failed to adequately show:

a. The sex/gender difference in child soldiers;
b. The intersection between the crimes of forced marriage, enslavement and recruitment of child soldiers, and that between rape and recruitment of child soldiers.

[71] *Prosecutor v Brima, Kamara & Kanu* (Amended Consolidated Indictment) SCSL-2004-16-PT, 18 February 2005, 5391–5412.

[72] Exhibit P-33, "Report on the Situation in Sierra Leone in Relation to Children with the Fighting Forces." Exhibit D-37, O Gbla, "Research Report: The use of child soldiers in the Sierra Leone Conflict, and witness testimony: Witness TF1-296", Transcripts 4 and 5 October 2005.

[73] Witness TF1-157, Transcript, 22 July 2005, 55, 25 July 2005, 3 & 26 July 2005, 16.

[74] Witness TF1-158, Transcript 26 July 2005, 2.

[75] Article 19, CRC.

60. The range of witnesses called forward and the evidence presented by the Prosecution are inadequate, because they provided only a partial understanding of the experience of child soldiering. The Prosecutor, in his Pre-Trial Brief, promised that the evidence would demonstrate that: 'Thousands of children were abducted from all over Sierra Leone; thousands of children underwent military training at AFRC/RUF camps; children were formed into Small Boys Units and Small Girls Units; and Armed Small Boys Units and Small Girls Units were used in combat'.[76] Yet, the evidence presented pertained primarily to the experiences of boys, focusing on the combat and military activities linked to combat thus assuming that the community of children who suffer harms are predominantly boys trained and used for fighting purposes. For instance, witness TF1-157, a boy, testified that he was forced by his captors to participate in military training.[77] However, children include girls and boys and child soldiering covers a broader range of experiences, including sexual violence, abuse and domestic labour and such experiences should have been brought to the attention of this Court.[78] All such experiences is equally contrary to the best interest of the child and prohibited under the crime of recruiting children into armed forces.[79]

61. Further, the lack of female witnesses and female child soldiers presented during the trial reinforces the narrative that women and female children were only victims of sexual violence or related crimes, but did not actively participate during the civil war in Sierra Leone. The use of female child soldiers should have been properly researched by the Prosecutor and addressed by the Trial Chamber. The inclusion of more female witnesses, while beneficial to the case in underlining some of the more gendered experiences of child soldiers, would also have benefited future court cases and dispelled gendered assumptions about passive females, even if their actions were coerced. Likewise, male child soldier's experiences were limited by heterosexual gendered notions and did not address the possibility of sexual violence against them,[80] which should be seen as distinct from torture.

62. As a consequence, firstly, the Prosecution failed to explore the scope and nature of any differences in the experience of child soldiering for girls and boys. As the emergence of soft law instruments such as the 1997 Cape Town Principles and Best Practices on the Prevention of recruitment of Children into Armed Forces and on Demobilization and Social Reintegration of Child Soldiers in Africa demonstrate, there are multiple dimensions to the use of children in

[76] Prosecution Supplemental Pre-Trial Brief, paras 182, 465, 748.

[77] TF1-158, Transcript 26 July 2005, 39–41.

[78] Report by the Truth and Reconciliation Commission to the United National Security Council, Volume B, Chapter 4 on Children and the Armed Conflict in Sierra Leone, 2004, para. 131.

[79] Article 19, CRC.

[80] Machel Report, 29, para.93: "cases of young boys who have been raped … are under-reported".

armed conflict.[81] The Cape Town Principles' definition of child soldiers makes specific reference to 'girls recruited for sexual purposes'. In this respect, the failure to address girls' experience of recruitment into armed forces is problematic. Furthermore, the 1999 Report of the Special Representative of the Secretary-General for Children and Armed Conflict highlighted that in the month of January 1999, 4,000 children were abducted during incursions into Freetown by the RUF and AFRC, of which 60 per cent were girls and the vast majority of whom were reported to have been sexually abused.[82] The harms suffered from sexual violence, as part of the child soldier experience and perpetrated by members of the children's own armed groups is covered by the prohibition not to recruit children under the age of 15 into armed forces and children's human rights law. Not to address this gendered aspect of child soldiering results in unequal application of the law.

63. Secondly, the Prosecutor's limited approach to the crime of recruitment in order to use children under the age of 15 to participate actively in armed conflict discards the possibility of linkage between this crime and other crimes, such as forced marriage, or rape and other forms of sexual violence. The Trial Chamber, having heard a wealth of evidence on conflict-related rape and sexual slavery, questions whether sexual violence was also part and parcel of the child soldiering experience. Witness TF1-085 testified that she was conscripted and also forced into marriage. The lack of evidence by the prosecution did not allow the Trial Chamber to expand on this intersection between crimes, and her testimony relating to the crime of conscription was dismissed. The prosecution missed a vital opportunity to present further information and other testimony pertaining to similar instances. The Trial Chamber recognises that further examples of this kind were present within the conflict, but unfortunately was not presented with adequate evidence in order to expand this connection.

64. The Trial Chamber is thus unable to examine whether the Accused were guilty of the crime of recruiting children under the age of 15 for sexual purposes under Article 4 SCSL Statute. The Trial Chamber deems an inclusive approach which takes sex/gender difference into account when interpreting the crime of recruitment and use of child soldiers avoids marginalisation of girls and their experiences of child soldiering. Indeed, within children's human rights, the rights of the girl-child are inalienable, integral and indivisible.[83]

[81] UNICEF, Cape Town Principles and Best Practices on the Prevention of recruitment of Children into Armed Forces and on Demobilization and Social Reintegration of Child Soldiers in Africa, 27–30 April 1997.

[82] OA Otunna, Report of the Special Representative of the Secretary-General for Children and Armed Conflict, 1 October 1999, A/54/430, 22.

[83] Vienna Declaration and Programme for Action' World Conference on Human Rights (Vienna 14–25 June 1993) (12 July 1993) UN Doc. A/CONF.157/23.

Reflections

When Olga Jurasz brought the feminist international judgments project (FIJP) to my (Solange Mouthaan) attention, it was an opportunity not to be missed to (a) work collaboratively and (b) offer a feminist voice to a judgment in which the woman question had so blatantly been ignored. It has proven to be a positive experience to work collaboratively for the first time. As a group we have found it to be an invigorating, challenging and educative, a hugely enjoyable process that enabled detailed discussion and criticism of the law not through an academic, but judicial prism (prison, perhaps, as it was ultimately more a constrictive process than we had anticipated).

Our chamber was composed of four members. We had the privilege and advantage to know each other through other networks and to be geographically well-situated to meet face-to-face. In addition, we resorted to Skype meetings to discuss our work in progress. We divided the topics between two groups in order to work individually and in tandem to produce specific parts of the judgment before bringing it together. One of the pitfalls of our approach was the different voices that emerged in the judgment. Little did we know that that in itself would highlight possible different feminist approaches. Whilst our approaches were different, what 'united' our judgment was the common goal in sight: asking the 'woman' question in the context of a judgment that highlights highly gendered realities and impacts of modern armed conflict. Therefore, the end-product reflects our different feminist voices.

In addition, the project's meetings and workshops were very useful in setting out clear parameters for the project, hearing about previous similar projects and their challenges as well as sharing experiences with other chambers on the project. We have met some wonderful people and listened to thought-provoking discussions around our shared feminist project. In this sense, such feminist spaces and discussions are conducive to stimulate a more holistic approach to feminist research and scholarship which incorporates affective responses.

At its outset, the FIJP presented itself as an excellent opportunity to engage with feminist legal scholars and add fresh insight into an international criminal judgment; however, after moving through the process, it is clear that its main benefit was actually its ability to create a unique learning experience. The first point we would make is about how the process challenged hierarchical ideas about knowledge. For instance, Sheri, who began working on this judgment in the first year of her (now completed) PhD, noted that her perspective may be different from more senior academics. Nonetheless, her thoughts and ideas were viewed as equally relevant and her contributions were treated with the same regard as the other members of the group. Despite the fact that we all came from different feminist backgrounds, had different end goals, and often fundamentally disagreed as to what the project was truly meant to do, our group was still able to create a judgment that mirrors all our key points and balances very different strands of feminist thought. Each group member saw a 'feminist project' as a space for multiple voices, this fundamental belief underpinned our work and made it possible to create this chapter. This is not an easy task and it is this aspect that distinguishes itself from other projects. The dynamics within the group and the exchange of knowledge often reflected feminist methods taught in the classroom, such as critical thinking and the integration of multiple viewpoints outside mainstream legal analysis. The work of this chapter gave grounding to their importance, and offered a real-life example when teaching such methods to undergraduate and masters students.

The Process of Judgment-writing

Among the useful feedback received about process and writing during the judgment-writing workshops was the advice to write our judgment as a group. However, for pragmatic reasons, we had already split into two sub-groups. As a result, once we had completed a first draft we met face-to-face or on Skype to discuss and write the judgment together. As each section was already written, rather than re-write together we decided to adopt the tone, pace and style of the section on forced marriage.

One of the frustrations that members of our group voiced many times is that an international criminal law judgment offers limited opportunity to strike a balance between a legally plausible feminist judgment and the need for a feminist narrative which enables empathy and acknowledges diversity. The difficulty is to identify and adopt an empathetic tone which gives due emphasis to the horrendous experiences of armed conflict and applies the law (mechanically). For instance, in the section on forced marriage, the challenge was to write a feminist judgment that was based on the state of the law and facts as they were at the time. As judges we were charged with upholding the key principles of international criminal law rather than 'reinventing the law' retrospectively. This is not necessarily specific to international criminal law, but the issue of forced marriage really brought the issue into sharp focus.

Re-writing the part of the judgment dealing with forced marriage brought to light the fact that prior to the SCSL's jurisprudence there was hardly any commentary on that subject. This posed a degree of difficulty as we tried to inform our understanding of marriage (and the implications of forced marriage) in a Sierra Leonean, rather than a European or Western, context. It was important to understand the 'local' context in which the events charged in the indictment took place rather than transplant the Western ideas about marriage, in particular the customary marriages, into the judgment.

On the other hand, it highlighted the fact that the Chamber at the time would also in all likelihood have had a limited knowledge of the characteristics of marriages in Sierra Leone. However, we relied on a couple of academic works addressing legal as well as customary marriages in Sierra Leone in our judgment. We treated these as a starting point for building our understanding of marriage in

Sierra Leone, which in turn assisted us in constructing our own definition of the term 'forced marriage'.

At the same time, it was necessary to put ourselves in the shoes of the tribunal at the time and to distance ourselves from the wealth of post-2007 academic literature on the work of SCSL in prosecuting forced marriage as an 'other inhumane act' under Article 2(i) of the SCSL Statute. The vast majority of research addressing the long-term impact of forced marriage on women was also carried out and published after 2007, therefore rendering it impossible for us to rely upon it in the re-written judgment under the project's rules.

Challenges Posed by the Structures and Norms of International Law

Judges do not deliver their judgments in isolation from other actors. There is an intricate interplay in International Criminal Law cases between the Prosecutor and the Judges and it is only when both work in symbioses that a coherent re-written feminist judgment can be delivered. Indeed, we decided to re-write parts of the judgment that addressed gender-based crimes. However, even if we wanted to explore broader understandings of gender, the confirmed indictment and the case presented by the Prosecutor became the confines within which we were obliged to work. So, for instance, when addressing crimes relating to the recruitment and use of child soldiers, we offered an alternative interpretation of the crime, one that embraces gendered aspects and experiences of child soldiers. However, the limited range of witnesses and evidence presented, which in itself was already a feminist critique of the stance taken by the Prosecutor, only enabled us to allude to what might have been if the Prosecutor had (a) done what he had set out to do (to present evidence pertaining to the experiences of boys and girls) and (b) had himself asked the 'girl' question (is the child soldiering experience similar, partially similar or different for girls and boys). This demonstrated to us that international (criminal) law operates on gendered assumptions and prioritises masculine stereotypes. The narratives surrounding child soldiers focused on the military experiences of child soldiers without exploring their broader experiences or, in this context, asking the 'girl' question. As a consequence, we felt unable to use the facts in order to retell the story in a way that was more sensitive to how gender shapes and informs experience.

In re-writing the judgment on forced marriage, we were immediately faced with the challenge of effectively addressing a crime that has not been previously been defined or prosecuted under international criminal law. This challenge has also been true for other international criminal tribunals that were breaking ground in relation to the international prosecution of gender-based crimes. In the indictment, forced marriage was categorised as a crime against humanity, specifically as an 'inhumane act' within the scope of Article 2(i) of the SCSL Statute. This provision has attracted a lot of criticism, especially in relation to its open-ended nature.

Because there has been no prior codification or jurisprudence that has recognised the crime of 'forced marriage' (understood as a phenomenon specific to the war in Sierra Leone, rather than given its common legal meaning), we found that the prosecution of this crime under Article 2(i) of the Statute would violate the principle of legality. Instead, we held that 'forced marriage' was a form of enslavement – an international crime that had been successfully prosecuted before the acts charged in the *AFRC* case took place. Whilst we were not able to secure a conviction in relation to these defendants (as forced marriage was not charged as enslavement in the indictment), we were happy that our categorisation of forced marriage as enslavement satisfies the underlying principles of international law and human rights law.

This example is a good illustration of some of the tensions that exist in the prosecution of gender-based crimes in international law. Unlike other international crimes, gender-based crimes were generally not defined or prosecuted by international courts before the mid-1990s. Landmark cases prosecuted by the ad hoc international criminal tribunals as well as the coming into force of the ICC statute have somewhat changed this position. However, as illustrated by the *AFRC* case, challenges still remain regarding the prosecution of 'new' international crimes that have not been codified or prosecuted before. It was particularly difficult to provide a gender analysis of the crimes while remaining mindful of the broader societal implications of gendered norms in daily life. Balancing the local perspective with our own positionality was challenging.

In addition, the re-writing of the judgment highlighted the shortcomings surrounding sentencing in cases involving gender-based crimes. Feminist international criminal law literature criticises the fact that whilst gender-based crimes are included in indictments issued by international criminal courts, the gravity of these acts is often inadequately reflected at the sentencing stage. In our re-written judgment, we viewed forced marriage as a form of enslavement rather than as an other 'inhumane act' (as charged in the indictment), therefore leading to a somewhat dissatisfactory absence of a sentence for the gender-based crime of forced marriage. The judgment recalls the principles of equality and dignity that are foundational to international human rights law: within a trial, human rights apply to all involved – the victim, the witness and the accused. However, this also highlighted the need for careful and adequate charging of gender-based crimes, which reflect the gravity, nature, as well as contextual aspects of the acts in question.

About Feminist Methods and Theory

The interpretation of the law applied in the initial judgment prioritises a male perspective in which men were the benchmark norm, privileging the experiences of men and boys. Within the parameters set by the initial judgment, we challenged gender stereotypes and assumptions by, for instance, questioning why the Prosecutor addressed the combat-related experiences of boys only. We went on to offer a more diverse understanding of the child soldiering experience that included discussion of rape and forced marriage.

Working on a feminist approach to international criminal law allowed for deeper reflection as to whether feminism and international criminal law are compatible. Within the confines of a criminal judgment, bound by certain legal rules, inserting a feminist narrative proved challenging at times, even for a chamber composed entirely of feminist judges. Asking questions such as: does international criminal law leave room for a more empathetic tone?; is it possible to show understanding of the crimes and give weight to the extent of the crimes committed while using the language usually employed by the court?; from a feminist viewpoint, is it more valuable to have a project that speaks the language of law or one that completely reworks the way judgments are presented? These questions seemed to return again and again: we are not sure we have the answers, but we definitely have a greater understanding of our own perspectives as well as our own strengths and limitations as feminists working in international law. Whatever the reasons that someone reads a copy of our judgment, our hope is that it inspires the same sort of debates and frustrations about the larger meanings of feminist methods and international criminal law as it did among our chamber. That unique learning experience happened through confronting uncomfortable thoughts about our own positionality, and to that end this project is much larger than just a collection of judgments.

International Criminal Court

15

The Prosecutor v Thomas Lubanga Dyilo

YASSIN M BRUNGER, EMMA IRVING AND DIANA SANKEY

Authors' Note[1]

The Factual Background

The Democratic Republic of Congo (DRC) has a prolonged and complex history of conflict. While there are historical antecedents to violence in the DRC dating back to the brutal colonial rule of King Leopold II of Belgium in the late nineteenth century,[2] the roots of the more recent conflict can be traced back to the aftermath of the 1994 Rwandan genocide when forces from Rwanda and Uganda invaded the DRC to quash exiled Rwandan Hutu genocidaires who had fled into the region. The DRC is one of the richest countries in the world regarding natural resources.[3] Ethnic fragmentation and competition for the region's precious natural resources are both causes and consequences of the hostilities, and it is estimated that more than 3.9 million people died between 1998 and 2003, either as a direct or indirect result of the conflict.[4] The mineral wealth of the DRC is concentrated in the northeast of the country, including North and South Kivu provinces and Orientale province, which includes the district of Ituri. The significant economic, natural wealth of Ituri, with deposits of gold, diamonds, oil and timber, have caused bloody violence amongst the armed groups and militias operating in the area.[5]

[1] The authors would like to acknowledge and express thanks to Clare Hayes and Nuria Vehlis for their contribution to earlier drafts and Eithne Dowds, Kathryn McNeilly and the editors of this volume for their invaluable feedback.

[2] A Hochschild, *King Leopold's Ghost: A Story of Greed, Terror, and Heroism in Colonial Africa* (Boston MA, Houghton Mifflin Harcourt, 1999).

[3] The mineral wealth of the DRC includes copper, gold, diamonds, cobalt, tin, coltan, zinc and lead. G Nzongola-Ntalaja, *The Congo from Leopold to Kabila: A People's History* (London, Zed Press, 2002) 28.

[4] International Rescue Committee, *Mortality in the Democratic Republic of the Congo: An Ongoing Crisis* (May 2007).

[5] See 'Report of the Panel of Experts on the Illegal Exploitation of Natural Resources and Other Forms of Wealth of the Democratic Republic of Congo', (12 April 2001) UN Doc S/2001/1072.

The occurrence of sexual and gender-based violence has been a defining characteristic before, during and after the hostilities in the DRC. In 2010, Margot Wallström, the UN Secretary-General's Special Representative on Sexual Violence in Conflict, condemned the use of rape as a weapon of warfare and declared that the DRC was the 'rape capital of the world'.[6] Perpetration of sexual and gender-based violence occurs in both private and public spaces in the DRC and the devastating physical, psychological and social effects on individuals, families and communities are well documented by both the UN and civil society.[7] Evidence points to how Congolese women and girls have been disproportionately victimised; for instance, a report in the American Journal of Public Health in 2011 found that somewhere between 407,000 and 434,000 women reported having been raped in the preceding 12 months.[8] Further, there is growing recognition that men and boys have also been victims of sexual violence in the DRC.[9]

Another feature of the violence in the DRC is its effect and impact on children. Hostilities and regular attacks on civilians have resulted in the displacement of tens of thousands of children who have been recruited by many armed forces or militia groups operating in the country.[10] The UN Secretary-General's annual reports on children and armed conflict have listed several groups in the DRC responsible for the recruitment and use of child soldiers.[11] Precise figures are hard to find, but UNICEF reported that the DRC could have the largest concentration of child soldiers in the world, and in 2006 suggested that as many as 30,000 children were

[6] 'Tackling sexual violence must include prevention, ending impunity – UN official' (UN News Centre, 27 April 2010), available at www.un.org/apps/news/story.asp?NewsID=34502#.VNKYQZ3F_kU; 'UN official calls DR Congo "rape capital of the world"' (BBC News, 28 April 2010), available at http://news.bbc.co.uk/1/hi/world/africa/8650112.stm.

[7] See, for example: Human Rights Watch, 'Soldiers who rape, commanders who condone: sexual violence and military reform in the Democratic Republic of Congo' (2009), available at: www.hrw.org/sites/default/files/reports/drc0709web.pdf; 'Secretary-General Calls Attention to Scourge of Sexual Violence in DRC' (United National Population Fund, 2009), available at www.unfpa.org/public/News/pid/2181; Medecins Sans Frontiers, '"I have no Joy, No Peace of Mind": Medical, Psychosocial and Socio-Economic Consequences of Sexual Violence in Eastern DRC' (2004), available at www.doctors-withoutborders.org/publications/reports/2004/sexualviolence_2004.pdf.

[8] A Peterman, T Palermo and C Bredenkamp, 'Estimates and Determinants of Sexual Violence Against Women in the Democratic Republic of Congo' (2011) 101(6) *American Journal of Public Health* 1060.

[9] C Dolan, 'War is Not Yet Over – Community Perceptions of Sexual Violence and its Underpinnings in Eastern DRC' (2010) *International Alert*; ME Baaz, 'Why do Soldiers Rape? Gender, Violence and Sexuality in the DRC Armed Forces' (2009) 53 *International Studies Quarterly* 495; E Mechanic, 'Why Gender Still Matters: Sexual Violence and the Need to Confront Militarized Masculinity. A Case Study of the Conflict in Democratic Republic of the Congo' (2004) Insights Series, Partnership Africa Canada.

[10] These groups have included the Democratic Forces for the Liberation of Rwanda (FDLR); Mai-Mai groups; National Congress for the Defence of the People (CNDP); Patriotic Forces for the Liberation of Congo (FPLC); Allied Democratic Forces/National Army for the Liberation of Uganda (ADF/NALU); Lord's Resistance Army (LRA); Front for Patriotic Resistance in Ituri/Popular Front for Justice in Congo (FRPI/FPJC); Alliance of Resistant Congolese Patriots (PARECO); Enyele/Independent Movement of Liberation and Allies (MILIA); Armed forces of the DRC (FARDC); and M23.

[11] See, Security General's reports to the Security Council on children and armed conflict, 2002, 2003, 2005, 2006, 2007, 2009 and 2010.

fighting or living with armed forces or militia groups.[12] Other reports point to the widespread incidence of rape and sexual exploitation against both girls and boys by commanders and other soldiers. In 2008, the UN Population Fund reported that more than 65 per cent of victims of reported sexual violence during that period were children, many of which were adolescent girls.[13] Undoubtedly the experiences of child soldiers can be devastating, complex and multi-layered. Child soldiers risk medical, psychological and social damage resulting from their experiences in conflict. The treatment and living conditions of children within armed forces and militia groups are sources of these risks, in addition to the dangers child soldiers face from enemy forces. Regardless of the source, the damaging effects of the recruitment and use of children in the DRC in various combat and non-combat roles have severe consequences for their physical and emotional well-being and their reintegration into civilian life.[14]

The Legal Background

The situation in the DRC was referred to the International Criminal Court (ICC) by the President, Joseph Kabila, in 2004, and the first suspects to be arrested and surrendered to the ICC were Thomas Lubanga Dyilo, Germain Katanga and Mathieu Ngudjolo.[15] Since the opening of investigations, the ICC has focused on Eastern DRC, the Ituri region and the North and South Kivu Provinces. The case against Thomas Lubanga Dyilo relates to crimes committed within the Ituri region. The prosecutorial strategy of the ICC concerning the DRC situation indicated that attention would focus on violations in Ituri. Investigations were opened in June 2004, with the Office of the Prosecutor justifying its concentration on Ituri on the basis that the alleged crimes in that region were deemed to be some of the gravest in the conflict.[16] The serious, widespread and systematic crimes that were reported

[12] M Bell, UNICEF: 'Child Alert: Democratic Republic of Congo' (2006), available at www.unicef.org/childalert/drc/content/Child_Alert_DRC_en.pdf; Amnesty International: 'Democratic Republic of Congo: Children at War: Creating Hope of their Future' (October 2006), available at www.refworld.org/docid/4538df414.html.

[13] Human Rights Watch, 'Soldiers who rape, commanders who condone' (July 2009), available at www.hrw.org/en/node/84366/section/7#_ftnref4.

[14] United Nations Organisation Stabilisation Mission in the Democratic Republic of Congo/MONUSCO, 'Invisible survivors: Girls in Armed Groups in the Democratic Republic of Congo From 2009 to 2015' (November 2015), available at https://childrenandarmedconflict.un.org/wp-content/uploads/2015/11/151123-Girls-in-Armed-Groups-2009-2015-Final.pdf; The Office of the Special Representative of the Secretary-General for Children and Armed Conflict, 'The Six Grave Violations against children during armed conflict: The legal foundation' (November 2013), available at http://childrenandarmedconflict.un.org/effects-of-conflict/six-grave-violations/child-soldiers.

[15] 'Prosecutor Receives Referral of the Situation in the Democratic Republic of Congo' (ICC Press Release, 19 April 2004), available at www.icccpi.int/legalAidConsultations?name=prosecutor+receives+referral+of+the+situation+in+the+democratic+republic+of+congo.

[16] ibid.

in Ituri had not resulted in national prosecutions in the DRC legal system, and it took the Office of the Prosecutor two years before the first indictment was issued in 2006.

On 12 January 2006, the Prosecutor applied for a sealed arrest warrant against Thomas Lubanga Dyilo, the former President and founding member of the of the *Union Patriotes Conglais* (UPC) and alleged leader of the *Forces patriotiqués pour la liberation du Congo* (FPLC), the military wing of the UPC. Mr Lubanga Dyilo was charged with war crimes committed from 1 September 2002 to 13 August 2003 in the Ituri region, specifically with the crimes of conscripting and enlisting child soldiers (children under the age of 15 years) into the FPLC and using them to actively participate in hostiles under Article 8(2) (e)(vii) and 25(3)(a) of the Rome Statute. On 14 March 2012, Mr Lubanga Dyilo was found guilty by Trial Chamber I of the war crime of conscripting and enlisting child soldiers and using children to participate actively in hostilities.[17] Mr Lubanga Dyilo appealed both the conviction and the sentence, which was rejected by the Appeals Chamber on 14 December 2014.[18]

The *Lubanga* Judgment: A Significant Case for Feminist Re-writing

The trial verdict, delivered by Judges Fulford (Presiding), Odio Benito and Blattmann, was the first determination of the guilt or innocence of an accused at the ICC. It was the culmination of a trial that generated controversy from the moment the accused made his first appearance before the Court on 20 March 2006. The trial itself, which started on 26 January 2009, lasted 38 months from start to finish. Sixty-seven witnesses testified before the court, with several victims and witnesses travelling from the DRC to The Hague to participate in the legal proceedings.[19] The Court's treatment of its first case, concerning a single accused on a single charge, included the judges' summaries of the submissions of the Prosecutor, the Defence and the Victims representatives on the legal and factual issues. The original judgment includes extensive arguments on some issues and more cursory consideration of others, and much academic attention has focused on the significance of the case from a variety of perspectives, such as the approach

[17] *Prosecutor v Thomas Lubanga Dyilo* (Judgment pursuant to Article 74 of the Statute) ICC-01/04-01/06 (14 March 2012) ('Lubanga Trial Chamber Judgment'). On 10 July 2012, Lubanga was sentenced to 14 years' imprisonment, to include eight years of time already served. *Prosecutor v Thomas Lubanga Dyilo* (Decision on Sentence pursuant to Article 76 of the Statute) ICC-01/04-01/06-2901 (14 July 2012).

[18] *Prosecutor v Thomas Lubanga Dyilo* (Judgment on the appeal of Mr Thomas Lubanga Dyilo against his conviction) ICC-01/04-01/06-3121-Red (01 December 2014). Judge Ušacka dissented and submitted that the conviction should have been reversed. *Prosecutor v Thomas Lubanga Dyilo* (Dissenting Opinion of Judge Anita Ušacka) ICC-01/04-01/06-3121-Anx2 (01 December 2014).

[19] *Lubanga* Trial Chamber Judgment, above n 17, para 11.

to witness evidence and victim participation.[20] Ultimately, the Lubanga judgment was, and will continue to be, a critical moment for establishing the reputation and credentials of the ICC.

Among the reasons the Lubanga trial was considered a landmark for the ICC, three have been drawn upon for this feminist judgments project. Firstly, the case focused exclusively on crimes relating to the recruitment and use of child soldiers, which represented a significant opportunity to directly address harms experienced by children, both girls and boys, in armed conflict. Customary international law and many international treaties, including the Rome Statute, speak of the illegality of recruiting children to armed groups and using them to participate in hostilities.[21] While consideration of the plight of children in conflict has featured heavily in jurisprudence before the Special Court for Sierra Leone, as discussed in the previous chapter in this collection, the choice by the ICC to bring its first case on this matter could be understood as a deliberate pronouncement in support of the rights of children.[22] In focusing on the war crimes of enlisting or conscripting children under the age of 15 or using them to participate actively in hostilities under the Rome Statute, the trial inevitably raised important issues around the experiences, needs and rights of child soldiers and the violence perpetrated against them.[23] In particular, it highlighted the nature of recruitment of children to armed groups, regarding levels of consent and coercion, and raised challenging questions as to the extent of the agency and vulnerability of children during armed conflict. Another important issue in the trial was the interpretation of 'using children to participate actively in hostilities', which had particular implications for the breadth of the offence and who obtains recognition as a victim. The extent to which the judgment reflected the diverse and gendered experiences of children and the multiplicity of harms perpetrated against them has obvious significance from both a child-centred and feminist perspective.

Some of the important critiques of the case have focused on its limitations regarding the recognition of harms experienced by girl child soldiers and whether gendered experiences and roles were sufficiently reflected.[24] Law plays a unique

[20] See K Ambos, 'The First Judgment of the International Criminal Court (Prosecutor v. Lubanga): A Comprehensive Analysis of the Legal Issues' (2012) 12(2) *International Criminal Law Review* 115; R Graf, 'The International Criminal Court and Child Soldiers an Appraisal of the Lubanga Judgment' (2012) 10(4) *Journal of International Criminal Justice* 945.

[21] See MA Drumbl, *Reimagining Child Soldiers in International Law and Policy* (Oxford, Oxford University Press, 2012); MD Rosen, 'Child Soldiers, International Humanitarian Law, and the Globalization of Childhood' (2007) 109(2) *American Anthropologist* 296.

[22] *Prosecutor v Alex Tamba Brima, Brima Bazzy Kamara and Santigie Borbor Kanu* (Judgment) SCSL-04-16-T (20 June 2007) ('The AFRC Case'); *Prosecutor v Moinina Fofana and Allieu Kondewa* (Judgment) SCSL-04-14-T (2 August 2007) ('The CDF Case'); *Prosecutor v Sesay, Kallon and Gbao* (Judgment) SCSL-04-15-T (2 March 2009) [1623] ('The RUF Case').

[23] Art 8(2)(e)(vii).

[24] S Merope, 'Recharacterizing the Lubanga Case: Regulation 55 and the Consequences for Gender Justice at The ICC' (2011) 22 *Criminal Law Forum* 311; N Hayes, 'Sisyphus Wept: Prosecuting Sexual Violence at The International Criminal Court' in W Schabas, N Hayes And Y Mcdermott (eds), *Ashgate Research Companion To International Criminal Law: Critical Perspectives* (London, Routledge, 2013).

role in naming harm and in condemning the perpetration of certain forms of violence. International criminal law has the power both to recognise selective harms and silence others.[25] The ICC system allows for different harms caused to individual victims to be recognised, as well as providing legal recognition for collective harms. International crimes cover collective crimes carried out against specific groups as well as individual violations. How judgments identify and define harm, therefore, shapes the types of experiences recognised and the way victimhood is framed.

Secondly, leading on from this, the case is notable for its marginalisation of the harms of sexual violence. Despite initial investigation of the use of sexual violence against child soldiers, the Office of the Prosecutor (OTP) eventually chose only to bring charges relating to the recruitment and use of child soldiers. Given the widespread evidence of the use of sexual violence against child soldiers, particularly girls, in the DRC this decision has been widely criticised.[26] Attempts by victims' legal representatives to have the charges re-characterised to include the war crime and crime against humanity of sexual slavery and the war crime of cruel and inhumane treatment were ultimately rejected by the Appeals Chamber.[27] Despite the lack of separate charges of sexual violence, there remained opportunities for the Trial Chamber to address sexual harms within the charges relating to the use of child soldiers. However, while sexual violence committed within the context of the use and recruitment of child soldiers was deemed relevant to reparation and sentencing decisions, the Majority held that sexual violence did not constitute an aspect of the legal definition of the crime.[28]

The judgment not only silences the perpetration of sexual violence against boy child soldiers, but it can also be seen as potentially discriminatory to girl victims, who may have been particularly affected.[29] It is still possible for victims of sexual violence to benefit from the activities of the ICC's Trust Fund for Victims concerning the provision of collective reparations, which may begin to address some victims' needs.[30] However, given how experiences of sexual violence have continued to be marginalised in the case, many victims may continue to feel that

[25] F Ní Aoláin, DF Haynes and N Cahn, 'Criminal Justice for Gendered Violence and Beyond' (2011) 11 *International Criminal Law Review* 425.

[26] Hayes, above, n 24.

[27] *Prosecutor v Thomas Lubanga Dyilo* (Judgment on the appeals of Mr Lubanga Dyilo and the Prosecutor against the Decision of Trial Chamber I of 14 July 2009 entitled 'Decision giving notice to the parties and participants that the legal characterization of the facts may be subject to change in accordance with Regulation 55(2) of the Regulations of the Court') ICC-01/04-01/06 (8 December 2009).

[28] Lubanga Trial Chamber Judgment, above n 17, para 896.

[29] Women's Initiatives for Gender Justice, 'ICC issues first appeal judgment on reparations The Prosecutor v. Thomas Lubanga Dyilo' (March 2015), available at http://4genderjustice.org/icc-issues-first-appeal-judgment-on-reparations-in-the-lubanga-case/; see also L Chappell, 'The Politics of Gender Justice at the ICC: Legacies and Legitimacy', EJIL:Talk! 16 December 2016), available at www.ejiltalk.org/the-politics-of-gender-justice-at-the-icc-legacies-and-legitimacy/.

[30] *Prosecutor v Thomas Lubanga Dyilo* (Judgment on the appeals against the 'Decision establishing the principles and procedures 'to be applied to reparations' of 7 August 2012 with Amended order for reparations (Annex A) and public annexes 1 and 2, ICC-01/04-01/06-3129 (3 March 2015).

justice has not been served.[31] Not only did the approach of the Majority in the Trial Chamber result in the silencing of the range and complexity of harms predominantly experienced by girls, but it also presented a hierarchy of harms; those that were recognised within the substantive offence, and those that were only deemed relevant for sentencing or reparations stages.[32]

The final landmark feature of the *Lubanga* judgment was the participation of victims during the trial proceedings. As provided for by the Rome Statute, a total of 129 individual victims were authorised to participate in the trial proceedings, which included 34 females and 95 male victims.[33] The Rome Statute of the ICC was hailed as a victory for the rights of victims in international criminal proceedings, and it was anticipated that the inclusion of participatory rights would empower victims to have a voice in the procedural aspects of the criminal proceedings. The rhetoric surrounding the ICC process and procedure is that it recognises the importance of witness protection and the vulnerability of victims, as well as understanding the critical role of victim support in facilitating and encouraging victim participation within its cases. The high threshold for witness credibility and reliability of evidence adopted by the ICC in the *Lubanga* trial presented clear obstacles for severely traumatised child witnesses. Due to concerns over the reliability of testimony and overreliance on intermediaries who were not adequately vetted, the majority decided to remove the victim status of several victim-witnesses. This decision raises concerns as to how the legal process can address the needs of vulnerable witnesses whose trauma may impact their testimony. While trying to balance the Court's responsibilities to provide a fair trial to the accused, the needs and experiences of child victims should not be minimised.

The gendered shortcomings epitomised by the *Lubanga* case have fed into alterations at both the policy and practice level of the ICC. At a policy level, the ICC issued a Policy Paper on Sexual and Gender-Based Crimes (June 2014) and a Policy on Children (November 2016) both of which can provide valuable guidance for integrating a gender-sensitive approach towards crimes pertains to the experiences of child soldiers, within the limits of the Rome Statute of the ICC.[34] The conviction of Jean-Pierre Bemba for rape as both a crime against humanity

[31] Women's Initiatives for Gender Justice, above n 29; see also Chappell, above n 29.

[32] See R Rubio-Marín, *The Gender of Reparations: Unsettling Sexual Hierarchies while Redressing Human Rights Violations* (Cambridge, Cambridge University Press, 2011).

[33] Art 68(3) governs victim 'participation in proceedings' and provides when and how victims may participate. See also: T Markus Funk, *Victims' Rights and Advocacy at the International Criminal Court* (Oxford, Oxford University Press, 2010).

[34] ICC Office of the Prosecutor, 'Policy Paper on Sexual and Gender-Based Crimes' (June 2014), available at www.icc-cpi.int/iccdocs/otp/OTP-Policy-Paper-on-Sexual-and-Gender-Based-Crimes--June-2014.pdf; ICC Office of the Prosecutor, *Policy Paper on Case Selection and Prioritisation* (September 2016), available at www.icc-cpi.int/itemsDocuments/20160915_OTP-Policy_Case-Selection_Eng.pdf; ICC Office of the Prosecutor, *Policy on Children* (November 2016), available www.icc-cpi.int/iccdocs/otp/20161115_OTP_ICC_Policy-on-Children_Eng.PDF. See also Y Brunger, *Investigations and Prosecutions of Sexual and Gender-based Violence by the International Criminal Court* (The Institute for Justice and Reconciliation No. 23, March 2017), available at www.ijr.org.za/home/wp-content/uploads/2017/03/IJR-Brief-No-23-Updated-version.pdf.

and a war crime in March 2016 was widely hailed as a victory for victims of sexual violence and is a further step towards rectifying the Court's record on sexual and gender-based violence crimes.[35] Nonetheless, there remains much work to be done to fully integrate a gendered perspective across the work of the Court, including the judiciary.[36] This feminist judgment inspires further thought into how the ICC could use feminist approaches to interrogate the law's ability to acknowledge and make visible the gendered experiences of victims.

The Contribution of the Feminist Judgment

The feminist judgment differs from the original Trial Chamber judgment in several important ways. The original is much wider in scope, and the feminist judgment was only able to focus on a few key concerns surrounding the definition of the substantive offences of conscripting or enlisting children under the age of 15, using children to participate actively in hostilities and the application of the law to the facts.

First, the feminist judgment seeks to re-open the relationship between conscription and enlistment much more fully than the original judgment and to reflect on the nature of consent and coercion. The Majority in the Trial Chamber examined the difference between conscription and enlistment regarding the voluntariness, or lack thereof, of recruitment to armed groups, focusing on the lack of capacity of children to consent. The feminist judgment more fully problematises and explores the issues of consent and coercion to foreground the diverse experiences of child soldiers and to balance understandings of vulnerability with the rights and agency of children. Thus, while the original judgment presents a rather one-dimensional view of the capacities and vulnerabilities of children, the re-written version explores the complexities surrounding the recruitment of children in the DRC and how different situations and experiences of children may have impacted on the harms they suffered.

Second, the feminist judgment provides a slightly different approach from the original in its interpretation of the offence of 'using children to participate actively in hostilities'. The original judgment of the majority focused on examining the roles undertaken by children and the risk of them being targeted, providing a test that can be used on a case-by-case basis. The feminist judgment moves beyond this approach, to more explicitly acknowledge the multiplicity of roles undertaken by children within armed groups and complexities of their experiences. Moreover, rather than focusing on the risk to children regarding their targeting by enemy forces, the feminist judgment includes the risks to children from the armed groups

[35] *Prosecutor v Jean-Pierre Bemba Gombo* (Judgment pursuant to Article 74 of the Statute) ICC-01/05-01/08 (21 March 2016).

[36] Brunger, above n 34.

themselves, which aligns with the dissenting opinion of Judge Odio Benito. The guiding principle of the feminist judgment was to more fully explore the varying experiences of children and the different forms of violence suffered.

Third, the feminist judgment foregrounds a gendered perspective in explicitly including the experiences of and harms suffered by girl child soldiers. While the original judgment includes some aspects of girl child soldiers' roles, namely domestic work, there remains a clear sense that the judgment reifies the experiences of boy child soldiers and does not sufficiently recognise the gendered nature of roles within the armed groups. Crucially, the feminist judgment illustrates how the offence can be interpreted in a gender-sensitive way to include experiences of sexual violence. Overall, the feminist judgment provides a more contextualised and gender-emphatic approach than the original, that enables recognition of the varying experiences of child soldiers and gendered nature of the violence suffered.

JUDGMENT

SITUATION IN DEMOCRATIC REPUBLIC OF THE CONGO IN THE CASE OF

THE PROSECUTOR v THOMAS LUBANGA DYILO

No: ICC-01/04-01/06

Trial Chamber I:

Judge Yassin M. Brunger (Presiding Judge), Judge Diana Sankey and Judge Emma Irving

14 March 2012

THE FACTS

1. On 12 January 2006, the Prosecutor applied for a sealed arrest warrant against Thomas Lubanga Dyilo, the former President and founding member of the *Union Patriotes Conglais* (UPC) and alleged leader of the *Forces Patriotiques pour la Liberation du Congo* (FPLC), the military wing of the UPC. Mr Lubanga Dyilo is charged with war crimes committed from 1 September 2002 to 13 August 2003 in the Ituri region of the Democratic Republic of Congo (DRC). Specifically, Mr Lubanga Dyilo is charged with the crimes of conscripting and enlisting child soldiers (children under the age of fifteen years) into the FPLC and using them to actively participate in hostilities in the DRC pursuant to Articles 8(2)(e)(vii) and 25(3)(a) of the Rome Statute.

APPLICABLE LAW

2. Articles 8(2)(b)(xxvi) and 8(2)(e)(vii) of the Rome Statute comprise three separate offences:

a. Conscripting children under the age of fifteen; or
b. Enlisting children under the age of fifteen; or
c. Using children to participate actively in hostilities.

3. This formulation of the crimes as alternates follows from the wording of the Articles themselves, namely their use of 'or'. Although it will generally be the case that more than one element is present, the commission of one element of the offence is not dependent on the commission of another. As such, the meaning of the terms 'conscripting', 'enlisting', and 'participate actively in hostilities' must be determined individually.

[Extract from judgment ...]

A. Conscription or enlistment of children under the age of fifteen

31. While neither the Rome Statute nor the Elements of Crimes document set out the meanings of conscription and enlistment, it is clear that they are both forms of recruitment, in that they refer to the incorporation of a child under the age of fifteen into an armed group. The Report of the Preparatory Committee to the Rome Statute only referred to '[r]ecruiting children under the age of fifteen years into armed forces', the Rome Statute instead articulated the separate crimes of conscription and enlistment. The Pre-Trial Chamber in the Confirmation of Charges Decision in this case set out the meanings of conscription and enlistment.[1] Following the distinction outlined in the Commentary to the Additional Protocols to the Geneva Conventions between forcible and voluntary recruitment, the Pre-Trial Chamber held that conscription constitutes 'forcible recruitment' and enlistment 'pertains to more voluntary recruitment'.[2] The Pre-Trial Chamber was also clear that both offences are 'continuous' in nature in that they continue to be committed throughout the period that the children remain with the armed group and are under the age of fifteen years.[3]

32. The Special Court for Sierra Leone (SCSL) has followed a similar approach. According to the Trial Chamber in the *AFRC* case, conscription 'encompasses acts of coercion, such as abductions and forced recruitment by an armed group against children, committed for the purpose of using them to participate actively in hostilities', while enlistment 'entails accepting and enrolling individuals when they volunteer to join an armed force or group'.[4] The Appeals Chamber of the SCSL has further emphasized that enlistment does not simply involve a formal process in relation to a conventional military force, but includes 'any conduct accepting the child as a part of the militia'.[5] The SCSL has therefore recognised that the contemporary context of recruitment extends beyond traditional understandings of state conscription or enlistment, which is a view that this Chamber endorses.

33. The distinction between conscription and enlistment therefore lies in whether the recruitment was forced/coerced or voluntary. The consent of a child to his or her recruitment does not provide an accused with a valid defence to the charge of enlistment, as was clearly set out by the Pre-Trial Chamber in this case.[6] The SCSL has also consistently denied any possibility of consent acting as a defence.[7] The crimes of conscription and enlistment together, as interpreted by the SCSL,

[1] ICC-01/04-01/06-803-tEN.

[2] ICC-01/04-01/06-803-tEN, para. 246.

[3] ICC-01/04-01/06-803-tEN, para. 248.

[4] *Prosecutor v Alex Tamba Brima, Brima Bazzy Kamara and Santigie Borbor Kanu* (Judgment) SCSL-04-16-T (20 June 2007) ('The AFRC Case') paras 734–35.

[5] *Prosecutor v Moinina Fofana and Allieu Kondewa* (Appeals Chamber, Judgment) SCSL-04-14-A (28 May 2008) ('CDF Appeal Judgment'), para. 144.

[6] ICC-01/04-01/06-803-tEN, para. 247.

[7] CDF Appeal Judgment, para. 140.

cover the recruitment of all children under the age of fifteen years into armed forces or groups, regardless of the method of recruitment or the consent of the child.

34. The applicability of conscription or enlistment is to be determined using a case-by-case approach, depending on the method of recruitment of the individual child and the surrounding circumstances. Where the recruitment appears to be voluntary and involves the consent of the child, the crime of enlistment would be applicable, whereas forcible and coercive forms of recruitment should be charged as conscription. As the United Nations (UN) Special Representative of the Secretary-General on Children and Armed Conflict has highlighted:

> The case-by-case determination of which kind of recruitment will be relevant in a particular case will require evidence that focuses on the acts children are required to perform, the circumstances on how the child was enrolled and the circumstances surrounding the child's separation from family and community.[8]

35. The evidence provided by the UN Special Representative provides significant insights into the broad coercive contexts that impact on children's recruitment into armed groups.[9] Her written submissions highlight that the reality of many children's recruitment into armed groups involve elements of both compulsion and voluntariness. Dr Elisabeth Schauer's expert evidence on the psychological impact of child soldiering also illustrates some of these coercive elements and the complex push and pull factors influencing child recruitment.[10]

36. The factors impacting on children's ability to make a voluntary choice include: children believing 'that they have to "stand up" against an enemy, who would otherwise kill them or hurt their loved ones'; parents enlisting children due to the 'powerful influence of militia leaders of their own ethnic group'; and children lacking adult care or being orphans and therefore struggling to survive in a context of 'social, emotional and economic hardship'.[11] Dr Schauer also highlighted that children may perceive enlisting into an armed group as a way of protecting themselves in a context of armed violence and that girls 'might think that joining an army might protect them from being raped or harmed' by other armed groups.[12]

37. The Chamber notes that the Trial Chamber in the *CDF* case found the distinction between forced and voluntary recruitment 'somewhat contrived' in the context of the violent conflict and 'of questionable merit'.[13] It is evident that elements of

[8] Written Submissions of the United Nations Special Representative of the Secretary-General on Children and Armed Conflict Submitted in application of Rule 103 of the Rules of Procedure and Evidence, ICC-01/04-01/06-1229-AnxA, para. 16.

[9] ibid, paras. 13–14.

[10] Report of Dr Schauer (CHM-0001), The Psychological Impact of Child Soldiering, ICC-01/04-01/06-1729-Anx1 (EVD-CHM-00001).

[11] ibid, p.7–8.

[12] Report of Dr Schauer (CHM-0001), The Psychological Impact of Child Soldiering, ICC-01/04-01/06-1729-Anx1 (EVD-CHM-00001), p.8–9.

[13] *Prosecutor v Moinina Fofana and Allieu Kondewa* (Judgment) SCSL-04-14-T (2 August 2007) ('The CDF Case'), para. 192.

coercion and abuse are often so pervasive in situations of armed conflict, that it may be unrealistic to present a clear-cut demarcation between enlistment and conscription. However, the separation of recruitment into two different modes of the offence under the Rome Statute was clearly intended to cover various modes of recruitment and to acknowledge some distinction between forced and more voluntary forms of recruitment. Importantly, the separate nature of these crimes enables the Court to acknowledge the context and complexity of children's recruitment, and the multiple ways that children can be exploited and harmed and become involved in an armed group.

38. While there are often evident constraints acting upon the agency of children, particularly of very young children, the Chamber is mindful of the dangers of completely denying any possibility of voluntariness on the part of any children in any conflict situations. Clearly, children under the age of fifteen are protected from joining armed groups under international law due to their vulnerability and continuing physical and psychological development. Children will have differing capacities and levels of psychological maturity to fully understand the consequences of their decisions or the implications of joining an armed group.[14] Nevertheless, it is important to acknowledge that international law also emphasises the importance of children's 'evolving capacities' in relation to their rights.[15] Although children cannot legally decide to join armed groups, nor should they be in any way held criminally responsible for their actions when they do, it is clear that many children, both boys and girls, do enlist, with varying degrees of consent. The Chamber emphasises that to completely deny any voluntariness in relation to the facts surrounding enlistment of children, particularly young adolescents, in all cases, would be to obscure the realities of child recruitment and hide the very issues and experiences that need to be tackled to prevent such crimes in the future.

39. Rather, the particular circumstances of the individual child should be examined on a case-by-case basis. Dr Schauer's evidence also suggests some criteria for establishing in specific cases whether recruitment was forced or voluntary: asking children 'what would have been a likely alternative to joining' and 'what, in the child's view is likely to have happened if they would not have joined the group'.[16] The Chamber is also informed by the work of anthropologists and legal scholars in characterising children as potentially circumscribed actors:

> A circumscribed actor has the ability to act, the ability not to act, and the ability to do other than what he or she actually had done. The effective range of these

[14] Report of Dr Schauer (CHM-0001), The Psychological Impact of Child Soldiering, ICC-01/04-01/06-1729-Anx1 (EVD-CHM-00001), 7–8.

[15] UN Committee on the Rights of the Child, 'General Comment No. 4: Adolescent health and development in the context of the Convention on the Rights of the Child' (2004) UN Doc HRI/Gen/1/Rev.9 (Vol II).

[16] Report of Dr Schauer (CHM-0001), The Psychological Impact of Child Soldiering, ICC-01/04-01/06-1729-Anx1 (EVD-CHM-00001), 9.

> abilities, however, is delimited, bounded, and confined [...] Circumscribed actors exercise some discretion in navigating and mediating the constraints around them.[17]

40. This approach emphasises circumscribed action as a *spectrum* or *continuum* along which children may be aligned according to their individual qualities and experiences, such as their age, development and circumstances.[18] The Chamber is satisfied that acknowledging children as potentially circumscribed actors on a case-by-case basis constitutes an appropriate and realistic application of the law. This is clearly not to say that all children, particularly young children, are capable of being characterised in this way, but merely that application of the crimes of conscription and enlistment needs to be determined according to the circumstances of the individual children and the level of coercion to which they were subjected. This interpretation allows the Chamber to consider the complex interrelationships of force, coercion and consent and to reflect the broader contexts underlying child recruitment. Importantly, it enables the different experiences of individual child soldiers, boys and girls, and the harms of recruitment of children to be carefully examined and exposed.

41. To conclude, conscription or enlistment were articulated as separate offences in the Rome Statute in order to acknowledge various forms of recruitment and the possibility of voluntary enlistment. These offences need to be carefully applied in order to acknowledge both the various abusive, exploitative and coercive factors that may be operating on children in situations of armed conflict and the possibilities of some degree of (often circumscribed) agency in relation to enlistment. The Chamber is satisfied that the correct application of the law requires careful examination of the particular circumstances in order to apply the distinction on a case-by-case basis.

B. Using children under the age of fifteen to participate actively in hostilities

42. Key to the crimes under Articles 8(2)(b)(xxvi) and 8(2)(e)(vii) of the Rome Statute is establishing the meaning of the term 'participate actively in hostilities'. Neither the Statute nor the Elements of Crimes documents provide guidance in this regard. However, there are a number of other international legal instruments that deal with child soldiers and which offer a starting point.

43. International humanitarian law and international human rights law both proscribe the use of child soldiers in hostilities. Under international humanitarian law the recruitment and use of child soldiers was first prohibited with the adoption of the 1977 Protocols Additional to the 1949 Geneva Conventions. Article 77(2) of Additional Protocol I requires that the parties to an international

[17] MA Drumbl, *Reimagining Child Soldiers in International Law and Policy* (Oxford, Oxford University Press, 2012) 17.

[18] ibid, 99.

armed conflict 'take all feasible measures in order that children who have not attained the age of fifteen years do not take a direct part in hostilities and, in particular, they shall refrain from recruiting them into their armed forces'. Under international human rights law, the 1989 Convention on the Rights of the Child, one of closest to universal ratification of the human rights treaties, prohibits the recruitment of persons under fifteen years of age into armed forces and explicitly obliges states to 'take all feasible measures to ensure that persons who have not attained the age of fifteen years do not take a direct part in hostilities'.[19]

44. The Chamber notes that the meaning of the term 'direct' in relation to the prohibition of the use of child soldiers is considered to have some equivalence to the term 'active' in the Rome Statute definition of the crime. Support for this view can be found in the ICRC Interpretative Guidance, which highlights that both terms are often used synonymously in international humanitarian law.[20] Further support can be derived from Common Article 3 of the 1949 Geneva Conventions which states that '[p]ersons taking no active part in the hostilities including members of armed forces who have laid down their arms and those placed "hors de combat" by sickness, wounds, detention, or any other cause, shall in all circumstances be treated humanely [...]'. The synonymous usage of these terms is particularly evident in the French versions of Common Article 3 and the Additional Protocols, where the term '*participent directement*' is used throughout.[21]

45. However, the Chamber considers that the formulation of 'participate actively' in the Rome Statute encompasses a broader range of conduct and usage of children than direct participation. The Report of the Preparatory Committee on the establishment of an International Criminal Court makes clear that the object and purpose of the offence in Articles 8(2)(b)(xxvi) and 8(2)(e)(vii) is to cover a broad range of uses to which children can be put in conflict. The Report sets out the acts that were intended to be covered by Article 8(2)(b)(xxvi) and 8(2)(e)(vii):

> The words "using" and "participate" have been adopted in order to cover both direct participation in combat and also active participation in military activities linked to combat such as scouting, spying, sabotage and the use of children as decoys, couriers or at military checkpoints.[22]

[19] Convention on the Rights of the Child, (adopted 20 November 1989, entered into force 2 September 1990) UNTS 1577. The 2000 Optional Protocol on the Involvement of Children in Armed Conflict raised the age limit for compulsory recruitment and direct participation from 15 to 18 years of age for armed forces, but did not reflect customary law at the time the ICC Statute was adopted and thus was not incorporated. Optional Protocol to the Convention on the Rights of the Child on the Involvement of Children in Armed Conflict, (adopted 25 May 2000, entered into force 12 February 2002).

[20] ICRC, *Interpretative Guidance on the notion of direct participation in hostilities under International Humanitarian Law*, (Geneva, 2009).

[21] ibid. p.43–44 and footnotes. ICC-01/04-01/06-T.207-Red2-ENG, p.18. and ICC-01/04-01/06-T-125-Red3-ENG, 66.

[22] 'Report of the Preparatory Committee on the establishment of an International Criminal Court' UN Diplomatic Conference of Plenipotentiaries on the Establishment of an International Criminal Court (Rome 15 June–17 July 1998) (14 April 1998) UN Doc. A/CONF.183/2/Add.1, p.21, footnote 12.

46. The Pre-Trial Chamber in its Confirmation of Charges Decision in the present case has followed this approach.[23] While noting the Closing Submissions of the Defence on this issue, the Chamber cannot agree with the claim that this interpretation is 'excessively broad'.[24] This Chamber is acutely aware of the potential risks of adopting a broad interpretation of active participation in terms of the possible impact on protections afforded to children under international humanitarian law. However, one of the objectives and purposes of the Rome Statute is a prohibitive message with respect to the recruitment and use of child soldiers, and as a response to the harms committed to children and by children during hostilities. This also seeks to prohibit practices that have a detrimental effect on the welfare of children during armed conflict. The intent of the drafters of the Rome Statute was clearly to ensure a broad criminalisation of the recruitment and use of child soldiers.[25]

47. While agreeing with the Pre-Trial Chamber that the scope of 'participate actively' is broader than direct combat roles, this Chamber has reservations regarding the Pre-Trial Chamber's approach to interpreting 'participate actively'. The Pre-Trial Chamber's approach is similar to the jurisprudence of the SCSL (whose Statute also makes reference to active participation in relation to child soldiers) in cataloguing the particular activities undertaken by children in the course of conflict in order to determine whether or not each activity constitutes active participation in hostilities.[26] Within this approach the type of activity is the sole determinant of whether the use of the child counts as 'actively participating'. An example of this 'activities' approach is the Trial Chamber Judgment of the SCSL in the *AFRC* case:

> carrying loads for the fighting faction, finding and/or acquiring food, ammunition or equipment, acting as decoys, carrying messages, making trails or finding routes, manning checkpoints or acting as human shields are some examples of active participation.[27]

48. This Chamber respectfully departs from this approach on the grounds that it is both unsuitable and unworkable. Determining the scope of 'participating actively' on the basis of the particular activity would be overly restrictive and would not reflect the realities of the use of children in armed conflict situations. This Chamber

[23] ICC-01/04-01/06-803-tEN, para. 261.

[24] ICC-01/04-01/06-2773-Red-tENG, para. 39.

[25] A broad understanding of active participation is also supported by both the Cape Town and the Paris Principles. Cape Town Principles and Best Practices on the Prevention of Recruitment of Children into the Armed Forces and Demobilization and Social Reintegration of Child Soldiers in Africa (30 April 1997); The Paris Principles and Guidelines on Children Associated with Armed Forces or Armed Groups, (February 2007).

[26] Statute of the Special Court of Sierra Leone (2002), UN Doc. S/2002/246, appendix II, Article 4(c).

[27] *Prosecutor v Alex Tamba Brima, Brima Bazzy Kamara and Santigie Borbor Kanu* (Judgment) SCSL-04-16-T (20 June 2007) ('The AFRC Case'), para. 737. See also the detailed analysis of what activities do and do not constitute active participation in hostilities in the RUF case. *Prosecutor v. Sesay, Kallon and Gbao* (Judgment) SCSL-04-15-T (2 March 2009) [1623] ('The RUF case'), paras. 1710–1748.

has heard evidence from the UN Special Representative of the Secretary-General on Children in Armed Conflict that this approach excludes a great number of child soldiers, in particular girls.[28] The Chamber is cognisant that usage of girl child soldiers may go unpunished and this category of victims unjustly denied recognition of the offences committed against them if the approach of the Pre-Trial Chamber is followed.

49. Instead of the 'activities' approach, this Chamber adopts an experience-led approach in order to determine the meaning of active participation in hostilities. The experience-led approach considers both the changeability of roles undertaken by children in hostilities and the external/internal sources of risks confronted by children in armed groups. Rather than being determined by the level of support provided to the armed group by a particular activity, this approach looks at the experience of the child as a whole in terms of the range of activities undertaken within the armed group and the risk of various forms of violence. This approach examines the overall experience of children, including the various roles undertaken within the armed group and the risks of violence and harm they are exposed to both from enemy forces and their 'own' armed group.

50. Children often play diverse and multiple roles in armed groups. These range from active fighting, to guard duty, to acting as cooks and sexual slaves. These roles are not fixed; children can act as a guard one moment, cook the next, or as an active combatant at other times.[29] As the UN Guidelines for the Demobilisation of Child Soldiers has emphasised, 'children, and girls in particular, perform numerous combat support and noncombat roles that are essential to the functioning of the armed force or group'.[30] This Chamber is mindful that when examining the experiences of child soldiers it is critical to recognise that those experiences are not gender-neutral. The nature and experience of being a child soldier, either as a girl or a boy, will inevitably vary in different situations of conflict, but more importantly, will also vary based on the gendered elements within the perpetration of child soldiering. To ensure consistent practice and fulfil the objective and purpose of the offence, it is necessary that the Chamber interprets this offence in a way that reflects such realities.

51. Taking an experience-led approach does not mean that 'participating actively' is determined simply by the activities conducted by a particular child at a particular time. Rather, this requirement is concerned with the level of risk that the child is exposed to over the course of the various activities they are required to undertake. The question of whether the child was placed in the situation where they were

[28] Written Submissions of the United Nations Special Representative of the Secretary-General on Children and Armed Conflict Submitted in application of Rule 103 of the Rules of Procedure and Evidence, ICC-01/04-01/06-1229-AnxA, para. 24.

[29] ibid, para. 22.

[30] United Nations, Operational Guide to the Integrated Disarmament, Demobilization, and Reintegration Standards, para 5.30, 218 (1 August 2006), available at www.unddr.org/iddrs/iddrs_jguide.php, 230; Report of the Secretary-General 'Disarmament, demobilization and reintegration' (2006) UN Doc A/60/705.

at risk of violence is therefore crucial in determining whether they were used to 'participate actively in hostilities'. Alongside the recruitment offence, the crime of using children to 'participate actively in hostilities' seeks to criminalise conduct that places children at risk of harm in armed conflict situations, beyond simply the risks of combat roles. The use of children in hostilities is prohibited by international law, not merely because children are at risk of being targeted by enemy forces, but due to the manifold harms that children may experience as a direct result of their use within armed groups. Children associated with armed groups are placed at particular risks of violence and are vulnerable to harm in ways that differ from the treatment of other populations. The notion of 'violence' is to be understood broadly in relation to the harms caused by child soldiering. As highlighted by the Paris Principles, the 'recruitment and use of children violates their rights and causes them physical, developmental, emotional, mental, and spiritual harm.'[31]

52. In determining whether children were used to 'participate actively', the Chamber recognises both external risks of violence, i.e. the placing of children in situations where they are at risk of targeting by the enemy, and internal risks of violence, i.e. from violence perpetrated by the armed group in which they are being used. The external risks relate not simply to direct participation in fighting, since children not in direct combat roles may still be at considerable risk of being targeted by enemy forces. The internal risks also constitute a central feature of the reality of children's experiences within armed groups. The environment within an armed group can be particularly dangerous for children.

53. The Chamber is acutely aware of the importance of acknowledging and recognising the perpetration of sexual violence against children in armed conflict. The UN Special Representative of the Secretary-General on Children in Armed Conflict has stressed that 'during war, the use of girl children in particular includes sexual violence'.[32] Dr Schauer's Report also highlights that 'girl's participation is central to sustaining a force because of their productive and reproductive labour'.[33] The inclusion of the use of children for sexual purposes within the meaning of 'participate actively' is consistent with the approach of the Cape Town Principles, which included 'girls recruited for sexual purposes and forced marriage' in its definition of child soldiers, and with the subsequent approach of the Paris Principles.[34]

[31] The Paris Principles and Guidelines on Children Associated with Armed Forces or Armed Groups, (February 2007), para. 1.0.

[32] Written Submissions of the United Nations Special Representative of the Secretary-General on Children and Armed Conflict Submitted in application of Rule 103 of the Rules of Procedure and Evidence, ICC-01/04-01/06-1229-AnxA, para. 25.

[33] Report of Dr Schauer (CHM-0001), The Psychological Impact of Child Soldiering, ICC-01/04-01/06-1729-Anx1 (EVD-CHM-00001), 27–28.

[34] Cape Town Principles and Best Practices on the Prevention of Recruitment of Children into the Armed Forces and Demobilization and Social Reintegration of Child Soldiers in Africa (30 April 1997); The Paris Principles and Guidelines on Children Associated with Armed Forces or Armed Groups, (February 2007), para. 2.1.

54. The Chamber also notes the Closing Submissions of the Legal Representative of Victims a/0047/06, a/0048/06, a/0050/06 and a/0052/06 on this issue and recognizes that susceptibility of children to sexual exploitation and forced marriage is a crucial internal risk experienced by children in their membership of an armed group.[35] By acknowledging this internal risk to children, it is critical to emphasise that sexual violence is not a 'natural' or inevitable feature of armed conflict. Rather, children, particularly girls, are at risk of sexual violence due to the militarised violence and gender discrimination often inherent within armed groups. As the Paris Principles acknowledge, '[g]ender inequalities, discrimination and violence are frequently exacerbated in times of armed conflict.'[36] The evidence from the UN Special Representative further highlighted 'the multiple roles of these girls and the need to protect them in every context'.[37]

55. In conclusion, in deciding whether or not a particular child was used to 'participate actively' this Chamber adopts an experiential approach that considers children's particular experiences of the internal and external risks posed during their period of involvement within an armed group. This Chamber is of the view that such an approach would more readily capture the multiple roles of children in order to assess the totality of the child's experience and the overall conduct of the armed group in relation to that child.

LEGAL FINDINGS

A. The conscription or enlistment of children between September 2002 and 13 August 2003

56. As established, the crimes of conscription or enlistment involve the recruitment of children under the age of fifteen years, either through forcible or coercive means, or on a more voluntary basis. This section of the judgment will summarise the evidence on the recruitment of children under fifteen in relation to the applicable law and conclude with the overall findings. While the Chamber has confirmed that conscription and enlistment constitute separate offences, it deals with these crimes together in this section in order to examine in depth the complex relationships between force, coercion and consent in the Ituri region.

57. The reasons why armed groups may wish to recruit children, including young children, are complex and multiple, and are dependent on the circumstances in a particular case. However, the Chamber has heard expert evidence from Dr Schauer outlining some of the factors that may influence the willingness of armed groups to recruit children.[38] In particular, her evidence highlighted how children may constitute a readily available population for armed groups to use and

[35] ICC-01/04-01/06-2744-Red-tENG, paras.10–11.

[36] The Paris Principles and Guidelines on Children Associated with Armed Forces or Armed Groups, (February 2007), para. 6.0.

[37] ICC-01/04-01/06-T-223-ENG, 14.

[38] Report of Dr Schauer (CHM-0001), The Psychological Impact of Child Soldiering, ICC-01/04-01/06-1729-Anx1 (EVD-CHM-00001), p.6–7.

exploit, particularly in the context of mass displacement. She also highlights that children, due to their level of maturity, may be more easily indoctrinated by leaders of armed groups and are cheaper to train and arm.[39] It is clear from the totality of the evidence presented that many of those factors played out in the recruitment of children under fifteen by the UPC/FPLC.[40]

58. The UN Special Representative has highlighted that there 'is not one objective when a child is recruited'.[41] Rather, children are often recruited for multiple purposes and to play multiple roles. For girls, in particular, part of the purpose of their recruitment may be sexual, but they may also be recruited in order to perform various roles, including combat or body-guard roles.[42] While girls were often recruited by the UPC/FPLC for similar purposes to boys, the Chamber is aware that there were gendered dynamics in the processes and purposes of recruitment. The evidence presented to the Chamber clearly indicates that the UPC/FPLC recruited girls to play multiple roles in the armed group, but that girls were often also recruited for the purposes of sexual slavery or to be used for other forms of sexual abuse.[43] As such, the experiences of girls and boys of the processes and outcomes of conscription or enlistment may have been different, but, equally, all children will have had varying experiences that depend on their own circumstances. One of the roles of this Court is to acknowledge and to make findings about the divergent experiences of individual children, while prosecuting a crime that has been perpetrated against a collective group. While it is patently outside the scope of the ICC to investigate and prosecute on behalf of individual victims, we recognise that we prosecute on behalf of many thousands of child victims, survivors and their families, and that they each suffered individual harm, from which they now seek to move forwards.

59. The Chamber has heard evidence that the UPC/FPLC used various methods to recruit children.[44] There have been some horrific stories presented of forcible recruitment and abduction of children into the UPC/FPLC. While noting the concerns of the Defence regarding the reliability of certain of these witnesses, the Chamber is satisfied that forcible abductions constituted a feature of child recruitment into the UPC/FPLC, employed against both boys and girls.[45] Evidence has been presented of the deliberate targeting of children through abductions at and around schools, as well as in other places, such as markets.[46] The Chamber also notes the closing submissions of the Legal Representative of Victims a/0047/06, a/0048/06, a/0050/06 and a/0052/06 regarding evidence of abductions of victims and their forcible recruitment into the UPC/FPLC.[47]

[39] ibid; ICC-01/04-01/06-T-223-ENG, p.11, line 19 to p.12.
[40] See, for example, ICC-01/04-01/06-T-113-Red2-ENG, p.36.
[41] ICC-01/04-01/06-T-223-ENG, p. 30.
[42] ibid.
[43] ICC-01/04-01/06-2744-Red-tENG, para. 51.
[44] ICC-01/04-01/06-2748-Red, para. 170.
[45] ICC-01/04-01/06-2773-Red-tENG, para.757–760. ICC-01/04-01/06-2748-Red, para. 171.
[46] ICC-01/04-01/06-T-207-Red2-ENG, 18.
[47] ICC-01/04-01/06-2744-Red-tENG, paras. 34–37.

60. The contribution of witness and victim statements show that children were coerced and exploited in multiple ways.[48] Evidence has been presented of the active use of recruitment drives and mobilisation campaigns by the UPC/FPLC to recruit children. Such recruitment processes involved varying degrees of coercion and force. In some circumstances families and communities were directly pressured and coerced into handing over their children to UPC/FPLC. Witness P-0041 testified that families were sometimes under an obligation to send one of their boys to enlist in the UPC, or face possible fines.[49] In some circumstances, boys may have been at greater risk than girls of being sent to an armed group by their families, due to traditional gendered roles and perceptions of masculinity, but families may also have sent girls. Due to the level of coercion in such circumstances, it is clear that there may have been little or no consent from the child or family, and that such methods constitute conscription.

61. Other methods of coercion were also used, such as propaganda drives and instilling in children and their families' perceptions of the need to protect the community through joining the group.[50] The UPC/FPLC used emissaries to persuade families to enlist their children, or the children themselves to enlist. The Chamber has heard evidence from witness P-0055 that village elders along with senior UPC officials persuaded the population to enlist children and young people in order to protect their ethnic group.[51] Given the circumstances of the conflict in the region, particularly the ethnic elements, the social pressure to enlist from family and peers may have been particularly strong.[52] In such situations, children under the age of fifteen may be more easily manipulated, particularly by adults, due to their level of maturity and respect for the opinions of elders and family members.[53] Children and their families were therefore often under considerable pressure, although much depends on the nature of the propaganda and coercion used in the individual circumstances that results in children joining armed groups. This Chamber is mindful of the complexities inherent in the relationship between the presence of coercive circumstances and consent that leads to the enlistment of boys and girls in armed groups.

62. The recruitment of children also included more subtle forms of coercion through the exploitation of underlying social, economic and psychological factors to encourage enlistment. The UN Special Representative has highlighted, based on her visit to the DRC, that:

> [t]he recruitment and enlisting of children in DRC is not always based on abduction and the brute use of force. It also takes place in the context of

[48] ICC-01/04-01/06-T.207-Red2-ENG, 18.
[49] ICC-01/04-01/06-T-125-Red3-ENG, 66.
[50] ICC-01/04-01/06-T-113- Red2-ENG, 39.
[51] ICC-01/04-01/06-T-174-Red3-ENG, p.32; ICC-01/04-01/06-T-175-Red3-ENG, 58.
[52] ICC-01/04-01/06-T-223-ENG, 24.
[53] ICC-01/04-01/06-T-223-ENG, 12–13.

poverty, ethnic rivalry and ideological motivation. Many children, especially orphans, join armed groups for survival to put food in their stomachs.[54]

63. Poverty, mass displacement and loss of family members and communal structures were important in shaping the contexts surrounding child recruitment in the region. Lack of basic resources and loss of family and care structures made children particularly vulnerable to recruitment drives. The Chamber has heard evidence that recruitment drives specifically targeted children who had lost family members or whose communities had been attacked during the fighting. While such recruitment has elements of voluntary action, the Chamber also notes the elements of coercion involved which undoubtedly shaped the choices of the children. The factors above highlight the difficult choices facing children and the limited options that were often available to them. The evidence presented by the UN Special Representative highlights that the line between voluntary and forced recruitment can be difficult to draw in such circumstances.[55] The Chamber finds that such circumstances of indirect coercion by the UPC/FPLC fall more easily within the crime of enlistment than the crime of conscription. However, the Chamber notes the limited choices available to such children and the limitations on voluntary action, such that a careful assessment is required to apply the distinction on a case-by-case basis.

64. In addition to the push factors of poverty and loss of family members, the UPC/FPLC were also able to provide pull factors to induce children to join the armed group. In particular, the UPC/FPLC were able to capitalise on the coercive circumstances faced by children, offering the attractions of being a member of an armed group and access to resources, weapons and the protection of a militarised group.[56] The UN Special Representative in her oral evidence highlighted that children may perceive militia leaders as 'glamorous role models', particularly in the absence, due to the conflict, of other male role models.[57] In the difficult circumstances that many children faced, joining the UPC/FPLC may therefore have appeared to be the best – or only real – option available to them. In such circumstances, children may be seen as circumscribed actors, in that there was some degree of agency involved, but also that their choices and options were often limited. However, this also depends on the maturity and development of the individual child and their overall experience and circumstances.

[54] Written Submissions of the United Nations Special Representative of the Secretary-General on Children and Armed Conflict Submitted in application of Rule 103 of the Rules of Procedure and Evidence, ICC-01/04-01/06-1229-AnxA, para. 13.

[55] Written Submissions of the United Nations Special Representative of the Secretary-General on Children and Armed Conflict Submitted in application of Rule 103 of the Rules of Procedure and Evidence, ICC-01/04-01/06-1229-AnxA, para. 14.

[56] ICC-01/04-01/06-T-223-ENG, 22.

[57] ICC-01/04-01/06-T-223-ENG, 22.

65. The Chamber emphasises the harms suffered by children who were conscripted or enlisted into the UPC/FPLC and forced to serve with the armed group. The forcible or coercive nature of some of the recruitment not only meant that the children had no choice as to their future, but that they were deprived of whatever remnants of a normal life they may have had, such as schooling and growing up with their families or communities. As we have established, conscription and enlistment do not simply occur at the moment of recruitment, but continue throughout the period that the child is with the armed group or until they have reached the age of fifteen. The Chamber therefore notes that the harms of conscription were on-going, with the child continuing to experience the suffering of separation from families and communities, the harsh realities of living and serving with an armed group and the possibilities of threats to life and physical integrity if they attempted to escape.

66. Children who enlisted or were enlisted by their families were often not aware or not fully aware of the nature of the experiences and harms they would face.[58] This raises concerns with regard to consent, and questions around informed consent, not only in terms of capacity to consent but also in terms of awareness of the activities being consented to. The Chamber notes that regardless of whether there were elements of voluntariness in the enlistment, once recruited children were often subject to the same forms of harm as those who had been forcibly taken into the group. The level of consent therefore may have been subject to change over time, depending on the nature of their circumstances or experiences. In some circumstances, children may have effectively withdrawn their initial consent once the reality of their circumstances became evident. Children who enlisted, or were enlisted by family members, were not free to decide to leave once they had joined the group, and were subject to the same threats and punishments if they tried to leave.[59]

67. The distinction between conscription and enlistment should not therefore suggest a hierarchy of harms, although the nature of the harms as a whole will be considered at the sentencing stage. Rather, this distinction exists in order to recognise the contexts and multiple methods of recruitment and to broadly criminalise all forms of recruitment of children.

68. In light of the range of evidence presented, the Chamber concludes that the UPC/FPLC used various methods to recruit children under the age of fifteen, and that varying degrees of force, coercion and consent were present. The Chamber finds that both conscription and enlistment were perpetrated by the UPC/FPLC in the Ituri region. While the dividing line between conscription and enlistment has been difficult to draw in this context, some distinction can and has been made, which illustrates the complexity of children's experiences of recruitment.

[58] Report of Dr Schauer (CHM-0001), The Psychological Impact of Child Soldiering, ICC-01/04-01/06-1729-Anx1 (EVD-CHM-00001, 7–8.

[59] ICC-01/04-01/06-T-207-Red2-ENG p.20; ICC-01/04-01/06-T-113- Red2-ENG, 68–69.

B. The use of children to participate actively in hostilities

i) Multiple roles of children in armed groups

69. As outlined above, the Chamber has determined that an interpretation of the 'use of child soldiers to participate actively in hostilities' requires an experience-led approach, which considers both the changeability of roles undertaken by children in hostilities and as manifested by external and internal risks confronted by children. By employing this approach, the Chamber will therefore embrace a broader interpretation of 'active participation' than the Pre-Trial Chamber. This develops the jurisprudence of the SCSL in the *CDF*[60] and *AFRC* cases.[61] In particular, it develops SCSL jurisprudence drawing from the interpretation note of the ICC draft Statute by the ICC Preparatory Committee. The note sets out that 'use' does not necessitate that the acts put children's lives directly at risk during frontline combat, but also includes labour or support that gives effect to or helps maintain operations in a conflict.[62]

70. The Chamber has heard evidence of the diverse and multiple roles that children in the UPC/FPLC undertook including active fighting, guard duty, domestic roles and acting as sexual slaves. The UN Special Representative of the Secretary General on Children and Armed Conflict testified that children were used for roles such as cooks, porters, nurses, translators and for sexual exploitation, which were considered essential support for the armed group.[63] Some of these roles involved considerable risk to the safety of the child, either from the enemy on the frontline or from their treatment within the armed group itself.

71. Despite some common experiences between girls and boys, there are also gender-based differences in the experiences of child soldiers. Evidence has been presented to this Chamber that the use of child soldiers by the UPC/FPLC was not gender-neutral. As such, it is important that the particular experiences of girls and boys in the armed group are acknowledged in the interpretation of the offence. The Paris Principles highlight that the situation for girls can be very different in relation to: the reasons and manner in which they join the armed forces or armed groups; the potential for their release; the effects that the experience of being in the armed force or armed group has on their physical, social and emotional

[60] *Prosecutor v Moinina Fofana and Allieu Kondewa* (Judgment) SCSL-04-14-T (2 August 2007) ('The CDF Case').

[61] *Prosecutor v Alex Tamba Brima, Brima Bazzy Kamara and Santigie Borbor Kanu* (Judgment) SCSL-04-16-T (20 June 2007) ('The AFRC Case').

[62] The CDF Case, para. 193 and The AFRC Case, para. 736. See also 'Report of the Preparatory Committee on the establishment of an International Criminal Court' UN Diplomatic Conference of Plenipotentiaries on the Establishment of an International Criminal Court (Rome 15 June–17 July 1998) (14 April 1998) UN Doc. A/CONF.183/2/Add.1, p.21, footnote 12.

[63] Written Submissions of the United Nations Special Representative of the Secretary-General on Children and Armed Conflict Submitted in application of Rule 103 of the Rules of Procedure and Evidence, ICC-01/04-01/06-1229-AnxA, paras. 17–26.

well-being; and the consequences this may have for their ability to successfully adapt to civilian life or reintegrate into family and community life after their release.[64]

72. Evidence has been presented to the Chamber that girl child soldiers routinely fulfilled domestic roles for commanders, such as cooking and cleaning, as well as sexual roles, in addition to acting as bodyguards or fulfilling combat roles.[65] Witness P-0017 stated that girl child soldiers were usually assigned household tasks and Witness P-0016 also provided evidence that a number of very young girls were tasked with cooking at the camp at Mandro.[66] Witness P-0016 testified that the UPC/FPLC trainers and guards in the Mandro training centre raped the girl recruits, whom he said were of 'all ages'.[67]

73. This Chamber also heard evidence that 'the condition the girls were in was worse than the condition the boys were in very often'.[68] Witness P-0038 testified that girls undertook cooking twice a day in addition to the other tasks that all children undertook. Witness P-0046 described the situation of girls in the following terms: '[a]part from the fact that they would often participate in all the activities that the boys participated in, they also had to cook, prepare food for the officers. They had to spend the night with them. So, the situation the girls was in was a lot more worrying. It was terrible'.[69] This is in line with the expert witness testimony of Dr Schauer, who highlighted the multiple roles of girls in armed groups, but also the particular gendered roles they fulfil.[70]

74. This Chamber has determined that sexual violence can be included within the legal definition of what it means to 'participate actively in hostilities' as a manifestation of the internal risks posed to children. Sexual violence constituted one of the central features of the violence of the conflict in the DRC, including in the Ituri region, and was widely perpetrated against child soldiers. While sexual violence may constitute an aspect of more general inhumane treatment of children by the UPC/FPLC, this Chamber emphasizes the importance of separate legal recognition of the particular nature and harms of sexual violence.

75. The harms of sexual violence are distinct from other forms of violence and have particular implications for victims, such as possible stigmatisation and social exclusion. As such, harms of sexual violence cannot be fully encompassed or subsumed within other offences. It is particularly important that separate

[64] The Paris Principles and Guidelines on Children Associated with Armed Forces or Armed Groups, (February 2007), para 4.0.

[65] ICC-01/04-01/06-T-178-Red3-ENG, p.77–78; ICC-01/04-01/06-T-160-Red3-ENG, p.60; ICC-01/04-01/06-T-207-Red2-ENG, p. 21.

[66] ICC-01/04-01/06-T-189-Red2-ENG.

[67] ICC-01/04-01/06-T-191-Red2-ENG CT, 15, lines 13, 15 -16; ICC-01/04-01/06-T-189-Red-ENG, 26, line 8 to 28, line 12.

[68] ICC-01/04-01/06-T-207-Red2-ENG, 21, lines 12–13.

[69] ICC-01/04-01/06-T-207-Red2-ENG, 21, lines 13–17.

[70] ICC-01/04-01/06-T-166-ENG, 95–6.

charges of sexual violence are brought before international courts, where sufficient evidence is found. Separate charges ensure the recognition of the experiences of sexual violence and the condemnation of its perpetration. It is therefore regrettable that separate charges were not brought in this case, as this has potentially limited the range of evidence presented and meant the experiences of victims of sexual violence has not been fully heard. However, despite this failure, this Chamber has already determined that sexual violence could be included within the legal definition of 'participate actively in hostilities' as a manifestation of the internal risks posed to children.

76. The Chamber has heard substantial evidence of the widespread and systematic perpetration of rape and other forms of sexual violence against child soldiers, particularly of girls, by adult UPC/FPLC commanders.[71] All but a few girls suffered sexual abuse in the camps of the armed group. Witness P-0046 stated, '[t]he sexual abuse perpetrated against young girls was quite prevalent'.[72] This witness also spoke of the sexual abuse as 'systematic conduct', and described how '[t]he girls had to systematically spend the night in a separate area, and they were forced to spend the night with the officers'.[73] Various forms of sexual violence were employed within the UPC/FPLC, including rape, sexual slavery, forced marriage, forcible impregnation and other forms of sexual assault. Children, particularly girls, were often used as sexual slaves or 'wives' for commanders. Witness P-0038 testified to the use of girls for sexual services for the commanders.[74] In this way, sexual violence was a key feature of the use of children during hostilities, particularly girls, by the UPC/FPLC. It has been made clear to this Chamber that providing sexual services was a central function of the labour provided by girls and was crucial to the functioning of the UPC/FPLC.[75]

77. Some of the girls used for sexual purposes who fell pregnant were given abortions, sometimes on multiple occasions. Witness P-0046 testified that some girls had abortions, while others miscarried due to the harsh living conditions.[76] Others who became pregnant were thrown out of or felt rejected by the armed group.[77] When they tried to return to their families, they were often stigmatised and excluded, particularly if they had had a child as a result of the sexual abuse.[78] It is important to acknowledge the damage that this causes to the young girls' health and lives and eventually to the lives of their own children. Indeed, the harm inflicted on young girls can in turn affect a new generation, especially when they are cast out of both their families and the armed group, leaving them with no

[71] ICC-01/04-01/06-T-207-Red2-ENG, 30–31, 35–39.
[72] ICC-01/04-01/06-T-207-Red2-ENG, 30, lines 16–17.
[73] ICC-01/04-01/06-T-207-Red2-ENG, 31, lines 6–7.
[74] ICC-01/04-01/06-T-114-Red3-ENG, 23.
[75] Report of Dr Schauer (CHM-0001), The Psychological Impact of Child Soldiering, ICC-01/04-01/06-1729-Anx1 (EVD-CHM-00001), 28.
[76] ICC-01/04-01/06-T-207-Red2-ENG, 37.
[77] ICC-01/04-01/06-T-207-Red2-ENG, 37.
[78] ICC-01/04-01/06-T-207-Red2-ENG, 39.

support. The physical and psychological impact of this on these girls has been described as 'catastrophic'.[79]

78. The Chamber is also cognisant of the potential long-term impact of sexual violence on child soldiers, and indeed on wider society in the DRC. The Chamber is particularly concerned about the impact of the widespread use of sexual violence within the UPC/FPLC in terms of the normalisation of sexual violence. Children undoubtedly learn about sex and relationships through their own experiences and the experiences of those around them. The widespread use of girls, in particular, by older commanders in the UPC/FPLC for sexual slavery has a potential wider impact on the experience of all child soldiers in terms of their perception of the norms of sex and relationships and how girls and women can and should be treated.

ii) The overall impact of the conditions and treatment on child soldiers.

79. The Chamber has heard disturbing evidence of the widespread and systematic exploitation and abuse of children under the age of fifteen by the UPC/FPLC. The facts outlined above have illustrated the horrific conditions often endured by child soldiers and the multiple manifestations of abuse and harm they experienced. In particular, the Chamber notes the extensive physical, sexual and psychological harms suffered by many of the children recruited and/or used by the UPC/FPLC. The Chamber is particularly concerned about the possible long-term impacts of these harms on the children involved.

80. The evidence of Witnesses P-0014, P-0016, and P-0017 demonstrates that children endured inhumane treatment and brutal punishments perpetrated at the UPC/FPLC camps. Children were subject to harsh training conditions and were threatened if they tried to leave the group.[80] The militarised culture of the UPC/FPLC perpetuated aggressive and violent behaviour towards child soldiers. The Chamber accepts the closing submissions of the V01 group of victims, which highlighted evidence that 'the conditions in the camps were closer to those found in a concentration camp than in a barracks, and were completely unacceptable for children'.[81]

81. Violence from the armed group had clear physical and psychological effects on the children and their development.[82] Evidence from Witness P-0046 stated that:

> [t]hey would have to get up very early. They wouldn't be given food. They'd have to do physical exercises throughout the day without a break. Some said

[79] ICC-01/04-01/06-T-207-Red2-ENG, 31, line 18.

[80] Witness P-195 testified that if children ran away and were then caught they would be whipped and return back to the training centre, ICC-01/04-01/06-T-195-Red2-ENG, 39. There was further evidence from the Witness P-207 ICC-01/04-01/06-T-207-Red2-ENG, 20–21.

[81] ICC-01/04-01/06-2746-Red-tENG, para 64.

[82] ICC-01/04-01/06-T-207-Red2-ENG, 25.

> that they were forced to go and fetch food outside the camp. In villages inhabited by the civilian population. They had to go there so that they could obtain food […] The children told us about the daily living conditions. They said they couldn't sleep. Sometimes they couldn't have clothes. They weren't authorised to return to their families.[83]

82. This Chambers accepts the evidence from Witness P-0017, that recruits also did not have access to medical or sanitary facilities to maintain personal health or hygiene and this exacerbated the overall poor health of the child recruits.[84] This Chamber also heard evidence from Witnesses P-0017 and P-0041 and the Victims represented by the V01 legal team of the widespread consumption of cannabis amongst children as a means of giving them courage. The Chamber is persuaded that the persistent lack of food, medical or sanitary facilities, combined with the use of cannabis would have cumulatively created an environment that was detrimental to the physical and psychological welfare of the children recruited.

83. The Chamber found compelling the evidence from Witness P-0046 in respect of the psychological state of the children when they testified that:

> the younger ones were quite lost. The looked lost and they had been traumatised by the experience, in particular those who had lost members of their family, who had been victims before they were associated with armed groups. They had seen displacement. They had seen massacres. They had personal stories which were just not easy.[85]

84. The long-term effects of enduring physical, psychological and sexual trauma for children who have now reached adulthood are likely to linger for a life-time, particularly where there are minimal or non-existent after-care, rehabilitative or therapeutic services available in post-conflict society.

85. It is clear to this Chamber that the life in the UPC/FPLC in which the children lived not only isolated and ostracised them from their community and family members but also, and most significantly, made them reliant on their membership of the UPC/FPLC for continued survival. The UPC/FPLC were able to capitalise on the coercive circumstances faced by children, and offer the benefits of membership of an armed group in order to access resources, weapons and obtain the protection of a militarised group. The realities of the training camps for children that were either recruited voluntarily or forcibly were extremely damaging. The Chamber also observes that the regime in UPC/FPLC training camps would undoubtedly reflect the multiple ways in which children would then be used to participate actively in hostilities.

86. The Chamber would like to acknowledge the particular contribution of former child soldiers as victims and witnesses in this case. Their contribution illustrates

[83] ICC-01/04-01/06-T-207-Red2-ENG, 20–21.
[84] ICC-01/04-01/06-T-158-Red2-ENG, 23.
[85] ICC-01/04-01/06-T-207-Red2-ENG, 26, lines 1–5.

both the devastating harms experienced, as well as their resilience and ability to cope and survive in the most difficult of situations. This Chamber also wishes to emphasise the resilience of children in general and the need to balance understanding of the harms caused by the conscription, enlistment and use of children in hostilities with recognition of the ability of children to survive and to contribute to rebuilding their societies in the longer-term. The Chamber therefore highlights the importance of long-term measures, beyond the scope and role of this Court, to address the needs of child soldiers and promote societal reconciliation in the DRC.

OVERALL CONCLUSIONS

A. Conscription and enlistment in the UPC/FPLC

87. The Chamber finds that the UPC/FPLC conducted extensive recruitment directly targeting children and young people, including those under the age of fifteen, between 1 September 2002 and 13 August 2003. While the distinction between forcible and 'voluntary' recruitment has been difficult to draw in this case, the evidence has illustrated the various methods employed by the UPC/FPLC to recruit children and the varying experiences of the children it recruited. The evidence clearly establishes that the UPC/FPLC abused, coerced and exploited children in multiple ways in its recruitment strategies.

88. In addition to abducting children, the UPC/FPLC drew directly on the power and control it held over local communities in its mobilisation campaigns and applied considerable pressure to children and their families. The Chamber has also heard evidence of the subtle forms of coercion and exploitation utilised by the UPC/FPLC to encourage children to enlist, in circumstances where they may have had few other options open to them. The evidence has demonstrated the considerable harms experienced by children recruited by the UPC/FPLC, often regardless of the method of their recruitment. These harms were evident not only in recruitment but in the subsequent experiences of children serving within the ranks of the UPC/FPLC.

89. The Chamber is therefore satisfied beyond reasonable doubt that both conscription and enlistment were perpetrated by the UPC/FPLC between 1 September 2002 and 13 August 2003.

B. The use of children under fifteen to participate actively in hostilities

90. The Chamber finds that the UPC/FPLC used children under the age of fifteen to participate actively in hostilities between 1 September 2002 and 13 August 2003. The evidence has clearly established the use by the UPC/FPLC of children under the age of fifteen in a range of different roles, including active fighting, guard duty, domestic roles and acting as sexual slaves. The evidence has shown that children often had multiple roles and were subject to various risks of violence, both from enemy forces and from the armed group itself.

91. The evidence of various witnesses has shown the horrific treatment of children under the age of fifteen used by the UPC/FPLC to participate actively in hostilities and the inhumane conditions they experienced. Children were subject to extensive physical, sexual and psychological harms, many of which will have long lasting effects. The evidence has established that children were at risk of sexual violence and that many girls were used as sexual slaves or were subject to forced marriage.

92. The Chamber is therefore satisfied beyond reasonable doubt that the UPC/FPLC conscripted and enlisted children under the age of fifteen and used them to participate actively in hostilities between 1 September 2002 and 13 August 2003.

Reflections

The process and experience of re-writing the first judgment of the ICC from a feminist perspective was a challenging task that brings about a wide range of reflections.[1] The central question that anchored our mission was whether the *Lubanga* judgment advanced goals that align with feminist agendas and, if so, how this advancement can be sustained. A collaborative project such as the one at hand presents the challenge of dividing tasks among the authors/judges while asking individuals to take responsibility for the entire text and calls for constant scrutiny of whether the right balance has been struck. Imagining the strategy employed by international judges, with an array of staff employed to assist, research and produce the lengthy judgment, was not something we could reproduce. However, multiple conversations were had, and several drafts were circulated amongst the group, with discussions following, to facilitate insight into the deeper questions about the narrative that is being developed by our judgment and the wider implications of it.

A critical element of feminist approaches is to make visible gendered harms and label such harms accordingly.[2] In the *Lubanga* case, that lost opportunity is evident in the original Trial Chamber judgment at the ICC and thereby reflected in the re-written feminist judgment. The proceedings saw significant amounts of evidence related to sexual crimes; however, neither these crimes nor the specific types of victimisation inflicted on children were represented in the judicial narrative of the ICC. As trial judges, we were not allowed to revisit the charges, hence the need to work with whatever charges were brought by the Prosecution. In the case of *Lubanga*, this restriction was certainly great as there were no specific charges of sexual violence to be considered by our Chamber. Instead, we were limited to assessing crimes concerning child soldiers, rather than including related crimes that captured further victimisation suffered by both boys and girls. For example, had separate charges been brought for sexual slavery and exploitation, there may have been more scope to explore how sexual violence and sex crimes involve specific forms of coercion in the context of conflict. A separate charge for sexual offences would also have provided an opportunity to undertake a gendered analysis of the age-factor in the experience young children and adolescents. Whether age is an aggravating feature, and how the experiences of young girls and boys differ (or perhaps do not differ), from those of adolescent girls and boys was a lost opportunity for in-depth legal consideration. Another outstanding issue,

[1] See E Rackley, 'The Art and Craft of Writing Judgments: Notes on the Feminist Judgments Project' in R Hunter, C McGlynn and E Rackley (eds), *The Feminist Judgments: From Theory to Practice* (Oxford, Hart Publishing, 2010).

[2] See F Ní Aoláin, 'Rethinking the Concept of Harm and Legal Categorizations of Sexual Violence During War' (2000) 1 *Theoretical Inquiries in Law* 307; D Sankey, 'Recognition of Gendered Experiences of Harm at the Extraordinary Chambers in the Courts of Cambodia: The Promise and the Pitfalls' (2016) 24 *Feminist Legal Studies*, 7; D Buss, 'Performing Legal Order: Some Feminist Thoughts on International Criminal Law' (2011) 11(3) *International Criminal Law Review* 409.

resulting from the limited charges, was to problematise the question of consent in the context of sexual violence in conflict.

While the process of formulating sexual and gender-based harms within the confines of litigation can be problematic from feminist perspectives, particularly regarding how harms may be framed and shaped through law, legal recognition is important to contest the silencing of gendered experiences.[3] It is perhaps of some consolation that in the reparative work of the ICC the particular gendered needs of victims may be met when they fail to receive adequate attention from the Prosecution (in the framing of the charges) or the Majority of the Chamber (in its judgment in respect of the accused). However, this approach renders invisible both the range and complexity of gendered harms and it instead presents a hierarchy of victimisation; those that are recognised within the substantive offence, and those that are only deemed relevant as aggravating factors at the sentencing or reparations stages.

Nonetheless, our Chamber found much of interest in the dissenting judgment of Judge Odio Benito. In Judge Odio Benito's view, whether the Majority embraced the wider definition of the crime or whether the prosecution amended the charges is less relevant than the legal acknowledgement of these harms, many of which she notes are less visible than overt forms of harm affecting children who are forced or coerced to be 'soldiers':

> the Majority of the Chamber is making a critical aspect of the crime 'invisible'. Invisibility of sexual violence in the legal concept leads to discrimination against the victims of enlistment, conscription and use who systematically suffer from this crime as an intrinsic part of the involvement with the armed group.[4]

The acceptance of the range of 'multiple and different risks' of harm including 'ill treatment, sexual violence and forced marriage' or servitude could have resulted in a non-discriminatory analysis of harm towards predominantly girl victims of atrocity crime in this context.[5] Judge Odio Benito relies on the overarching 'object and purpose' of the Rome Statute, and her recognition of the potential for gendered discrimination towards child victims is entirely persuasive. She expertly articulates that the primary purpose in respect of the charges in Lubanga are 'to protect the life and personal integrity of children under the age of 15'.[6] The failure of the majority to include all manifestations of harm in the legal definition of the crime, instead leaving it open to a case-by-case approach, was considered a retrograde rather than progressive step by Judge Odio Benito.

[3] Hilary Charlesworth and Christine Chinkin have exhaustively discussed the many silences of international law, see H Charlesworth and C Chinkin, *The Boundaries of International Law: A Feminist Analysis* (Manchester, Manchester University Press, 2000).

[4] *Prosecutor v Thomas Lubanga Dyilo* (Judgment pursuant to Article 74 of the Statute) ICC-01/04-01/06 (14 March 2012) ('Lubanga Trial Chamber Judgment'). Dissenting Opinion, Judge Odio Benito, para 16.

[5] ibid, Dissenting Opinion, Judge Odio Benito, para 6.

[6] ibid, Dissenting Opinion, Judge Odio Benito, para 7.

Judge Odio Benito additionally questioned the legal validity of removing the victim status of individuals during the trial due to their failure to provide evidence to sufficiently determine the criminal liability of the accused. Regarding several child victims, she asserts that there is clear evidence (including corroborated evidence) that the victims were enlisted, but perhaps not in the way they testified. She further claims that they were predominantly still children when they first met with the Office of the Prosecutor. Regarding Witness P-0010 who experienced harm in the form of sexual violence, amongst other harms, she states that 'this life experience of a young woman has to be taken into account'.[7] Importantly, Judge Odio Benito articulates the effects of post-traumatic stress disorder on memory, intellectual and cognitive functioning, as well as the passing of time since the harms and the events experienced (ranging between two to eight years). She warns that 'with such elapses of time it would be suspicious if the accounts would remain perfectly alike and unchanged'.[8] There is an implication here that the children's statements were genuine and real (albeit inconsistent) recollections, rather than rehearsed stories of fictitious harm.[9] There may be an argument that the ICC system placed an impossible standard of proof upon traumatised child victims and this went against the balance of fairness afforded to their meaningful participation. A recurring concern for feminist scholars is that criminal processes should avoid further re-traumatisation to the victims who are central to its operation. One of the historical narratives that will be synonymous with the *Lubanga* judgment is the plight of child soldiers, yet the historical record must also show how the ICC fell short and silenced the experiences of girl child soldiers in the conflict.

Considering the above, the importance of adding context through feminist approaches throughout our judgment was evident.[10] This was to be instrumental in a better transition between the substantive criminal law issues and the experiences of children in conflict. Similarly, the re-writing of the judgment compelled the authors to establish and follow a clear line of argumentation. Defining what the authors considered feminist priorities was a critical step. This opened a set of questions that formed an integral part of our discussions, precisely what do 'we' understand by feminism and how can we use feminist approaches in this context while acknowledging the diversity and plurality of feminism itself? How far shall we go in our judgment? Questions of masculinity were also included in our debates.

[7] ibid, Dissenting Opinion, Judge Odio Benito, para 27.

[8] ibid, Dissenting Opinion, Judge Odio Benito, para 32.

[9] The effects of post-traumatic stress disorder were recognised by the International Criminal Tribunal for the former Yugoslavia in *Prosecutor v Dragoljub Kunarac, Radomir Kovac and Zoran Vukovic* (Judgment) IT-96-23&IT-96-23/1-T (22 February 2001) [679] and *Prosecutor v Dragoljub Kunarac, Radomir Kovac and Zoran Vukovic* (Judgment) IT-96-23&IT-96-23/1-A (12 June 2002) [324].

[10] C Dolan, 'Into the Mainstream: Addressing Sexual Violence Against Men and Boys in Conflict', Briefing Paper prepared for the workshop held at the Overseas Development Institute, *Refugee Law Clinic* (May 2014) 1; S Mouthaan, 'Sexual Violence against Men and International Law – Criminalising the Unmentionable' (2013) 13 *International Criminal Law Review* 665; D Couturier, 'The Rape of Men: Eschewing Myths of Sexual Violence in War' (2012) 6(2) *On Politics* 1; S Sivakumaran, 'Sexual Violence Against Men in Armed Conflict' (2007) 18(2) *European Journal of International Law* 253.

In the context of child soldiers, we did not want to override the acknowledgement given to experiences of boy child soldiers in the judgment, but were also cognizant of the norms of masculinity and hyper-masculinity perpetuated by that judgment. This was an approach that distinguishes our judgment from that of the Dissenting Opinion of Judge Odio Benito. We were keen to contest the stereotypical vision that boys are solely designated to combat roles that fall within the definition of the crime, whereas girls serve in non-combat roles outside of the definition or are only protected within the context of specific sexual violence charges. Furthermore, we wished to avoid the discourse that categorises men/boys as active perpetrators and women/girls as passive victims, for that would be devoid of reality and not true to the experiences of children as seen in the transcripts of the judgment.[11]

A significant contribution of our feminist judgment was to collapse the essentialist approach to experiences of child soldiers in the DRC, as the original Trial Chamber judgment often does. The authors were keen that the voices of victims/survivors themselves, particularly former child soldiers, should be able to be heard and reflected in the feminist judgment. However, the issues of victim/witness reliability raised in the original judgment posed a considerable dilemma regarding the use of former child soldier testimony. While the authors had clear reservations over the treatment of issues of witness reliability, in this case, we had not heard the original evidence or the arguments of the various parties on this matter, and therefore lacked the insights afforded to the Trial Chamber. As such, the only credible option was not to rely on any testimony that the original judgment had felt to be unreliable. Inevitability, this has impacted on the nature of our re-written judgment, as it has not been able to foreground the voices and lived experiences of victims/survivors in the way we had hoped. Our judgment relies in large part on the testimony of various experts and other witnesses, as well as the submissions of victims' legal representatives. Despite the undoubted value of such testimony and the important role of victims' legal representatives, we are mindful of the dangers that expert testimony and legal representation processes pose in translating victim/survivor experiences and shaping how such experiences are presented and understood.

While the re-written judgment was not able to centre the testimony of victims/survivors, we did seek to open the complexity and variety of children's experiences. In our treatment of the crimes of conscription and enlistment, we were keen to avoid negating all possibilities of children exercising any agency in any circumstances, and thus of perpetuating images of child soldiers purely as passive victims. Instead, we wished to engage with the complex issues of consent and agency operating in the case and the range of methods employed to recruit children, in a way the original Trial Chamber failed to. While consent and agency are key themes within feminist discourse, applying these to children under the age

[11] K Engle, 'Feminism and its (Dis)contents: Criminalizing Wartime Rape in Bosnia and Herzegovina' (2005) 99 *American Journal of International Law* 778.

of 15 in the context of conflict obviously requires care and sensitivity. Mindful of the significant coercive and exploitative factors operating in children's lives during the conflict, the authors sought to reflect the complex interrelationships between consent and coercion and the varying experiences of child soldiers.

Reflecting on our experiences as authors/judges, perhaps the question is not so much about the effectiveness of feminist theories and methods to transcend international law's biases, but rather the willingness to attract the attention of key stakeholders to consider the feminist agenda as an asset to the international justice agenda. This re-written judgment seeks to contribute to the conversation between feminism and international justice that needs to be increasingly amplified. Feminism is not just about asking the 'woman/girl question', but rather unveiling the way in which patriarchal constructions of gender elevate a dominant narrative that silences and neglects the lives of the some of the most marginalised within the international community. For the authors, it has been a challenging and enriching experience and reaffirmed their efforts to concretise feminist approaches to the operation of international law in conflicted societies.

International Criminal Tribunal for the Former Yugoslavia

16

Prosecutor v Radovan Karadžić

CELESTINE GREENWOOD

Author's Note

Introduction

On 24 March 2016, the International Criminal Tribunal for the former Yugoslavia (ICTY) passed judgment on Radovan Karadžić – former psychiatrist, poet, political leader and alleged perpetrator of atrocities amounting to genocide, crimes against humanity and war crimes. Karadžić had been the political leader and supreme military commander of the Bosnian Serbs during the Bosnian War which endured from 6 April 1992 until 14 December 1995 and claimed the lives of an estimated 100,000 people, 80 per cent of whom were Bosnian Muslims.[1] The war pitted the three major ethno-religious groups in the territory of Bosnia Herzegovina against each other, Croats (largely Roman Catholic), Serbs (mostly Orthodox Christian) and Bosnian Muslims. The ICTY convicted Karadžić of the genocide committed in Srebenica in July 1995, as well as nine other offences of crimes against humanity and violations of the laws or customs of war.[2] He was sentenced to a total of 40 years' imprisonment.[3] However, the Tribunal acquitted him of genocide in the seven named 'Municipalities'[4] of Bosnia Herzegovina during the period from the end of March to the end of December 1992,[5] finding that the requisite genocidal intent had not been proved.[6] The re-written feminist judgment, in the form of partly dissenting separate opinion, will demonstrate that Karadžić could and should have been found guilty with respect to the Count One charge of genocide. The original Tribunal's assessment of intent was flawed, and the evidence clearly

[1] United States Holocaust Memorial Museum, 'Bosnia-Herzegovina', www.ushmm.org/confront-genocide/cases/bosnia-herzegovina.

[2] *Prosecutor v Karadžić* (Prosecution's Marked-Up Indictment) ICTY-95-5/18-PT, (19 October 2009).

[3] *Prosecutor v Karadžić* (Judgment) ICTY-95-5/18-T (24 March 2016).

[4] The seven named Municipalities: Bratunac, Foča, Ključ, Prijedor, Sanski Most, Vlasenica and Zvornik.

[5] Count One of the Indictment: above n 2.

[6] Above n 3, para 2605.

supported a finding of genocidal intent. Had the ICTY both applied a feminist legal methodology, such as that espoused by Katherine Bartlett,[7] to its assessment of the evidence, and considered both the 'communicative value' and the 'pattern' evidence of sexual violence[8] in the case it would have found Karadžić guilty of this alleged offence.

Relevant Background and Facts

In the early 1990s, the world watched appalled as the nation state of Yugoslavia collapsed – fractured into various, mostly ethnically constituent, parts – and then descended into the chaos and bloodshed of war. One of those constituent parts was the territory of Bosnia Herzegovina. Radovan Karadžić was the political leader of the largely Serbian political party, the Serbian Democratic Party (SDS). On 9 January 1992, Karadžić declared an area of Bosnia Herzegovina, later called Republika Srpska (RS), to be an independent state for the Bosnian Serbs. By April 1992, Bosnia Herzegovina had descended into an internal conflict which endured until December 1995. On 6 August 1992, British journalists shared pictures of Bosnian Muslim and Croat men held by their former neighbours, Bosnian Serbs, in detention camps in the municipality of Prijedor,[9] inevitably raising the spectre of genocide.[10]

The phrase 'ethnic cleansing' soon entered into common use to describe the unfolding tales of atrocities, which included harrowing tales of systematic and mass rape.[11] In May 1993, the UN Security Council passed Resolution 827 (1993)

[7] KT Bartlett, 'Feminist Legal Methods' (1990) 103/4 *Harvard Law Review* 829.

[8] S SáCouto, 'Advances and Missed Opportunities In The International Prosecution Of Gender-Based Crimes' (2007) 15 *Michigan State Journal of International Law* 137.

[9] Having received authority from Radovan Karadžić, ITN journalists, Ian Williams and Penny Marshall and their film crew, together with Ed Vulliamy, journalist with The Observer newspaper, visited the Omarska, Trnopolje and Prijedor detention camps. Extended footage recorded by ITN and subsequently entered into evidence before the ICTY in various trials can be accessed at: www.youtube.com/watch?v=w6-ZDvwPxk8.

[10] The term 'genocide' was coined by international criminal law scholar R Lemkin, *Axis Rule in Occupied Europe: Laws of Occupation, Analysis of Government, Proposals for Redress* (Washington, Carnegie Endowment for World Peace, 1944). As a legal norm, it came to life in 1948 when the United Nations General Assembly (UNGA) adopted the Convention on the Prevention and Punishment of the Crime of Genocide. The Convention definition of genocide is repeated in the Rome Statute of the International Criminal Court at Art 6. Pursuant to this definition, genocide is the destruction (by various acts, including killing), in whole or in part, of a national, ethnical, racial or religious group. The crime of genocide did not exist as an international legal norm at the time of World War II and the alleged war criminals of the European Axis Powers were not prosecuted for this offence.

[11] On 25 August 1992, the United Nations General Assembly issued Resolution 46/242 addressing 'The situation in Bosnia and Herzegovina' in which it referred to the practice of "ethnic cleansing". See UNGA Res 46/242 (25 August 1992) UN Doc. Subsequently, on 18 December 1992, the UN General Assembly stated (a) that the Special Rapporteur of the Commission on Human Rights had reported on the situation in the Former Yugoslavia on 6 November 1992 and noted that 'ethnic cleansing' did not appear to be the consequence of war, but rather its goal, and (b) that 'ethnic cleansing' is a form of genocide, UNGA Res 47/121 (18 December 1992) UN Doc A/RES/47/121.

establishing 'an international tribunal for the sole purpose of prosecuting persons responsible for serious violations of international humanitarian law committed in the territory of the former Yugoslavia between 1 January 1991 and a date to be determined by the Security Council upon the restoration of peace …'[12] By July 1995, some five months before the war ended, the ICTY was already served by an operational 'Office of the Prosecutor', which filed an indictment charging Radovan Karadžić, the political leader of RS, together with Ratko Mladić, the military commander of its forces, with numerous offences, including genocide.[13]

At the conclusion of the war, both men went into hiding. Radovan Karadžić was eventually arrested some 13 years later in July 2008 in the Serbian capital, Belgrade.[14] He was immediately transported to the ICTY and – in the absence of Mladić, who was then still 'on the run'[15] – proceedings against him commenced. Karadžić's trial, which concluded on 24 March 2016 when verdicts were announced, lasted over seven years and occupied 499 trial days.[16]

Legal Context

The trial of Radovan Karadžić was the penultimate case to be heard by the ICTY, which had been conducting hearings since May 1996.[17] It is fitting, given the position that he held at the top of the political and military pyramid in RS, that Karadžić's trial represents the apex of the work of the ICTY. Although others lower down the chains of military command have been convicted of the genocide committed at Srebenica,[18] his is the only conviction of a recognised political leader

[12] UNSC Res 827 (25 May 1993), UN Doc S/RES/827.

[13] *Prosecutor v Karadžić and Mladić* (Indictment) ICTY-95-5-I, (24 July 1995). The indictment contained 16 specific counts, including one count of genocide (Count One) relating to the treatment of persons held in several named detention camps. An allegation of genocide relating to the killings at Srebrenica was not made in this July indictment.

[14] For contemporaneous news coverage of his arrest on 18 July see, for example, J Borger, 'Radovan Karadžić, Europe's Most Wanted Man, Arrested For War Crimes' *The Guardian* (London, 22 July 2008) and H de Quetteville, A Todorovic and S Adams, 'Radovan Karadžić Was Disguised As Doctor' *The Telegraph* (London, 22 July 2008).

[15] Ratko Mladić was arrested in a village in northern Serbia on 26 May 2011. He was subsequently transferred to The Hague and subject to trial under indictment number in respect of two counts of genocide, five counts of crimes against humanity, and four counts of violations of the laws or customs of war. Judgment was pronounced on 22 November 2017. He was convicted of 10 offences, including genocide at Srebrenica, but he was also acquitted of the alleged genocide in the Municipalities: *Prosecutor v Mladić* (Judgment) ICTY-09-92-T (22 November 2017). His case is now the subject of appeal proceedings.

[16] *Prosecutor v Karadžić* (Case Information Sheet) ICTY-95-5/18.

[17] The Court was established in 1993 pursuant to UN Security Council Resolution 827, above n 12. See also www.icty.org.

[18] For example, Radovan Krstić who was a Major General in the VRS, the Army of the Republika Srpska, and Commander of the Drina Corps, *Prosecutor v Krstić* (Judgment) ICTY-98-33-T (2 August 2001); and Dragan Obrenović who held the rank of Major at the time of the Srebrenica genocide, *Prosecutor v Obrenović* (Sentencing Judgment) ICTY-02-60/2-S (10 December 2003).

for that offence in the Balkans.[19] Indeed, he was prosecuted in his role as supreme political and military leader; he was found to be individually responsible for the crimes committed by Bosnian Serb forces; and he was also prosecuted for his role in 'joint criminal enterprises' with other political and military leaders, including Slobodan Milosevic, Biljana Plavšić and Ratko Mladić.[20]

Ultimately, the Tribunal acquitted him of genocide in the Municipalities (Count One of the indictment). Although the Tribunal found that members of 'protected groups' had been killed and subjected to serious bodily or mental harm, thereby satisfying the actus reus of the offence of genocide in two respects, the Tribunal did not find sufficient evidence to infer that those acts were carried out with the intention to destroy the groups in question.[21] In the Tribunal's judgment, an intention to commit genocide was not the only reasonable inference to be drawn. Instead, the evidence was 'consistent with the Bosnian Serb objective of ethnic separation and the forceful creation of an ethnically homogenous state.'[22] That is, the intention might have been to separate and displace Muslims rather than to commit genocide. That decision, and the sentence, are currently the subject of cross appeals.

Responses to the Original Judgment and its Consequences

Radovan Karadžić remains a highly divisive character and his trial controversial. His acquittal for genocide in the Municipalities, for some,[23] means that the systematic and mass killing, torture and sexual violence that ravaged those areas have not been adequately recognised, and remains unpunished, despite the fact that he was convicted of several counts of crimes against humanity based upon these same atrocities and convicted in relation to the genocide in Srebrenica.

Pending the decision of the Appeals Tribunal, his conviction is part of the closing chapter of the ICTY; part of a record of justice that at times has lived up to global expectations of fairness, transparency and appropriate punishment, while at other times, has fallen short. The Tribunal failed to hear and acknowledge the voices of women subjected to sexual violence, failed to thereby convict Karadžić on Count One (genocide), and then failed to mark the enormity of these offences

[19] Slobodan Milošević, the President of the Republic of Serbia, was charged, inter alia, with genocide in Bosnia Herzegovina. He died on 11 March 2006, and on 14 March 2006 the ICTY formally terminated proceedings against him: *Prosecutor v Milošević* (Case Information Sheet) ICTY-02-54.

[20] These individuals are three of the 11 persons with whom it was alleged Karadžić acted in concert as part of a criminal enterprise. For the full list, see Para 11 of the Third Amended Indictment: *Prosecutor v Karadžić* (Prosecution's Marked-Up Indictment) ICTY-95-5/18-PT (19 October 2009).

[21] above n 3, para 2626.

[22] above n 20, para 2605.

[23] The critical and disappointed reaction of Bosniak war victims has been recorded in various newspaper articles, interviews and websites. See, for example, D Dzidic, 'Karadžić Verdict: Mixed Reactions Reflect Divided Bosnia' (24 March 2016), www.balkaninsight.com/en/article/Karadžić-verdict-mixed-reactions-reflect-divided-society-03-24-2016.

by a sentence of life imprisonment. The prosecution of Radovan Karadžić was always going to be controversial, politically charged and capable of demonstrating that the law can sometimes be a blunt and unwieldy tool satisfying none of the parties involved.

The law can, however, fulfil three roles which are especially significant in the context of conflict-based crimes, roles that Phelps has referred to as the 'symbolic and communicative function.'[24] Firstly, the law can allow voices to be heard and stories to be told by recording and acknowledging the stories of those who have been violated. Secondly, it can acknowledge those wrongs by labelling them accurately. Indeed, both law and society rely on language and the labels that are created as the framework for their existence. Some words, such as 'rape', become loaded with social meaning and significance; acknowledging and labelling the crime can thus be the most important outcomes for victims.[25,26] Thirdly, the law has the power, and duty, to punish those who have committed crimes, to send a message to the individual offender and to wider society. In these ways, 'the trials themselves and the pronouncements of the tribunals also serve to symbolize and communicate powerful messages about women and about sexual violence.'[27]

In its assessment of Count One, the Tribunal completely failed in its duty to acknowledge the voices of those who were subjected to sexual violence. The ICTY failed to recognise how rape and other forms of sexual violence were used as a weapon of war and more specifically, as a means of committing genocide in Bosnia Herzegovina. Consequently, the ICTY also failed to label accurately the wrongs suffered by many, mostly women and girls. Disappointingly, it continued the practice common to other tribunals of ignoring offences committed against women during conflict and thus squandered a valuable opportunity to build upon the seminal finding in the International Criminal Tribunal for Rwanda case of *Akayesu*,[28] namely that offences of rape can constitute genocide. The *Akayesu*[29] decision represented a breakthrough in what feminist writers such as Copelon[30] have termed the 'surfacing', or bringing into the light, of the suffering of women,

[24] TG Phelps, 'The Symbolic and Communicative Function of International Criminal Tribunals' in MA Fineman and E Zinsstag (eds), *Feminist Perspectives on Transitional Justice, From International and Criminal to Alternative Forms of Justice* (Cambridge, Intersentia Publishing Limited, 2013).

[25] In the experience of the writer who practised as a barrister in the jurisdiction of England and Wales for 20 years primarily in cases of violence and child abuse, acknowledging what occurred can be a seminal and cathartic experience for the 'victim' (often one which leads the way to being a 'survivor' of sexual or other violence).

[26] Nowrojee recorded that women in Rwanda wanted public acknowledgement of the crimes that were committed against them: 'They want the record to show that they were subjected to horrific sexual violence …' (B Nowrojee, *Your Justice is Too Slow: Will the ICTR Fail Rwanda's Rape Victims?*, Occasional Papers 10 (Geneva, United Nations Research Institute for Social Development, 2005) 4).

[27] Above n 24.

[28] *Prosecutor v Akayesu* (Judgment) ICTR-96-4-T (2 September 1998).

[29] ibid.

[30] R Copelon, 'Surfacing Gender: Re-Engraving Crimes Against Women in Humanitarian Law' (1994) 5 *Hastings Women's Law Review* 243.

experiences previously unacknowledged by the law. The ICTY failed to build upon *Akayesu*.[31] It also missed a valuable opportunity to highlight the intersectionality of genocidal rape.

Further, the ICTY also failed in its duty to properly sentence offenders. By not sentencing Karadžić to life imprisonment, the tribunal communicated a message that denigrated, or at the very least, failed adequately to acknowledge, the suffering of the victims. To say that 40 years in prison amounts in practical terms to a life sentence for a man of his age misses the communicative role and impact of sentencing. Moreover, the ICTY damaged its credibility by sentencing Karadžić, the political leader and supreme military commander, to a lesser sentence than others convicted of the genocide at Srebenica.[32] The subsequent imposition of a life sentence on Ratko Mladić served to exacerbate that anomaly.[33]

This case was an opportunity for the law and the international criminal justice system to show its ability to deliver justice in the face of significant challenges: an enormous factual matrix, a complex legal framework and a politically charged environment. It was also an opportunity for the tribunal to build upon the work already done to 'surface gender.'[34] As Phelps notes, 'the international tribunals do not do "justice work" in a vacuum – they respond to and in turn affect the culture.'[35] It was an opportunity to air and bring to light the cultural norms and values that give sexual violence its communicative and symbolic value. The failure to convict Karadžić of genocide for the atrocities committed in the Municipalities amounts to a failure to hear the suffering of women, to acknowledge and punish rape as an act of genocide. In these respects, the case of Radovan Karadžić was something of a missed opportunity.

Aims and Contributions of the Feminist Judgment

This feminist judgment aims, by applying a feminist legal methodology and by using some of the legal analyses advanced by feminist legal scholars, such as 'communicative value'[36] and 'pattern evidence'[37] of sexual violence, to correct the failures identified above. The judgment will apply the feminist legal methodology formulated by Bartlett, specifically: 'asking the woman question'; adopting feminist

[31] Above n 28.

[32] Both Vujadin Popović and Zdravko Tolimir were convicted of genocide at Srebrenica and both were sentenced to life imprisonment. Their convictions and sentences were both subsequently upheld on appeal: *Prosecutor v Popović et al* (Appeal Judgment) ICTY-05-88-A (30 January 2015); *Prosecutor v Tolimir* (Appeal Judgment) ICTY-05-88/2-A (8 April 2015).

[33] *Prosecutor v Mladić* (Judgment) ICTY-09-92-T (22 November 2017).

[34] Above n 30.

[35] TG Phelps, 'Feminist Legal Theory in the Context of International Conflict' (2009) 39 *University of Baltimore Law Forum* 173, 176.

[36] F Ní Aoláin, 'Sex-Based Violence and the Holocaust – A Reevaluation of Harms and Rights in International Law' (2000) 12 *Yale Journal of Law and Feminism* 1. See also above n 24.

[37] Above n 8.

practical reasoning (otherwise referred to as 'story telling'); and through 'consciousness raising'. Bartlett also postulates 'positionality', which Weisberg describes as recognising that 'truth is partial and provisional' and that in response we need to seek and examine other perspectives.[38] In other words, the judgment will seek to do three things: 1) ask the woman question (put the woman at the centre of the story and tell the story from her perspective); 2) include women in the process; and 3) challenge gender bias in legal doctrine and judicial reasoning.

In contrast to the original judgment, this dissenting judgment, written by an individual feminist judge, will use the techniques of asking the woman question, telling women's stories and exploring background context to achieve a richer and more complete picture of the issues before the court. Coupled with a willingness to see and understand both the significance of pattern evidence of sexual violence and its deeply communicative purpose and impact, this judgment clearly finds evidence of genocidal intent and thus convicts Radovan Karadžić of genocide in the Municipalities.

[38] DK Weisberg, *Feminist Legal Theory: Foundations* (Philadelphia PA, Temple University Press, 1993) 534.

JUDGMENT

PROSECUTOR v RADOVAN KARADŽIĆ

Case No. IT-95-5/18-T

Judgment of the International Tribunal for the Prosecution of Persons Responsible for Serious Violations of International Humanitarian Law Committed in the Territory of the former Yugoslavia since 1991

Partly Dissenting Opinion of Judge Celestine Greenwood

24 March 2016

1. I shall start this opinion by setting out my findings. I will then proceed to elucidate each of these findings.

FINDINGS

2. I am satisfied so that I am sure beyond reasonable doubt that:

(i) Genocide of the Bosnian Muslims was perpetrated by their neighbours, the Bosnian Serbs. This genocide was not limited to the genocide of the Bosnian Muslims at Srebrenica in July 1995.

(ii) The Bosnian Muslim groups of Bratunac, Foča, Ključ, Prijedor, Sanski Most, Vlasenica and Zvornik were also the victims of genocide. These genocides were executed during the period from the end of March 1992 to the end of December 1992.

(iii) Genocide of the Bosnian Croat groups of Bratunac, Foča, Ključ, Prijedor, Sanski Most, Vlasenica and Zvornik was also perpetrated by their neighbours, the Bosnian Serbs. These genocides were also executed during the period from the end of March 1992 to the end of December 1992.

And that:

(iv) Radovan Karadžić was the architect and orchestrator of these genocides. He led his people, the Bosnian Serbs, in this orgy of extermination, depravity and cruelty, having, at all material times, the intention to destroy these groups in whole or in part.

3. Accordingly, I disagree with the Majority in relation to Count One of the Indictment concerning the alleged genocide in the Municipalities of Bosnia Herzegovina between 31 March and 21 December 1992. Instead, I would convict Radovan Karadžić of this offence.

4. Further, I disagree with the Majority as to the appropriate sentence for Radovan Karadžić. Instead, I would impose a sentence of life imprisonment. In my judgement, the overwhelming nature and scale of the offences of which the Majority has convicted him are such that only a sentence of life imprisonment can be countenanced. At the apex of our sentencing powers this Tribunal may impose sentences of life imprisonment. Such sentences should, of course, be reserved for only the most serious cases. In my judgement, the case of Radovan Karadžić is such a case. He has been convicted of offences that cover the whole range of criminal offending committed by Bosnian Serb forces throughout the duration of the war. As the supreme political and military leader, the orchestrator of these crimes, it is appropriate that he be sentenced to the maximum penalty. Moreover, this Tribunal has hitherto imposed life sentences on Zdravko Tolimir for his part in the genocide at Srebenica, on Milomir Stakić for his part in the crimes against humanity committed in the Municipality of Prijedor in the period 30 April to 20 September 1992 and, on Stanislav Galić for his part in the siege of Sarajevo. Given Radovan Karadžić's role in these crimes as supreme commander with overall responsibility, it is only fitting that he too be sentenced to life imprisonment. Further, taking his offences cumulatively, a life sentence is both justified and reasonable. Indeed, the nature and scale of the offences, whether taken separately or together, demand the most serious penalty.
5. Having set out the key points of my opinion, it is now appropriate to set out my findings in some detail, starting with a consideration of the law on genocide.

OBSERVATIONS ON THE LEGAL REQUIREMENTS FOR PROVING GENOCIDE

6. I respectfully adopt the exposition of the law relating to the offence of genocide set out in the Majority decision at paragraphs 537 to 555 inclusive. However, I think it helpful to consider one or two additional matters before moving on to discuss background and contextual matters that I consider to be relevant in the determination of this charge of genocide.
7. The offence of genocide is set out in Article 4 (2) of the Updated Statute of the International Criminal Tribunal for the Former Yugoslavia:[1]

> Genocide means any of the following acts committed with intent to destroy, in whole or in part, a national, ethnical, racial or religious group, as such:
>
> (a) killing members of the group;
> (b) causing serious bodily or mental harm to members of the group;
> (c) deliberately inflicting on the group conditions of life calculated to bring about its physical destruction in whole or in part;

[1] UNSC Res 1877 Updated Statute of the International Criminal Tribunal for the Former Yugoslavia (as amended 7 July 2009) UN Doc S/RES/1877f.

(d) imposing measures intended to prevent births within the group;
(e) forcibly transferring children of the group to another group.

8. In other words, before a finding of genocide can be proved, the Tribunal must be sure beyond reasonable doubt that members of a national, ethnical, racial or religious group, 'the protected group', were subjected to one or more of the five enumerated acts and that those acts were committed with an 'intent to destroy' that group in whole or in part.

9. I note that the International Criminal Tribunal for Rwanda (ICTR) in the landmark case of the *Prosecutor v Akayesu*[2] interpreted 'destroy' as equating to ruining someone emotionally or spiritually. In my judgement, this interpretation has particular resonance in cases of allegations of rape tried at the international tribunal level. The ICTR found that 'sexual violence was a step in the process of destruction of the Tutsi group – destruction of the spirit, of the will to live, and of life itself',[3] and that 'rapes resulted in the physical and psychological destruction of the Tutsi women, their families and other communities'.[4] In my judgement, this precedent is relevant and applicable when considering the Prosecution case that genocide was committed in the Municipalities by the causing of serious bodily or mental harm to members of the group (Article 4(2)(b)) and, when considering 'other culpable acts.'

1. *Interpretation of 'in whole or in part'*

10. It is now settled jurisprudence that any 'part' must amount to a substantial or significant part of the group and enough to have an impact on the group as a whole.[5] In respect of Count One, the Tribunal is entitled to consider whether the Muslim and/or Croat communities of each of the separate Municipalities was destroyed in whole or in part and, whether the mens rea in respect of each was present. Indeed, this Tribunal has previously endorsed such an approach in the

[2] *Akayesu* Trial Judgment, paras. 505 and 731.
[3] ibid, para. 732.
[4] ibid, para. 731.
[5] *Karadžić* Trial Judgment, para. 555. Earlier decisions of this Tribunal establishing this principle start with Jelisić, in which the Trial Chamber noted that, 'given the goal of the Genocide Convention to deal with mass crimes, it is widely acknowledged that the intention to destroy must target at least a substantial part of the group.' *Jelisić* Trial Judgment, para. 82.
The *Jelisić* Trial Judgment was reversed in part by the Appeals Chamber on other grounds: see *Jelisić* Appeal Judgment, para. 72. The Trial Chamber's definition of what constitutes an appropriate part of the group protected by the Genocide Convention was not challenged. The same conclusion was reached by the *Sikirica* Trial Chamber: 'This part of the definition calls for evidence of an intention to destroy a substantial number relative to the total population of the group': *Sikirica* Judgment on Defence Motions to Acquit, para. 65. Finally, in *Krstić*, the Appeals Chamber, when considering a finding of genocide in Srebrenica, endorsed a case-by-case approach, which means examining a number of factors such as the numeric size of the targeted part of the group, not only in absolute terms, but also in relation to the overall size of the entire group, the prominence of the targeted group within the overall group, and whether the targeted group is emblematic of the overall group, or is essential to its survival: *Krstić* Appeal Chamber, paras. 8–17.

cases of Prosecutor versus *Jelisić*,[6] *Krstić*,[7] and *Sikirica*[8] respectively. In this case, we have considered the genocide of a particular geographic group of Muslims within the territory of Bosnia Herzegovina, namely the Bosnian Muslims of Srebrenica; in my judgement, this approach is entirely in keeping with the case law of this Tribunal. It follows that this Tribunal should examine what happened in each of the seven Municipalities and whether the Accused had the intent to destroy the Muslim groups of Bratunac, Foča, Ključ, Prijedor, Sanski Most, Vlasenica and Zvornik. In my judgement, it is the destruction in whole or in part of the specific Muslim and/or Croat groups of each of the Municipalities that is important and that must be considered by the court.

2. *Genocidal intent*

11. When considering the requirements of mens rea, namely the presence of genocidal intent, it is not enough to be satisfied that the Accused knew that his actions would result in genocide, it must be proved that he *intended* them to have such effect – as has been said so often, intent is the distinguishing feature of the crime of genocide.[9]

12. In my opinion, it is this feature of specific intent, as well as the requirement for a significant number of people to be victims of the crime, that often results, erroneously, in a perception that there exists *de facto* a 'hierarchy of crimes', with genocide being the most 'heinous' of all. In my judgement, any tribunal dealing with a case in which genocide is charged in addition to crimes against humanity must take special care not to assign special status to the offence of genocide and, in doing so, to inadvertently raise the standard of proof either in respect of the actus reus or intent.

APPLICATION OF THE LAW TO THE EVENTS IN THE MUNICIPALITIES

13. I shall address each of the constituent parts of the offence of genocide in turn examining whether each is satisfactorily made out.

1. *Is there a 'protected group'?*

14. I share the Majority's findings, and adopt the reasoning elided at paragraph 2574, that Bosnian Muslim and Bosnian Croats living in the Municipalities of Bosnia Herzegovina were protected groups within the meaning of Article 4 of the Statute.[10]

[6] *Jelisić* Trial Judgment, para. 93.
[7] *Krstić* Trial Judgment, para. 590.
[8] *Prosecutor v Sikirica et al.* Judgment on Defence Motions to Acquit, para. 68.
[9] The Statute governing the ICTY lists the crime of genocide at Article 4 and crimes against humanity at Article 5. No specific intent is required for crimes against humanity. This mirrors the position in the Rome Statute governing the jurisdiction of the International Criminal Court.
[10] *Karadžić* Trial Judgment, paras. 2573 and 2574.

2. *Have the 'protected groups' been subjected to any of the acts enumerated under Article 4(2) of the Statute?*

a. Killing members of the group: Article 4(2)(a)

15. I share and endorse the findings, factual and legal, made by the Majority in respect of the killings of Bosnian Muslims and Bosnian Croats in the Municipalities by Bosnian Serb forces, namely that a large number of Bosnian Muslims and Bosnian Croats were killed. They were killed during the takeover of the Municipalities, they were killed in detention facilities and some died in such places as a result of the cruel and inhumane treatment inflicted upon them.[11]

16. Accordingly, I am satisfied so that I am sure that Article 4(2)(a) of the Statute is met.

b. Causing serious bodily or mental harm to members of the group: Article 4(2)(b)

17. I also wholeheartedly endorse the findings[12] and conclusions reached by the Majority in respect of this element of the case. However, these findings fail adequately both to acknowledge the suffering of the victims and to illustrate their stories with sufficient detail. In my judgement, the systemic and systematic use of sexual violence is one of the central aspects of the case in determining genocidal intent. With respect, the failure to adequately see this violence, to identify its pattern, and to recognise its intended communicative effect has, in part, led the Majority to err in its conclusions as to Count One of the Indictment.

18. I am satisfied beyond reasonable doubt that rape of women was both systemic and endemic in the Municipalities. As this Chamber has found, this included gang rape in detention facilities in Foča.[13] We have also found that women held in detention camps were regularly raped by guards, soldiers and paramilitaries given access to the camps.[14] Some of them were raped many times a day and with frequent, at times daily, regularity.[15] This Tribunal has heard evidence from one woman of being raped at least 150 times, of others being raped so many times that they simply cannot estimate the number.[16] Women held captive in the camps were at times taken out of the camps and raped by Bosnian Serb soldiers elsewhere. Some women were held in sexual slavery in private homes, forced into labour to support the men who abused them, and on some occasions sold to others like property, like slaves. Some women were subjected to public nudity and paraded through the streets, some were even raped in public.[17] In my judgement, all these

[11] ibid, paras. 2578 and 2579.
[12] ibid, paras. 2580 and 2581.
[13] ibid, paras. 920 and 2501.
[14] ibid, paras. 2500 to 2503.
[15] ibid, paras. 2500 to 2501.
[16] ibid, para. 2501.
[17] ibid.

acts of violence and degradation were committed with the aim of causing sustained and enduring terror, pain and suffering.[18]

19. Not surprisingly, many women who suffered and survived this violence have experienced long term physical and/or mental sequelae. According to the evidence heard by this Tribunal, some became pregnant as a result of the rapes they endured. Many have suffered and continue to suffer post-traumatic stress disorder or depression and their attendant symptoms.[19] Some have contemplated or attempted suicide.[20] Some have found it impossible, for fear of being shamed, stigmatised, and shunned, to tell their family and friends.[21] It is sad to say that those who have come forward have not yet received sufficient financial recompense or other support they truly need and deserve.

20. I have no doubt that these acts of sexual violence were committed in the knowledge, individual and common, that these acts would hurt, humiliate, defile, and degrade the individual, possibly destroying their psychological and emotional well-being, and their ostracisation from the group would contribute to the degrading and ultimately the destruction of the group as a whole.[22]

c. *Deliberately inflicting on the group conditions of life calculated to bring about its physical destruction in whole or in part: Article 4(2)(c)*

21. Unlike the Majority,[23] I am satisfied so that I am sure beyond reasonable doubt that Bosnian Muslims and Croats held in detention centres across the Municipalities were deliberately subjected to conditions of life calculated to bring about the physical destruction, in whole or in part, of the ethnic groups of which they are members.

22. As the ICTR held in the case of *Akayesu*:

> … deliberately inflicting on the group conditions of life calculated to bring about its physical destruction in whole or in part should be construed as the methods of destruction by which the perpetrator does not immediately kill the members of the group, but which, ultimately, seek their physical destruction.[24]

In other words, genocide can encompass a form of 'slow death.'

23. We have found that 'detainees were held in terrible conditions';[25] namely, that they were subjected to: (i) severe overcrowding; (ii) stifling heat and lack of ventilation; (iii) inadequate or non-existent medical care; (iv) insufficient access to adequate water and food; and, (v) inadequate access to sanitation and washing

[18] ibid, para. 2504.
[19] *Kunarac, Kovac and Vukovic, T. 1288* (29 March 2000).
[20] ibid.
[21] *Kunarac, Kovač and Vuković, T. 1253* (29 March 2000).
[22] *Karadžić* Trial Judgment, paras. 2504 and 2505.
[23] ibid, para. 2587.
[24] *Akayesu* Trial Judgment, para. 505.
[25] *Karadžić* Trial Judgment, paras. 2507 to 2510, and 2584.

facilities and inadequate hygiene. Diseases such as dysentery were rife. We also found that these living conditions had serious continuing and long-term effects on some of those who survived.

24. With great respect to my Learned colleagues, if these conditions of living do not amount to 'slow death', as they put it,[26] repeating the phraseology used in *Tolimir*,[27] I am hard-pressed to consider what might. These conditions were inhumane and must, ipso facto, have been intended to result in either slow and agonising death or permanent physical and/or psychological damage.[28]

25. Moreover, I note that in the *Akayesu* case the ICTR held conditions similar to those which men and women were subjected in the Municipalities to be capable of fulfilling the requirements of Article 4(2)(c).[29] Furthermore, this Tribunal has previously held in the case of *Prosecutor v Stakić*[30] that similar but slightly less severe conditions satisfy Article (2)(c).

26. It bears reminding ourselves of the evidence of journalist, Edward Vulliamy, one of three British journalists granted access to the Omarska and Trnopolje camps on 6 August 1992.[31] He and his colleagues, Penny Marshall and Ian William, were the first journalists to access any of the camps and did so following express personal authorisation from the Accused. Mr Vulliamy's oral testimony to this Tribunal, just as the video footage evidence recorded that day by his colleagues from International Television News does,[32] provides harrowing evidence of the physical state of men held at the camps, pictures reminiscent of the Holocaust.

27. Further, we have found that individuals held in detention centres in Foča, Ključ, and Vlasenica were forced to work at the frontlines clearing mines, recovering dead bodies from mined areas, being used as human shields and at times, coming under fire.[33] To say that these individuals must have been terrified every day sounds banal and insensitive. It must have been agonising beyond imagination waiting to be selected for such labour – every moment would have been filled with terror that it might be your last. Such is the gravity of the mental and emotional, as well as the physical, strain to which they were subjected that I am satisfied beyond reasonable doubt that they were caused serious mental harm and therefore that the criteria in Article 4(2)(b) has been met. I am satisfied that being detained in such conditions amounts to treatment calculated to bring about the physical destruction of those individuals who had to endure these conditions.

28. I would like to note the way in which the Tribunal has properly, in my opinion, analysed the genocide in Srebrenica under Article 4(2)(b) by focusing on the 'harrowing circumstances under which thousands of Bosnian Muslim males faced

[26] ibid, para. 547.
[27] *Tolimir* Appeal Judgment, paras. 228 and 233.
[28] *Karadžić* Trial Judgment, para. 2512.
[29] *Akayesu* Trial Judgment, paras. 505–506.
[30] *Stakić* Trial Judgment, para. 546.
[31] *Karadžić*, T. 21034-141 (9 November 2011).
[32] *Karadžić*, T. 21034-141 (9 November 2011).
[33] *Karadžić* Trial Judgment. paras. 2531 to 2536, and 2444.

the prospect of their imminent death.'[34] This Tribunal has noted that the suffering endured by those who were murdered in those final days and hours, faced with the knowledge of their imminent death, as well as those who managed to survive, constituted bodily or mental harm. I do not detract from this finding at all, but raise it now to support my judgement that those who were used for labour on the front lines, whether as human shields, to clear mines, or collect dead bodies, must have experienced similar terror and suffered serious bodily and/or mental harm, and not just once but on multiple, repeated occasions; in my opinion, the agony that must have been endured cannot be overstated.

29. Finally, I would like to address the labour that women held in the camps were forced to undertake. I noted a little earlier how many women were routinely and repeatedly raped by camp guards, soldiers and members of the various Bosnian Serb paramilitary groups. Some of them were also forced to work in the kitchens and canteens preparing and serving food, some were also forced to clean 'interrogation sites', often cleaning blood, skin and hair from the walls and floors.[35] The impact of witnessing the evidence of torture must have exercised a chilling and significant communicative effect upon them. The overriding message communicated to these women was that there would be no escape from the brutal horrors, including sexual violence, to which they were routinely subjected. In my judgement, being subjected to these conditions was in fact, a form of 'slow death.'[36] Indeed, life in these detention camps must have been a living hell from which death, at times, must have seemed like a release.

30. In conclusion therefore, I am satisfied so that I am sure that the actus reus of genocide under Article 4 (2) subsection (a): killing; subsection (b): causing serious bodily or mental harm; and subsection (c): inflicting conditions of life calculated to bring about the physical destruction of the group in whole or in part, is met in respect of both the Bosnian Muslim groups and the Bosnian Croat groups of the named Municipalities.

3. *Did the Accused intend the 'protected groups' to be destroyed in whole or in part?*

31. I note the observations of the Appeal Chamber when dealing with the Rule 98 issues that arose in this matter; namely, that specific intent can be inferred from indirect as well as direct evidence.

32. As the Appeal Chamber noted,[37] evidence that can and should properly be considered includes: (i) the general context; (ii) identified facts and the surrounding circumstances; (iii) whether any other culpable acts were perpetrated against the protected groups; (iv) the scale of the committed atrocities; and, (v) other evidence revealing systematic targeting of the group. I shall consider each in turn.

[34] ibid, paras. 5661, 5662.
[35] ibid, para. 1773.
[36] *Tolimir* Appeal Judgment, paras. 228, 233.
[37] *Karadžić* Rule 98 bis Appeal Judgment, para. 80.

(i) The general context

33. In my judgement, there are three contextual areas of particular relevance in this case: the historical context, and in particular the background of enduring ethnic and ethno-religious enmities; the operative sexual norms, attitudes and behaviours across the three societal groups as at 1991; and, the personal background history of the Accused.

a) Historical context – old and enduring enmities in the Balkans

34. Firstly, it is appropriate to set the alleged actions of Radovan Karadžić, and others implicated in the Joint Criminal Enterprise (JCE), within some historical and cultural context. To this end, I rely upon the evidence the Tribunal has heard from historians, including that of Professor Robert Donia,[38] and the findings as to the historical and geographical background made by this Tribunal in the case of *Dusko Tadić*,[39] the first contested case decided by the ICTY.

35. The history of the territories that were amalgamated to form the State of Yugoslavia after the First World War is long and rich, but also at times dark and violent, reflecting its occupation by a rich and diverse mix of ethnicities, religions, languages and cultures for centuries, if not millennia. Its history is also marked by colonialization by various of the dominant regional powers, as well as inter-ethnic and inter-religious disputes, divisions and violence. It is also an history stained with modern inter-ethnic and inter-religious atrocities that predate and foreshadow the wars of the 1990s.[40]

36. During the fourteenth and fifteenth centuries, the Ottoman Empire conquered most of the Balkans bringing Islam to the region. Following the battle of Kosovo in 1389, Ottoman Turkey ruled Bosnia Herzegovina and Serbia until 1878 and 1912–1913 respectively.[41]

37. By the time World War I (WWI) commenced in 1914, the area that was later to become Yugoslavia was inhabited by many ethnic groups, namely the Serbs (predominantly Orthodox Christians), the Croats and the Slovenes (both of which are predominantly Catholic Christian groups). There was also, of course, a significant Muslim population, including in Bosnia Herzegovina where the 'Bosniaks' – or 'Turks', as they were called – was the most numerous as well as prosperous and influential group. Following the end of WWI, the Kingdom of the Serbs, Croats and Slovenes, comprised of Croatia, Serbia, Bosnia Herzegovina and other territories, was formed. In 1929, it became the Kingdom of Yugoslavia.[42]

38. The Second World War (WWII) visited many atrocities upon Yugoslavia. I take judicial notice, in accordance with Rule 94(A) of the Rules of this Tribunal,[43]

[38] *Karadžić*, T. 3067 (31 May 2010).
[39] *Tadić* Opinion and Judgment, paras. 56–121.
[40] ibid, paras. 56–121.
[41] ibid, paras. 56–58.
[42] ibid, para. 58.
[43] Rules of Procedure and Evidence of the International Criminal Tribunal for the Former Yugoslavia, 14 March 1994, as amended.

that it is widely held amongst the Serbian population and accepted by the United States Holocaust Memorial Museum – that Jews, Roma, and Serbs were the victims of a genocide perpetrated largely by the Croat Ustasha, a political organisation supported by the Nazi regime, which ruled the newly declared Independent State of Croatia. The genocide of the Serbs during WWII is said to be exemplified by events at the notorious Jasenovac concentration camp.[44]

39. Following the end of WWII, Yugoslavia remained united under the leadership of Marshall Tito.[45] Following his death in 1980, however, old nationalistic divisions resurfaced that ultimately culminated in the wars of the 1990s.

40. Whatever the historical truths of the various ethno-religious enmities percolating in Bosnia Herzegovina and Serbia, I take judicial notice of the fact that many Serbs consider a genocide to have been committed against them and commemorate Holocaust Remembrance Day on 22 April, a date that remembers the escape of persons held during WWII in the Jasenovac concentration camp.[46] It is noteworthy, in my judgement, that this Serbian suffering was referenced by Biljana Plavšić when addressing this Tribunal following her plea of guilty to persecution as a crime against humanity.[47]

41. In my judgement, it is essential to any proper consideration of the events and motivations with which this Tribunal is concerned that this wider historical context is kept in mind. Wherever the truths of these hurts lie, it is undoubtedly the case that many Serbs, including Bosnian Serbs who were influential during the early 1990s, such as Biljana Plavšić, considered themselves to be members of an ethnic group that had suffered greatly at the hands of their neighbours.[48] In my judgement, this narrative, is significant and illuminates the collective Bosnian Serb view of the background context to the events that occurred from late 1991 to the end of 1995. More importantly, the evidence we have heard demonstrates that it was a narrative embraced and advanced fervently by the Accused.

b) Relevant societal norms, values and attitudes

42. Tragically, this case is replete with stories of sexual violence suffered by women and, to a lesser extent, by men. In my judgement, is impossible properly and adequately to understand, evaluate and weigh the evidence of such violence, its purpose, or its ramifications without having some understanding of the cultural normative context within which it was perpetrated, especially if we are to appreciate its power as a weapon. Moreover, when we weigh the evidence against this cultural normative background, the communicative and symbolic effects of the sexual violence can be plainly seen and understood.[49]

[44] *Tadić* Opinion and Judgment, para. 83.
[45] *Kordic* Trial Judgment, para. 444.
[46] R Israeli, *The Death Camps of Croatia: Visions and Revisions, 1941–1945* (Abingdon, Routledge, 2013) 128.
[47] *Plavšić* Sentencing Hearing, T. 609-14 (17 December 2002).
[48] ibid.
[49] *Karadžić* Trial Judgment, paras. 2504–2506.

43. Similar to the situation in Rwanda at the time of the genocide committed there against the Tutsis, each of the three communities – the Bosnian Serb, Bosnian Croat, and Bosnian Muslim communities – were patriarchal and patrilineal societies heavily influenced by religious norms and values. This was especially so in rural communities and in the Bosnian Muslim communities.[50] I take judicial notice of the fact that gendered attitudes as to the role of men and women predominated and gendered norms prevailed. In my judgement, these were certainly communities in which sex was regarded as the preserve of marriage and in which a girl was seen to be defiled if she had sexual intercourse before marriage. Consequently, to rape the women of another group is to insult, humiliate, and possibly destroy that group. Further, I note and adopt the reasoning of my learned colleagues sitting in the ICTR in the case of *Akayesu* and conclude that sexual violence was a step in the process of destruction of the Bosnian Muslims and Bosnian Croats.[51] Ostracisation of raped women, forcible impregnation, and permanent injury resulting in the inability to have children all have the potential to destroy the group. Rape was an act through which power, ownership, domination and control of one group was seized and demonstrated by the other.

44. This normative context is the foundation for what some scholars[52] term the 'communicative effect' of sexual violence. An inherent and intuitive understanding of these norms, both at the societal and individual level, ensures that members of the perpetrator group understand that the rape of women from another group will communicate various significant and potentially destructive messages. Herein lies the power of rape as a weapon. They intuitively understand that rape results in shame, stigma and possibly shunning of the victim. Shame is heaped upon and felt by the individual, as well as her male relatives and the group as a whole. Each victim is stigmatised. Each is at grave risk of being treated as defiled and regarded as 'unclean' and worthless by their family and community. Each victim bears the risk of being shunned. Each will be at risk of rejection by her family and community and subsequently, ejection or ostracisation from the community. The Tribunal has heard evidence that it was commonly believed amongst the Bosnian Serbs that the impregnation of Muslim women would result, not in the birth of ethnically mixed children but rather, of Serb children.[53] Consequently, in my judgement, rape was used as the ultimate weapon of conquest.

(ii) Identified facts and the surrounding circumstances

45. In my judgement, and applying the guidance of the Appeals Chamber, the relevant evidence to be considered includes: (a) the Accused's political speech;

[50] ibid, para. 5664.

[51] *Akayesu* Trial Judgment, para. 732.

[52] TG Phelps 'The Symbolic and Communicative Function of International Criminal Tribunals' in MA Fineman and E Zinsstag (eds), *Feminist Perspectives on Transitional Justice, From International and Criminal to Alternative Forms of Justice* (Cambridge, Intersentia Publishing Limited, 2013) and F Ní Aoláin, 'Sex-Based Violence and the Holocaust – A Reevaluation of Harms and Rights in International Law' (2000) 12 *Yale Journal of Law and Feminism* 1.

[53] *Karadžić* Trial Judgment, para. 1830.

(b) his speech, and attitudes as evidenced in his poetry; (c) evidence of Karadžić's grievance against the Muslims and Croats; (d) evidence of his knowledge of what was happening; (e) his failures to act; and, (f) evidence as to the intention and attitudes of others incriminated in the JCE may also properly be used to infer intention on the part of the Accused.

a) The Accused's political speech

46. Each of the two Chambers previously to consider evidence in this case has examined background threats and speeches made by Karadžić. For example, the Rule 61 Trial Chamber cited Karadžić's now infamous speech of 14 to 15 October 1991 to the Assembly of Bosnia Herzegovina when addressing those who favoured Bosnia Herzegovina's secession from Yugoslavia:

> You want to take Bosnia and Herzegovina down the same highway of hell and suffering that Slovenia and Croatia are travelling. Be careful. Do nothing that will lead Bosnia to hell and do nothing that may lead the Muslim people to their annihilation, because the Muslim cannot defend themselves if there is war. How will you prevent everyone from being killed in Bosnia?[54]

47. That Trial Chamber went on to note, 'From that moment on, resort to force seemed to have been envisaged by the President of the SDS as a way of separating the nationally diverse populations.'[55] I agree with and adopt this reasoning.

48. Even more significantly, as it relates to evidence that has been tested by cross-examination, the Rule 98bis Appeals Chamber noted evidence of a decision on the part of the Bosnian Serb leadership that 'one third of Muslims would be killed, one third would be converted to the Orthodox religion and third will leave on their own',[56] leading to the disappearance of Muslims from Bosnia. In my view, this decision is extremely significant, not least because it mirrors the policy operated in the genocide of the Serbs in WWII. In my Judgment, it is clear that the aim of this strategy was the elimination or destruction of the Bosnian Muslims as a distinct group. In other words, this was a decision to ensure the genocide of the Bosnian Muslims.

49. Further, the Appeals Chamber noted statements made by Karadžić and recorded in evidence that 'his goal was "to get rid of the enemies in our house, the Croats and Muslims, and not to be in the same state with them [anymore],"[57] and that if war started Muslims would be 'annihilated"'.[58]

50. In addition, during this trial hearing the Prosecution has submitted the following statements attributed to Karadžić: 'this is a fight to the finish, a battle

[54] *Karadžić and Mladić*, Review of the Indictments Pursuant to Rule 61, T. 942.
[55] ibid, T. 943.
[56] *Karadžić* Rule 98 bis Appeal Judgment, para. 97.
[57] ibid, para. 98.
[58] ibid, para. 98.

for living space'; and, referring to Bosnian Muslims, 'They should be trashed. That people will disappear from the face of the earth.'[59]

51. In my judgement, these statements, made or adopted by the Accused are clear and direct evidence of his intention that the Bosnian Muslims as a distinct ethnic and religious group should be destroyed. In turn, this is clear and direct evidence of genocidal intent on the part of Radovan Karadžić.

b) His 'speech' as evidenced in his poetry

52. In my judgement, his poetry – a passion of Dr Karadžić's which seems to have drawn him some notoriety and limited acclaim – also sheds significant light on the man and his motivations. During the Rule 61 proceedings, the Prosecution played and entered into evidence a video recording, taken by a BBC recording crew for use in the 1992 documentary 'Serbian Epics,' by Pawel Pawlikowski and Lazar Stojanovic, of Radovan Karadžić together with the Russian poet Edouard Limonov at a Bosnian Serb military gunpoint on Mount Trebevik overlooking the city of Sarajevo. In this recording, the Accused strides about the mountain reciting his poem entitled 'Sarajevo' as the guns around him pound the city below.[60] His Russian colleague appears, in my estimation, to be in thrall to the Accused and his poetry; Limonov even takes a turn at the guns and discharges rounds on the city below.[61]

53. In my judgement, the Accused's poetry is steeped in nationalism and bellicosity and reflects his sense of Serb history, the sense of Serbian subjugation since the Battle of Kosovo, and in particular the narrative of Serb as victim. The theme of conflict and armed struggle emanates throughout his body of work. His poetry also conveys a sense of Serb ethnic and cultural superiority. None of this of course makes him guilty of any of the allegations brought in this case, but this Tribunal is entitled to take it into consideration as part of the wider context and as indirect evidence of intent on his part, especially when taken together with his public warnings about the annihilation of the Muslims and his assertion that they 'will disappear from the face of the earth'.[62] In my judgement, this is a probative strand of evidence revealing the Accused's attitudes and evidence which supports the inference of genocidal intent.

c) Evidence of Karadžić's grievance against the Muslims and Croats

54. Observations of Karadžić during these proceedings suggest a man who still, despite the end of the War and his years spent in hiding, harbours and nurtures those long-held grievances and that sense of ethnic superiority. The Accused told this Tribunal at an early stage in these proceedings that rather than facing charges

[59] *Karadžić*, T. 514 (27 October 2009).
[60] *Karadžić and Mladić*, Review of the Indictments Pursuant to Rule 61, T. 902.
[61] *Krajisnik*, T. 16694 (19 July 2005).
[62] *Karadžić* Rule 98 bis Appeal Judgment, para. 98.

he should instead be thanked for what he had done. Whilst his nationalism does not prove genocidal intent it is a matter I take into consideration when putting together all the strands of evidence.

55. At other times his behaviour has ranged from dismissive of this Tribunal and the concept of any international tribunal having any power of judgment over him to active and vociferous engagement in proceedings. Whilst this Tribunal understands such sentiment, it is significant, in my judgement, that he has at times been dismissive of the suffering to which this Tribunal has borne witness.

d) Evidence of his knowledge of what was happening, and (e) His failures to act

56. I concur with and join in the findings of the Majority that the Accused had timely and adequate knowledge of the nature and scale of the crimes committed throughout the Municipalities and of the conditions and mistreatment of non-Serbs in the detention centres across the Municipalities.[63] Based on those findings, I am satisfied so that I am sure beyond reasonable doubt that the Accused knew of the acts of sexual and other violence being perpetrated. He did nothing to stop them. He did nothing to punish them. In my judgment, he knew of the forced deportations, just as he knew of the desecration and destruction of sites and symbols of religious significance. In my opinion, he failed to do either because he never had any intention other than to achieve the eradication of the Muslim and Croat communities from each one of the Municipalities.

f) Evidence as to the intention and attitudes of others incriminated in the Joint Criminal Enterprise

57. Evidence that is probative of genocidal intent on the part of other alleged members of the JCE has been admitted. For example, Ratko Mladić's alleged avowal to have the Muslims 'disappear completely'[64] and the reported alleged wish of Momcilo Krajisnik, President of the Bosnian Serb Assembly, 'to kill off all the [Muslims and Croats].'[65]

58. Biljana Plavsić, deputy president to Karadžić, and, following his resignation in 1996, President of Republika Srpska, was an advocate of the pseudoscience of racial genetics. I take judicial notice, in accordance with Rule 94(A) of the Rules of this Tribunal that on 6 September 1993, when refusing to negotiate with Bosnian Muslims, she told the Novi Sad newspaper 'Svet', 'It was genetically deformed material that embraced Islam. And now, of course, with each successive generation it simply becomes concentrated.'[66]

59. However, as I have noted earlier, Plavsić, when speaking on her own behalf during her sentencing hearing, did not demur from her stance during the war

[63] *Karadžić* Trial Judgment, paras. 3331–3375.

[64] *Karadžić* Rule 98 bis Appeal Judgment, para. 99.

[65] ibid, para. 98.

[66] M Shatzmiller, *Islam and Bosnia: Conflict Resolutions and Foreign Policy in Multi-Ethnic States* (Montreal/Kingston, McGill-Queen's Press, 2002) 58.

years that the Serbs had been victims and, in her ardour to prevent a repetition of such suffering, she herself became victimiser. In my judgement, these statements support the narrative that these three other members of the Serbian leadership shared an intention to eliminate, by whatever and variety of means necessary, the Bosnian Muslim groups from various municipalities.

(iii) Whether any other culpable acts were perpetrated against the protected groups

60. In my judgement, there are several compelling points which should properly be considered under these headings: namely, the pattern evidence of the near concurrent attacks upon and the takeover of each of the Municipalities; the forcible removal of members of the protected groups; and the evidence of the destruction of homes and sites of religious and cultural value to respective groups, such as their churches and mosques.

61. The story of the decimation of the Croats and Muslims living in the various towns in the Municipalities reads like some sort of manual for conquest and ethnic cleansing. The takeover of each of the seven Municipalities share a number of common features. Prior to the attacks, Serb-only institutions were created, non-Serbs were dismissed from employment in public institutions, and restrictions on their employment were imposed. On or about the same dates, Serbian forces attacked the towns of the Municipalities. During those military takeovers, numbers of non-Serbs were killed in public, others were raped or subjected to other sexual violence, homes and property owned by non-Serbs were destroyed or seized, and churches and mosques were destroyed. Numerous non-Serbs were then forcibly transferred out of the area and others were detained and held captive in terrible conditions in detention camps. As a result, the non-Serb populations in the seven Municipalities virtually disappeared.

62. The significance of these crimes is not only the systematic way in which the sequence of actions was employed, but also the communicative effect of each of these actions separately and taken together. For example, public killings and sexual violence instil terror and secure subjugation and obedience. Destruction of homes, property and sacred places of worship communicates the message that you are not welcome here, you should not attempt to come back and, there won't be anything for you to come back to – it will be as if you did not exist in this place.

63. It must be accepted that this message does not necessarily render these crimes genocide. However, in my judgement, the targeted and replicated nature of this criminality is probative of genocide, especially when taken together with the statements and stance of the Serbian leadership, the effectiveness of operations in eradicating Muslims and Croats from the Municipalities, and the use of sexual violence which was used with full communicative effect, namely, to destroy the Croat and Muslim groups in the Municipalities.[67]

[67] *Karadžić* Trial Judgment, paras. 3443–3447.

(iv) The scale of the atrocities committed

64. Indeed, evidence before this Tribunal shows that in 1991, the Muslim population of Bratunac accounted for 62% of the overall population of the municipality.[68] By the time the War ended in 1995, that figure had fallen to 2.4%.[69] In Foča, Muslims accounted for 52% of the population in 1991; by 1995 they only constituted 4.4% of the population.[70] Such drastic differences are reflected across the other five Municipalities as follows:

Ključ:	47% in 1991, down to 1.8% by the end of 1995;[71]
Prijedor:	44% in 1991, down to 5% by the end of 1995;[72]
Sanski Most:	49% in 1991, down to 9% by the end of 1995;[73]
Vlasenica:	55% in 1991, down to 0.2% by the end of 1995;[74] and finally,
Zvornik:	60% in 1991, down to 1% by the end of 1995.[75]

65. The combination of mass killings, wholesale forcible deportations and other heinous acts, including rape, were so effective in destroying the Bosnian Muslim population that it defies belief not to see these concerted crimes as part of a wider effort to commit genocide. It would be a tragic coincidence of unbelievable proportions for random crimes against humanity and war crimes to have resulted in the near destruction of certain ethnic groups. In my judgement, such a tragic coincidence did not occur in the Municipalities; rather, this almost complete eradication of Muslims from these areas occurred because it was a genocide.

(v) Other evidence revealing systematic targeting of the group

66. Pattern evidence, or evidence of the systematic and/or widespread use of violence of a certain kind, can be used to prove the actus reus of genocide. Indeed, the systematic and widespread use of rape can constitute genocide just as systematic and widespread killing can.[76] Further, this Tribunal has also stated that the systematic and/or widespread nature of abuses against a particular group can be a relevant factor in inferring genocidal intent.[77]

67. As we should be aware, actions commonly taken during armed conflict have, in my judgement, been gendered by the law. For example, rape has been seen, until very recently, as merely a by-product or 'spoil' of war to be inflicted by combatants,

[68] ibid, para. 685.
[69] ibid, paras. 788–9.
[70] ibid, paras. 839 and 933.
[71] ibid, paras. 1489 and 1567.
[72] ibid, paras. 1574 and 1913.
[73] ibid, paras. 1919 and 2040.
[74] ibid, paras. 1099 and 1220.
[75] ibid, paras. 1228 and 1365.
[76] *Akayesu* Trial Judgment, paras. 731–732.
[77] ibid, para. 523.

predominantly men, on vulnerable civilians, predominantly women. In this way, international law's treatment of offences committed during armed conflict has been gendered and has largely ignored the offences committed against women. Thus, a hierarchy of significance was created, with the suffering experienced by men being treated by the law as being more important and deserving of prosecution than that experienced by women. I take judicial notice, in accordance with Rule 94(A) of the Rules of this Tribunal, that, despite evidence of huge numbers of rapes being disclosed, there was little judicial notice of these crimes by the various post World War II Tribunals. Indeed, it is estimated that as many as 200,000 so-called 'comfort women' were subjected to systematic rape and sexual slavery by the Japanese Imperial army, but this evidence was wholly ignored in the Tokyo War Crimes trial.[78] It was this hierarchy that until recently rarely permitted rape to be recognised, investigated or prosecuted.

Several important points which inform my judgment in respect of the allegation of genocide in the Municipalities arise in this case. Firstly, the number and nature of the alleged acts of sexual violence in this case is vast and shocking.[79] Secondly, these offences are gendered in their nature and purpose. Thirdly, international law has now recognised that rape is used as a weapon of war. Fourthly, rape can be an act of genocide.[80] Fifthly and finally, that despite this Tribunal's recognition of the gendered aspect of the crimes committed in Foča,[81] one of the seven Municipalities subsumed within Count One, this aspect has neither been adequately advanced nor explored in the presentation of the case against the Accused.

68. In my judgement, my colleagues have reverted to the practice of assessing the crimes alleged to have been committed in the Municipalities through a male lens, and in doing so have failed to give sufficient attention to the crimes inflicted on women, the pattern that evidence of these alleged offences reveals, and the way in which they were committed in order to communicate a certain message and create a particular symbolism for the victims and the group to which they belonged. In my judgement, both the pattern of these crimes and the communicative and symbolic value of these crimes make a significant contribution to the inference of intent on the part of the Accused.

69. The incarceration of women in detention camps, the indiscriminate, brutal and repetitive use of sexual violence against them, the attempts to forcibly impregnate them, and forcing them to perform labour was communicative, and intended to be so. Again, the message was plain and stark: the Serbs owned the women, were free to use and abuse them, and could infiltrate their group by the creation of Serb children. As this Tribunal found in *Kunarac* when recognising the gendered

[78] Formally known as the International Military Tribunal for the Far East.
[79] See Judgment of the Majority, paras. 2500–2506.
[80] *Akayesu* Trial Judgment, paras. 731–734.
[81] *Kunarac, Kovač and Vuković* Trial Judgment, para. 867.

nature of these crimes, rape was used as an 'instrument of terror … Muslims, women and girls, mothers and daughters together, robbed of their last vestiges of human dignity, women and girls treated like chattels, pieces of property at the arbitrary disposal of the Serb occupation forces.'[82]

70. In my judgement, the nature, scale and context of the sexual violence committed in the Municipalities not only amounts to the actus reus of genocide, but also lays bare that the intent in committing crimes of rape, indecent assault, forced gross indecency and assault, sexual slavery, forced prostitution, forced nudity, and forcible impregnation, was to destroy in whole or in part the target groups. Through these crimes, domination and absolute control over members of the group was asserted and exercised. These crimes were committed across the length and breadth of the Municipalities, in villages and towns, in public and in private, in streets, in houses, and in detention camps. The number of victims is vast. In the context of patriarchal, patrilineal, religious and conservative communities – and against a backdrop of hundreds of years of ethnic and ethno-religious rivalries and violence, including the perceived genocide of the Serbs in WWII – the only, and compelling, inference to be drawn is that genocidal intent was present.

CONCLUSION

71. In conclusion, I am satisfied so that I am sure beyond reasonable doubt, that significant numbers of the Bosnian Muslim and Bosnian Croat communities of the Count One Municipalities:

a) Were killed;
b) Were subjected to rape and other sexual violence causing them serious bodily and mental harm; and,
c) Were deliberately subjected to conditions of life calculated to bring about the physical destruction of their groups.

Further, I am satisfied so that I am sure beyond reasonable doubt that Radovan Karadžić intended that these groups should be destroyed in whole or in part.

These findings of the most abject and harrowing inflicted human suffering warrant nothing less than life imprisonment; in my opinion, that is the sentence that should be imposed upon the Accused.

[82] *Kunarac, Kovač and Vuković*, T. 6559 (22 February 2001).

Reflections

In this final note, I reflect on the specific methodological issues and other challenges inherent in attempting to apply a feminist legal methodology to re-writing the judgment, in the form of a partly dissenting opinion, delivered in one of the most infamous, most eagerly watched and most significant trials in international law, and in doing so as a graduate student, and, effectively, as a solitary endeavour. My final reflection considers expanding the feminist judgments project to a serial discussion of seminal decisions of regional human rights tribunals, such as the European Court of Human Rights, and perhaps also specific international tribunals, such as the Committee on the Elimination of Discrimination against Women.

Collaborative Judging

Unlike most others in the collection, this feminist judgment was essentially a sole endeavour that arose from a paper I wrote in May 2017 as part of my postgraduate studies at American University Washington College of Law under the tutelage of Professors Teresa Godwin Phelps and Susana SáCouto. Unfortunately, neither this judgment nor my experience in writing it benefitted from the collaborative experience that is a hallmark of much feminist methodology and this project in particular.

The challenges of undertaking this task as a solitary endeavour have been daunting, at times overwhelming. Working alone deprived me of the opportunity to tease out and explore my questions and misgivings about the approach I was adopting, my interpretation of the evidence and my understanding of the law and feminist theory with others learned in these areas. The ability to interrogate all these issues, especially the application of feminist legal theory, with others undoubtedly strengthens the final judgment. Reflecting upon this experience has served to strengthen my belief in the value of collaborative judging, not least because it enriches the quality of the process and the final product.

Challenges of Process

I pondered at length the ethics and efficacy of writing a feminist judgment whilst the case is still sub judice, both sides having lodged notices of appeal. The appeal has now been heard by the International Residual Mechanism for Criminal Trials[1] – also known as the Mechanism for International Criminal Tribunals (MICT) – which assumed full responsibility for all outstanding cases upon the closure of the ICTY at the end of 2017. The decision of the MICT is awaited at the time of writing.

[1] *Prosecutor v Karadžić* (Appeals Proceedings), MICT-13-55 (ongoing).

It would not be appropriate for the decision of an appellate or any other judge to be influenced by outside opinions. That said, if this project results in judges of the MICT considering and applying a feminist legal methodology to their judgments in this appeal or others, then the project will have had a notable success. Indeed, being cognisant of the interest in the case against Radovan Karadžić and the potential impacts of this project as a whole to advance positive changes in the international criminal justice system, my concerns as to the quality of work I was producing were increased exponentially. Despite having practised at the Bar for 20 years, I am new to the academic study of feminist jurisprudence and also to the study of international criminal law. Attempting to produce a piece of work of the required quality has been a truly daunting task. Here again, the collaborative process would have useful both in easing such concerns and enhancing the quality of the final work. Perhaps my experience also serves to underline the importance of having one or more members of a judgment-writing chamber who, amongst other skills and attributes, have significant experience in technical legal writing.

Deciding upon the approach of the judgment, and the voice in which it was to be written, were significant considerations. One of my key aims in writing the judgment was to highlight the ways in which the Tribunal's decision would have been different if the judges had listened to the stories of women, had looked at the evidence through a different lens, and if they had honoured the principle espoused in the *Akayesu* case that rape and other sexual violence may amount to genocide. A dissenting opinion seemed the most appropriate vehicle for accomplishing this. This approach carries its own potential risks, namely that the judgment may instead read like an academic critique of the Tribunal's decision-making. I hope I have avoided this risk.

Finally, it is worth acknowledging the burden of sitting in judgement. Striving to bring the various strands of evidence together to form the whole in a way that is meticulous, intellectually rigorous and convincing has been onerous but rewarding. I have grown in the process of writing this judgment, and learned that the weight of delivering justice and of posterity are not easily done but must be done with humility and courage. I have also learned that recognising our internal biases and ensuring that they play no part in our reasoning when passing judgement is much more difficult in practice than it seems either in theory or from the vantage point of the advocate. Throughout the process, I have been reminded that it is not enough to be a woman engaged in the justice system, it is vital to be a feminist.

Writing the Judgment

In common, I imagine, with most of the other authors, I had very little previous experience of writing a judgment. However, I have engaged in voluminous legal writing over the course of 20 years in practice at the Bar of England and Wales, including drafting countless 'Final Submissions', parts of which would sometimes appear in the judgment of the Court in due course. I drew heavily on my experience listening to numerous judgments being delivered. I found, once I began, that I was magically transported back into court and seemed to be able to hear the voices of some of the judges I most respect. Many of those voices belong to women judges. I have reflected repeatedly during this process on the work of those formidable women in front of whom I was privileged to appear as an advocate. I value the fact that they brought their experiences as women to the work they did. However, I recognise that the presence of a woman judge doesn't necessarily mean that a feminist legal approach is applied: it is necessary to do more than simply be a woman advocate or a woman judge; we need to be feminist advocates and feminist judges.

Engaging with the Structures and Norms of International Law

The Tribunal's different treatment of the atrocities, in particular rape and other sexual violence, committed in the Municipalities and the mass murder in Srebrenica was the burning passion behind my engagement with this judgment. This different treatment led me to reflect upon the relative absence of women's voices in the creation and development of the jurisprudence of the offence of genocide. Consequently, I wanted to give voice to those thousands of women who were brutalised in the most intimate and communicative ways simply because they were women. Moreover, the fact that most findings of genocide have been based on mass killing, as opposed to any of the four other potential contributory acts, has ensured that genocide has become gendered and given a very masculine identity and meaning. Until the International Criminal Tribunal for Rwanda's decision in the case of *Akayesu*,[2] rape and sexual violence had not been recognised as a contributory act of genocide. Applying feminist theory reveals why this has been the case; namely, because law, including international criminal law, is a male institution. Applying a feminist legal methodology creates a space within which the experiences of women can be recognised and acknowledged. Doing so revealed that the Tribunal had failed to give adequate attention to the rape and sexual violence that was committed systematically and on a mass scale in each of the Municipalities.

Applying Feminist Methods and Theories

The absence of real stories of sexual violence in the original *Karadžić* judgment was a disappointment, reminding me of the observations of Mark Harmon, retired Senior Prosecutor at the ICTY: 'Building up the pyramid, … the trials become more sterile and lose the victims' voice, because trials at the top, with the likes of

[2] *Prosecutor v Akayesu* (Judgment) ICTR-96-4-T (2 September 1998).

Karadžić, are all about proving linkages, with the atrocities already established.'[3] Similarly, the description of genocide as 'the crime of crimes' articulated by the ICTR and the legal scholar, William Schabas,[4] seemed constantly to interrupt my thinking. The systematic creation and use of camps with the sole purpose of incarcerating women to be raped, defiled, humiliated and impregnated, in my opinion meets the description of 'crime of crimes.' I have tried, however, not to permit this visceral response to cloud my legal assessment of the evidence in writing my dissent; a judgment riven with a visceral response rather than an equanimous assessment is rarely convincing. Applying feminist legal methodology countered these problems by exposing the awful nature, scale and systematic commission of sexual violence across the Municipalities. Further, in requiring closer attention to the context of the crimes feminist legal methodology revealed the pattern of sexual violence and its symbolic and communicative purpose and effect. All these factors overcome the facial constraints of the masculine gendering of international criminal law and contribute to the finding that intent to commit genocide is the only reasonable conclusion to be drawn in this case, proven beyond reasonable doubt.

A finding of genocide that reflects the serious bodily and mental harm inflicted via the use of rape and sexual violence as a weapon in the case of Radovan Karadžić is necessary not just because it reflects a legally accurate and justified conclusion and acknowledges the victims, but because it sends a strong message that the approach adopted in *Akayesu* was not an legal aberration or a finding that can be limited to its individual facts but rather a reflection of long-overdue approach to justice that includes women, their experiences and their voices.

Contribution to International Criminal Law?

It is my hope that this judgment may, in some small way, contribute to international criminal law. I hope that by exposing and foregrounding the experience of women in the Municipalities it will encourage others involved in international criminal justice to give voice to women and fully acknowledge their experiences. Indeed, I would like to see those involved in investigating and preparing cases to actively seek out the experiences of women. Similarly, I have sought to advance the understanding that patriarchal attitudes, especially those related to the ownership of women's sexuality, give sexual violence its destructive power. I would like to see an understanding and acceptance that sexual violence is used as a weapon in conflict *because* of its potential to destroy – the individual, her intimate and family relationships, and, ultimately, the group – cemented in the processes of international criminal law.

[3] E Vulliamy, 'Face to Face With Radovan Karadžić' *The Guardian* (London, 4 December 2011).

[4] W Schabas, *Genocide in International Law: The Crimes of Crimes* (Cambridge, Cambridge University Press, 2000).

Finally, I would like to encourage, if not exhort, feminist legal academics and others to extend the revolutionary feminist judgment-writing methodology to projects that specifically focus on the decisions of other international tribunals, such as the decisions of regional human rights courts and decisions of the CEDAW Committee. The need to approach decision-making in a different, more comprehensive, and inclusive way – one that supports gender equality as well as equality of access to justice across the genders, while recognising that gender is a continuum rather than a binary framework – is pressing.

PART V

Conclusion

17

Prefiguring Feminist Judgment in International Law

HILARY CHARLESWORTH*

Prefigurative politics is a form of activism harnessing theories of social change. In essence, it means a group's adoption of structures and styles of reasoning that the group is promoting, a modelling of the desired political and social outcomes; the aphorism 'be the change you want to see' sums up the practice of prefiguration. The term 'prefigurative tradition' first emerged in the 1970s in the context of Marxist methods, describing them as a movement embodying 'within the ongoing political practice … those forms of social relations, decision-making, culture, and human experience that are the ultimate goal.'[1] The idea was that Marxist prefigurative politics would undermine 'the division of labor between everyday life and political activity.'[2] The women's camp at Greenham Common, established in 1981 to protest against the presence of Cruise missiles at a US Air Force base in the United Kingdom, was a prefigurative venture in challenging traditional family structures.[3] Another example is the Occupy! movement in 2011, which set out to establish public spaces in the heart of large urban areas where free food, medical care and education were available.[4]

As an approach, prefiguration is a challenge to 'realism', or a view that social reformers must work within prevailing dispensations of power and privilege.

* Many thanks to Jenny Morgan for valuable comments on an earlier draft of this chapter and Michael McArdle for helpful research assistance.

[1] C Boggs, 'Marxism, Prefigurative Communism, and the Problem of Workers' Control' (1977) 6 *Radical America* 99, 100. See also W Breines, *The Great Refusal: Community and Organization in the New Left 1962–1968* (New York NY, Praeger, 1982).

[2] Boggs, ibid, 104.

[3] S Roseneil, 'Queering Home and Family in the 1980s: The Greenham Common Women's Peace Camp' (Queer Homes, Queer Families: A History and Policy Debate, British Library, 17 December 2012) eprints.bbk.ac.uk/7874/1/7874.pdf. See generally F Frenzel, 'Exit the System? Anarchist Organisation in the British Climate Camps' (2014) 14(4) *ephemera* 901.

[4] Others prefigurative projects include workers' cooperatives, barter economies, community gardening, the creative commons and restorative justice movements. See F Cornish et al, 'Rethinking Prefigurative Politics: Introduction to the Special Thematic Section' (2016) 4 *Journal of Social and Political Psychology* 114.

Prefiguration is equally an alternative to revolutionary change, as it stimulates people to operate as if social structures were already transformed. If they are to have a chance of changing a system, prefigurative ideas must not only inspire, but also relate to existing institutions in some way. As Margaret Davies observes:

> … as theorists, we cannot make anything, since even a theoretical performance has to be meaningful and therefore relate at some point to existing constructions, even as it might attempt to move beyond them. The present and past are a constraint on what can be prefigured. At the same time, a thought of utopia – the motivation for a better if not a perfect world – is intrinsic to prefigurative theory.[5]

Prefigurative politics, then, asks us to suspend belief in the inevitability of current structures and to experiment with putting bold ideas into practice.

Prefigurative practices have also emerged on the international plane. Examples include the formation of 'Peoples' Tribunals' by civil society groups to model a form of accountability for misuses of power.[6] We could also understand workings of the United Nations General Assembly through the lens of prefigurative politics. The 'one State, one vote' system models the theoretical equality of States, whatever their relative political and economic power. Other parts of the UN system manifest a more realist approach; the veto held by the five permanent members of the UN Security Council is an example. Another counter illustration of prefiguration is the organisation of UN peacebuilding missions. For example, when the UN established the UN Transitional Authority in East Timor (UNTAET) in 1999 to guide the country into independence, it gave UNTAET an autocratic structure. The UN Secretary-General's Special Representative was effectively unanswerable to the people he was shepherding into democracy.[7]

I. Feminist Judgments in International Law

Feminist activists have used prefiguration in creative ways, from domestic cooking practices[8] to support for reproductive justice,[9] and this book is another example. The project of writing feminist judgments in already-decided cases is an intriguing form of prefiguration, modelling some of the changes feminists seek in

[5] M Davies, 'Material Subjects and Vital Objects – Prefiguring Property and Rights for an Entangled World' (2016) 22(2) *Australian Journal of Human Rights* 37, 39.

[6] See A Byrnes and G Simm (eds), *Peoples' Tribunals and International Law* (Cambridge, Cambridge University Press, 2017).

[7] T Hohe, 'Delivering Feudal Democracy in East Timor' in E Newman and R Rich (eds), *UN Role in Promoting Democracy: Between Ideals and Reality* (New York NY, United Nations University Press, 2004) 302, 315.

[8] SJ Williams, 'Personal Prefigurative Politics: Cooking Up an Ideal Society in the Women's Temperance and Women's Suffrage Movements, 1870–1920' (2017) 58 *The Sociological Quarterly* 72.

[9] CS Lin et al, 'Engendering the Prefigurative: Feminist Praxes that Bridge a Politics of Prefigurement and Survival' (2016) 4 *Journal of Social and Political Psychology* 302.

legal systems, while taking legal forms seriously. It contrasts with two prevalent modes of feminist legal scholarship: one type points to the inadequacy of law in responding to women's lives and argues for more tailored laws or stronger implementation of legal standards so that the law lives up to its promise of justice;[10] another type emphasises feminist critique without specifying measures of law reform.[11] Feminist judgments are a more restricted exercise. They have to deal with a specific situation and apply specific laws to it. The judgments are a form of 'as if' fiction, going back in time to expose paths not taken by the original tribunal.[12] This is a thorny exercise in terms of temporality as the judgments here are inevitably informed by current feminist ideas and sensibilities. Generally, they present what the tribunals *could and should* have done rather than what they *would* have done if exposed to feminist thought circulating at the time of the original judgment.[13]

Karen Knop has studied such temporal complexities in the context of the Tokyo Women's Tribunal, held in 2000 to respond to the failure of the International Military Tribunal for the Far East (1946–48) (IMTFE) to address Japan's wartime system of forcing women into sexual slavery as 'comfort women' for the Japanese army. Knop notes that the Women's Tribunal was constituted as the IMTFE, rather than as a modern 'people's tribunal'. She suggests that this fiction risks both obscuring the influence of women's movements at the time of the original IMTFE[14] and deradicalising later feminist developments, 'contributing to the impression that they were gradual next steps in the inclusion of women and issues of gender justice in international law and institutions.'[15]

While the judgments in this volume refer only to material available at the time of the original judgment, they are certainly informed by contemporary feminist thought. The risks that Knop has identified in the context of the Tokyo Women's Tribunal appear however less acute in this exercise. This is in part because the feminist purpose of this collection of judgments is explicit, and in part because of the form of each chapter, with an introduction and post-judgment reflection emphasising the fictionality, and destabilising the 'as if' quality, of the judgments themselves. Existing collections of feminist judgments in national legal systems offer an array of approaches to the judicial task. Common ones include the suggestion that the original judgment got the law wrong, or focused on a skewed account of the facts. These types of arguments are certainly present in this volume, but by venturing into the international legal arena, the judgments must also engage

[10] See, eg, A Dworkin and CA MacKinnon, *Pornography and Civil Rights: A New Day for Women's Equality* (Minneapolis MN, Organizing against Pornography, 1988).

[11] See, eg, B Cossman et al, 'Gender, Sexuality and Power: Is Feminist Theory Enough?' (2003) 12 *Colombia Journal of Gender and the Law* 601.

[12] K Knop, 'The Tokyo Women's Tribunal and the Turn to Fiction' in F Johns, R Joyce and S Pahuja (eds), *Events: The Force of International Law* (New York NY, Routledge, 2011) 145, 146.

[13] ibid 157–58.

[14] ibid 159.

[15] ibid 152.

with the complexity of international justice, more obviously tinted by politics than national legal systems.

Women have long held great faith in the international sphere as hospitable to their concerns. From the end of the nineteenth century, women's groups saw the international arena as a useful site for their campaigns, hoping that they would transcend the conservatism of national systems. A series of International Congresses of Women, held in various countries starting from 1878, promoted women's equality. Some focussed on women's right to vote, but others made broader claims about women's rights.[16] The 1915 Women's Congress, held in The Hague, emphasised women's critical role in ending international conflict and adopted proposals aimed at ending the Great War.[17]

Feminists called on the League of Nations, established in 1919, to counter moves against women's rights within states, prompted by economic instability and the spread of nationalist conservative movements.[18] Some women's groups mounted a campaign for the League to adopt an equal rights treaty in the 1920s and 1930s.[19] Other women's groups advocated for protective treaties to support working women's social roles as mothers and wives and saw an equal rights treaty as a threat.[20] While the move for an equal rights treaty was ultimately unsuccessful, the League adopted a number of specific treaties to deal with concerns relating to women, including slavery[21] and trafficking in women and children.[22] Women's groups have similarly regarded the United Nations as a valuable site for action. The UN adopted a series of treaties in its early years addressing discrimination against women in certain areas of public life, including political life,[23] nationality after marriage,[24] and on the conditions of marriage.[25] A significant outcome

[16] See L Beers, 'Advocating for a Feminist Internationalism Between the Wars' in G Sluga and C James (eds), *Women, Diplomacy and International Politics Since 1500* (New York, Routledge, 2016) 202, 203–04.

[17] See International Congress of Women, *Report of the International Congress of Women: The Hague – The Netherlands, April 28th to May 1st, 1915* (Chicago IL, Women's Peace Party, 1915) 11–17.

[18] C Miller, '"Geneva – The Key to Equality": Inter-War Feminists and the League of Nations' (1994) 3 *Women's History Review* 219.

[19] ibid, 220–21.

[20] ibid, 222–24; 233–34. See also C Jacques, 'Tracking Feminist Interventions in International Legal issues at the League of Nations: From the Nationality of Married Women to Legal Equality in the Family, 1919–1970' in SL Kimble and M Röwekamp (eds), *New Perspectives on European Women's Legal History* (New York NY, Routledge, 2017) 321.

[21] Convention to Suppress the Slave Trade and Slavery (adopted 25 September 1926, entered into force 9 March 1927) 60 LNTS 253.

[22] International Convention for the Suppression of the Traffic in Women and Children (adopted 30 September 1921, entered into force 15 June 1922) 9 LNTS 415; International Convention for the Suppression of the Traffic in Women of Full Age (adopted 11 October 1933, entered into force 24 August 1934) 150 LNTS 431.

[23] Convention on the Political Rights of Women (opened for signature 20 December 1952, entered into force 7 July 1954) 193 UNTS 135.

[24] Convention on the Nationality of Married Women (opened for signature 20 February 1957, entered into force 11 August 1958) 309 UNTS 65.

[25] Convention on Consent to Marriage, Minimum Age for Marriage and Registration of Marriages (opened for signature 10 December 1962, entered into force 9 December 1964) 521 UNTS 231.

of the UN's International Decade for Women (1976–85) is the Convention on the Elimination of all Forms of Discrimination against Women (CEDAW), adopted in 1979.[26] Catharine MacKinnon has summarised feminist confidence in the international realm in arguing that 'the further away from home women go, the experience has been, the more rights they get … making it more likely that women's violations … will be recognized as real'.[27] As this collection shows, however, the international judicial sphere has been slow to address women's lives and social orders based on gender.

By its nature, a feminist judgments project limits the horizons of prefiguration. At the broadest level, the genre of a legal judgment, or advisory opinion, builds towards a decision or statement of the law. It must set out the 'facts' as they are deemed relevant and the law that it considers applicable. Dealing with judgments precludes reference to the non-textual realm of law, for example its visual or auditory resonances. Judgment-writing also dictates a detachment in voice, and a masking of the emotional, subjective, speculative or imaginative. A judgment that uses satire, irony or humour would breach the rules of the genre. It can only be in prose, rather than in poetry, sound or music. Another limit, imposed by the terms of the project itself (as noted above), is the stipulation that the feminist judges included here can refer only to materials available at the time of the original judgment. In the case of the international criminal tribunals, the feminist benches had to accept the charges as originally formulated by the prosecutors. Despite these restraints, the judgments in this volume model fruitful alternatives to familiar international judicial decisions.

II. Prefigurative Practices

A. Women as Judges

The most obvious element of feminist prefiguration in the judgments included in this volume is that of participation of women judges in equal or greater proportions compared to men in international judicial institutions. Even the simple device of recording the names of women scholars as judges in these renderings seems subversive and inspiring. Although male scholars are co-authors in some judgments, they are in a distinct minority. Some national judicial systems have increased women's participation over the past two decades, but the international sphere is deeply resistant to change. In the case of the International Court of Justice, for example, in 2018 just three out of 15 elected members of the Court

[26] Convention on the Elimination of All Forms of Discrimination against Women (opened for signature 1 March 1980, entered into force 3 September 1981) 1249 UNTS 13.

[27] C MacKinnon, 'Creating International Law: Gender as Leading Edge' (2013) 36 *Harvard Journal of Law and Gender* 105, 120.

are women and this is the highest number to date. In the International Law Commission, membership of which often serves as a precursor to nomination to the ICJ, there are four women of 34 members in 2018. The prestige of these institutions means that States tend to nominate people whose careers have followed a particular trajectory – of full-time legal work, replete with public activity and recognition – in other words, based on typical professionally successful male lives. Women can of course qualify as '*des hommes comme les autres*' but they are rarer.[28] Research has also shown that international judgeships can be a form of reward for political loyalty, or based on ties of personal camaraderie, or a way of bolstering a particular political agenda,[29] factors less likely to result in the nomination of a woman. The opacity of the nominations process, relying on professional networks, increases the likelihood that States will nominate male 'insiders' for judicial office.[30]

A study of nine international and regional courts from a range of sizes and subject-matter jurisdictions shows that in 2015 women comprised 20 per cent or less of the judiciary. This percentage was not increasing over time; indeed, it had declined in two-thirds of the courts surveyed.[31] In international courts whose statutes require or call on states to take sex into account when nominating or voting for judges, notably human rights and international criminal courts, the percentages were higher. For example, in 2015, women formed 39 per cent of the bench of the International Criminal Court (seven out of 18 judges).[32] By 2018, the percentage has dropped to a third, with six women members of the Court. In the case of the European Court of Human Rights (ECHR), a 2004 Resolution of the Parliamentary Assembly of the Council of Europe stated that the Assembly would not consider national lists of candidates for election to the Court unless there was at least one candidate of each sex among the three nominations.[33] Stéphanie Hennette Vauchez has chronicled the 'sustained, organized and successful hostility' the resolution encountered,[34] and its effective undermining in 2008 by a further resolution.[35] Hennette Vauchez's analysis of the curricula vitae of women candidates for election to the European Court indicates that states nominate either women who were 'replica[s] of [a] male international elite'[36] or women

[28] S Hennette Vauchez, 'More Women – But Which Women? The Rule and Politics of Gender Balance at the European Court of Human Rights' (2015) 26 *European Journal of International Law* 195, 215–18.

[29] See N Grossman, 'Achieving Sex-Representative International Court Benches' (2016) 110 *American Journal of International Law* 82, 86, 90.

[30] ibid 90.

[31] ibid 83.

[32] ibid. See also Rome Statute of the International Criminal Court (opened for signature 17 July 1998, entered into force 1 July 2002) art 36.8(a)(iii): States Parties shall take into account the need for '[a] fair representation of female and male judges.'

[33] Parliamentary Assembly of the Council of Europe, Resolution 1366: Candidates for the European Court of Human Rights (adopted 30 January 2004).

[34] Hennette Vauchez, above n 28, 209.

[35] Parliamentary Assembly of the Council of Europe, Resolution 1627: Candidates for the European Court of Human Rights (adopted 30 September 2008).

[36] Hennette Vauchez, above n 28, 215.

who were complete outliers in terms of international judicial office, with little prospect of election.[37] In any event, the notion that 40 per cent is the threshold for equality of participation of women and men[38] has become in practice a ceiling for women's participation on the ECHR.[39] Indeed, in September 2018, there were 14 women judges on the Court, just 30 per cent of the bench.

The presence of women judges has symbolic significance. The perception of representativeness increases the democratic legitimacy of a judiciary.[40] It also indicates that entry to the judicial profession is open equally to both women and men.[41] There is a considerable literature on the question of whether women judges make a difference to the types of decisions that are made, however. Studies of national jurisdictions differ, and the area of law in question is also relevant.[42] Given that, in order to be appointed, or elected, to the bench, women will be steeped in the culture of the relevant legal profession, their judgments typically hew closely to established forms.[43] Women judges may display more empathy with human litigants,[44] but they do not tend to challenge legal structures or the style of legal reasoning.[45] The pressure to conform to a judicial persona honed over centuries of exclusively male judiciaries is strong. Some women judges and prosecutors in international justice systems have recorded the difficulties they have faced.[46] If women judges use feminist vocabularies and ideas, they face a backlash that they are biased and prejudiced against men,[47] or that they will introduce unpredictability into the judicial process.[48] So, gendered ideas influence both the

[37] ibid 219–20.

[38] Parliamentary Assembly of the Council of Europe, Resolution 1426: Candidates for the European Court of Human Rights (adopted 18 March 2005). This means 19 out of a total of 47 judges.

[39] Hennette Vauchez, above n 28, 209.

[40] SJ Kenney, 'Thinking about Gender and Judging' (2008) 15 *International Journal of the Legal Profession* 87; E Rackley, *Women, Judging and the Judiciary: From Difference to Diversity* (New York NY, Routledge, 2013).

[41] See R Hunter, 'More than Just a Different Face? Judicial Diversity and Decision-Making' (2015) 68 *Current Legal Problems* 119, 123.

[42] See, eg, B Wilson, 'Will Women Judges Really Make a Difference?' (1990) 28 *Osgoode Hall Law Journal* 507; R Graycar, 'The Gender of Judgments: An Introduction' in M Thornton (ed), *Public and Private: Feminist Legal Debates* (Melbourne, Oxford University Press, 1995) 262.

[43] H Sommerlad, 'Let History Judge? Gender, Race, Class and Performative Identity: A Study of Women Judges in England and Wales' in U Schultz and G Shaw (eds), *Gender and Judging* (Oxford, Hart Publishing, 2013) 389.

[44] See, eg, K Mack and S Roach Anleu, 'Skills for Judicial Work: Comparing Women Judges and Women Magistrates' in U Schultz and G Shaw (eds), *Gender and Judging* (Oxford, Hart Publishing, 2013) 211, 227–29.

[45] Kenney, above n 40. Compare P Wald, 'Six Not-So-Easy Pieces: One Woman's Journey to the Bench and Beyond' (2005) 36 *University of Toledo Law Review* 979, 989, where Judge Wald argues that women judges at the international level may understand the facts of a case in a different way to men, and decide the cases in a different way.

[46] See F Tulkens, 'Parity on the Bench: Why? Why Not' (2014) 6 *European Human Rights Law Review* 587.

[47] L Chappell, *The Politics of Gender Justice at the International Criminal Court* (New York NY, Oxford University Press, 2016) 91.

[48] F Ní Aoláin, 'More Women – But Which Women? A Reply to Stéphanie Hennette Vauchez' (2015) 26 *European Journal of International Law* 229, 235.

opportunities for entry to and the outcomes from international judicial institutions in a circular manner.[49]

The politics of women's presence, while still a contested arena, does not of itself achieve change in institutional cultures, nor achieve transformative accounts of equality.[50] This is nicely illustrated in this collection by *Kell v Canada*, re-writing the views of the treaty body that monitors CEDAW, the Committee on the Elimination of Discrimination against Women. This was a communication under the Optional Protocol to CEDAW made by an Indigenous woman who had lost title to her home. The Committee's 23 members at the time of the original decision were all women, but the feminist version here demonstrates how different the reasoning could be if the treaty were read in light of the realities and particularities of women's lives.

In this volume, the feminist judges are self-appointed. As academics and activists, they are less confined by professional expectations and freer to engage in prefigurative politics. Indeed, assuming a judicial role can amplify the confidence of feminists. For example, in this collection, Amal Ali reflects on participating in a re-writing of the *Leyla Şahin v Turkey* case:

> I … [felt] a power dynamic when writing the judgment. When I took on the voice of a judge, armed with both legal reasoning and professional, political clout I found it easier to write the judgment. I started off referencing in my judgment writing in order to write a more convincing argument supported by the ideas of others, but did so less and less.

Ali observes that resuming her own, non-judicial, voice made writing the reflection much more taxing than preparing the judgment itself.

B. Expanding the Judicial Lens

A second prefigurative feature of the feminist judgments in this volume is attention to context. Margaret Davies has pointed to the way that law is typically presented as a type of superstructure, distinct from morality, politics and the real lives of people. She argues for a recovery of human life in law, in other words for 'the primacy of the subject in the construction of law'.[51] This collection amply responds to this challenge. All the chapters widen the aperture of the judicial focus, resisting the abstract and often depersonalised version of 'the facts' that the original judgments presented. The judgments rely on a greater range of materials than the original tribunals to build a fuller account of the background of the case. Humans, rather than States, are at the centre of the story. This is particularly striking in those judgments in cases that do not directly implicate the situation of women.

[49] ibid 231.

[50] ibid 234.

[51] M Davies, 'Feminism and the Idea of Law' (2011) 1 (1) *feminists@law* journals.kent.ac.uk/kent/index.php/feministsatlaw/article/view/9/66.

Take the original version of the ICJ's judgment in the case of *Germany v Italy*, addressing the scope of state immunities in national court cases, which featured a traditional, disembodied analysis of state immunity. The feminist judges, by contrast, draw on a variety of sources to acknowledge the human suffering that gave rise to the case. The feminist Court quotes a historical commission report to provide a firsthand account of the inhumane transfer of Italian military internees to German labour camps, and draws on memoirs to chronicle the violence of the German army against Greek civilians during the Second World War. Similarly, in the feminist re-writing of the World Court's decision in the *Lockerbie* case, the victims of both the United States bombing of Tripoli in 1986 and of the downing of Pan Am flight 103 over Lockerbie in Scotland in 1988 are brought to the fore. The authors resist the original ICJ account of the Lockerbie incident as if it were 'a standalone event without antecedents'. They tell us that they set out to write a judgment that was 'answerable to the dead'. The *Bozkurt* case (the renamed decision of the Permanent Court of International Justice in the *Lotus* case) also addresses the lives of the people directly affected by the maritime disaster, rather than simply the rights and obligations of France and Turkey.

A comparable expansion of the judicial lens is evident in cases in which women are litigants. Examples include *Ruusunen v Finland*, a case challenging the criminal conviction of Susan Ruusunen for publishing private information about her affair with the Finnish Prime Minister, Matti Vanhanen, in a memoir. The feminist panel of the European Court of Human Rights challenges the stereotype of gold-digging women found in the original decision. It offers a fuller picture of Ms Ruusunen's relationship with the former Finnish Prime Minister, the nature of the revelations she made about it, and the imbalance in their social and economic positions. The identity of the author as a single mother of limited means is emphasised, and the difficulty she would have in paying even a modest fine. The Court emphasises the autobiographical style of the book which it argues should attract a greater measure of artistic freedom than a news report. This casts Ms Ruusunen's publication of a memoir about her relationship with Mr Vanhanen in a more complex light than acknowledged in the original decision, and results in the success of Ms Ruusunen's case, unlike the original version of the judgment.

In *Burden v United Kingdom*, Nicola Barker's feminist opinion, concurring with the ECHR's original decision, refers to the social, political and economic context of the United Kingdom's inheritance tax rules. She differs from the Court in insisting that marital relationships should not be given a protected status for the purposes of exemptions from inheritance tax. Barker also adverts to the wealth of the Burden sisters and the fact that they are unlikely to be forced to sell their family home in order to pay inheritance tax. Another feminist ECHR decision in *Goodwin v United Kingdom* challenges the rigidity of the female/male binary used by the original bench, even though it had found that the United Kingdom had breached the European Convention on Human Rights by failing to recognise Christine Goodwin's sexual identity. The feminist version of *Goodwin* considers the social harm a female/male binary causes, including pathologising transsexuality, creating pressure to have corrective surgery and undermining relationships. *Leyla Şahin v Turkey* addresses the context of women in higher education in Turkey in rejecting the original ECHR decision upholding Turkey's ban on wearing head scarves in universities. The re-written ECHR judgment in *Opuz v Turkey* presents the phenomenon of domestic violence as a patriarchal structure, in contrast to the fleeting interest paid to it by the original bench. In *Gómez-Limón*, a case about how parental leave intersects with social security payments, the feminist bench of the European Court of Justice finds that a broad context is crucial for an analysis based on indirect discrimination. It criticises the 'blind approach' of the equal treatment model of non-discrimination used in the actual decision.

But the judicial or legal form can also restrict feminist benches. The feminist panel of the ECHR in *A, B and C v Ireland* gives greater detail of the lives of the three women bringing the case about access to abortion. It shows how the idea that Irish women must 'travel abroad' to receive an abortion mischaracterises the concrete experiences of the women litigants. The feminist Court regrets however that it could not give greater consideration to patterns of female poverty in the case because it would go beyond 'the realms of credibility.' In the CEDAW communication under the Optional Protocol, *Kell v Canada*, the feminist account uses film theory to model a richer response to Cecilia Kell's plight, placing her Indigeneity at the forefront. The film theory concept of 'space off' brings attention to 'the imperceptible margins and background [of the case], very real and very present, but by their nature not within the frame …', that had been overlooked by the CEDAW Committee. The authors note nevertheless the difficulties of according weight to intersectionality in their views, given the way that they are structured sequentially around the provisions of the treaty. They reflect ruefully that '[our] ability to write about the totalising effect of the operation of the law over an indigenous single woman subject to violence in the home, and unable to assert her legal rights before the courts, kept slipping from our grasp.'

C. Hearing the Voices of Outsiders

A related prefigurative element to that of context is the prominence the feminist judgments accord to women's and other outsiders' lives and voices. The feminist Permanent Court of International Justice in the *Bozkurt* case identifies silences in the facts presented to the Court, for example the identities and stories of all those who drowned. It also looks at the situation of women in the litigant states, France and Turkey, and criticises those 'who cannot see beyond the artificial entity of the State to understand the living human beings who feel its effects.' In the same case, the feminist Court addresses the inequalities at the heart of Franco-Turkish relations ('France epitomises an out-dated masculine model of sovereignty'). Expanding the traditional sources of international law, it invokes the resolutions of the International Congress of Women held in the Hague in 1915 and in Zurich in 1919 as a basis for an alternative version of sovereignty based on co-operation and solidarity. The feminist PCIJ also in turn reminds Turkey of the plight of the Kurdish people and calls on Turkey to change its policies with respect to minorities. In *Lockerbie*, the feminist judges of the International Court of Justice point to the unstable distinction between terrorism as a harm and sanctions as an appropriate response to it in terms of their effects on human lives, particularly the lives of women.

Feminist revisions of international criminal law judgments also attend to the women and girls affected by the alleged crimes: Bosnian women in the *Karadžić* case, Congolese women in *Lubanga* and Sierra Leonian women in the *AFRC* case. The authors of these chapters point out that the original benches had significant evidence of sexual crimes before them, but that this was not reflected in their judgments. In the case of *Lubanga*, however, the feminist bench of the International Criminal Court records its dismay that it cannot 'foreground the voices and lived experiences of victims/survivors in the way we had hoped' because the original bench had considered this testimony unreliable. Similarly, the feminist *AFRC* bench was constrained by the witnesses and evidence presented in the original case. In *Karadžić*, Celestine Greenwood invokes the concept of the communicative effect of sexual violence to explain why it should be understood as genocidal in that context.

D. Attending to the Politics of Law

More generally, the style of the feminist judgments in this volume often prefigures an expansive judicial agenda, blurring the traditional separation of law from politics. In this respect, the international feminist judgments differ from some nationally-based feminist judgments. For example, one feature of some of the judgments included in the Australian project was adherence to legal formalism as a method.[52] One feminist judge reflected that she wanted the original bench 'to take note of the fact that within the same paradigm as black letter law they could reach a different decision.'[53]

While some of the international feminist judgments in this volume rely on standard legal techniques, such as treaty interpretation, to establish that the original courts simply got the law wrong, the international feminist judges seem more prepared overall to abandon black letter law. In the *Bozkurt* decision we encounter unfamiliar judicial language such as '[t]he Court wishes to disrupt' particular doctrines of international law. In other cases, the authors re-write international judgments to avoid specific rules that they regard as hierarchical, such as the doctrine of *jus cogens* in *Germany v Italy*, concerning state immunities. The feminist concurring judgment in *Burden* concludes with a resounding call

[52] See H Douglas et al, 'Reflections on Rewriting the Law' in H Douglas et al (eds), *Australian Feminist Judgments: Righting and Rewriting Law* (Oxford, Hart Publishing, 2014) 19, 32–34.
[53] Quoted in ibid 34.

to the United Kingdom to abolish privileges attached to marriage in its taxation laws. And the *AFRC* bench excoriates the Prosecution for its lack of research into the use of female child soldiers in the civil war in Sierra Leone and into the links between recruitment of child soldiers and sexual crimes.

In the feminist version of the ICJ's advisory opinion in the *Reservations* case, the Court branches out from treaty interpretation to propose that independent dispute settlement bodies be included in human rights treaties that are likely to attract broad State reservations. For the Genocide Convention, the feminist ICJ bench establishes a two-pronged mechanism to deal with the impact of reservations that are objected to by other States: all Contracting States must specifically accept or reject a reservation, with objecting States clarifying the legal basis of their objection. In the case of an arguably impermissible reservation, a dispute resolution process is engaged. The Court also introduces the notion of placing a time limit on a reservation's effectiveness, with review at least every five years. The feminist ICJ bench in the *Lockerbie* case imagines a more activist World Court, and a more accountable UN Security Council.

The feminist revisions of ECHR cases wrestle with that Court's recourse to a State's 'margin of appreciation'. This doctrine acknowledges that States have a measure of discretion in fulfilling their obligations under the European Convention.[54] It is linked to the notion of a 'European consensus' on the scope of human rights. The general approach has been that the greater the degree of regional consensus, the narrower is a state's margin of appreciation.[55] The concept of subsidiarity also operates to restrain the European Court's jurisprudence by giving primary responsibility for the protection of human rights to domestic authorities.[56] The feminist bench in *Goodwin*, by contrast, insists on greater international judicial activism. It calls on the Court to abandon its deference to State margins of appreciation in the context of Article 8's guarantee of the right to privacy and Article 12's guarantee of the right to marry and found a family, even though there is no European consensus on these matters. The feminist judgment in *Burden* winds back States' margins of appreciation with respect to preserving the special status of marriage; *Leyla Şahin* limits the margin of appreciation in the area of freedom of religion; and the feminist bench in *Ruusunen* envisages a much narrower scope for national restrictions on the right to freedom of speech.

The feminist version of *A, B and C v Ireland* presents a different approach to consensus. The bench challenges the consensus analysis in the original decision, used to uphold Ireland's restrictive abortion laws, and instead points to a European consensus on the need to protect a pregnant woman's health. It also

[54] See generally A Legg, *The Margin of Appreciation in International Human Rights Law* (Oxford, Oxford University Press, 2012).

[55] See E Benvenisti, 'Margin of Appreciation, Consensus, and International Standards' (1999) 31 *New York University Journal of International Law & Politics* 843, 851.

[56] See A Mowbray, 'Subsidiarity and the European Convention on Human Rights' (2015) 15 (2) *Human Rights Law Review* 313.

counters what it describes as the Irish government's 'historic' antipathy to abortion with data from opinion polls in Ireland, challenging the government's representation of Irish moral beliefs. Relying on consensus analysis is however complicated from a feminist perspective as it is unlikely to deliver a transformative form of equality. For example, linking reproductive rights to women's health is not the same as respecting women's autonomy to make reproductive choices.[57]

E. Unsettling the Determinacy of Law

The form of the chapters, with both the authors' introductions and reflections on the writing process juxtaposed with the re-written judgments, deploys a feminist technique to destabilise claims to determinacy inherent in traditional court judgments. It allows quite different voices to be included in the judgment 'package'; the doubts and uncertainties of the authors about what they have written stand cheek by jowl with their more confident judicial voices. For example, in the *Germany v Italy* case, one of the authors, Zoi Aliozi, reports that she was 'discouraged by the inevitability of compromising with and in a twisted way contributing in upholding the patriarchal morality. … I felt frustrated by the necessity to use the same masculine legal tools that make sense only in an androcentric legal world.' A co-author, Ekaterina Yahyaoui, indeed wonders if poetry would be a better medium to express the law than a judgment. The feminist *AFRC* Trial Chamber of the Special Court for Sierra Leone refers to the 'judicial prism/prison' and the difficulties of producing a 'legally plausible feminist judgment' at the same time as a feminist narrative. The *Goodwin* bench ends up finding that international law is 'an essentially anti-queer tool' and unable to achieve radical feminist change. The feminist Court's reflection concludes poignantly with the words of Christine Goodwin's daughter after Goodwin's death: she 'was broke, the road to recognition [of her rights] had taken their toll physically, mentally and financially.' Other reflections refer to earlier versions of the feminist judgments and the negotiations that took place to finalise them arriving at, in the words of the *A, B and C v Ireland* judges, 'a roughly shared goal through compromise, collective effort, and feminist debate.'

Some of the reflections describe the feminist judges' hopes and uncertainties about the task they are undertaking. This acknowledgement redefines the nature of the judicial role as one engaging emotions, such as empathy, as much as detached reasoning. The *AFRC* Trial Chamber judges speak of 'confronting uncomfortable thoughts about our own positionality' during the drafting process. Contestation about the outcome of a case is inevitable, although the genre of a written judgment

[57] See Guaranteeing Sexual and Reproductive Health and Rights for All Women, in Particular Women with Disabilities: Joint statement by the Committee on the Rights of Persons with Disabilities and the Committee on the Elimination of All Forms of Discrimination against Women (adopted 29 August 2018).

requires a decision. The *Bozkurt* Court avoids this however by postponing delivering an order. The feminist ICJ in *Germany v Italy* re-writes the original order by identifying a series of joint obligations on the parties, such as calling on them to establish a compensation scheme.

Another element of feminist prefiguration occasionally surfacing in the judgments is playfulness. This may have been easier in cases that did not directly involve the situations of women. The best example is the *Bozkurt* decision from the feminist PCIJ. Its subtitle, 'ships that go bump in the night', references a traditional Scottish poem which included 'things that go bump in the night' in a list of imagined supernatural phenomena. Aspects of this judgment border on the rollicking, subverting the particular style of seriousness judicial pronouncements rely on for their authority. The form of a judgment however ultimately limits the irreverence. Indeed, other judicial benches in this book emphasise that they wanted their decisions to be recognisably the work of a particular court.

III. Conclusion

Feminist international lawyers have generally found it easier to identify feminist messages than feminist methods.[58] The prefiguration of feminist judgments, as illustrated in this volume, offers a powerful method of engaging with the gendered form of the international legal system, enacting changes that feminist theorists have long argued for. The project is a constructive form of activism in its assumption that feminists can already shape the legal system. This process is complicated however by the fact that feminists are often ambivalent about legal norms and institutions: they both challenge the masculine structures of law and yet rely on law as one means of achieving equality. Ratna Kapur and Brenda Cossman articulate this dilemma in their study of feminist engagement with the Indian legal system:

> The law has constructed women as … passive and weak, as subordinate and in need of protection. … At the same time, law is a site where these roles and identities have been challenged. … [S]ocial reformers and feminist activists have sought … to reconstruct women's roles and identities as more full and equal citizens.[59]

Law and legal institutions play an important role in shaping women's lives, but they cannot achieve social change in isolation. The judgments in this volume illuminate not only the significance of an expanded referential universe to judicial activity but also the limits of international adjudication in achieving transformative equality for women.

[58] See H Charlesworth, 'Talking to Ourselves? Feminist Scholarship in International Law' in S Kouvo and Z Pearson (eds), *Feminist Perspectives on Contemporary International Law: Between Resistance and Compliance* (Oxford, Hart Publishing, 2011) 17, 32.

[59] R Kapur and B Cossman, *Subversive Sites: Feminist Engagements with Law in India* (New Delhi, Sage Publications, 1996) 12.

What can a collection of feminist judgments achieve that a collection of feminist analyses of international cases cannot? I think that this volume offers a creative form of feminist practice, engaging closely with the object of critique and putting flesh on the bones of feminist theory. Prefiguration is, as Margaret Davies has described in a different context, a way of moving between utopian imaginings and the material world in which we find ourselves, 're-creat[ing] present law in a manner that gestures towards a different and possibly more expansive future.'[60] In a similar spirit, the judgments in this volume keep their feet firmly on the ground, dealing with existing legal structures and doctrines, but also presenting a rich trove of feminist speculation and experiments.

[60] Davies, above n 5, 55.

INDEX

www.ingramcontent.com/pod-product-compliance
Ingram Content Group UK Ltd.
Pitfield, Milton Keynes, MK11 3LW, UK
UKHW020225290926
15470UKWH00001B/384

9 781509 91445